W9-CMR-366

THE GOLDEN WARRIOR

The Life and Legend of Lawrence of Arabia

Lawrence James

THE GOLDEN WARRIOR

The Life and Legend of Lawrence of Arabia

Marlowe & Company

NEW YORK

For Andrew and Cherry

Second Edition, 1994

Published in the United States of America by
Marlowe & Compnay
230 Fifth Avenue
New York, NY 10001

Distributed by Publishers Group West

Copyright © 1990 by Lawrence James
Preface Copyright © 1993 by Lawrence James
All rights reserved. No part of this book may be
reproduced, in any form, without written permission
from the publishers, unless by a reviewer who wishes
to quote brief passages.
Originally published in Great Britain by
George Weidenfeld & Nicolson Limited.

Manufactured in the United States of America

Library of Congress Cataloging-in-Publication Data

James, Lawrence
     The golden warrior : the life and legend of Lawrence of Arabia /
Lawrence James. —
     p.   cm.
     Originally published: London : George Weidenfeld and Nicolson
Ltd., 1990.
     Includes bibliographical references and index.
     ISBN 1-56924-861-3
     1. Lawrence, T. E. (Thomas Edward) 1888–1935.   2. Soldiers—Great
Britain—Biography.   3. Great Britain. Army—Biography.   4. World
War, 1914–1918—Campaigns—Middle East.   5. Middle East-
History—20th century.   I. Title.
D568.4.L45J36   1993
940.4'15'092—dc20
[B]   92-31944
                                                                CIP

Contents

ILLUSTRATIONS

Between pages 116 and 117

For King and Empire   (Merton College, Oxford)
Eagle on the Crescent
Ready for action
Desert raiders
Brothers-in-arms
Deutschland über Allah
Intruder
Robes for a Prince
The terrible Turk
The Sultan's Arabs
Intelligence briefing

Between pages 276 and 277

Turkey's lifeline
A lifeline destroyed
Master of Damascus   (Rolls-Royce plc)
Sir Ronald Storrs   (National Portrait Gallery, London)
Lord Lloyd of Dolobron   (National Portrait Gallery, London)
Medina falls
Warriors turned peacemakers
Lawrence at Miramshah   (National Portrait Gallery, London)
Man of letters   (National Portrait Gallery, London)
Death of a hero   (*Daily Sketch*)
Sleeping Galahad   (Tate Gallery, London)

Photographs are from the Imperial War Museum, London, except where otherwise
identified.

Maps drawn by John Gilkes

ACKNOWLEDGEMENTS

I am grateful to the Scottish Arts Council for a grant to meet my expenses when I undertook research in Paris. I would also like to thank Mr Toby Buchan, Dr John Charmley, Air Marshal Sir Edward Chilton, KBE, CB, Dr Martin Edmonds, Mr Michael Ffinch, Professor M.R.D. Foot, Professor John Gaskin, Mr Michael Hodges, Dr Jeffrey Keith, Mr Phillip Knightley, Mrs Hilary Laurie, Mr Andrew Lownie, Mr and Mrs Christopher Rathbone, Dr Ken Robertson, Mr Jeffrey Richards, Mrs Laura Ridings, M. and Mme. Serge Soudaplatoff, Mr David Vernon-Jones, Mr and Mrs Andrew Williams, Mr and Mrs Philip Williams, and Mr Vivian Williams for advice, suggestions and assistance. I am especially grateful to Dr Maarten Schild for his kindness in sharing with me his clinical and historical knowledge and insights into Lawrence's behaviour and for presenting his information in such an agreeable and often humorous form. Thanks are due to my wife, Mary, and sons, Edward and Henry, for their good humour and assistance.

Special thanks are also due to Mr Sam Clayton for permission to consult and quote the papers of his father, Sir Gilbert Clayton, and to his sister, Mrs Patricia Marshall, for their hospitality and answers to my questions about Lawrence. Likewise, I would like to thank Mrs William Roberts and her son, Mr John Roberts, for their generosity and sharing with me their recollections of Lawrence.

I am also indebted to Miss Gillian Grant and her staff at the Middle East Centre, St Antony's College, Oxford; to Mrs Lesley Forbes and the staff of the Sudan Archive at the University of Durham; to Miss Elizabeth Bennett and the staff of the Churchill College Archives Centre, Cambridge; to Mr Roderick Suddaby and the staff of the Department of Documents at the Imperial War Museum; and the staff of St Andrews University Library, the National Library of Scotland, the Metropolitan Police Archives, the Public Record Office, the Ministry of Defence, the India Office Library, Le Service pour l'Histoire de l'Armée de la Terre and Dorsetshire County Constabulary. All have shown great generosity of spirit and time, and their help has been invaluable.

I acknowledge with thanks Lady Lloyd and The Master, Fellows and Scholars of Churchill College in the University of Cambridge for permission to use and quote from the papers of the first Lord Lloyd; Durham University Library for the Wingate Papers and *The Seven Pillars of Wisdom* Trust for passages from Lawrence's published and unpublished letters. At no stage in the preparation of this book have I received assistance from the Trust or the Lawrence family.

Quotations from the Crown-copyright records of India Office Records and the Public Records appear by permission of the Controller of Her Majesty's Stationery Office.

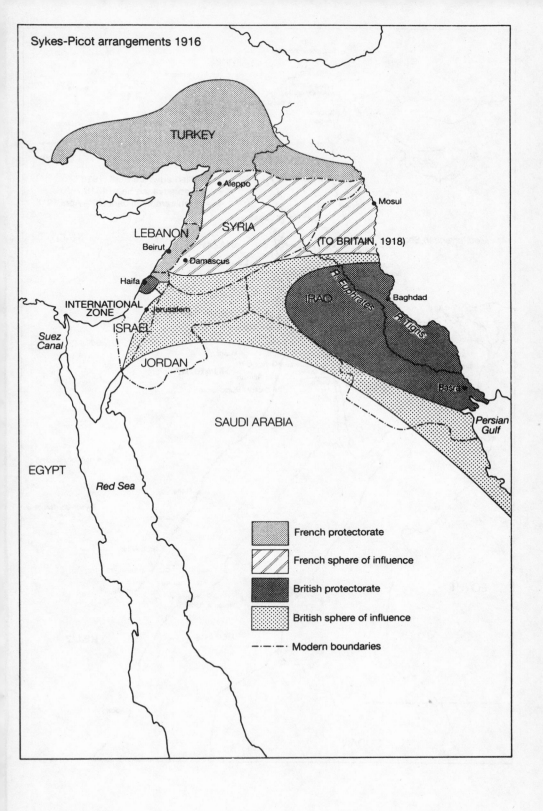

Sykes-Picot arrangements 1916

TURKEY

Aleppo

Mosul

LEBANON

SYRIA

(TO BRITAIN, 1918)

Beirut

Damascus

Haifa

INTERNATIONAL
ZONE

Jerusalem

ISRAEL

Suez
Canal

JORDAN

R. Euphrates

IRAQ

Baghdad

R. Tigris

Basra

Persian
Gulf

SAUDI ARABIA

EGYPT

Red Sea

	French protectorate
	French sphere of influence
	British protectorate
	British sphere of influence
–·–·–	Modern boundaries

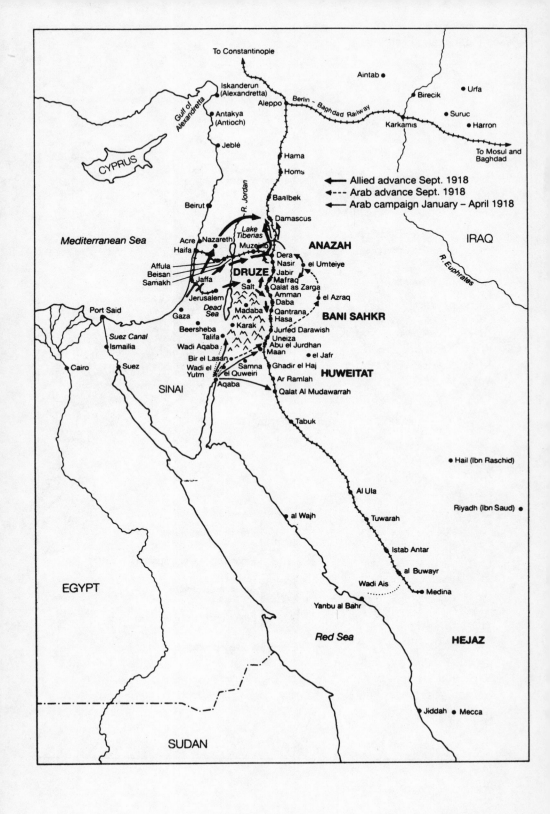

To Constantinople

Aintab •

Iskanderun
(Alexandretta)

Berlin – Baghdad Railway

Birecik •

• Urfa

Antakya
(Antioch)

Aleppo

• Suruc

Karkamis •

• Harron

*Gulf of
Alexandretta*

CYPRUS

Jeblé •

Hama •

To Mosul and
Baghdad

Homs •

Beirut •

Baalbek •

IRAQ

R. Jordan

Damascus •

R. Euphrates

Mediterranean Sea

Lake
Tiberias

Acre • Nazareth •

Muzeirib

ANAZAH

Haifa •

Affula
Beisan
Samakh

Jaffa •

Jerusalem •

Dera
Nasir • el Umteiye
Jabir
DRUZE Mafraq
Salt • Qalat as Zarga
Amman
Dead Daba
Sea Madaba Qantrana
Hasa

• el Azraq

BANI SAHKR

Port Said •

Gaza •

Beersheba •

Karak •

Talifa

Wadi Aqaba

Bir el Lasan

Wadi el
Yutm

Samna
el Quweiri

Jurfed Darawish
Uneiza
Abu el Jurdhan
Maan •

Ghadir el Haj

• el Jafr

Ar Ramlah

HUWEITAT

Cairo •

Suez Canal

Ismailia •

Suez •

SINAI

Aqaba •

Qalat Al Mudawarrah

• Tabuk

Hail (Ibn Raschid) •

Al Ula •

Riyadh (Ibn Saud) •

al Wajh •

Tuwarah •

Istab Antar •

al Buwayr •

Wadi Ais

• Medina

EGYPT

Yanbu al Bahr •

Red Sea

HEJAZ

Jiddah • • Mecca

SUDAN

→ Allied advance Sept. 1918
⇢ Arab advance Sept. 1918
→ Arab campaign January – April 1918

PREFACE

The story of Lawrence of Arabia, hero of the Arab revolt, was an American creation. It was the concoction of Lowell Thomas, an academic turned newspaperman with a taste for hyperbole and a flair for publicity. During the spring of 1919 he enthralled audiences at New York's Century Theatre with a dramatic presentation of what was popularly called 'The Last Crusade', the recent campaign for the liberation of the Holy Land. Slides, newsreel footage of Beduin horsemen, and the backing of a full orchestra gave immediacy and vividness to an exciting tale, but it was the romantic Colonel T.E. Lawrence, dubbed by Thomas 'the uncrowned King of Arabia', who captured the imagination of New York theatregoers. Like the showman he was, Thomas recognised what his audiences wanted and responded accordingly. When his extravaganza opened in London in the late summer it had become the story of adventures of Lawrence of Arabia. Thomas's instinct was right; his show was not only a box office success, he had discovered and promoted a hero.

Every generation has its own heroes and, thanks to Lowell Thomas, Lawrence filled this role for the 1920s and 1930s. His reputation rested upon his prowess and his deeds which were remarkable by any standard. According to the Thomas version of events, Lawrence was a modern paladin who, between 1916 and 1918, had won the confidence and admiration of Beduin; led them into battle against the Turks; risked his life in daring missions behind enemy lines; and masterminded the Arab liberation of Damascus. The man of action was not only a gallant and resourceful warrior, but an intellectual whose self-questioning and literary talents set him apart from the conventional war hero. Lawrence was—and it is hard to know whether Lowell Thomas fully understood this—the right man for his times. The survivors of the killing fields of the Western front and the generation that followed were stunned by four years of seemingly futile mass slaughter. Lawrence emerged the hero of a nobler struggle for the emancipation of a country and its peoples from tyrannical Turkish rule. His war could be romantised without any sense of guilt; it had been waged in the desert, an environment that Lawrence called 'clean'. Moreover, as Lawrence himself proved, his war had been one in which the individual could still dominate the battlefield.

Lawrence outlived the hero worship of his own generation. Long before he died in 1935 people spoke about the 'Lawrence legend', and its essential features became fixed in the national consciousness of Britain and America by David Lean's film *Lawrence of Arabia*. Crammed with dramatic incident, with dazzling shots of the desert and a Bruckneresque score, the film entertains and reassures. Like the ancient ballad or epic poem, it recreates history as it ought to have been rather than as it was. At the same time the film offers an insight into Lawrence the man, exploring, not always convincingly, his internal struggles and private apprehensions.

While the cinematic Lawrence entranced audiences, his historical counterpart was being found wanting. In 1955, Richard Aldington's biography broke a twenty-year tradition of Lawrence hagiography by arguing that its subject was a sham and that his reputation had been artificially preserved by a coterie of admirers. To judge by the roars of rage provoked by this book, Aldington had damaged his target. His foray was the prelude to a broader and more sustained assault on the values and heroes of a previous generation that was undertaken by writers and intellectuals in the late 1950s and 1960s. It was open season for those like Lawrence who was now identified as a scheming intelligence officer concerned with the extension of British imperial power in the Middle East. How he did so and how he underrated the part played by the Arabs in their own liberation were revealed by Professor Suleiman Moussa and by Phillip Knightley and Colin Simpson whose biographies appeared in 1966 and 1969.

Lawrence still had his champions, including Lowell Thomas, who challenged the findings of the 'revisionists'. The most formidable was John Mack, an American psychologist who had been allowed free access to the closed files of Lawrence's papers in the Bodleian Library, Oxford. Mack's 1976 biography attempted to rehabilitate Lawrence and invest him with a fresh significance that would be relevant for late twentieth-century man. Following a line first suggested by Christopher Isherwood, Mack proposed that Lawrence's inner turmoil and contradictions somehow reflected in microcosm those of his generation. Not only did he illuminate a pandemic of modern neuroses which, Dr. Mack asserted, had yet to run its course, he was a hero of non-war fit to join an American liberal pantheon alongside such figures as Gandhi. So, within twenty years, Lawrence had come full circle: mountebank, Hollywood super-hero, imperialist manipulator, neurotic, and pacifist.

Legends survive because they are worth hearing and because they are continually being re-examined, reinterpreted and retold; there is Malory's Arthur as well as Tennyson's, Hollywood's and the Romano-British warlord of the archaeologist and historian. What is important is that Lawrence, like

Arthur, lies at the heart of a legend that seems set to enjoy some sort of permanence and universality.

It is possible to distinguish two Lawrences, one a historic figure and the other a creature of mythology, in part created by Lowell Thomas. The separation of the two is difficult, not least because Lawrence willingly and sometimes guiltily helped embellish his own myth. His motive was the hope that posterity would revere him as an artist, and to that end he made his own life into a work of art.

In this book, I have tried to unravel the threads of the legend and separate the authentic from the fanciful. Since what Lawrence became was solely the consequence of what he did and what he said he had done during the First World War, I have concentrated on a reconstruction and analysis of the events in which he was involved. For reasons which became clear during the narrative, I have been deliberately cautious about accepting without question his own words and have turned to other sources, some hitherto unknown or little used. I have also devoted much space to that other aspect of Lawrence which demands close investigation, his legend. Here and elsewhere, I have endeavoured to place Lawrence within the context of his times and draw attention to the activities of others who worked with him but whose efforts have too often been overlooked.

Some time after the completion of this book, Jeremy Wilson's *Lawrence of Arabia*, a biography authorised by Lawrence's surviving brother, appeared. Its approach was radically different from mine and having read it I felt no need to revise my conclusions. I hope that I have offered new perspectives on Lawrence as a figure from history and a historical phenomenon. Whether his stature has been enhanced or reduced is for my readers to judge.

St Andrews, St George's Day, 1992.

One

FROM BIRTH TO MANHOOD

August 1888–August 1914

All Arabic and Turkish place-names are as rendered
in the current *Times Atlas*.

I

ANCESTRY AND INHERITANCE

T.E. LAWRENCE'S birth, upbringing and education were not an obvious
preparation for his later life. What he ultimately became was decided
by the outbreak of war in August 1914. By offering himself to the British
army, he put aside his private ambitions and, like millions of others, surrendered his future to forces beyond his control.

At this time, Lawrence was at a loose end. He was twenty-six, a gifted,
personable scholar who had travelled extensively in Syria and Palestine;
he was competent in Arabic and well along a road which seemed to lead
towards a distinguished academic future. He was not sure whether he
wanted to continue the journey. 'I am not going to put all my energies
into rubbish like writing history, or becoming an archaeologist,' he had
written three years before. 'I would rather write a novel even, or become
a newspaper correspondent.' These dreams suddenly evaporated. He
became a soldier and was posted to Military Intelligence where he proved
useful to his commanders and found an outlet for energies and talents
which had been hitherto hidden. He had a quick mind, relished his new
tasks and exploited the chances which they offered. But the forces which
a public emergency released in him were already there, implanted by heredity and the influences of family, friends and tutors, who in turn embodied
the attitudes and preoccupations of the age in which Lawrence grew to
manhood.

Thomas Edward Lawrence ('Ned' to his family and companions) was
born on 16 August 1888 at Tremadoc in North Wales where his parents
had rented a small house. His father, who called himself Thomas Lawrence,
had the immediately recognisable bearing and manners of a gentleman,
which he was. He had been born in 1846, Thomas Robert Chapman, grandson of an Irish baronet, and on the death of an elder brother had inherited
a country house and estate at South Hill, two miles from the small town
of Castletown Devlin in Westmeath. His family had counted for something in Westmeath since the Elizabethan conquest and colonisation of
Gaelic Ireland. Then the Chapmans had been granted lands through, it
was believed, the backstairs influence of a courtier kinsman, Sir Walter
Raleigh. They were already a family on the move, having in a few
generations risen from the counting house to the squirearchy of Tudor
Leicestershire.

At some stage in his youth, Lawrence had discovered his father's family history and all his life he set some store by his gentle blood and Irish ancestry. He also knew something about his maternal grandmother's family, the Vansittarts, and took an interest in their activities. Lawrence's attachments to his lineage and roots were strong and sentimental. In 1927 he had a daydream about buying some acres in Westmeath 'to keep some of Walter Raleigh's gift in the family of which I have the honour of being not the least active member'. Two years later he told the Labour MP Ernest Thurtle that his 'experience in many camps' had convinced him he was 'a very normal sort of Anglo-Irishman'. Just what qualities this stereotype might possess, Lawrence hinted elsewhere. Irishmen, he thought, were generally a disappointing breed. 'They go so far, magnificently, and cease to grow,' but there were exceptions like the playwright Sean O'Casey.

Lawrence could freely romanticise his Irishness, but he was unable to enjoy the prestige of his pedigree openly, or assume his father's patrician port. He was illegitimate. In 1873 Thomas Chapman had married a cousin, Elizabeth Hamilton Boyd, the daughter of a neighbouring squire. In nine years she gave her husband four daughters and much distress. A mean-spirited and vixenish woman, Mrs Chapman suffered from a manic religiosity which drove her to hand out Protestant tracts to the local Catholic peasantry. Their priests nicknamed her the 'Holy Viper'.

By the beginning of 1885, Chapman had taken a mistress, Sarah Junner. Sarah, a fine-featured and strong-willed Scottish girl, had entered South Hill in 1879 as a nanny. A capable body, she soon took over the management of the household from Mrs Chapman, whose mind was elsewhere, and introduced some joy into what must have been a gloomy ménage. Sarah had been born in Sunderland in 1861, the illegitimate daughter of Elizabeth Junner and John Junner, a shipwright who may have been a kinsman. After her mother's death (from drink when she was eight or nine) Sarah was placed with her grandparents in Perthshire, and when they died, she was passed to an aunt, the wife of a Scottish Episcopalian minister at Blairgowrie in the same county. She followed this couple to Skye from where she was recruited to the Chapman household, no doubt recommended by her links with the kirk. Until her death in 1959 she spoke with a slight Scottish burr.

When Victorian gentlemen became dissatisfied with their wives, they often found mistresses from the lower classes whom they would establish in discreet homes. Thomas Chapman went further; he abandoned his wife and South Hill and set up house with Sarah thirty miles or so away in Dublin. Here their first son, Montague Robert, was born at the end of December 1885. Chapman family tittle-tattle alleged that the couple, pretending to be man and wife, had been discovered by a former servant who overheard Sarah call herself Mrs Chapman when ordering groceries. What is certain is that the pair could not hope to sustain the pretence of being man and wife in Ireland and so fled to anonymity in North Wales.

Divorce was impossible. The 1857 Matrimonial Causes Act permitted legal separation on the grounds of one act of misconduct by the wife, and two by the husband. Mrs Chapman's life was impeccable, so her husband could not start proceedings; nor would he abandon Sarah. His own desertion and infidelity gave his wife adequate grounds for a suit, but her religious views ruled out such an action. The problem was simply but illegally resolved by Thomas and Sarah who took the surname Lawrence and behaved to the world as if they were married.

Soon after Ned's birth, his parents embarked on a nomadic life which lasted eight years. From Tremadoc they passed to Kirkcudbright, where their third son, William, was born in 1889, and then into exile at Dinard on the Normandy coast. There was a brief excursion to Jersey in 1894 for the birth of their fourth son, Frank, who, if he had been born on French soil, would have been liable for conscription. By the end of the year, the Lawrences were back in England and set up house in a red-brick villa at Langley in the New Forest. Their travels ended in 1896 when they settled at 2 Polstead Road, a newly built villa in North Oxford, where their fifth and last son, Arnold, was born in 1900.

This restless way of life was forced on the Lawrences by fear of public exposure. Had they been Bohemians or radicals embracing the novel and outrageous doctrines of free love, they could have cocked a snook at the mores of the rest of society and flaunted their liaison. But they were not. Mr and Mrs Lawrence were conservative and conventional by temperament, and upheld the prevailing morality. Once, when T.E.Lawrence mentioned Oscar Wilde, he was rebuked by his parents, who shared the widespread revulsion against a writer whose vices had made him a moral outcast. Yet while they might have reviled Wilde, the Lawrences must have been uncomfortably aware of two other recent scandals, the Dilke and Parnell affairs, both of which involved adultery and triggered spasms of typically British prurience and sermonising. In order not to fall victim to their own morality, the couple always had to be wary.

Even after they had put down roots in Oxford, Mr and Mrs Lawrence were circumspect. Over-intimate social contacts could have led to the exposure of their secret and so were avoided. Mr Lawrence was always polite but aloof, and his wife did not make the customary social calls. She was also noticeably uneasy in the company of those whom she had been brought up to regard as her 'betters', but more at ease with workmen who came to her house. As a result those acquainted with the Lawrences remarked on what seemed the social disparity between the pair. When he was old enough to understand such matters, T.E.Lawrence also sensed it.

He had been born into a society which was deferential and hierarchical, but not rigid. The able and determined could move up, while the feckless slipped down. Lawrence came to believe that his father had been socially diminished by his liaison with his mother while she had been elevated. He was aware of the lowliness of her origins and made no attempt to gloss over or glamorise them. In a confessional letter written in 1927 to Mrs Bernard Shaw, he described his mother as 'a child of sin' nurtured on Skye by a 'bible-thinking Presbyterian', and in another he caller her 'a charity child'. She had risen in the world and, impelled by motives of possession, had ensnared and tamed a wild Irish milord. Or, in Lawrence's words, 'She was wholly wrapped up in my father, whom she carried away jealously from his former life and country, against great odds; and whom she kept as the trophy of her power.' His father had been degraded by these events. Lawrence had contrived for himself a picture of his father's previous existence which came straight from the pages of R.S.Surtees or Somerville and Ross. For his son, at least, Thomas Chapman of South Hill was a boisterous Irish squireen whose life was a harum-scarum rout of hard riding, shooting and drink, but not, it seems, womanising. By the time he had reached suburban Oxford, this fellow had been recast by his wife into a benevolent, passive bourgeois.

Thomas Lawrence had not only been forced to jettison his pastimes and indulgences; his standard of living had fallen. His rents and investments were still his, but they had to be divided between two households. This was a thin time for Irish squires, a period of agrarian wars between landlords and tenants (Westmeath was a major centre of disorder in the 1870s and 1880s), Gladstone's Land Acts and an agricultural depression. Thomas Lawrence did not suffer the full effects of a dwindling rent roll for, like others of his kind, he had shifted capital into industrial and government stocks. When deductions had been made for the upkeep of Mrs Chapman and his daughters at South Hill, he was left with about £400 a year to support his Oxford household. Yet his son believed that the burden of the two establishments had 'reduced his means to a craftsman's income'. This was not only untrue but showed how little Lawrence understood of other people's lives. In the years when he was growing up, a skilled artisan lucky enough to be in permanent employment earned between £75 and £100 and was considered to be among the aristocracy of labour. Wherever Thomas Lawrence the elder stood in the social order of Oxford, he kept his family without having to work. He was, as he called himself when his sons were enrolled at Oxford High School, of 'independent means', and his annual income placed him securely in the ranks of the professional middle classes who lived around him in North Oxford. But what social position did he bestow on his sons?

The question was an important one for the young Lawrence. The private knowledge of his gentle ancestry meant much to his self-esteem, which was understandable in an age which set store by the medieval notion that moral virtue was inherited with nobility of blood. The cult of the English gentleman was at its height when Lawrence was growing up. Its dogmas would have been familiar to him from the example and advice of his father, the counsel offered in the popular boys' magazines available at home and what he heard from clergymen and schoolmasters. As a Church Lads' Brigade leader, in his teens, he would have been responsible for broadcasting these ideas to young men from the working classes. In essence they were simple and derived from a late-Victorian appreciation of the principles of Christian knighthood, so the English gentleman was expected to show a respect and reverence for women, and generosity and protectiveness towards the poor and weak, and above all to live according to high principles of honour and truth. These virtues were the natural inheritance of those born gentlemen and it was not surprising that men on the make often concocted noble ancestors. Oscar Wilde invented a kinship with a Cromwellian swashbuckler, Colonel de Wilde, and Sir Arthur Conan Doyle wove fantasies about the ancient Doyles, whom he believed were Norman warlords. This sort of fancy was taken to characteristic extremes by Lawrence's first biographer Lowell Thomas, who embellished the Lawrence family tree with a Crusader and a brace of Victorian warrior proconsuls, Sir Henry and Sir John Lawrence. This fiction was further evidence that noble blood conveyed more than quarterings: it transmitted nobility of character and courage.

Lawrence was unsure where exactly he fitted in. From his first days in Oxford, if not earlier, he had been fascinated by the chivalric past and its trappings, and so the blood links with Raleigh and his Chapman forbears, with their seat at Killua Castle, must have had a special significance for him. As a schoolboy and undergraduate, he was profoundly interested in the highest expressions of the chivalric ethic, the Crusades and the *chansons de geste* which extolled the bravery and honour of semi-legendary knights who, like Sir Galahad, incidentally offered models for late-Victorian and Edwardian boyhood. As a historian, Lawrence was never blind to the greed and inhumanity of the Crusaders, whose activities he studied with the cold eye of the historian of war. Yet his admission that he had been driven by 'impulses' deep within him suggests a belief that warrior adventurousness could be carried in the blood.

Gentle blood may have contained rare essences of leadership and knightly courage, but for Lawrence it could not ensure entry into the gentlemanly caste. His birth was one disbarment, his early education another. The public schools, temples of the cult of the gentleman, were beyond the purse of

Mr Lawrence, whose boys were sent to Oxford High School to learn alongside the sons of tradesmen. Oxford University followed and, with it, the everyday company of men who by birth and public school education had acquired the status of gentlemen. Then and later at army headquarters at Cairo, Lawrence penetrated their society. Their reactions to him were mixed; those, like Sir Ronald Storrs and George Lloyd, who were impressed by his perceptiveness, charm and learning became his friends. Others had misgivings. There was, according to Mrs Winifred Fontana, the wife of the British Consul at Aleppo, 'something uncouth in Lawrence's manner contrasting with a donnish precision of speech'. 'He had none of a gentleman's instincts,' remarked Henry ('Chips') Channon, a minor Tory politician and social butterfly, who resented Lawrence's 'strutting about the [Versailles] Peace Conference in Arab Dress'. Flamboyance together with unmuted cleverness were not gentlemanly traits. In fact they were just the sort of affectations which public schools existed to excise.[1]

There was always something socially incongruous about Lawrence. His father had given him the blood of the gentry, the class which traditionally bore arms and ruled. He was proud of his connections, and could even joke about how they were flawed. 'Bars Sinister', he told Lionel Curtis, 'are rather jolly ornaments. You feel so like a flea in the legitimate prince's bed.' He could also stand back and make fun of some features of the gentlemanly code. He mocked the punctilious rituals of the army, jesting which was shared by a handful of public school brothers-in-arms. Yet he had to fight back an urge to enforce the code when, in 1922, he was confronted at Uxbridge with an RAF Commanding Officer who brutally hectored new recruits. Lawrence was appalled 'that an officer should so play the cad', and wanted to strike him. By then he had found himself a satisfactory social position, a gentleman ranker who divided his life between the barrack hut and the salons of the nation's literary and political elite. It was oddly fitting for a man who, as a child, had listened to details of his noble pedigree and witnessed his mother's familiarity with workmen.

Mrs Lawrence could offer her son no distinguished family tree. Her blood, as Lawrence knew, was Scottish with a trace of Norse, presumably from her father, who may have been Norwegian. There were some faint grounds for speculation about a kinship of blood and spirit with General Gordon, with whom Lawrence was sometimes compared. When Bernard Shaw made the link, fearful that Lawrence might reveal the same fanaticism, he replied, 'There is only a superficial likeness I think: though my mother was a Gordon.' This may have been so, but Sarah Lawrence gave her son something more formidable than a tenuous connection with a famous clan.

Throughout her life, Mrs Lawrence bore the stamp of the Evangelical creed she had absorbed in Scotland. Her profound religious faith, which gave her an inner strength and sense of purpose, rested upon a simple theology. Like all who felt the saving Grace of Christ, she served Him, and ordered her life according to the ordinances of the Bible, whose literal truth was unquestionable. As an Evangelical, she was bound to spread the Word and reveal its power by the example of her own life.

Yet, when tempted, Sarah Lawrence had followed her instincts and taken a man from his wife, another devout woman. Her action had been sinful, cutting her off from the community of believers and even, if she failed to repent, from salvation itself. In the language of her own faith, Sarah Lawrence was a licentious woman. By becoming and remaining Thomas Chapman's common law wife – preachers used a blunter word – she was living in breach of God's law. She found the weight of sin unbearable. All her life, she was haunted by this anguish. In her eighties and during a bout of flu, she was heard to murmur several times, 'God loves the sinner, hates the sin. God hates the sin, loves the sinner.'[2]

Mrs Lawrence's inner suffering was eased by the spiritual comfort of an Anglican Evangelical, Canon Alfred Christopher, the Rector of St Aldate's, Oxford. Mr and Mrs Lawrence first encountered this determined clergyman in 1895 at Ryde where he was on one of his many missions of conversion. He not only offered comfort, but probably encouraged the Lawrences to make their permanent home in Oxford. The city had much to offer; the new high school gave the boys the chance of a good academic education which would not stretch the family income, and the Lawrences would be welcomed into the St Aldate's congregation.

Ever since he had taken the incumbency of St Aldate's in 1859, Canon Christopher had followed the central tenet of Evangelicalism and looked for converts, especially among undergraduates. Young men, saved for Christ, would, at the canon's bidding, become teachers, clergymen and missionaries and disseminate the Evangelical gospel. This pattern was followed by three of Mrs Lawrence's sons. Her eldest, Robert, qualified as a doctor and after front-line war service became a medical missionary in China in 1925, where she joined him. William, the third son, followed a successful Oxford career as a historian and athlete by taking up a teaching post at the boys' school in Delhi. Before his enlistment in the army in September 1914, the fourth son, Frank, had been deeply involved in the Church Lads' Brigade as an organiser and leader of their summer camps.

Mrs Lawrence actively encouraged her sons in these vocations, which were as spiritually satisfying for her as they were for them. Although her guide, Canon Christopher, would have rejected the Anglo-Catholic doctrine of confession, he may well have discovered the truth about the

Lawrences' union. Whether or not at his prompting, Mrs Lawrence came to believe that she could redeem her own sin through service to God as a Christian mother. Though her sons had been conceived in wickedness, they would grow to manhood in godliness. Then, in accordance with Evangelical doctrine, they would be ready to serve God's purpose.

The regime at 2 Polstead Road was typical of that in contemporary Evangelical households in Britain and the United States, and had its roots in the traditions of English and Scottish Puritanism. Family prayers, which were believed to be a bulwark against moral waywardness, were held daily, and there were frequent readings from the annotated family Bible. The byways to vice were blocked by Mrs Lawrence's strictures against strong drink (Mr Lawrence appears to have been allowed an occasional glass of claret), the non-Shakespearean theatre, and dancing. Flirtation was impossible. Girls were kept at a distance and Mrs Lawrence saw to it that her sons stayed clear of such opportunities for dalliance as the annual St Giles Fair or Christmas parties. There were no incontinent words or thoughts. The domestic moral tone was such that, when Frank found himself a junior subaltern in the mess of the 3rd Gloucesters, he was horrified by what he heard. 'I cannot describe the language, sentiments and thoughts freely expressed here by the officers,' he told his brother William. 'It is beyond words abominable.' In a letter written to be delivered to his parents if he were killed in action, he admitted to having lived 'through indescribable depths of infamy' from which he emerged unsoiled thanks to what he had learned at home. 'If I had been accustomed to going to theatres, music halls etc. in the seemingly harmless way other boys go I should have found it trebly hard to have kept myself clean.'[3]

Mrs Lawrence's Puritanism was not just a barricade against vice. There was a strong vein in contemporary religious thought which insisted that moral weaknesses could be passed from one generation to another like the cast of the jaw or the colour of eyes. In terms of moral heredity, her sons had a baleful pedigree. Their mother lived in sin, their maternal grandmother had borne an illegitimate child and died from drink, and, if T.E. Lawrence's version of his father's life in Ireland contains even a shadow of truth, there was a tendency to loose living on his side of the family. Mrs Lawrence would have her work cut out to prevent recidivism, and there could be no sparing the rod or the sermon.

There was a positive side to the Puritan regimen of Lawrence's childhood. Learning was held in high regard by Evangelicals, who saw ignorance as the yoke-devil of vice. Education had to be at the centre of the Lawrence boys' lives if they were to develop intellectual gifts necessary for their future callings. Much energy therefore was concentrated on their education; reading was encouraged, they were exhorted to work hard at school and, to judge by the family letters, the household was a place of intellectual stimulation in which books and ideas were commonly discussed. In consequence all the young Lawrences flourished at school, passed exams and proceeded to the university at Oxford or Cambridge. Their achievements were, in the eyes of Mrs Lawrence, stepping-stones towards future vocations in the service of God.

On 20 July 1919, while attending the Paris Peace Conference, Lawrence admitted his bastardy to his friend and fellow guest at the Continental Hotel, Colonel Richard Meinertzhagen. The colonel's reply, a characteristic mixture of common sense and flippancy, was that 'In these enlightened times, it mattered little and anyway he shared something in common with Jesus Christ.' Lawrence had already confided the circumstances of his birth to several close friends and by the time of his death they were widely known, although never publicised. It seems to have been common knowledge among Lawrence's brother officers at Aqaba, one of whom was overheard to remark, 'He's a bastard, did you know?', much to the irritation of some other-ranks who were near by. According to Robert Graves, 'he was not informed of the "guilty secret" until he was so emancipated that, as he told me, "My mother was shocked that we weren't shocked at her news and that we took it lightly."' Lawrence told Mrs Bernard Shaw that he had uncovered the truth when he was about ten, but delayed letting his mother know of his discovery until his father's death in April 1919.[4]

How Lawrence had unravelled the 'guilty secret' when so young can only be guessed. Like all children, he must have questioned his parents about their own childhoods and enquired after relations. He was a quick-witted, observant boy and so may have deduced something from the correspondence to and from Ireland and meetings with land agents and lawyers. His father's exciting tales about Land League terrorism may have led him to wonder why the family never visited Westmeath. An acute and thoughtful listener might have been puzzled by Mrs Lawrence's linguistic precision, which made her call Mr Lawrence 'Tom' or 'the boys' father' rather than the usual 'my husband'. Somehow, Lawrence evaluated the evidence and came to a correct conclusion. Whether he shared it with his other brothers is not known, although he did tell Arnold.

Lawrence's initial reaction must have been coloured by moral attitudes which had been instilled by his parents. Their relationship flew in the teeth of all that they publicly professed. They were defaulters against their own moral code, and maybe something worse, since they condemned others such as Wilde. Like their spiritual predecessors, the Puritans known to Samuel Butler, they:

Compound for sins they are inclined to
By damning those they have no mind to.

If the young Lawrence wholeheartedly accepted his parents' dogmas, then he was devalued by their sins, and they became hypocrites. Yet his own experience, before and after his discovery, made it abundantly clear that their union was a loving one. They were affectionate and attentive parents who loved him and cared for his welfare.

When he finally came to terms with the implications of what he had found out, Lawrence condemned the morality and faith of his parents rather than their behaviour. Knowing too well that 'living in sin' had brought them much inner torment, he developed a revulsion against all religious fanaticisms and their attendant urge to convert. 'Religious theories are the devil, when they are ridden too hard, and begin to dictate conduct,' he wrote of the Muslim Wahabbis. The same was true of the doctrines on which his parents had built their lives, and which, as their son knew, had given them endless miseries of guilt. News of the funeral service for Thomas Hardy in 1927 provoked Lawrence to sudden anger. 'I grow indignant for him, knowing that those sleek Deans and Canons were acting a lie behind his name. Hardy was too great to be suffered as an enemy of their faith: so he must be redeemed. . . . I wish these black suited apes could once see the light with which they shine.' The sentiments were those of one who, in his youth, had been on the receiving end of such proselytising. Men, Lawrence later told Liddell Hart, should be spared the attentions of converters and be left in peace.

Lawrence's brothers-in-arms, the Sunni Muslim Arabs, managed these matters better. 'The Beduin could not look for God within him: he was too sure that he was within God,' Lawrence wrote in *The Seven Pillars of Wisdom*. Looking back perhaps to the faith and observances of his family, he added:

There was a homeliness, and everyday-ness of this climatic Arab God, who was their eating and their fighting and their lusting, the commonest of their thoughts, their familiar resource and companion, in a way impossible to those whose God is so wistfully veiled from them by despair of their carnal unworthiness of Him and by decorum of formal worship. Arabs felt no incongruity in bringing God into the weaknesses and appetites of their least creditable causes.

How different from his mother's austere god, who was revealed through suffering. Lawrence's own faith in that god, learned from her, evaporated.

When it went he did not say, but in a letter to Liddell Hart he admitted that, after it had gone, he scarcely noticed the loss.

Faith might slip away unnoticed, but Lawrence could not shake off his Evangelical inheritance of thought and behaviour. All his life he adhered to that ascetic Puritanism which considered sensual indulgence an obstacle to mental concentration. Physical pleasures were to be shunned. He very rarely drank alcohol. Touring southern France in August 1908 he told his mother, 'My water-drinking is the subject of general amazement, by the way, far beyond what I had thought possible,' and hotel staff were astonished when he asked for water rather than wine. This must have pleased Mrs Lawrence, although her son overheard waiters call his choice *blague* [humbug]. Lawrence's abstinence set him apart from those of his wartime friends for whom the bar at Cairo's Shepheard's Hotel was a second home. On campaign, he disapproved of his brother officers' whisky-drinking and, long after, he found knowledge of Hilaire Belloc's drinking habits a barrier to the enjoyment of his writing.

Lawrence did not smoke, which was unusual when the habit was all but universal, especially in the Forces. Food seems not to have interested him and between sixteen and nineteen he was a vegetarian. These were the years of his French excursions and his attitude to the local cuisine was fiercely practical. Once he wrote home, 'We had déjeuner in one of the embrasures of the gateway: our déjeuner was an innocent one: nothing had to be killed to feed us. Milk, bread, butter was our total. Price 4d [two pence].' While he later relented and learned to enjoy Middle Eastern cooking, his diet was usually spare. In the 1920s and 1930s visitors to his cottage at Cloud's Hill discovered that he had perfected a form of culinary minimalism which involved their being presented with a tin-opener and cans of pre-cooked food. Those so victualled had to prop themselves up against the fireplace, since their host's Spartan regime did not permit an abundance of furniture. There were additional discomforts: cups and saucers were scarce before 1934, when Lawrence set to making some at a local pottery.

The Puritan virtue of simplicity in all mundane, physical things, which had its roots in medieval asceticism, appealed deeply to Lawrence and lay at the heart of his love affair with the desert. There was, as well, the form if not the spirit of intense Christian meditation in his interminable self-analysis. While the pietist looked within himself to uncover the nature of his soul and explore its relationship with God, Lawrence's end was the discovery of a quintessential self which was independent of any god. In the *Seven Pillars*, he presents himself as an instrument of Providence, who gave the vital impulse to the Arab national movement, rescued it and gave it direction. In this guise he became an apostle of what he called 'our creed', a secular religion which he claimed would bring political salvation to the Arabs, but the threads of self-sacrifice, single-mindedness and an urge to enlighten which run through his narrative unconsciously reflect elements of the Evangelical creed to which he had been introduced as a child.

II

BOYHOOD AND SCHOOLING, 1888–1907

L AWRENCE appears to have had a happy childhood, to judge from the accounts of his early years written soon after his death by his mother, elder brother, boyhood chums and schoolmasters. He preferred to think otherwise. The sight of the tin bath in which he had been washed as an infant, and which Mrs Lawrence had kindly passed to Robert Graves' family, gave him a 'violent revulsion to recall such physical dependency'. In his later letters, Lawrence grumbled about the constraints of family and schoolroom life and the deflection of his energies into boring tasks. 'Schools are queer places,' he warned a godson just before he went up to Eton in 1929. 'I was very happy when I finished with them all. Oxford was like a heaven to finish up with.' A few years before, he had told Robert Graves that he had been educated 'very little, very reluctantly, very badly' at school and not at all at Oxford.

Before he joined the first form at Oxford High School in September 1896, Lawrence's education had been disjointed. It had begun in France where he attended a Jesuit academy and the St Malo junior gymnastic class, and after his parents' return to England in 1894 he was taught by a governess and tutor. In those eight years, he made considerable headway. He had learned to read before he was five and practised his new skills on the police reports in the newspapers – reading matter which suggests that his parents were either unvigilant or less strict than they became in Oxford. At Oxford High School, Lawrence showed himself a well-read, apt and biddable pupil who picked up prizes for English Language, Literature, Scripture and History. The final measure of his academic achievement was a Meyricke Exhibition to Jesus College, Oxford, to read Modern History, awarded in January 1907 and worth £40 a year.

During his eleven years at school, Lawrence took great pride in his evasion of team games. When his youngest brother Arnold was about to begin his first term at the high school, Lawrence urged him to 'carry on our tradition: "no games"', forgetting for a moment that his other brother Frank was making his mark in cricket and soccer. Had Lawrence been at public boarding school, his avoidance of team games would have been a source of interminable misery, for membership of an eleven or fifteen was a passport to general acceptability; outstanding prowess on the pitch automatically won popularity with masters and boys. As it was, whenever he was coerced into a match, he would find a chance to sidle off to the edge of the playing field from where he would watch the game with a fixed grin on his face. He was not a weakling: he relished the rough and tumble of boyish horseplay and wrestling and proved himself a good distance runner. His quirkiness was discounted by his school mates who found he could take care of himself, was good-natured and had a sense of fun. All the Lawrence boys embodied the ideals of manliness, then so prized by schoolmasters. One later observed that they were 'an ideal family of boys', each 'clean in limb and life'. At one stage their brotherhood was emphasised by their mother, who dressed each for school in striped, Breton-style sweaters. Yet for Ned, in this conspicuous dress, the shift from home to school may not have been easy for, as both his teachers and fellow pupils noticed, he seemed on first meeting to be a shy and self-contained boy.

All the boys were well kempt and in good shape physically, thanks to the diligence of Mrs Lawrence. She breast-fed her first four sons, and all her life tirelessly fulfilled her responsibilities as a mother and housewife. She had control over all household routines and servants, although, unlike other women in her position, she preferred to do some of the chores herself. When her boys were young, however, she was helped by nannies. Every particular of their welfare was given careful attention. During the summers of 1906, 1907 and 1908 when Ned was bicycling through France, his mind full of matters Gothic, he was chased by anxious notes from his mother, who was concerned about the state of his health and wardrobe. He could not have cared less, and thought her obsessions trifling: 'Mother was always caring (to my mind) too much about such essentials as food and clothes,' he told Mrs Bernard Shaw in 1927. 'Life itself doesn't seem to matter, in comparison with thought and desire.' Maybe not for an adult determined to live within himself on his own terms, but the eighteen-year-old in France took care to assure his mother that all was well with his laundry. In turn, he cautioned her not to overstretch herself with housework, and also warned his father not to weary himself with domestic repairs. 'Do nothing rather than too much,' he advised; 'you are worth more than the house.'

Maternal care and Mrs Lawrence's wholesome but very plain cooking made sure that her son was a robust, sturdy boy, but small for his age and class, at least when set alongside his brothers. At fifteen he was five foot four and a half inches, and a year later he was just under five foot six, the height he remained for the rest of his life. The average height for a middle-class boy at the time would have been nearer five foot nine, and many were taller; brother William topped six feet. Mrs Lawrence mistakenly blamed her son's shortness on a broken leg, gained in a schoolyard tussle when he intervened to rescue a victim of bullying, probably in his sixteenth or seventeenth year. The spare diet which he was following could not have stimulated either growth or girth. Between 1905 and 1908 he limited himself to vegetables, milk (drunk by the litre in France), eggs, fruit, cakes and abundant helpings of porridge, which he believed reinstated energy lost in exercise. His small frame got plenty of this, running and bicycling. Just after his eighteenth birthday, the sight of his biceps, seen when he was sea-bathing, amazed a French mademoiselle. 'She thinks I am Hercules,' he told his mother.

Inside the Lawrence household, the boys' moral welfare and correction were Mrs Lawrence's province. She was untroubled by the theories of child psychology to be laid down by the pundits of a later generation. For boys there was simply right and wrong, so when her sons misbehaved or flouted her authority they were whipped on their bare bottoms. Ned was the most wilful and suffered more chastisement than his brothers. Among his misdeeds were a refusal to persevere with piano lessons, and indulgence with a friend in that schoolboy vice known to Edwardian clerics and educators as 'beastliness'. Many years later Mrs Lawrence was still sticking to her code for she advised Lord Astor that his horses would win races only if they were whipped. Her views and actions were commonplace at a time when all but a handful of parents and pedagogues were guided by that bleak principle, Castigo te non quod odio habeam, sed quod amam (I beat you not from hatred, but out of love). Mr Lawrence disagreed. According to his son Arnold, he found the infliction of such punishment distasteful and against the grain of his nature. Nevertheless, he allowed his wife to usurp what was generally considered a duty of fatherhood – Prince Albert had thrashed his sons at least once. Ned Lawrence did not openly resent this form of repression, although he later admitted a deep fear of punishment at school, which no doubt explains why he behaved so well there.[1]

Nothing of this appears in Mrs Lawrence's short memoir of her son, written soon after his death. She recalled a small, strong infant, who from the moment he could crawl was recklessly exploring the world around him.

She also remembered a cheerful, warm-hearted lad, who was always helpful. What he became remained a source of puzzlement to her. Anxious to probe her mind on this subject, Thomas Jones, a senior civil servant, quizzed her at a lunch party in February 1936. She could only answer, 'He was a genius.' Later, Jones noted in his diary, 'The old lady, I imagine, was much more at home with the Chinese medical missionary than with Ned, who had travelled in worlds beyond her gaze.'[2]

Meeting her a few months before at another lunch, a formal affair given in her son's honour, Colonel Meinertzhagen was impressed by Mrs Lawrence's bearing. She was 'a pathetic little figure with all the pluck and character of her son and some of his looks', who sat through the speeches 'with a very charming smile on her face, looking very young and terribly proud'. She had, as everyone recognised, bequeathed to Ned her clear, blue eyes, strong jaw line and crop of almost Nordic blonde hair. There were too, as she and he were aware, interior likenesses, for each possessed iron willpower and single-mindedness.

After his final return from the Middle East in 1922, Lawrence knew that he had irrevocably parted company from his mother. 'I have a terror of her knowing anything about my feelings or convictions or way of life,' he told Mrs Bernard Shaw, since such knowledge would leave her 'damaged: violated: no longer mine'. Mrs Lawrence had already been distressed by what she had read of the draft of the *Seven Pillars*. 'The horrors of the book shake her painfully,' Lawrence wrote, 'and she hates my having noted, or seen such things.' In time Lawrence dreaded the arrival of her letters and felt uneasy when she asked to hear from him as 'we haven't a subject we dare to be intimate upon.' What he feared most was a reassertion of her possessiveness and a revival of attempts to dominate him. He was forced to resist 'letting her get ever so little inside the circle of my integrity; and she is always hammering and sapping to come in.' The deaths in 1915 of her sons Frank and William and of her husband four years later had made her intensify her efforts. 'She has so lived in her children, and my father, that she cannot relieve herself on herself at all. And it isn't right to cry out to your children for love.'

To some extent these were the reactions of a disturbed man wanting only to create his own world and live inside it, but they also contained an element of childhood emotions recollected at the onset of middle age. The battle which was still flickering on as Lawrence approached forty had started in the nursery. Its features were recalled in another letter to Mrs Bernard Shaw: 'No trust ever existed between my mother and myself. Each of us jealously guarded his or her own individuality, whenever we came together. I always felt that she was laying siege to me and would conquer, if I left a chink unguarded.'

Twice, Lawrence chose words from the vocabulary of siegecraft to explain their relationship. He was a fortress, she the investing army, ever seeking some weak point which could be exploited. He knew much about sieges. The close study of medieval fortification was one of his ruling passions between his eighteenth and twenty-first years. His painstaking examination of curtain walls, barbicans and flanking towers, and analyses of the advantages and disadvantages of defenders and assailants, in a curious way touched on his own life.

Lawrence knew that prolonged sieges were marked by alternate periods of lassitude and violent activity. Presumably his mother's efforts to penetrate his defences followed the same pattern, otherwise family life at 2 Polstead Road would have been a continuous wrangle, which it was not. From what is known of her own and Evangelical views in general, Mrs Lawrence wanted to get control over all her sons' minds so that they would understand how to fight temptation and prepare themselves for lives in which their Christian values would bring benefit to others. With Robert, William and Frank she accomplished her end, but with Ned things were different. So they were with Arnold, who, encouraged by Ned, ignored efforts at conversion.

Yet Ned was not a complete disappointment. Mrs Lawrence must have approved of his austerity and schoolboy seriousness but, as he would remember, there was never trust between them. Either she suspected Ned of dissembling or else she detected a shallowness in his sincerity. There was certainly something about his peculiar smile, which looked like a smirk, that might have troubled her and perhaps for good reason. Unknown to her, he knew her 'secret' and therefore how far she had fallen short of the standards she tried to impose. That smile certainly vexed others. Seeing him grin in 'that typical Mona Lisa manner', a fellow undergraduate immediately assumed that Lawrence was secretly laughing at him. This was not so, Lawrence assured him; 'Everything amuses me.'[3]

When Lawrence was small, his mother had quite literally held the whip hand, so skirmishes were one-sided, but not decisive. Her son's will stayed unbroken and, as he grew into manhood, physical coercion was replaced by a more subtle kind, based on affection. The outlook was not completely unpromising for Mrs Lawrence. Ned's school progress must have been cause for satisfaction, just as a few years later she was keenly interested in his decorations for gallantry and even hoped that he might get the Victoria Cross.[4] Yet achievement was not a goal in itself: it took on a greater worth when it was harnessed to some higher ambition. This Lawrence lacked when he left school in 1907.

In fact, by this time, Lawrence's character was being moulded into a recognisable shape, but it was not one which his mother could comprehend. As its outlines became clearer to her, a clash was inevitable. Unlike many others in the long siege which must have occurred inside 2 Polstead Road, this engagement was conducted by letter.

The opening shot was fired by Mrs Lawrence and its weight and trajectory can be judged from Ned's reply, written at the beginning of August 1908 when he was at Aigues Mortes on the shores of the Mediterranean. He wrote, 'You are all wrong, Mother dear, a mountain may be a great thing, a grand thing, "But if it is better to be peaceful, and quiet, and pure", pacata posse omnia mente tieri [Lucretius V 1203], if that is the best state, then a plain is the best country.' In such a landscape 'one can sit down quietly and think, of anything, or nothing which Wordsworth says is best.' Beauty and calm were absent from mountain peaks where 'there is always the feeling that one is going up or down: that one will be better, will see clearer from the top than from the valleys; stick to the Plains, Mother, & all ye little worms [family argot for the brothers], you'll be happiest there.' Mrs Lawrence hoped that her sons would soar, overcome spiritual heights and fulfil a mission in the world, not enjoy self-indulgent, sedentary dreams.

Contemplative exile had for some time been on Lawrence's mind. Among poems he had strongly recommended to an undergraduate friend, Vyvyan Richards, had been Tennyson's 'The Palace of Art', in which the aesthete builds himself a 'pleasure house' of art and artefact on a high mountain.

> My soul would live alone unto herself
> In her high palace there.
> ... I sit as God, holding no form of creed,
> But contemplating all.

Finally isolated hedonism cloys, and the builder descends to 'make a cottage in the vale' where he repents of his selfishness. Remoteness is the theme of the few lines from Shelley's 'Julian and Madallo: A Conversation', which were the prelude to Lawrence's letter from Aigues Mortes.

> I love all waste
> And solitary places; where we taste
> The pleasure of believing what we see
> Is boundless, as we wish our souls to be....

It was an appropriate piece, in that these had been the thoughts of another young English exile on the shores of the Mediterranean. There may, however, have been more to Lawrence's choice of this poem than mere geographical appositeness. He read verse carefully and, while his tastes were wide, Shelley does not appear to have enjoyed the same favour as Tennyson, Christina Rossetti, the medieval sagas and *chansons*. What may have drawn Lawrence to 'Julian and Maddallo' was Shelley's preface, which lays out the temperaments of the two protagonists. Each was a man capable of action who had confined himself to the world of the spirit. Count Madallo, based upon Byron, was an Italian nobleman 'of most consummate genius', a word spinner, a traveller, contemptuous of all lesser men, and aware of the nothingness of human life. Had he chosen, he could have been 'the redeemer of his degraded country'. Julian, like Shelley an atheist, believes in the power of man over his own mind, and of the possibility that society can improve itself. 'We know', he argues,

> That we have power over ourselves to do
> And suffer – what, we know not till we try;
> But something nobler than to live and die –
> So taught those kings of old philosophy
> Who reigned, before Religion made men blind;
> And those who suffer with their suffering kind
> Yet feel their faith, Religion.

Lawrence, by his rigorous physical exercise and diet, had shown he had a power over himself and that he could be a doer as well as a thinker. Many years later he confessed to having had passing dreams of doing something 'nobler'. At the end of the *Seven Pillars* he wrote, 'I had dreamed, at the City School in Oxford, of hustling into form, while I lived, the new Asia which time was inexorably bringing upon us.' Learning about Garibaldi and the Risorgimento aroused a schoolboy ambition to lead a national movement, or so Lawrence told Liddell Hart. If this was so, his reaction was understandable. The colourful tale of the unification of Italy in the 1860s was presented in British schools as a high adventure in which courageous visionaries overcame huge obstacles and won a triumph for the noble cause of liberal nationalism. Reading of this, whether in a school textbook or in the vivid pages of G.A.Henty, an imaginative boy could easily identify with Garibaldi and his guerrillas, and invent a destiny for himself. The same impulse made Lawrence mislead his schoolfriends with the claim that he shared a birthday, 15 August, with another man of destiny, Napoleon.

At the age of twenty, Lawrence had set his mind on another ideal, that of the contemplative, introspective life. As he insisted to his mother, he had no desire to ascend the heights. Fulfilment of this ambition would require physical detachment from the routines of the household and its noise. Lawrence had developed an intense loathing for noise. The nocturnal barking dogs of southern France irritated him intensely– 'my brain would go if I lived here long,' he complained in a letter of August 1908. When he returned to Oxford, he asked for and obtained a divorce from his family. After discussions and advice from Canon Christopher and his academic mentors, Mr Lawrence agreed to provide his son with a study and bedroom in a bungalow built late in 1908 at the bottom of the garden.

Lawrence got his way and achieved self-imposed exile. Not only was he cut off from the rumpus of the household and his three brothers aged eight, fourteen and eighteen, but he had secured an additional defence against his mother. Family life played an important part in the Evangelical regime, and Lawrence's wish to distance himself from it must have been a blow to her. Nevertheless she could console herself with his continued performance of his duties at St Aldate's, even if she was unsure whether his heart was in them. There was already a strange duality about her son: he could and did quote an atheist poet to her yet, at the same time, extol the value of Christina Rossetti's 'The Martyr' in which the Christian virgin seeks and finds perfection through God.

The decision to pander to Ned's wish for solitude and silence had been his father's. He had always fostered his sons' intellectual interests and saw it as his duty to inspire and direct their enthusiasms. As small boys they had learned to sail, ride and cycle under his instruction, and they had read boys' magazines with him. Ned learned how to ride his bicycle and to maintain it from his father, who also passed on to him his considerable skills as a photographer.

Encouraged by his father, Ned had become addicted to antiquarianism which, by his sixteenth birthday, had all but taken over his life. His enthusiasm was total and all-consuming – of energy, thought and time. Walking around Oxford his curiosity had been aroused by tiles and shards, uncovered as workmen dug the foundations for new buildings. Coins and bones were also revealed, and he was soon offering his pocket money to labourers for their finds. Into his hands came medieval artefacts, pieces of pottery, fragments of glass, and brass jettons (trading tokens) which aroused his enthusiasm for the Middle Ages. Brass-rubbing expeditions into the Oxfordshire countryside followed, on which he was often accompanied by another budding antiquary, his schoolfriend, C.F.C.('Scroggs') Beeson.

By 1905, Lawrence was an accomplished brass-rubber, to judge from examples of his work which remain among the Ashmolean collection; they include a beautiful copy of an early fifteenth-century knight, nearly seven feet tall, from Wisbech in Cambridgeshire. Passion soon developed into fanaticism. There was an element of ruthlessness in his antiquarianism: box-pew floors in Waterperry church, five miles from Oxford, were torn up in the quest for a hidden knight. As an undergraduate, he bicycled out to churches with a screwdriver in his pocket, and while a friend kept 'cave', he unscrewed Tudor brasses and looked at their reverses to discover if they were re-used spoil from the dissolved monasteries. In August 1905, accompanied by his father, he cycled through East Anglia, rubbing brasses, examining churches and castles, and touring museums. The forty-nine-year-old Mr Lawrence was well up to the cracking pace, as his son noted when they reached Colchester on the last leg of the trip. 'We came here from Ipswich over a rather hilly road 18 miles long. Still we took two hours over it; and walked about six hills; a proceeding Father does not like. We are feeding splendidly.'

The end products of these excursions finished up hung on the walls of Lawrence's room, which was soon covered with rubbings, all numbered. He took a special joy in the bizarre figure of Ralph Hamsterley, a Tudor parson from Oddington, Oxfordshire, who was shown as a cadaver riddled with eel-like worms. Knights and ladies looked down on him as he pored over and mastered the literature of armour, heraldry and architecture. The rubbings offered a tangible link with medieval men and women, showing them as they looked at court or on the battlefield.

What captivated Lawrence were the flowers of medieval civilisation, the world of courts and courtliness, tournaments, sieges, coloured glass and manuscripts, the ballads of chivalry and the architecture of castles. He cared nothing for the roots of medieval society, and never showed any interest in the drudgery of the peasantry or manorial routines. By his nineteenth year, he had settled on castles as a subject for detailed investigation. They had a double attraction, offering scope for purely antiquarian research, measuring, examining stonework, drawing sketches and taking photographs, which Lawrence enjoyed most. There was also the intellectual challenge of piecing together evidence collected on the spot and using it to explore the minds of the castle-builders. What considerations of general strategy dictated the siting of a castle, how did the builders exploit inaccessible places created by nature, and how did novel architectural ideas travel across Europe? It was a study which fused the romantic with the intellectual. At Château Gaillard, set on an outcrop above the Seine, he was impressed by how Richard I had exploited the site. 'The whole construction bears the unmistakable stamp of genius,' he told his mother. 'Richard I must have been a far greater man than we usually consider him; he must have been a great strategist and a great engineer, as well as a great man-at-arms.' At Chepstow, Lawrence was reminded of Yniol's castle in Tennyson's 'Geraint and Enid'. Other literary associations made him take a detour in August 1908 to Hautefort, the Périgord seat of the twelfth-century balladeer, Bertrand de Born, whose verses in praise of war he must have known well.

And my heart fills with gladness when I see strong castles besieged, and the stockades broken and overwhelmed, and the warriors on the bank, girt about by fosses, with a line of strong stakes, interlaced. . . .

Such poetry, and the courtly culture which produced it, was, like the art of fortification, international. To understand both, Lawrence had to travel. He pleaded for and got his parents' backing for an excursion to Normandy in August 1906, which he toured with 'Scroggs' Beeson. A further trip followed in August 1907 when he crossed the province with his father, and then, alone, penetrated the former Angevin domains as far as the Loire. He went alone for his final and most ambitious expedition during July and August 1908. By then an undergraduate at the end of his first year, he had in mind writing a thesis on castles as part of his final degree, and his route took him southwards beyond the Loire into Provence as far as the Mediterranean coast and back through the Marches of Gascony.

On each trip, Lawrence travelled by bicycle. He could, he told his family, average 10 m.p.h. over long distances, making ninety miles a day but, since he muddled miles and kilometres, some of his claims were exaggerated. Once, in August 1906, he showed signs of flagging and he suggested that a motorbike would best suit his purposes. His parents seem to have ignored this oblique request and for the rest of his journeys he made do with a bicycle. Each excursion was carefully planned beforehand, and so his family and friends were able to write to him, addressing their letters to post offices along his projected route. His parents financed him, and on every trip he sent them details of his careful husbandry of their funds. Thanks to his vegetarian diet, Lawrence seems to have managed on between six and seven francs a day (about thirty to thirty-five pence), spending about four on an evening meal and bed for the night and the rest on postcards, postage and occasional tips. His cash, in sovereigns and five-pound notes, was kept in hidden pockets and he took care not to eat in out-of-the-way and therefore risky cafés. He was puritanical about accommodation, and when confronted in August 1908 by carpets and a spring mattress at Montoire, he told his parents, 'I prefer my polished boards in the "midi" to extra pile carpets & extra piled bills.' Back in Oxford, he duped a fellow undergraduate, Vyvyan Richards, into believing that he got by on fifty centimes (about three pence) a day.

On each excursion, Lawrence wrote extended letters home (taking great care to get exactly twenty-five centimes' worth of news in each envelope and save extra postage). He outlined where he had been, what he had seen in the way of churches and castles, exchanged gossip and gave incidental details about his meals, spending, Frenchmen encountered and local customs. The whole collection conveys a delightful impression of a dogged, hardy English schoolboy overcoming headwinds, punctures and an alien diet in his determination to see for himself and record the splendours of Gothic France. The wonderment of discovery is infectious, but always toned down a little by the practical need to record every antiquity in scholarly detail. Lawrence sought both to share his serendipity with his family and create a set of working notes for future study. One passage, describing monuments in Lenon Abbey, examined in August 1906, may stand example for many others.

> Her [Tiphaine, Countess de Beaumanoir's] face was perfect, without any mutilation and exhibited the calm repose and angelic purity which the mediaeval sculptor knew so well to blend, with a certain martial simplicity and haughtiness. . . . Opposite her on the other side of the church lay her husband assassinated in 1385. He is chiefly remarkable for two gigantic curls, each supported by a sturdy angel. He has a beard, and wears a jupon, gorget, pauldrons, brassarts, coutes, and a large sword.

Each August, the Lawrence family read much more in the same vein; they were, one assumes, as well versed in the arcane vocabulary of the antiquary as Ned. There was also room for less weighty matters, even humour, but no frivolity. At Dinard, Lawrence noticed a Pomeranian dog wearing goggles seated in his mistress's motor car; in Brittany he disparaged local over-eating, and elsewhere he noted that many Frenchmen were stout. The Limousin village dogs 'whose duty is to bark at all tourists, above all motorists, & people in knickers' (that is, shorts as worn by Lawrence) annoyed him, as did the dozen American tourists ('twangs') whom he came across at Chinon and who made him, out of national pride, tip the guide a franc (six pence). His family also heard news of old friends at Dinard, including the Chaignons, who were good-hearted hosts on each tour. Other acquaintances were followed up, and the eighteen-year-old boy recorded an earnest conversation with the Jesuit father with whom he discussed the English Anglo-Catholic movement and Oxford. His own French improved steadily and he congratulated himself on being mistaken for a native at least once on his third trip.

In May 1927, Lawrence told Liddell Hart that he had, at the age of eighteen, run away and joined the army as a private soldier. Fascinated, Liddell Hart pressed him for further details, but was disappointed, getting some inconsequential remarks about the Friday and Saturday night loutishness of his barrack mates. The same observations occurred in *The Mint*, but Lawrence was very wary of revealing the exact date of his service or his *nom de guerre* (no Thomas Edward Lawrence left the army during 1905–6), aware no doubt that they could be checked from official records. His friends and family never indicated that he was away from home for several months and he was uncertain about how long he was away, once telling Liddell Hart that it was six months. Liddell Hart was perplexed by this confession and soon after Lawrence's death made enquiries at the War Office. An examination of enlistment and discharge papers for 1905–6 drew a blank and later investigations similarly failed to trace Lawrence's service record, even though he claimed to have been attached to the Royal Garrison Artillery unit at St Mawes near Falmouth.

On one level, this fiction was an attempt by Lawrence to give his boyhood an adventurousness and glamour which it lacked. On another, it indicated his strong-mindedness and refusal to be overridden by his parents, since he gave a family quarrel as the reason for his flight. These qualities, confirmed by his insistence on a private bolt-hole in the garden, were certainly present in the young Lawrence. The resistance to his mother, the tireless pursuit of antiquarian lore and the resolution with which he sought withdrawal from domestic distractions were evidence of a formidable will. If he did not actually beat a path to the recruiting sergeant after having been thwarted, he may well have considered it.

III

OXFORD AND THE ORIENT, 1907–1910

ACCORDING to Dr David Hogarth, the true antiquary needs a 'mind which is more curious of the past than the present, loves detail for its own sake, and cares less for ends than means'. In 1908, Hogarth, a fellow of Magdalen College and newly appointed Keeper of the Ashmolean Museum, felt sure that he had found such a creature in Lawrence. What he had seen of him, first as a schoolboy who brought finds to the Museum and later as an enthusiastic undergraduate who helped catalogue pottery, convinced Hogarth that here was an interesting young man worth cultivation. Hogarth's patronage changed Lawrence's life, giving it a direction it had hitherto lacked. Academic doors would be opened for him and, guided by Hogarth, he was set on a course towards the Middle East and a career as a field archaeologist.

Lawrence's final debt to Hogarth was more than that of a scholar to his master. Soon after his death in November 1927, Lawrence wrote: 'Hogarth was a very wonderful man. . . . He was first of all human, and then charitable, and then alive. I owed him everything I had, since I was 17, which is the age when I suddenly found myself.' He counted Hogarth's death among his greatest losses, and confessed to Edward Garnett that 'He was really to me the parent I could trust, without qualification, to understand what bothered me.' Hogarth possessed 'the most civilised wisdom I've ever met'. Lawrence turned to this urbane, worldly and tolerant man as to a father – 'His advice was always the last I asked for whenever I had a question to decide.' At first, Hogarth had seen Lawrence as a potential academic like himself, who could be steered along a conventional course of scholarship towards a seat at college high table. It was a path which Hogarth had followed, but not without misgivings, for he had a restless spirit that was never at home within the confines of the common room or library. At heart he was an adventurer, a wandering antiquary driven by the search for 'hidden treasure' or the chance to uncover some 'lode of antiquarian lore'.[1] Lawrence sensed this and after his death remarked, 'His career did not fit his character.'

Hogarth had begun what he called his 'arduous apprenticeship' as an antiquary in 1887 when, twenty-five years old and fascinated by the life of Alexander the Great, he enrolled at the British School at Athens. Its routines bored him so he went off, revolver on hip, to see Macedonia for himself. He travelled widely across Turkey, Syria and Palestine, living cheaply. He excavated in Cyprus (alongside M.R.James, another embryonic don and the future writer of ghost stories) and in Egypt under the direction of Professor Flinders Petrie, the most celebrated British archaeologist of his day. In 1897 he took a turn as *The Times*'s correspondent in Crete, where he reported the Graeco-Turkish war. He became a don and wrote academic studies including *Devia Cypria*, which, to his amusement, stimulated ill-founded excitement amongst collectors of erotica.

For Hogarth, direct experience of the Middle East, 'whose ancient monuments conspicuously exalt the past at the expense of the present', was essential for any aspiring antiquary since it would both quicken and fix his enthusiasm. Lawrence, whom he realised was more at home in the past than the present, was very susceptible to such persuasion. By August 1908 his mind was made up. He gave exuberant notice of his decision in a letter home written at Aigues Mortes, an appropriate place for such a resolve since it was from here that St Louis and his Crusaders had taken ship for Egypt in 1249:

I felt that at last I had reached the way to the South, and all the glorious East; Greece, Carthage, Egypt, Tyre, Syria, Italy, Spain, Sicily, Crete ... they were all within reach. ... I fancy I know better than Keats what Cortes felt like, 'silent upon a peak in Darien'. Oh I must get down there, – farther out – again! Really this getting to the sea has almost overturned my mental balance. ...

Lawrence's imagination may have run wild, but there was a practical reason for him to undertake an expedition to the Middle East. An examination of the then little-known Crusader strongholds in the Lebanon, Syria and Palestine was a natural outcome of his studies of fortification in England, Wales and France. Furthermore, Oxford's examination statutes permitted historians to submit a thesis as part of their Final Examinations. Supported by Hogarth, Lawrence planned to offer such a study in which he would explain and demonstrate the exchange of ideas about castle-building between the Crusader states and the West. It was an ambitious project which required extensive field work in a remote region, but, if successful, it could do much to advance Lawrence's academic career.

This certainly needed promotion. The most outstanding feature of Lawrence's progress through Oxford had been his eccentric behaviour. His arrival at Jesus in October 1907 was a moment of liberation which released him from the chafing bonds of schoolmasters and parents. Like many other undergraduates he felt that now he could do as he liked and his new freedom was marked by a regime of waywardness. Fortunately, Edwardian Oxford was essentially a benign and tolerant society in which all kinds of unconventionality were more or less accepted. Even so, his quirkiness stood out and irritated some. A.G.Prŷs-Jones, a contemporary, recollected an exchange which followed one of Lawrence's visits to his rooms and which provoked the ire of one of the college 'hearties'.[2]

In his blunt Anglo-Saxon way he said 'I've just passed that lunatic Lawrence on the staircase. What's he been doing in our territory?' 'Seeing me' I replied. 'My God, Prŷs, the man's barmy. Don't you know that?' 'Well' I said 'either that or some kind of genius. I can't tell yet. Give me time, old man: I've only just met him.' 'You Welshmen do seem to have a knack of picking up the queerest fish. I know he's barmy. He doesn't run with the boats, he doesn't play anything. He just messes about on an awful drop-handled bicycle. And if he ever wore a bowler hat he'd wear it with brown boots.'

Lawrence's activities gave plenty of cause for such outbursts. Although he had rooms in college, he lived at home where, after the autumn of 1908, he used his garden bungalow as study and bedroom. He ignored established college routines by which men read and attended lectures in the morning, took athletic exercise after lunch, and between tea and dinner either worked or chatted. 'No gentleman works after dinner' was the custom, but Lawrence often studied well into the early hours of the morning. He seldom dined in college, indeed he was rarely seen to eat a square meal. Sustained by nibbling biscuits, cake, apples and raisins, Lawrence went in for occasional bouts of endurance, once working and fasting for forty-five hours at a stretch. Another bizarre form of self-discipline involved at least one nocturnal dip in the frozen Cherwell, which must have been particularly astringent for a man who had a passion for hot baths.

At night, Lawrence came alive. He would wander around Oxford after dark for some unknown purpose: he claimed that sometimes he navigated the city's sewers in a canoe. These had some attraction for him, since he descended them on another occasion with a revolver which he fired to disturb those walking above. This revolver was used at other times, once in the street to celebrate the end of his forty-five-hour fast, and again outside Prŷs-Jones's rooms to announce Lawrence's return from Syria. Strangely, Lawrence avoided the attentions of the university proctors and bulldogs, who were more accustomed to dealing with collective under-graduate rowdiness than with the pranks of a solitary night-walker.

Lawrence was a man apart, at least in outlook and behaviour. He kept clear of communal ragging and social junketings such as Eights Week. He avoided such regular college activities as rowing; he drank water rather than beer or wine; he showed no interest at all in women and so stayed silent when his companions discussed sex, and he never swore. Yet men were drawn into his company. There were undergraduates, willing to over-look Lawrence's oddities or finding them refreshing, who became part of his small circle. For them, his presence was intriguing. He arrived without warning at their rooms, shunned chairs and sofas, and chose instead to sit cross-legged on a cushion. Often he would remain frozen in the same position for hours on end, listening carefully to the flow of conversation with an enigmatic, sometimes unnerving smile fixed on his face.

There were some regular features in Lawrence's university life. In the Michaelmas Term 1908 he joined the cyclist detachment of the university Officers' Training Corps. His elder brother Robert had taken the same course while reading medicine at St John's and Ned may have been keen to exploit the opportunities for cycling and shooting. He was an apt cadet who proved himself a good shot and capable scout, although his failure to master the skills of tying puttees vexed his sergeant-major. His volunteer-ing was a reminder that he came from a patriotic family for whom service to their country was a natural duty. For some years, like his brothers, he had been a leader in the St Aldate's Church Lads' Brigade. The Boys'

Brigade movement had been started in 1883 as a vehicle for the moral regeneration of working-class youth and by 1909 it had over 60,000 members. Lawrence and other middle-class young men acted as leaders and guides, steering their charges towards Sunday School and Bible classes and away from street-corner gangs, public houses, music halls and cheap sensational newspapers. Each unit wore uniform, performed military-style drill and held summer camps. By 1910, Lawrence had abandoned his duties both to the Church Lads and their Sunday School. According to a friend, his departure had been occasioned by his reading to his class a religious story by the unmentionable Oscar Wilde.[3] Mrs Lawrence may have been upset, but she had some consolation in the knowledge that her son was doing his duty by his country, if not God, in the ranks of the OTC.

Undergraduates who had contact with Lawrence at Oxford were all taken aback by the depth of his knowledge about the Middle Ages. He told them that it was a 'real' period, unlike its successor, which was heralded by the twin demons of gunpowder and printing. Others were bowled over by his antiquarian passions. Warren Ault, an American Rhodes scholar, and Vyvyan Richards, a Welsh–American, neither of them run-of-the-mill Jesus men, were among those who found in Lawrence something worth knowing. Each was converted to brass-rubbing, and Richards recalled being relentlessly badgered into seeing the prehistoric Rollright Stone Circle twenty miles north-west of Oxford. Meeting Lawrence was 'love at first sight' for Richards, who would compose a warm memoir soon after his friend's death. Lawrence, as a freshman, was flattered by the admiration of the third-year man whom he later described as an 'unworldly, sincere, ill-mannered Welsh philosopher'.[4] They quickly became intimates although it was an association of which Mr and Mrs Lawrence did not approve.

Richards guessed that Mrs Lawrence was dimly aware of Ned's under-graduate escapades. Nothing of this sort marred her other sons' passages through university. Robert, a medic, went through St John's without a hitch; William, a Classicist who turned Modern Historian, followed him with a scholarship worth £100 a year and gained a Half-Blue as a miler: while Frank, who went up to Jesus as an exhibitioner, made his mark in the college soccer eleven and as a rifle shot. Their wholesome manliness was not to Richards's taste and he found Ned's brothers 'a dull lot'.

Ned was very different. Richards thought him an exotic original who 'lived in a world of old things' and who opened his mind to the beauties of medieval art and literature. Lawrence released his previously repressed aestheticism and, in return, received utter devotion. Together they dreamed about a joint future in which they would live together in contrived Gothic surroundings as creative artist–craftsmen in the manner advocated by the visionary William Morris. The dream combined both the traditional,

Victorian pattern of manly friendship, which had its roots in the Platonic ideal of love between young men in ancient Greece, and a shared passion for Morris's Gothic idealism. The present, industrial, capitalist world was unbearable and its tastes an abomination. Intelligent, sensitive men could escape from its hideousness by returning to an idealised Middle Ages in which were produced works of beauty and integrity. Richards did find Lawrence physically attractive, but the essential bonds between the two were intellectual rather than carnal.

Women of his own age were all but unknown to Lawrence, whom Richards found strangely without any interest in sex. His home life had been deliberately masculine thanks to his mother, who kept girls at bay. So too and with equal vigour did the Oxford collegiate authorities. Lawrence may not have needed these artificial barriers for he cared little for girls, either in the abstract or in the particular, and was hazy about just what was involved in heterosexual behaviour. Such gaps in the knowledge of middle-class youths were not uncommon. Years later, Lawrence, by turns shocked and fascinated by the coarse ribaldry of his RAF hut-mates, sought enlightenment from Robert Graves. Graves was surprised and in February 1930 informed Siegfried Sassoon, 'It doesn't take long to fuck: but perhaps you don't know about it. T.E.[Lawrence] is similarly ignorant.'[5]

Yet, according to Janet Laurie, the daughter of a Hampshire land agent who had known the Lawrences since childhood and sometimes stayed with them in Oxford as an honorary sister, Ned – aged twenty or twenty-one – proposed to her. The question was popped without preliminaries after dinner when the rest of the family had withdrawn. Flummoxed by this off-the-cuff offer, Miss Laurie said no, a refusal that did not trouble her suitor. Soon after, she developed an attachment to his younger brother Will, which displeased Mrs Lawrence. If this incident occurred, and there is only Miss Laurie's word for it, it appears more an instance of Lawrence's whimsicality than of his passion.

Passion of another kind permeated Edwardian Oxford and touched Lawrence. When he was about sixteen he became friendly with Leonard Green, a homosexual and contemporary of his brother Robert at St John's. In defiance of college rules, Lawrence was a guest at Green's rooms, where they talked about common aesthetic interests which included fine printing. They planned to set up their own press which would print elegant editions of such suitable works as Pater's essays. Lawrence imagined himself destined to keep alive the traditions of William Morris and, in the summer of 1909, he went so far as to buy some costly Tyrian purple dye in the Lebanon with which he and Green proposed to stain the vellum covers of their limited editions.

Green was a poet as well as aspirant printer. Early in 1910 he invited

Lawrence's comments on his verses and was encouraged by the response. Lawrence suggested that Green would not find a publisher easily, but thought that they were suitable material for the projected press. He cautioned Green not to bow to conventional morality and 'develop a sense of sin or anything prurient', which was prudent advice since Green, a member of the secret homosexual order of Chaeronea (founded in 1890 and including Laurence Housman in its brotherhood), also belonged to a circle of poetasters and fiction writers who would be known as Uranians. Their most notorious member was Lord Alfred Douglas (Oscar Wilde's 'Bosie') and their most distinguished F.W.Rolfe ('Baron Corvo'). The common inspiration of the Uranians was the innocence and sensuality of young boys. The titles of Green's small volumes, *Dream Comrades* (1916) and *The Youthful Lovers* (1919), suggest the thinly disguised pederasty of the Uranian muse. Uranian verses were erotic and voyeuristic, for instance Corvo's 'The Ballade of Boys Bathing':

> White boys, muddy & tanned & bare
> With lights and shadows of rose and grey
> And the sea like pearls in their shining hair
> The boys who bathe in St Andrew's Bay.

Corvo's lines were strangely reflected in two paintings acquired by Lawrence in 1922 from the artist Henry Scott Tuke. They show young soldiers bathing and one, undressing, looks uncommonly like Lawrence. Certainly Corvo would have been personally known to Lawrence. Between 1900 and 1909 he regularly stayed in rooms at Jesus when he came to Oxford to act as secretary to Dr E.G.Hardy of St John's. Lawrence was drawn towards his writing and read *Don Tarquino* (1905) which he warmly praised for its 'fleshiness'.[6] It is an overripe tale of young men at the late fifteenth-century Roman court. One passage, which describes the arming of Tarquino and Cesare Borgia, may explain why Lawrence was attracted to a novel which oddly mingles antiquarianism with homoeroticism.

> The Paparch's [Pope Urban VI] son watched me glittering in the pliant
> steel, while I was buckling on my sword belt; and said that I was as
> comely in the mail falling in escallops round mine haunches as I was
> in silk or velvet. Thus he spoke; and, finding on the tray another mail
> shirt so fine that his two hands plump, juicy with heat, completely
> covered it, he let my pages do it to him.

As an undergraduate, Lawrence was a figure on the fringes of the Uranian circle, and when he compiled his own anthology of minor poetry in the 1920s he included two Uranian pieces by William Johnson and J.B. White. Uranian preoccupations were reflected in his own writing and there is a strong vein of homoeroticism throughout the *Seven Pillars*. True to the Uranian canon, Lawrence's young Arabs turn aside from women and seek friendship and more from each other.

> The public women of the rare settlements we encountered in our months of wandering would have been nothing to our numbers, even had their raddled meat been palatable to a man in healthy parts. In horror of such sordid commerce, our youths began indifferently to slake one another's needs in their own clean bodies – a cold convenience that, by comparison, seemed sexless and even pure.

Uranian pederasty was for the greater part confined to the imagination and expressed through words. The prosecution of Wilde had served to remind such men that, even in private and with mutual consent, homosexual acts were felonies. The Uranians were free only to give voice to their suppressed longings, and what they wrote was accepted at face value by readers who were wholly innocent of the emotions behind such works. Public morality fiercely damned any open revelation of 'the love that dared not speak its name'. It was reported that George V, on hearing that an acquaintance was a homosexual, exclaimed, 'I thought such men shot themselves.'

Lawrence's interest in Uranian writing and his friendship with Green had an element of daring, shared aesthetic interests aside. There was nothing in his demeanour which indicated even latent homosexuality, or so two fellow Jesus men recalled. By taking up with Green and approving of Corvo, Lawrence was flirting with the outrageous and trespassing in a world where the slightest hint of his presence would have aroused the Puritan frenzy of his parents (there was a strong Anglo-Catholic element among the Uranians) and the indignation of the stiffer elements in his college. As it was, Mr and Mrs Lawrence were uneasy about their son's friendship with Vyvyan Richards, whom they suspected might be a homosexual. Yet as Lawrence's friends were swift to notice, he had a streak of devilment in him.

After he left Oxford, Lawrence admitted to having spent most of his time there reading the imaginative literature of early and high medieval France. He read quickly and boasted a facility by which he could absorb the gist of a book within half an hour. He could also steel himself to read for up to eighteen hours at a stretch. These energies were concentrated on the lyrics of the thirteenth-century Provençal *trouvères* (a taste he passed on to his brother Will) and contemporary French *gestes*, lengthy heroic poems which chronicled the adventures of legendary and semi-legendary paladins. This passion was a natural fusion of his childhood enthusiasm for Tennyson's Arthurian verse and his later interest in the feudal world.

When immersed in these tales, Lawrence suspended all contact with the outside world. The mundane and uncongenial were excluded from his garden bolt-hole, where he would withdraw into a reverie of pure imagination. In August 1910 he told his mother of his 'joy in getting into a strange country in a book'. The wonderment began 'when I have shut my door and the town is in bed' and would last throughout the night beyond an unnoticed dawn. 'It is lovely too', he added, 'after you have been wandering for hours in the forest with Percivale or Sagramors le Desirous, to open the door, and from the Cherwell to look at the sun glowering through the valley mists.' His companion on this excursion into the dream-world was Sir Thomas Malory whose *Morte d'Arthur* he read again and again when he was on active service in 1917 and 1918. Its appeal, like that of the other chivalric literature which he consumed, was to the imagination. 'Imagination', he assured his mother, 'should be put into the most precious caskets, and that is why one can only live in the future or the past, in Utopia or the wood beyond the world.'

Lawrence was addicted to a literature which had been created to illustrate the knightly virtues and to entertain a sophisticated, aristocratic audience. As he read, he heard the voices of the men and women who had lived in castles talking about love and war. Medieval political and satirical verses were 'the only things not dry in history', he told his brother Will in 1911 and urged him to read them in preference to modern texts.

Courtly medieval literature was full of models for human conduct. Caxton, who first printed the *Morte d'Arthur,* aimed to give his fifteenth-century readers a code of conduct for their own lives. In the story of Arthur and his knights, 'Noble men may see and learn the noble acts of chivalry, the gentle and virtuous deeds that some knights used in those days, by which they came to honour, and how they that were vicious were punished and oft put to shame and rebuke.' Lawrence learned from what he read. Prolonged exposure to medieval romances inevitably had a profound effect on his thoughts and behaviour.

His self-esteem was satisfied by knowing that in the legendary medieval past his own birth carried no moral stigma nor hindered advancement. In the *Morte d'Arthur,* Galahad, the illegitimate son of Elaine and Lancelot, who was, it seems, bewitched at the moment of conception, is automatically given his father's status. 'He must be a noble man', announces Queen Guinevere, 'for so is his father.' The 'passing fair and well-made' Galahad is also recognised as 'he by whom the Sangreal [Holy Grail] shall be achieved'. In another of Lawrence's favourite romances, the early thirteenth-century French epic poem *Huon de Bordeaux*, one of the hero's adversaries was 'a young knight named Gerard, right hardy and valiant in arms, he was bastard son to the emperor [Charlemagne]'.

This tale had an incidental appeal for Lawrence since Huon and his knightly band travel to Arabia, where they suffer fatigue, hunger and thirst in the desert before defeating the 'Emir of Babylon' and his paynims. Victory comes from their stamina and willpower and from the help of a friendly magician prince, Auberon, who is host to Huon in his enchanted kingdom on the shores of the Red Sea and provides him with a horn with which he can summon supernatural assistance when in peril. Like all the stereotypes in such epics, Huon is skilled in arms, possesses almost superhuman powers of endurance, and never shrinks from a challenge.

In William Morris's *The Story of Sigurd the Volsung*, which captivated Lawrence in 1912, the hero calls out, 'I am ready; and what is the deed to win?' In different forms, it is the war-cry of all those warrior heroes who held Lawrence's imagination. Moreover, like Sir Galahad, many carry with them a peculiar force of destiny. They are driven into sundry adventures by impulses within themselves and their own sense of vision, although the exact nature of these powers is often beyond their understanding. Lawrence was intoxicated by these possibilities; perhaps he too had such forces within him. After the war, when asked by George Kidston, a diplomat, why he had become so closely involved in the Arab movement, Lawrence offered four reasons. 'Intellectual curiosity' was the fourth. He had wanted to know how it felt 'to be the mainspring of a national movement'. There was also the element of the knightly quest: 'Being a half-poet, I don't value material things much. Sensation and mind seem to me greater, and the ideal, such a thing as the impulse that took us into Damascus, the only thing worth doing.'

The imaginative, like the historical chivalric world, was male-dominated. Women existed as two broad stereotypes. They were either embodiments of virtue, beautiful creatures set on pedestals, their honour guarded by their knightly lovers, or else creators of mischief through their lustfulness and scheming. In the *Morte d'Arthur*, Sir Bors is nearly distracted from his quest by a devil in the form of a seductive gentlewoman, and Guinevere's illicit love for Lancelot undoes the bonds of the Round Table. The ties of male loyalty were more enduring. Huon is sustained by his loyal companions in arms, who shared his exile and fight alongside him. A certain heroic resilience came from the bonds and common purposes of men. Lawrence already understood something of this from his experiences as one of a close-knit band of brothers, as a leader in the Church Lads' Brigade and a cadet in the OTC. Such ties could not withstand the pull of the individual will; when Arthur's knights, moved by the vision of the Grail, swear to seek it, the King laments the loss of 'the fairest fellowship and the truest of knighthood that ever were seen together'.

He was mesmerised by the idea of the quest. His regimen of diet, self-discipline, exercise and, from 1909 onwards, training with firearms suggests a young man making himself ready for some adventure. There was also a need for mental preparation and, in March 1912, he told his family that 'I have for the second time assimilated Thompson's "Mistress of Vision".' Lines from Francis Thompson's poem, in which the imprisoned 'Lady of fair weeping' reveals her secrets, give an indication of what might be expected of Lawrence when the moment came to fulfil his aspirations:

> Pierce thy heart to find the key;
> With thee take
> Only what none else would keep;
> Learn to dream when thou dost wake,
> Learn to wake when thou dost sleep
> Learn to water joy with tears,
> Learn from fears to vanquish fears.
> To hope, for thou dar'st not despair,
> Exult, for that thou dar'st not grieve;
> Plough thou the rock until it bear;
> Know, for thou else couldst not believe;
> Lose, that the lost thou may'st receive,
> Die, for none other way can'st live.

Beyond his private world of knights, magicians and quests in distant lands was that of the Oxford History Syllabus, to which Lawrence had committed himself when he entered Jesus. Naturally he liked best the period from 918 to 1273 and had the good luck to find that the first three Crusades were one of the Special Paper choices. He approached his studies with a gusto which was not always applauded by his tutors. 'Your matter is passable, but you write in the style of a two-penny-halfpenny newspaper' was how R.L.Poole, a Magdalen medievalist, summed up one of Lawrence's essays. He was not disturbed and, on leaving, remarked cockily to his tutorial partner, Warren Ault, 'I thought that it would stir the old boy up a bit.'

But Lawrence was uneasy about the thinness of his knowledge, especially in areas of history which bored him. Finals were due in June 1910 and, as they came nearer, he thought it prudent to join forces with Prŷs-Jones and procure the services of a coach, Cecil Jane, who in 1907 had crammed him for his scholarship exam. 'I should not call him a scholar by temperament and the main characteristic of his work was always that it was unusual without the effort to be unusual' was Jane's circumspect summary of Lawrence's essays. What worried Jane was his pupil's overriding wish to explain historical events through the character of those involved. Lawrence lacked the academic detachment which was considered laudable among historians; this, with his taste for satire, convinced Jane that he was not a scholar in the narrow Oxonian sense. Lawrence's indirect retort to such criticisms was delivered in a letter to Will in which he asked, 'Do you really expect a history don who is abstract and constitutional political to understand the mysteries of tattooing and the origin of the impi?'

While he may have been exasperated by the limitations of the Oxford historical imagination, Lawrence was grateful to Jane. When he was in Syria during 1911 he asked Will to visit Jane and do what he could to dispel his periodic moods of gloom and isolation. It was a kind gesture and well deserved since, with Jane's help and backed by his thesis on Crusader castles, Lawrence survived the six-day ordeal of Finals and achieved a first-class degree.

Lawrence's first, which R.L.Poole celebrated with a dinner, owed much to his research thesis on castles. It was a remarkable accomplishment for an undergraduate, since it rested on field work done by him in the Lebanon and Syria during the summer of 1909. The castles, which he systematically photographed, sketched and measured, were all but unknown to British scholars and his conclusions were novel. Hogarth had been godfather to the venture which he believed would open Lawrence's eyes and mind to the monuments of Middle Eastern antiquity and stimulate him to further travel in the region.

Preparations were well in hand by the beginning of 1909. At Hogarth's bidding, Lawrence had written for advice to the Victorian explorer and author, Charles Doughty. The response was tepid; travelling on foot in the hot season across a remote landscape whose inhabitants mistrusted Europeans would be hazardous. Doughty added, prophetically, that 'Insufficient food, rest and sleep would soon tell.' Undaunted, Lawrence turned at Hogarth's suggestion to a young archaeologist, Harry Pirie-Gordon, an Oxford dandy who shared his interest in Corvo. It was a sensible move, for Pirie-Gordon and the author Compton Mackenzie had as undergraduates spent their summer vacation in 1901 in another inaccessible region, Morocco. More to Lawrence's immediate purpose, Pirie-Gordon had lately been exploring in Syria, possessed a useful map and had examined castles there. 'Some Arabic is of course necessary,' Doughty insisted, so Lawrence began lessons with the Reverend N. Odeh, a Syrian Protestant cleric. By July, when he disembarked at Beirut, Lawrence knew less than a hundred words, or so he told Robert Graves, but his letters home record that he could manage well enough in simple conversations.

Physical necessities for the journey were provided by Mr Lawrence, who gave his son £100. Forty pounds went immediately on a camera and a smaller sum on a Mauser automatic pistol, over three pounds weight of the latest German technology and the most efficient sidearm of its time – Churchill had carried one at the battle of Omdurman. Like the questing warrior heroes, Lawrence had to equip himself with the finest weaponry. He also needed the equivalent of magical protection, since the final stages of his journey would bring him into bandit country around Aleppo. Through the good offices of his college Principal and Lord Curzon, a former Viceroy of India and Chancellor of the university, the British Embassy in Constantinople procured *iradehs* which Lawrence picked up at the Beirut Consulate. These documents commanded all local officials to do everything within their power to assist and protect a British subject as he passed through the Sultan's provinces. They had a talismanic quality which enabled Lawrence to enlist help from governors and policemen and even got him a cavalry escort for one dangerous leg of the journey.

The camera, its tripod and magnesium flares, and the heavy pistol with its wooden holster were Lawrence's basic baggage. His wardrobe was minimal; a light suit with abundant pockets, two thin shirts and one change of socks. In Beirut, Lawrence bought a solar topee and a water bottle. As things turned out, he was inadequately equipped for his task.

His walk had three aims. The first was the inspection of the fortifications of the Crusader states, including those at Urfa, a remote town in eastern Syria which, as Edessa, had been the capital of a Crusader county that had flourished between 1099 and 1147. During this stage of his peregrination, he intended to carry out a commission from Hogarth and visit Jerablus, a township on the upper Euphrates close to the mound under which lay the Hittite city of Karkamis (known then as Carcemish). Hogarth had given Lawrence a further assignment, buying Hittite clay seals. Since 1905, Hogarth had been laying plans to restart the Karkamis diggings under the auspices of the British Museum and, in 1908, he had made formal application for permission from the Ottoman government.[7]

Knowledge of the Hittites and their civilisation was still fragmentary. Written historical references were scarce to what archaeologists believed was a Hittite empire which had dominated Anatolia and northern Syria between 1350 and 1250 BC. A growing number of artefacts which could be ascribed to the Hittites had been appearing in Europe since the 1870s and had stirred up much interest. What most intrigued scholars were the seals with their inscriptions in either cuneiform script or hieroglyphs, which were studied in Britain and Germany. The beginning of the century saw a fresh and determined effort to solve the mysteries of the Hittites. As the pace of research quickened, the lead was taken in 1905 by Dr Hugo Winckler of the Royal Museum in Berlin, who began digging at Boghazköy, which was considered to be the choicest site. In the following year, Professor

John Garstang and a team from Liverpool University started work at Sakca-gozu, northwest of Aleppo.

Karkamis, once a thriving city on the southern marches of the Hittite empire, had been neglected after some amateurish probing by the British Consul in Aleppo in the late 1870s. He had uncovered remains of a royal palace and had taken the precaution of buying a third of the site for a bagatelle on behalf of the British Museum. Hogarth believed that Karkamis had potential and hoped that discoveries there would enable him to trace connections between Hittite and early Greek art. While his prime motive was the extension of knowledge about an obscure culture, there was an underlying element of rivalry with the Germans. Filling state museums with objects recovered from remote lands was a prestigious form of cultural imperialism. From the turn of the century, German scholars had taken advantage of their government's growing political friendship with the Otto-man empire to get official permits to dig up the choicest archaeological sites.

Lawrence's assignment to gather Hittite seals, his examination of the Karkamis site in 1909 and his extended periods excavating there between 1911 and 1914 have been the subject of much recent speculation. This has given rise to a theory that his archaeological investigations were a red herring with which he drew the Ottoman authorities away from his real purpose, which was to spy on the railway works just south of Jerablus. Not that there was anything to see in 1909, since operations to build a bridge over the Euphrates did not begin until January 1912. The finished bridge carried the Aleppo-to-Baghdad link of the Berlin-to-Baghdad railway, an enter-prise largely financed by the French-controlled Imperial Ottoman Bank, undertaken by German engineers and using German-made track, engines and rolling-stock. The commercial and strategic potential had been immedi-ately appreciated in Britain, where there had been apprehension about a line which directly connected Germany with the heart of a region which was considered a buffer zone between Europe and the Indian empire. Yet the line was being built by a public company (which was running short of funds by 1913) whose activities were well known and could be read about in its annual reports. If, during 1912 and 1913, Lawrence took it upon himself to spy on the German surveyors and civil engineers he would have found out nothing that was not already well known to the British government.[8]

Central to the contention that Lawrence went to Syria as a secret agent is the assumption that his academic sponsor, Hogarth, was a spymaster whose scholarly sightseeing and excavations were a cover for intelligence-gathering in the Ottoman empire. In this guise, he had singled out Lawrence as a likely recruit who would in time, like him, masquerade as an archaeol-ogist and spy on the Turks and their German friends. This is quite simply absurd.[9]

In the first place, Hogarth had a deeply rooted distrust of all governments and bureaucracies. More importantly, the British government had no need of him on its payroll. At the beginning of the twentieth century, the Admiralty and Foreign and War Offices possessed intelligence departments with tiny staffs which were mainly concerned with cataloguing military, naval, political and economic information which came into their hands from various sources. Among these were loyal British subjects who travelled abroad and reported anything which they believed ought to be known to their government.

Lawrence was one of these sources. At least once in 1912 he passed on local hearsay to Raff Fontana, the British Consul in Aleppo, arrogantly claiming that what he gathered from his regular dragomen was 'rot'. Even so, Fontana in his reports to the Ambassador in Constantinople preferred to set down what had been collected in remote districts by the dragomen. Lawrence also claimed to have carried out another patriotic duty in 1913 when he addressed Lord Kitchener, then High Commissioner in Egypt, and revealed his fears about the extent of German penetration in Syria. He was dismissed with a prophecy that a general European war was imminent and that the best thing he could do was to get back to his diggings. What he had to say was well known anyway.[10]

Lawrence clearly felt impelled to bring such scraps of information as came his way to the attention of the government. Others went further and indulged in active sleuthing, like the fictional yachtsmen in Erskine Childers's spy thriller *The Riddle of the Sands* (1903). Laurence's future intelligence colleague Philip Graves, another Englishman on the loose in Syria, went in for private espionage. In 1905 he had taken a train on the newly opened Damascus-to-Maan line and kept his eyes and ears open for any hints of future Turkish military plans. A drunken German railway engineer told him that when completed the line would carry soldiers as well as pilgrims bound for Mecca, which would have surprised no one. In Maan, Graves snooped about and overheard Italian railway workers gossip about a projected branch line to the Red Sea port of Aqaba, from where a reinforced Turkish garrison might menace the Suez Canal. So blatant were Graves's enquiries that a Greek café owner asked him whether he was a spy. So he was, and so also were other watchful British tourists, many of them army and navy officers on extended leave. What they stumbled across sometimes had its value. In February 1915, when Lawrence and the rest of the intelligence staff at Cairo were collating information about Alexandretta (Iskanderun) for a projected invasion of Syria, they were assisted by Captain Boyle, a naval officer who before the war had navigated the offshore shoals 'for sporting purposes'.[11]

As to Hogarth, he was always conscious of the strategic and political

importance of the Middle East and as a traveller in the area, he was aware
of the chronic instability of the Ottoman empire and its vulnerability to
foreign penetration. These were the everyday preoccupations of British
diplomats and soldiers and were frequently vented in the serious press.
Hogarth had been at Winchester with Sir Edward Grey, who from 1906
was Foreign Secretary, and he had remained in contact with him, no doubt
proffering advice and suggestions. A patriot, he volunteered his services
as an adviser to Admiralty Intelligence and in this capacity was canvassed
by Lawrence to represent the views of Military Intelligence in Cairo. At
the time, Hogarth had no official post or rank. During the summer of
1915, he approached Compton Mackenzie, then running a Naval Intelligence
office in Athens, and asked him for an 'Intelligence job'. Like Lawrence,
Mackenzie was attracted to Hogarth's 'very rich and abundant personality',
but could only suggest that he open an office in Sofia. The idea of
Bulgaria dismayed Hogarth, whose face took on the 'expression of a drama-
tist being invited to go out to Hollywood and work for the movies'. A
further disappointment followed in August when Hogarth failed to get an
intelligence post with the Gallipoli expeditionary force. His fortunes soon
changed; on 25 October he was commissioned as a lieutenant-commander
in the Royal Navy Volunteer Reserve, in spite of being fifty-three, and
two months later was appointed Director of the new Arab Bureau in Cairo.
If Hogarth had been a key figure in pre-war intelligence, his slow and
haphazard recruitment in 1915 is scarcely believable.[12]

Like Lawrence, Pirie-Gordon and many others, Hogarth was part of
a stock of travellers, newspapermen, archaeologists and businessmen on
which the government called in an emergency. Their pre-war knowledge
of the Middle East instantly qualified them as intelligence officers and
they were hurriedly enlisted by the War Office and Admiralty. Their sudden
precipitation into wartime intelligence bureaus was not a sign of any previous
connections with espionage, but rather a token of a desperate official need
to get together as many well-informed experts and linguists as possible.

Lawrence's quest in the Lebanon and Syria in 1909 was for evidence of
the region's past, not its present or future. All travellers about to embark
on a journey to a new country set out with some conceptions about what
it will be like when they arrive. In June, when Lawrence joined the SS
Magnolia bound for Port Said, he was similarly encumbered.

At the time, the Middle East was occupying more and more European
attention. It was an area which seemed in the first stages of transition from
supine backwardness to active modernity. Lawrence had been closely following events there for some time. In July 1908 he had read vague accounts
in French journals of the Young Turk revolution in Constantinople and

had pressed his parents to send him some hard news from British newspapers. His own political opinions were heterodox and fickle. 'I am an anarchist,' he told Mrs Bernard Shaw in 1928, 'convinced that there is no moral basis for the authority which some men assume.' As a schoolboy and undergraduate, he was a Tory, an allegiance inherited from his father, who as an Irish landowner had every reason to detest the Liberals, because their laws had dissolved the economic and political power of his class. Politics were discussed in the Lawrence household and the tenor of Ned's contributions may be judged from his remarks on Lloyd George's Old Age Pension Bill written in 1908. For Lawrence, the measure was 'an impudent pauperisation of all its old wasters, and penalisation of all its old workers', which ignored the principles of political economy and had been devised to catch votes.

When confronted with the Orient, Lawrence's political reactions were simple and conventional. As a European, he knew that he came from a continent whose achievements in every field of human activity entitled it to be called 'civilised'. He was about to walk through a land, which for all its other attractions was 'uncivilised'. Lawrence wrote home approvingly of the achievements of the American University at Beirut, where such modern subjects as Medicine, Pharmacy, Law, Agriculture and Dentistry formed the curriculum. There was praise too for the scattered American Protestant missions where on occasions he was a well-treated guest. He spent three days at Qalat al Husa with a 'new man', a Turkish provincial administrator whose conversation revealed him as 'a-most-civilised-French - speaking - disciple - of - the - Herbert - Spencer - Free - Masonic - Mohammedan-Young Turk'.

The traditional, backward Orient was despised. In Galilee, Lawrence contrasted what he imagined to have been the state of the country when Jesus and his disciples wandered through it and what he had just encountered. 'They [Jesus and his disciples] did not come upon dirty and dilapidated Bedouin tents, with people calling to them to come in and talk, while miserable curs came snapping at their heels.' Instead they enjoyed the luxuries of 'the most Romanised province of Palestine'. The area cried out for civilisation. Lawrence was glad to report that rebirth was at hand when he described some of the recently established Zionist settlements, peopled by European Jewish immigrants. 'The sooner the Jews farm it [Galilee] all the better: their colonies are bright spots in the desert'.

Beyond the major cities of Beirut and Aleppo, Lawrence discovered that there were some compensations for backwardness. The rural peasantry were open-handed and hospitable. 'There are common people,' he told his father, 'each one ready to receive one for a night, and allow me to share in their meals: and without a thought of payment from a traveller on foot.

It is pleasant, for they have an attractive kind of native dignity.' On entering a Syrian house, Lawrence was greeted, sat on a thick quilt, asked many times about his health and sometimes given coffee. All villages had some arrangement for the accommodation of travellers. There were *hans* (inns), to which travellers had to bring their own bedding but where they received a meal from the owner, and village guest rooms which were often carpeted and in which counterpanes and cooking fuel were ready for the visitors. The counterpanes were a bane for Lawrence as they were always flea-ridden, even that offered by the Young Turk official. No payment was asked for use of the guest room, and when none was available a villager seemed always on hand to put a room in his house at the disposal of a visitor.

Lawrence's route had been planned beforehand and fell into three stages. The first took him inland from Beirut towards Galilee and back. The second, which he began on 6 August, took him northwards to Tripoli, Latakia and Antakya (Antioch) and inland into the uplands of the Jebel Ansariye. This journey included the most formidable of all Crusader castles, Krak des Chevaliers, the Knights Hospitaller fortress where he spent three days. Then he plodded across country towards his next goal, Aleppo, where he arrived on 6 September. For part of this trek he had a guard of Turkish cavalrymen, who like everyone else were astonished to find a European travelling on foot. Lawrence discourteously refused a mount. 'They couldn't understand my prejudice against anything on four legs,' he wrote to his mother. He had been walking for up to thirteen hours a day, so he said, and had gone without washing for ten.

Lawrence preferred to walk: he thought it the best means of getting to understand the lie of the land, which was essential if he was to explain the geographical siting of castles. These exploited naturally inaccessible places and they were placed strategically to guard frontiers or block access to territory. So Lawrence appreciated the strategic problems of the Crusaders; and he saved money. Furthermore, he believed that his gruelling regime had given him an immunity from that intermittent looseness of the bowels which normally bedevilled Europeans in the Middle East.

However, hitches were occurring. Although he had been well looked after at various missions along his route and found the largely farinaceous local diet to his taste, Lawrence was in a physically parlous condition by the time he reached Aleppo. Malaria, first picked up in southern France a year before, had sapped his strength and he was on the verge of a fourth bout when he got to Aleppo. He was therefore forced to take a carriage for the next leg of his journey and the return fare of £14 to Urfa knocked his budget askew. When he returned to Aleppo on 22 September he announced to his family, 'I am coming home at once, for lack of money.'

His suit was falling apart, his boots had given up an unequal struggle and were leaking, and, in spite of regular treatment with boracic powder, his blisters and sores refused to heal.

He had shown considerable pluck, but his stamina, so rigorously built up and tested, had not matched the strain of his programme. He had covered 1,100 miles in eighty-three days, mostly on foot, had purchased twenty-four Hittite seals and examined three dozen castles. The last stage of his quest, which would have taken him south from Aleppo to the strongholds around the Dead Sea, had to be called off. Unlike his knightly heroes, he had failed to measure up to the demands of his undertaking and the blow to his self-esteem must have been heavy.

How could all this be explained when he returned to Oxford? On the road to Aleppo, Lawrence had been shot at by a mounted tribesman. He fired back with his Mauser and the tribesman's horse bolted. Lawrence attached the wooden holster to the pistol as a stock and fired a second round at 800 yards which sent the man packing. He had tangled with a Tartar and a well-armed one at that. Such ambushes were common in this district and Europeans were cautioned to be wary of bandits. Lawrence was not, at least at Surruc on his way back from Urfa where his camera was stolen from his carriage. The previously invaluable *iradehs* failed to get a helpful response from the local police, whose lassitude Lawrence blamed on Ramadan.

The theft of the camera spawned several different stories which, when told to friends, revealed Lawrence's forced abandonment of his expedition in a new light. On 24 September he wrote to Sir John Rhys, the Principal of Jesus, with an explanation as to why he would be starting term late. Pleading with him to keep the matter from his father, Lawrence said that he had been 'robbed and rather smashed up' in the past week. 'The man was caught,' Lawrence continued, thanks to the precious *iradehs*. Pirie-Gordon heard how Lawrence had been attacked by several Kurds who beat him, stole his clothes and camera, and left him for dead. As proof, Pirie-Gordon got his map back, its cover stained with blood.

Friends in Jesus were told how Lawrence had been stalked by a single robber, a bold fellow apparently undeterred by the massive Mauser, who struck him on the head with a rock. In another version of the tale, the robber grabbed a Colt revolver, which Lawrence was holding as he told the story, pressed the barrel against his head and squeezed the trigger. As luck would have it the safety catch was jammed, so the thief threw away the gun and ran off. Years later Robert Graves heard a further elaboration of the incident. This time Lawrence was bushwhacked close to the Euphrates, where he was looking for seals. His assailant stole his copper watch, thinking it gold, and fled when a shepherd appeared. Lawrence turned the tables on the rogue. Waving his *iradehs*, he called out the local police, who persuaded the elders from the robber's village to hand him over with his loot. Later, to round off the story neatly, Lawrence had the thief working under him as a labourer at Karkamis.[13]

Brigandage was common in this poor area, where the peasantry supplemented scant incomes by robbery and the authorities' grip was weak. In 1911, Professor Garstang's excavators exchanged shots with villagers near Aintab who were furious about the removal of an antiquity which might have fetched a high price with an Aleppo dealer. Details of this incident were swiftly passed to the Consul in Aleppo, who forwarded them to the Embassy in Constantinople. Strangely, nothing was reported of Lawrence's mishap. Yet he had told his mother that a local newspaper had an account of the murder of 'Mr Edvard Lovance' near Aintab during the second week in September. 'The hotel people received me like a ghost,' after having read this news story, which seems to have been completely missed by the British Consul and his normally vigilant staff of dragomen. This was still the age of gunboat diplomacy, in which the murder of a British subject was interpreted as an act of war against Britain and when British consuls vigorously goaded local authorities into punitive action at the slightest affront to one of their countrymen.[14]

It was obviously better for Lawrence that his college Principal believed that his failure to keep term was the consequence of a bloody ambush rather than exhaustion, sickness, tattered clothing and an empty purse. Parental doubts could be dispelled by their son's praiseworthy wish not to alarm them with letters describing his ordeal. University chums were no doubt fascinated to hear about their friend's courage and resourcefulness.

Lawrence's letters home and the recollections of those who knew him at the time show that he was an observant, intelligent and fluent teller of stories about himself and his travels. He had also assimilated the artifices of his medieval poets, and so his quest for antiquarian knowledge in the Lebanon and Syria was soon overlaid with invented flourishes. After all, he had completed a risky undertaking and, in private, egotistical yarn-spinning was a harmless diversion. What he said in college rooms and later to such sympathetic listeners as Lowell Thomas, Robert Graves and Liddell Hart had a veracity in his own imagination where it shared a place with the deeds of Huon de Bordeaux and Sir Galahad. Moreover, the acceptance of such tales was gratifying, for it enhanced his own standing in the eyes of his audience. Yet in some aspects of human affairs an adherence to truth, although hard to achieve, is essential. On the public stage which Lawrence would shortly occupy, his concoctions of reality and fancy would prove dangerously misleading for those around him and, ultimately, for himself.

IV

WANDERING SCHOLAR: THE
MIDDLE EAST, 1910–1913

LAWRENCE spent most of the four years between his going down from Oxford and the outbreak of the First World War in the Middle East. Except for four short visits to England, most of his time was taken up with the excavations at Karkamis, which became his second home. In the summer of 1911 he made a second excursion on foot in Syria which ended, like its predecessor, with him sick and exhausted. The following winter he was in Egypt for a short lesson in archaeological methods from Professor Flinders Petrie and, at the beginning of 1914, he joined a small official party surveying Sinai.

All these activities were directed by Hogarth, who in the autumn of 1910 had secured Lawrence a four-year demyship (scholarship) from Magdalen College which gave him an annual income of £100 and the independence to travel and study. Hogarth also procured him a daily payment of fifteen shillings (seventy-five pence) for his sustenance during the 1912, 1913 and 1914 digging seasons at Karkamis. Lawrence was therefore free to follow the course set by Hogarth, that of a professional archaeologist.

There were three parallel paths open to him which he followed fitfully. The first was as a historian of the Crusades who would merge his knowledge of contemporary texts with what he had discovered walking across the landscape of the former Crusader states. The ideas for 'my monumental work on the Crusades' were coalescing in January 1911 when he wrote at length to Leonard Green about the tactical problems which beset Crusading armies. Much of what he had to say was based on his first-hand observations in Syria, which had convinced him that 'the extreme difficulty of the country' hampered the deployment of armoured cavalry. Lawrence dropped this project and plumped for fiction instead. Since the beginning of 1911 he had in mind a book to be called 'The Seven Pillars of Wisdom' which he later dismissed as 'a youthful indiscretion'. He burned what he had written in November 1914 just before he joined the army. What was destroyed were 'adventures in seven type-cities of the East (Cairo, Baghdad, Damascus etc.)', which he had presented as 'a descending cadence: a moral symphony'. Beyond this outline of its form and pretensions nothing is known of the work.[1]

Lawrence also toyed with a third form of creative art. At the end of 1910 he was laying plans with Vyvyan Richards, then schoolmastering, for the setting up of a printing press which would revive the traditions which William Morris had founded at Kelmscott. The venture depended upon Richards learning how to print and on Lawrence capital, money earmarked from his scholarship and a £100 loan from his father. Land close to Morris's birthplace in Epping Forest was purchased, but the additional funds needed to build a house and install a press could not be found. Mr Lawrence was sceptical of the enterprise and suspected that Richards would prove an unsatisfactory businessman. His coolness and his son's increasing absorption in archaeology brought progress to a halt. In December 1913 Lawrence admitted to Richards that 'I cannot print with you when you want me' as the draw of his present work at Karkamis was too strong. 'I have got to like this place very much: and the people here ... and it is great fun to be with them.' The work would continue for at least five years, after which he expected that he would 'go after another and another nice thing'.

Virtual exile in Syria suited Lawrence and he recalled it with pleasure. 'Carcemish [Karkamis]', he told Mrs Bernard Shaw, 'was a wonderful place and time: as golden as Haroun el Raschid's in Tennyson.' 'The best life I ever had' was how he summed up these four years to Liddell Hart. Several things contributed to his sense of well-being. The excavations were engrossing – 'Digging is tremendous fun, and most exciting and interesting.' Furthermore, he had the adulation of the local Syrian peasantry and enjoyed a status and authority which he could never have experienced at home. Above all, in Syria he was completely cut off from English social conventions, and his freedom to behave as he wished was limitless. There were also people and places to be discovered and books to be read during extended periods of leisure.

These years of indulgence were also those of his apprenticeship as an archaeologist. In between distractions, Lawrence had to direct himself towards the serious business of learning how to uncover the buried past and interpret what he found. Training had started in Oxford after his Finals when he began to classify pottery in the Ashmolean. That same summer he made a fourth visit to France, accompanied for some of the time by his brothers Frank and Will, where he was on the look-out for pottery shards. The study of pottery offered the key to many archaeological mysteries. Lawrence hoped to learn from the patternwork of shards how Oriental designs passed into Europe at the time of the Crusades. In Constantinople in December 1910, he noticed that the glaze of local pottery on sale in the bazaars was identical to the fifteenth-century ware he had dug up in Oxford.

Examining pots in a museum was both a mental exercise and a preparation for field work in Syria, where Lawrence was given charge of the cataloguing and reconstruction of pottery. In June 1910 Hogarth had heard from the Foreign Office that the Ottoman government had finally given permission for the dig to begin at Karkamis. It was too late to begin that year, so he planned to start once the cold, wet north Syrian winter had passed. Lawrence went ahead of him by an unreliable French steamer whose meandering route gave him a chance to see Athens and Constantinople before making landfall in Beirut. At Athens he enthused over the Acropolis and imagined that he heard echoes of Aristophanes in the street banter of the Athenians. At Constantinople he renewed his *iradehs* which would officially guarantee his privileged status and smooth passage through the Ottoman empire.

Waiting for Hogarth's arrival, Lawrence renewed his acquaintance with Miss Holmes, the Principal of the American Protestant mission at Jeblé, and stayed several weeks as her guest; his Evangelical connections had their uses. There he practised his Arabic with the 'wonderful' Miss Fareedah el Akle, a young Syrian who found him an apt pupil: he bathed in the sea, pottered after antiquities and read two-week-old copies of *The Times*. Hogarth joined Lawrence in February 1911 and, avoiding routes closed by snow, they took a steamer to Haifa and then went by rail to Damascus. They were already late, for the excavations had been scheduled to begin that month.

Hogarth had been given £1,700 by the British Museum (Lawrence was unpaid but made do on his scholarship) and he expected the diggings to continue until November. At Aleppo, he, his deputy Reginald Campbell-Thompson and Lawrence received their licences to carry firearms and an escort of Turkish troops which had been requested by the Foreign Office. On 9 March, they set off for Jerablus with a convoy of over twenty camels, mules and donkeys, which carried their supplies. Hogarth demanded comfort and his boxes included three blends of tea and nine varieties of jam. The seventy-mile journey was a dismal tramp through rain and snow showers and took two days. When they arrived at Jerablus, the party found lodgings available in the vacant house of the manager of a licorice plantation.

Labour was recruited from the village, whose forty households yielded between 90 and 120 labourers. Hogarth offered good wages, eight piastres a day (four pence), and there was never a shortage of willing recruits. For the peasantry of Jerablus, the archaeologists provided a welcome supplement to their sparse incomes.

During each of the four seasons of digging from 1911 to 1914, Lawrence had direct control over the workforce, with power to hire and fire men, which explains much about his relations with them. No one could afford to cross his path and all had to treat him with respect. Overall direction of operations was in the hands of Hogarth and, in his absence, Campbell-Thompson, hitherto a sedentary scholar of linguistics whose specialism was the deciphering of Hittite seals. Lawrence found him agreeable company. Like him, Campbell-Thompson would join Military Intelligence; in 1917 this 'curious old bird with an amazing inventive brain' was decrypting Turko-German wireless messages in Iraq.[2]

Initial progress with the dig was sluggish and the finds unremarkable. After two months, Hogarth proposed ending work in August when most of the labourers would have to harvest their crops. There was a further snag when the local owner of two-thirds of the site began grumbling and threatened to impede the work. On 24 June, the Trustees of the British Museum, disappointed by the yields and uncertain whether legal hitches might prevent further digging, decided to call a halt.

A month before, Campbell-Thompson and Lawrence had been visited by the explorer Gertrude Bell, who turned up well escorted by troops. She had hoped to meet Hogarth and her criticism of his principles of digging irritated Lawrence and Campbell-Thompson. She further ruffled their feathers by praising the techniques of the German archaeologists whose site at Qalat Surgar she had just visited. They not only dug up remains but tried to reconstruct the buildings which had been uncovered. 'We had to squash her with a display of erudition,' Lawrence wrote home, but in spite of a barrage of pedantry she left in a good humour. Lawrence, then aged twenty-three, she thought 'a pleasant boy' who 'is going to make a traveller'.

She had heard of Lawrence's plans for an excursion eastwards to re-examine Urfa and Harran. The expedition began in the second week of June with Lawrence taking a boat down the Euphrates to El Tell el Ahmar and then going cross-country, with a police escort, to Harran and Urfa. From Urfa he returned westwards to Birecik, from where he went down river to Jerablus. His objectives were, as they had been in 1909, an examination of castles and the purchase of seals. Again, he ran into difficulties. On 17 July at Harran he was troubled by a painful abscess on his tooth, and when he reached Jerablus twelve days later he had contracted dysentery.

He was nursed by his boy servant, Dahoum, and Haroun, the site foreman, and treated with arrowroot and milk. After five days he had a false recovery which was followed on 8 August by a relapse. Four days later he set off for England.

After convalescence, Lawrence returned to the Middle East in December 1911, this time to Egypt, where at Hogarth's suggestion he offered his services to Professor Flinders Petrie, then excavating a large cemetery at Takhan, south of Cairo. Petrie was a querulous, brusque and opinionated scholar who, in 1885, had broken away from the Egypt Exploration Fund and set up his own British School of Archaeology, which was privately funded. Petrie's experience and knowledge were unequalled. So was his way of life. In horror, Lawrence reported, 'A Petrie dig is a thing with a flavour of its own: tinned kidneys mingle with mummy-corpses and amulets in the soup.' What was worse, especially for a man lately recovered from dysentery, many of the opened tins had been festering for a week in the Egyptian heat. For his part, Petrie had been astonished by Lawrence, who turned up at the site in shorts and a white Magdalen blazer. He was indignantly asked if he had come for cricket. This must have been galling for Lawrence, who loathed team games, and he was firmly told that no Englishman in Egypt ever wore shorts. Still, master and pupil did eventually get on and Lawrence came to appreciate Petrie's pawky humour. He did not, however, like his 'too highly organised methods'. In short, Lawrence was soon bored by the painstaking examination and cataloguing of 1,500 Egyptian corpses.

After a few weeks with Petrie, Lawrence was recalled to Karkamis. A gift of £5,000 to the British Museum and a further £2,000 from the Trustees made it possible for the excavations to be reopened and, in February 1912, Lawrence was sent by Hogarth to Aleppo to handle the problem of the site's ownership. He was also to investigate reports that German railway engineers, then beginning their bridge over the Euphrates, intended to lay foundations for a depot and workshops on the southern side of the mound. They had been temporarily deflected by a false rumour that the British Museum owned the whole site. It fell to Lawrence, assisted by a consular dragoman, to sort out the business and persuade the local landowner, Hassan ibn Hussain el Maqale, to sell his portion of the site to the British Museum. Matters were further complicated by the Ottoman Ministry of Public Instruction, which wanted rights to the site, although it lacked the cash to pay for it.[3]

Lawrence was temperamentally unsuited to play the part of diplomat, but he was immeasurably more qualified than his new senior, Leonard Woolley. The confident, mercurial Woolley was eight years older than Lawrence, whom he had briefly met in Oxford. He had excavated in Nubia, experience which qualified him to take charge of operations when Hogarth was in England. In general, Woolley believed that the best way to handle the local peasantry and the Turkish authorities was by browbeating them and, when this failed to produce acceptable results, a revolver was brandished in their faces to a background of harsh words about gunboats off Beirut. Lawrence wholeheartedly endorsed such bluster. Beset by the lawsuits of Hassan ibn Hussain el Maqale, by official doubts about whether Woolley could excavate with a permit which named Hogarth, and by obstruction from local officials in Aleppo and Birecik, Lawrence was buoyant. 'But good heavens don't you know that no Turkish officer or policeman or government official can lay hands on an Englishman, or enter his house? Much less imprison him,' he reminded his family in June 1912. 'There would be a warship in Beirut if anyone in Birecik insulted us.'[4]

Mr and Mrs Lawrence needed such an assurance. On 17 March at the onset of the legal rumpus, their son had written from Birecik:

> Have come up here with Woolley to fight the Kaimmakam [local
> commissioner]: we have done it: threatened to shoot any man who
> interrupted the digs, whether soldier or not. The Kaimm[akam] collapsed
> and sends strict orders to allow us to do our pleasure.... Woolley came
> out exceedingly well: he explained that he was not declaring war on
> the Turkish government, but on Birecik only. We are very well amused.

There were few smiles at the Consulate in Aleppo, which had to clear up the mess. It was arranged for Woolley and Lawrence to discuss their difficulties with Fakhri Pasha, the Governor of Syria. The upshot of this interview with the Turkish officer, who as commander of the Medina garrison was to be one of Lawrence's wartime adversaries, is not known. The *iradehs* and the invidious system of capitulations by which all Europeans were immune from civil or criminal actions in Ottoman courts ensured that, when the dust had settled, the Karkamis diggings proceeded unhindered. As to the Germans, the foundations of their bridge were built beyond the edge of the mound, perhaps as a result of a few words of Hogarth's, uttered when he was a dinner guest on the Kaiser's yacht.[5]

While Lawrence, pistol at hip, and Woolley, revolver in trouser waistband, swaggered and squared up to Turkish functionaries, the Ottoman empire was suffering graver and more wounding assaults. Italy, greedy for the Ottoman province of Libya, had declared war. Just after Lawrence disembarked at Beirut, Italian men-of-war had sunk two Turkish warships in the harbour. As he passed through Aleppo, Muslim crowds, inflamed by preaching in the mosques, were clamouring for arms with which to fight for Islam against the infidels. The war, which was soon to be followed by a wider conflict in southern Europe when Greece, Montenegro, Serbia, Bulgaria and Roumania combined to invade Turkey's last remaining Balkan provinces, was one of a series of convulsions which had been shaking the empire since 1908.

Lawrence was the chance witness to a society in its last days. In 1908 the Young Turk coup had ushered in an era which promised modernisation and the general application of the democratic ideal. Lawrence had already learned something of the dreams of the new movement during his 1909 visit. His charming Arab tutor, Miss Akle, told him more about the aspirations of her people, how they were groping towards a historic, national identity and their hopes for a partnership with the Turks or even independence. Even in the backwater of Jerablus there were inklings of the ferment and tension created by new ideas and awakened hopes. These were always more detectable in the cities and towns of the coast, but they crept slowly inland. In June 1911, while Lawrence was digging at Karkamis, the consular dragoman at Birecik reported an upswell in restlessness among the local Kurds and Armenians. There was also for the first time organised political activity in the shape of a newly formed Kurdish Reactionary Club.[6]

As a highly intelligent young man whose interest in his surroundings and their inhabitants was growing, Lawrence sensed the forces of historic change which were spreading through Syria even though his immediate experience of them was limited. His stamping ground around Karkamis was largely populated by illiterate peasant farmers and nomads who were only dimly aware of the world beyond their villages and camps. The ignorance of rural Arabs startled a Jewish conscript in the Turkish army who found that 'Napoleon Bonaparte and Queen Victoria are still living figures to them.' In normal circumstances, Lawrence's feelings towards such people and his reactions to the forces which were about to transform their lives would have been unimportant. After all he had come to Syria as a scholar whose primary concern was the country's distant past. But the outbreak of war turned him into one of the gravediggers of the Ottoman empire and, in time, he occupied a position in which he had considerable influence over the future of its former provinces. What he had seen and learned in Syria suddenly assumed a formidable importance.

Between 1911 and 1914, Lawrence was willingly, even enthusiastically, drawn into the complex and turbulent political life of Syria. As a medievalist, he would have recognised many features of Syrian life which were the same as those of medieval Europe. Rural and desert society was still dominated by feudal sheiks, who had armed retinues, shepherds and tenantry and levied *khawah* (protection money) on the peasantry. The ancient rights of these autocrats were underwritten by the Ottoman government, which allowed them to collect official taxes and levy private imposts on caravans and traders who crossed their lands. Lawrence had had his first, noisy introduction to this system at work in 1909 when, as a guest in a Lebanese village, he had been woken by his hosts and asked to keep watch against marauding landlords who were after their cut of the local harvest. At Karkamis in May 1912 he discovered that 'Our donkey-boy till last week was only getting 15 of the 45 piastres we pay him: the percentage of the sheik accounted for the rest: since he was a boy and helpless.'

Helplessness was the common condition of most Syrians. As an Englishman, Lawrence was repelled by the unfreedom of the Jerablus peasantry, who endured 'the hideous grind of forced labour' or were fettered to debts they could never repay. His reaction was true to the chivalric code of his warrior heroes, which enjoined the knight to protect those too weak to fend for themselves. His situation may also have reminded him of that shared by so many young English heroes of the G.A.Henty adventures he had read as a boy. In foreign lands and on the empire's frontiers, these stout fellows stood up for the downtrodden and carried with them their country's principles of fair play and honest dealing. Faced with the wretchedness of the Jerablus peasantry, victims of landlords and moneylenders and, from 1912, the bullying of German overseers, Lawrence cast himself in the role of a guardian justiciar. When news reached him in December 1911 that the diggings at Karkamis would be reopened, he looked forward to making himself the local squire. 'I feel on my native heath,' he told his parents, 'and am on the pitch of settling in a new Carcemish as Sheik.' Six months later, this ambition was within his grasp, for the British Museum committed itself to buying more land on the site. Lawrence wanted to make these acres an estate which would offer sanctuary to his labourers. 'Our workmen can move on to it, and live away from the clutches of their sheiks and mukhtars,' and in his absence, Haj Wahed, a trusted cook, would act as land agent.

Another contemporary traveller in this region had been pleased to find that the 'Ingleez' enjoyed a high prestige among the peasantry. Lawrence's wild behaviour, which included organising his labourers into competing teams and firing his revolver into the air when one had made a find, made the Jerablus Arabs think him 'mad', but they also gave him unstinted admiration and affection. His brother Will, who visited him during the summer of 1913, described him as 'a great lord in this place'. Like all sympathetic squires, Lawrence was a good listener to his tenants' stories. The conversation of uneducated Arabs was confined to recitals of family connections, sagas of blood feuds, and religion. Pedigrees and tales of rivalries and skirmishes were the stock-in-trade of Lawrence's medieval romancers, so he was fascinated by all that he heard. He also came to appreciate the quality of the storytellers, who were 'very curious and very simple, and yet with a fund of directness and child-humour about them that is very fine'. They were not, he was glad to say, like the Egyptian workmen he had met when digging with Petrie, who presumed too much and lacked deference. There was always a gulf between Lawrence and his protégés.[7]

Lawrence was also drawn into the affairs of the nomadic Kurds. A race with their own language, they occupied a region which spread from northern Syria across eastern Turkey and northern Iraq and over the Persian border. Their tribal organisation, unlike that of the Syrian Arabs, was still more or less intact. Like other races within the Ottoman empire, the Kurds were feeling their way towards a national identity and thinking of future independence. There was a sprinkling of Kurdish labourers at Karkamis, and by 1913 Lawrence had won the friendship and respect of the local Kurdish chief, Busawari Agha, and was starting to learn Kurdish.

Traditional Kurdish life, like that of the nomadic Bedu of the deserts south and east of Karkamis, was little touched either by regulations framed by the government in Constantinople or by the twentieth century. Tribal feuding and stock rustling were endemic in a region of chronic instability. In May 1911 a Jerablus village sheik had kidnapped a young girl and Lawrence watched her kin leave the diggings, pick up their guns and ride off in pursuit. He had also to be careful at the excavations to keep apart men from feuding families, and in June 1913 was forced to lock quarrelling workmen in his darkroom until they came to their senses. The Kurds were more fearsome. In June 1912, Lawrence saw a body of Kurds launch a half-hearted attack on some villagers which was repelled after a harmless exchange of revolver fire. During the autumn there were rumours that a larger tribal force was ready to attack and loot the railway works. There had been a poor harvest that year and, early in 1913, Lawrence and Woolley reported to Raff Fontana, Consul in Aleppo, that local Kurdish chiefs were planning a plundering raid on the city. Lawrence was sent down to Beirut to assist two naval officers from HMS *Duke of Edinburgh* smuggle ten rifles to the Consulate for use in the event of an attack. Whether this precaution was against the Kurds, who never turned up, or Pan-Islamic demonstrators incensed by Turkish setbacks in the Balkan Wars is not clear either from Fontana's despatches or from his wife's memories of the event.[8]

Later in the year, neutral Karkamis was the scene for a reconciliation between emissaries from Buswari Agha and a rival which Woolley and Lawrence supervised. The choice of place owed something to the desire of some Kurdish sheiks for closer relations with Britain. They were impelled by contradictory motives. If, as many suspected, the Ottoman empire was about to fall apart, the Kurds needed friends and the best candidates were Russia, whose empire bordered Turkey in the East and whose influence was creeping into northern Persia, or Britain, which dominated southern

Persia and the Persian Gulf. On the other hand, if the new rulers of Turkey achieved their goals of rejuvenation and modernisation, which would make the Ottoman empire the 'Japan of the East', then the power of Kurdish sheiks and their tribal customs would be swept away. A party of pro-British Kurdish chiefs from the Turco-Persian border region called on Fontana on their way back from Mecca and asked him to tell his government that they would 'hail British occupation as a blessing'. A fortnight later, on 27 March 1913, he reported a deputation of Arab sheiks who told him that they were convinced that there was 'no hope of improvement under the Ottoman Government'. Knowing 'that those of the faith in Egypt and India enjoy a Government preferable to this', their people 'were praying for a British Government in the country'.[9]

Behind such pleading were the fears of traditionalist Muslims that new provisions for political equality would give rights and privileges to the Greek and Armenian Christian minorities. Shortly before Lawrence had arrived in Beirut in 1909, there had been massacres of Armenians to the north in Adana which the local British Vice-Consul, Major Doughty-Wylie VC (a future intelligence colleague), had tried to stop by taking command of the Turkish garrison. The wars in Libya and the Balkans were widely interpreted as acts of Christian aggression against Islam. Lawrence was conscious of the tension during his walk through eastern Syria in the summer of 1911 and thought it imprudent to ask for food from Muslim households. Religious disturbances flickered on during 1912 and 1913, although insignificant in scale compared to the officially backed genocide which would be launched against the Armenians by Mehmed Talaat Bey, the Minister of the Interior, in January 1915.

As a neutral Englishman, Lawrence was able to have contacts with both Kurdish and Armenian nationalists, and he had learned something about Arab national dreams from Miss Akle. He was broadly sympathetic to these movements, and Woolley remembered him as an 'enthusiast' for Syrian nationalism. 'Down with the Turks!' he proclaimed to Mrs Rieder of the Jeblé mission school in April 1913, just after their defeat by the Balkan League. 'Their disappearance would mean a chance for the Arabs, who were at any rate once not incapable of good government.'[10] He offered no hint as to whether he believed this facility was recoverable.

Hogarth would have seen that self-determination for Arabs and Kurds had obvious drawbacks. He believed that backward peoples were automatically excluded from democratic processes, which he viewed with much distaste even in Britain. His Coriolanus-like disdain for the hustings made him decline Sir Mark Sykes's suggestion that he stand as Tory candidate for Oxford in December 1918.[11] Taking a historical perspective, Hogarth argued in *The Ancient East* (1914) that the Middle East, 'lost to the west' with the collapse of the Roman empire, would inevitably return to European domination.[12] Although Lawrence may have succumbed to the emotional appeal of local nationalism, his background inclined him towards Hogarth's view. Perhaps as a consequence of the ideas passed down to him from his father, Lawrence was an instinctive paternalist. The self-appointed British 'Qonsolos' (Consul) at Karkamis who settled tribal disputes and spoke to the Turkish Commissioner in Birecik 'in a lordly fashion' saw himself as agent of a benevolent imperialism. He was, in his own words, 'the protector-of-the-poor-and-enemy-of-all-the-rich-and-in-authority'. Knight errant and umpire combined, Lawrence brought peace and justice to the oppressed and fulfilled one of the highest ideals of the late-Victorian and Edwardian empire. Whether or not his behaviour at Karkamis contributed to the feeling among some Kurds and Arabs that they would be better off under British rule is not known. Nevertheless, in April 1914, Sir Edward Grey, the Foreign Secretary, had to deny publicly that there were agents abroad in Syria canvassing local support for British annexation.[13]

As patron of the natives of Jerablus and its environs and the upholder of British principles of fair-dealing and justice, Lawrence saw it as his first duty to keep all foreign influences at bay. In day-to-day terms this involved taking a strong line with the team of German engineers working a few hundred yards away on their railway bridge. Lawrence found them 'rather unpleasant creatures'. One, a senior engineer called Contzen, he told Robert Graves, was particularly odious. He had a fleshy bull's neck which overhung his collar; this was of course the hallmark of the stereotype Prussian officer which Walt Whitman had called 'the mark of the beast'. Together Contzen and his colleagues drank too much rakis, contaminated the village of Jerablus with what Lawrence called 'the sweepings of Aleppo', and treated every native with brutal contempt.

There were between 1912 and 1914 a number of clashes which had started with the row over whether part of the site would be covered with engine sheds and workshops. Lawrence and Woolley always took the labourers' part against their employers and their guards. In one incident, which Lawrence recounted to Graves, he took up the cudgels on behalf of his servant Dahoum after the boy had asked the Germans for back pay and received a beating for his presumption. Lawrence demanded and got an apology after threatening to thrash the man responsible. Prestige rather than legal principle seemed to have been at stake for, when Lawrence caught some dynamite poachers on the Euphrates, he urged the local police to have them flogged. British prestige soared in the neighbourhood in May 1914 when Woolley and he restored order after an unpleasant affray between the Germans, their Circassian and Turkish guards and local villagers and

Kurds. The trouble started when a Circassian guard shot dead a Kurd during a quarrel over unpaid wages. Site workers seized guns, pickaxes and hatchets and attacked the German offices and there was some shooting in which Woolley was nearly hit. Between them, Woolley and Lawrence calmed the natives and later used their influence with the Kurds to arrange payments of blood money for the man killed and others wounded.

Relations with the Germans were not always acerbic. Some engineers were invited to the archaeologists' lodgings and borrowed books. Lawrence entertained the agreeable Heinrich Meissner, who had built the Damascus-to-Medina line and directed the operations of the Baghdad railway. Another, more sinister guest at Karkamis was the Freiherr Max von Oppenheim, a Bavarian Jewish millionaire who divided his time between archaeology and political intrigue. 'I hardly was polite,' remarked Lawrence after the meeting, 'but was interesting instead.' Oppenheim could not be trusted and was under partial surveillance by consular dragomen. In October 1911 he was purchasing land for 'colonisation' near Tel Halaf on the Baghdad line and bribing Arab sheiks near Mosul. No doubt Oppenheim thought Lawrence was a man who should be watched. He constantly meddled in the affairs of the German railway builders and generally behaved in a manner which suggested that his object was to demonstrate to the local Kurds and Arabs that Britain, not Germany, was their true friend.

For Lawrence, the railway symbolised the penetration of Syria by foreign influences and the wider forces of change which were altering the way of life of its people. He resented both. The Germans whom he encountered at Karkamis represented a country which was fast developing close political and economic ties with the Ottoman empire. Even so they were comparative latecomers on the Middle Eastern scene and in 1914 their share of Ottoman trade was still a fraction of Britain's. In terms of finance, Turkey was beholden to France, which in 1914 had 800 million francs (£40 million) invested in the empire and controlled 60 per cent of the Ottoman national debts. Since the 1840s, France had followed a programme of systematic infiltration of the Lebanon and Syria through state-subsidised mission schools. By 1914 French schools had a roll of 100,000 pupils, a tenth of the entire school population of the Ottoman empire. This attempt to dominate the region's culture and capture the minds of its middle classes through an educational monopoly had been devised to yield political returns.[14]

France sought to enter Syria through the *bourse* and the classroom and by 1912, when the Foreign Minister Cambon believed that the Ottoman empire was on its last legs, prepared for annexation. A department was set up in the Quai d'Orsay to draw up plans for occupation and, in February 1914, a conference of French and German businessmen discussed economic partition of the region. France came out of it rather well with a promise of paramountcy in Syria, while Germany went away free to develop concessions along the track of the Baghdad railway. British influence in the Persian Gulf was to remain unchallenged. In the House of Commons, Sir Mark Sykes, who knew the area intimately, was indignant. 'Cosmopolitan harpies', he announced, 'are now preparing in the most legitimate way to rob the inhabitants [of the Ottoman empire] under the guise of introducing them to the benefits of civilization.'[15]

If he read an account of Sykes's speech, either in *The Times* or in the Parliamentary summaries in *Punch*, which was regularly posted to Karkamis, Lawrence would have applauded. After six months in Syria, he had changed his tune. He had now utterly abandoned his earlier belief that its people needed improvement and civilisation. In June 1912 he had written from Karkamis:

> Fortunately there is no foreign influence as yet in this district: if only you had seen the ruination caused by the French influence, and to a lesser degree by the American, you would never wish it extended. The perfectly hopeless vulgarity of the half-Europeanised Arab is appalling. Better a thousand times, the Arab untouched. The foreigners come out here always to teach, whereas they had very much better learn, for in everything but wits and knowledge, the Arab is generally the better man of the two.

Although the previous January he had accepted the hospitality of the American mission school at Jeblé and would do so again in the summer of 1912, he confided his contempt for such institutions to Woolley.

Lawrence's conversion to the quintessentially conservative dogma that Arab society and customs should remain inviolate from external influences was emotional rather than intellectual. During the first digging season at Karkamis, he developed close ties with Selim Ahmed, an Arab boy of about fourteen or fifteen, whom he called by his nickname 'Dahoum' or the dark one. The name was a local joke since Dahoum was rather light-skinned and Lawrence thought he might have had a dash of Armenian blood. He first met Dahoum when he was employed carrying water to the labourers, but once his aptitude was apparent he graduated to houseboy. By June 1911, when Lawrence set off for Urfa, Dahoum had become his servant. He attended Lawrence when he took a holiday on the coast in the summer of 1912 (he was 'cheaper than local labour'), was with him when he was in Beirut arranging the shipment to England of Karkamis finds in January 1913. Then, Lawrence got a lift to Alexandretta on board the cruiser *Duke of Edinburgh*, whose officers were so impressed by Dahoum's qualities that they 'made him offers to come with them permanently'. Perhaps as a reward for his loyalty and to satisfy his curiosity, Lawrence took Dahoum together with Haroun, the site foreman, to England in the summer of 1913. Dahoum was also Lawrence's servant during part of the Sinai expedition in 1914.

A good-looking, intellectually curious but, by reason of his upbringing, naive young Arab, Dahoum was to Lawrence as a squire was to a knight. The boy had first come to Lawrence's attention because, unlike the other villagers, he could read and write a little and was keen to go to school in Aleppo. The boy had a natural wit and ingenuousness which appealed to Lawrence. He also presented his patron with a dilemma. The fulfilment of Dahoum's ambitions for self-improvement would mean the corruption of his endearing innocence which Lawrence found so refreshing. Dahoum's education would have to be carefully controlled, even censored. In July 1911, Lawrence asked Mrs Rieder for some books for Dahoum, but he insisted that 'Nothing with a taste of Frangi [that is, French influence] was to enter Jerablus by my means.' Not long after, Lawrence played with setting up his own school in the village and for a time was running classes for Arab youths in multiplication tables, local history and geography. Dahoum was also given instruction in photography.

Dahoum's attentions were very flattering. Although Woolley considered that the boy's gifts were limited, Lawrence could record some intellectual progress. Dahoum 'is beginning to use his reason as well as his instinct', Lawrence told his parents in July 1911. Of course, Lawrence did not dissent from the common view expressed by another traveller in the region that 'All Orientals are children, and the average native of Anatolia and Kurdistan is not only a child, but one with very limited intellectual capacity.' Once, as part of a trick to deter a Turkish gendarme from scrounging brandy under guise of sickness, Lawrence had forced Dahoum and another boy to drink water aerated by aperient Seidlitz powder. The fizziness terrified Dahoum, who went about saying, 'I drank some of that sorcery, it is very dangerous, since by it men are turned suddenly into the forms of animals.' Lawrence was amused, as he was by Dahoum's wonderment at the gadgetry on the British man-of-war and the London Underground, on which he travelled during his holiday in England. His and his master's reactions were a reminder of the vast gulf of experience and understanding which separated them.[16]

Yet Lawrence could find much in common with him. He was deeply grateful to him for opening his mind to the peerless solitude of the desert. The memory of the moment was recalled in the *Seven Pillars*:

> But at last Dahoum drew me: 'Come and smell the very sweetest scent of all,' and we went to the main lodging, to the gaping window sockets of its eastern face, and there drank with open mouths of the effortless, empty, eddyless wind of the desert, throbbing past.

This revelation came to a man already converted to a belief that the ideal environment was silent and empty and that absolute simplicity was the highest virtue.

Not only could Dahoum teach Lawrence, they could share in boyish amusements. They exchanged clothes and, for the first time, Lawrence began to dress in Arab costume. Once, during 1912 when the archaeologists' house was being built, Lawrence persuaded Dahoum to pose naked for him for a sculpture which was eventually set on the roof. The villagers were scandalised; any representation of the human form was forbidden to Muslim artists and the Quran condemned homosexuality. There was a whiff of the Uranian about the companions and Woolley, in his memoir of Lawrence, felt obliged to say that he was in 'no sense a pervert'. Woolley added that 'He liked to shock,' which is in all likelihood the most accurate explanation of Lawrence's careless disregard of local prejudices.

Lawrence and Dahoum also shared a frightening adventure. The story was told by Lawrence to Graves and Liddell Hart, who were given no dates. Alerted by reports that a large, possibly Hittite carving had been unearthed in a region north of Birecik, Lawrence set off to investigate, accompanied by Dahoum. The pair were arrested at Halfati as suspected draft dodgers and thrown into a noisome dungeon from which they escaped the next morning by means of a bribe. In one version, Lawrence was man-handled, possibly whipped, but not robbed since he had cash on him for a *douceur*.[17]

During October 1912, Turkish police and soldiers were sweeping the country around Aleppo for reluctant reservists and Woolley and Lawrence had to use their letters of protection to get immunity for their labourers. The countryside was scoured again in September 1913. If Lawrence had been unlucky enough to get ensnared in one of these nets, he never mentioned his mishap to his family, Woolley or the British Consulate. This reticence seems strange considering his zeal in making full use of all the official privileges to which he was entitled. Stranger still was his utter folly, since he went off unarmed and in native dress into a region where brigandage was commonplace. Even if Lawrence followed a reckless impulse, it is hard to believe that Turkish officials mistook him for a native, even a light-skinned Circassian. According to an American who met him in 1914 he was 'a clean-cut blonde with peaches and cream complexion which the dry heat of the Euphrates Valley seemed powerless to spoil'. Much later and in the context of the desert war, Lawrence felt sure that 'No easterner could have taken me for an Arab, for a moment,' and in September 1912 he had admitted that he was still a long way from fluency in Arabic. As in earlier tales of hairbreadth escapes, it is impossible to distinguish invention from reality. Nor were there any bounds to his capacity for expanding a tale. In September 1918, he pointed out to Private Rolls a cellar in the ruined castle at el Azraq (far to the south of Karkamis) and said, 'Once I was kept prisoner in that dungeon for months,' and showed him scratchings on the wall which represented his efforts to break free.[18]

Whether or not Lawrence shared the perils of imprisonment and rough usage with Dahoum, his passion for the Arab boy had far-reaching consequences. The intensity of Lawrence's feelings and their eventual expression in action were reflected in the dedicatory poem to the *Seven Pillars*, 'To S[elim]. A[hmed].':

> I loved you, so I drew these tides of men into my hands
> and wrote my will across the sky in stars
> To earn you Freedom, the seven-pillared worthy house,
> that your eyes might be shining for me
> When we came.

This emotion was deeply felt and sincere. When, in 1919, George Kidston, a professional diplomat, asked Lawrence to explain why he had become so closely involved in the Arab national movement, he was given four reasons. The first was personal, 'I liked a particular Arab very much, and I thought that freedom for the race would be an acceptable present.'[19]

Lawrence's answer begs many questions. Leaving aside his assessment of his motives during the war, what were the ingredients of his 'freedom' and why did he think an unsophisticated Arab youth would want it? Between 1911 and 1914 Lawrence had developed a powerful attachment to Dahoum and may have been conscious of a wish to do something for the Arabs, an ambition which at the time would have seemed beyond fulfilment. Dahoum embodied what Lawrence liked best about the Arabs and illustrated their present predicament. He was the heir to values and traditions which Lawrence believed should be preserved from outside interference. He cherished ambitions of self-improvement which, by their very nature, involved opening his mind to ideas from the West, and these, Lawrence thought, were ultimately destructive. Scepticism, which lay at the heart of so much Western thinking, had no place in Dahoum's world. The Arabs 'were a dogmatic people, despising doubt, our modern crown of thorns', he later wrote in the *Seven Pillars*.

Emancipation of the Arab mind was, for Lawrence, dangerous. Its consequence would be the extension of European ideologies and the uprooting of tradition. Yet, to judge from what he had to say on the matter, Lawrence found the Arabs' helplessness in the face of sheiks, landlords, officials, policemen and moneylenders repugnant. He hoped to achieve a well-nigh impossible balancing act, liberating the Arabs from their everyday tyrannies but preserving the integrity of their culture. That one was perhaps a part of the other did not strike him. Furthermore, Lawrence never cared to ask Dahoum or any other Arab whether they wanted his or any other form of deliverance. There seemed no point, for, as he remarked in the *Seven Pillars*, 'They were a limited, narrow-minded people, whose inert intellects lay fallow in incurious resignation.'

Beyond Lawrence's Arcadia at Karkamis were small groups of Arabs who were stumbling towards national self-realisation. They largely belonged to that Western-educated class which Lawrence despised, and drew on European liberal philosophers for some of their ideals. Like him, many were apprehensive about European political and economic imperialism, which they believed could only be kept at arm's length as long as the Arabs stayed under Ottoman rule.

Arab nationalists had been exultant at the news of the Young Turk coup in 1908 and threw themselves wholeheartedly into the subsequent constitutional experiment. When the first Ottoman parliament assembled at Constantinople in December 1908, 72 of its 260 members were Arabs. In the years which followed, Arab cultural and political societies sprang up in Constantinople, Beirut, Damascus, Aleppo, Baghdad and Basra, drawing members from the professional classes. The largest, al Fatat, looked on Europe as a source of ideas, but stayed firm to the principle that the best interests of Arabs would be served by a partnership with the Turks. The Jammiyyat al Nahda al Arabiyya (Arab Renaissance Society) founded in 1907 concurred, but saw the creation of an educated, enlightened middle class as the Arabs' most pressing need. This elite would be the dynamic force which would regenerate their people from above.

Other Arabs, who knew little of and cared less for Western political thought, were taking tentative steps towards independence. Since 1902, Ibn Saud of Riyadh had been making approaches to the Indian government which he hoped would back him as he established himself as a semi-independent ruler in central Arabia. Early in 1914, Abdullah, one of the sons of Hussain, the Sharif of Mecca, had called on Lord Kitchener in Cairo. He was seeking more than British patronage for he directly requested machine-guns which, the British rightly guessed, were intended for use in tribal wars and against Turkish garrisons in western Arabia.[20] He was following the example set by el Idrissi, the Yemeni rebel, who had courted the Italians in 1912 and received arms and naval assistance in his campaign against the Turks.[21] These were straws in the wind, but together they indicated the willingness of traditionalist Arab rulers to make secret deals with the imperial powers and to beg for material help with which to defy their overlord, the Sultan.

Like the Kurdish chieftains whom Lawrence knew in Syria, these Arab rulers were nervous about the policies of the government in Constantinople. A resurgent and confident Ottoman government would, in time, strip them of their feudal powers and local authority. Moreover, as deeply conservative Muslims, they were offended by the secular principles which the Young Turks were embracing.

Between 1911 and 1914, the government inaugurated by the Young Turk revolution drifted into dictatorship. The democratic ideal first proclaimed in 1908 failed to survive the buffets of external war and the pressures of minority nationalism. Control of the empire passed into the hands of the Committee of Union and Progress (CUP). It comprised the more radical Young Turks and was dominated by such 'new men' as Mehmed Talaat Bey, a former postal clerk, and the pro-German Enver Pasha, a junior officer who had become Minister of War. They were faced with an immediate need to preserve Ottoman unity and to instil a sense of imperial pride in the Sultan's subjects. Their fumbling approach and contradictory policies succeeded in making matters worse. Radicals, Muslim conservatives and religious and ethnic minorities were even more apprehensive and confused than before.

Minority nationalism was countered by the encouragement of purely Turkish nationalism. Genghis Khan was actively promoted as a Turanian [i.e. Turkish] hero and the teaching of the Turkish language was enforced in schools throughout the empire. In 1916 Turkish became the official language for all business transactions. This upsurge in aggressive Turanian nationalism dismayed educated Arabs who, with good reason, feared that their own, embryonic national identity would be stifled. Conservatives were indignant at plans to translate the Quran into Turkish even though, as Muslims believed, Allah had spoken to Muhammad in Arabic. The orthodox interpreted Turkish defeats in Libya and the Balkans as indications of Allah's displeasure with their impiety. Untroubled, the CUP pressed on with the imposition of secular legal codes throughout the empire (civil marriage was instituted in 1917) in place of the traditional Muslim *sharia*.[22]

While with one hand the CUP broadcast Turanian propaganda and insisted on secularisation, with the other it promoted Islamic unity. Whatever their political differences, Turks and Arabs were brothers in the faith and their secular ruler, the Sultan Medmed V, was also Caliph, the spiritual head of Islam and successor to the Prophet. The CUP appreciated that religion was still a powerful cement which could bind together the two largest racial groups in the empire. At its Salonika Conference in 1911, the CUP resolved to harness and exploit Pan-Islamic forces not only within the empire but beyond. Muslims under Russian rule in the Caucasus and Central Asia and under British rule in India were publicly reminded that the last-remaining Islamic power, the Ottoman empire, was their natural protector. The message was understood by Arabs. Severed from Turkey, they would fall prey to France, Britain and Russia, the acquisitive Christian imperial powers which over the past hundred years had overrun North Africa, Egypt, the Sudan, Central Asia, and northern India. 'The Arab Umma [nation] does not want to separate itself from the Ottoman empire,' insisted Iskaner Amman, al Fatat's Vice-President. Other nationalists concurred. If the Turks would make concessions and allow them a fair share in the government, the loyalty of the Arab people was assured.[23]

Lawrence would review these developments from a post-war perspective. In the *Seven Pillars* he wrote dismissively of the educated Arab elites of Syria and the Lebanon who were 'full of Herbert Spencer and Alexander Hamilton' and wanted 'freedom to come by entreaty, not by sacrifice'. Since some were already, by 1914, making clandestine approaches to the French, his contempt is understandable. Likewise his irritation with those Arabs who throughout the war were unwilling to sever ties with the Ottoman empire. Their caution and backsliding was contrasted with the determination and courage of Lawrence's Arabs, the armies of the ultraconservative Sharif Hussain, who was prepared to shed his allegiance to the Sultan and ally himself with Britain and France.

For the Turks, Lawrence had nothing but vilification. Three years in Syria had left him convinced that what he called the 'blight' of the Turkish government had to be removed from the province. He had, however, in 1913 been prepared to be employed by the Turkish government as an excavator at Rakka. Four years of war transformed him into an implacable hater of Turks. An intemperate and bitter hatred of the Turks runs through the *Seven Pillars* which is unequalled in any other account of the war on this front. While he could have found abundant support for his views from the well-known evidence of the Armenian massacres, Lawrence chose instead to base his vituperation on a bogus assertion that half the Turkish army was infected with venereal diseases transmitted by sodomy.

There is little to support such a distasteful contention. Venereal infection increased in Turkey as it did in other countries whose moral codes were upset by the war. The Ottoman army's medical system had all but collapsed by 1917 and records are therefore incomplete. Those available suggest that out of a total of 446,000 recorded Turkish casualties, 27,000 died as a result of venereal infection. British medical records, drawn from examinations of Turkish prisoners taken during the 1917 and 1918 campaigns in Palestine, recorded an epidemic of pellagra and large amounts of malaria, dysentery and influenza. Prisoners taken on the Iraq front suffered from cholera and relapsing fever. All these maladies were the obvious consequence of dietary deficiencies and lack of basic medicines. Turkish logistics, not Turkish morals, had fallen apart.[24]

The passion with which Lawrence blackguarded the Turks after the war probably owed little to his experience of them before. He would have got to know very few and most whom he encountered would have been from the official classes. Such men, another traveller in Syria observed, tended to treat the English as equals, which would not have recommended them to Lawrence. Furthermore Lawrence's attachment to what he regarded as the Arab cause made him look on the Turks as an alien, occupying power in Syria.

Three years in that country, admittedly as a foreigner hedged by official privileges which placed him above the law, taught Lawrence much. His experiences in Karkamis led him to believe that he possessed a facility to command the affections of the ordinary Arabs. In England, he had established no close personal ties with anyone outside his family, but in Syria he had become attached to an Arab boy who reciprocated his devotion. Hogarth had guided Lawrence towards the Middle East in order that he could learn to become an archaeologist. He may also have been aware that Lawrence, whose birth and unconventional behaviour made it hard for him to fit into English society, might find himself more at home in a world whose values were different. Certainly Syria gave him an opportunity to behave flamboyantly; and paradoxically his extravagance, which had been frowned on in England, delighted the Arabs.

Lawrence was living in a region which was entering a period of revolution. The prospect both excited and frightened him. His reactions to change were accordingly hesitant and confused; he wished both to see the Arabs emancipated from Turkish rule and to quarantine them from modern thought and commerce. The villagers of Jerablus enchanted him and he wanted to keep them just as they were, as much for his own satisfaction as for their benefit. Lawrence had been converted to Arab nationalism, but on his own and not Arab terms. On a small scale he had made himself a benefactor to the Arabs and his dreams may have encompassed gestures on a grander scale. The chances of their translation into action seemed extremely remote. As 1914 opened, the Ottoman empire lumbered on, and Europe was outwardly tranquil. All that Lawrence could be certain of was a further five or even six years dedicated to unearthing Hittite remains and sticking together broken pots.

V

FOR KING AND COUNTRY, 1914

THE digging season at Karkamis stopped in December 1913 as cold and wet weather closed in. Thanks to Hogarth, Woolley and Lawrence had been assigned as archaeologists to the Egyptian military survey of western Sinai. Their brief was to trace ancient caravan routes, identify Biblical sites, and generally find out what they could about the historical development of a hitherto seldom explored region. Their work was to be concentrated in the central Negev around the Zin watercourse, and their joint account of their discoveries, which Hogarth edited, was called *The Wilderness of Zin*.

This was Lawrence's first serious published work and appeared in the summer of 1915 under the imprint of the expedition's sponsor, the Palestine Exploration Fund. It was, according to Hogarth, 'a very faithful, discerning, and picturesque description of natural features and social character'. Hogarth also praised the 'zeal and aptitude' of his two protégés and acknowledged Lawrence's unrivalled knowledge of Crusading and Hittite history. Hogarth concluded his recommendation of the book to Fund subscribers by drawing attention to its fluency and wit. 'The style of the descriptive chapters is eminently readable, and the serious matter is relieved by lighter touches here and there, mostly in the vein of irony which close contact with Orientals seldom fails to encourage in the Western mind – and, perhaps, equally in the Eastern.'[1]

The book was well received at the Fund's annual general meeting in June 1915 when the President, Colonel Watson, an engineer, noted, 'It is satisfactory to think that our explorers, civil as well as military, are under the flag.' A former balloonist, he added that 'Mr Lawrence was at one time, as a lightweight, used as an observer in an aeroplane – very useful for a man who surveys the country.'[2]

The background to the Sinai expedition of January 1914 was military. In 1905, the Turkish government decided to make a gesture designed to remind the Egyptians that they were Muslims and, in theory, still subjects of the Sultan, although their government had been controlled by Britain since 1882. Turkish patrols turned back a British surveying party, shifted frontier posts westwards towards the Suez Canal, and temporarily increased the Aqaba garrison to 4,500. Britain found this sabre-rattling intolerable and responded by sending a cruiser to Aqaba while warning the Turks that their provocation could lead to war. This stern reaction was dictated not so much by fears of the Turkish army marching into Sinai as by the knowledge, passed on by Lord Cromer, formerly Consul-General Egypt, and Kitchener, who had commanded the Egyptian army, that a Turkish attack would certainly trigger popular uprisings and mutinies inside Egypt. The crisis passed but the threat lingered. The purpose of Captain New-combe, the expedition leader, was not merely the extension of geographical knowledge: his maps would be invaluable in the event of a war with Turkey, which Britain's strategic planners knew would involve an invasion of Egypt across the Sinai desert.

Lawrence liked Newcombe; the two men would serve together during the war and remain close friends until Lawrence's death. They soon found they had much in common, for Lawrence admired the stark simplicity of the soldier's camp and the Spartan rigour of the expedition's routines. Newcombe was an audacious, restless and unorthodox soldier. Years later, Colonel Edouard Brémond, who served alongside him in Hejaz, recalled him as 'un soldat plein d'allant, mais dont la nervosité inquiétait ses chefs; l'un d'eux le qualifiait de "wild man".' Newcombe's manner did not blind his superiors to his professional talents. General Sir Reginald Wingate, anxious to secure his services in Arabia, described him as 'a first-rate soldier and a man of boundless energy and resource'.[3]

Newcombe directed five survey parties, which charted the region south of Gaza. At first, the local Arabs were uncooperative and hostile but, thanks to Newcombe's tact, relations improved. Lawrence found the Negev land-scape and its inhabitants uniformly depressing. 'The wearing monotony of senseless rounded hills and unmeaning valleys' made 'this southern desert of Syria one of the most inhospitable of all deserts'. The tribesmen were wretched creatures, 'few in number, poor in body, and miserable in their manner of life'.[4]

One of the tasks assigned to Woolley and Lawrence was the investigation of Ain Qadeis, which had been identified as the Biblical Karnesh Barnea, one of the Israelite resting-places during their forty-year migration through Sinai. What the two found was completely at odds with the eyewitness description published in 1884 by an American preacher H. Clay Trumbull. The discrepancies between what they saw and what the cleric said he had seen was an excuse for some dry pedantic humour: 'Lastly, the pool into which Trumbull's Arabs, after stripping, plunged so rashly to have a bath, is only about a foot or eighteen inches deep, and full of very large and sharp stones. Our guide also washed his feet in it.' This led into a wider criticism of those who rather too easily linked modern places with those named in the Bible. 'That glib catchword "The unchanging East" has blinded writers to the continual ebb and flow of the inhabitants of the desert' and encouraged a mistaken faith in the continuity of place-names. Modern archaeologists knew better, and they pointed out that there were very good strategic and agrarian reasons why the region around Ain Qadeis could have served as an Israelite headquarters 'during forty years of discipline' in Sinai. As intended, these gibes provoked an academic row. An irritated partisan of the worthy Trumbull wrote from an American university to rebuke Lawrence and Woolley and insisted that the Palestine Exploration Fund excised their 'objectionable statements' from future editions of *The Wilderness of Zin.*[5]

Lawrence not only had fun at the expense of an earnest American clergyman; he teased the Turks in Aqaba. He had left Woolley and moved southwest across the Negev towards the Wadi el Araba and Aqaba. His search was for archaeological remains which might indicate for how long and by whom the township had been occupied. The commander of the small Turkish garrison suspected him of being a spy, forbade him to take photographs and refused him permission to cross to the small island of Gez Faraun. Lawrence constructed three makeshift rafts from zinc tanks and paddled himself, Dahoum and the camera across waters which he believed were shark-infested. Thwarted, the Turkish officer took no further action. Aqaba was, in 1914, an insignificant outpost whose garrison of sixty showed no stomach for a fight when, on 2 November, a naval landing party came ashore.[6] Still, Lawrence was taking a risk, more dangerous for Dahoum, who was an Ottoman subject, than for himself. Free to leave Aqaba, he travelled northwards, examined Petra and caught a train to Damascus at Maan.

After paying off his servants at Maan, where Dahoum generously agreed to forgo his wages, Lawrence found himself short of cash. This happened often to him and this time he was rescued by the lucky appearance of another English traveller, Lady Evelyn Cobbold, who advanced him some money. His charm served him well as it had in the spring of 1912 when he had thrown himself on the mercy of Raff Fontana, the Consul in Aleppo. Fontana cashed his cheques but was annoyed at the depletions of consular funds and the bad impression created locally by two Englishmen out of pocket – Woolley was in the same predicament. At other times Lawrence borrowed from Woolley in anticipation of remittances from home. Like many spendthrifts he was generous, and letters home indicate that he constantly bought presents for his family.

Lawrence was back in Karkamis by the beginning of March for a fourth season of digging. The lodgings he shared with Woolley, Hogarth and any visitor who had come to inspect the workings were sumptuous. They had been built in the spring of 1912, when Lawrence had arranged the removal and relaying of a Roman mosaic pavement of 250,000 pieces for the floor of the main room. Fittings included an abundance of fine carpets, and furnishings were carefully purchased in Aleppo. Unglazed Hittite cups were used for tea and coffee and Lawrence, who still abjured spirits, began to take wine with his meals. The decorations may have been Oriental, but the ambience was donnish. An American student visitor recalled Hogarth smoking his pipe and Woolley an after-dinner cigar, in an atmosphere which was elegant and academic. What his hosts thought of their guest, who turned up in a football sweater marked with a large 'K', is not known.[7]

Another, perhaps less agreeable feature of Oxonian life had been transplanted to Karkamis, Lawrence's taste for undergraduate pranks. Once, Woolley, ailing from a fever, was given a disturbed night after Lawrence rigged up a device with a nail and a tin plate which rattled continuously. Hogarth was peeved to discover that Lawrence had scattered a pink cushion, hairpins, scent bottles and other female knick-knacks in his bedroom to remind him that he was forgoing married domesticity. It was Lawrence's turn to fume when he was the victim of some playful Kurdish girls who tried to strip off his clothes and discover whether he was white all over. Woolley waspishly commented that Lawrence's sense of humour was all one-sided, and that he was quick to anger when he found himself the butt of another's joke.

When he came to Karkamis for a 'peep' at the railway, Captain Hubert Young, a real spy, found Lawrence a shy, quiet scholar who looked about sixteen or eighteen. Joined by Lawrence's brother Will, the three spent much time target-shooting with rifles and revolvers.[8] The sound of gunfire regularly broke the stillness of Karkamis as Lawrence kept his eye in. Just as the heroes of his medieval romances exercised with sword and lance, he practised with their modern equivalents. Skill with each was of course invaluable to a European resident in an ungovernable part of the Middle East and surrounded by armed tribesmen.

Pistols and their use were on Lawrence's mind again at the outbreak of war in August 1914 when he ordered a brace of .45 Colt automatics from Mrs Rieder, who had returned to America from the Jeblé mission. They were destined for the battlefield, not the range, and soon after they arrived Lawrence gave one to his brother Frank, who was then in training camp prior to embarkation for service on the Western Front.

Lawrence had been brought up in an intensely patriotic, conservative family. As a child his father had taken him, no doubt dressed in his sailor suit, to watch Queen Victoria review the fleet at Spithead in 1897. As much as Rupert Brooke, he and his brothers Frank and Will represented that generation which volunteered with light, adventurous hearts and lofty sense of duty. Their response to the call to arms was an awesome and profoundly moving phenomenon. An insight into Lawrence's mind at this time comes from two letters written to his parents after Frank's death in action on the Western Front in May 1915.[9]

> I hope that when I die there will be nothing more to regret. The only thing I feel a little is that there was no need surely to go into mourning for him. I cannot see the cause at all – in any case to die for one's country is a sort of privilege : Mother and you will find it more painful and harder to live for it, than he did to die : but I think that at this time it is one's duty to show no signs that would distress others. . . .

This appeal troubled Mrs Lawrence, so her son wrote again.

> You *will* never understand any of us after we have grown up a little. *Don't* you ever feel that we love you without our telling you so? – I feel such a contemptible worm for having to write this way about things. If only you knew that if one thinks deeply about anything one would rather die than say anything about it. You know men do nearly all die laughing, because they know death is very terrible, and a thing to be forgotten till after it is come.

Lawrence urged his mother to show the stoic impassiveness of a caste whose duty it was to show others a lead. 'In a time of such fearful stress,' he wrote, 'it is one's duty to watch very carefully lest one of the weaker ones be offended; and you know we were always the stronger, and if they see you broken down they will all grow fearful about their ones at the front.' When it was Lawrence's turn to see action, he took care that his mother never knew the perils he was exposed to behind enemy lines.[10]

Frank Lawrence, already destined for the army, had been commissioned in the 3rd Gloucesters in September 1914. Like Ned, he had held to a high sense of purpose, but he had not been blind to his possible fate. 'I didn't go to say good-bye to Frank', Lawrence explained to his mother, 'because he would rather I didn't, and I knew that there was little chance of my seeing him again; in which case we were better without parting.' Will Lawrence, who was following the course of the war from Delhi, was also keen to volunteer. By November, he was serving as an officer in the 9th Gurkha Rifles, and four months later he returned home to join the Oxfordshire and Buckinghamshire Light Infantry. He briefly met Ned at Port Said in March 1915, and in October was killed serving as a Royal Flying Corps observer.

Lawrence later claimed that he had gone to the army recruiting officer, but had been turned down as too short. In fact his abilities were needed elsewhere. During the autumn of 1914, the War Office was desperately casting about for young men whose talents could be used by Military Intelligence. Priority was naturally given to those who spoke German or had travelled in France, but there was a need for other specialists. Hogarth, who realised Lawrence's potential value to intelligence in the event of Turkey throwing in her lot with Germany, pulled strings, and by October Lawrence was attached to the Geographical Section of the War Office.

Still a civilian, he was ordered to classify roads and tracks on the army's new map of Sinai. He was a diligent worker who impressed his section's commander, Colonel Coote Hedley. On 1 November, the Ottoman empire declared war on the Allies, and soon after Lawrence was commissioned. He was ordered to proceed to Cairo with Newcombe (whose help he had sought to secure a swift commission) and Woolley and join the expanding intelligence section attached to General Headquarters. For a time, his mother contemplated going out with him, but abandoned the idea, no doubt because of her husband's bronchial disorders.[11] Lawrence and Newcombe crossed to France in the first week of December and at Marseilles took ship for Alexandria.

Lawrence was glad that the chance had come for him to do something to bring about the downfall of the Ottoman empire. Throughout September and October he had been hoping that the Turks would make common cause with Germany and Austria–Hungary. Once Turkey took the plunge, he felt her eventual defeat was assured and her empire would be dismantled to the benefit of all. He found the announcement that capitulations had been abolished 'amusing' and was indignant that the Ottoman government now had legal control over and the right to tax foreign property. This gesture of independence was welcomed throughout the Ottoman empire, whose subjects duly celebrated the outbreak of war with the same wild enthusiasm as those of the European powers.

The crisis of 1914 had put Turkey in an impossible position. In June, her diplomats had proposed an alliance with Britain, which they hoped might guarantee the immunity of Ottoman provinces from seizure by Russia or France. Britain, unwilling to be tied to an alliance which would harm her *ententes* with Russia and France, rebuffed the Turkish approach. She then went further and showed her indifference to Turkey by seizing two Turkish battleships which were nearing completion in British yards. They had been paid for by public subscription and their confiscation provoked a wave of anti-Allied agitation. The way was now open for Enver Pasha and his pro-German war party. Ottoman neutrality, they argued, would be disastrous since, if Britain, France and Russia won the war, they would be free to dismember the empire. An alliance on equal terms with Germany and Austria–Hungary would boost the standing of Turkey. In the event of a victory, Ottoman survival would be assured and there would be substantial rewards, including Egypt and the Caucasus. In effect, the Turkish empire had no choice but to join Germany.

When he had left Karkamis in June, Lawrence had expected to return to the Middle East, continue his career as an archaeologist and work on his projected book. Giving way to the pressure of external events and impelled by his own concepts of duty, Lawrence found himself six months later a junior officer attached to the staff of the British army in Egypt. It was a turning point in his life marked, significantly, by the burning of the draft of his projected 'Seven Pillars of Wisdom'. His ambitions as a creative writer remained and, the war over, he resurrected the title for a new book based upon what he had seen and done with the Arab armies. Of course when he volunteered, Lawrence had resigned control over his life to the army, and he could have had no inkling of what it would do with him.

The Karkamis idyll had ended and with it a period of enjoyable, indulgent drifting. It had been a satisfactory existence which Lawrence would never experience again. The nearest he came to a summary of what he wanted from himself and from the world was an admission, made in December 1913, to Vyvyan Richards: 'I fought very hard, at Oxford and after going down, to avoid being labelled.' As a result, at twenty-six he was an elusive butterfly who flitted between extremes of mood and behaviour. He could be alternately animated and withdrawn, ostentatious and unobtrusive. He had a perceptive intellect and was considered a promising scholar, but his academic energies were easily diffused. He dreamed of silent, contemplative retirement, but relished spasms of intensive activity in which he stretched his body beyond the point of exhaustion. Above all, he sought and generally got what he wanted on his own terms.

It must have been very bewildering for his friends and family. Yet he possessed an infinite charm and often revealed a warm nature which made it easy for his friends to overlook his eccentricities. Many, then and later, wondered whether he had ever really outgrown his schooldays.

Two

INTELLIGENCE OFFICER

December 1914–June 1916

I

WAR AND DUTY

'IT promises to be good fun' was Lawrence's reaction to his first few days on the staff of the intelligence section at General Headquarters in Cairo. Rooms at the Savoy Hotel had been commandeered for offices and were being filled by a company of regular soldiers, ex-consuls, travellers, a former journalist and archaeologists like Lawrence. All knew something about the Middle East, its peoples, politics, economy, topography and languages. Rich in ideas and experience, the band of professionals and amateurs was commanded by two capable officers, Colonel Gilbert ('Bertie') Clayton, the Director of Intelligence, and his assistant, Major Newcombe.

Lawrence was doubly fortunate since both were highly intelligent, flexible-minded officers who came to respect his talents and overlook his quirkiness. Newcombe was already known to him from the Sinai survey earlier in the year and, as the war progressed, their friendship deepened through a shared loathing for the Turks and a common sympathy for the Arab cause. Lawrence was further blessed with a sympathetic commanding officer. Thirteen years Lawrence's senior, Clayton was an imaginative soldier whose charm, sound sense and cleverness impressed all who worked with him. Lawrence recalled him as 'a man with whom independent men could bear' for his mind was open to unorthodox ideas and he was never a stickler for those niceties of military decorum which Lawrence overlooked. In time, the men became friends and Lawrence visited Clayton's house, where his willingness to play won him the affection of Clayton's young family. Their parents sometimes found his anti-authoritarian postures too much, but Mrs Clayton was always firm. Lawrence took her reprimands like a chastened schoolboy.[1]

Clayton was a professional intelligence officer who, before the war, had managed the internal security section of the British-controlled Egyptian army. He also represented the interests of the Governor-General of the Sudan, Sir Reginald Wingate, and confidentially reported Egyptian affairs to him. Ability and experience made Clayton the natural choice to take charge of all the army's intelligence services under the local commander, General Sir John ('Conkie') Maxwell. Clayton was indispensable to Maxwell and his successors, Generals Sir Archibald Murray and Sir Edmund Allenby. By 1916, Clayton had been promoted to brigadier-general and

Lawrence sensed the quiet power of his hidden hand. Clayton, he wrote later, 'was like water, or permeating oil, creeping silently and insistently through everything. . . . He never visibly led; but his ideas were abreast of those who did.' Clayton prevailed because he was a permanent official whose breadth of local knowledge was wider than that of the transitory generals and proconsuls he served. For Lawrence, Clayton was an influential patron and useful ally, the more so since the junior officer accepted many of the assumptions and doctrines of his superior.

The web of personal connections and competing influences which enmeshed the rulers of the British empire, the inner mysteries of intelligence and the high priests who presided over them were scarcely known to Lawrence in 1914. His ignorance was such that with greenhorn brashness he assured Hogarth that before his and his brother officers' irruption into the Savoy Hotel, 'There wasn't an Intelligence department ... and they thought that all was well without it.' This was nonsense. The department was over six weeks old when Lawrence arrived and already had agents in the field in Palestine and Syria.[2] Nevertheless, Lawrence could have been forgiven his innocence in such matters. Intelligence-gathering bureaucracies were still a novelty in Britain, where MI5 and MI6 were in their infancy, the offspring of pre-war spy scares and the need to have skeletal organisations in readiness for a war against Germany.

They ordered things differently in Egypt. There, as in India, the smooth operation of imperial government demanded far-reaching and omniscient intelligence agencies. Lawrence was soon aware of this need. In the streets he was conscious of 'the most burning dislike' of the Cairenes for their British masters. He wore the uniform of an alien power which had deposed the Khedive Abbas Hilmi, replaced him with a puppet, and dragged Egypt into the war against her people's will. On his desk he saw intelligence reports which revealed that Turkish and German officers in Syria confidently predicted that the Egyptians would turn on their overlords the moment the first Ottoman soldier appeared on the banks of the Suez Canal. Turco-German agents encouraged Egyptian nationalist revolutionaries, ran a network of saboteurs and paid tale-bearers who spread inflammatory rumours in the streets and bazaars. Clayton's secret war against subversion was unending, but he was always a move ahead of his adversaries. Yet in the spring of 1916 he still feared that the enemy's underground was strong and capable of stirring up revolutionary disorders of the kind which had just been seen in Ireland.[3] Lawrence played no part in counter-subversionary activities, although he was intrigued and amused by the back-stairs entries and exits of Clayton's informers, who came to the Savoy Hotel to trade revelations of anti-British plots for cash.

'Our Intelligence', Lawrence boasted to Hogarth, 'has a capital "I", and is a very superior sort of thing.' He was attached for general duties to Cairo's Section Ia, which was run by Newcombe and was solely concerned with information about the enemy; spy-catching and sniffing out subversion was Ib's responsibility. Lawrence's unit existed to tell those who shaped strategy and commanded armies what they needed to know about the strengths and weaknesses of the enemy. Lawrence's duties were cynically summed up by another intelligence officer, Compton Mackenzie, in his novel *Extremes Meet* (1928):

> A good agent tells you that a lack of coffee and contraceptives among the Turks will make them sue for peace in less than a month. The fighting arms ... are always thirsting for an intellectual tonic. That is what the secret service is intended to provide. That, and a little mild mental recreation from the stern realities of war.

There was much truth in this. Arab, Greek, Armenian and Jewish field agents, all animated by a passionate hatred for the Turks, never missed a chance to relay information which suggested that their enemies were in deep trouble. This was what they wanted to believe. It was also, they thought, what their controllers liked to hear and so intelligence assessments were often unrealistically optimistic.

Intelligence officers like Lawrence were assigned to collect information from every available source, including spies, assess it and compile reports which were circulated to those for whom it would be useful. Recipients of Cairo's analyses included Lieutenant-General Sir George Macdonogh, who was Director of Military Intelligence at the War Office, General Maxwell and his staff, the British High Commission in Egypt, the Admiralty and the Foreign Office. As the scope of the war widened, Cairo circulated its reports to commanders in the Western Desert, Iraq, the Dardanelles and Salonika, and to Major Marsh, the British intelligence officer attached to Russian forces on the Caucasus front.

Lawrence's department quickly expanded. A special unit, commanded by Kitchener's nephew, Colonel A.C.Parker, was based at Ismailia to handle the canal sector and Sinai. By January 1915, the Athens bureau had been set up in neutral Greece under 'R' (Major Louis Samson, a former consul in Adrianople), to which Compton Mackenzie of Naval Intelligence was attached. The breaking of German wireless codes required new specialist sections to man listening stations in Egypt and Cyprus, which were set up in March 1916. These in turn grew when, in October 1916, Turkish codes had been cracked. By the end of the war, Cairo's Military Intelligence had a staff of over 700.[4]

Other intelligence agencies flourished alongside the army's. The British High Commission had its own intelligence department which ran a network of native spies, some of whom were giving the army information on gun-runners during the 1915–16 campaign in the Western Desert. The Royal Navy had its own Middle East intelligence section under the Commander-in-Chief East Indies which ran its own agents and was responsible for landing them and the army's agents on the Palestinian and Lebanese coast-lines. In January 1915, when Churchill, the First Lord of the Admiralty, passed control of naval operations in Syrian waters to the local French commander, Admiral D'Artigi de Fourneir, a special French intelligence unit came into being. In October 1915, the French occupied Arwad Island, a mile off Tripoli, which became the forward base for the Agence des Affaires de Syrie. Like the British, the French were busy creating a network of spies, recruited largely from Lebanese and Armenian exiles, who were regularly put ashore and picked up by warships.[5]

Second-Lieutenant Lawrence was, therefore, part of a machine whose several working parts were expected to function in harmony, each backing and helping the other. In terms of his immediate duties, Lawrence was through-out 1915 a jack-of-all-trades in intelligence. His time and his talents were disposed wherever Newcombe needed them. Most of his assignments were humdrum and boredom came easily, as he told his family in June:

> I got a letter yesterday asking for more details of what I am doing. Well, drawing, and overseeing the drawing of maps: overseeing printing and packing of the same: sitting in an office coding and decoding telegrams, interviewing prisoners, writing reports, and giving information from 9 a.m. till 7 p.m. After that feed and read, and then go to bed. I'm sick of pens, ink and paper: and have no wish to send off another telegram.

Lawrence's brief experience with Newcombe's survey party had marked him out for duties with the cartographic section under Commander L.B. Weldon, a professional surveyor who had worked in Sinai. Less than a month after Lawrence's arrival in Cairo, Newcombe detached Weldon for propaganda work with the Arabs of northern Sinai. He was also attached as a liaison officer to the *Anne Rickmers*, a captured German merchantman turned seaplane-carrier from which reconnaissance and surveying flights were made over Palestine and Syria. It may have been at Weldon's suggestion that Lawrence made a survey flight over Sinai in one of these machines, probably a Henri Farman on loan from the French.[6] (Lawrence seems to have made no impression on Weldon, who did not mention him in his account of his adventures, *'Hard Lying': The Eastern Mediterranean, 1914–1919* (1925).) While Weldon had an exciting time at sea, Lawrence was left in uneasy harness with the professional map-makers of the Egyptian Government Survey under Ernest Dowson. Together they had to draw accurate charts of Sinai, of the Dardanelles hinterland and of Syria.

Production was marked by a series of squabbles. Lawrence's tactless suggestion that he alone knew the correct way of rendering Arabic place-names into English and his advice on how they could best do their jobs tried the patience of his colleagues. Dowson remembered the interloper's flippancy. Some maps of Cilicia were found to lack indications of high ground, and Lawrence, when asked what ought to be done, answered, 'Oh, do let us have some hills. It would be such fun to have some hills.' The amendments were catastrophic. Such whimsies and the demands of the Gallipoli campaign hindered production of the Sinai maps. When, in the summer of 1916, General Murray was planning his advance into that region, he complained, 'I am surprisingly short of topographical information.' A systematic aerial survey had to be made hurriedly by the Royal Flying Corps and Murray had to get a map of Aqaba from the Royal Navy, which confounds theories that Lawrence's visit there in January 1914 had been to draw a map for Military Intelligence.[7]

When Lawrence was not overseeing the making and distribution of maps, he was busy gathering, sorting and collating information about the enemy. This was published in a daily mimeographed bulletin which was edited by Newcombe. From April 1915, he alternated with his brother officers, M.S.MacDonnell, Philip Graves and Kinahan Cornwallis, as a stand-in editor when Newcombe was away. What he put together was a ragbag of intelligence material made up of statistics, memoranda, background surveys and analyses and snippets of information from every conceivable source, reliable or not.

Lawrence's own contributions included pieces on the condition and deployment of Turkish army units. Overall responsibility for the regular reports on the Turkish army had rested since November 1914 with Philip Graves, a butterfly collector who had travelled extensively in the Middle East and had been *The Times* correspondent in Turkey. His first report opened with a diffidence rare among his colleagues, for he cautioned readers that it was the work of an author 'whose only military knowledge is derived from reading and service in public school and later University Volunteer Corps'.[8] Graves had, in fact, seen the Turkish army in action during the Balkan Wars of 1912–13 and soon became a master in his field.

Graves's authoritative articles on the Turkish army appeared in the bulletin under his own name. Other contributions were usually anonymous, although Newcombe's survey of the hostile Beduin sheiks of Sinai, which was based on his own experience and the reports of a spy, was signed.[9] Lawrence's specialism was the people and topography of Syria and he claimed that his knowledge was unequalled, or so he later told Robert Graves (who was Philip's younger half-brother). Syrian notes updating the 1911 official army handbook of the region appeared regularly and may well have been processed by Lawrence. Certainly much raw intelligence out of Syria was coming his way and he mentioned it in his letters home. His parents, who were familiar with pre-war Syria from their son's exhaustive letters, learned during 1915 about shortages of sugar and paraffin and the effects of conscription, which had sent many men from the Jerablus district to the Gallipoli front.

In one of his few post-war revelations about this period of his life, Lawrence claimed that he often ornamented his routine reports with vivid asides and sharply drawn vignettes of personalities. This habit irritated some of his superiors, although Sir Mark Sykes at the Foreign Office enjoyed his flourishes and urged his colleagues to read his Hejaz report of January 1917 'for the sake of its local colour'.[10] Lawrence must therefore have been the author of a piece on men and women of importance in Syria which appeared, unsigned, in GHQ Cairo's Intelligence Bulletin in August 1915.[11] Herr Foellner, the local director of the Berlin–Baghdad railway, was rendered as a 'pale, fish-like man, very timid and crooked in his ways'. The portrait of Madame Koch, an amateur archaeologist and collector of antiquities who had crossed Lawrence's path in 1912, ended with a comment that she fancied herself as the mistress of a *salon*. To this end, 'Her daughters helped her greatly for a time, but one got married suddenly, and the other one is plain.' Lawrence was also fond of historical analogies and so tribal sheiks would be likened to medieval German robber barons, which was probably an exact comparison.

Lawrence handled raw material which had come from spies. During November 1914, Clayton had hired agents who crossed Sinai into Turkish territory and found out what they could about garrison strengths, troop movements and the location of German officers, who were regarded by the British as the mainstays of the Turkish army. One spy, sent into southern Palestine on 1 November, returned with vivid details which suggested that he had studied his quarry at close quarters. 'Many [Turkish infantrymen] had not changed their underclothes for the last two months or more,' he reported. 'They are in a filthy state and stink badly when they march in a strut.'[12]

However unwholesome, these men were expected to attack the canal, and so the network of agents in Palestine and Syria had to be extended in order to discover as much as possible about the projected invasion. On his arrival, Newcombe had taken charge of the recruitment of agents and ran what Lawrence called 'a gang of most offensive spies'. They included 'Egyptian Boy', who kept an eye on anti-British Egyptian exiles in Damascus, and a resourceful Lebanese commercial traveller, Serkis Awad. He watched and listened during his business trips and mixed in the same circles as Jamal Pasha, the Governor of Syria.[13] Agent 'Maurice', a wealthy Damascene, also had influential contacts among senior Turkish officials which enabled him to travel to Athens and neutral Switzerland where, in December 1916, he was keeping the deposed Khedive Abbas Hilmi and his French mistress under surveillance.[14]

Venal neutrals were tempted into British service by the sovereigns doled out in the Savoy Hotel. Among them were hashish smugglers, professionally adept at dodging the authorities and disregarding frontiers. They were hired to discover the whereabouts of Austrian and German U-boats, which they did at the same time as running fuel and victuals to them in return for German cash. Early in 1915 GHQ intelligence in Cairo boasted that it had recruited the entire eastern Mediterranean dope-peddling community, although a year later a few were taking German fees in return for laying mines on roads near the Canal.[15] Private Rolls met one of these characters, Ali the Smuggler, in the Western Desert. 'All our agents', he found, 'were low characters from the mingled fringes of East and West,' since 'Arabs look upon spying as a dirty trade, especially on their own race in the interests of aliens.'[16]

Lawrence not only handled information collected by such men; he was, at least once, responsible for the recruitment of a spy. The agent in question, Charles Boutargy, an Armenian refugee from Haifa, recalled being passed to Lawrence after applying to Clayton for an interpreter's job early in 1915.[17] Lawrence offered him sovereigns in return for undertaking a mission in Haifa, where he was to draw his father into British service. This enterprise flopped, but Boutargy was retained by Military Intelligence, which despatched him to travel around the eastern Mediterranean in steamers keeping his ears open for gossip.

Along with other Arabic- and Turkish-speaking officers, Lawrence was called upon to interview prisoners of war. These Arabs were taken after the February 1915 offensive against the canal or after subsequent small-scale raids across Sinai, or were brought back from Gallipoli. Many were Syrians, like the soldiers from the 129th Regiment, captured near the canal during a skirmish in March 1915, and later interviewed by Lawrence's colleague, George Lloyd.[18] Lawrence's local knowledge and mastery of Syrian dialects qualified him for this task, and in mid-July 1915 he interrogated some Gallipoli prisoners, probably Syrians from the Aleppo V Corps, which had been deployed there the previous month.[19] It was a duty which needed alertness and there were plenty of pitfalls for the unwary, which were outlined in a manual written at the end of 1916 based on previous experiences.[20] Arab NCOs proved 'the most intelligent and communicative prisoners', but were easily fuddled by figures and were over-keen to tell their questioner what they imagined he wanted to hear. A 'friendly manner and offer of a cigarette' would break the ice and establish an early rapport. Lawrence, who never smoked, relied on his recondite knowledge of Syrian dialects to pinpoint where his prisoner once lived, and then chatted familiarly about local personalities and gossip. The technique always worked, he later told Robert Graves, for 'they told me everything.'

In twelve months, Lawrence had been a report-writer, editor, spymaster, interrogator and cartographer. Occasional gripes about drudgery apart, he relished his work and attacked it with energy and dedication. His letters to his family, who were very curious about what he did, show that he took a pride in his labours. They offered him an intellectual challenge which he was well prepared to overcome thanks to his training as a historian and archaeologist. Compton Mackenzie had noticed how the antiquarian mind was easily attuned to the painstaking tasks of sifting, weighing and putting together small pieces of evidence from widely differing sources. In his novel *Extremes Meet*, Henderson, an Oxford don and sometime archaeologist (loosely modelled on Hogarth), is called on to fit together torn scraps of paper stolen from a waste-paper basket in the German legation at Athens: 'These fragments were always pieced together with marvellous patience by Henderson. They took for him the place of the Minoan potsherds he used to piece together just as patiently in the days before the war.'[21]

Lawrence's equivalent industry and attention to detail impressed his superiors. Early in August 1915, Newcombe recommended him as a reliable officer who could help Major Samsom sort out some administrative difficulties in Athens. These probably involved his rather unsatisfactory counterespionage officer, Major Monréal, although at the time there were three visitors to Athens in whom Cairo was interested.[22] Two Arabs, Riza Jeghem and Hamid Hamdi, were making suspicious visits to the Turkish Embassy, and Ali Samy Bey, a Cairene businessman who had once been chief photographer to the Sultan Abdul Hamid, was frequenting the French Embassy.[23] Lawrence spent a few days with the Athens section and returned to Cairo with secret despatches on 14 August.

There is nothing in Lawrence's letters to his family which explains his visit, although he mentioned that he could see the Acropolis from his office window. Throughout this period, his letters home and to Hogarth are littered with indiscretions which suggest that Lawrence was utterly indifferent to the demands of security. He seems to have had no difficulty in evading military censorship, which was carried out in an adjoining office by a fellow intelligence officer. It was probably very easy for him since GHQ Cairo intelligence section was extraordinarily casual about secrecy. In February 1915, Maxwell issued a general reprimand about laxness in the censorship of correspondence but its effect seems to have been minimal. Over two years later officers in the Iraq intelligence section complained that their colleagues in Cairo were not keeping to themselves highly secret information about the decipherment of German wireless codes.

'We cannot all go fighting,' Lawrence wrote to his mother after hearing the news of his brother Frank's death in May 1915. Maybe he felt a spasm of guilt about remaining behind a desk while others risked and lost their lives. He had hoped in April 1915 that he and Newcombe would be appointed as advisers to the Yemeni insurgent el Idrissi, but the plan came to nothing. At the same time several of his brother officers were being detached for active service with the intelligence section of the Gallipoli expedition. Lawrence seems not to have been disappointed by his omission. 'I haven't any training as a field officer,' he told Hogarth, 'and I don't know that I want to go fighting up to Constantinople. It would be bad form, I think.'

After the war, Lawrence did try to invest this period of mundane but useful office work with some glamour. He told Robert Graves that he had undertaken a mission into the Western Desert to seek information about the crews of the *Tora* and *Morine*, who had been taken prisoner by the Sanussi after their ships had been sunk by U-boats off the Libyan coast in November 1915. GHQ intelligence native spies were closely involved in the search for the seamen, but the War Diary of the Western Desert Force makes no mention of Lawrence.[24] Exact information about the prisoners' whereabouts was obtained from an ex-Turkish soldier Osman Abdul, who had been taken prisoner at Rhodes by the Italians in 1912 and subsequently found himself fighting alongside the Sanussi.[25] His revelations enabled Captain Royle, formerly of the Egyptian coastguard, to organise a spectacular rescue dash which was carried out in March 1916 by the Duke of Westminster's squadron of Rolls-Royce armoured cars. If Lawrence was involved at all, it must have been indirectly through the supervision of native agents from Cairo.

Lawrence also told Robert Graves that in February 1916 he had forwarded vital information about Arab officers in the Erzurum garrison who were ready to defect and hand over their positions to the Russian besiegers. This was at a time when GHQ Cairo was cultivating dissident Arab officers in the hope that they could be employed to enkindle mutinies among Arab units in the Turkish army. Telegrams which confirm this amazing coup are lacking and there is nothing in the flow of messages from Major Marsh at Tiflis to suggest that the Russians had any help from Arab renegades. The whole affair is, however, extremely close to the climax of John Buchan's *Greenmantle*, in which British agents deliver information about gaps in the Turkish defences to the Russian staff. In fact, General Yudenich's decisive assault passed through an undefended section of the Turkish line and there was a precipitate abandonment of one outpost, Coban-dede, at the end of the siege. Nevertheless the final Turkish collapse on 16 February was clearly the result of intense cold, hunger, demoralisation and the pressure of the Russian attack rather than Arab treachery.

As with the stories of his escapades in Syria, Lawrence may either have exaggerated his peripheral role or else have embellished the truth to a point where it became unrecognisable. Given the abundance of official records, it is strange that there are no indications of Lawrence's part in these two incidents beyond his own word.

Lawrence's mention of communication with Petrograd is a reminder that throughout 1915 and half of 1916 he was well placed to see how war was waged from the top. Through the decipherment of telegrams and the reading of confidential files, memoranda and minutes he gained an overview of the war. He understood the general considerations which were the basis of Allied strategy and the preoccupations and prejudices of the statesmen, diplomats and generals who decided policy. His natural alacrity of mind and historical training made it easy for him to grasp the drift of affairs on all fronts, although his overriding interest was always the Middle East. As a result of eavesdropping at Headquarters, he was able to convey what he had picked up to the discreet Hogarth and to his parents. One hopes that early in October 1915 they did not pass on to their friends and neighbours in Oxford their son's news, hot from Headquarters, that 'The Dardanelles expedition wasted a great chance' and was now running into grave difficulties.

In simple terms, all Lawrence's labours were to one end, the defeat of Turkey. When he first reached his desk in Cairo, everyone was concerned with an expected Turkish attack on the Suez Canal. Since the Ottoman government's partial mobilisation in September 1914, Cairo had been receiving a steady flow of information which suggested that a large-scale invasion of Egypt was impending. 'Reliable' agents in Syria warned that German and Turkish commanders were confident that their attack would trigger a local rebellion with possible help from the Sanussi in Libya.[26] Kitchener, the Secretary for War, ordered Maxwell to concentrate his 6,000-man garrison along the canal's banks. It was absolutely vital to the Allied war effort that the canal stayed open since it was the conduit through which passed troopships filled with British, Indian, Australian and New Zealand reinforcements then desperately needed in France.

An attack on the canal was imminent, but it was not the major offensive which Cairo dreaded. Enver Pasha had decided to direct the bulk of the Ottoman armies eastwards against Russia, where they suffered severe reverses in January 1915. Maxwell and his staff were not only ignorant of the broad thrust of Turkish strategy, they were unclear as to how many soldiers were earmarked for the invasion of Egypt and had no idea about the timetable of the attack. Only a chance aircraft sighting of Colonel Freiherr Kress von Kressenstein's columns crossing Sinai alerted Maxwell that the attack was under way. Forewarned, the Anglo-Indian detachments defending the canal easily threw back the undermanned invasion force, which withdrew into southern Palestine in February 1915. As they trudged back, Arab conscripts blamed 'infidel' (that is, German) leadership for their setback. 'The Turks are off for the time being,' Lawrence told his family, but like everyone else in Cairo he knew they would be back. It was up to him and his colleagues to find out from their minute examination of reports of troop movements, transport facilities and the availability of grain supplies when and with how many men.

The defensive strategy imposed on Maxwell passed the initiative to the Turks. This was repugnant to him and to all professional officers of his generation. They had served their apprenticeships in arms fighting 'Orientals' (a category which embraced the Turks) in India, Egypt and the Sudan. Their experience and the wisdom handed down from an older generation of imperial soldiers convinced them that aggressive audacity always got the best results. Boldness in the offensive established moral authority, which was the basic ingredient of prestige, that mystical abstraction which every general and proconsul knew made it possible for Britain to rule unchallenged over wide areas of Africa and Asia.

This philosophy had two determined advocates in the Cabinet, Kitchener and Churchill. Swayed by these adherents of the prestige school of strategy, their colleagues rubber-stamped a display of awesome imperial temerity, the forcing of the Straits. Constantinople was the goal and, when it fell, the whole Muslim world would realise that Allied power was invincible and that of Turkey a sham. Furthermore an overpowering blow against Turkey offered a way out of the seemingly fruitless embroilment of masses of men in France where, in spite of both sides suffering heavy casualties, the German army doggedly held its ground. Throughout the war, politicians and generals remained mesmerised by Turkey, an apparently weak prop to Germany which, if knocked away, would bring down her ally. By April 1915, Lawrence had been converted to the view that the Ottoman empire would fall apart easily. 'Poor old Turkey is only hanging together,' he wrote to Hogarth. 'Everything about her is very very sick, and almost I think it will be good to make an end of her, although it will be very inconvenient to ourselves.'

As he wrote, his new friend Ronald Storrs, Oriental Secretary to the High Commissioner, was under orders to get a khaki uniform from his tailor to be worn when he took up a new post in the military administration of Constantinople. Yet Lawrence, while expecting Turkey's swift disintegration, had misgivings about the Gallipoli expeditionary force which was mustering in Egypt. On 20 April, he told Hogarth that the army which was soon to land on the Gallipoli peninsula was 'beastly ill-prepared, with no knowledge of where it was going, or what it would meet, or what it was going to do'.

His later letters, composed with the knowledge of what passed in and out of Headquarters, were a barometer of the fortunes of the Gallipoli campaign. On 27 July he thought that the 'Dardanelles show' would shortly end, but a month later he realised that it had been bungled after early advantages had been thrown away. Just over a month later, on 23 November 1915, his apprehension was justified when the War Cabinet agreed to call off the operation and withdraw all forces from Gallipoli. Having failed to gain a decisive victory in the East, the government turned its attentions and new reserves of men from 'Kitchener's army' of volunteers towards the West and a major offensive against the German lines in northern France. The Middle Eastern theatre reverted to a sideshow, with British forces sitting and waiting on the Suez Canal while Lawrence and his brother officers in Cairo endeavoured to find out the Turks' intentions.

II

MEN AND IDEAS

LAWRENCE found life in Cairo congenial. He made himself a circle of stimulating friends and deliberately steered clear of the stilted social life of the city's British community. He urged Robert Graves to do the same. 'Englishmen in these small colonies abroad are snobbish to a degree: the smallness of their colony makes them smaller.'[1] What he had in mind was the rigid pecking order of the civil and military communities and their clubs. He happily admitted that he had entered these only twice during his 'magnificent' years in Cairo. Luckily, he was able to find refreshmen from a small body of companions who were his intellectual equals and shared his literary tastes.

The greatest source of serendipity in Cairo were Lawrence's colleagues in intelligence. They were an effervescent crowd whom he described in a sequence of pen portraits written for his parents in February 1915. George

Lloyd was 'Welsh, but sorry for it; small, dark, very amusing ... quite pleasant, but exceedingly noisy', and Aubrey Herbert 'is a joke, but a very nice one'. This happy picture was completed by General Maxwell, who delighted Lawrence:

> He is a very queer person: almost weirdly good-natured, very cheerful, with a mysterious gift of prophesying what will happen, and a marvellous carelessness about what might happen. There couldn't be a better person to command in Egypt. He takes the whole job as a splendid joke.[2]

A year later, in January 1916, Lawrence was pleased with the arrival of Captain Wyndham Deedes ('Deedez Bey'), a man of sturdy independence who had once told Churchill to his face that the Gallipoli expedition would fail. 'A very excellent man,' Lawrence told his parents, 'I like him best of the bunch.' There were also old friends in Cairo: Newcombe, Woolley, who from January 1915 was based in Port Said as liaison officer with the French navy, and Hogarth, an occasional bird of passage who dropped in to discuss intelligence matters with Lawrence as part of his unofficial roving commission on behalf of the Admiralty.

Lawrence did not stray beyond his knot of old and new friends for there was nothing in Cairo's wartime society to beckon him. The city's pre-war social life went on as before. When General Murray arrived there in January 1916 to take up his command on the canal front, he was shocked to discover that the city was 'at peace not war'.[3] So it must have seemed to an officer straight from London: the winter season was in full swing, adorned by fashionable ladies, including Lady Evelyn Cobbold, who had rescued the penniless Lawrence on Maan station, and some officers had brought out their wives. Colonel Leachman, a priggish officer fresh from the Iraq front, was offended by the abundance of 'MPs and sprigs of the nobility' whom he encountered 'waging war from Shepheard's Hotel'. No doubt he had come across Lawrence's colleagues, Aubrey Herbert and George Lloyd, both MPs who regularly haunted Shepheard's bar, and the Marquess of Carisbrooke and Lord Hartington, two officers on Maxwell's staff. 'More like a carnival' was Deedes's description of Shepheard's in January 1916. It was even too much for Maxwell, who officially rebuked those responsible for 'the very undesirable state of affairs now existing in Cairo when crowds of idlers in military uniforms throng the streets from morning to night'. Many were back from Gallipoli and they were soon sent packing to the Western Front by Murray. The relaxed atmosphere persisted; a year later Hogarth was taken aback when he discovered officers accompanied by ladies without wedding rings staying for weekends at his hotel near the Pyramids.[4]

Further diversion was provided by the harum-scarum Australian contingent. One staff officer described them as 'a most lawless, turbulent and undisciplined crowd who really break out and commit fearful atrocities' in Cairo. These included a riot in February 1915 when the brothels of the Wassa district of the cities were wrecked, much to the amusement of some staff officers, who called the affray 'the battle of Warsaw', a joking reference to a recent engagement on the Eastern Front. The refractoriness of the Australians made Murray apoplectic and he was glad to send many off to France where General Sir William Robertson, the Chief of the Imperial General Staff, felt certain 'the Germans will soon put them in order.'[5] Lawrence was unmoved by the wild scenes in Cairo, which he never mentioned in his letters; maybe he had a secret sympathy with the Australians' collective rejection of military discipline or else he thought his mother would be distressed by reports of debauchery. Much later, in September 1918, he noticed that alone of Allied troops, they were always friendly towards the Arabs, cheerily calling each Arab soldier 'Mecca'.

The round of dances, race-going, card-playing, drinking, flirtation and seduction was shunned by Lawrence. His relaxation remained what it had always been, intellectual. He wrote home for new books (*The Seven Golden Odes of Pagan Arabia* or *The Moallakat*: translated by Lady Anne Blunt, and put into English verse by Wilfred Scawen Blunt: published at the Chiswick Press 5/- in 1904 probably') and was reassured by the old. 'All the relief I get [is] in *The Greek Anthology*, Heredia, [William] Morris and a few others!' he told his brother Will in July 1915.

Lawrence's duties introduced him to men with similar passions. A glimpse of him off-duty is revealed by the vain, fastidious and talkative Ronald Storrs, the Oriental Secretary to Sir Henry McMahon, the High Commissioner, with whom he soon struck up a close friendship, based at first on shared literary tastes. 'I would come upon him in my flat, reading Latin or Greek,' remembered Storrs, who added that whenever Lawrence borrowed books they were always returned, a very rare virtue. Conversation would follow in which Lawrence would propose the merits of Homer against Dante or Aristophanes against Theocritus. Relaxation was simple. 'He loved music, harmony rather than counterpoint, and sat back against the cushions with his eyes half-closed, enduring even that meandering stream of musical consciousness which I have dignified by the name of improvisation.' These were intimate indulgences, for when Storrs formally entertained guests whom Lawrence believed were 'smart', he kept well away. Storrs was a valuable friend in other ways. An ambitious official, he was a behind-the-scenes intriguer, determined to set the stamp of his own ideas on British policy, and, like his colleague Clayton, he enjoyed the confidence of Kitchener, whom he had once briefly served.

Lawrence did not drink, so he was not a habitué of Shepheard's, but he did treat himself to coffee and chocolates in Groppi's tea garden, which he later recommended to Robert Graves. He now had more money than he had ever had before; his salary was £400 a year, from which ten shillings (fifty pence) was deducted daily to cover his room and meals at the Savoy. By September 1915, he had saved over £60, which he offered to his father to help meet the costs of his younger brother Arnold's schooling.

As in Oxford, Lawrence strived to keep himself a man apart. Not only did he openly avoid the expatriate clubbishness and pastimes of his brother officers, he was indifferent to military formalities. Ten years after the war, he told Robert Graves that his dishevelment was a public declaration of his independence. To wear a khaki uniform was to accept a label, a thing hateful to Lawrence, who wished always to be his own man. His hair was always too long and resisted grooming, his uniform was crumpled and, on the few times he remembered to wear it, his Sam Browne belt was loosely buckled. He never wore the correct shoes. Once Deedes asked General Murray, 'What did you think of Lawrence?' 'I was disappointed,' was the reply, 'he did not come in dancing shoes.' His reputation as the most unkempt officer in Egypt had run before him. Just before Christmas 1917, when he was the guest of Sir Reginald and Lady Wingate at the Residency in Alexandria, he went about happily in a subaltern's tunic with 'badges somewhere between a Lieutenant and a Captain, and no decorations and no belt'.[6] He did, however, remember a year later to tell the editors of *Who's Who* that he had been awarded the Companionship of the Bath and the Croix de Guerre with oak leaves.

This contrived nonchalance mattered less than has been imagined and its impact was muted. In the first place General Maxwell was not bothered about smartness, which was one of the reasons why Murray confidentially told General Robertson that 'Maxwell is not a soldier.'[7] Neither, in a conventional sense, were Lawrence and the other wayward amateurs on Maxwell's staff, at least two of whom cared nothing for their appearance. Aubrey Herbert's canary-yellow uniform had been made by his wife from curtain material and was worn with a dented topee and Turkish slippers. His Cairo lodgings, borrowed from Lord Howard de Walden, had what Deedes called 'a very untidy picnicky look' about them which seemed somehow right for their occupant, who, in January 1916, 'looked madder and more untidy than ever'.[8] Storrs was amused by Philip Graves's inability to control his wardrobe.

In spite of his claim that his carelessness about dress was a gesture against military conformity, Lawrence's scruffiness probably owed as much to his natural carelessness in such matters, the insouciance of Maxwell and the aristocratic *déshabille* of Herbert, whom he admired. Lawrence's Bohemianism may have raised a few eyebrows and distended some spleens, especially of the older professional officers. It was, however, endured as the sort of behaviour expected from the kind of civilian who would find his way into such a rum department as intelligence.

Yet sloppy dress was an outward sign of the tension which existed between officers like Lawrence and some, but not all, of his superiors. When he wrote to Lloyd in June 1915 with the blunt comment, 'We think the staff above the rank of captain are shits,' Lawrence spoke for other tyros in Cairo who were impatient with hidebound superiors with closed minds. (Incidentally, unlike his brother Frank, Lawrence seems not at this time to have had an aversion to everyday mess language.)[9] Deedes concurred and confided to Compton Mackenzie his 'despair of the brains of professional soldiers'. Mackenzie also spoke to a civilian official in Cairo who could not understand the 'primitive society' of professional officers with its irrational 'taboos and totems'.[10]

By and large, pre-1914 army officers were not noted or promoted for their intellects and they lived in an exclusive world governed by arcane codes of conduct which were beyond the comprehension of civilians. Cleverness too openly displayed was ungentlemanly and therefore to be avoided. The outbreak of war had forced these officers into close working contact with unashamedly bright and sometimes outspoken young men like Lawrence for whom their conventions seemed pointless and their habits of mind obtuse. What was unforgivable to the likes of Lawrence was the dullness of so many of the old guard. 'I am nearly dead with boredom at his eternal Anglo-Indian talk about himself, his pay allowance, his grievances, and his colleagues,' complained the normally even-tempered Hogarth after some enforced hours in the company of one professional officer.[11] The real problem, which emerged as the war progressed, was not tedious military small-talk, but the unwillingness of professional men at arms to see things in the same way as Lawrence and his fellow amateurs.

There were clever men in Lawrence's circle in Cairo whose conversation was urbane and scholarly. They included men from that caste which considered itself destined through birth, upbringing and education to serve and govern Britain and its empire. Lawrence had encountered them before at Oxford and had shied away. Writing to his friend Mrs Rieder in September 1912 he said how glad he was she would not be sending her son to a public school – 'I don't like the type they produce.' Nearly all his brother officers in Cairo were public schoolmen and, after mixing intimately with them, Lawrence revised his judgement. He soon found that several were men of literary discernment and intellectual liveliness. He came to appreciate the company of cultured, gifted men of patrician birth and bearing, and they were fascinated by him. His affability, his unorthodox but lively mind combined with his out-of-hand rejection of convention aroused their interest and, in time, affection. Two, Aubrey Herbert and George Lloyd, whom he first met in Cairo in December 1914, he counted as among his best-loved friends.

Herbert was amazingly eccentric. Seven years older than Lawrence, the son of an earl, and Unionist MP for South Somerset, Herbert had travelled widely in the Far and Near East before the war. Wounded in France, he transferred to Cairo's intelligence section in December 1914. Soon after, he was serving as a liaison officer on board warships patrolling the Syrian coast and later he was transferred to the staff at Gallipoli. In March 1916 he was assigned to Admiral Sir Rosslyn ('Rosie') Wemyss, the new commander of the East Indies station, as army liaison officer. The Admiral found him 'extremely intelligent, very agreeable' and useful since he possessed 'just that touch with the F.O., etc. which may be invaluable to me a little later on'.[12] Herbert's exotic past and reputation made him the model for Sandy Clanroyden in Buchan's *Greenmantle*.

When they first met, Herbert was already what Lawrence would become, a figure about whom amazing tales were told. It was not easy to reconcile the short-sighted, untidy and shambling reality with the man who, during a Gallipoli truce, had taken command of a Turkish company and in their own tongue ordered them back to their trenches. Something about Herbert drew Lawrence to him. After the war he placed him alongside Hogarth as a profound influence on his life, although he never revealed the exact nature of this influence. Each man disdained social 'form' and cultivated individuality, an easier task for the aristocrat than for Lawrence, a man from the middle classes, who preferred to live within the boundaries of social convention.

Some clue to Herbert's appeal may lie in Lawrence's obsession with chivalric legends. His life had been crowded with picaresque adventures which bordered on the fantastic, just like those experienced by the heroes of medieval epics. Furthermore, Herbert came from a family which had won glory for itself on the battlefields of the Wars of the Roses and the Civil War. He had upheld the warrior tradition and, for all his physical incongruity, displayed coolness and cavalier bravado in the face of the enemy. For Lawrence, this likeable aristocrat may have appeared a living embodiment of the ancient warrior virtues he had read about. Still untested under fire, he may well have hoped that he could live up to his example and prove himself as honourably as his friend.

Lawrence's other patrician friend, George Lloyd, was a man of ideas rather than action. Lloyd, an Etonian and Cambridge rowing Blue, had been a businessman with strong Middle Eastern links and, from 1910, Conservative MP for West Staffordshire. Together Lloyd and Lawrence shared such routine intelligence duties as POW interviews and report-writing on Syria. Lloyd's pre-war connections marked him out for higher duties. He served at Gallipoli (having already put himself to the test under fire by hurrying to the canal when the Turks attacked) and on missions to Russia and, in August 1915, to the Greek Prime Minister, Venizelos.[13] Lawrence found the mercurial Lloyd a diverting and generous-hearted brother officer, and common intellectual interests cemented a friendship which lasted until Lawrence's death. When Lawrence was on active service, Lloyd felt a brotherly concern for his welfare which revealed itself in his fears for his mental stability during the trying days of October 1917. Then, for a short time, Lloyd was Lawrence's companion in the field.

Lloyd was an imperialist, and a persuasive one. After hearing him, Compton Mackenzie realised that 'Imperialism could touch a man's soul as deeply as Religion' and was almost converted. Another staff officer at Gallipoli, Colonel Guy Dawnay, found Lloyd a 'most keen Imperialist (of the Jingo type rather, I think)'. Political conversations with Lloyd, Deedes and another Cairo intelligence officer, Major Doughty-Wylie (who was killed soon after), left Dawnay convinced that they were 'mad keen' on exploiting the war to extend Britain's imperial power across the Middle East. The Foreign Office and Sir Edward Grey, the Foreign Secretary, were contemptuously dismissed, and Dawnay, who was unmoved by this vision of imperial expansion, was branded a 'dreadful little Englander'.[14]

Lawrence may have been more open to Lloyd's arguments than Dawnay. In December 1914, his own views on the future of the Middle East and the part Britain was destined to play there were unformed. He had much to learn from Lloyd, Clayton and Storrs, and they would find him an enthusiastic and receptive pupil.

The first lesson which Lawrence learned was that, while the war was being waged to defeat Turkey, intelligence officers like himself had to look far ahead and lay the ground for a post-war settlement in the Middle East. A colleague, James Cockerell, who arrived in Cairo at the same time as Lawrence and died shortly after, sensed that his colleagues would not stay satisfied for long as mere servants who submitted dispassionate advice to their military masters.[15] Their natural talents and the power of their private convictions would make them find ways in which they could impose their individual wills on the creation of policy. Moreover, as civilians with political and consular backgrounds, they would think in political rather than military terms and press for the concoction of strategies which would achieve political as well as military goals.

Cockerell's prognosis was correct. In February 1915, Lloyd wrote to his wife that his and his colleagues' thoughts were concentrated on 'what kind of result for the future we are going to fashion out of all this hurly-burly in Asia'. Buoyed up by a feeling that they were in a position to lay the foundations for a new order in the Middle East, Lawrence and his colleagues buried themselves enthusiastically in their work and soon lost touch with the outside world. Soldiers and public officials in Cairo viewed the war from a Middle Eastern perspective, an astigmatism which blighted Lawrence's vision. 'It seems to me that attention is so fixed on the Belgian front that our interests in the East are being sacrificed,' he wrote to his parents in February 1915. 'It will go against us very heavily some day.' At the same time, Lloyd told his wife, 'We soon become very self-centred in our Oriental backwater here,' where only the 'dimmest echoes' of the Western front were heard.[16]

Outsiders noticed and regretted the tunnel vision of the luminaries of Cairo. After dining with some, including Gertrude Bell, in December 1915, Guy Dawnay concluded that in what he called 'Egyptian Hall (the home of mystery)' they 'set far too much importance on this part of the world as a factor in the main war'. Admiral Wemyss agreed. Conferences with Cairo's civil and military experts convinced him that 'like all specialists they are inclined to think only of their own specialization and ignore other factors.'[17]

Empire-building was uppermost in the minds of the well-established 'specialists' in Cairo and they quickly passed on their preoccupations to their new staff. Officials like Sir Henry McMahon, the High Commissioner in Egypt, Wingate in the Sudan, Storrs, Clayton and generals like Maxwell had dedicated their lives to the protection and extension of British territory and influence in the Middle East. Over all loomed the figure of Kitchener, now Secretary of State for War, who, as Commander-in-Chief of the Egyptian army in the 1890s and High Commissioner in Egypt between 1911 and 1914, was their patron and mentor. Master and pupils were of one mind. They accepted unquestioningly Britain's imperial mission as an agent of civilisation and stability. The ultimate success of this mission and the safety of Britain's land empire depended upon her survival as a maritime and global power. This, in turn, required a firm grip on Egypt and the Suez Canal and a tranquil Middle East. Until 1914 a benevolent Ottoman empire had imposed sufficient order across the Middle East to give the region stability and Egypt had been safeguarded by 4,000 British soldiers backed by the formidable Mediterranean fleet.

In November 1914 the old system collapsed. Turkey was now a hostile power and the canal lay in a war zone under threat of Turkish attack. In spite of fears that Egypt might be invaded, there was a strong body of official opinion in Cairo which was convinced that Turkey's war effort would soon fall into disarray and her empire disintegrate. Exaggerated hopes for the Gallipoli expedition added to the euphoria which infected Lawrence. Consequently those who employed him had been devising ways in which to fill the vacuum which would be created when the Ottoman empire fell apart. There was no coherent overall government policy for this eventuality, just a series of competing suggestions all drawn up by officials and soldiers anxious to extend Britain's control over vital strategic areas.

All concerned, including Lawrence, constantly referred to Britain's 'interests', but there was no agreement about what these were or how they might best be served. Iraq, invaded early in November 1914 by an Anglo-Indian army, was seen by the India Office in London and the Viceregal government in Delhi as a future colony of India. A fortnight into the campaign, Colonel Arnold Wilson, soon to be a senior administrator in occupied Iraq, was building colonies in the air. 'I should like to see it announced', he wrote, 'that Mesopotamia [Iraq] was to be annexed to India as a colony for India and Indians, that the Government of India would administer it, and gradually bring under cultivation its vast unpopulated desert plains, peopling them with martial races from the Punjab.'[18] This was welcomed in London, where one official saw the project as a way of diverting Indian immigrants away from such 'white man's colonies' as Kenya and South Africa and it was supported in Cairo by George Lloyd.[19] In time, Lawrence condemned the scheme, which, if enforced, would irrevocably turn Arab opinion away from Britain by confirming latent fears that her Middle Eastern ambitions were purely annexationalist.

Cairo's policies for the post-war Middle East rested primarily on the need to provide a secure, defensible frontier and buffer zone for the Suez Canal. A secondary requirement was provision for safe land communications from the Mediterranean to the Persian Gulf which was traditionally seen as India's advance frontier. From the start, the achievement of these aims was complicated by the rival claims of Britain's wartime allies, France and Russia, who cherished ambitions in this area which had to be taken into account, however unwillingly, by officials in Cairo.

Obligations to France could not be ignored, although Lawrence and those of similar mind soon began looking for ways in which they could be by-passed. Before the war, Lawrence had been dismayed by the extent of French penetration in Syria and he was no doubt well aware that French loans and French mission schools were preparing the way for eventual occupation, as indeed they were. Once the war was underway, France and Russia lost no time in putting forward their claims to what the British Prime Minister, Asquith, called Turkey's 'carcass'. Negotiations continued during 1915 which resulted in the Sykes–Picot agreement in March and its amendments in October, which pledged France territory along the Syrian and Lebanese coastlines and political and economic hegemony over a wide hinterland which stretched across northern Iraq to beyond Mosul. Russia was promised control over the Straits. This collection of promises, which would soon loom large in Lawrence's dealings with the Arabs, were supposedly secret. Whether or not as a consequence of Cairo's relaxed attitudes towards security, rumours were current in the city in January 1915 that the French would be given Syria.[20]

The prospect of the French installed in Syria disturbed Kitchener and his acolytes in Cairo. On 16 March 1915, he warned the Cabinet that once the war had ended 'old enmities and jealousies which had been stilled by the existing crisis in Europe may revive,' and he predicted that Britain might again find herself at 'enmity with Russia or with France' as she had been before the *entente cordiale* of 1904. France had been deeply aggrieved by Britain's occupation of Egypt and in 1898 an expedition led by Colonel Marchand had challenged Britain's control of the Nile at Fashoda. Kitchener with superior forces had politely expelled the intruder and for a few months a war had seemed likely. Wingate and Clayton, both officers in Kitchener's army, had been eyewitnesses to the clash. For six years after there had been fears that the French would seek revenge for the humiliation. Tucked away in Cairo's military files were contingency plans for the defence of Egypt against a Franco-Russian invasion, drawn up in the early 1900s with Kitchener's advice. The Egyptians would welcome the invaders and the British garrison would be overwhelmed, but final rescue would come in the form of the men-of-war from Malta, which would destroy the enemy's fleet in a second battle of the Nile.

Lawrence appears to have seen these plans; certainly, he knew of them. A revised version was offered to Hogarth in a letter of 18 March 1915 in which Lawrence foresaw the terrifying consequences of France being let into Syria:

> In the hands of France it [Alexandretta on the Syrian coast, now Iskanderun] will provide a sure base for naval attacks on Egypt – and remember with her in Syria, and compulsory service there [since the 1840s France had used her colonies in Senegal and Algeria as reservoirs of soldiers], she will be able any time to fling 100,000 men against the canal in 12 days from declaration of war.

This was the nightmare which was haunting Kitchener and officials in Cairo. Lawrence had been completely swept away by their strategic dogma and, like all converts, he preached his new faith with a wild zeal. His parents were told on 20 February 1915, 'So far as Syria is concerned it is France and not Turkey that is the enemy.' On 22 March, Hogarth was told that if successful, which it was not, an alliance with Idrissi of the

Yemen would mean that 'we can rush right up to Damascus and biff the French out of all hope of Syria.' Lawrence had both swallowed the ideas of Cairo's imperialists and picked up the Hentyesque slang of the subaltern empire-builder.

Private apprehension mingled with public fears for the future safety of the empire. Lawrence's objections to French paramountcy in Syria rested ultimately on his older fear that the Syrians would be irredeemably diminished by imported French culture and commercial exploitation. His views on this were reinforced by what he had seen in Egypt. 'I only hope', he told Hogarth in April, 'that Aleppo and Damascus will escape a little the fate that has come upon Cairo. Anything fouler than the town building, or its beastly people, can't be.' How unlike Karkamis, undefiled by the West, 'a village inhabited by the cleanest and most intelligent angels'.

At about this time, Lawrence may have written his 'Fragmentary Notes' on Syria, destined presumably for the intelligence bulletin but never circulated, presumably on the advice of either Clayton or Newcombe, who may have been taken aback by their vehemence.[21] According to Lawrence, francophile Beirut 'produces nothing' and was just a sewer through which 'shop-soiled foreign influences flow into Syria'. The city was crammed with 'Mohammedans talking and writing like the doctrinaire cyclopaedists who paved the way for the Revolution in France'. Many of these, political exiles, were already in Egypt but they spoke for no one since their home, Beirut, 'is as representative of Syria as Soho is of the Home Counties'. So much for the French-educated elite who talked about the Rights of Man and wanted to modernise their country along Western lines. Worse still were the German Jews of the Zionist settlements who were 'the most foreign, most uncharitable parts of the whole population'. Another immigrant community, the Algerians (expelled by Napoleon III in 1860), were lawless ruffians. Only the rural, patriarchal villages (like Jerablus) were praised. As to the future, Lawrence believed that Damascus, 'a lodestone to which Arabs are naturally drawn' and 'a city which will not easily be convinced that it is subject to any alien race', should become the centre of the region. Foreign protection was ruled out and Lawrence hoped that the area would be given just enough central government to preserve public order.

These views broke surface again and again whenever Lawrence was asked to give his opinions on the future of Syria. They were reactionary in so far as Lawrence wished to keep the region quarantined from external forces even though, as he had admitted, they already dominated Beirut. There was also a dash of true Toryism, since Lawrence wished to preserve existing religious and social institutions and his admiration for rural village life may have owed a little to his reading of William Morris's idealised versions of medieval times. Implicit throughout was Lawrence's assumption that, even in the form he desired, the new Syria would be created from above and by outsiders, not by Syrians.

While Lawrence's formula for the new Syria may not have found many sympathisers among his colleagues, they all shared a common apprehension about the establishment of French colonies and bases in the region. The lead here came from Kitchener, whose views were transmitted through Maxwell and Clayton. Yet unlike Lawrence, who could indulge in reckless francophobia, his seniors had to be more circumspect since they had to deal personally with French officials and commanders. Furthermore, as Lawrence never appreciated, Britain depended heavily on French naval co-operation in the Mediterranean as her own fleet, by common consent, had been concentrated in home waters to face the German navy.

All these strands of intrigue came together during the spring and autumn of 1915 when military and naval intelligence officers were ordered to produce extensive plans for an Allied landing at Alexandretta. Lawrence was a fierce partisan of the project and was involved in various stages of its preparation. It became something of an incubus, making him lose touch with reality. In 1929 he went so far as to tell Liddell Hart that 'the Alexandretta scheme ... was, from beginning to end, my invention', which was untrue. Liddell Hart knew this and prudently omitted Lawrence's claim from his biography.[22]

Kitchener, not Lawrence, was the begetter of the Alexandretta scheme. Shortly before he left Egypt in 1914, he had discussed with Maxwell possible strategies in the event of a war with Turkey, which both men knew would imperil the Suez Canal. Kitchener favoured a swift, aggressive blow delivered against the newly modernised port of Alexandretta which, if successful, would enhance British prestige, humble Turkey and divert Turkish troops away from the canal. The plan had a further attraction since, once Alexandretta was taken, British forces would be well placed to move inland and sever the Berlin–Baghdad railway. Ottoman armies in Syria, Palestine, Arabia and Iraq would be cut off from Constantinople and a wedge would be driven into the Ottoman empire which could bring down the whole gimcrack structure.[23]

Maxwell, keen to take the offensive, reminded Kitchener of the plan in December 1914 but was told to be patient. Every reserve of men and energy was needed on the Western Front. In the meantime, Kitchener canvassed the Cabinet with the Alexandretta project, presenting it as a valuable secondary operation which would draw Turkish troops away from Gallipoli.

While Kitchener was persuading the Cabinet to approve the landing,

Maxwell ordered his intelligence staff to gather information about the port and its hinterland. There was close co-operation with Naval Intelligence, which undertook offshore reconnaissance of possible landing sites, a task carried out by Lawrence's Oxford acquaintance and sometime traveller in Syria, Harry Pirie-Gordon, now a commander. Lawrence was also busy with topographical work and on 15 January 1915 asked Hogarth for photos of the Beilan Pass which Maxwell was hoping he could seize by an inland cavalry dash after Alexandretta had fallen.

All involved were encouraged by a stream of reports which suggested that the local people would welcome the invasion and do all they could to assist the landing force. Pirie-Gordon had watched the *opéra bouffe* scene on 23 December when Arab soldiers, based at Alexandretta, fired charges laid by bluejackets from HMS *Doris*, which blew up engines and rolling-stock. This extreme case of benevolent neutrality not only heartened intelligence staffs, but raised the question of whether dissident Arabs would desert en masse. Naval Intelligence was receiving reports early in January which revealed that dissatisfaction among Arab conscripts was so deep and widespread that they would throw down their arms the moment the British came ashore.[24]

Similar information was coming the army's way. Clayton, who had taken charge of intelligence-gathering in the area, was told that there was much pro-British feeling among local communities. His Armenian agent, Joseph Catoni, formerly the Beirut Vice-Consul who had helped despatch the crates of antiquities excavated at Karkamis, was certain that local help would be forthcoming. He controlled Nasariyah chiefs and one of his ablest spies, 'a Monocular Armenian', had collected so many pledges of assistance from village headmen that GHQ intelligence were considering a campaign of guerrilla warfare to coincide with the landings.[25]

Catoni and his henchmen were also contributing to a body of evidence which suggested that there was a 'widespread' local wish for British occupa-tion.[26] Cautiously, Clayton approached the Foreign Office on 15 January to enquire what arrangements had been negotiated with France and Russia for the region's political future. He did not think that the Syrians would accept a permanent British occupation and did not want Alexandretta in Russian hands. Neither did Lawrence, who on 18 March was pressing Hogarth to wake up the Admiralty to the dangers of Russian or French occupation of the port. There was no need to ring the alarm bell: Churchill, Lord Fisher, the First Sea Lord, and Lloyd George were well aware of the necessity to hold Alexandretta and in principle were sympathetic towards the operation to take it.

Clayton understood the military and propaganda value of swinging local Syrian opinion behind Britain, but he also thought that 'partition of the

Arab country between different powers would be deeply resented,' a judgement he may have owed to Lawrence.[27] Lawrence may also have been the author of a memorandum which argued that 'there is amongst all classes and religions a very widespread desire for interference by Great Britain.' A further report prepared in January 1915 reflected views which Lawrence would hold later on Arab national feeling: 'Judiciously nurtured, this national sentiment might in a few generations create an Arab-speaking nation, prepared to claim in the British Empire, such a part as India is now beginning to take.'[28] With the Arabs under British tutelage, imperial strategic needs would be met. Furthermore, and this would have appealed to Lawrence, French claims would be utterly confounded.

Planning ahead for Alexandretta brought the possibility of an alliance with the Arabs into the forefront of intelligence thinking. Clayton, with a background of practical administration, was opposed to a burdensome protectorate which might meet resistance.[29] Lloyd was instinctively annexationalist. Where did Lawrence stand? He agreed that Alexandretta had to become a British naval base which would serve to guard the canal, and he wanted Syria closed to French influence and left to what amounted to her own devices. If this was impractical, the only alternative was indirect British control, which might be more sensitive to local customs than French.

All these solutions were in the end pipe-dreams. In mid-March the Cabinet decided to shelve the scheme. The French had deep misgivings about the plan and their approval and co-operation were essential for the larger operation against the Straits. Furthermore, neither ally possessed enough warships, transports and reserves to mount two simultaneous seaborne landings. The Gallipoli invasion would go ahead; the Alexandretta diversion was abandoned. It had, however, given the French food for dark thoughts about the sort of *coup de main* the British might deliver in an area pledged to them. On 4 May, Woolley repeated to Newcombe a conversation he had just had with Admiral D'Artigi de Fourneir in which the Frenchman said that, as soon as men could be spared from the Dardanelles, a landing force of 30,000 would be put ashore to occupy the hinterland of Alexandretta and Adana, a region he believed the British wanted for themselves.

In September 1915, when he realised that the Gallipoli expedition was running out of steam, Clayton suggested the revival of the Alexandretta project to the Foreign Office. He had already put the idea to naval colleagues and had been told they favoured an assault on Ayas Bay, twenty-eight miles north of the original landing place.[30] His plea was ignored, but by the end of October, when the time had come for a clear-cut decision on the future of the Gallipoli front, the Syrian project was again on the agenda. On 4 November Kitchener, then at Marseilles on his way to the eastern Mediterranean, ordered Colonel Guy Dawnay to collect the old

Alexandretta plans from Cairo. It was a fool's errand, since GHQ intelligence had mislaid the relevant files, but, as Dawnay recalled, Clayton and Lawrence came forward with a fresh project. 'I was put on to Ayas Bay by Bertie Clayton and T.E.Lawrence ... owing to the fact that we could not find a copy of the official Alexandretta scheme in Cairo.'[31] In a hugger-mugger rush, Dawnay, Clayton, Lawrence and Philip Graves cobbled together a completely new operational plan. What Lawrence called the 'unnecessary' effort took thirty-six hours, which gave Dawnay enough time to take ship from Alexandria on 8 November. Two days later the papers were read over and approved by Kitchener, Maxwell, Generals Monro and Birdwood (the Dardanelles commanders), Admiral de Robeck and McMahon at their conference on Mudros Island.

They had been pondering gloomily on the prospects of the Gallipoli campaign, which Monro wanted to terminate and whose lack of headway was provoking public criticism of the government. More was at stake than reputations, since Kitchener believed that evacuation from Gallipoli would indelibly tarnish Britain's prestige throughout the Muslim world. Another aggressive gesture, this time against the Syrian coast, would therefore be a timely reminder that Britain still held the initiative. The War Cabinet was not impressed. On 17 November the Ayas Bay plan was dismissed without discussion at a conference of Allied ministers and commanders in Paris. Militarily it squandered men and resources needed in France and Flanders, and politically it created a rift between Britain and her ally. The French suspected that the project was a thinly disguised piece of legerdemain designed to promote British interests in Syria at the expense of theirs. The French Commander-in-Chief, Marshal Joffre, was particularly incensed and threw a tantrum, threatening to resign if the plan was adopted. The ruffled French demanded and got British assistance for another gamble: reinforcement of the expeditionary force at Salonika, which was there to shore up the faltering Serbs (who were soon knocked out of the war) and to encourage Roumania and Greece to join the *entente*. It was Kitchener's turn for fury and he warned Asquith by telegram that the decision would cheer the Germans and Turks and dishearten the Arabs, who would now think again before seeking Britain's friendship.[32] Other voices, from Cairo and the Admiralty, joined the chorus of dismay. For a further six months a persistent lobby, which included Lawrence, kept up the backstairs pressure in Cairo for opening a Syrian front through Alexandretta.

Lawrence was not only galled by what he regarded as mistaken deference to any ally; his pride was bruised. Soon after the news reached Cairo that the Ayas Bay project was off, the War Office staff sent out a detailed criticism of its planning. Cairo's HQ staff were out of touch with the realities of modern war since they seemed unaware that experience on the Western Front proved that at least 160,000 and not 100,000 men would be needed to defend the proposed perimeter around the beachhead. There was also, the War Office noticed, vagueness about just how many Turkish troops would be deployed to throw back the invaders. Lawrence later shifted the blame for miscalculations on to Clayton, who, he said, had reduced his and Graves's estimates. He could not sidestep the final criticism of the plan which questioned its broad strategic aims. A landing in Syria 'offended against the fundamental principle of strategy' since, even if it succeeded, it would have done nothing to harm the Allies' most formidable adversary, the German army. Moreover the plan created mischief because, if carried out, it would drive a wedge between Britain and France. For the first but not last time, the War Office called in question the competence and reasoning of officers in GHQ Cairo and in its intelligence section in particular.

III

A SECRET WAR

B Y the beginning of 1916 Lawrence found himself increasingly immersed in the secret war of subversion and counter-subversion being waged between Britain and Turco-German intelligence services in the Middle East. Hitherto his routine duties had brought him into only occasional contact with this struggle. It offered exciting opportunities for adventure and he was keen to join in. The chance had almost come in March 1915 when he believed he was about to be ordered to the Yemen and he was full of schoolboy enthusiasm. 'It's a big game, and at last one worth playing,' he told Hogarth. The players were secret agents who penetrated their enemy's territories with gold, guns, promises and propaganda with which to stir up unrest and tribal rebellions. Turco-German agents appealed to the religious zeal of Muslims, their British counterparts preached Arab nationalism. Those who waged this new kind of warfare needed courage, daring and imagination, and were free to make their own rules.

The contest had begun on 23 November 1914 in Constantinople, where the Sultan Mehmed V had declared a jihad or holy war against the Allies. He spoke as Caliph, the successor to Muhammad and spiritual leader of the world's Sunni Muslims. He called on them to unite and make common cause with Turkey in defence of their endangered faith. The 'Muscovite government' and its allies had unleashed a war for the destruction of Islam. The past record of British, French and Russian colonisation was clear evidence of their malevolence.[1] 'The Alliance which calls itself the Triple Entente has during the past century stolen the political independence, governments and freedom of the Muslims of India, Central Asia and much of Africa.'

Now all Muslims could fight back. When the jihad was publicly proclaimed in Aleppo in June 1915, listeners heard that henceforward 'The killing of infidels who rule over Islamic lands has become a sacred duty.'[2] Any doubts which believers may have had about Turkey's alliance with Germany were dispelled by the simultaneous announcement that the Kaiser had been converted. His new name, Gulliam Haji, revealed that he had already made his pilgrimage to Mecca, presumably incognito. This news and the proclamation of the jihad were widely welcomed by Muslims throughout the Ottoman empire. Many Turkish and Arab conscripts copied Enver Pasha and grew bristly *kaiserlich* moustaches in honour of Islam's new champion.

Jihadic propaganda had two general aims. Inside the Ottoman empire, Turks and Arabs were exhorted to forget racial and political differences and draw together as brothers in the faith, a process which would make it easier to enforce the unpopular conscription laws. Muslims outside the empire faced a dilemma. Did they stay loyal to their infidel British, French and Russian rulers or did they rise up against them as the Caliph had demanded?

Properly directed by German and Turkish intelligence, the jihad had enormous potential as a source of mischief. The effects of what Wingate called 'the Turco-German poison' were soon apparent: in January 1915 there was an anti-British revolt by 3,000 Arab tribesmen in Muscat, and more ominously a serious mutiny by Muslim sepoys at Rangoon in November 1914 and another at Singapore the following February. In Cairo, Lawrence felt the ripples of these disturbances for, in March 1915, he wrote to Hogarth that British troops were being sent to Iraq to stiffen 'shaky' Indian units. During 1915 and 1916 there was a disturbing trickle of desertions to the Turks, self-inflicted wounds and malingering, all of which indicated that Indian Muslim troops were deeply unhappy about fighting their co-religionists.[3] Even more alarming for the British was the fact that these were spontaneous outbursts and not the result of direct enemy propaganda or subversion.

In fact the Turco-German campaign of subversion got under way slowly. From the start it was hampered by Turkish suspicions that the Germans were conducting undercover operations in furtherance of their own rather than the Alliance's interests. This apprehension was symptomatic of the wider unease felt by many Turks about their country's growing subjection to Germany, which was expressed by Constantinople wits as 'Deutschland über Allah'.[4] What General Liman von Sandars called 'German order and control' were resented by Turks at all levels. Proposals for the distribution of German bribes among Arabian sheiks and the establishment of a German propaganda newspaper at Medina were blocked in March 1916 by Enver Pasha, who suspected that their real purpose was to prepare the ground for post-war German influence in the region.[5] These Turco-German tensions were, paradoxically, similar to the Franco-British bickering during 1916 and 1917, when the French believed that their ally was directing the Arab revolt solely in her own interests.

General direction of the Turco-German programme of subversion was in the hands of Max von Oppenheim, the Bavarian archaeologist whom Lawrence had encountered at Karkamis before the war. As an adversary, GHQ intelligence in Cairo did not rate him very highly. According to a report on his activities sent to the War Office early in 1916, von Oppenheim was out of touch with the Syrian population, preferring to keep the company of tradesmen and 'Mahomedan paramours'.[6] Aware that Britain was bidding for Arab friendship, he had set up an anti-British news agency in Aleppo and was doling out bribes, but his converts were confined to the educated, urban Syrians. Lawrence's beloved villagers appeared to have been untouched by German efforts to keep Muslim fervour at a high pitch. The Kurds were a different matter and intelligence reported that the Germans had enjoyed some success in whipping up their fanaticism. At the end of December 1916, Lawrence heard further details of von Oppenheim's propaganda machine from the Amir Faisal, who had visited Damascus the previous March. What had struck him particularly had been a film which opened with a view of the Pyramids surmounted by a Union Jack. Below Australians knocked down Egyptians and raped their wives, while far away Turkish columns advanced towards the Suez Canal. In the final scene the Turks suddenly appear, trounce the Australians, tear down the flag and receive Maxwell's surrender. The Australians' reputation was a bonus for von Oppenheim's propagandists who, during the spring of 1916, were broadcasting a tale in which Indian Muslim soldiers mutinied in thousands after a brutal Australian officer had shot his Indian servant.[7]

India, with its 57 million Muslims, was the area where Britain was most vulnerable to Pan-Islamic subversion, although Berlin's Eastern Intelligence Section also encouraged Bengali and Sikh nationalist revolutionaries. It was von Oppenheim's task to convince Indian Muslims that Germany was the friend of their faith and to raise an anti-British jihad on the

North-West Frontier, where Islamic resistance to British rule was traditionally strong. Unrest on the North-West Frontier would distract the government in Delhi and beat the drum for Muslim uprisings across northern
India. By the summer of 1915 preparations for this ambitious project were
in hand. A team of twenty-five Austrian and German officers had assembled
in Constantinople; some were detailed to make contact with the Amir of
Afghanistan and bribe him to join the jihad, while others were ordered
to assist colleagues who were spearheading a tribal revolt in Persia. There
were also a handful of Afridi tribesmen, deserters from the Indian army,
who were to return to the Tirah and sound the jihadic trumpet there.[8]

Intelligence reports of the mission created near panic in Delhi. Faced
with the prospect of unrest among native troops and a recrudescence of
warfare on the North-West Frontier, the Viceroy, Lord Hardinge, had
cabled Kitchener in March 1915 with the plea, 'I want every white soldier
I can get.' A further spasm of viceregal nervousness made itself felt in
the Cabinet, which in April 1916 agreed to earmark two divisions of British
troops, then stationed in Egypt, for service on the North-West Frontier.[9]

Covert German operations were also panicking the generals in Iraq. By
exploiting local resentment against Anglo-Russian domination, German
agents had contrived a series of tribal uprisings in Persia. The long-term
aim was to push the country into an alliance with Germany and provide
a safe springboard for sedition in India. The spadework was largely in
the hands of Wilhelm Wassmüss, a former consul, who by May 1915 had
gathered an army of over 3,000 tribesmen and deserters from the gendarmerie with which he harassed centres of British and Russian control. Wassmüss was an inspiring and resourceful commander whose spectacular coups
earned him the title the 'German Lawrence'. Yet his successes were deceptive. He made a nuisance of himself and led British and Russian forces
a dance, but his ability to do lasting harm in Persia was limited because
he was starved of arms and cash.

All von Oppenheim's schemes suffered from one fundamental flaw, which
had been recognised by Liman von Sandars when the Kabul mission
reached Constantinople. It seemed, to the professional soldier, wasteful
to send men, arms and money over vast distances into regions where they
were cut off from any hope of further assistance. Enver Pasha was also
unhappy about the plans because he thought the German and Austrian
officers were all skipping front-line service and drank too much. Von
Sandars knew that British and Russian control over Central Asia and
Persia was too tight to allow the unhindered flow of the supplies of arms
and cash in the amounts which would be needed to keep tribal revolts
alive. Moreover, like his British counterparts later, he was sceptical about
the value of tribal armies without a stiffening of trained, regular troops.

In essence, von Sandars was correct. Wassmüss's gadfly campaign was a war waged in isolation by unsupported forces which, in the end, could be contained by local British and Russian units. The Amir of Afghanistan warily set a high price on his co-operation. Jihads preached by local holy men broke out on the North-West Frontier in 1917 and spluttered on for four years but, without direct assistance from Turkey, their suppression presented no serious problems for British forces.

At GHQ intelligence, Lawrence and his colleagues traced the fortunes of the Kabul mission. On 12 February 1916 they received details of the interrogation of one of its members, Lieutenant Winckelmann, who had been taken prisoner in Persia. Once employed by von Oppenheim as a propagandist in Aleppo, Winckelmann told British intelligence how he had taken eight boxes of gold to Kirmanshah, the centre of Turco-German subversion in Persia, and there had witnessed a quarrel between Raouf Bey and German officers over what were their exact orders. In acrimony the party fragmented into five units which dispersed into Persia and Azerbaijan.[10] It all added up to a missed opportunity thanks to muddled staff work, and it could have been no comfort that von Sandars had predicted this kind of outcome when the officers had been in Constantinople.

In spite of faulty planning and confused objectives, the Turks and Germans had made the running in the secret war of subversion. They had shown their enemies what could be achieved by determined and imaginative officers able to exploit latent Muslim passions. In terms of military objectives achieved, the net gains had been negligible: nowhere did the Allies lose territory or suffer serious setbacks. Still, von Oppenheim's operations had panicked the government of India and, most importantly, had forced Britain to divert forces urgently needed on the battlefronts in France to colonial garrison duties.

GHQ intelligence Cairo learned further lessons in the value of sedition as a weapon of war during the winter of 1915–16. After nearly twelve months of coaxing, Turco-German agents persuaded the Sanussi of Libya to invade Egypt in November 1915. A month later, Lawrence wrote off their incursion as 'a damp squib', although it took until the following spring to bring the Sanussi to heel and British forces had to guard Egypt's western border until the end of the war. Some Egyptians had deserted to the invaders, and in May Clayton had to deal with a new anti-British conspiracy, this time involving Egyptian army officers. There was trouble further south in the Sudan in June 1916 when, after nearly a year of procrastination, Ali Dinar, the Sultan of Darfur, rebelled in the name of the jihad. Local forces supported by aircraft ruthlessly crushed the uprising. Wingate was full of trepidation; it was less than twenty years since an Anglo-Egyptian army had overthrown the Islamic Mahdist state, there had been a mutiny by Sudanese troops at Khartoum in 1900, and eight years later a small-scale Mahdist rebellion. The Sudan was an unstable region where British control was neither fully effective nor totally accepted. Not surprisingly, Wingate badgered Cairo for European troops to be held in readiness in case of a local emergency.[11]

Wingate was soon disturbed by fresh alarms from an unexpected quarter. In Ethiopia, the twenty-year-old Emperor, Lij Eyasu, had converted to Islam, proclaimed himself a descendant of Muhammad and not of Solomon and Sheba, and made public overtures to the Turkish Sultan. German consular officials were quick to offer him their country's friendship and during February and March 1916 Italian sources informed GHQ intelligence Cairo of a mission to Ethiopia by six German agents, whom they claimed, somewhat improbably, had been landed from a U-boat.[12] Other visitors to Lij Eyasu included emissaries from Abdullah ibn Hassan, the 'Mad Mullah' of Somaliland, who was given arms with which to reopen his twenty-year-old war against the British. In Cairo and Khartoum there were fears that the Emperor, egged on by Turkish and German agents, would make himself a figurehead for an Islamic revolt in the Sudan.

Unsubstantiated rumours which later circulated in Ethiopia linked Lawrence's name with propaganda devised in Khartoum to blacken Lij Eyasu in the eyes of his Christian subjects. These included the printing and circulation of lewd postcards which showed the Emperor in sexual poses with his several wives.[13] These and other forms of propaganda helped prepare the ground for the rebellion by Zauditu and her son, Ras Tafari (Hailie Selassie), which toppled Lij Eyasu in December 1916. French machine-guns, smuggled through Djibouti, helped Ras Tafari, who had unsuccessfully approached Wingate for aircraft.[14]

Lij Eyasu's apostasy was an unlooked-for piece of good luck for von Oppenheim which he was quick to exploit. In December 1915, the German High Command was keen to seize the initiative in the Middle East before the Allies had time to recover from the Gallipoli débâcle. On 21 December 1915, Enver announced a new offensive against the Suez Canal, but GHQ intelligence believed that it would take Turkey at least a year to muster the necessary men and logistical support. The invasion of Egypt was scheduled to coincide with a series of diversions in the Red Sea area which, if successful, would drain British manpower.

A mission commanded by Major von Stotzingen arrived at Damascus on 26 March 1916 under orders from Berlin to extend jihadic propaganda into Arabia and to make contact with anti-British elements in Ethiopia. This was the task of Karl Neufeld, 'a very low-down individual' according to GHQ intelligence in Cairo, whose older members were probably well aware of his bizarre career.[15] A sometime trader, he had fallen prisoner to the Mahdi in 1885, turned Muslim, and before his release in 1898 had helped the Dervishes manufacture bullets. On his way to Arabia in 1916 he married a third wife. Wireless technicians attached to the German party were detailed to build a transmitting station at Sana in the Yemen to make contact with German forces in East Africa. Von Oppenheim hoped that the mission's eventual base at Medina would become a powerhouse for Pan-Islamic subversion in the Sudan and Somaliland. At the same time it was hoped that the German presence would put some ginger into the Turkish offensive against Aden.

As in Persia and Afghanistan, von Oppenheim was hindered by fragile lines of communication since the Royal Navy's control of the Red Sea made gun-running to the Sudan and Ethiopia risky. Still, there were German plans to distract the navy by a campaign of mine-laying from bases at Aqaba and Jiddah. News of this and of German efforts to build small mine-layers began to filter through to Naval and Military Intelligence during the spring of 1916 and created new alarms.[16]

So far the British response to the Turco-German initiative had been fumbling. Each disturbance and the expectation that others were imminent made local administrators clamour for more troops, usually British battalions whose loyalty was beyond question. Half-buried in the minds of many men on the spot was the dread of a general Muslim uprising which, gathering irresistible momentum, would become uncontrollable. Their fears were voiced by Bullivant, the intelligence chief in John Buchan's *Greenmantle*: 'There is a dry wind blowing through the East, and the parched grasses await the spark. And the wind is blowing towards the Indian border.'

The War Office's response to this sort of scare-mongering was cool. Giving way to demands for extra troops depleted vital reserves which were needed to hold the line in France. This was the view held by General Sir William Robertson, who had become Chief of the Imperial General Staff on 23 December 1915. His influence was soon felt in every theatre of war, while that of Kitchener, discredited by the Gallipoli shambles, waned. Robertson's rise marked the ascendancy in London of the 'Westerners', those politicians and commanders who were convinced that the war would be won only when the German army in France and Belgium had been decisively beaten. Their logic seemed unanswerable. Germany was the keystone of the Central Powers, all of which depended upon her manpower, money (by November 1918 Germany had loaned Turkey 50 billion marks) and industry. As the War Office criticism of the Alexandretta scheme insisted, even the heaviest blows against Turkey did nothing to weaken the German army. Rather, the Westerners' philosophy ran, such offensives indirectly assisted Germany because they deflected manpower and resources away from France and Belgium: Lawrence was never converted to this view and, even towards the end of the war, remained certain that Turkey's defeat would fatally undermine Germany.

One of Robertson's first duties at the War Office was to fend off demands for extra men in the Middle East. He attached little importance to arguments based upon prestige. 'Prestige', he wrote later, 'no doubt carries much weight in eastern countries, but in war it is apt to become a bogy.' He deplored the hitherto supine response of the authorities in the Middle East, who, it seemed to him, had taken 'no effective steps' to scotch Turco-German subversion. The remedy was clear to him and his staff. 'What was needed was to despatch to centres of intrigue and disaffection a few Englishmen of the right type to give our version of the state of affairs, and furnish them with money to pay handsomely for intelligence and other services.'[17]

There was nothing novel in this. 'A few officers who could speak Arabic' were all that Lord Cromer, a sometime consul-general in Egypt, thought necessary to raise Arabia in arms against the Turks. In October 1915, Kitchener had asked Cairo to consider recruiting and training Armenian exiles as guerrillas for use in Syria and his idea was later revived by Admiral Wemyss.[18] Intelligence in Cairo had come up with ideas along these lines, and in March 1915 a plan was in hand to send Newcombe and Lawrence to the Yemen as military advisers to the insurgents there. This fell through since the India Office claimed that the area was under its jurisdiction, but, soon after, Wyndham Deedes had formed small guerrilla units for some behind-the-lines forays during the Gallipoli campaign.[19]

Cairo could not be blamed for its concentration on defensive, preventative measures against Turco-German subversion. Professional soldiers were never altogether happy with such projects and were always quick to point out the drawbacks of guerrilla warfare by loosely disciplined irregular units. Moreover, as long as there was a chance of success for the Gallipoli campaign, there was no immediate need to give serious consideration to active subversion. Beneath the surface, many officials found the concept of this kind of warfare distasteful. Until 1914, the imperial powers had shared a common front when it came to facing resistance to their rule; for instance, in East Africa, Britain, Germany and Italy had helped each other out in the suppression of native revolts. There were practical as well as moral reasons why Britain, an imperial power, should be cautious about the promotion of unrest within the Turkish empire. As officials in India repeatedly pointed out, even limited encouragement offered to Arab separatists could have unlooked-for repercussions after the war. Indians might justifiably contrast the treatment accorded to the Arabs with their own government's coolness towards demands for self-determination.

Faced at the end of 1915 with failure at Gallipoli, an enforced retreat in Iraq and prospects of a new Turkish assault on the Suez Canal, the British government had little choice but to press ahead with plans to subvert the Turkish empire through an Arab alliance. The creation of a fissure between the Arabs and the Turks would be a masterstroke which would divide the Ottoman empire and blunt the Pan-Islamic sword.

There were several stumbling-blocks in the way of an Arab–British understanding. Arab nationalists were by no means universally convinced of the long-term value of co-operation with Britain, an aggressive imperial power which over the past century had made no secret of its ambitions to dominate the Middle East. Moreover, as Lawrence soon discovered, many educated Arabs followed the course of the war in Europe through newspapers, and what they read was not always reassuring. Throughout 1916, 1917 and most of 1918 an Allied victory over Germany did not seem predetermined, and prudent Arabs realised that it was in their interests to hedge their bets by keeping lines open to Turkey and Germany.

Inside the India Office and in Delhi the prospect of an Arab alliance caused deep consternation. Lord Hardinge called it 'a Frankenstein Monster,' predicted that like the original it would plague its creators, and refused any contribution to the costs of the Arab revolt, which, he hoped, would swiftly collapse.[20] It was dangerously absurd for Britain to foster Arab nationalism on one hand and on the other allow India to annex Iraq, where by the winter of 1915–16 there were already pockets of Arab resistance to the new British imperial order.

There were French as well as Indian objections to the Arab alliance. These emerged during the extended Anglo-French discussions in late 1915 which attempted to settle what could and what could not be offered as inducements to the Arabs. The French were inflexible over Syria and even demanded additional territory in northern Iraq as the price for their consent to the Arab alliance. French greed appalled Asquith, but it had to be stomached by his Cabinet. The ministers were under pressure from the War Office, which saw the Arab alliance as a quick way out of Middle Eastern difficulties and an end to fears about Pan-Islamic agitation. This was the case laid before the Cabinet on 23 March 1916 by General Macdonogh, who urged the signing of an immediate agreement with Hussain, the Sharif of Mecca. He spoke with the voice of Cairo, where in January Lawrence drew up a memorandum on the benefits which would follow an Arab uprising led by Hussain.[21] It pleased Clayton, who on 1 February forwarded it to the Foreign Office, where it would serve as ammunition to be used against those who held back for fear of offending France.

Lawrence's contribution to the debate on the Arab alliance was boldly written and sweeping in its arguments, too much so for one Foreign Office official accustomed to bland departmental prose, who labelled the piece 'Partial and highly coloured'. Perhaps for these reasons he thought Gertrude Bell the author. Lawrence offered a clear analysis of Meccan politics and an explanation of the motives of Hussain. He pictured him as a princeling who expected to harness Britain to his private ambition, which was to make himself Caliph and emancipate the Arabs 'from their present irritating subjection'. A foe to both the Young Turks and Pan-Islamic agitators, Hussain's 'activity seems beneficial to us, because it marches with our immediate aims, the break-up of the Islamic "bloc" and the defeat and disruption of the Ottoman Empire'.

Hussain had already shown tokens of his goodwill by attempting to persuade the Imam Yahya not to join the Turkish attack on Aden and restraining the 'Mad Mullah' of Somaliland – not for long as it turned out, for he was on the warpath in March 1916. More to Britain's advantage, Hussain had refused the proclamation of the jihad in Mecca and restricted Turkish army recruitment in Hejaz. In the short term, Hussain sought the expulsion of the Turks from Hejaz, where a revolution would suit Britain. 'If', Lawrence argued, 'we can arrange that this political change shall be a violent one, we will have abolished the threat of Islam, by dividing it against itself, in its very heart. There will then be a Khalifa in Turkey and a Khalifa in Arabia, in theological warfare, and Islam will be as little formidable as the Papacy when Popes lived in Avignon.' The theology but not the imagery had been provided by Wingate, whose adviser, Sayyid Ali al Murghani, had told him that Hussain could lay a justifiable claim to the caliphate.[22]

As for the outcome of these manoeuvres, Lawrence concurred with Indian views about the Arabs' administrative ineptitude, but claimed that their anarchic tendencies would be to Britain's post-war advantage. The Arabs were 'even less stable than the Turks', he observed. 'If properly handled they would remain in a state of political mosaic, a tissue of small jealous principalities incapable of cohesion and yet always ready to combine against an outside force.' Throughout his paper, Lawrence assumed that political power within the Arab movement would remain the monopoly of tribal autocrats like Hussain. He never mentioned republican and democratic nationalists. Foreign annexation of Arab land was abhorrent and, Lawrence warned, harmful to Britain's future interests. 'Colonisation by a European power other than ourselves' (that is, France) would lead straight to 'conflict with the interests we already possess in the Near East.' That the Arabs would accept some form of British control was taken for granted and Lawrence offers no suggestions as to how the French could be persuaded to forgo their post-war colonial consolation prize in Syria.

When he wrote this memorandum, Lawrence was still assigned to the cartographic section of intelligence and was continuing with his routine office duties. It shows that he was keeping in touch with everything which passed through his office (for example, the reference to the activities of the 'Mad Mullah') and that his thinking was in tune with the official line taken by Macmahon, Wingate and Clayton. If his treatment of Hussain appears cynically Machiavellian, it must be remembered that in January 1916 Britain was fighting for her life in a war where final victory seemed elusive and distant. At the time Cairo was jammed with officers and men just back from Gallipoli – Lawrence said he once counted fifty-four generals – and the news from the Iraq front was chilling. Any device which could hurt the enemy and accelerate victory deserved careful examination. Furthermore, as Lawrence recognised, if an anti-Turkish revolt in Hejaz could be engineered, then the credibility of Turco-German, Pan-Islamic propaganda would be irreparably damaged.

At the beginning of 1916 everything depended on Hussain, who had been bargaining by letter with Sir Henry McMahon since the previous June. He was a hesitant revolutionary who intended to show his hand only after he had wrung the best possible terms from Britain. On 9 March 1916, the Cabinet approved the payment to him of a monthly subsidy of £125,000, and he was promised Royal Navy assistance and arms. Orders were given on 14 March for the shipment of 5,000 rifles and a quarter of a million rounds of ammunition to Port Sudan, where they were to be handed over to Hussain's agents.[23] As to what Hussain would get in the way of territory, the issue would be clouded by later claims and counter-claims over Syria, a province which he already cherished. At least as early as June 1916 he had got some inkling of the agreements for shared spheres of influence and annexation in the area, which is hardly surprising given that they had long been the subject of speculation in the French press.[24]

Not that this mattered greatly in 1916. Then the Arab Revolt was a gamble for all concerned. The final stakes were less important than when and how the first die was thrown. Hussain could not afford to haggle over-long. Time was running out for him since Turkish intelligence had uncovered evidence of his underhand dealings with the British by mid-January 1916.[25] News that the von Stotzingen mission would arrive in Medina in April, accompanied by an escort of 3,000 men commanded by Khari Bey, concentrated Hussain's mind. The return from Damascus of his son Faisal would have also helped bring the Sharif nearer to the moment of truth, since he brought with him news that Jamal Pasha, the Governor of Syria, was beginning a crack-down on local nationalists. Details of the wave of arrests, courts martial and public hangings during April and May suggested that a limit existed to Turkish tolerance of dissent.

The evidence of these measures, the German mission and reinforcements for the Hejaz garrison, which already stood at 16,000, convinced Hussain that he could no longer safely run with both the hare and the hounds. His untrustworthiness exposed, he was faced with the possibility that the Turks would introduce coercive measures and replace him as sharif. He appealed for direct British assistance in the form of a diversionary attack on Alexandretta which would force the Turks to pull troops out of Hejaz, but this was refused. As it was, his fears were inflated. Neither the Turkish government nor its German advisers were troubled by Hussain's treachery and his uprising was confidently expected to flop. The Germans believed, with some justification, that he was bribable, and Enver Pasha predicted that his fanaticism would quickly exasperate the British. If his activities became a serious nuisance, then he was to be assassinated.[26]

On the British side, the directions of arrangements for the Arab Revolt were in the hands of a new agency, the Arab Bureau, which had been set up in January 1916. It had been the creation of a committee of officials from the War, Foreign and India Offices which had been formed to work out how best Britain's future policy towards the Arabs could be co-ordinated and implemented. The Bureau's godfather had been Sir Mark Sykes, the mercurial thirty-seven-year-old baronet and MP who had travelled in the Middle East before the war. After raising a battalion from his estates on the Yorkshire wolds, he had been appointed to liaise between the War and Foreign Offices on all aspects of Middle Eastern policy. A Roman Catholic and Zionist, Sykes had negotiated the Anglo-French agreement, known as the Sykes–Picot Treaty, which set out the boundaries of the post-war Middle East. Sykes also recognised the value of an alliance with Hussain and he took care to staff the Bureau with men of like mind. The pro-Turkish Wyndham Deedes was therefore kept out.[27]

Sykes was a frequent visitor to Cairo, where, according to Hogarth, he 'inspired, encouraged and always taught us something'. Lawrence mistrusted him and his policies. In the *Seven Pillars* (written after Sykes's death in 1919) Lawrence portrayed him as 'a bundle of prejudices, intuitions, half-sciences', and then went on to describe him in terms which could easily have applied to himself:

> His ideas were of the outside; and he lacked the patience to test his materials before choosing his style of building. He would take an aspect of the truth, detach it from its circumstances, inflate it, twist and model it, until its old likeness and its new unlikeness together drew a laugh; and laughs were his triumphs. His instincts lay in parody: by choice he was a caricaturist rather than an artist, even in his statesmanship. He saw the odd in everything, and missed the even.

At root of this criticism was Lawrence's refusal to forgive Sykes for his accommodation of French interests in Syria and his backing for the Zionists which, during late 1917 and early 1918, threatened to create a rift between Lawrence and Faisal. There may also have been an element of jealousy in Lawrence's reaction to Sykes. Brilliant men are often suspicious of each other and Lawrence may have envied Sykes his self-assurance and extensive connections in Whitehall, which enabled him to impose his own views on government policy.

Whether or not Lawrence was aware of it, Sykes was also a romantic Tory anxious to protect the Arabs from the corruption of the modern world and its ideas. He disliked those Arab radicals who dreamed of bringing 'European Jacobinism to Sunni Mohammedanism' and was disgusted that Iraq, 'this land of poetry and ignorance', would be swamped by 'the ideas of the lowest Anglo-Saxon savages' which included 'respectability and over eating'.[28] Lawrence would have approved.

It was with Sykes's creation, the Arab Bureau, that Lawrence's future lay. It ran all Arab propaganda, collected and recorded all Arab intelligence and acted as an instrument of British policy towards Arabs everywhere. It was housed in three rooms in the Savoy Hotel, adjacent to the GHQ intelligence offices, and cost £4,000 a year. Its director answered to the Foreign Office through the High Commissioner in Egypt and through Clayton to the Director of Military Intelligence at the War Office. It was an Admiralty intelligence officer, Lieutenant-Commander Hogarth, who was appointed director over Clayton's candidate, Colonel Parker, and after a briefing in London he took up his duties on 25 March 1916. An ex-Sudan civil servant turned army intelligence officer, Kinahan Cornwallis, was Deputy Director, Philip Graves attended to Turkish business and the press, A. B. Fforde represented the interests of India, and Gertrude Bell was sent to Basra as the Bureau's temporary agent in Iraq. There was a small staff of typists.

Lawrence was never on the payroll of the Bureau, although like his brother intelligence officers he was frequently assigned to work for it. Much of its work overlapped with that of GHQ intelligence and Hogarth was always free to secure the services of army intelligence specialists like Lawrence. In the first weeks of the Bureau's existence, Lawrence contributed material to a dossier on Arab 'personalities', leading figures whose future allegiance had to be ascertained. For a time in January 1916 he was helped by Gertrude Bell, whose particular expertise was the tribes of Iraq which she knew from her pre-war travels. Soon after, he presented a report on the Syrian camel trade.

The genesis of the Arab Revolt and the Arab Bureau are covered in early sections of the *Seven Pillars*. Next to nothing is said about the extent and success of Turco-German subversion during 1915 and 1916, which the revolt was designed to frustrate. Nor are there any signs of the hard-headed perception and appeal to self-interest which marked Lawrence's Hussain memorandum. Instead the manipulators of the Arabs reappear as nation-builders.

> We called ourselves 'Intrusive' [actually the telegraphic code-name of GHQ intelligence, Cairo] as a band; for we meant to break into the accepted halls of English foreign policy, and built a new people in the East, despite the rails laid down for us by our ancestors.

The brotherhood of visionaries, Lawrence, Clayton, Storrs, Lloyd, Hogarth, Cornwallis, Newcombe, Parker, Herbert, Philip Graves and the wavering Sykes, move into action and enlighten their superiors. Thanks to their persuasiveness, Britain adopts the Arab cause and it thrives because of their dedication. In fact, it was the so-called converts, Kitchener, Macmahon and Wingate, who were the first and most influential advocates of an Arab alliance, but for reasons which had to do with winning the war and preserving the British empire.

There is no room for such base motives in Lawrence's narrative and they are deliberately excluded. The wary procrastinator Hussain becomes an idealist in arms:

> The Young Turks in his eyes were so many godless transgressors of their creed and their human duty – traitors to the spirit of the time, and to the highest interests of Islam. Though an old man of sixty-five, he was cheerfully determined to wage war against them, relying on justice to cover the cost.

In fact it was the British taxpayer rather than 'justice' who footed the bill, as Mark Sykes drily remarked in June 1916, soon after hearing the news of Hussain's rebellion. 'The Sharif', he wrote, 'has hitherto regarded us as an unfailing source of Bakshish and rifles,' and his action had been prompted solely by the fear that his plots had been uncovered by the Turks, who were set on bringing him to heel.[29]

The omissions and distortions of the first part of the *Seven Pillars* set the pattern for much which is to follow. Since Lawrence was not writing an orthodox history he saw no need to adhere to the truth. The chicanes of the secret war of ideologies, the manipulation of nationalism and the backstairs trafficking in territory, concessions and bribes which were the real background to the Arab Revolt had no place in an epic written to illustrate the triumph of an idea and the sufferings and tenacity of its followers. By their own determination and sacrifice on the battlefield, Lawrence's Arabs would regenerate themselves and find dignity and nation-hood. If Lawrence had such visions at the beginning of 1916, he kept them to himself and dispassionately presented the Arab Revolt as a stratagem which would bring Britain untold advantage in her struggle to deflect the wave of Islamic fanaticism which Turkey and Germany were bent on unleashing.

The prospect of the Arab Revolt had a further attraction for Lawrence. Once under way it would have to be an unorthodox war since it would be months, even years before the Arabs could train and field a conventional army. There would therefore be openings for an imaginative, adventurous young officer who had long hoped that he might be able to do something for the Arabs.

IV

ADVENTURES IN BLUNDERLAND: IRAQ, APRIL 1916

ON 20 March 1916, Lawrence went by train to Port Said, and joined the liner *Royal George* bound for Kuwait. There he embarked on the fast mail steamer *Elephanta* for Basra. He was travelling under orders from Sir Henry Macmahon and Clayton, who had entrusted him with a mission which required experience of everyday intelligence work, a detailed knowl-edge of the preparations then in hand for Hussain's rebellion and, most importantly, considerable forbearance and tact. Lawrence showed all these qualities even though he would claim in the *Seven Pillars* that at this time, 'I was all claws and teeth, and had a devil.'

Lawrence had been given three connected assignments. The first was to explore and report back on how two defectors from the Turkish army, Major Aziz Ali al Mizri and Captain Muhammad al Faruqi, might be used to foment mutinies among Arab troops in Iraq. He was also, on their and the Arab Bureau's behalf, to make contact with local Arab nationalists and discover their reactions to the imminent uprising in Hejaz. Lawrence's second task was to meet Colonel Percy Cox, the Chief Political Officer with the Anglo-Indian forces in Iraq, and explain to him the policies and areas of responsibility of the new Arab Bureau. This required much patience and diplomacy since Cox's employer, the Delhi government, distrusted the Bureau and feared that its sponsorship of Arab nationalism would harm Indian interests in Iraq. Lastly, Lawrence had to hold discussions with his opposite numbers in the intelligence section of D Force (the Anglo-Indian army in Iraq) and find ways in which they could work in tandem with Cairo. Here he would again have to act as a spokesman for the Arab Bureau and outline what was expected from the Arab Revolt.

All were difficult tasks. There could be no effective Arab policy until there was understanding and co-operation between Cairo and Basra. The present sourness owed much to the 'bitter and outspoken anti-Indian attitude' displayed all too publicly by Mark Sykes.[1] Among his gaffes was a galling aside in which he declared that Muslims were better off under Turkish than British rule. One consequence of his insensitivity had been the treatment meted out to Gertrude Bell on her arrival in Basra at the beginning of March. She was lectured on the Indian Secrets Act and her correspondence was censored.[2] To avoid such embarrassment, Lawrence was equipped with an Arab Bureau cipher book.[3]

From his personal standpoint, the first part of Lawrence's mission was the most challenging. For over a year GHQ Intelligence in Cairo had been mesmerised by the possibility that disruptive mutinies could be kindled among Arab troops in the Turkish army. Throughout 1915 and early 1916 there had been an encouraging trickle of information from all fronts that Arab officers and conscripts were disheartened and restless. During January and February 1915 there had been reports that Arabs stationed near Alexandretta would throw down their arms. During the autumn Russian sources revealed widespread Arab desertions on the Caucasus front and Turkish officers placed in charge of suspect Arab and Kurdish battalions. Two Arab deserters, questioned at Gallipoli, told their interrogator that Arab battalions were riddled with insubordination and had to be kept back from the front. There was news of Arab desertions from Aden and, in March 1916, reports of general disaffection among Arabs serving with the 35th Division in Iraq. Two captured officers from this unit gave an indication of their feelings by their willingness to reveal all the military information they knew.[4]

These strands were pulled together by the extensive revelations of Captain al Faruqi of the 142nd Regiment, who gave himself up at Gallipoli on 20 September 1915. After hearing and believing what he had to say, General Sir Ian Hamilton immediately sent him to Cairo, where he was examined by Clayton, Sykes and McMahon. All were impressed by his sincerity; more significantly some of his disclosures were confirmed by independent

For King and Empire: signals section of the Oxford University Officers Training Corps, c. 1910. Lawrence is seated at the far left.

Eagle on the Crescent: Kaiser Wilhelm II (waving), Sultan Mehmed V (centre) and Enver Pasha (right); Constantinople 1917.

Ready for action: Lawrence mounted on one of his racing camels, Aqaba 1917.

Desert raiders: Colonel Stewart Newcombe (second left in Arab dress),
Lieutenant Hornby (far right in British uniform), Major al Mizri (second right
in Arab dress) with Arab irregulars, 1917.

Brothers-in-arms: Three of Lawrence's fellow officers attached to the Arab
armies: from left to right, Major Davenport, Colonel Pierce Joyce (who
commanded at Aqaba) and Colonel Cyril Wilson (in charge of the mission at
Jiddah).

Deutschland über Allah: General Liman von Sandars greets Turkish officers
and officials while an Austro-Hungarian officer in gala uniform looks on;
Palestine 1917.

Intruder: Colonel Cadi of the French Military Mission wearing sharifian robes,
1917. Cadi angered Lawrence and others by hoisting the tricolour over the
French quarters in Jiddah.

Robes for a prince: Lawrence in 1917 in the white robes of a sharif with golden-hilted dagger, a costume which immediately suggested to the Arabs that he was a man of wealth and authority.

The Terrible Turk: Lawrence blamed Turkish lancers for the massacres of civilians around Tafas in September 1918. Four years earlier, British propaganda had condemned German lancers for similar atrocities in Belgium.

The Sultan's Arabs: Fakhri Pasha, commander at Medina, (seated right) consults with Ibn Raschid of Hail (seated next to him); behind, Raschid's Beduin and Turkish officers, dressed like their British counterparts in Arab head dresses.

Intelligence briefing: Lawrence (left) consults Commander Hogarth while
Colonel Alan Dawnay, who directed operations against Qalat al Mudawarrah
in March 1918, listens; Army HQ, Cairo 1918.

sources.[5] He bore out earlier prognoses about the unrest among troops at Alexandretta and he described how one engineer had deliberately botched work on the defences there and how other officers were busy spreading sedition and encouraging desertions. His assertion that officers from his own regiment were urging their men to desert was supported by a decrypt of a Turkish wireless message which described such activities.[6] Lawrence was among those utterly convinced by al Faruqi's confessions and the workability of his plans, which, he later told Liddell Hart, would have culminated in a general Arab mutiny and uprising. As a result, the whole of Syria and Iraq could have been liberated from Turkish rule in February 1915.

Al Faruqi's extravagant claims rested upon the hidden strength of al Ahd (the Covenant), an underground organisation of Arab junior officers bound together by Islamic oath and dedicated to the nationalist cause. All were men with a service grievance since senior ranks were a Turkish monopoly and their political loyalty was to al Fatah, a wider movement which embraced the educated middle classes of Syria and Iraq. These clandestine organisations were looking to Britain for backing, but if this was not forthcoming, al Faruqi ruefully admitted, they would turn to Germany and Turkey. In brief, Arab co-operation was open to all bids, although Britain's would be most welcome.

This was also the message of Major al Mizri, the founder of al Ahd, who had fled from Constantinople to Cairo in April 1914. By August he was seeking British assistance and, sensing his value, Sir Edward Grey, the Foreign Secretary, placed £2,000 at his disposal.[7] Al Mizri saw Britain as the champion of people straining for freedom, well aware no doubt of her past assistance to Greece and Italy. Idealistic young Arabs looked to Britain as their friend, he wrote to Kitchener in February 1915.[8] 'C'est cette jeunesse qui vous demande une amitié noble et franche et non pas une domination ou protectorat,' he pleaded. He contrasted the present plight of the Arab people with the position of the Irish, who had just been given self-government by magnanimous, freedom-loving Britain; apparently he was unaware that the Home Rule Act had been suspended several months before. Al Mizri predicted that with British support the Arabs would rise up, form an army and fight the Turks in the Caucasus. If Britain held back, he warned that they would seek an understanding with the Turks. Kitchener passed the plea to Maxwell, who did nothing about it until 11 October when, alerted by the news of al Faruqi's revelations, he asked the Foreign Office to issue a proclamation of support for Arab nationalism.

Al Mizri and al Faruqi were members of that class of educated Arabs which Lawrence despised for their reliance on Western political philosophies, but even he acknowledged that they had their uses. His job in Iraq was to discover just how useful they could be. McMahon, won over by the two Arab officers, had persuaded Grey and Austen Chamberlain, the Secretary of State for India, to sanction their employment as agents behind Turkish lines in Iraq, where they would mobilise their contacts in al Ahd and al Fatah and trigger a series of mutinies and tribal uprisings.

It was a desperate stratagem devised in an emergency. Since 3 December 1915, General Townshend and 14,000 British and Indian troops had been besieged at Kut and attempts to relieve them had been beaten back. On 7 March 1916, the Turkish commander, Khalil Pasha, had suggested sur-render terms. Three days later, Townshend, a keen student of Napoleonic campaigns, replied with a proposal that an agreement might be reached along the lines of that made between Marshal Masséna and the Austrians in 1800. This would involve, among other things, a cash payment to the Turks. General Lake, the commanding officer of D Force, was scandalised and, after reading Townshend's telegrams on the subject, Asquith con-cluded that 'he was off his head'.[9] Everything had to be done to save Kut and prevent its surrender on terms which, while they were thought honourable by Townshend, would humiliate Britain.

Lawrence was therefore sent out to save Kut by means of subversion behind Turkish lines, or, in his words, 'to see what could be done by indirect means to relieve the beleaguered garrison'. His mission was, as he knew, a forlorn hope, but the situation was so desperate that any stratagem was worth trying. His authority came from Robertson and Austen Chamber-lain, who, on 24 March, cabled the Viceroy and General Lake with an outline of the project.

In view of [the] Sharif's intention to make an attempt at once to detach [the] Arab element from [the] Turkish army in Arabia and Syria, it is thought desirable that [a] corresponding move should be made in Mesopotamia [that is, Iraq]. Authority has been given [by] Macmahon to send Faruqi and possibly al Mizri also to get in touch with [the] Turkish army there with this object.[10]

The plan was abhorrent to Lake, who found Cox of like mind, so on 30 April he protested to Robertson. Al Mizri and al Faruqi were nationalists whose 'political views and schemes are too advanced to be safe pabula for the communities of occupied territories'. Their presence in Iraq would be 'inconvenient and undesirable' and two of their proposed contacts, Nuri es Said and Dr Shahbandah, had already been deported by Cox as subver-sives. Lake doubted whether they could get through Turkish lines, and added that previously when Arabs claimed 'to be able to influence their compatriots in the Turkish ranks' they had been 'unable or unwilling to face the risks and practical difficulties involved'.[11]

McMahon vainly tried to placate Lake with a telegram of 1 April in which he pointed out that it was not his intention to send al Mizri into Turkish territory.[12] What he had in mind was a propaganda exercise, since the presence of al Mizri in Iraq would advertise the new Anglo-Arab 'unity of interest' to Arab soldiers in the Turkish army. He might even swing the Iraqi Arabs behind Hussain.

In London, Robertson, already certain that Kut's fall was imminent, had come up with an ingenious scheme to buy off one of the Turkish commanders in Iraq. Something of the sort had been tried a year before when Admiral Hall, the Director of Naval Intelligence, had employed agents to offer £4 million to the various Turkish officials for free passage through the Straits. There had been an indication that venal Turks might be susceptible to such bribes when, in April 1915, Jamal Pasha had secretly enquired whether Britain would recognise him as independent ruler of Syria in exchange for taking the province and the Fourth Army out of the war.[13] Robertson had in mind a £1 million incentive and Lawrence was to find a suitable go-between.[14] Kut might be saved and Robertson spared the unwelcome duty of having to despatch to Iraq troops needed on the Western Front.

Lawrence was ignorant of these exchanges, the controversy generated by his mission and Robertson's hare-brained scheme. He reached Basra on the evening of 5 April, was met by Gertrude Bell and Campbell-Thompson, his one-time Karkamis associate, now employed to decipher Turkish telegrams, and taken straight to Cox at Headquarters. Cox found Lawrence extremely vague about how he could fulfil his orders, which he understood as giving 'assistance ... to a certain project' which had been proposed by the War Office.[15] Cox cabled Colonel W.H.('Bill')Beach, the officer commanding D Force's intelligence section, for exact instructions. Beach replied, ordering Lawrence to report to him at D Force's forward HQ at Wadi, having first discussed the business with Cox and obtained an Arab officer on parole from Captain More, an intelligence officer stationed in Basra.

It was an awkward and probably frosty exchange. Cox ended the interview by telling Lawrence how strongly he disapproved of his orders. The proposed exercise in sedition could not be kept secret and, when known, would injure local British interests. What he meant was that anti-Turkish agitation among the Arabs might easily rebound on its creators and make Iraq ungovernable in the future. But he was a servant of the government, and so he delivered to Captain More the names of local Arab nationalists who might co-operate.

Lawrence had set his hopes on enlisting Sayyid Talib Pasha, whom he later called the 'John Wilkes' of the Arab independence movement, presumably on account of his arrant opportunism. Before the war, Sayyid Talib had been first a supporter of the Young Turks and then an Arab nationalist. A feudal landowner in Basra, he had, on the eve of the Anglo-Indian landings in Iraq, offered his services to the invaders, whom he hoped would appoint him amir of Basra. Cox believed him untrustworthy and a source of future resistance to British occupation, so he was deported to India along with another local nationalist, Lieutenant Nuri es Said. All that Cox could offer Lawrence were two of their former cronies, whom he interviewed the following day at More's house. Without revealing why their help was needed, Lawrence asked if they would be willing to cross Turkish lines and approach certain officers. They refused because of the danger.

Disheartened but not surprised, Lawrence returned to Cox and candidly admitted that the project was unworkable. 'To bring off a coup by sending an Arab prisoner on parole across Turkish lines' was impossible and none of the local nationalists dared take the risk. He had been placed in an invidious position by superiors wildly casting about to find ways in which to avert a disaster at Kut. He had been sent to Iraq to investigate ways in which the loyalties of Arab soldiers and civilians could be undermined and had arrived to find that he was also expected to procure an agent bold enough to cross Turkish lines, approach a Turkish general and secretly offer him £1 million. No such fools could be found in Basra, nor were there any signs of Arab nationalist fervour. On 9 April, Lawrence wired Clayton with the bleak result of his canvass of local feelings. 'Sayyid Talib and some jackals' made up the nationalist faction, and 'There is no Arab sentiment and for us [the] place is negligible.'[16]

In compliance with Beach's orders, but without an Arab renegade, Lawrence left Basra for Lake's front-line headquarters at Wadi on 9 April. Supplied with ration biscuits, ten loaves and ten tins each of bully beef and jam, Lawrence was put aboard an Irrawaddy paddle-steamer which had been pressed into the King Emperor's service. The Tigris was in flood and cold winds and rain blighted the cruise, although at Headquarters it was confidently believed that these conditions would hamper the Turkish army investing Kut. When the rain stopped, swarms of flies emerged to plague everyone.

For the first time in his service career, Lawrence witnessed life at the front. His arrival at Basra had coincided with Lieutenant-General Sir George ('Blood Orange') Gorringe's attempt to relieve Kut. Among Lawrence's fellow passengers was a detachment of 'Cumberland territorials' (in fact men from the Lancashire battalions of the 38th Brigade) on their way to reinforce Gorringe's division. When, on 19 April, he arrived at Lake's headquarters on the river gunboat *Waterfly*, a battle was in progress. Kut was twenty miles to the west and the British front was five miles off.

Lawrence's reception on board the *Waterfly* was dusty. 'The local British had the strongest objection to my coming; and two Generals of them were good enough to explain to me that my mission (which they did not really know) was dishonourable to a soldier (which I was not).'[17] One was certainly Lake and what stuck in his throat was not Lawrence's mission as the corrupter of a Turkish general, but his orders to encourage disobedience among Arab soldiers and rebellion among Arab civilians. On the Iraq front the Arabs were widely seen as despicable, craven and malevolent neutrals. They murdered the wounded, ambushed small units and plundered both British and Turkish supplies. In January, Lake had commanded punitive operations against them, and in Basra Lawrence would have heard the common joke that the British and the Turks ought to declare a truce, join together and set about the Arabs.[18] Lawrence's assertion that 'conditions were ideal for an Arab movement' in Iraq would have been greeted with disbelief and ridicule. What was more, the Anglo-Indian army was not fighting its way through Iraq so that it could be delivered into Arab hands when the war was over.

Moreover, Lake and his brother officers were Victorian and Edwardian soldiers (Lake had fought Afghans and 'Fuzzy-Wuzzies') whose gentlemanly code was violated by the notion that the military crime of mutiny could be considered a legitimate instrument of war. Lawrence's plans may also have been an uncomfortable reminder that the loyalty of Indian sepoys was becoming more and more brittle.[19]

What the staff at Wadi thought about Robertson's project for buying off an enemy commander is not known. Certainly Lawrence's position as an officer under Robertson's orders would have assured him brusque treatment by Lake and his staff. Robertson considered their performance had been disgraceful. 'Very little courage and determination' had been shown in Iraq and he was keen, in his own words, to inject some 'ginger' into those in charge.[20] Since he had taken full control of the Iraq front on 16 February, Robertson had tormented Lake and the aptly named General Sir Beauchamp Duff, Commander-in-Chief of the Indian Army, with a series of telegrams in which he made it clear that he regarded Lake as an incompetent dotard unfit for active command.[21]

Lawrence was not completely isolated among the blunderers. He got on well with Colonel Beach, with whom he had useful discussions on intelligence techniques and procedures. There was also the consolation of Aubrey Herbert's company, although his outspoken remarks on maladministration added to the general tension. Herbert had left Cairo as Admiral Wemyss's army liaison officer on 22 March and he had arrived at Wadi on 14 April. Wemyss had been there for three days and, like Herbert, was blunt in his observations about the Indian government and its generals.

'This expedition', he wrote, 'has been most scandalously starved and in my opinion the troops have been asked to perform the almost impossible.' He and Herbert were there to oversee arrangements for river transport and riverine operations to save Kut, although neither held out any hope for its defenders.[22] Herbert tried to wire Austen Chamberlain with a warning that the town would fall, but his message was censored by Indian officers who already sensed that their ill-conducted campaign would soon be a national scandal.

Between 19 and 21 April, Herbert and Lawrence were kept busy with routine intelligence activities, although Lawrence may not have been able to give them his closest attention since he suffered a bout of malaria. Herbert interviewed some Arab POWs, taken during the recent fighting. One confessed that he was unhappy about his capture because 'his own people might think he hadn't fought well', which was perhaps not what Lawrence had hoped to hear. He later reported to Clayton the more cheering news that there was widespread defeatism among the 35th and 38th Divisions, a conclusion which rested on evidence collected at Kut.[23]

Just before midnight on 22 April, headquarters at Wadi received a message from Gorringe. His exhausted army had been fought to a standstill at Sanniyat, twelve miles short of Kut. He had lost 9,700 dead in just under three weeks and what remained of his forces could not maintain the offensive.[24] This news, long dreaded in London and Wadi, began a series of bizarre events which ended with Herbert, Lawrence and Beach being ordered to conclude negotiations for the surrender of Kut. It has been assumed that Lawrence and Herbert had been kept at Wadi for this purpose, but in fact they were called in at the last moment. Their value in the emergency rested on Herbert's fluency in Turkish and Lawrence's in Arabic, although in the end their talks with Khalil Pasha were in French. As Lawrence observed in his report on D Force's intelligence section, in Iraq all interviews with POWs were conducted through native interpreters and the only Arabist, Captain More, was based at Basra.[25]

Gorringe's admission of defeat was followed four hours later by a message from Townshend.[26] In essence it repeated one sent on 13 March in which he outlined the terms he believed he could secure from Khalil, whom he 'was delighted to find ... was a soldier and a gentleman'. Such a good fellow, Townshend thought, would accept the surrender of the town and all his artillery pieces, but would allow the garrison to withdraw to British lines. If, however, his 10,000 men became POWs, then a payment would have to be made.

> It will cost some money. I expect to get Khalil to agree, but it is well
> worth it, besides the Turks have no money to pay my force in captivity

and cannot feed them. The force would all perish from weakness and be shot by the Arabs if they had to march to Baghdad and the Turks have not enough ships to take us there.

He added that the fall of Kut would be a disaster, equalled to that of Yorktown, and might bring down the government. It was regrettable that 'No message has come from King and country' in expression of sympathy for his army's plight. He concluded that 'money might easily settle the question'.

Lake procrastinated. The débâcle could no longer be staved off; British prestige would be damaged and there would be scandal and sackings, including his own. 'The interest of Empire ... demands another attempt at all costs,' Lake trumpeted, and then proposed playing his 'last card', a dash upriver by the steamer *Julnar* crammed with a month's provisions.[27] Lake's rhetoric was empty and the gesture futile. On 24 April, while brave men were volunteering to crew the *Julnar*, Lake wired Kitchener for permission to open talks with Khalil along the lines set out by Townshend.[28]

Kitchener and Robertson had rejected Lake's initial proposition in March, although it may have opened Robertson's mind to the possibility that a Turkish general could be bribed. Kitchener was adamant and on 26 March warned Lake that Kut's surrender 'would be for ever a disgrace to our country' and 'our prestige in the East would undoubtedly be gravely prejudiced by such a disaster'.[29] Faced with Lake's telegram, both he and Robertson relented. In his version of the affair, Robertson said that after consultations with Kitchener and fearful that the garrison would starve, he wired Lake with permission to negotiate, all military alternatives being exhausted. Kitchener's sanction reached Lake on the morning of 26 April with a reminder that 'ample funds [are] at your disposal'. Robertson's concurrence followed soon after.[30] Both were uneasy and when they announced the decision to the Cabinet on the 28th, they distanced themselves from it. The ministers heard that Townshend was already in contact with Khalil 'and the use of money in conducting these negotiations was quite possible, and the money was there'.[31] There had been no time to call a special session of the Cabinet and the responsibility to negotiate rested ultimately with the men on the spot, who knew just what the military situation was. Although Robertson claimed to have secured Asquith's approval beforehand, the Prime Minister expressed his disagreement with the proceedings. Not that this mattered now, for it was too late to stop them.[32]

During the night of 24/25 April, the *Julnar* was intercepted and forced aground by Turkish shellfire after a gallant sally. Lake, certain of War Office approval for talks, sent Beach to Herbert in the morning with orders that he and Lawrence were to stand by in case they were needed as emissaries to Khalil.

Talks began on the morning of the 27th, when Townshend offered Khalil all his artillery and £1 million in return for his men being allowed to leave Kut on parole. Khalil immediately referred the terms to his uncle, Enver Pasha. 'Money is not wanted by us' was the reply. Townshend then sought and got Lake's permission to double the sum to £2 million on the ground that 'The nation has certainly saved that amount by our defence of Kut.' All along, Townshend had regarded the money as a payment to cover the costs of his men in captivity, but Enver and Khalil interpreted it as either a bribe or a gesture of contempt. For a moment Townshend contemplated letting Herbert, Beach and Lawrence take over the negotiations, but Lake thought that they would have had no more success. The Turks were resolved on unconditional surrender and on the evening of the 28th Townshend gave way and began destroying his guns.[33]

The next morning, Herbert, Beach and Lawrence were ordered by Lake to go to Khalil's HQ and ask his permission for the evacuation of over 3,000 sick and wounded men.[34] They were empowered to offer Arab POWs in exchange, but only as a last resort since Robertson feared that the released men would be exploited later by Turco-German propagandists.[35]

Lawrence had hitherto been a spectator during these events. He had travelled independently of Beach and Herbert, whom he met at the HQ of Lieutenant-General Younghusband's 7th Division near Sanniyat just before they set off to the front-line trenches. What followed was set down by Lawrence in a letter to his parents and a report to the Arab Bureau. In this he reported what he had heard about Arab morale in the Turkish army during negotiations with Khalil. This was a breach of military etiquette, so he ended his report with a statement that its details had been obtained 'under privilege from the Turks' and could not be disclosed.

A white flag was raised over the trench parapet and the three stepped into no-man's land, where they were met by Turkish officers who agreed a local truce. Early in the afternoon, they were taken, blindfolded, to Khalil's HQ, a journey of ten miles. Khalil was, Lawrence surmised, in his early thirties, 'very keen and energetic but not clever or intelligent'. Herbert later told Wemyss that Khalil had a mouth 'like a steel trap'. It was Herbert who began the talks since he had met Khalil before the war at an Embassy ball in Constantinople. As Lawrence realised, 'the cards were all in his hands' and it was, he regretted afterwards, impossible to save all the wounded and sick men in Kut. As it was, 1,000 Indian invalids were exchanged for Turkish POWs.

Lawrence probed circumspectly for gossip about the morale of Arab soldiers. His cue came when discussions turned on the exchange of Indian wounded for Arab POWs, of whom there were over 3,000 in Indian camps, already segregated in case a deal was made.[36] Khalil seemed interested at first, but then changed his mind. Nine out of ten Arab soldiers were worthless since 'their desire was only to get taken prisoner, and ... the whole lot of them were unreliable'. Lawrence fenced delicately by pointing out that in campaigns against the Russians in the last century the Arabs had proved their fighting qualities. Khalil reconsidered his judgement and admitted that the 'Turkised' Arabs from Mosul and Syria were better material. Lawrence found that Khalil's views were shared by his Chief of Staff and several junior officers present, one of whom branded the Kurds lacklustre fighters. It was a neat exercise in discreet but effective intelligence-gathering and striking proof that Lawrence knew his job.

Before dinner, the three British officers withdrew to the tents which Khalil had put at their disposal, wrote their reports and 'sat and smoked' – even Lawrence, it appears. Then they were entertained by Khalil and his staff, who had laid on 'a most excellent dinner in Turkish style' which Herbert and Lawrence relished. Beach was less happy with the unfamiliar cuisine. For all Khalil's courtesy there was an acerbic moment which Lawrence described to Robert Graves. Khalil remarked with great percipience that Britain and Turkey ought not to be enemies, 'after all, gentlemen, our interests as Empire builders are much the same as yours. There is nothing that need stand between us.' 'Only a million dead Armenians,' Herbert riposted. Graves suspected with good reason that the answer had been Lawrence's.[37]

On the morning of 30 April, Lawrence and Beach returned to their lines, leaving Herbert behind to clear up outstanding details. Kut was already in Turkish hands and Lawrence heard that in spite of his pleas Arabs were being hanged by the Turks as collaborators. Lawrence was told how one condemned man had thrown his *musbah* (Muslim rosary) to a nearby British medical officer. The gesture seemed full of political and religious significance for Lawrence, who thought it might be exploited as propaganda.

Lawrence left Wadi for Basra, where he had further discussions with Cox and his staff. The sombre events he had just lived through made him prickly and he spoke frankly in the political officers' mess. Hubert Young, once a visitor to Karkamis and now serving with a Mahratta regiment, met him there and recalled that 'Lawrence was already suffering from that passion of contempt for the regular army which was to attract certain politicians in later years ... but the time for its sublimation into glorious irregularity had yet to come.' It was a strange observation, since Young was equally biting in his censure of the staff in Iraq and their utter ignorance of local conditions. Herbert, who followed Lawrence to

Basra, was burning with rage. He spoke in the Commons debate on the catastrophe at Kut on 26 July, drawing on what he had seen for himself of the haphazard commissariat and slack staff work. 'This expedition has been starved,' he claimed, and called for the 'judgement of Byng' (court martial and execution) to be delivered on those Indian government officials responsible. In the same vein, Kipling wrote:

> They shall not return to us, the resolute, the young,
> The eager and whole-hearted whom we gave:
> But the men who left them thriftily to die in their own dung,
> Shall they come with years and honour to the grave?

Of course they did, and with their pensions too.

It was left to Lawrence to spend his last days in Iraq explaining to Cox and his political staff the responsibilities of the Arab Bureau and what was expected from the forthcoming revolt of Hussain. On a personal level, Lawrence soon got to like Cox, whom he found 'delightful to work with', and Cox was impressed by Lawrence's talents as an intelligence officer and hoped he would stay. Lawrence found that Cox was well served by a staff of experts who were doing 'magnificent work' winning respect for the new administration and keeping in touch with local Arab opinion.[38]

The sticky business was convincing officials who were laying the grounds for an Indian administration in Iraq that there was no conflict between their interests and British support for Arab nationalism. Cox was hostile to the Arab Bureau and was unwilling to accept one of its officials on his permanent staff. He feared that the Bureau wanted unfettered control over every aspect of British policy in the Middle East. Lawrence eased his mind somewhat by emphasising that the Bureau was the creature of the Director of Military Intelligence. Cox then assumed that it was purely a wartime measure and would have no say in the management of post-war affairs in the Middle East, and he was persuaded by Lawrence to take Gertrude Bell on to his staff as the Bureau's corresponding officer.[39]

Lawrence was faced with the task of reconciling Cairo's alliance with Arab nationalism to the Indian government's plans for the colonisation of Iraq. Cox was deeply suspicious both of the Arab Bureau, which he feared was an anti-Indian clique dominated by Sykes, and of its plans to foster Arab national feeling. Mandarin politeness and natural reserve prevented him from revealing his apprehension to Lawrence. As a consequence of this and perhaps because Lawrence paid attention only to what he wanted to hear, Lawrence misunderstood the attitudes of Cox and his staff. He left confident that they were almost in step with Cairo. Cox 'does not know how Cairene he is', he concluded, in the belief that the pro-consul would co-operate with attempts to convince Iraq's Arabs that Britain was their ally. Lawrence imagined him willing to allow British and Arab flags to fly side by side over Baghdad when it was occupied and a joint Anglo-Arab city government afterwards. Moreover, Lawrence told Clayton, Cox welcomed Cairo's programme for the creation of a 'united Arabia', presumably the cluster of petty states which Lawrence had described in his memorandum on Hussain.[40]

It was all wishful thinking on Lawrence's part; fundamental differences of approach and policy remained. Nevertheless he had achieved something, even if it was not the harmony he imagined. George Lloyd, who arrived in Basra soon after Lawrence's departure, had known Cox for some years and was able to uncover his actual feelings. Distrust of the Arab Bureau lingered, but Lloyd wrote, 'Lawrence's visit did something to allay it.' Good reports of his activities reached Clayton, who told Wingate, 'Lawrence was evidently of the greatest assistance and I have had great appreciations of his services.'[41] Not from General Lake though, who wrote in June in condemnation of 'the experiment made in attempting to handle [the] affairs of Iraq through Cairo without previously consulting us'.[42] This referred to Lawrence's mission to foment Arab mutinies and uprisings. Still, Lake hoped he had learned something in Iraq, which he had – how not to run a war.

Lawrence was a collector of information and he drew on local officials and files for details of Iraq's Arabs which were delivered to Clayton. It was largely routine stuff but racily written with occasional private asides. The Marsh Arabs of the Lower Tigris 'are impure savages, without any code of manners or morals to restrain them', which no doubt reflected local hostility to tribes of marauders and murderers.[43] The Arabs of the Shatt al Hai were natural anarchists who loathed all forms of government. They were Lawrence's kindred spirits – 'only conquest they are afraid of. I rather sympathize with them.' Still, the local British authorities were just in their dealings with these people and Lawrence heard no serious complaints about the administration. It would be well, he thought, if the British explained that they were not invaders.

Lawrence produced a further report on D Force's intelligence services which was for Clayton alone.[44] Beach and his staff were all 'good men' although, not unlike Cairo in the early days, they were 'all beginners or amateurs at Intelligence work'. They suffered from a lack of linguists and their local topographical knowledge was thin. The Indian government cartographers were good and flattered Lawrence by seeking his advice on lithography, but their technical services were poor and they had not begun aerial surveys. There was a shortage of aircraft in Iraq; at Wadi the Germans and Turks had air supremacy and, as Lawrence saw, there were too few machines to supply the garrison at Kut. In all, he concluded, Iraqi field intelligence was manned by 'very excellent' officers struggling under intolerable conditions which were the fault of their superiors. Clayton found that Lawrence wrote 'very good and interesting' and forwarded a copy to Wingate.

When Lawrence got back to Cairo a story went the rounds that this very fair, professional and diligent report was an excoriating indictment of the Anglo-Indian army in Iraq and its management of the campaign; it was so savage that staff officers had to censor it before it was passed to Murray. The tale was circulated by another staff officer, Captain Walter Stirling, and was repeated by Liddell Hart, who used it to embellish his picture of Lawrence as an unorthodox soldier at loggerheads with the establishment.

The explanation for this canard is probably Lawrence's shipboard meeting with Lieutenant General Sir Webb Gilmann, whose congenial company he enjoyed on the steamer between Basra and Port Said. Gilman had been sent out to Iraq by Robertson in March to discover the extent of local incompetence and draw up a report for the War Office. Like Lawrence, he had been coolly received at Wadi and may have drawn on his companion's experiences for his report. Back in Cairo, Lawrence told Clayton what he had seen in Iraq. Clayton wrote to Wingate that Lawrence's saga of 'mismanagement on all sides and muddle of the worst' was 'sad hearing'.[45]

In retrospect, Lawrence felt bitter about his experiences in Iraq. His mission to foster Arab national feeling there had failed. Cox had bluntly told him that the plan to employ al Mizri and al Faruqi was no more than a device to get a couple of 'gas bags' out of Cairo.[46] He and the generals at Wadi were wrong and their obstinate refusal to listen to Lawrence and act on his advice lost Kut. Or so he argued in the *Seven Pillars*:

> The conditions were ideal for an Arab movement. The people of Nejef and Kerbela, far in the rear of Halil Pasha's army, were in revolt against him. The surviving Arabs in Halil's army were, on his own confession, openly disloyal to Turkey. The tribes of the Hai [the anarchists of Lawrence's report to Clayton] and Euphrates would have turned our way had they seen signs of grace in the British. Had we published the promises made to the Sharif, or even the proclamation afterwards posted in captured Baghdad, and followed it up, enough local fighting men would have joined us to harry the Turkish line of communication between Baghdad and Kut. A week of that, and the enemy would either have been forced to raise the siege and retire, or have themselves suffered investment outside Kut.

Such a prediction would have stunned officials in Basra and staff officers in Wadi. They had discovered no evidence that the Iraqi tribes were prepared to throw in their lot with the British, rather the contrary. Up to 5,000 Muntafiqs joined Turkish forces blocking the advance towards Hayy in January 1916. They continued, with other tribes, to hamper British operations until February 1917, when the scale of British successes made their sheiks switch sides. Until then, Sheik Ajaimi of the Muntafiq had been taking German money. Like his countrymen elsewhere in Iraq, he saw the war as an opportunity for his people to prosper either from the combatants' subsidies or by looting. It was an attitude which Lawrence would soon discover, but never reveal, among the Arabs of the Hejaz and Syria. A reconnaissance and intelligence unit was created, manned by Arabs from the Nasiriya district, and some irregular tribal units sold their services, but their combat value was negligible.[47]

Of course, as Lawrence realised, the Indian government's policy for Iraq's future would easily have been compromised by enlistment of Arab support, even had it been readily available. At the outbreak of the war an alliance of a kind had been made through Captain Shakespeare with Ibn Saud of Riyadh, but he wanted British backing only for his private tribal war against Ibn Rashid, who was the Ottoman government's pawn.[48] Subsequent claims that Ibn Saud might have been employed against the Turks in the same way as Hussain rest on the assumption that he would have been happy to fight the Sultan, which he was not.

The evidence of ambivalent Arab loyalties and a common willingness to fight alongside the Turks was found on the Sinai front as well as in Iraq. Arabs had attacked reconnaissance patrols in November 1914 and their continued hostility provoked a small-scale punitive expedition in February 1916. The Turks took heart from this and were arming them with modern rifles. On the eve of the first British advance into the region, intelligence at Ismailia assessed the local Arabs as 'a source of danger rather than security', a conclusion which no one in Iraq would have quarrelled with.[49]

A further clue to why the Iraq political and military authorities challenged Lawrence's scenario for an Arab uprising against the Turks lay in its sources. There was there, if not in Cairo, a healthy scepticism about pledges of Arab support. On 3 April, Beach examined a report, forwarded by Cairo, compiled by agent 'Mustafa' who had just completed a tour of Syrian and Palestinian towns and cities. What he had heard and seen convinced him that the anti-Turkish sentiments of the Syrians and Beduin were sapping the loyalty of Arab officers and that local sheiks were willing to help the British. Nuri Shalaan of the Rwallah had written to the Iraqi Beduin and urged them to restrain their attacks on the British. Beach wondered whether 'the natural wish of the Agent to make out a case for allied action in Syria' had coloured his conclusions.[50]

Turning to the Arab mutinies, a careful appraisal of interviews with Arab deserters on all fronts shows that the usual reasons for their flight were sparse rations and maltreatment by officers. 'I deserted because I was tired of having little to drink and not sufficient to eat' was the explanation of one determined man who had crossed Sinai in April 1915 and was probably questioned by Lawrence or Lloyd.[51] For every man who crossed to British lines in January 1917, many more crept off to their homes and families.[52] A general unwillingness to endure the harsh regime of the Turkish army was not the same thing as a desire to fight against the Ottoman empire alongside Britain and France. This was soon obvious during the winter of 1916–17 when efforts were under way to recruit Arab POWs for Hussain's army.

This truth was understood by von Sandars. By the end of 1917, when desertions were put at 300,000, he commented that the truants were 'not men that go over to the enemy, but for the most part return to the country in the rear to rob and plunder'. The Arabs were no worse than any other race. 'A large part of the Arabs may be made into good usable soldiers', he wrote, 'if from the very beginning of their service they are treated with fairness and justice.'[53]

Lawrence and his colleagues were both easily misled and anxious to believe any snippet of information which seemed to confirm general Arab disaffection. Even the plausible and in part substantiated evidence of al Faruqi that his regiment, the 142nd, was defeatist and disaffected was deceptive. In November 1915 it fought hard and well in the battle of Ctesiphon.[54] Those like Lawrence who placed their faith in the Arab Revolt almost always took it for granted that the Arabs' exasperation with Ottoman government automatically meant that they wanted British assistance to overthrow and replace it. Once the revolt had started, they assumed that every discontented Arab would identify with Hussain and his movement.

Lawrence had been sent to win converts in Iraq and had come away with none. Nor had he ignited Arab uprisings or mutinies. But in terms of routine intelligence duties, he had been successful and he had handled the local officials calmly and sensitively. He now held the local rank of captain and had measured up well to the duties of gathering and collating intelligence. As a man, he remains an obscure figure during this period, something of a recluse who had chosen to cut himself off from the common pastimes of his brother officers. Little of his personality emerges from the private letters and diaries of Deedes, Lloyd or Dawnay, and Weldon never mentioned him. What emerges from fragments in these sources and his letters home is a clever, agreeable and hard-working officer given to eccentricities.

This would soon change, for a few days after his return to his Cairo desk uprisings occurred in Jiddah and Mecca. Undismayed by his setback in Iraq, Lawrence was impatient to get to Hejaz and set his mark on the movement. At last the chance had come for him both to take the field and to help the Arabs, although he was far from clear how. He was, however, confident in his abilities and the opportunities open for unorthodox warfare. He was certain of one thing: fresh amateur ideas would serve better than the stale, conventional thinking he had encountered in the 'blunderland' of Iraq.

Three

WITH THE ARABS AT AQABA

June 1916–July 1917

I

A MAN OF DESTINY

WHEN Captain Lawrence came ashore at Rabigh on 16 October 1916, the Arab Revolt was four and a half months old and languishing. His commanding officer, General Murray, believed that the Arab movement was on the point of extinction. Lawrence disagreed; he had followed its wayward course, analysed its problems and was convinced that he was its saviour. Recounting his arrival in the *Seven Pillars*, he presented himself as a man of destiny who alone understood the historical forces he was about to encounter and knew how they could be effectively harnessed. To fulfil his private vision, Lawrence had to discover another man of destiny whom, like Merlin, he would identify and then guide as the 'once and future' king of the Arabs. Hitherto they had lacked a leader with 'the flame of enthusiasm' which 'would set the desert on fire'. 'My visit', Lawrence continued, 'was mainly to find the yet unknown master-spirit of the affairs, and measure his capacity to carry the revolt to the goal I had conceived for it.'[1] This was the liberation of Syria and the establishment there of an independent Arab kingdom under British tutelage.

In his version of the beginning of his Arabian quest, Lawrence had engineered the time and place of his decisive arrival in Hejaz. After a summer of sulking during which he had made himself intolerable to his colleagues, he got ten days' leave and unofficially attached himself to Ronald Storrs, then about to embark from Suez for Rabigh. While full of dramatic effect, this narrative is misleading.

The truth was that, disappointed by the failure of his Iraq mission, he had been desperately eager to become directly involved in the Hejaz campaign, which for all its shortcomings offered the only means by which he could help the Arab national movement. Nevertheless when he finally got his way, he went to Hejaz as a result of circumstances beyond his own control and he travelled, not as a free agent guided by his own will, but as the instrument of others. He was sent to Rabigh by Murray and Clayton with specific orders to collect vital information about the situation in Hejaz, the Arab armies and their leaders. The revolt had lurched from crisis to crisis and his superiors were striving to find the means by which it could be kept alive without the commitment of British troops.

According to Lawrence's version of his first visit to Hejaz, he was still employed as a staff officer based in Cairo where, after his return from

Iraq, he continued his now despised routine duties. In his absence there had been a number of changes which were not to his liking. His section, Ia, had been split between Cairo and operational HQ at Ismailia, and from 20 June he was under the command of an ex-gunner, Major G.V.W. Holdich.[2] Lawrence had previously got on well with Holdich, but the continued thwarting of his wish for secondment to Hejaz made him testy and they soon squabbled. He also showed his pique by correcting the spelling, punctuation and grammar of reports written by his superiors.[3]

Lawrence kept in touch with developments in Hejaz throughout these months of frustration, making special use of the on-the-spot reports sent back by Ruhi, Storrs's Persian agent. He had a further, tenuous link with the affairs of the province since, as the officer responsible for printing the army's maps, he was given charge of the production of a set of Hejaz postage stamps which appeared in October. As they were officially regarded as propaganda which advertised to the world the birth of an independent Islamic state, Lawrence had traditional Muslim patterns included in the designs as well as the inscription 'Mecca the Blessed' in Arabic.

While he oversaw the printing of the Hejaz stamps and bickered with his colleagues, a more serious row was under way over the future of the Arab Revolt. This wrangle between generals and pro-consuls gave him the chance he had been waiting for, an opportunity to visit Hejaz. The issue in question was how far Britain should go to help the Arabs when they faced a counter-attack from Turkish forces known to be regrouping at Medina. The matter had first been raised at a policy conference at Ismailia on 12 September attended by Murray, Admiral Wemyss, McMahon, Storrs, Clayton and Colonel Cyril Wilson, the British Consul at Jiddah and Hussain's chief military adviser. Wilson had first-hand knowledge of what was happening, was strongly pro-Arab and served as Wingate's mouthpiece. He told the meeting that the Arabs would be swamped by the Turkish offensive, a disaster which could be prevented only if a brigade of British infantry was sent to Rabigh. Murray was furious; he challenged Wilson's assessment of the situation and pointed out that he needed every man he could get in Egypt for operations in Sinai. He added that an Arabian side-show would inevitably get out of control. 'You start with a brigade, that brigade wants some artillery, then aeroplanes,' and then 'comes a request that the force may be moved to another point which it is absolutely essential to hold'.[4]

Robertson stood by Murray's refusal to send men to Hejaz. His first reaction was to draw attention to the unhappy experiences of the Gallipoli and Iraq campaigns, which 'should have been quite enough proof of this futility'. He also queried whether the presence of Christian troops so close to Mecca would not provoke a fanatic response from the local Arabs which would wipe out for ever the propaganda value of the revolt. This was later Lawrence's view and it made sense, since Hussain had already banned a company of the Warwickshires from landing at Jiddah to pick up Turkish POWs and was very reluctant to allow British staff officers to travel inland.[5]

Murray and Robertson prevailed, but they had to resist continuous pressure from Macmahon and Wingate. Wingate was coming more and more to the forefront on Arab affairs. On 4 October he took full charge of the small group of technicians, staff officers and Egyptian troops which comprised the Hejaz Force and, in December, he was appointed High Commissioner in Egypt in succession to McMahon. By the end of the year this forceful pro-consul had secured control over both the political and military affairs of the Arab movement, which he wanted to prosper. What always mattered most to Wingate was the imperial dimension: if the Arabs faltered or were stifled, British prestige would plummet and Mecca would become the powerhouse for Pan-Islamic subversion against the Sudan and Egypt. For this reason Wingate ceaselessly badgered Murray and Robertson for British troops.

Lawrence followed the exchange of memoranda and telegrams with deep interest. As a partisan of the Arabs he was dismayed by the indifference to their fate shown by his fellow staff officers, whose minds were concentrated on operations in Sinai. Murray was dismissive of the Arab movement and doubted whether its forces, which had already fired 2 million rounds of ammunition to kill less than 2,000 Turks, would ever amount to much.[6] Robertson disagreed and reminded him that he had a duty to succour 'our enthusiastic and somewhat uncivilized allies', for 'it is better that they should be on our side than partners of the Huns.'[7] His view was shared by Lawrence's former chief, Clayton, who now combined the posts of Murray's adviser on Muslim affairs and Wingate's Chief of Staff for the Hejaz Force. Trapped between the contending sides, Clayton privately endorsed Murray's stand against direct British intervention in Hejaz.[8]

Both factions agreed that the intelligence available from Hejaz was unsatisfactory. Wemyss was exasperated by 'The usual streams of contradictory telegrams ... from political and military officers in Jiddah and Rabigh' which confused rather than enlightened. The principal sources were Colonels Wilson and A.C. Parker, both keen Arabists whose judgements were mistrusted by Murray. Clayton did not trust Wilson, whom he suspected of doctoring the evidence in his reports in order to give weight to his own opinions.[9] One answer to the problem of flawed and partial intelligence was to send a reliable officer to Hejaz who could reveal the exact military position of both the Arab and Turkish forces there. On 9 October Clayton suggested that Lawrence should be assigned to this task and Murray agreed.[10]

Lawrence's single-minded and passionate zeal for the Arab cause must have been well known in Cairo. Yet Murray and Clayton considered him sufficiently professional in his approach to observe impartially and draw up a balanced and authoritative report. Furthermore, Lawrence was an excellent choice in so far as his own inclinations made it likely that his report would uphold their own views. Thoughout his involvement with the Arab movement, Lawrence always maintained that its ultimate success would depend upon the Arabs' ability to help themselves rather than relying on foreign troops. These were no doubt his views when he set off for Jiddah on 13 October and, on his return to Cairo, he did unreservedly condemn the proposal to land a British brigade at Rabigh.

Whether or not his mind was filled with dreams of finding the hidden leader of the Arab people, Lawrence was pleased with his assignment and full of optimism. Just before he left Cairo, he told Captain Doynal St Quentin, the French military attaché, 'Abdullah is coming to talk with us about his future Arab kingdom which will embrace Palestine and Syria. We will advise him first how to take Medina.'[11] This was an impudent challenge, since both officers knew that Syria was already pledged to France. Lawrence, his mind running far beyond the immediate problems of Hejaz, was already laying plans for the extension of the Arab movement to Syria, where its ultimate success would check French territorial ambitions.

Lawrence's official brief was to accompany Storrs and Major al Mizri, now Hussain's Chief of Staff, who had recently been recruiting Arab POWs in Egypt, to Jiddah. There they would discuss the military situation with Wilson and the Amir Abdullah and afterwards confer with Parker at Rabigh. If permission to travel inland had been wrung from Hussain, Lawrence was to make contact with the Amir Faisal, whose army was about to take the brunt of the Turkish offensive. Once with Faisal, Lawrence would assess the numbers and quality of his men and the strengths and positions of their Turkish adversaries. He would also set up a network of trustworthy native agents who would replace Faisal's unreliable spies and guarantee the Arab Bureau a flow of accurate information from the Medina region. To judge from his reports, Lawrence was also asked to prepare a profile of Wilson, who was believed to be on the verge of a breakdown, and to find out al Mizri's ambitions and future operational plans.

Lawrence's military and civilian colleagues were pessimistic about the future of the Arab movement. Even the most sincere and dedicated adherents of the Arab alliance had been disappointed by their military performance since June. Once the serious fighting had begun, it was obvious that Hussain and his tribal forces had bitten off more than they could chew. According to the captain of HMS *Fox*, which was giving close support to the Arabs besieging Jiddah, their leaders were 'discouraged at not having a walkover'. The port fell on 10 June after a naval bombardment of the Turkish trenches which the Arabs had been most unwilling to storm. Five days later, Arab morale rallied when the sea-plane carrier *Ben-my-Chree* hove to off the Hejaz coast; for the next few weeks, its machines carried out vital reconnaissance and bombing missions without which the Arabs would have suffered serious reverses. This heavy dependence on British men-of-war and aircraft was officially kept secret, since Allied propaganda demanded that the revolt be advertised to the world as a purely Arab affair.[12] Although Lawrence did much to perpetuate this myth, he did acknowledge the crucial assistance rendered the Arabs by Wemyss and his ships during the first months of the uprising.[13] Arab historians have been less generous.

The summer campaign in Hejaz set the pattern for the future. Arab irregulars could never hope to engage, let alone overcome, Turkish troops in open battle without substantial assistance. Until the end of the war the Arabs would depend upon endless transfusions of Allied arms and ammunition as well as British gold to keep their forces in the field. In combat they were sustained by British, French, Egyptian and Indian specialists such as engineers, gunners, signallers and supply officers as well as artillery, armoured cars and aircraft. Their bases at Jiddah, Rabigh, Yanbu al Bahr and later al Wajh and Aqaba would be protected by British and French men-of-war.

With the aid they had received between June and October, the Hejaz Arabs had made some gains, although their position remained precarious. During June tribal forces supported by aircraft and warships had secured Jiddah, Rabigh and Yanbu al Bahr, and on 9 July Mecca was taken. Subsequent fighting was desultory and the initiative passed to the Turkish commander, Fahkri Pasha, who concentrated his forces around Medina in readiness to recover the ground lost during the summer. Enver Pasha had not been unduly troubled by the Arabs' gains and, contrary to British intelligence predictions, thought it unnecessary to divert troops from Syria or the Caucasus for a counter-attack.[14] Fahkri appeared able to cope without reinforcements. Assured of the benevolent neutrality of Ibn Rashid on his eastern flank, Fakhri's army could be supplied from Damascus by the Hejaz railway, which the Arabs had been unable to sever because of their ignorance of explosives.

A breakdown of Fakhri's command, prepared by Lawrence's Cairo section at the end of September, gave him 12,000 men and two aircraft based on Medina.[15] A division of 2,400 infantry and 1,000 camelry held Bir Abas to the south-west, and a unit of 800 with two field pieces and four machine-guns occupied Bir al Mashi. These outlying detachments were thought to be the advance guard for offensives against Rabigh and

Mecca which were expected in the last week of November. To oppose the Turkish advance, there were three Arab armies, commanded by Hussain's three eldest sons, the amirs Ali, Zaid and Faisal. Each army was in a permanent state of deliquescence, since the tribal warrior insisted on bouts of extended leave with his family. Morale was low. The Arabs were short of artillery and machine-guns and, in spite of a stiffening of Egyptian infantry and gunners, Wilson and Parker believed they would crumble before a Turkish attack. Lawrence was setting out for Hejaz when the Arab movement faced its gravest crisis.

The steamer *Lama* took two days to reach Jiddah. Lawrence enjoyed the relaxation of the cruise, during which he explained the mysteries of cipher to Storrs and listened while the diplomat discussed the merits of Debussy and Wagner with al Mizri. Then and later Lawrence talked with al Mizri and gently questioned him about his plans for the future. These largely concerned Syria and Lawrence passed on what he heard to Clayton.

Aziz [al Mizri] has not taken me into his confidence, but is enormously interested in the Hejaz railway *North of Maan*. I cannot get him worked up to consider the Ula–Medina stretch at all. Also his questions are about the Hawran, Karak, and the Nabk–Salamieh region: even Aleppo sometimes. I fancy he may be trying to get up into the Rwallah–Hawran country, not to do very much perhaps, but to sound out the people, and cut the line. He will not take troops with him from Hejaz.[16]

What is remarkable about this revelation was that al Mizri had outlined the very programme of railway sabotage and canvassing support for the Arab movement in Syria which Lawrence undertook during the second part of 1917. He approached the Syrian Arabs as the emissary of Faisal, whereas al Mizri, if he had stayed true to his ideals, would have represented the radical nationalists whom Lawrence held in contempt. For this reason, as well as the present impracticality of long-range operations, Lawrence tried to deflect al Mizri towards attacking the railway closer to Medina, which was what Murray and Wingate wanted.

Once al Mizri had represented a dynamic force within Arab nationalism, and when Lawrence made his foray into Iraq on his behalf he was regarded as a future leader with extensive influence. With his taste for Irish whiskey and soda and modern ideas, al Mizri felt uncomfortable in orthodox and feudal Hejaz. He confided to Storrs that he really wanted to pull out and marry his German fiancée, who lived in Switzerland. Hussain and his sons distrusted al Mizri's ambitions, fearing that he might push them aside and become another Enver. They were therefore pleased when he resigned in 1917 and returned to Cairo, where he proffered his services to the British and promised to foment mutinies among Turkish troops in Syria and

Palestine.[17] The offer was turned down, partly because of suspicions that it was a vehicle for al Mizri's personal ambitions.

Lawrence was in buoyant mood when he landed at Jiddah. His new surroundings fascinated him. In a letter to Clayton he classified the local architecture as 'gimcrack Elizabethan exaggerated' and noted that 'The tone of public opinion in Jiddah is rollicking good-humour towards foreigners.' Bad humour marked his first encounter with Wilson. Within two days of his arrival, he wired Clayton, 'There are some personal remarks here about Colonel Wilson which I won't write down. Will you please ask Storrs a few leading questions about him? Consider me as prejudiced.'[18] Wilson did not pussy-foot and on 22 October cabled Clayton:

> Lawrence wants kicking and kicking *hard* at that, then he would be [illegible] all present. I look on him as a bumptious young ass who spoils his undoubted knowledge of Syrian Arabs &c. by making himself out to be the only authority on war, engineering, HM's ships and everything else. He put every single person's back up I've met from the Admiral [Wemyss] down to the most junior fellow on the Red Sea.[19]

The immodest, doctrinaire young man was also a slovenly soldier. When they first met at Port Sudan at the beginning of November, Colonel Pierce Joyce, one of the team of staff officers newly appointed to the Hejaz Force, was appalled by Lawrence's appearance. He recalled 'an intense desire ... to tell him to get his hair cut and that his uniform and dirty buttons sadly needed the attention of his batman'.[20] Cairo's forbearance towards clever graduates masquerading as soldiers did not extend to the Arabian war zone.

While he offended some by his dogmatism, Lawrence carried out his instructions thoroughly in a way which would eventually impress Murray. On 18 October he joined a conference at Jiddah attended by Storrs, Wilson and the Amir Abdullah. The main purpose of the meeting was to inform Abdullah that, guided by Robertson, the War Committee in London had turned down the request for a British brigade at Rabigh. The news upset him: as Lawrence tartly observed, he showed every sign of having suffered a 'heavy blow (mostly I think to his ambition)'. However, its harshness was softened by £10,000 in gold sovereigns delivered by Storrs. As the exchanges progressed, Lawrence learned how power was exercised in Hejaz. Abdullah had twice to consult his father by telephone and Lawrence concluded that the 'old dear' Hussain 'looks upon his sons as boys not quite fit to act independently'.

For his part, Abdullah was amazed by Lawrence's disclosures about the activities of the Turkish army, which were based upon British intelligence material. 'Is this man God to know everything?' was the Prince's reaction, and Lawrence, then re-reading the *Morte d'Arthur*, may have been reminded of how Merlin had used his supernatural powers to reveal to Arthur what his enemies were doing.[21] As the conversation turned towards the situation in Rabigh it soon became clear that 'Nobody knew the real situation,' and so it was agreed that Lawrence and al Mizri would visit the port the next day.

In the *Seven Pillars* version of the conference, Lawrence wrote that by the time it was over he had realised that Abdullah, Hussain's Foreign Secretary and Commander-in-Chief, was not the leader he sought. This charming, sophisticated sybarite with a taste for European opera acquired in Cairo was not the Arab Garibaldi. He was:

> too cool, too humorous to be a prophet: especially the armed prophet, who, if history is true, succeeded in revolutions. . . . During the physical struggle, when singleness of eye and magnetism, devotion and self-sacrifice were needed, Abdullah would be a tool too complex for a single purpose.

Having found that Hussain's second son did not match up to his rigorous standards, Lawrence was left with the choice between his eldest, Ali, and third, Faisal. The fourth, Zaid, was too young and his mother's Turkish blood disqualified him as an Arab nationalist leader. There were no other alternatives, since Hussain's uprising was a revolution from the top, led by the aristocratic Hashemite family which was determined to keep power in its own hands. Of course if Lawrence went beyond the traditionalist Hashemites, he would be forced to consider Syrian and Iraqi nationalists, whose modernism and European radicalism were distasteful to him. What he really wanted was a pliant Arab susceptible to his own peculiar views of the national movement and what it should achieve.

After the conference, Lawrence's party joined Abdullah for dinner at the French Consulate, where their host was Colonel Edouard Brémond, the head of the French military mission which had arrived in Hejaz five weeks before. Brémond 'is a *sahib* and I like him' was Wilson's reaction to his counterpart. The burly, bearded veteran of several North African campaigns found Wilson 'a most agreeable brother-in-arms', which was something of a distinction, since nearly every other British officer he had met in Egypt and Hejaz offered him a façade of politeness which never quite covered their francophobia.

With Lawrence there was no attempt to hide his anti-French feelings. Looking back on their acquaintanceship, Brémond wrote, 'He had an abundance of antipathies: he disliked armies; the occupation of the English soldier seemed to him "abject". He did not like the French, nor the Catholics, nor Jerusalem.' Lawrence was not to be trusted. When he returned from his visit to Faisal's camp, Lawrence told Brémond that the Arabs were not unnerved by Turkish aircraft, but the Colonel, who had heard otherwise from reliable eyewitnesses, was not convinced and suspected an attempt to mislead him.[22]

When he had first come to Hejaz, Brémond had hoped that Anglo-French co-operation would be the basis for the advancement of civilisation throughout the Middle East. What he heard and saw in Cairo and Jiddah soon disillusioned him. By the time he met Lawrence, he secretly feared that the Arabs would renege on their agreements with the Allies and do a deal with the Turks, and he was alarmed that, if Medina fell, the Arabs would move northwards and fan the nationalist fires in Syria, which would make it impossible for his government to assert its claims there after the war. Although Lawrence repeatedly claimed in the *Seven Pillars* that the Arabs were innocent of Anglo-French agreements on the future of Syria, the possibility of partition and French occupation was well known in Hejaz. Shorty before Lawrence's visit, Brémond complained that Egyptian troops were disseminating anti-French propaganda, presumably picked up from the Cairo press, which speculated freely and usually accurately about what was in store for Syria.[23]

Lawrence and the anti-French party (which included Macmahon, Wingate, Wemyss, Murray and Clayton) objected to what they considered to be French meddling in a British affair. Brémond's mission had been foisted on them by the Foreign Office in the interests of the alliance and its thinly disguised purpose was to ensure that French imperial interests in the Middle East would not be ignored or overridden. The French government considered Syria its legitimate prize, already won by the 26,000 French casualties during the Gallipoli campaign. This feeling was ignored by British officers like Lawrence who tried to pretend that the French dimension was immaterial or could be by-passed. For this reason, Brémond had not been invited to the conference with Abdullah, even though his government was offering the Arabs the service of Algerian Muslim troops.

On 19 October, Lawrence and al Mizri took ship for Rabigh. When they landed the next morning, they found Colonel Parker at his wits' end and expecting a catastrophe. There was, he told Wingate, an 'utter lack of any organisation and co-ordination among the Arabs' and they would shortly be overcome by the Turks, who 'have the advantage of cohesion and single command as well as the custom of defeating Arabs'.[24] Only British troops could save the port. The local Arab commander, the Amir Ali, was not, Lawrence quickly discovered, the natural leader he was seeking. He was a 'pleasant gentleman, conscientious, without any great force of character, nervous and rather tired' – which exactly fits a general having the utmost difficulty in getting his men to dig trenches. Nevertheless, had Faisal failed to fulfil Lawrence's ideal of a national leader, he confessed that he would have chosen Ali.

Thanks to Abdullah's intercession, Hussain had granted Lawrence permission to travel inland and meet Faisal. It was an extremely risky enterprise, since Lawrence would have to pass through the lands of the pro-Turkish Masruh Harb, and the Turks had been encouraging Arabs to assassinate British officers, whom they rightly identified as the mainstay of Arab resistance.[25] The journey was also very uncomfortable, for Lawrence, still unused to such transport, rode a camel.

He reached Faisal's camp at al Hamra after an eighty-mile journey, and by 24 October his first report was being wired from Rabigh to Cairo with details of Turkish preparations for their march on Rabigh. Three identified regiments were massing south-west of Medina and arrangements were in hand to lay a road between Medina and Bir Abas, the main Turkish base fifteen miles north-east of Faisal's camp. The morale of Faisal's 4,000 irregulars was sagging for, despite help from an Egyptian artillery battery, they were outgunned by the Turks. 'Turkish artillery', Lawrence noted, 'appears the most formidable to Faisal's Arabs and they fear aeroplanes.' The Arabs' immediate requirements were mountain guns and Lewis light machine-guns with which they could arm mobile units that would harass the extended Turkish lines of communication.[26] As Lawrence knew from the Arab Bureau wireless decrypts, Fakhri was disturbed by the vulnerability of his communications, especially his lifeline to Damascus, the Hejaz railway.[27]

In subsequent reports, Lawrence evaluated the Arab forces, assessed their potential and emphasised the harmful consequences which were bound to follow direct British intervention.[28] Taking first the condition of the Arab armies, his confidence contrasted with the gloom of Parker and Wilson:

> Their morale is excellent, their tactics and manner of fighting admirably adapted to the very difficult country they are defending, and their leaders fully understand that to provoke a definite issue now is to lose the war, and to continue the present *guerre de course* is sooner or later to wear out the Turkish power of resistance, and force them back on a passive defence of Medina and its railway communication.

Rabigh would fall only if the hill tribes who occupied the territory between it and Medina collapsed or shifted sides. At that moment they were 'terribly afraid of the English occupation of Hejaz' and so, if British troops landed, the movement would in all likelihood fall apart. If this happened, Lawrence feared that the French would intervene and make themselves sole protectors of Hussain. The Arabs, Lawrence insisted, 'are our very good friends while we respect their independence', but their knowledge of recent Middle East history was enough to make them apprehensive about British imperialism. This fear did not extend to British technology and they were ready to welcome all kinds of material assistance. Aeroplanes were 'delightful toys' which they wanted, as well as artillery and armoured cars, an addition to the Arab arsenal which had already been proposed by Colonel Parker.[29]

Passing to political matters, Lawrence stressed the Arabs' sense of political identity. 'Tribal opinion in Hejaz struck me as intensely national, and more sophisticated than the appearance of the tribesmen led one to expect,' and there was 'little trace' of Muslim fanaticism. Such observations were reassuring to his superiors who, like him, had hoped to divert Arab passions away from potentially harmful religious enthusiasm towards secular nationalism, which it was safe for Britain to patronise. Wearing his khaki uniform and, like all other European officers attached to the Hejaz Force, an Arab *qalifeh*, Lawrence found that some Arabs mistook him for a Syrian officer who had defected from the Turkish army. Exploiting their misunderstanding and speaking Arabic with a Syrian accent, Lawrence acted the part and talked to them about Syrian nationalism. 'In my capacity as a Syrian', Lawrence offered a sympathetic account of the recent executions of nationalists in Damascus, but got a stony response from his audience. 'These men had sold their country to the French' was their common reaction.

As to future tribal loyalties, Lawrence considered the Harb and Juheina lukewarm towards Hussain while their neighbours, the Billi, held back 'because they fear that the sharif means the British', which of course strengthened his case against direct intervention. Disunity remained a stumbling-block and Hussain's overall control was weak, since 'One thing of which the tribes are convinced is that they have made an Arab Government and consequently each of them is it.' Maybe Lawrence with his anarchist tendencies privately approved, but he felt obliged to add that, without careful British direction, the outcome of the rising might be a 'discordant mosaic of provincial administration'.

Lawrence found Faisal chary about allowing the creation of an Arab Bureau intelligence network in the region. This was a nuisance, but Lawrence thought that, if he stayed in the camp, information would be passed to him directly by Faisal's spies. Faisal was '*very* difficult' to advise, but his confidence and co-operation could be obtained with patience.[30]

So much for Lawrence's appreciation of what he had seen and heard in Hejaz. Clear, informative and freshly written, his reports had the authority of a perceptive man on the spot and therefore carried much weight with his superiors. They also did much to put Lawrence in the way of the career he had chosen for himself as Faisal's military and political counsellor. Their first meeting was described in the *Seven Pillars* in a passage heavy with historical significance.

I felt at first glance that this was the man I had come to Arabia to seek – the leader who would bring the Arab Revolt to full glory. Faisal looked very tall and pillar-like, very slender, in his long white silk robes and his brown head-cloth bound with brilliant scarlet and gold cord. His eyelids were dropped: and his black beard and colourless face were like a mask against the strange watchfulness of his body. His hands were crossed in front of him on his dagger.[31]

The formalities of introductory small-talk over, Lawrence tested the warrior's mettle.

'And do you like our place here in Wadi Safra?'
'Well: but it is far from Damascus.'
The word had fallen like a sword in their midst. There was a quiver. Then everybody present stiffened where he sat, and held his breath silent for a minute. Some, perhaps, were dreaming of far-off success: others may have thought it a reflection of their latest defeat. Faisal at length lifted his eyes, smiling at me, and said, 'Praise be to God, there are Turks nearer us than that.'

This was the answer of the authentic paladin, the man whom Lawrence had been seeking. Whatever the truth of this exchange, the Prince, whom Storrs described as a personification of the 'legendary noble Arab', appealed to the romantic in Lawrence, who once compared his features to those of his hero, Richard the Lionheart, as they appeared on his tomb in Fontere- vault Abbey.

Lawrence also sensed Faisal's latent qualities of leadership, especially over Arab tribesmen. He was not the first to recognise them for, as Faisal later told him, in October 1915 he had been singled out by von Oppenheim as a potential figurehead for a directed Pan-Islamic movement and the leader of an anti-British revolt in the Sudan. As late as March 1915, Faisal was considered sufficiently sympathetic to the Turco-German cause to be entrusted with letters of introduction to his father on behalf on the von Stotzingen mission.[32]

During his few days in Faisal's camp, Lawrence became completely immersed in the convoluted tribal politics of Arabia and Syria. He quickly recognised one essential truth: Arab success alone would generate support. Tribes now wobbling would be coaxed to throw in their lot with the insur- gents only when they saw that the rebels were winning. The point was made plainly to Lawrence by an agent sent to Faisal by the Syrian sheik, Nuri Shalaan of the Rwallah. Nuri's covert pro-British sentiments were well known to British intelligence, but his messenger told Lawrence that his master would remain 'cautious and shy' of open commitment to Hussain until he was 'assured of armed support' from either Arab or British forces.[33] Murray was particularly pleased with this news, since the Rwallah's lands abutted the Hejaz railway, which they could easily disrupt. Their co-operation was considered vital when British forces pushed northwards through Palestine and, in November, Murray prepared a plan to use them as guerrillas. The Rwallah would co-operate with a flight of aircraft which would operate from an airstrip in their territory deep in the Syrian desert and far behind Turkish lines.[34] It was a daring stratagem which caught Lawrence's imagination. Within eighteen months he would conduct a similar campaign against the Hejaz railway using Arab tribesmen and RFC bombers based in Aqaba.

When he parted from Faisal, Lawrence promised that he would lay his demands before Murray on his return to Cairo and urge him to send the desperately needed artillery and instructors, a measure which he knew was already in hand. Inwardly, Lawrence was exhilarated. The 'irregularity' of the Arabs excited his imagination as much as it exasperated such professional soldiers as Parker, whose only experience of tribal armies had been as opponents in India and Africa where they were easily beaten by the discipline and firepower of regular troops. Lawrence had found an army whose concepts of warfare were akin to those of his chivalric heroes. Each Arab fought as a free individual seeking battle on his own terms, unlike the constrained modern soldier who waged war as part of a tightly controlled machine. What Lawrence perceived as the virtues of the Arab fighting man were the despair of his superiors, who would need to be convinced that Faisal's army was not a rabble in arms. Lawrence believed that, correctly guided, adequately armed and allowed to fight in the way they knew best, they could beat the Turks.

When Lawrence returned to Jiddah on 4 November, he found that Wemyss, perturbed by the crisis facing the Arabs, was about to consult with Wingate at Khartoum. He could not afford to wait on events so he persuaded the Admiral to let him go as well and report in person to Wingate. Wemyss was ready to overlook Lawrence's recent peevishness and grant him this favour since he was in full agreement with his conclusions. He was convinced that British troops at Rabigh would create rather than solve problems and, if the Turks attacked, they could be repulsed easily by naval landing parties.[35] Lawrence crossed the Red Sea aboard the Admiral's flagship, HMS *Euryalus*, and in his dishevelled state no doubt relished the drollery of being welcomed at Port Sudan by a formal guard of honour of Sudanese *askaris*.

The emergency conference with Wingate was held at the Khartoum Residency on the afternoon of 6 November. The effluxion of Lawrence's opinions on Arab nationalism and guerrilla strategy took the pro-consul by surprise. He judged his effervescent guest 'to be a visionary and his amateur soldiering has evidently given him an exaggerated idea on the soundness of his views on purely military matters'. Nevertheless, Wingate was left with the impression that Lawrence agreed with him that British troops should be landed at Rabigh once it was clear that the Arabs had their backs to the wall.[36] This was not so: as in his conversations with Cox in Basra a few months before, Lawrence had revealed a knack for making his superiors think that he was of their mind when he was not.

Lawrence returned to Cairo on 11 November, where he presented his report against a Hejaz expeditionary force to Murray. The General was delighted and immediately passed it to the War Office, from where a copy was forwarded to Sir Edward Grey, the Foreign Secretary. Murray drew all readers' attention to Lawrence's 'strongly expressed opinion that no British or foreign forces should be sent to Hejaz', which was 'strongly supported by soldier and civilian residents in this country'.[37] Arab morale was good and they were capable of repelling any Turkish offensive against the coastal towns. This assessment pleased Robertson, whose views had been vindicated, and Hogarth was glad that Lawrence had squashed 'a bad and uneconomical venture'.[38] The judgements of Lawrence and Wemyss, both men with first-hand information, naturally carried weight with the Cabinet War Committee, although it was displeased that Lawrence's memorandum had not been passed through the correct channel, which was Wingate. Wingate himself was piqued at Lawrence's temerity and Murray's opportunism, but was placated by Clayton, who pointed out that the report had accelerated the flow of equipment to the Arabs.[39]

Some of Lawrence's recommendations were already being acted on before his report reached Murray. On 2 November, Robertson approved the transfer of Egyptian and Sudanese troops to Hejaz if they were needed, and a day later Murray released additional artillery for deployment there. Both were reactions to a false intelligence report that the Turks were within three days' march of Rabigh. Lawrence's plea for aircraft was also accepted. On 13 November, six machines from 14 Squadron were unloaded at Rabigh and a makeshift runway was levelled. It was guarded by an Egyptian battalion and all RFC personnel were armed for fear of attacks by Muslim fanatics: Lawrence had not dispelled Cairo's jumpiness about local religious zeal. The War Office also looked kindly on his request for armoured cars and offered Wingate two for the Hejaz Force.[40]

As Lawrence knew when he spoke with Faisal, a team of British specialist advisers was already being formed. Members of the British Military Mission

had been selected by Wingate and were approved by the War Office on
11 November. They were Colonel Newcombe, Captains A.J.Ross of the
RFC, A.G.Neill, C.E.Vickery and C.H.F.Cox, who were gunners and
engineers and all Arabic speakers, and Major W.E.Marshall, a medical
officer. Others like Joyce and Major H.Garland were already on their way
to Hejaz to take up posts as instructors.

Lawrence, still inexperienced as a field intelligence officer, had not
expected to be chosen either as a member of the mission or as a technical
expert. He had told Faisal when he left al Hamra that it was unlikely that
he would be back. Undoubtedly he wanted to return and had already emphasised in his report of 18 October the need for a 'really reliable' intelligence
officer to be posted permanently at Rabigh and for another officer to remain
with Faisal. Robertson, already alerted to these needs by Major N.N.Bray,
an Indian officer who had served in Hejaz during the summer and was
then in London, concurred. On 12 November he wired Murray with the
suggestion that either Lawrence or George Lloyd be sent immediately to
Rabigh to take over intelligence from Parker, who was needed in Sinai.
Wingate accepted both and proposed that Lloyd be sent to Rabigh and
Lawrence to Yanbu al Bahr, where, pending the arrival of Newcombe from
France, he 'would do the work excellently'. Clayton protested: Lawrence
ought to stay in Cairo because 'his great knowledge and experience' of
Arab affairs had made him 'almost indispensable' at Headquarters. His
objection was overruled by Wingate since the needs of Hejaz were greater
than those of Cairo. 'It's vitally important to have an officer of his exceptional
knowledge of [the] Arabs in close contact with Faisal at this ̃critical
moment.'[41]

Unwittingly, Wingate had offered Lawrence the chance to transform his
visions into reality, even though in the *Seven Pillars* he admitted to an
uncharacteristic diffidence about accepting the post. It was, as he knew,
a temporary assignment since Newcombe would arrive from France within
a few weeks. Still, it was an additional opportunity to enjoy close access
to the man whom he believed was best qualified to inspire and regenerate
the Arab movement. Lawrence's reputation with the Arabs would have risen
in his absence, since the first consignments of arms and aircraft which
he had promised were not flowing into Rabigh. The credit was not wholly
his, but his personal standing with Faisal would have been advanced.

There was still much for Lawrence to do to win Faisal's full confidence.
He had already appreciated that any British officer attached to Faisal, Ali
or Abdullah would have to urge them to act independently of their father
Hussain, 'of whom they are all respectfully afraid'. Financial liberation
would have to come first, since Lawrence had noticed that 'The old man

is frightfully jealous of the purse strings and keeps his family annoyingly short.' By offering himself as a conduit through which arms would flow directly from Egypt to Faisal's army, Lawrence had begun the process of releasing him from paternal control which would end when he took over the distribution of cash to the Amir and his adherents.

Just before he left Cairo on 25 November, Lawrence strengthened his position by the procurement of a wireless set, disdaining Wilson's suggestion that he use carrier pigeons for his messages. When the set became available, Lawrence was a swift link with the Arab Bureau, which could facilitate the despatch of arms to Faisal. Moreover wireless contact gave him access to the Bureau's intelligence which since mid-October included deciphered Turkish signals. He was therefore well placed to suggest how Faisal could anticipate his adversaries' moves. In the end it was Lawrence's tact and charm which won him Faisal's trust and, in a letter of 17 January 1917, he counselled Newcombe to act the same way. 'By effacing yourself for the first part and making friends with the headmen before you start pulling them about, you will find your way much easier.' It must have been hard for Lawrence, since deference and diffidence were not part of his nature, but within three months he had made himself indispensable to Faisal.

II

LAWRENCE AND THE ARABS

A T this point it is useful to pause and examine Lawrence's motives for plunging into the Arab movement, and the wider political considerations which dictated his actions and its course during 1917. He stayed with Faisal and his army from the end of November 1916 until the fall of Damascus at the beginning of October 1918. During this time he was Faisal's political and military adviser and recruiting officer in Syria, as well as a commander of Arab guerrilla units. From July 1917 he served as liaison officer between Faisal and General Sir Edmund Allenby, the new Commander-in-Chief of British forces in Egypt, and was responsible for Anglo-Arab operational planning.

Each duty required Lawrence to adopt a double identity since he was the servant of both the British government and one of its allies. The question of ultimate loyalty came to torment him, because he was well aware that his British masters had already agreed to deliver Syria to France once it had been conquered. 'You know,' he told Clayton in September 1917, 'I'm strongly pro-British and also pro-Arab. France takes third place with me: but I quite recognise that we may have to sell our small friends to pay our big friends, or sell our future security in the Near East to pay for our present victory in Flanders.'[1] Lawrence's appreciation of this unpalatable truth did not mean acceptance and he did everything he could to render this policy unworkable, even to the point of undertaking anti-French subversion in Syria.

Service to and with the Arabs presented further moral problems. In the broadest terms, Lawrence portrayed himself in the *Seven Pillars* as an almost messianic liberator of the Arabs, who awakened and fostered their sense of national identity and guided them towards a goal which he had set. As an outsider he considered himself peculiarly fitted for these tasks, although he believed that their accomplishment diminished his own national identity. While he was the Arabs' saviour, he was never one of them:

> A man who gives himself to the possession of aliens leads a Yahoo life, having bartered his soul to a brute master. He is not of them. He may stand against them, persuade them of a mission, batter and twist them into something which they, of their own accord, would not have been. Then he is exploiting his old environment to press them out of theirs.

This life, Lawrence claimed, deprived him of his Englishness and left him with nothing to put in its place, for 'I could not sincerely take on an Arab skin.'

Yet without Lawrence the Arabs were helpless, unable to coalesce or secure their own freedom.

> Arabs could be swung on an idea as on a cord; for the unpledged allegiance of their minds made them obedient servants. None of them would escape the bond till success had come, and with it responsibility and duty and engagement. Then the idea was gone and the work ended in ruins. . . . They were as unstable as water, and like water would perhaps finally prevail. Since the dawn of life, in successive waves they had been dashing themselves against the coasts of the flesh. Each wave was broken. . . . One such wave (and not the least) I raised and rolled before the breath of an idea, till it reached its crest, and toppled over and fell at Damascus.

Lawrence had surrendered himself to the service of a volatile race in order to make them do what was beyond them or their leaders. He would make himself the motor force of the Arab revolt, generating its impulses and driving it towards ultimate victory at Damascus.

Like many intellectuals who enter politics, he was driven by an over-whelming urge to control, simply because he knew what was best for the Arabs. Without him the Arabs could neither understand what they wanted nor summon up the necessary mental and physical energy to achieve it.

> Their mind was strange and dark, full of depressions and exaltations, lacking in rule, but with more ardour and more fertile than any other in the world. They were a people of starts, for whom the abstract was the strongest motive, a process of infinite courage and variety, and the end nothing.

The Arabs could not make their own history. The inadequacies of the collective Arab mind required continual injections of Lawrence's vision.

Up to a point, Lawrence's programme for Arab regeneration coincided with his government's policies, which enabled him to accommodate both. Through his association with the Arab movement he was helping to break Islamic unity and prepare the way for a new Middle East, which he hoped would be made up of a 'mosaic' of petty client states watched over by Britain. In Lawrence's mind France had no right to play any part in this process or to expect any reward when it had been completed. On this issue he was out of step with his government's policy, although many of his superiors privately endorsed his views.

When, in May 1917, Lawrence undertook his first excursion into Turkish-held Syria he faced a crisis of conscience and became convinced that he was procuring future allies for Faisal with false claims. Putting on one side what he actually promised and what the Arabs knew about Anglo-French plans for Syria, he convinced himself that he was guilty of gross deception. From then on he became increasingly acerbic in his dealings with his superiors, who he believed were exploiting the Arabs' simple faith. More and more, Lawrence revealed a high degree of intolerance towards anyone whose views on the Arab question disagreed with his own. There was a strong flavour of evangelical self-righteousness in the expression of his opinions, combined with academic quarrelsomeness which made him dismiss opponents as obtuse fools.

The same vein of all-knowing dogmatism coloured his thinking about the Arabs. Accepting the common prejudice of his time, he took for granted the existence of closely defined racial stereotypes. His 'Arab' was a cipher, conditioned to behave in a predictable manner and constrained by deeply rooted patterns of thought and morality which made him psychologically incapable of joining with his fellows in pursuit of a common purpose. Stead-fastness, Lawrence believed, could only be understood by one group of Arabs, the nomadic desert Beduin. They alone could carry out what he required of their race because of their ability to grasp an abstract principle, and, tempered by the rigours of desert life and imbued with a fierce Puritanism, they would accept the necessary suffering and self-sacrifice.

Nothing of this sort could be expected from the deracinated, soft-living town Arabs whose heads had been filled with corrupting ideas from the West. In his official reports and later in the *Seven Pillars*, Lawrence never missed a chance to vent his contempt for these Arabs, whom he had first learned to despise before the war. Again he revealed himself to be a child of his age. He shared the classic imperial attitude which made his country-men admire such proud, independent warrior races as the Pathans and Sikhs of India or the Zulus of South Africa. Their courage, nobility and stark life commanded respect, and generations of Englishmen, including Lawrence, felt themselves highly honoured when they discovered that they had in turn won the respect and loyalty of such warriors. The townsman, with his smattering of learning and sophistication, was generally more criti-cal and less tractable.

The love affair between Lawrence and the Beduin was instantaneous. At Faisal's camp in October 1916 he felt stirred by the 'spirit of these roman-tics of the hills'. They were lean, hard men, 'a tough-looking crowd ... physically thin but exquisitely made, moving with an oiled activity altogether delightful to watch. . . . They were wild spirits, shouting that the war might last ten years.' Like the Crusading Knights Templar, these warriors disdained luxury and embraced a Spartan life; they would, Lawrence believed, submit themselves to the pursuit of his creed, which offered secular salvation.

The Beduin fighting men aroused his historical imagination. Here in the twentieth century were armies of mounted warriors commanded by warlords who carried swords and rode into battle under colourful embroid-ered banners. Lawrence had found an army which might have been the host of Saladin as depicted in an illuminated manuscript. Its captains were figures of heroic proportions, speaking and acting like their medieval counterparts:

There entered a tall, strong figure, with a haggard face, passionate and tragic. This was Auda. . . . His hospitality was sweeping; except to very hungry souls, inconvenient. His generosity kept him always poor, despite the profits of a hundred raids. He had married twenty-eight times, he had been wounded thirteen times; whilst the battles he provoked had seen all his tribesmen hurt and most of his relations killed. He himself had slain seventy-five men, Arabs, with his own hand in battle. . . . Of the number of Turks he could give no account.

Reading through this catalogue of prowess it is hard not to think of

Chaucer's knight – 'Thrice in the lists and always slew his man'. It was easy for Lawrence, the avid absorber of chivalric literature and values, to identify with such figures. He could even become, like them, a source of legend. During his cross-desert trek in May 1917, he heard from his companions how the deeds of two of his brother officers were passing into Beduin myth. 'Arabs told me Newcombe would not sleep except head on rails, and that Hornby [another engineer officer] would worry the metals with his teeth when gun cotton failed. They were legends. . . .' Older legends still preoccupied Lawrence at this time for he continued to re-read his *Odyssey* and *Morte d'Arthur* on campaign. Perhaps he was already conscious that his own deeds of arms might become the seeds of legend, not only among the Arabs but in his own country.

Lawrence's familiarity with medieval concepts of war and warrior codes made him feel a close affinity with the Arabs. He had no qualms about looting, an Arab habit which angered many of his colleagues because it stopped the fighting man from pursuing his broken adversaries and engendered indiscipline. Once he admitted to plundering a Baluchi carpet from a wrecked train, and at other times he stood by while his men indulged themselves more lavishly. Intervention would not have squared with his philosophy, which insisted on unqualified acceptance of the traditional Arab ways of fighting. They did not conform to King's Regulations or to the theories evolved by modern Western strategists but, with marginal adjustments, could be adapted for war against the Turks.

Lawrence recited Arab poems and sang Arab songs as he rode with them, and he could hold his own in everyday camp gossip about tribal politics and family pedigrees.[2] One junior officer who joined him at Aqaba in 1918 noticed that he chose Arab company, shunning his own countrymen. Yet Lawrence, in a letter of July 1918, was cautious about the extent of his understanding of the Arab mind: 'I can understand it enough to look at myself and other foreigners from their direction,' but an impassable gulf existed between him and the Arabs. 'I know I am a stranger to them, and always will be.'

His experiences at Karkamis probably gave him a deeper knowledge of Arab patterns of thought and behaviour than was possessed by other British officers. For all the sweeping racial presumptions revealed at the beginning of the *Seven Pillars*, Lawrence was more sensitive to the habits and manners of his hosts than most of his countrymen, who measured Arab achievement, or more usually its absence, in European terms. Unlike such men, accustomed to treating the empire's subject races in the manner of the drill-sergeant or the schoolmaster, he was prepared to take cognisance of Arab sensibilities and forgo the normal assumption that the European always knew best. This philosophy was at the heart of his twenty-seven-point guide to relations with the Arabs, which he based on his own experience and compiled for circulation among British staff during 1917.[3]

Three points were emphasised by Lawrence. To see the world through Arab eyes, the noviciate must first shed his European ways of thinking and then he might penetrate the Arab mind. This process required circumspection, since Arabs set great store by first impressions. In practical terms, the British officer had to understand the arcane mysteries of the Arab command structure and realise that the Arab warrior's reactions to battle were utterly different from those of the disciplined British soldier. 'If the objective is a good one (booty) they will attack like fiends,' but 'strange events cause panic', a euphemism for the precipitate routs that commonly ended engagements against determined Turkish forces.

Lawrence also stressed the need to work entirely inside the existing Arab social and political structure. 'Magnify and develop the growing conception of the Sharifs as the natural aristocracy,' he urged. The Arab Revolt was always an aristocratic movement, a revolution from the top in which all initiative and command flowed downwards. The sharifs were the tribal elite whose members claimed authority based upon descent from Muhammad through his daughter Fatima. They were identified by their distinctive rich robes. A sharif expected deference and thrived on flattery. 'Strengthen his prestige at your expense before others when you can,' Lawrence advised. Even when the sharif's plans were faulty, he must not be corrected but, instead, guided gently towards the right path. 'Keep a tight grip' over his mind but so subtly that neither he nor those about him ever realised the extent of his indebtedness. This had obviously been Lawrence's approach with Faisal and it had worked, turning Lawrence into a courtier whose invisible influence dominated his prince. It was a form of political control which a medieval scholar would have understood more readily than a pro-consul or general.

'Guide, philosopher and friend' was how Major Hubert Young summed up Lawrence's position at Faisal's court during 1918. During the winter of 1916–17 Lawrence had used the methods he was to outline for others to break down Faisal's reserve and establish a close harmony with him. In January he told Newcombe that the Prince was 'an absolute ripper' and, more soberly, informed his family that 'He is charming towards me, and we get on perfectly together.' Most importantly, Lawrence provided Faisal with the moral resolution which he usually lacked. 'Faisal is very jumpy and difficult,' observed George Lloyd in October 1917, 'but so long as Lawrence is here all goes well.'[4]

In a bleak, often opaque chapter of introspection towards the end of the *Seven Pillars* entitled 'Myself', Lawrence characterised his relationship with Faisal in terms of the strong and the feeble.

Feisal was a brave, weak, ignorant spirit, trying to do work for which only a genius, a prophet or a great criminal, was fitted. I served him out of pity, a motive which degraded us both.

These remarks were part of a stream of thoughts which passed through Lawrence's mind on 15 August 1918, his thirtieth birthday. An urge for self-abasement underlay much of this reverie, which may have had its source in private passions unconnected with the performance of his public duties. Nevertheless, Lawrence later confessed to Liddell Hart that he had been forced to deceive his superiors by false advertisements of Faisal's bravery and resolve.

An independent account of Faisal as a commander, written by an Egyptian officer who had served with him during 1916, revealed an inept muddler.

Faisal has no notion whatever of military tactics, and being afraid to rely on anyone else, as does his father and brothers, he loses much of the money and ammunition entrusted to him, as well as the energy of his followers, by continued movements which are often unnecessary and by his inability to take advantage of the enemy.[5]

The most vital of Lawrence's duties was to protect Faisal from his own follies without, according to his own code, ever letting the Prince know that he had committed or was about to commit them.

Lawrence advised all who served alongside the Arabs to wear the *qalifeh*, which was already common practice before Lawrence first came to Hejaz. The Arabs regarded the usual British topee as a device which shaded the infidel from the eye of Allah. Full Arab costume was essential for those who needed to acquire the complete 'trust and intimacy' of the Beduin, but wearing it obliged a British officer to conform wholly to his hosts' manners and customs. 'You will be like an actor in a foreign theatre,' Lawrence noted, 'playing a part day and night for months, without rest, and for an anxious stake.'

Faisal had first suggested that Lawrence wore the robes of a sharif when he returned to Hejaz at the end of November 1916 and was vexed whenever he appeared in khaki.[6] Lawrence in British uniform was a reminder that his clever, omniscient courtier was the representative of a foreign power with which he was in unequal alliance. Sharifian robes, as Lawrence knew, gave him an enormous authority over tribesmen, who immediately identified him as a man of wealth and importance, to be accorded respectful treatment. Lawrence also revelled in his new wardrobe and welcomed any opportunity to be photographed wearing it.

His gear was always fancy dress, never a disguise. 'No easterner could have taken me for an Arab,' he told Liddell Hart, and only Indian lancers 'and similar ignorant foreign soldiery' in Egypt and Dera ever mistook Lawrence for an Arab. Leaving aside the question of whether the Turkish soldiers at Dera were 'easterners', Lawrence was correct. British troops, at first taken in by his clothes, soon changed their minds when they saw his reddish face, for like so many fair-skinned people Lawrence never tanned. Colonel Meinertzhagen was briefly duped when he first encountered Lawrence in December 1917 and wondered whether this 'Arab boy, dressed in spotless white', was possibly 'somebody's pleasure boy'.[7]

What always distinguished Lawrence was his beardless face. Other British officers attached to the Arab armies went unshaven; water was scarce and the Arabs prized the beard as a token of manly virility. Lawrence only needed to shave every few days and was 'always recognized as a British officer' by the Arabs. Lawrence knew this and, like those of his colleagues who affected full Arab costume, took the precaution of packing 'a soldier's cap, shirt, and shorts' in his saddlebag ready for an emergency change if it seemed likely that he would be taken prisoner.[8] Captured as a spy in civilian dress, a British officer would face court martial and certain execution. The same standards applied to both sides: a disguised Turkish officer taken in the Sudan in 1914 was sentenced to death.

The flamboyant, exhibitionist streak in Lawrence first seen at Karkamis endeared him to his Arab followers. He did not hector or preach to them in the way of some of his countrymen, which must have been surprising, even endearing. He was distinctly unEnglish, as Major Bray recalled in an account of a conference at al Wajh early in 1917 which he attended with Faisal, Lawrence and Colonel Gerard Leachman, a caricature proconsul from Iraq.

> Lawrence in full Arab robes, richly embroidered, a gold dagger at his waist, speaking as softly as Faisal, carefully choosing his words and then lapsing into long silences. Leachman, clothed in fading khaki, inscrutable, with that puzzling smile of his lurking at the corners of his mouth, but straightforward and decisive in his speech. The contrast between the two Englishmen was patent: Lawrence acting the Arab and maintaining his prestige through the medium of his magnificent clothes. His servility to Faisal and his seeming unreality form a picture which still lingers in my mind. Leachman on the other hand was obviously and unashamedly the Englishman, and a masterful one.

More than clothing separated the intelligent amateur who persuaded from the professional who commanded. As Lawrence remembered, Leachman 'had an abiding contempt for everything native', an outlook nurtured in

India. His brutishness towards his servant was such an embarrassment that the Colonel had to be packed off back to his ship. Lawrence was appalled – 'any decent servant would have shot him.' As it was, an Iraqi Arab assassinated Leachman four years later.[9]

Leachman's behaviour was a result of pure imperial arrogance, and other officers queried Lawrence's insistence on a patient approach towards the Arabs on the ground that they were unworthy of such accommodation. Major Henry Garland, who jibbed at military protocol, was very much an officer in Lawrence's mould. His breezy informality put the back up of a senior in Cairo, who reported that Garland had 'no manners, never says "Sir"; but "righto!" dresses in breeches and gaiters, leans across his chair with his hands in his pockets and talks of all officers by their names'.[10] In August 1917, Garland complained to Colonel Wilson about the hopelessness of instructing the Arabs along the lines prescribed by Lawrence.[11] 'The politic way of treating the Arabs is to praise all their war work, good or bad.' This was impossible and intolerable since 'It is not given to every British Officer to be able to sink his identity or see the Arab through rosy glasses, and those of us who cannot help draw attention to waste, neglect and disobedience must not expect to remain popular with the rank and file.' This outburst was the culmination of several months of unhappy experiences in the field. Reporting after a raid on the Hejaz railway in February, Garland described himself as 'helplessly in the hands of the Arabs', who endlessly pestered him for baksheesh.[12] Unlike Lawrence, he felt Arab clothing was restrictive and found it hard to turn a blind eye to pillaging. The Arabs' insolence was unbearable and they exposed themselves and Garland to 'unnecessary risks by their stupid conduct, such as singing and shouting within hearing of the enemy'.

Major Vickery, whom Lawrence wrote off as a medal-hunter after a row at al Wajh, was shocked by the Arabs' graft and laziness and in particular the 'life of sloth and indulgence' followed by their leaders.[13] His and Garland's experiences and reactions were not exceptional and gave backing to Lawrence's own contention that service to an alien race was a 'Yahoo' existence. Others who fought alongside the Arabs during 1917 and 1918 were dismayed by their allies' faint-heartedness and downright cowardice in battle which often endangered the lives of British, French, Egyptian and Indian personnel. Corporal Rolls of the Armoured Car Squadron and an admirer of Lawrence spoke for many when he wrote: 'We hated the Arabs. Turkish prisoners, with their sense of order, with their European uniforms and their understanding of military discipline, are like dear friends to us compared to our Arab allies.'[14]

His passion was understandable. In May 1918 a member of his unit, Lance-Corporal Lowe, had been murdered by Arabs near Aqaba.[15]

Lawrence glossed over the incident with the bland statement that he had been 'accidentally killed doing amateur policework off his own bat'. Not long after, a sergeant was set upon and robbed by a gang of Arabs.[16] Yet Lawrence continued to find virtue in such men when others could see only flaws.

For all that he wrote of the trust and understanding which existed between them, Lawrence's relationship with Faisal and the Arabs in general depended upon money. In February 1917, Garland had asked one Arab whether he was fighting for Hussain. 'No,' he replied, 'not for the Sharif; for British Gold.'[17] The cynical Brémond observed that Lawrence, 'a man who had the use of two hundred thousand pounds sterling and who could deliver two thousand harnessed camels', would never lack Arab admirers. An outright enemy, Colonel Arnold Wilson, insisted that Lawrence could have achieved nothing without the gold sovereigns. They certainly gave him one of his Arab nicknames, Abu Khayyal, 'the father of the horsemen', that is St George, who appears on the obverse of the coin. The sovereigns Lawrence distributed in Syria were being called 'the Cavalry of St George' at the end of 1917, in much the same way as their equivalents, used as subsidies to Allies during the French Revolutionary wars, were called 'Pitt's Grenadiers'.[18]

Lawrence wrote little about the economics of the Arab Revolt in the *Seven Pillars* and what he had to say was deliberately deceptive. At the onset of the uprising, Hussain 'was cheerfully determined to wage war against them [the Turks], relying on justice to cover the cost', which was untrue; he received a monthly subsidy of £125,000 paid from Foreign Office funds in sovereigns delivered from the Egyptian Treasury. Even the most cursory discussion of this matter could have drawn Lawrence's readers to wonder whether the army of Beduin idealists might have included a few mercenaries, an understandable conclusion given their admitted passion for plunder.

Lawrence was not so fastidious during his first visit to Hejaz in October 1916 when he reported to Clayton, 'The money question is going to be decisive; the Turks have been trying to circulate paper money lately which will be the end of them.'[19] He was absolutely right; like so many backward people, the Hejaz and Syrian Beduin mistrusted banknotes and instinctively preferred silver and gold currency. Even so, many had been retained by the Turkish government before the war to guard the Hejaz railway, a service which they undertook up to the moment of Turkey's defeat. Some, probably Bani Sakhr, encountered by a Gurkha unit attached to Faisal's army on 14 September 1918, were clearly willing to earn their wages. 'We came across a party of hostile Arabs, hostile in the sense that if we attacked the Turkish line, they would fight on behalf of the enemy. If we did not attack the line, these tribesmen numbering 2,000 were our friends.'[20] It would be interesting to know whether this contingent had ever taken British gold or whether they discarded their loyalty to their former masters and joined in the general pillage of the remnants of the Turkish Fourth Army at the end of September.

They probably did. Between 1916 and 1918 the war presented the tribal sheiks of Arabia and Syria with an opportunity to supplement their thin incomes and enhance their status. Over the past fifty years the Ottoman government had become less and less willing to purchase Beduin obedience with subsidies and had instead attempted coercion. Now, the Turks, their German allies and Britain were all anxious to pay for Beduin goodwill and co-operation. 'The Germans poured gold upon us,' remembered one sheik from northern Syria, and in October 1918, when the Turks evacuated Aleppo, they distributed 30,000 gold lira to local tribesmen in return for a safe passage.[21]

This flow of gold came at a time of severe regional economic crisis created by the Syrian famine of 1915–16, the breakdown of the food distribution system, hyperinflation and the widespread commandeering of camels and other pack animals by the Turkish army. As the shortages worsened, more and more entrepreneurs accepted payment only in gold. The nomadic Beduin were among those hardest hit, since their survival depended upon grain purchased from the settled districts of central Syria and Palestine. One of the chief concerns of the Rwallah Sheik, Nuri Shalaan, was his tribe's inability to secure grain from the Hawran and his overtures to the British included demands for alternative corn supplies from Iraq. Lawrence's sovereigns were welcome to him and others like him, since the Hawran corn dealers were insisting on payment in gold.[22] Whatever their political loyalties, the Syrian Beduin needed British gold to survive.

Other Arabs exploited the war for personal gain. In 1917 British intelligence became aware that rifles originally sent to Hussain were being traded in southern Persia and the Gulf.[23] At least one shipment of arms was hijacked by a Hejazi sheik for his own use, even though he claimed to be Hussain's ally.

As Lawrence discovered on his first visit to Hejaz, Hussain coveted his subsidy and kept his sons and their tribal forces short. His allowance was raised in May 1917 to £200,000 monthly, and by August, fourteen months after the start of the rebellion, he had received £2.2 million. By this time Faisal was independent of his father and, as commander of the northern section of the Arab armies, was receiving through Lawrence £75,000 a month, which was raised to £80,000 in October 1918. These remittances were his main source of income even after the fall of Damascus and were intended to cover his private expenses, the wages of his regular troops and allowances paid to tribal sheiks for the hire of their followers. The distribution of these funds was haphazard. On 10 May 1918 there was 'slight trouble' when regular Arab soldiers protested that they had not been paid for four months. Faisal calmed them, but the next day two companies mutinied and refused to march out of Aqaba for an attack on Abu el Jurdhan.[24] Those who went were in a sour mood, which explained why the assault was so halfheartedly pressed.

Arab forces, tribal or regular, would not fight without payment. This was understood by Wingate and Allenby, who in July 1918 faced a crisis when Egyptian gold reserves had dwindled to £30,000 with just over £4,000 available in sovereigns. Hussain agreed to take some payment in silver, but Allenby had to have £400,000 in sovereigns hurriedly shipped from the Melbourne mint to avert a complete halt to all Arab activity.[25] The Hejaz Arabs were so heavily dependent on their monthly allowance that in January 1919 Wingate feared that Hussain would face widespread tribal restlessness unless his full wartime subsidy were extended.[26] Reporting on conditions in Aqaba during the bitterly cold weather in January 1918, the French Attaché St Quentin felt certain that British cash was the chief prop to Arab morale.[27] His countrymen knew this from experience, for a party of Algerian soldiers had been robbed by tribesmen near Yanbu al Bahr in October 1917. The excuse offered by the Arab Bureau was that 'the sharif Ali has not been paying his Arabs lately and some of the discontented are out to loot anything,' which must have been a comfort to their victims.[28]

Lawrence acted as direct paymaster to the tribal sheiks of Syria and the desert region east of the Jordan with whom he had first established dealings during May and June 1917. After he had taken Aqaba and his reports had been examined in Cairo and London, the Foreign Office allocated £200,000 in gold which he was free to distribute among the sheiks whose lands lay close to the Hejaz railway between Dera and Maan. On 12 August he was given a further, secret service allowance of £200 a month, also in gold.[29] A month later, he asked for £20,000 for a party of Syrian sheiks who were due to visit Faisal, no doubt to help sway their future allegiance.[30] By 18 October, he had disposed of £97,000 and was asking Clayton to release the remaining £103,000 of his allowance for future special operations which already had Allenby's approval. This proved inadequate for what he had in mind, so on 18 November Robertson sanctioned an additional £20,000 to be sent to Lawrence at Aqaba. Three weeks later, Faisal allocated his entire monthly allowance of £80,000 to subsidies for tribal forces at Lawrence's insistence, which may explain why Arab regular troops were starved of wages for the next six months. A further £30,000 was delivered to Gedua el Sufi at Beersheba in January 1918 on Lawrence's instructions.[31]

Between August 1917 and January 1918, £320,000 had been handed over to tribal sheiks in Syria and east of the River Jordan at Lawrence's instigation in return for attacks on the Hejaz railway and future adherence to Faisal. Lawrence clearly recognised that there was a price for Arab co-operation in Syria; his 'ideal' was not enough to sustain the momentum of a national movement. During operations alongside tribal forces in 1918, Captain Peake of the Imperial Camel Corps noticed that there was 'no trouble about a satisfactory muster when it was a question of pay or food'.[32]

For Lawrence, the money was a means to an end and he was careless in handling it. In October 1917 he forgot to sign a receipt for £10,000 delivered to him at Aqaba, and during his post-war service in Jordan his accounts included the entry '£10,000 – lost, I forget how or where'. Harry St John Philby later found the missing cash in a buried safe near Aqaba. On campaign, Lawrence carried his sovereigns in bags of 1,000 or else had them conveyed by armoured car. The residue was held in a safe aboard the Aqaba guardship, HMS *Humber*, for fear of theft. This was a needless precaution, since throughout all the time he spent in remote country behind enemy lines Lawrence was never robbed, which says much for the awe and respect felt for him by the Beduin. Captain Hubert Young, his comrade-in-arms and most honest critic, remarked after the war that 'Lawrence could not have done what he did without the gold, but no one else could have done it with ten times the amount.'[33]

Tribal loyalty had its price and Lawrence could pay it. In effect he had taken over and exploited the old Ottoman system which had created a network of more or less dependable clients among the Beduin sheiks. Furthermore, his gold reached the sheiks at a time of extreme need and provided them with the only currency with which they could purchase the basic foodstuffs their people needed for survival. The prospect of starvation more than attachment to a national idea drove the Beduin to him, as well as the prospects he offered for looting Turkish trains and stations. Yet this policy of buying support proved self-defeating, at least as far as the promotion of Faisal's interests was concerned. Through Lawrence's liberal disbursement of British gold, Faisal had assembled a formidable tribal following in Syria by October 1918, but its strength was illusory. By July 1920, when it was clear that Britain was no longer underwriting him, Faisal's authority evaporated. When his gold ran out, his sometime retainers turned elsewhere and soon discovered that the French colonial administration was willing to continue the custom of tribal subsidies. Nuri Shalaan preferred French gold to nationalist slogans and, in 1925, when the Druze rebelled against the French and were joined by the Damascus nationalists, the Beduin readily accepted French bribes and stayed neutral.[34]

Lawrence played down the money as a factor in deciding Arab allegiance. To have revealed how essential it had been would have invited the question of how far he was the commander of a mercenary army. He found the concept abhorrent and in 1928 wrote scathingly of the Indian army, 'No native troops are loyal to their foreign masters: or rather, only those who had no self respect would be loyal, and men without self respect aren't capable of loyalty. The better the Indian, the less happy he could be as an agent of repression.' It was an unthinking piece of dogmatism which indicated that either Lawrence understood nothing about the Indian Army or else he could not forgive it and its officers for wartime slights during the final Damascus campaign. As for the Arabs, he went to elaborate lengths to convince his contemporaries that they were fighting for national sentiment and not for cash. From his first visit to Faisal in October 1916 he continually repeated the contention that the Arabs represented a truly national movement, motivated by the highest sentiments. In his official report on the march to al Wajh in January 1917, he repeated a conversation which supported this conviction. Sheik Awda Tayi, sometime brigand and chief of the Huweitat, amazed by the numbers around him, remarked, 'It is not an army but a world which is moving on al Wajh.' His neighbour agreed and added, 'Yes, we are no longer Arabs, but a nation.'[35] If the rank and file were animated by such feelings, and Lawrence believed they were, he was the midwife at the birth of a new nation which, in time, he would guide through its infancy.

He may have flattered himself, but everything he wrote during and after the Arab campaign was based on the assumption that the Arab uprising was a popular movement which embodied the historic aspirations of all Arab peoples. His interpretation of events suited Allied propaganda and carried weight in London and Cairo, since his first-hand experiences had given what was seen as an unequalled insight into the Arab mind. 'Major Lawrence's opinions demand the most serious consideration,' insisted William Yale, the US Consul in Cairo, when he forwarded an account of them to the State Department in March 1918.[36] 'No other westerner' was in a position to offer a more accurate evaluation of Arab attitudes and aspirations. This was so, yet as Harry St John Philby noticed, Lawrence, like other partisans of the Hashemites, was prone to mould his evidence to fit his opinions. As with his own and Military Intelligence's prognoses about the mutinies in the Turkish army, there was a strong element of wishful thinking in Lawrence's assessments of the Arab movement.

From the first the Arab movement, which had Hussain as its figurehead, had been an uneasy alliance. Its adherents were united only by a common wish to break free from Ottoman rule. They had been thrown into partnership by peculiar wartime conditions and even before these had disappeared differences broke surface. At the root of these disagreements lay divergent opinions about the kind of Arab state which would emerge once Turkey had been defeated. This was unavoidable since Hussain's movement had attracted supporters and prospered because it could call upon substantial Allied resources. For nationalists of all political complexions it offered the only means by which Turkish rule could be overthrown. For this reason Hussain's adherents included Syrian and Iraqi nationalists who had no truck whatsoever with his reactionary political ideas.

The final success of the Arab movement rested with an Allied victory. This was understood by Faisal and Abdullah, Hussain's most politically sophisticated sons, who closely followed newspaper reports of the campaigns on the Western Front, which they knew were the key to Allied victory and, with it, Arab release from Turkish government. Lawrence found Abdullah well informed about the course of the Somme offensive and Faisal told Brémond that 'The Arabs were helping to secure for France the coveted provinces of Alsace and Lorraine, just as France at Verdun was confirming Arabia for the Arabs.'[37] The news of Russia's armistices with Germany and Turkey in December 1917 and the German advance in the following spring shook Arab confidence in their allies and for a time made Faisal seriously consider Turkish peace overtures. In what was an alliance of convenience rather than conviction, one of Lawrence's regular duties was to convince Faisal that his allies would eventually win.

When they joined the rebellion against Turkey, Arabs in both Hejaz and Syria were embarking on a dangerous course. There were widespread fears that, in the event of a Turco-German victory, the Turkish government would exact a terrible retribution on those who had defected to the Allies. The systematic massacres of Armenians which had begun in January 1915 on the ground that they were secretly pro-Russian, were evidence of how far the Turks would go to coerce and punish resistance. Incidentally, this barbarism convinced many devout Arabs that the Young Turks had finally discarded Islamic principles and were deliberately inviting the vengeance of Allah.

The Armenian atrocities were referred to in Hussain's second proclamation of independence issued in November 1916. In this and its predecessor of June, he accused the Committee of Union and Progress of rejecting Muslim traditions and ideals and of inhuman treatment of the empire's subjects. Measures to advance the status of women were singled out for special censure. 'Arab matrons were conscripted and trained in barracks,' and in Damascus Jamal Pasha had patronised a women's society and permitted women to speak publicly in front of men. Hussain was a reactionary alarmed by the policies of modernisation and reform which threatened the traditional, hierarchical society of Hejaz. He favoured the countryside, from where his Beduin followers were drawn, over the town. On his first visit to Jiddah, Lawrence heard how Hussain had replaced Turkish civil law by the Muslim *sharia*, a move which benefited the Beduin and hurt the townsmen. As well as putting the clock back, Hussain actively discouraged any spread of the democratic ideal among his subjects. His newspaper, *al Qibla*, in a report on the opening of a military academy in September 1917, noted approvingly that its students would be 'educated in moral qualities and reverence for Arab virtues, more especially in the display of obedience and submission to their Gracious Sovereign'.

Hussain had declared himself King of the Arabs in November 1917 and he boasted that his overlordship extended right across Arabia. This claim was stoutly contested by Ibn Rashid of Hail, who remained a Turkish client until the end of the war, and by Ibn Saud of Riyadh, who loathed Hussain more than he did the Turks. Before the war Ibn Saud had been courted by the Indian government, whose agent, Captain Shakespeare, had hoped to create an anti-Turkish Arabian alliance which would bring together Hussain, Nuri Shalaan, the Imam Yahya and Sayyid el Idrisi of the Yemen. The private ambitions and mutual suspicions of the parties ruled out any cohesion and, after Shakespeare's death at the beginning of 1915, the plan languished. In the meantime Cairo pressed forward with its scheme for an alliance with Hussain.

Ibn Saud refused any co-operation with Hussain despite appeals from Sir Percy Cox and his agent St John Philby. He had good reasons, for in November 1916 Hussain revealed to Colonel Wilson that his long-term ambition was to make himself sole ruler of all Arabia. Ibn Saud repudiated his pretensions and, by July 1918, felt confident enough to challenge Hussain openly. His forces invaded Hussain's territory and in a skirmish at Khurma defeated his British-armed tribesmen, inflicting over 200 casualties. Hussain's British advisers naturally discouraged this private war, which deflected Arab energies away from the main war effort. The Turks were delighted; Fakhri Pasha congratulated Ibn Saud and French intelligence sources heard that he was supplying him with arms. Abdullah, anxious to draw Britain into his family's war, spread disinformation to the effect that Ibn Saud had entered into a secret agreement with Fakhri. Hussain's other rival, Ibn Rashid, victualled the Medina garrison and in February 1918 supplied Fakhri with tribal irregulars for an offensive against Abdullah.[38]

In his narrative of the Arab Revolt, Lawrence ignored Hussain's tribal adversaries. Their existence and activities were an uncomfortable reminder that the Beduin were disunited and in many cases deeply suspicious of Hussain's dynastic ambitions. From the beginning, Hussain and his sons believed that they could use the Arab movement to propel their family, the Hashemites, into a position of pre-eminence in the Middle East. Hussain imagined that with British backing he could make himself supreme in Arabia, and Abdullah was haunted by dreams of founding his own kingdom. Before the revolt Abdullah had considered making himself King of Hejaz and, once it was successfully under way, his ambition increased. In June 1916 he was considering a kingdom in Iraq and in October he told Brémond that, after he had captured Medina, he intended to conquer Syria. Eight months later, sitting in his tent, Lawrence and an Algerian officer, Lieutenant Raho, heard that he had in mind conquests in the Yemen, Syria and even Anatolia.[39]

Lawrence never mentioned his host's dynastic daydreams, although he did record in the *Seven Pillars* his own comments on monarchy which must have pleased Abdullah greatly.

> I remarked again how much the comfortable circumstance that we still had a King made for the reputation of England in this world of Asia. Ancient and artificial societies like this of the Sharifs and feudal chieftains of Arabia found a sense of honourable security when dealing with us in such proof that the highest place in our state was not a prize for merit or ambition.

The ambitious and meritocratic ruled in Constantinople (Enver had been a junior officer and Talaat a postal clerk) and they seemed bent on uprooting the ordered, layered society of the Beduin.

This was to Hussain's advantage, as it brought into his camp Syrian tribal sheiks whose authority and way of life were endangered. Two powerful tribal groups, the Anazah and the Bani Sakhr, were making tentative approaches to Hussain and Faisal during the winter and spring of 1916–17. The Anazah, of whom the Rwallah were the most numerous, were scattered across eastern Syria and the Bani Sakhr were spread to the south of Amman. Both were pushed into Hussain's camp, not out of a sense of national identity but because, for the past fifty years, they had been under pressure from the Ottoman government. Administrative centralisation, greater efficiency, permanent garrisons, dwindling subsidies and the enforcement of taxation and conscription were eroding tribal independence and livelihoods.

The Bani Sakhr were particularly vulnerable. The completion of the Hejaz railway in 1908 deprived them of income earned from escorting parties of pilgrims, which explains their enthusiastic participation in raids aimed at its destruction. They were also suffering economically from the new colonies of Circassian settlers planted by the Turkish government in southern Jordan. Like the Anazah tribes, the Bani Sakhr had a long history of armed resistance to Ottoman government which made them natural allies of Hussain. So too were such freebooters as Awba Abu Tayi of the Huweitat, a brigand and tax-avoider for whom adherence to Hussain was a continuation of a long struggle against Ottoman officialdom.

The final group in Hussain's coalition was drawn from the remnants of pre-war Syrian and Iraqi Arab nationalist parties. Most were exiles and all were from the educated professional classes. Their talents, in particular those of former Turkish officers, were essential for the creation of an Arab state. The most pressing need was for a trained, regular Arab army which cou'd undertake conventional operations alongside Allied forces.

The backgrounds and sympathies of the regular officers were varied. Their European tastes and habits, which included a common liking for whisky and, in the cases of al Mizri and al Faruqi, European mistresses, made them unwelcome in orthodox Hejaz. Politically many were liberal and republican. Jafar al Askari, an extremely able Iraqi who commanded Arab regular units at Aqaba, had been a member of al Ahd before the war. Another Iraqi, Nuri es Said, had been described by Sir Percy Cox as a 'highly Europeanised delicate Arab, aloof, about 25, apparently a visionary socialist'. Not surprisingly, neither felt comfortable in the service of Hussain, although both were happy under the more tolerant Faisal. Others shared their distaste for Hussain's ultra-conservatism. In August 1917 an Iraqi nationalist wrote from Zurich to the Labour MP Arthur Henderson (the letter was intercepted by Military Intelligence) with their complaints.[40] 'The rascally and hypocritical' Hussain was an autocrat in the mould of the former Turkish Sultan Abdul Hamid, who would back Allies 'so long as the money lasts'.

Mistrust was mutual. Hussain and his sons feared that the cadre of radical officers might be tempted to follow the example of the Young Turks and manage a coup. The behaviour of the rank and file of the Arab regular army gave cause for misgivings, mostly among British and French officers. Nationalists like al Faruqi and the Syrian Dr Abd al Rahman Shahbandah encountered indifference and hostility when they toured POW camps in Egypt in search of recruits. One party of volunteers marched away from the camp followed by a barrage of catcalls – 'You are going to fight for England and France! We will have none of it and we are going back behind barbed wire.' A contingent shipped from Indian prison camps mutinied at Aden in protest against having to undergo training in Egypt, and there was another mutiny at Ismailia in October 1918 against the employment of British and French instructors. At Aqaba there was ceaseless bickering between Syrian regulars and tribesmen. Once brawlers were brought to order when an officer threatened to open fire on them with a machine-gun. An attempt to form a mixed Christian, Jewish and Arab battalion ended in disorder when the Christians and Jews refused to soldier and demanded civilian occupations. Listening to their grumbling, Colonel Brémond thought he heard 'echoes of the soviets'.[41]

The problems of the Arab regular army were a symptom of the deeper malaise which infected the Arab movement. It possessed no common purpose beyond a general desire to be rid of Turkish rule. This bond was itself a collection of contradictory ambitions. Hussain and his family hoped that the Turkish twilight would be followed by a Hashemite dawn; tribesmen like the Bani Sakhr wished to reverse the flow of Ottoman reforms which disrupted their way of life, while Syrian and Iraqi nationalists wanted regeneration and modernisation, but on Arab terms. Palestinian Arabs who joined Faisal's forces during 1918 later claimed they had been told that they would become liberators of their homeland. The tribesmen who rode with Lawrence were fighting for gold and loot. In terms of political conviction the nationalists were deeply divided. There were those, held in contempt by Lawrence, steeped in the ideas of Western enlightenment and liberalism who looked to the French Revolution for inspiration. By contrast, Hashemite political thought was firmly rooted in the *ancien régime*.

Lawrence favoured Hashemite patriarchalism, which he sincerely believed offered the best future for the Arabs. The liberation of Syria would be achieved by an alliance between Faisal the aristocrat and the Beduin, supported by the settled peasantry. By harnessing these essentially conservative forces, Lawrence imagined that he could preserve the traditional Arab way of life from dislocation. He explained his creed in a letter written to Clayton early in September 1917.[42]

> You say they [the Syrians] will need French help in the development
> of Syria – but do you really imagine anyone in Syria (bar Christians)
> wants to develop Syria? Why this craze for change? A slow progress,
> utilising only the resources of Syria itself, seems to me more desirable
> than foreign borrowing and a forcing bed of public enterprises.

Lawrence appreciated that his romantic Toryism applied to Syria would not be welcomed in many quarters. Defending Faisal in February 1918, he wrote, 'The sacred words Progress and Nationality are to be ranged against him' by those who challenged his right to the throne of Syria and regarded him as 'a Meccan obscurantist'.[43]

By guiding Faisal towards Damascus, Lawrence was fulfilling his private dream to liberate Syria and his self-imposed obligation to give 'freedom' to his beloved Dahoum. The overlordship of Syria was obviously attractive to an Arab prince and, long before Lawrence's arrival in Hejaz, the Hashemites had been cherishing ambitions in that direction. Damascus brought with it a rich province whose possession would enhance their power and status within the Arab world. For Lawrence, the city represented a positive goal after which the largely negative and friable Arab movement could strive. Its capture in October 1918 marked the symbolic climax of the Arab Revolt and of Lawrence's version of it as set out in the *Seven Pillars*.

Lawrence never offered a convincing moral or political justification for the replacement of an Ottoman governor in Damascus by a Hejazi prince, beyond conquest and Faisal's tenuous links with some Syrian nationalists. Even the argument of conquest does not bear close scrutiny since the city was first entered by Australian cavalry and the Arab units which followed them were a fragment of a larger Allied army which had borne the brunt of the fighting. Nevertheless, in the light of the quest he had set himself at the beginning of the *Seven Pillars* Lawrence's version of the fall of Damascus to Faisal's Arabs forms a fitting outcome to his struggles.

These had first been undertaken for motives as mixed as those which agitated the Arabs. Lawrence was the historian who had found a chance to make history, the intellectual able to use his ideas to control others and the romantic visionary who turned the dreams of his childhood and youth into reality. He felt a kinship with nomadic Beduin and was flattered by their affection; he satisfied his curiosity, did his bit for his country and served a cause which be believed could bring happiness to the Arabs. He also won fame for himself, which he relished or despised as the mood took him. No single urge impelled Lawrence on his course, instead he followed a sequence of often contradictory reactions to ideas, people and circumstances which in retrospect he found hard to explain or rationalise.

III

TRIUMPH AT AQABA

'THIS show is splendid: you cannot imagine greater fun for us, greater vexation and fury for the Turks', was Lawrence's summary of his first seven weeks of active service with Faisal's army. It was an exciting and invigorating life which he felt certain Newcombe would enjoy – 'you'll find it as good as I say and better.'[1] Lawrence's exuberance stayed at the same high pitch even after the novelty of active service had worn off. 'It is all such sport,' he would often remark during operations around Aqaba, and as Colonel Joyce remembered, 'his enthusiasm must have been infectious for the hours of sport were few and the days and months of dust and sun were long and weary.'[2] One mainspring of Lawrence's jaunty resolve was his dedication to a cause in which he had confident faith. After a conversation in Cairo in August 1917, the French Military Attaché St Quentin was forcibly struck by Lawrence's 'almost mystical zeal for the Arab cause, an unwavering faith in its success so long as European help was neither too obvious or hasty, and a sincere attachment to the fortunes of Faisal'.[3]

As a leader who had to enthuse and encourage those around him, Lawrence could not afford the indulgence of public moods of self-doubt or depression. But the mask did slip and, at least once, he confidentially admitted that the strain of command and action was almost unbearable. During their ride from Aqaba at the end of October 1917, he talked about his secret fears to George Lloyd, who reported the conversation to Clayton:

> Lawrence is quite fit but much oppressed by the risk and magnitude of the job before him. He opened his heart to me last night and told me that he felt there was so much for him to do in the world, places to dig, peoples to help that it seemed horrible to have it all cut off as he feels it will be, for he feels that while he may do the job, he sees little or no chance of getting away himself.... He is really a very remarkable fellow – not the least fearless like some who do brave things, but as he told me last night, each time he starts out on these stunts he simply hates it for two or three days before until movement, action and the glory of scenery and nature catch hold of him and make him well again.[4]

This reliance on his surroundings as a distraction may explain the abundance of long descriptive passages of closely observed landscape in the *Seven Pillars*. Taking account of his surroundings was a luxury, since Lawrence's mind was almost exclusively given over to his duties:

> On a show so narrow and voracious as this, one loses one's past and one's balance, and becomes hopelessly self-centred. I don't think I ever think except about shop, and I'm quite certain I never do anything else.[5]

Lawrence's normal human reactions were suspended in battle. 'This killing and killing of Turks is horrible. When you charge in at the finish and find them all over the place in bits, and still alive many of them, and know that you have done hundreds in the same way before and must do hundreds more if you can.'[6]

One way in which he justified the awfulness of what he had done was by depriving his victims of their humanity. So in the *Seven Pillars* the Turkish soldiers are depicted as amoral and wantonly brutal creatures who slavishly obeyed their 'showy-vicious Levantine officers'. 'Ordered to be kind, and without haste they were as good friends and generous enemies as might be found. Ordered to outrage their fathers or disembowel their mothers, they did it as calmly as they did nothing, or did well.' Lawrence would press the point further when he described his own torture and depraved abuse at the hands of a Turkish officer and his men at Dera.

From the moment he returned to Hejaz at the very end of November 1916, Lawrence had needed all his reserves of energy and dedication. In his first weeks with Faisal's army he had acted as a field intelligence officer who collected and reported evidence of the enemy's movements, co-ordinated naval and aerial support for Faisal's army and maintained a constant flow of up-to-date information about the situation at the front to Wilson at Jiddah and the Arab Bureau in Cairo.

This was a hectic period for Lawrence since the long-expected Turkish offensive was in full swing and Arab resistance was crumbling. At the beginning of December a small Turkish advance guard pierced Faisal's lines, created panic and occupied his bases at al Hamra and Bir Said unopposed. Lawrence's report of the débâcle confirmed the axiom that tribal forces were no match for trained regulars. During an engagement at Nakhl Mubarraq, Faisal's 'centre and right wing held and repulsed the enemy, the left wing (Juheina) retired suddenly behind the centre without hostile pressure'. As Lawrence explained, the deserters had run off 'to find opportunity for brewing a cup of coffee undisturbed'.[7]

Hemmed in at Yanbu al Bahr and separated from his brother Ali's army which had been badly mauled and was retreating to Rabigh, Faisal's nerve broke. On 12 December he pleaded with Lawrence for British troops.[8] Wilson passed on the request to Wingate, who on 15 December got permission from Arthur Balfour, the new Foreign Secretary, for a British brigade to be sent to Hejaz if the situation deteriorated further. Meanwhile Wilson was laying plans for the evacuation of Arab forces from Rabigh and Yanbu al Bahr.[9]

No British troops were needed. Sea and air power were sufficient to save the day and, for that matter, the Arab Revolt. The long-range guns of the monitor *M31* kept the Turks away from the approaches to Yanbu al Bahr, and aircraft summoned by Lawrence from the flight at Rabigh and the *Suva* spotted and bombed Turkish formations inland. These attacks tipped the balance for, as Lawrence knew from an Arab Bureau decrypt, Fakhri's aircraft were grounded for lack of spares. Subsequent intelligence gained by Lawrence from his field agents and interviews with POWs revealed that the cautious Fakhri dared not risk pressing on with his attack without air cover and that he was anxious about the lack of fodder for

his vast train of transport camels.[10] By the last week of December he prudently withdrew his forces to defensive positions around Medina. British
sea power, a small but decisive advantage in the air and Turkish logistical
problems had saved the Arab movement.

Fakhri's retreat provided a breathing space for the Arab forces and a
chance for them to implement plans for an offensive which, if successful,
would pen the Turks inside Medina and sever their rail links with Damascus. Having survived six months and, with British assistance, frustrated
all efforts by local Turkish forces to break them, the Arab armies were
now free to play a part in the wider Allied war effort. The question how
they could most effectively be deployed was decided in London and Cairo
by General Staff planners who were largely dependent on the advice of
men on the spot like Lawrence. It also fell to Lawrence to explain to Faisal
and his staff what was expected of their forces and make them understand
that close co-operation with the Allies was in the best political interests
of the Arabs.

In London the Arab movement was now seen as a vital factor in the
Middle East war. The Lloyd George coalition had come to power in
December 1916 with a cabinet which included Lords Curzon and Milner
and later Churchill, all imperialists keen to use the war as a means of
extending British power in the Middle East. For advice on Arab affairs,
the Cabinet looked to Sir Mark Sykes, who was given the rank of Under-
Secretary and controlled the flow of intelligence from the Middle East.
One of the first acts of the new ministry was to approve, on 29 December
1916, a major offensive against Turkey which would involve a large-scale
invasion of Palestine and Syria in conjunction with renewed Russian pressure in the Caucasus. Together these hammer blows would weaken Turkey
and force her to sue for terms. This represented a significant shift in government policy which, after Gallipoli, had restricted operations on the Palestine
front to cautious, small-scale advances across Sinai. Concentration of men
and material for a knock-out blow against Turkey naturally aroused opposition from the Westerners, who repeated their old argument that the war
would be won only when the German army was beaten in France. This
had not been achieved by the Somme offensive and some, like Milner,
doubted whether the Germans could ever be defeated, so that in the end
a peace would have to be negotiated. Turkey was a different matter and
her defeat would open the way for annexations. Nevertheless Robertson
and the Westerners prevailed; the Syrian offensive was officially postponed
until the autumn so that reserves could be drafted to France to back up
General Nivelle's offensive at Verdun. Schemes for a grand assault on
Turkey received a further setback in March 1917 with the overthrow of
Nicholas II and the subsequent dissolution of the Russian army.

The new emphasis on an all-out attack on Turkey forced GHQ in Cairo to find ways in which the Arabs could be used on the projected Syrian front. The options were limited. There could be no question of using irregular Arab forces in conventional front-line actions since they lacked the necessary training, discipline and nerve for that kind of fighting. This would be the province of the Arab regular army formations, which would not be ready for this type of warfare for at least a year, probably longer. There remained the tribal forces which at the beginning of 1917 mustered three armies, respectively commanded by Abdullah, Faisal and Ali.

Since the first days of the revolt, Wingate, Clayton and Murray's staff had wanted these forces to be deployed in a sustained campaign against the Hejaz railway. This railway exerted a peculiar fascination for GHQ Cairo and the War Office staff planners, all of whom regarded its destruction as essential for the success of the Hejaz campaign and the Syrian offensive. Two methods were possible. The first involved bombing from the air, but a long-range sortie against the line near Maan on 24 November 1916 by two Martinsyde bombers, armed with hundred-pounders, had disappointing results. The alternative was an unremitting guerrilla campaign in which British engineers, supported by Arab irregulars, demolished bridges, culverts and sections of track to render the railway unusable. By November a small nucleus of sapper officers, including Newcombe, Hornby and Garland, had been ordered to Hejaz to prepare the Arabs for this work.

Lawrence always vigorously supported this strategy and after instruction from Garland led many daring raids against the line in Hejaz and Syria. Like all the men involved in the planning and execution of these raids he defended them on two grounds. As long as the Turks had unimpeded use of the Damascus-to-Medina line they could shift men and munitions through an area which would eventually become the eastern flank of General Murray's Syrian front. To keep the line open, the Turkish High Command had to deploy between 15,000 and 16,000 men in Medina and its hinterland and a further 6,000 disposed in a chain of fortified stations and outposts which stretched northwards to Maan, where there was a garrison of 7,000. In all about 27,000 men were tied down guarding the line, although the figure fluctuated because of wastage through disease and desertions, which was made good with periodic reinforcements.

According to Lawrence's analysis of the situation, set out in the *Seven Pillars*, this force could, by using the railway, intervene at any time to menace British operations in Syria. This had been Murray's fear and there had been a spasm of nervousness in March 1917 when two Turkish prisoners claimed that Fakhri had been ordered by Enver to abandon Medina and bring his forces back to Syria.[11] This proved to be untrue, but it highlighted a peril which would remain as long as the line stayed open. Moreover,

Lawrence argued, a guerrilla war of attrition against the railway would injure Turkey where she was most vulnerable. 'In Turkey things were scarce and precious, men less esteemed,' and so the destruction of scarce war materials did more lasting harm than the killing of men. Such a war of tip-and-run raids was the only possible option open to his Beduin irregulars with their brittle morale, dread of casualties and inability to take, hold and defend positions against disciplined Turkish troops.

This was certainly the best way to use the Arab irregulars, but was the Turkish war effort as seriously damaged as Lawrence imagined? His assumption that the Medina garrison would have been a valuable reinforcement for the Syrian Fourth Army was shared by von Sandars. In February 1918 he sought Enver's permission to evacuate Medina and redeploy its garrison in Syria, where Turco-German forces were already outnumbered. Enver refused. From the first days of the Arab Revolt he had resolved to hold the holy city of Medina for propaganda purposes and as a bargaining counter in the event of peace talks.[12] So long as Enver remained Minister of War there was no chance that Fakhri's forces would be committed to Syria. Inside Medina, Fakhri was not unduly troubled by the persistent attacks on the railway. The blockade by Abdullah's army was never tight enough to cut off supplies of food from Ibn Rashid.

Nor was Fakhri inconvenienced by the destruction of track, as Garland discovered:

> In fact, Fakhri Pasha said to me after the armistice, that whenever he heard the detonations of railway destruction in the night, he chuckled to himself and said, 'My lazy troops will not be able to loaf tomorrow.'[13]

Supplies of track and sleepers were plentiful in Medina, where they had been stored before the war in readiness for laying a branch line to Mecca. These were used by the excellent Turkish railway troops to repair the line, which remained open to trains from the north. After six months the results were disappointing, as Wemyss reported to the Admiralty: 'In spite of persistent raids by British officials against the Hejaz Railway the enemy has succeeded in getting munitions, supplies and reinforcements into Medina.'[14] Results apart, the railway campaign waged between January 1917 and the end of the war at least kept the Arab irregulars occupied, and reports of their demolitions were assiduously forwarded by Wingate to the War Office and Cabinet where they no doubt reassured those who read them that the government was getting a return on its subsidies.

Lawrence strenuously defended the guerrilla campaign and his views were later echoed by Liddell Hart, who used evidence drawn from the works of professional strategists such as Saxe, von Clausewitz and Foch to support the contention that a war could be waged in which one army deliberately shuns engagement with its adversary. The Arabs, moving freely as only they knew how, could use the desert as a ship uses the sea and it gave them immunity to retaliation from a conventional army whose mobility was curtailed by cumbersome columns of transport animals. More importantly, although neither Lawrence nor Liddell Hart mentions the fact, the Turks lacked sufficient aircraft and motor vehicles to reconnoitre and patrol vast areas of desert. This point was fully understood by Lawrence, who at the end of 1918 suggested that with a handful of tanks he could take on and destroy the Wahabbi camelry of Ibn Saud. Two years later Lawrence whole-heartedly backed proposals to employ RAF aircraft rather than conventional ground forces as the agents of imperial peace-keeping and punishment in Iraq, Jordan and Aden. Against the Turkish army, without armoured cars or enough aircraft, the sort of guerrilla war envisaged by Lawrence stood a chance of success. It could not beat the enemy but it could annoy him and force him to waste men and resources. This is what the diehard Boers had discovered between 1900 and 1902, when small commandos of mounted men had tied down over a quarter of a million British and Dominion soldiers. Lawrence's Arabs were more fortunate than the Boers for they had access to such modern weaponry as aircraft, armoured cars and artillery provided by their allies. Furthermore, Lawrence and the Arabs would never have to face more than a small fragment of the Turkish army, the bulk of which was concentrated on the Syrian front to resist a more formidable adversary, the Egyptian Expeditionary Force, which totalled 156,000 men at the beginning of 1917.

Lawrence did not invent the concept of the Arab guerrilla war, although after the war he provided it with an elaborate intellectual justification in terms of military theory. The general idea of using Arab irregulars as guerrillas had been bandied about in Cairo and London since the start of the revolt. It was discussed when Major Bray met Robertson and Austen Chamberlain in London in November 1916. Robertson opened the exchange:

> 'I hear you are one of those fellows who think the Arab is no damn good at all?'
> 'No, Sir,' I answered, 'I think that you cannot expect them, in their present state of organisation, to hold trenches against disciplined troops, but as guerrilla fighters they will be splendid.'[15]

Robertson snorted; he had fought the Boers, who had also been excellent guerrillas but, in the end, their campaign had just extended a war whose result had been a foregone conclusion. Clayton had no such misgivings about a guerrilla campaign. At the end of December, he wrote to George

Lloyd, 'There is only one key to the success of the Arab revolt and that is the cutting of the Hejaz railway, as has been persistently dinned into the ears of all and sundry from the beginning.'[16]

For Clayton such a campaign could proceed only under the direction of 'a guiding spirit who will see issues with a clear eye'. This man would have to be bold and unorthodox, unfettered by the hidebound military thinking which so far had held up progress on the Arab front. Lawrence had the stamina for the job, his imagination had been stirred by the possibilities of a guerrilla war and he was keen to demonstrate its potential. Clayton discarded his old view that Lawrence was most valuable behind a desk in Cairo and supported him as the man most likely to transform general concepts into reality. As Wingate's Chief of Staff he was in a position to ensure that Lawrence's attachment to Faisal's army became permanent. It was Faisal who tipped the balance by his insistence that Lawrence stayed.[17]

From January to July, Lawrence was Faisal's political officer, working alongside Newcombe, who advised on operations, and answerable to Wilson in Jiddah and through the Arab Bureau to GHQ intelligence and Murray. His first duty was to accompany Faisal's forces on their march northwards from Umm Lajj to al Wajh. The Red Sea port had been designated in October as a base for Arab attacks on the Tabuk-to-el-Ela section of the Hejaz railway line, but operations for its capture had been postponed by the Turkish offensive during November and December.[18] The attack on al Wajh opened a new, offensive phase in the Arab campaign. The overall strategy shaped by Wingate, Wilson and the Arab leadership involved the encirclement of Medina by Abdullah's army, which would keep up pressure on the southern section of the Hejaz line while Faisal's and Ali's forces mounted raids further north from their base at al Wajh.

The capture of al Wajh on 23 January 1917 was a fiasco which underlined the fears of many British observers that, when it came to fighting, the Arab movement was more farce than force. The plan had been for Faisal's army of 3,000 tribesmen with four cannon and a dozen machine-guns to move north on 15 January accompanied by Lawrence and Newcombe. Nine days later they would assault al Wajh from the south and east, while Royal Navy warships shelled the Turkish trenches before sending ashore 500 Arab irregulars and 250 bluejackets. Faisal's forces dawdled and were soon in difficulties when it was discovered that someone had forgotten to bring enough transport camels. By 23 January the Arab army was twenty-five miles from its objective without any hope of carrying out its part in the attack.

The Turkish commander at al Wajh was aware of Faisal's plans and withdrew himself and his mounted men rather than face naval bombardment and assault by overwhelming numbers. Wemyss, concerned about the sanitary risks involved in keeping 500 Arabs on board his three men-of-war and with no clear indication of Faisal's whereabouts, ordered a landing on the afternoon of the 23rd. The bluejackets carried the town and, once victory was certain, the Arabs plucked up courage and rushed in to plunder. Captain Vickery, who commanded their contingent, was dismayed by their cravenness and thought gloomily 'of the British taxpayer, who supplied those bottomless bags of gold sovereigns for Eastern potentates to squander'. The looters were also shocked, but by the ladies' underwear they found in the quarters of the Turkish commander. One British observer in a sea-plane had been killed and five Arabs while the Turks suffered twenty casualties.[19]

Faisal's forces trooped into al Wajh and seemed to Major Bray, an onlooker, to be 'extremely light-hearted' in spite of their lateness. To all but Lawrence the bungling at al Wajh was the Arabs' fault. Misinformed by an Arab youth that the taking of the town had cost twenty lives, Lawrence blamed Vickery.

> Vickery, who directed the battle, was satisfied, but I could not share his satisfaction. To me an unnecessary action, or shot, or casualty, was not only waste but sin. I was unable to take the professional view that all successful actions were gains. Our rebels were not materials, like soldiers, but friends of ours, trusting our leadership.

Had the seaborne forces waited for Faisal, the garrison could have been starved into surrender. This was a convenient gloss that drew attention away from Arab mismanagement, which at the time Lawrence clearly ack-nowledged. In his report on the march to al Wajh he lamented the Arabs' inability to adhere to schedules, the shortage of capable subordinate com-manders, inadequate provision of water camels and the fact that to keep spirits high Faisal brought with him more men than were needed.[20]

Recriminations after the al Wajh muddle created a rift between Lawrence and two Indian army officers, Bray and Vickery. The recriminations conti-nued after the war. Lawrence privately described Vickery as a 'vulgar' fellow who 'lowered white prestige', and Vickery, in a lecture to the Royal Asiatic Society in 1923, wrote off the Arabs as a cowardly, venal rabble, many of whom, despite Islamic prohibitions, drank too much.[21]

Vickery could not share Lawrence's tolerance for the Arabs; Bray ques-tioned Lawrence's military judgements and accused him of hijacking the Arab movement, dissipating its energies and thinking too much of his own glory. These charges appeared in Bray's autobiographical *Shifting Sands*, which appeared in 1934. Old rancour was getting a fresh airing. By March 1917 Bray had expressed deeply felt misgivings about the way in which the Arab movement was being handled by British officers, presumably including Lawrence, and on account of these secured his transfer back to France. His public challenge to Lawrence eighteen years later was contemptuously dismissed. 'Bray', Lawrence wrote, 'is quite an honest muddle-headed sort of chap, who believed everything he wrote,' and his criticisms were a publisher's device to sell more books.[22]

With his public reputation at its height and his version of the Arab movement almost universally accepted, Lawrence could afford to be off-hand. In the beginning of 1917 he could not be so blasé. To professional officers, accustomed to commanding natives, Lawrence's softly-softly approach and respect for the Arabs seemed ludicrous. Moreover as a political officer his intrusions into purely military affairs were resented. The events before and during the taking of al Wajh were plain evidence that the Arabs, on whom he pinned so much faith, would never amount to much. A spectacular demonstration of Arab prowess was needed to prove Lawrence's assertion that, directed on their terms and fighting in their own way, they could make headway. If he could be the instrument of such a coup, then he would no longer be dismissed as a meddler with a bee in his bonnet. His chance came in May 1917 when Faisal despatched him with a party of emissaries under orders to penetrate Syria and sound out the loyalties of tribal leaders there.

Syria was Faisal's goal as well as Lawrence's. In December 1917 a report filed at GHQ intelligence in Cairo, presumably by Lawrence, indicated that Faisal was already entertaining ambitions to move north and put himself at the head of a Syrian national movement.[23] Secret exchanges between representatives of Nuri Shalaan of the Rwallah and Faisal had been under way since October and Lawrence was allowed to be party to them. In January 1917 he told Wilson that Nuri, his son Nawaf and other Anazah sheiks had gathered at al Jawf and read Faisal's letters. They agreed to make an open breach with the Turks the moment Arab forces occupied el Ela and Tayma.[24] There were snags, since Ibn Rashid would resist any move against Tayma, and there was no harmony among the tribes around al Jawf.

The prospects for a Syrian revolt were promising. During 1917 GHQ intelligence in Cairo had accumulated evidence of widespread discontent generated by the after-effects of the 1915–16 famine, the repressive measures taken against local nationalists, high food prices, taxation and the continued exactions of the Turkish army. The exploitation of these grievances depended on the ability of Faisal and the Allies to suborn tribal and community leaders, of whom the majority still favoured the Turks or who would only make up their minds once it was clear which side would win. In the meantime the Arab Bureau stepped up the circulation of pan-Arabist propaganda.

Faisal needed little prodding in the direction of Syria. He was jealous of his brother Abdullah, whom he knew had Syrian aspirations and whose successes in the field contrasted with his own setbacks. Lawrence, now a close neighbour to Faisal's counsels, encouraged his ambitions and suggested means by which they could be accomplished. Early in April Adjutant Lamotte, the French representative at al Wajh, found Lawrence and Faisal totally preoccupied with Syrian enterprises.[25] By this time plans were well developed for a programme of subversion designed to draw the Syrian Beduin into an alliance with Faisal.

At the beginning of April, Faisal and his Syrian counsellor, Dr Nasib al Bakri, had further meetings with emissaries from the Anazah, including Nuri Shalaan's brother. They were told that in June Faisal intended to lead a small force into the Jebel Druze and then move against Dera and Afule, presumably having won over the Druze and with active assistance from the Anazah. Faisal added that he had the approval of his English advisers (Lawrence and Newcombe), who had said that these operations would not hinder the campaign against Medina. Faisal warned his listeners that the French with 60,000 men were about to land in Syria, which was nonsense, and added that, without Arab help, France would never subdue the province. If they tried to, he would fight them once the Turks had been beaten. This bullishness may have been designed to impress his audience, but Faisal had already bluntly told Brémond that he was soon to enter Syria. Brémond took him at his word and feared that the 'dull and headstrong' Faisal would give greater trouble to his government than Abdullah.[26]

In Faisal, Lawrence had found a willing accomplice for his private schemes to scotch a post-war French takeover of Syria. Colonel Brémond and the French mission were well aware of this, although Faisal had been chary of any direct confrontation over the Syrian issue. In a charming speech to Brémond and his colleague Colonel Cadi, he 'begged that they would make me party to their plans and intentions so that I could help them as far as lay in me'. Recounting the conversation to Lawrence, whom he allowed to take notes, Faisal continued, 'While saying this I saw their faces become parti-coloured and their eyes confused.'[27] The Frenchmen's response must have delighted Lawrence. Brémond replied, 'The firmness and strength of the present bonds between the Allies did not blind them to the knowledge that these alliances were only temporary and that between England and France, England and Russia lay such deep-rooted seeds of discord that no permanent friendship could be looked for.' If Faisal was telling the truth, his revelation to Lawrence that the French were already thinking in terms of post-war manoeuvres conceived to further their own national interests against those of their former ally would have confirmed what he had already surmised. For him, Wilson and Wingate, this candid admission justified the pursuit of secret stratagems against France in Syria.

This may have been just what Faisal wanted, for he claimed he told the French officers that 'treaties were made and unmade and not in the West only – but that between Great Britain and the Arabs were unwritten bonds of mutual understanding which had probably as strong an influence as the innate sympathy of a civilised man for the success of a small and oppressed people.' Britain, not France, would be the partner of his ambitions.

Lawrence would have endorsed all that Faisal said. Newcombe too, for he was thought by the French to have been of Lawrence's mind, even though he favoured a British occupation of Syria.[28] Wingate, Murray and Clayton concurred, at least in so far as they were prepared to do all that they could to exclude the French from active co-operation with Faisal's forces in Syria. What the French took as curmudgeonly British obstruction could be justified on strategic grounds. If Faisal was to make headway in Syria and harass the northern section of the Hejaz line and thereby assist Murray's operations to the west, he needed a port close to the front through which men and materials could be landed. Only Aqaba could satisfy his needs, although it lay within the *vilayet* (Turkish administrative district) of Syria and, therefore, in an area allocated by the Sykes–Picot agreements to France. If the French gained Aqaba they would never permit it to be used by the Arabs to foment a Syrian national movement, and so Arab assistance to Murray's forces would be severely limited.

Hussain had urged the capture of Aqaba in December and, on 31 January, Brémond heard that Newcombe and Faisal were discussing how it could be taken. With Aqaba as a springboard, Faisal would be free to canvass Syria on his own and the nationalist movement's behalf. To forestall this, Brémond visited Murray at Ismailia on 5 February and proposed a British landing at Aqaba and the establishment there of an aerodrome which would be guarded by French Muslim units then on standby at Port Suez.[29] He was politely rebuffed, but before leaving he warned Murray that if Britain would not co-operate he would seek Italian assistance. On his way back to Hejaz, Brémond ordered the captain of his ship to heave to off Aqaba so that he could estimate its garrison and assess the strength of its defences. He saw no one. At the end of June the Italian Military Mission to Hejaz on board the cruiser *Calabria* also spied out Aqaba.[30]

Aqaba had interested British strategists since the beginning of the war, when naval landing parties had temporarily occupied the port. Less than a hundred miles from the Hejaz railway, it was the obvious base for sabotage operations and even a permanent occupation of the line. For this reason Sir Edward Grey, the Foreign Secretary, recommended the seizure of Aqaba in June 1916 in order to isolate Medina, but Mcmahon ruled out such an operation on the ground that the Egyptian Expeditionary Force could not spare the men. The same kite was flown by Murray a month later, and he was warned off by Robertson, who dreaded another sideshow which would eat up reserves and possibly become another Gallipoli.[31] Still, Murray authorised an aerial survey of Aqaba and its hinterland during August which revealed that the port was thinly defended and that Wadi et Yutm to the east offered good sites for landing strips.[32]

Brémond's proposition had put Murray in a quandary. Shortly before the Frenchman presented himself at HQ, Murray had turned down Wingate's request for an Aqaba expedition because it would deprive him of a brigade needed for the forthcoming Gaza offensive.[33] Now he was faced with the likelihood that a Franco-Italian force would occupy the port, which they would then deny to the Arabs. This would have suited Brémond, who openly hoped that the Arab Revolt would stagnate in Hejaz. Matters were further complicated in April when Naval Intelligence got word that a unit of German mine-laying specialists were operating out of Aqaba. On 19 April Wemyss despatched three warships to the port which sent ashore landing parties. Three-quarters of the eighty-man garrison ran off, leaving the sailors free to demolish the mine-laying facilities.[34]

It was imperative to pre-empt the French, so early in April Faisal, with Wingate's backing, agreed to seize the port as part of his projected armed excursion into eastern Syria. Faisal and Newcombe were the principal architects of a plan which was finally settled on 20 May.[35] Newcombe was to take charge of 1,500 Arabs who would be mustered at al Wajh on 24 June and then transported to Aqaba by RN warships. Their disembarkation on 15 July would coincide with a landward assault on the port by Huweitat irregulars, who had already eliminated the chain of Turkish posts between Aqaba and Maan. Faisal, leading a larger force, would already have ridden cross-country to al Jawf in the Syrian desert, which he was scheduled to reach by 7 July. From there he would turn northwards to el Azraq where Lawrence and Awda would be waiting with supplies which would include the 3,000 camels promised by the Anazah at the beginning of April.[36] Then Faisal would proceed towards the Hawran and fulfil his promise to raise the Druze.

The success of the plan rested on the unproven ability of Arab forces to synchronise their movements and on a belief that Turkish forces in eastern Syria would be thrown into confusion by the attack on Aqaba and by the presence in the desert of large Arab contingents. Furthermore, it was intended that the sudden appearance of Faisal's Beduin would trigger local uprisings which the Turks would be too thinly spread to handle. There was no way of calculating the Turco-German response to this audacious stratagem. They were not totally unprepared. A report from

Damascus sent by agent 'Maurice' which reached Cairo on 27 May noted a recent increase in the hand-outs of gold among the Anazah and Rwallah. Nuri Shalaan's son Nawaf was reportedly pro-Turkish and it was feared he might sway his father in that direction.[37] A Turkish agent, probably close to Faisal and possibly the same man who had given the warning of the attack on al Wajh, reported the departure of Lawrence's column on 9 May with an indication of its destination.[38] Ten days later military posts between Maan and Aqaba were being reinforced.

Lawrence knew that the French were considering a coup against Aqaba and that Faisal intended to seize the port as part of his proposed armed demonstration in eastern Syria. The outlines for these operations had been first laid by Clayton in November 1916 shortly before Lawrence's return from Khartoum.[39] Both men appreciated that possession of Aqaba was vital, although Lawrence had deep apprehensions about Faisal's Syrian diversion. In the *Seven Pillars* he recalled fears that precipitate action by Faisal and the Syrians could easily end in a disaster which would cripple all future attempts to liberate the area. Lawrence favoured a piecemeal campaign in which the occupation of Aqaba would be the opening move.

He was attached to the party of thirty-six men which left al Wajh as the representative of the British government, whose prestigious endorsement was needed to give Faisal the authority he needed to convert the Syrian sheiks. As a token of British backing for the Prince, Lawrence carried 20,000 gold sovereigns, of which half were earmarked for Druze leaders, or so Adjutant Lamotte heard. Before the group set off, Lamotte took their photograph and was told that they would be back in five weeks, which was not so.

Lawrence's party was commanded by the Sharif Nasir, a kinsman of Faisal whom Lawrence found 'most capable, hard working and straight-forward'. Less to his liking was Nasib al Bakri, Faisal's Interior Minister, who had been entrusted with negotiations. He 'is volatile and short-sighted, as are most town-Syrians' and Lawrence suspected he would not carry out his orders.

Lawrence left two accounts of what passed. The first comprised a bundle of secret official reports written in Cairo during the second week of July 1917 (some of which were published in 1938), and the second was set down in the *Seven Pillars*.[40] According to his reports, the first phase of the expedition was an eastwards trek towards an Kabk which was interrupted by the demolition of the section of railway track at Kilo 810. The party of thirty-six reached an Kabk and the point of rendezvous with Awda and his Huweitat warriors on 2 June. For the next fortnight Nasir and Nasib camped there and at nearby Kaf, where they used Lawrence's sovereigns to recruit Huweitat, Shararat and Rwallah tribesmen for the attack on Aqaba.

According to the reports he wrote in Cairo, the second phase of the expedition began on 4 June, when Lawrence and two servants rode north-east into the Syrian desert on the first leg of a circular tour through Turkish-held Syria. On 8 June the trio approached Tadmor and then turned east-wards towards Baalbek Yarmud in eastern Lebanon. Returning southwards, Lawrence passed near Damascus, entered the Jebel Druze and then con-tinued through el Azraq to an Kabk. The journey lasted fourteen days.

At each stage of the expedition, Lawrence met local notables. Near Tadmor he had planned to arbitrate a feud between the Bishr and the Huweitat, but one party failed to appear. A small railway bridge was blown up in the Baalbek Yarmud region to please local tribesmen. 'The noise of dynamite explosions we find everywhere the most effective propagandist measure possible.' Outside Damascus he spoke with Aziz al Ridha al Rikabi, a former Turkish general and Mayor of the city, a future Hashemite adher-ent as yet unwilling to risk an open statement of his loyalties. Passing through the Laja district Lawrence met a local sheik, and at Salkhad he had discus-sions with the Druze Sultan Salim al Atrash, another secret Hashemite sympathiser who delivered the terms on which his followers would rise. The Druze would not rebel until British forces occupied Nablus in northern Palestine, a line they consistently followed until October 1918. They were a hard-hearted people disinclined to throw away their considerable privi-leges, including exemption from conscription and taxation. At el Azraq Lawrence faced more trimming, this time from practised hands: Nuri Shalaan and his son Nawaf repeated their old plea that they would take the plunge the moment the Druze declared themselves for Faisal. They were 'playing a double', but Lawrence felt assured they would join the Allies when 'we require them'.

None of this could have given much comfort to Faisal. It was intelligence of limited value, which merely affirmed what Lawrence and his superiors already knew. Hedged promises of future support were common currency in wartime Syria. The month before, agent 'Maurice' had acquired some which added to the reassuring impression that there was a groundswell of pro-British and pro-Faisal sentiment in Syria. There was always a draw-back: direct action against the Turks would only follow the victorious advance of Allied armies. As Lawrence had discovered, inter-communal jealousies were still strong and any stepping out of line by townsfolk and villagers invited chastisement of the kind which was still being meted out to the Armenians. Lawrence fully appreciated this and always emphasised that sabotage operations had to be confined to Beduin, whose desert home-land offered a degree of immunity to Turkish retaliation not available to sedentary communities.

Lawrence did not expect much open resistance from the settled regions he had visited. In his programme for future guerrilla operations, submitted to the War Office on 16 July, he concentrated on activities centred on the desert bases of el Azraq and el Jefre which would be directed against the Damascus–Maan section of railroad. He also proposed the use of these bases for long-range raids against the Dera–Haifa line which would be aimed against the bridges in the Yarmuk Valley. Further north he suggested attacks on the line below Aleppo by Beduin based in the Jebel Shomariye. Unremitting pressure on these lines would hamper Turkish troop movements and might even encourage local resistance once it was clear that the Turks could not long shift men for punitive actions. Even the Hawran Druze might be nudged towards a descent on Dera. Again everything hinged on the Druze.

There is nothing of all this in the *Seven Pillars* beyond a reference to Lawrence's unquiet state of mind on the eve of his journey: 'A rash adventure suited my mood' which, to judge from an all but erased note in his campaign jottings, was almost suicidal.[41]

> Clayton. I've decided to go off alone to Damascus, hoping to get killed on the way: for all our sakes try and clear up this show before it goes further. We are calling them to fight for us on a lie.

This is all very perplexing. Soon after, in the *Seven Pillars* version, Lawrence admitted to the haziest knowledge of what McMahon had offered Hussain and how the boundaries of French and British concessions in the Middle East had been drawn by Sykes and Picot. In the *Seven Pillars* he also confessed to bewildered shame when Nuri Shalaan proffered 'a file of British documents' allegedly filled with official promises, and asked which one he ought to believe. Lawrence remained silent about their contents and who had drawn them up. What is more bewildering is that, in his report to Clayton, Lawrence claimed he met Nuri and his son at el Azraq towards the end of the Syrian trip. Maybe then he briefly succumbed to a mood of despair. It would have been understandable, not in terms of what others had or had not promised the Arabs, but because all his Syrian contacts, including Nuri, had responded to his calls for bold commitment with wary procrastination.

Lawrence was taking enormous risks by penetrating enemy territory where pro-Turkish sympathies were still widespread. There was, he claimed, a £5,000 reward for his capture, which, if true, suggests that Turkish intelligence was aware of his activities. In fact, the head money was a general reward first announced some months earlier by Fakhri Pasha for British officers taken dead or alive.[42]

Whether he travelled in search of intelligence or whether to get killed,

Lawrence's exploit won him great respect in Cairo and London. What Robertson called his 'adventurous and successful journey', together with the Aqaba coup, established Lawrence's reputation as an able, daring and gallant officer.[43] Fifty years later this was challenged by al Nasib, who was adamant that Lawrence remained at an Kabk and Kaf during the fortnight of his passage through Syria. Moreover al Rikabi denied ever having met Lawrence during 1917: the entire episode was a figment of his imagination, a fantasy akin to those he had concocted during his pre-war Syrian excursions.[44]

In 1917 Lawrence had not lost his taste for tale-telling. Soon after he returned to Cairo, St Quentin sent a report to Paris which included stories of how, before the war, Lawrence had ridden about Syria on horseback or motorbike disguised as a Beduin (a bizarre fancy), had spied on the Hejaz railway with Woolley, had been arrested and spent three weeks locked up in Urfa before he escaped.[45] These were all falsehoods and must have come directly from Lawrence or else from what he had told others. A wide gulf separates such petty perjuries from the submission of a bogus report which deceived close friends like Clayton as well as general officers in Cairo and London and whose conclusions were later embodied in General Staff plans. However much Lawrence disliked the army as an institution, he was a loyal soldier and not untouched by the gentlemanly codes of honour which bound officers together. These embraced many of the chivalric virtues he admired.

To turn to Lawrence's accusers, whose evidence has been accepted by two biographers, Moussa and Stewart: although al Rikabi entered Faisal's service after the war, he and his family may have felt uneasy about the admission of treason against his former Ottoman masters and colleagues. Moreover, in the post-Suez era in the Middle East, few Arabs would have been willing to admit conspiracy with a British officer who was now widely regarded as a cunning agent of imperialism. Nasib in particular had every reason to mistrust Lawrence and blackguard him. At an Kabk Lawrence made very clear his scepticism about Faisal's intended Syrian coup, which, with good reason, he feared would misfire and jeopardise all future operations. In the *Seven Pillars* he accused Nasib of treachery because he had considered putting himself rather than Faisal at the head of the Syrian revolt. Nasib remembered their rows. 'Lawrence', he recalled in the 1960s, 'was inclined to double-dealing, slander and dissemination of discord.' One bone of contention was al Atrash and the Druze, to whom Nasib secretly delivered £7,000 of Lawrence's hoard, which he felt would be better spent on the proven Awda and his Huweitat.

Other British agents were busy in Syria while Lawrence was abroad, although he had no contact with them. A synopsis of their recent findings was passed from the Directorate of Military Intelligence in London to Cairo on 14 July.[46] There was news of tribal unrest near Baalbek Yarmud, where Lawrence had blown up a bridge, of extensive troop movements through Dera towards Damascus and rumours of 20,000 reinforcements, including Austrians, who were shortly due in Syria. There were also the commonplace reports of quarrels between Turkish and German officers which always heartened the British. Strangely for such an assiduous gatherer of intelligence, Lawrence's report includes no mention of this kind of information. Given the hazards he was facing, he made very limited use of his trek through enemy territory.

The French were given no details of Lawrence's incursion into what was to be their post-war sphere of influence, although an account of operations near Maan and the taking of Aqaba was later passed to Brémond and St Quentin. They were able through their own agents and sources to follow his party's activities, but got no indication of their whereabouts between 8 and 29 June when they heard reports of him in the desert east of Maan.[47] Lawrence's version of what he did between 4 and 18 June ultimately hangs on his word against those of two eyewitnesses, one of whom disliked him. For Lawrence to have created a completely untrue report based on a fictional mission would have been an act of supreme folly. If his deception had been uncovered, and given the presence of a network of agents already in Syria this was a possibility, he would have been discredited and removed from any position from which he could fulfil his dream of helping the Arabs to nationhood. Yet the question must also be asked whether his post-war addiction to masochistic guilt derived solely from his sense of having misled the Arabs. Here Professor Falls provides a small clue. As co-author of the official history of the Middle East campaign, he was in one of the best positions to appreciate what happened there. Falls admired Lawrence's 'genius' but warned that his version of events needed to 'be treated with caution, since he occasionally exaggerated without shame or scruple'.[48]

No shades of ambiguity cloud Lawrence's exploits during the final phase of his mission. Between 20 June and 7 July he was present with Arab irregular forces who undertook a brief and highly successful campaign which ended with the capture of Aqaba. Wingate was delighted. He had cherished Aqaba as a base for Faisal for six months and after reading Lawrence's report he cabled the War Office. Captain Lawrence had passed through enemy lines, moved among a 'highly venal population' with a price on his head, which 'considerably enhances the gallantry of his exploit', and had taken an enemy port. 'I strongly recommend him for an immediate award of the Victoria Cross, and submit that this recommendation is amply justified by his skill, pluck and endurance.' It was, but the regulations governing the award dictated that brave deeds must be witnessed by another British officer. Furthermore, though this was and is less well known, the medal could be awarded only if the recipient had a 90 per cent chance of losing his life. Instead Lawrence received a Companionship of the Bath. What mattered most to him was that he had shown what the Arab irregulars could achieve on their own and fighting in their own way. His faith in them had been tested and proved; they were a force to be reckoned with.

The account of the small campaign which Lawrence compiled for GHQ Cairo was a vindication of the type of guerrilla warfare which he and Clayton believed the Arabs were best suited to perform. Just over 700 irregulars had been enrolled, of whom 200 were detailed to guard the base camp in the Wadi Sirhan, and others joined up during the campaign. Against them were five battalions of Turkish infantry at Maan and a cavalry force of 400 at Dera. Turkish intelligence at Maan was not very efficient, but evidence that wells had been destroyed suggests that the local commander was aware of the presence of hostile Arabs north-east of the town.

The campaign opened on 23 June with a series of reconnaissance sorties and small-scale demolitions along the line north of Maan. Lawrence also claimed, and this was later denied by Arab sources, that he had led an expedition to examine the bridges on the Yarmuk Valley section of the Haifa–Dera line, which he later specified as targets for sabotage in his report to the War Office. The second stage of the campaign followed a successful attack by a small force on a gendarmerie outpost at el Fuweila, seventeen miles south-west of Maan. Given that the authorities in Maan were already alerted to the possibilities of an advance against Aqaba and had reinforced units between there and Maan, the response was quick and designed to be overwhelming.

A column of the 178th Regiment, lately drafted to Maan and numbering about 550 men, moved towards el Fuweila, and accordingly the Arabs withdrew. With probably just less than that number, the Arabs pulled back to a defensive position on high ground overlooking Bir el Lasan on 2 July. Their opponents foolishly refused to contest the high ground and camped on the valley floor close to some springs. The well-chosen reverse-slope position gave the Arabs safety from artillery fire. Just after sunset Awda charged the camp with fifty camelry while the rest of the army rode down the hillside firing from the saddle. Lawrence, astride a racing camel, was in at the kill, firing his revolver. One shot hit the camel, which fell dead and he was catapulted through the air. Dazed and unable to do anything but repeat to himself some half-remembered verses, he was found later. He was told that in the mêlée the Turks' nerve had broken and that 160 had surrendered. A further 300 were dead, many killed by Arabs enraged by the killing of some Huweitat women and children near el Fuweila a few days before.

The advance to Aqaba was now under way. At el Quweira the garrison of 120 surrendered on 4 June, while further down the Wadi el Yutm the 300 or so men of the reinforced Aqaba garrison had retreated inland. They had heard the news of the fighting to the north and clearly feared that it was the prelude to another seaborne attack. In their efforts to keep out of the range of possible naval gunfire the garrison found themselves surrounded by local tribesmen encouraged by reports of Turkish defeats. The men who had scurried off eight weeks ago when British warships had come over the horizon had little stomach for a fight. After Lawrence and Nasir had assured them that their lives would be spared, they surrendered. On the morning of 6 July Lawrence, Awda and Nasir led their small army into the abandoned port, where they discovered a German engineer NCO who had been boring wells.

Immediate measures had to be taken to forestall a counter-attack by the five battalions in Maan. The Arabs and their 600 prisoners had few rations beyond dates. Straightaway Lawrence set off across Sinai to Port Suez with an escort of eight men, and on the 9th he reached el Shatt, having covered 150 miles. Four days later HMS *Dufferin* anchored off Aqaba, unloaded food and picked up the Turkish prisoners. In Jiddah, Hussain ordered all public buildings to be illuminated in honour of a great Arab victory.

When he returned to Cairo in July 1917, Lawrence said he had taken Aqaba at 'Sharif Faisal's instructions'. In fact he had jumped the gun, since Faisal had intended to take the town nine days later as part of a combined land and sea operation. After the engagement at Bir el Lasan he had had little choice but to fall back on Aqaba, take it and get help from Egypt. A return to bases in the eastern Syrian desert would have been risky since the Turks, now fully alert to the presence of his small army, could easily have intercepted it with overwhelming forces. Even so, it seems likely that Wingate and Clayton were not taken by complete surprise when they heard that Lawrence had captured Aqaba. 'With few close exceptions', Lawrence's superiors had not known the plans he intended to carry out when he had left al Wajh on 9 May. This much Lawrence was prepared to tell St Quentin when they discussed the operation a few weeks later.[49] Arab possession of Aqaba suited their and Lawrence's plans for the future of the Arab movement.

Four

THE ROAD TO DAMASCUS

July 1917–October 1918

I

THE RAILWAY WAR

THE Aqaba coup made Lawrence the man of the moment in Cairo. He was 'the most remarkable figure in the army and British government in the East', noted St Quentin. 'His reputation has become overpowering,' Hogarth told his wife.[1] His resourcefulness, daring and bravery won him the sincere respect of those senior army officers he had once affected to mock, and he now had the supreme pleasure of having been proved right about the despised Arabs. What Lawrence had done at Aqaba and what he would do again in a series of raids and missions behind enemy lines had a *Boy's Own Paper* and 'deeds which won the Empire' quality which appealed to young and old officers alike. Hubert Young thought Lawrence afflicted with the same splendid madness as Wolfe of Quebec.[2]

Wingate was full of Lawrence's praises. 'His magnificent achievement', he told Wilson, was 'in my opinion one of the finest done during the whole war'.[3] The High Commissioner's career stretched back to the Sudan campaigns of the 1880s and to a more romantic kind of war. In his youth, lion-hearted British officers had, by the example of their courage and the force of their personality, commanded wild tribal forces on the empire's battlefields. How different from the present war in which men hid themselves underground in an unequal struggle against machines, chemicals and explosives. Lawrence's Arabs, as they were soon to be called, seemed to have strayed from the lost world of Rattray's Sikhs or Gordon's 'Ever Victorious' Chinese army.

What really mattered for Lawrence, and for the future of the Arab cause, was that after Aqaba his stature as a fighting soldier was unequalled. Everyone had known him as a very clever and often peevish intelligence officer; now he was a byword for courage, the most prized martial virtue. From now on generals would respect him as a man who had proved himself on their terms and would take seriously what he had to say. This was true of General Sir Edmund Allenby, the new Commander-in-Chief of the Egyptian Expeditionary Force, who had superseded Murray on 27 June. After meeting Lawrence and reading his reports, Allenby told Wingate, 'He strikes me as being a very fine soldier and I think our military operations could not be in better hands.'[4] Until the end of the war Allenby clung to this opinion, although Lawrence's behaviour at Damascus and what he wrote in the *Seven Pillars* shook the General's certainty. Once, after the war, when General Sir George Barrow called to see him, Allenby remarked, 'Lawrence goes for you in the book, George.' Barrow answered that he thought it best to take no notice of the matter. Allenby agreed, 'No, that would be a mug's game. Besides we know Lawrence. He thinks himself a hell of a soldier and loves posturing in the limelight.'[5] Still this show-off was able, and in July 1917 Allenby saw ways in which his energies and ideas could be used.

Lawrence offered Allenby not only Aqaba but a coherent programme which laid out ways in which Faisal's Northern Army could help him towards his goal, the conquest of Palestine and Syria. A more flexible and imaginative general than Murray, he inherited his predecessor's preparations for a crushing offensive which, if it succeeded, might force the Turks to sue for peace. On 8 October 1917 he received formal Cabinet approval for an advance as far as a line between Jaffa and Jerusalem, whose capture would be a boost to Allied morale. By July he was making plans for this strategic eventuality and was receptive to what Lawrence proposed.[6]

In brief, Lawrence envisaged an Arab campaign which would distract Turkish forces on Allenby's eastern flank and play havoc with Turkish railway communications in eastern and central Syria. The key to these operations was Aqaba, which would serve as the main Arab base and a conduit through which arms and money would flow to the Beduin of the eastern Syrian desert. These tribes, operating from the hilly regions east and north-east of the Dead Sea and from bases deep in the desert, would demolish sections of track between Dera and Maan. With the railway continuously fractured, Maan and Medina would become dangerously isolated outposts. Subsidiary raids would be undertaken against three other lines, between Aleppo and Baalbek Yarmud, between Damascus and Dera, and along the Yarmuk Valley section of the Haifa-to-Dera branch line. This line, which carried traffic for Jerusalem as well as Haifa, was of special concern to Allenby, who had already ordered it to be surveyed from the air.[7] If it could be severed, Turco-German units opposing him in southern Palestine would be denied reinforcements, supplies and a line of retreat. Once Turkish communications were in disarray, Lawrence predicted that 8,000 Arabs and Druze would attack Dera. The campaign could open at the beginning of September when the harvest had been gathered. Lawrence believed a later start during the October rains would be less productive as the Beduin would be migrating eastwards for camel grazing.

Allenby grasped the significance of Lawrence's stratagem and approved it on 16 July. So too did Wingate and Robertson. 'The advantages offered by Arab co-operation on [the] lines proposed by Captain Lawrence are, in my opinion, of such importance that no effort should be spared to reap [the] full benefit,' Allenby wrote, adding that this plan 'may cause the collapse of Turkish campaigns in the Hejaz and in Syria'.[8] It was essential, Allenby insisted, that Lawrence be placed directly under his command. Accordingly, on 9 August, he was formally appointed 'to serve with Beduin troops and advise and, as far as possible, direct operations'.[9]

Lawrence wisely appreciated that, alone, his irregulars could not hold Aqaba. On 27 July there were rumours that the port might be attacked from Maan, and the *Humber* was immediately assigned as the harbour guardship and remained there until January 1918, when she was replaced by another monitor, the *M31*. More than one man-of-war was needed to protect the port and its expanding camps and depots. By the time he laid his plans before Allenby, Lawrence had slightly shifted his position on British participation in an Arab 'show'. Aqaba's security rested on strong forces holding el Quweira and Bir el Lasan at the head of the Wadi el Yutm. Arab operations against the railway needed the backing of mobile regular units and aircraft which would inspire confidence and provide additional firepower. Lawrence requested and got from Allenby X Flight of 144 Squadron, a squadron of Rolls-Royce armoured cars and a motorised Royal Field Artillery battery, as well as such specialists as supply officers, signallers, armourers, medical staff and weapons instructors.

These units arrived slowly during the summer and autumn of 1917 and proved vital. Lawrence was never entirely happy about this dependence on external help and he argued against overloading the Arabs with too much assistance, however much it was needed. He feared that too great a foreign presence would make them anxious and that there would be friction. Always, he upheld the lie that he and the rest of the British, French, Egyptian and Indian personnel who were eventually posted to Aqaba were in some way of secondary importance in what was an Arab campaign. Events revealed it to be otherwise. During the next fifteen months these detachments bore much of the brunt of the heavy fighting and, unlike the Arab irregulars, never proved unreliable.

In terms of strategic theory, Lawrence's proposals offered much of value to Allenby. The strength of Faisal's Northern Army, with its expanding regular units, was now added to the Egyptian Expeditionary Force and, so long as Faisal heeded Lawrence's advice, was under Allenby's control. More importantly, Lawrence's forecast that the irregulars could play a decisive role in forthcoming operations in Syria was unquestioningly accepted by Allenby and Robertson. Staff assessments of the course of the campaign took for granted the fact that the advancing British forces would be welcomed by Syrians keen to lend a hand.[10] If the Arabs could tear apart the Syrian rail network, Robertson believed that the subsequent logistical chaos would render it impossible for the Turks to maintain 100,000 men south of Damascus. With their communications in disarray, they would be forced to pull back.[11]

As always, Robertson was worried about manpower. Lawrence's programme offered him some comfort, since it predicted that during the autumn campaign 14,000 Turkish troops holding Dera, Maan and the intervening line would be kept away from the Palestine front by the irregulars' attacks on the railway. These raids would also effectively leave stranded a further 17,000–20,000 Turkish troops occupying positions between Tabuk and Medina.[12] Looking ahead to the winter, Robertson knew that he would have to deplete forces in the Middle East to reinforce the line in northern France, where a formidable German offensive was expected in the spring. With Allied forces reduced, the more Arabs, regular and irregular, in the field the better. Lawrence's suggestions for the deployment of the Arabs had come at the right time, and because they satisfied both general strategic and specific tactical needs were accordingly welcome. With his promises accepted at face value, it remained for Lawrence to deliver the goods.

Once his plans had been rubber-stamped in Cairo and London, he turned all his energies towards their implementation. They were neither new nor original. He had listened in October 1916 to al Mizri's schemes for the mobilisation of the Syrian Druze and Beduin; the suggestion that armoured cars could be employed effectively in the desert came from Parker (they had already proved their worth in Libya), and Murray had first mooted the idea of using aircraft in co-operation with Arab irregulars. All this was by the way; what mattered was Lawrence himself. The force of his passion for the Arabs and the cogency and persuasiveness of his arguments had swayed Allenby, who had wondered momentarily whether the little man in his office was a mountebank. What was most convincing was Lawrence's knowledge of the Arabs and his proven ability as their leader. Clayton knew this better than anyone and he played his part in changing the General's mind. Just before Lawrence returned to Aqaba, Clayton felt certain that 'his presence will probably do much to maintain the confidence of the Arabs', which had plummeted after his departure and the arrival of rumours that the Turks were about to retake the town.[13]

Lawrence then had to induce Faisal to move himself and the bulk of his forces from al Wajh to Aqaba. For the moment Faisal had dropped all plans for a sally into Syria, perhaps deterred by reports that the Druze and their neighbours were havering or because the hazards were too great. He was none too happy about proceeding to Aqaba, but was reassured when Lawrence told him that the port would be protected by a warship. In the end he was swayed by political ambition. He told Lawrence that he had corresponded with his father over the issue and that Hussain had confessed himself too old-fashioned to adopt the new ideas and attitudes which would be necessary for a ruler of Syria. Sensibly he admitted that 'the educated Syrian would never have accepted government from Mecca on *sharia* lines', and so it was up to Faisal to make his bid, having first reached an accommodation with the French and local political factions.[14] On 31 July, Lawrence and Faisal disembarked at Aqaba.

Lawrence immediately threw himself into honouring the pledges he had made to Allenby. He had voluntarily taken on himself tasks which demanded prodigious physical and emotional energies and strength. For the next fifteen months he was a diplomat charged with keeping Faisal's goodwill and convincing him that his and the Allies' interests were the same; a staff officer responsible for operational co-operation between British and Arab forces; and a field commander leading Arab units behind enemy lines. At the same time he continued to gather intelligence and manage a network of field agents.

The railway war was Lawrence's first concern during the summer and autumn of 1917. He had assured Allenby that the concerted efforts of Arab saboteurs would paralyse the Turkish army in Syria and therefore weaken its resistance to his offensive. So far there was little evidence that this kind of warfare, which had been waged for the past six months against the southern section of the Hejaz railway, had achieved much.

The Damascus-to-Medina pilgrim railway had been sturdily built by German engineers; it had a 1.05 metre gauge and was served by between 30 and 50 wood-burning engines, 180 passenger carriages, 240 covered and 600 open wagons and 40 water tankers. Its major stations at Dera, Amman, Maan, Tabuk, el Ula and Medina were entrenched and garrisoned and its length was guarded by blockhouses and small fortified posts, many overlooking vulnerable bridges and culverts.

There was never any question of seeking a full-scale engagement with the concentrations of Turkish troops. Lawrence, defending his principles of guerrilla war in the *Seven Pillars*, justified avoidance of pitched battles on the ground that the overriding purpose of the attacks was to wear down the enemy without suffering losses. This was making a strategic virtue out of a tactical necessity. Whenever the Turks, even in small numbers, fought back, the Arabs flinched, despite the advantage of numbers. British and French officers serving with raiding parties were dismayed by frequent displays of Arab cowardice and panic. On 14 April 1917, during an attack on the line between Muadham and Sana, 1,000 tribesmen backed by artillery had run off rather than engage a blockhouse manned by 100 Turks. During the confusion Garland found numbers of Agayl tribesmen skulking in a ravine. After several experiences of this kind, Newcombe reported in May that he would prefer operations with just Hornby and their servants rather 'than with a gang of men who will abandon us'. A month later, Adjudant Lamotte and his British colleagues were left in the lurch by Beduin and Egyptians once it was clear that the Turks were ready for them.[15] It was one of the greatest marks of Lawrence's courage that he led such men from the front.

Even if raids went to plan, their effect was limited. Lawrence and the staff-planners in Cairo and London assumed that, like European armies, the Turkish army was heavily reliant on railway transport. This was not strictly true. Until early 1918 there were two gaps in the main line from Constantinople to Aleppo so that men and supplies had to be ferried by German-supplied motor lorries. This inconvenience may not have troubled the Turks, who were accustomed to waging war far from railheads, making use of animal transport and local supplies. They had done so during the 1911–12 Yemen campaign and again in 1914–16 in Sinai and Iraq. Contrary to Lawrence's prediction that its garrison would be slowly starved into surrender, Medina held out until February 1919 thanks to victuals provided by Ibn Rashid and, according to Garland, a few venal tribesmen in Abdullah's army.[16] Garland, whose experience in this area was at least equal to Lawrence's, concluded that the railway campaign in the south had not achieved its goal.

> I do not think the raids inconvenienced them until their communications were finally severed between Maan and [Qalat al] Mudawarrah in April 1916, by Imperial armoured cars and camel corps who destroyed 60 miles of line which were never repaired.

The date is a mistake; only on 10 August 1918, when Qalat el Mudawarrah station was put out of action, did Fakhri Pasha concede that his rail link with Damascus was finally broken. He instructed the local army authorities to cancel any further purchases for his garrison.[17]

Seen from the other side of the firing line, the railway war was a nuisance. Von Sandars believed the line was militarily valueless, but Enver insisted that it be held along with Medina for political reasons. For von Sandars, the intermittent fracturing of the Hejaz line was just one of many factors which contributed to the slow but steady corrosion of the Fourth Army's logistics. Others included administrative lassitude, corruption (coal supplies were hijacked and then sold to private contractors) and wider brigandage by bandits and deserters who were so numerous in southern Turkey that German troops had to guard trains and convoys.[18]

Newcombe, after three months of railway raiding, concluded that it was not doing much harm.[19] The derailment of trains and destruction of track 'does no serious damage, as trains are now so few and no food is being sent', and disruptions merely delayed trains for half a day. Such hitches did not disconcert the Turks, for whom timetables meant nothing, as von Sandars was painfully discovering. Newcombe concluded that if Medina were to be isolated the line had to be occupied permanently, which was impossible since 'to sit on a railway and prevent trains passing requires regular troops'. The Turks had plenty of these, including railway battalions which dutifully went out under protection and repaired the damaged track or replaced the missing rails. Surveillance of the Hejaz line was spasmodic and so it is impossible to measure exactly the volume of traffic before or after the beginning of the railway war. On 28 April 1917 an aeroplane was successfully transported from Medina to Damascus; on 4 May a battalion was said to have been carried from Damascus to el Ula, but during July and early August the Saleh–Medina section of the line was closed. It had reopened by September when Lawrence intercepted a Damascus-bound train carrying refugees from Medina.

Lawrence had already served a brief apprenticeship as a railway saboteur during March and early April when he was undertaking liaison duties between Faisal and Abdullah. It was then, while tormented by boils and a victim of the dysentery epidemic which was gripping Abdullah's army, that he formulated his theories of guerrilla warfare. He translated theory into practice on the night of 29/30 March when he derailed a train, one of whose two engines was damaged by the shellfire of Egyptian gunners. The attack was not pressed home since tribal machine-gunners had deserted their posts because they were lonely, but their behaviour did not discountenance him, for he had never subscribed to the professionalism of his colleagues Newcombe and Garland. Shortly after, he undertook two further demolitions.

Free of sickness, he reported to Wilson that he found the work congenial. 'The results of the trip were to show me the rare value of the Dakhilallal. Their humour makes railway breaking a pleasure to them.' So it was for all Beduin whose lands bordered on the railway. For them it was a hateful innovation which stripped them of the incomes they had formerly enjoyed from pilgrims, and it was an instrument of tighter Ottoman control. A derailed train presented wonderful opportunities for plunder which Lawrence, even if he had wished to, could not prevent.

Always an enthusiast for gadgetry, he began to pick up the recondite skills of the demolition engineer, thanks in part to the tuition of Garland, whom he found an agreeable instructor. Over the next fifteen months he learned on the job and, in January 1919, published a brief paper on railway demolition in the *Royal Engineers' Journal*. It was crammed with practical details on gun cotton, gelatine, mines, electrical detonators and the wayward habits of fuses, as well as advice on the best places to lay charges. Lawrence's experience had also taught him that damage to or removal of track was a fruitless enterprise. 'Speaking as a rule,' he wrote, 'rail demolitions are wasteful and ineffective unless the enemy is short of metal or unless they are only made adjuncts to bridge-breaking.' This was an acknowledgement of the efficiency of Turkish repair gangs.

In September 1917 Lawrence began his systematic campaign against the northern sector of the Hejaz line in fulfilment of his obligation to Allenby. His first objective was a stretch of track north of Qalat el Mudawarrah station. Attached to him and under the command of Awda were 116 Beduin from various tribes whose squabbling and cussedness gave the expedition the flavour of an outing by an unruly class of schoolboys. Tribal antics, Lawrence reported, 'threw upon me a great deal of detailed work, for which I had no qualifications and throughout the expedition I had more preoccupation with questions of supply, transport, tribal pay, disputes, division of spoil, feuds, march order, and the like.'[20] The 'cranky, quarrelsome' Huweitat gave the most trouble and Lawrence had to settle fourteen tribal feuds, a dozen assaults, four camel thefts, a row over a marriage portion, one case of bewitchment and two of the evil eye. Also in the company were two specialists, Sergeant Yells, a Lewis-gun instructor, and Brooks, an Australian who managed the Stokes mortar. They spoke not a word of Arabic and were nicknamed Lewis and Stokes.

The company may at times have been irksome, but the scenery was magnificent. The party passed up the Wadi Yutm and headed eastwards towards the line, finding on the way that the Turks had soured a water hole with the corpses of camels. A crepuscular reconnaissance of Qalat el Mudawarrah station revealed a garrison of about 200, which ruled out a direct attack by Lawrence's small, disharmonious force. Instead Lawrence chose to place an electronically detonated mine under the double-arched bridge. Setting the device and hiding his traces took five hours. The following morning, 16 September, brought a bonus for the company: a northward-bound train was seen getting up steam in the station. At the same time Turkish patrols fanned out and, to draw them away from the mine, thirty Arabs were detached to engage them in an extended skirmish.

Lawrence mistakenly feared that the discovery of hostile Arabs near the station might make the local commander delay the train, but he took no notice of the nearby marauders and the train of twelve carriages, pulled by two engines, steamed out of Qalat el Mudawarrah on its journey north towards Maan. Lawrence pressed the detonator and blew up the bridge under the second engine. The Arabs, deployed on a ridge overlooking the line, opened fire and then rushed the wagons under cover of Lewis-gun and mortar fire. Resistance crumbled and they got down to the looting.

There were many prisoners [Lawrence reported] and women hanging on to me, I had to keep the peace among plunderers, and the Turks from the south opened fire on us at long range just as the train surrendered, since our covering fire on that side came in to share the booty.

There were seventy Turkish dead and ninety prisoners of whom sixty-eight reached Aqaba alive. Two German officers were among the captured, and five Egyptians who had been taken a month before during a raid further south. It had been a close-run thing and disaster had been averted only by the coolness of Yells and Brooks. Afterwards Lawrence wrote, 'I do not think the Arabs could possibly have carried the train before Turkish relief came, had they not been present.' Their fire accounted for half the enemy's casualties.

The *Seven Pillars* included a few adornments to the plain tale of Lawrence's official report, with a grim account of how the prisoners, including women and Austrian officers and NCOs, pleaded for their lives. Recognising him as a European, several clung to Lawrence – 'A Turk so broken down was a nasty spectacle: I kicked them off as well as I could with my bare feet, and finally broke free.' A row broke out between the prisoners and Lawrence's Agayl bodyguard, presumably over loot, and a shot was fired at an Arab which was the signal for a massacre from which only two or three Austrians were saved. Something of the same sort had occurred when a train had been derailed in February, which no doubt explains the terror of the passengers who sought Lawrence's protection. Arab pitilessness may also explain but not excuse Turkish cruelty to captured or wounded guerrillas. There was no mention of this incident in Lawrence's official report.

A second raid followed, this time against Kilo 475 south of Maan. On this expedition Lawrence was joined by Captain Pisani, a Corsican ex-ranker who 'looked like a brigand disguised, unconvincingly, as a French officer'. Brave and lusty, he spoke freely about his sexual adventures, which entertained his British colleagues but must have vexed Lawrence, who abhorred ribaldry.[21] Pisani's crudeness apart, he was peeved by the presence of French officers at Aqaba, even though they had been requested by Faisal. Pisani's courage impressed Lawrence, who recommended him for a Military Cross after he had seen him lead the Arabs in a charge against a derailed supply train.[22] During the fighting, a Turkish officer recognised Lawrence and Pisani as European officers and deliberately fired at them. One shot grazed Lawrence's hip. In the *Seven Pillars* he wrote ungallantly of his adversary's percipience: 'I laughed at his too-great energy, which thought, like a regular officer, to promote the war by the killing of an individual.'

The attack over, Lawrence returned to Aqaba to start preparations for the next and most vital phase of his programme, railway sabotage and mischief-making in Syria to coincide with Allenby's imminent offensive. First, he had to visit HQ to receive Allenby's orders and discuss his plans with Clayton and Hogarth. Time was now short; the offensive was due to begin on 27 October, so Lawrence left Aqaba for Ismailia on 11 October in one of the newly arrived aircraft of X Flight.

When he arrived on the 12th, later than expected thanks to engine trouble, he set to work on future arrangements for Arab forces at Aqaba. Affairs there had languished over the past eight weeks. Faisal was gloomy and, in Lawrence's absence, had unburdened his woes to Commander Snagge of the *Humber*. He was fearful that Aqaba would be retaken by the forces based on Maan and was disheartened by the attitude of the Syrian tribes, who refused to move until he did. Hussain and Abdullah had both urged him not to go to Aqaba and he now wished he had heeded their words. If he failed, he would have to kill himself.[23] So much for the man whom Lawrence would later call 'A Modern Saladin'.

Taking their cue from their leader, his soldiers were in poor heart. Aqaba was suffering a cholera epidemic and there was endless wrangling between Syrian and Iraqi regulars which exploded into violence when a Syrian tried to assassinate Jafar al Askari.[24] Colonel Joyce, doing his best to impose order on what he called a 'Harry Lauder' show (music-hall comparisons were commonly used by regular officers when seeking ways of describing the Arab armies), realised that it would take time to transform Jafar's men into 'a fighting unit of much military value'.[25] He and Lawrence knew Jafar's qualities, and their faith in him, if not his men, was vindicated on 27 October when 350 mounted infantry under his command were attacked near Petra. In an inconclusive engagement, they endured artillery fire and aerial bombardment and held off their attackers.

The first Turkish response to the seizure of Aqaba had been to bring three Pfalz bombers of the Ottoman Air Force to Maan from the Caucasus front and use them for intermittent raids against Arab encampments. These attacks continued throughout September and worried Joyce, not so much for the casualties they inflicted as for the harm they did to fragile Arab morale. At Lawrence's request, counter-attacks were launched against Maan by RFC machines based on Kuntilla. He took a keen interest in these air raids, showing the pilots specific targets.[26] The resolution of the Turkish pilots was not matched by that of the Maan commander, Muhammad Jamal Pasha, whose thrust towards Aqaba lacked sufficient momentum to get far. By early November and the onset of cold weather, warfare south and west of Maan came to a temporary halt, allowing the Arabs some respite.

Lawrence and Allenby's staff appreciated that the future security of Aqaba rested on the presence of the promised armoured cars, motorised artillery and flight of bombers, whose transfer had to be accelerated. Turning to the campaign against the Hejaz railway, Lawrence was optimistic. Clayton reported his views to Wingate:

> As regards Lawrence's proposals for future action, he has paved the way and gained the necessary experience by means of his recent train breaking raids and his plan now is to make a serious attack on [Qalat el] Mudawarrah with three forces – one to the north and one to the south to prevent the arrival of reinforcements, and the third to attack [Qalat el] Mudawarrah station and destroy it and its water supply which is essential to that section of railway.[27]

The timing of this operation lay with Allenby, who would need Lawrence for behind-the-lines sabotage in Syria. If, as Clayton guessed, this would take precedence, then the Qalat el Mudawarrah 'stunt' would have to be left to Joyce. Still, Lawrence was keen to be there to see it 'thoroughly and successfully done'. He predicted the swift fall of Medina once the station had been knocked out and he hoped that Hussain would accordingly increase Faisal's allowance to £100,000 monthly.

Lawrence's recent experiences had taught him that tip-and-run raids by Beduin achieved little, save filling Beduin saddlebags with loot. Larger, more substantial forces were needed to do damage which could not be repaired by the 1,500 railway troops the Turks were now deploying along the line. This had already been affirmed by Newcombe further south after a successful raid undertaken by Indian and Algerian regular troops.

II

A Covert Operation

Two behind-the-lines operations were planned to coincide with Allenby's offensive in Palestine. The first, undertaken at his own suggestion, was by Newcombe. On 30 October, he took twenty Arabs, got behind Turkish lines and briefly severed the Beersheba–Hebron road before being taken prisoner. The second operation was Lawrence's attempt to destroy a bridge on the Haifa–Dera railway at Tell el Shehab. While it was impossible to keep to an exact timetable in such hazardous operations,

Lawrence had been briefed to carry out the demolition on 5 November in order to cause the maximum damage to Turkish communications during a crucial stage in the campaign. According to GHQ plans, the attack on Beersheba would begin on 30 October and that on Gaza on 1–2 November and, once they had fallen, mounted forces would chase retreating Turkish units northwards and prevent them from regrouping. If Lawrence destroyed the bridge the line would be closed for at least fourteen days. Reinforcements would be delayed and fleeing troops thrown into greater confusion.

His tactical objective achieved, Lawrence was free to turn his attentions towards the second stage of his mission. This involved an attack by Druze and Anazah irregulars on Dera which would distract Turkish forces in the region and hamstring their communications with Damascus. Such a coup, and the knowledge that British forces were advancing northwards, might encourage a rash of uprisings across Palestine and southern Syria which would further hinder the Turks.

These plans were discussed by Lawrence, Clayton, Wingate and Allenby during a series of meetings on 16 and 17 October. The general arrangements having been made, it was up to Lawrence to devise his own operational plans and schedule. 'Lawrence's venture is a side show which of course must be undertaken entirely independently and timed by him,' Clayton told Joyce on 24 October.[1] The responsibility was intimidating, the hazards vast, and Lawrence, already overworked, feared he might not measure up. Clayton sensed his secret apprehensions:

> I am very anxious about Lawrence. He has taken on a really colossal job and I can see that it is well-nigh weighing him down. He has a lion's heart, but even so the strain must be very great. Well, he is doing a great work and as soon as may be we must pull him out and not risk him further – but the time is not yet, as he is wanted just now. The first real issue in this theatre of the war is at hand and much will depend on the doings of the next month. We shall then see the future and its possibilities more clearly.[2]

Lawrence was also looking forward: his vision extended beyond military victory to its political aftermath. For him his Syrian mission offered an unequal chance to carry out a spectacular *coup de main* which would wreck French plans for the province, give Faisal a kingdom and Britain a naval base. He opened his mind to his friend and colleague George Lloyd, who at his own request had been assigned to accompany Lawrence on this mission. Lloyd heard the details of Lawrence's secret plans at Aqaba while the final preparations for the expedition were being made.[3]

Once the Yarmuk Valley bridge had been demolished, Lawrence intended to return with his party to el Azraq, which would become the centre for pro-Faisal sedition in Syria and the Lebanon. First, the Syrian Abdul al Qadir and Sharif Hassan would foment uprisings in a region bounded by Saida, Acre, Nazareth and Hasbaiya. There would be simultaneous revolts by the Druze and Leja and further insurrections to the south between Karak and Amman and to the north in the Jebel Liban. Lawrence himself would ride northwards to Tadmor and contrive the seizure of Aleppo, which, once taken, would be the base for uprisings across northern Syria that would culminate in the capture of Alexandretta, the prize denied by the Cabinet and War Office in 1915.

If Lawrence failed to blow up the Yarmuk bridge, he would enter the al Leja district, mine the railway south of Dera and then return to el Azraq and carry out the plan he had outlined. The result of this astonishing sequence of popular insurrections was explained by Lawrence and noted by Lloyd:

> Sharif's [that is, Hussain's] flag flies along coast from Acre northwards: French protests? Our attitude? Faisal's attitude will be non negotiatory – 'What I have taken I keep' – L[awrence] not working for Allenby but for Sharif – Had no instruction except hamper communications –
>
> Neither Faisal or Sharif [Hussain] ever seen text of S[ykes]–P[icot] agreement and claim never had its contents put before them –
>
> Nothing in writing – anyway not parties to it – agreement at best between France and England for partition of a country in armed occupation of forces of sharif of Mecca –
>
> Alexandretta must be obtained for G[reat] B[ritain]. This can be done but can only be done by Sharif's goodwill –
>
> Who gave Alexandretta to the French?
>
> On what claims: no railways: no politics, not Syria –
>
> Do we partition Arab countries without consulting the Arabs?

Lawrence ended his justification by arguing that McMahon had pledged Hussain Arab territory as far as Alexandretta and this ought to supersede the earlier Sykes–Picot agreement.

This was tantamount to a private policy concocted by Lawrence to deprive his country's ally, France, of post-war territorial and political rewards that had been formally promised by the British government. On one level Lawrence was defying his government, on another he was following the principles of a strategy endorsed by his superiors, who wanted anti-Turkish uprisings to precede the British advance into Syria. Furthermore, although Lawrence takes the point for granted, the overall willingness of the Palestinians, Syrians and Lebanese to rebel would depend ultimately on how far the British advanced and the extent of Turco-German military collapse.

Clayton saw Lloyd's report of Lawrence's hidden programme of sharifian sedition and was 'much interested'. No attempt appears to have been made to reprimand Lawrence, who remained convinced that his intended master-stroke had the stamp of genius. On 28 October 1918 he boasted to Lord Robert Cecil, the Assistant Secretary of State at the Foreign Office, that Damascus could easily have been taken by the Arabs in November 1917, presumably as a result of the local uprisings he had planned.[4]

In purely military terms what he had in mind could have been an immeasurable assistance to Allenby, even though the insurgents in the settled districts of the Lebanon, Syria and Palestine would have been dangerously exposed to Turkish retribution. Moreover there was an influential anti-French lobby among senior officers and administrators in Cairo which would have privately applauded Lawrence's coup. Their mood was detected by William Yale, who reported to the State Department on 12 November that there was a 'general feeling, unsupported by any tangible evidence, that Great Britain would welcome any solution of the Syrian question which eliminated a French occupation or protectorate'.[5]

Clayton was certainly hostile towards post-war French claims to Syria. While he urged Sykes not to be perturbed by manifestations of 'Fashoda-ism' in Cairo, he added that he could not imagine how the French would actually achieve their political aspirations in Syria when the war ended.[6] When Lawrence had tackled him in September about the precise terms of the Sykes–Picot agreement, Clayton deflected him with an assurance that changed political and military circumstances meant that it was now a dead-letter and could be ignored. He did, however, warn Lawrence against 'any violent action, such as George Lloyd and those of his school had advocated'. The caution was unheeded, and instead Lawrence took heart from Clayton's suggestion that Britain need not fear 'an exhausted France whose veins have been bled white'.

French officers in Cairo, Hejaz and later Aqaba had long known about Lawrence's opposition to their country's post-war occupation of Syria. With the opening of the Aqaba front and the prospect of Arab forces undertaking operations in Syria, French suspicions turned to alarm. St Quentin believed Lawrence 'wholly loyal to his superiors' and therefore willing to accept Anglo-French co-operation in spite of his passionate adherence to what he conceived as the 'higher interests of the Arab race'. Even so, it was considered prudent to keep an eye on Lawrence, especially since his missions north of Maan were taking him into areas set aside for France. This need to supervise him became urgent when, at the end of September, French officers heard rumours of British plans to engineer anti-Turkish uprisings in Syria. On 13 October, St Quentin formally asked Allenby for Lawrence to be joined by a French officer. He was refused.[7]

In explanation, St Quentin was told, 'Lawrence must not be hampered while engaged on delicate and dangerous tasks which are purely tactical, which may be of great importance to the success of any operations, and which he alone can carry through.' Wingate was pleased and congratulated Allenby on his firmness, adding, 'I should like to say a great deal more about my views in regard of some of our Ally's methods, but I had better refrain.'[8] The War Office also approved Allenby's stance. The French drew their own conclusions and pressed ahead with plans to raise and train their own Syrian army, largely drawn from Armenian refugees.

Lawrence's dreams of a sequence of Arab coups were utterly unrealistic and doomed to failure. As a historian he knew that small groups of single-minded men could make revolutions in the face of mass inertia and indifference, but the odds against this happening in Syria were very long. Only when it was clear that Turkish power was on the verge of extinction would the Syrian nationalists show their hand, and this moment would come when a British army overran the province. This is what happened in October 1918. Furthermore, as many Syrians realised, there was no reason why they should risk their lives and property to replace a Turkish governor in Damascus with a prince from Mecca.

In political terms, Lawrence's scheme was wildly irresponsible. Even if attempted, let alone carried through, it might easily have created a rift between Britain and France and jeopardised the alliance when absolute solidarity was essential. It was easy at the end of 1917 to consider France a spent force, especially after the disastrous Nivelle offensive of the spring and its sequel, the army mutinies of April and May. This view of a crippled France which prevailed in some quarters in Cairo was deceptive. French assistance was still vital to meet and throw back the German offensive expected in the spring of 1918. Lawrence was dimly aware of this, recalling in September 1917 how he and his colleagues 'were told unofficially that the need of bolstering up French courage and determination in the war made it necessary to surrender to her part of our own birthright'.[9] For him this birthright encompassed the right to take over the Ottoman empire and dispose of its provinces as Britain wished.

Lawrence's manic enthusiasm for the Arab cause and his obsession about Syria had impaired his judgement to a point where nothing else mattered. He knew he was right and his overpowering sense of rectitude made him forget that he was the servant of the British government and obliged to implement its policies even when he believed them mistaken. A man in Lawrence's place had the right to persuade his superiors that they were wrong, which he did, but he went further. By planning a campaign of subversion in Syria, paid for by British gold and backed by his authority as a British officer, Lawrence was using his position to indulge his private passion and thwart the wishes of his government. His revelations to Lloyd revealed a man who obeyed orders only when they suited him and who was therefore temperamentally unfitted to act as an agent of his country.

Lawrence's mission to Yarmuk was foredoomed. It ran into unforeseen difficulties, not least of which was the presence in his party of a Turkish agent, Abdul al Qadir. Al Qadir had arrived at Aqaba with a small party of Syrian nationalist refugees on 5 September. Lawrence reported to HQ that he had escaped from house arrest at Bursa, south of Constantinople and, keen to promote Faisal's cause in Syria, had made his way to Aqaba. Al Qadir's family had been expelled from Algeria by the French sixty years before and were influential in Syrian political life. His nationalist credentials appeared beyond question; he had refused to participate in a Turco-German propaganda campaign and his uncle had been hanged in 1916 for treason. Lawrence was no doubt pleased with his forthright anti-French views. These were muted when al Qadir visited Jiddah on 6 October and told Brémond that he would co-operate with the French in Syria with promises to do all in his power to suppress anti-French propaganda there. He also boasted that there would be 40,000 Arabs at the gates of Damascus within a month, which probably amused Brémond, who had heard much talk of this kind over the past few months. Less diverting was al Qadir's insistence that he had the right to pillage Christian villages when fighting the Turks.[10]

Faisal and Lawrence were completely fooled by al Qadir. He was selected for Lawrence's party and was entrusted with winning support for Faisal among the Druze and in northern Palestine. Al Qadir was also expected to use his contacts in the villages of the Yarmuk Valley to assist the passage of Lawrence and the sabotage party. He played his part remarkably well, although Clayton was aware that Turkish intelligence had placed an agent inside Faisal's immediate circle. 'There seems little doubt', he wrote to Lloyd on 25 October, 'that Faisal has a traitor in his councils and one who is well informed, as the enemy seem to get excellent information on Arab plans.'[11] This must have been al Qadir, although von Sandars admitted that his intelligence staff had broken British wireless codes.[12]

Lawrence realised al Qadir's real purpose on the morning of 4 November when it was discovered that he had fled from el Azraq. He rode to Dera and alerted local commanders to the presence of Lawrence's party and its purpose. A month later French intelligence had word that he was back with the Turks.[13] In the *Seven Pillars* Lawrence recalled him as a quarrelsome companion and religious fanatic. George Lloyd's reaction to him was that of the Englishman: 'He is a soft Syrian. I never met a good one yet. How suitable the French and Syrian dispositions will be to one another. Both look futile on a horse and wear extravagant gaiters.' His instinct was right and it is surprising that al Qadir never aroused suspicions even though his brother, Muhammad Said, had been identified as a German agent by Lawrence's own section in January 1916.[14]

The party for the Yarmuk Valley raid comprised Lawrence; his servant boys Farraj and Dawd; Lloyd; Lloyd's batman, Trooper Thorne of the Warwickshire Yeomanry; and Captain Wood of the Royal Engineers, who was to undertake the demolition if Lawrence suffered a mishap. Ahead were a party of Indian sappers, all veterans of railway raids and equipped with two Vickers and two Lewis machine-guns. The operational base was to be el Azraq and en route the parties met up with Sharif Ali, the overall commander, al Qadir and various tribal forces.

Lawrence's section left Aqaba on 24 October, two days later than he had planned. Wood soon got lost on the journey up the Wadi Yutm and was discovered the following morning 'grousing and refusing to eat' after having been frightened by some Arabs. Some of Lloyd's Scotch bucked him up but he remained sulky for some time. Lawrence was in a sombre mood, oppressed by the responsibility placed on him and by the dangers ahead. Lloyd was a cheerful and attentive companion who did all in his power to raise Lawrence's spirits. 'I had a conspicuous success in making Lawrence eat a real European breakfast, tea, bully beef and biscuits,' he wrote in his diary. 'He is only too ready to behave like a Christian – gastronomically at all events – if he is taken in the right way.' The pair talked as they rode; Lawrence described his parents, undergraduate days and diggings at Karkamis and the two pledged themselves to make a post-war crossing of the Arabian Desert. 'We would defy Victorian sentiment and have a retinue of slaves and would take one camel to carry books only.'

Beyond Abu al Lasan they got lost. 'Lawrence who had professed to know the way was in reality completely ignorant of it,' Lloyd observed. After a supper of Maconochie (tinned meat and vegetables), which he relished, Lawrence set off in the dark to find the railway line. This would be easy, he assured his companions, so long as they kept the constellation Orion in front of them. An hour's fruitless march followed. By midnight and with the help of Lloyd's compass, the track was found and Lawrence ran off to find a kilometre post which would fix their position. Meanwhile Lloyd climbed a telegraph pole to cut the wires, fell off and passed the job to Thorne, who discovered that the cutters were blunt.

By now, Sharif Ali had joined the party. Lloyd described him as a 'young Meccan, very eager for adventure and a pleasant and good type of Arab'. He thought that as he rode ahead of the party he 'looked like some modern

Saladin out to meet the Crusaders'. More Arab horsemen appeared on the morning of the 28th and at a distance were mistaken for Turkish cavalry and fired on. Later in the day the expedition reached the Arab camp, which had been moved some way from el Jawf, now attracting the attentions of Turkish aircraft flying from Maan. Here Awda was waiting, full of gratitude for the new set of false teeth which Lawrence had procured for him in Cairo. Lawrence immediately got down to work selecting men for the mission, collecting intelligence and dealing with the usual rows about cash. This completed, he kindly but firmly suggested that Lloyd went back to Aqaba. 'He would like me best to go home to England for he felt that there was a risk that all his work would be mined politically in Whitehall and he thought I could save this.' If Lloyd chose not to support the Arabs in the House of Commons (Faisal, who had been an MP in the pre-war Ottoman parliament, had considered it bad form for Lloyd, a British MP, to blow up trains), he was welcome to join Lawrence further north or in Karak once the bridge had been destroyed. Lloyd returned to Aqaba, proud to have ridden a camel 300 miles in seven days.

On 31 October Lawrence, Wood, the Indians and Arabs set off for el Azraq, where they arrived on 4 November. The defection of al Qadir ruled out the use of his well-wishers at Wadi Khalid and Umm Keis. Lawrence chose to go for the Tell el Shehab bridge, which was reached by the 8th. As he was preparing to lay charges, the noise of a dropped rifle alerted a Turkish sentry, who called out the picket. After a short exchange of fire the party drew off.

Acutely aware that he had failed in his mission, a feeling which extended to the rest of his men, Lawrence looked for a small consolation prize. While Wood and the Indians returned to el Azraq, he and the sixty or so Arabs turned their attentions towards the main Hejaz line. On 11 November they derailed a train travelling from Dera to Amman which was carrying Jamal Pasha, the Governor of Syria and commander of the 4th Army corps, and his staff. Lawrence was wounded in the arm by metal splinters from the exploding boiler. He had also suffered five or six grazes from bullets and a broken toe. On 12 November he and his party were back at el Azraq.

III

DERA: DEGRADATION OR DECEPTION?

By 21 November 1917 Lawrence had returned to Aqaba. On that day he and Colonel Joyce went on a motor reconnaissance into the Wadi Yutm. They travelled in one of the cars of the 10th Motor Section of the Royal Field Artillery which had been unloaded from the transport Ozarola that had berthed at Aqaba the previous morning.[1] One of the unit's officers, Lieutenant Samuel Brodie, later recalled that, after coming ashore 'the previous evening', he went to HQ and met Joyce and Lawrence.[2] These minor incidents in a sideshow of the war have a strange significance for Lawrence since they occurred on 21–22 November. He would later insist that on the night of 21–22 November he had been taken prisoner in Dera where he had been manhandled, whipped and buggered by Turkish soldiers, at the bidding of one of their officers, before escaping.

Lawrence remained silent about this appalling incident for over eighteen months. His first admission of what had occurred was in a letter written on 28 June 1919 to his friend Colonel Walter Stirling, then Chief Political Officer attached to GHQ Cairo.[3] His purpose was the exposure of Abdul al Qadir's treachery at el Azraq and his later duplicity after Damascus had been liberated. Al Qadir's career of double-dealing had ended on 7 November 1918 when he was shot dead by Faisal's police, an incident which the French had tried to link with Lawrence even though he was in London.

Lawrence correctly described al Qadir as a Muslim fanatic who resented Faisal's dependence on Britain. After his flight from el Azraq on 4 November, he had ridden to Dera where, three days later, he revealed details of Lawrence's mission to the Turco-German authorities. Cavalry patrols immediately began to comb the countryside close to the Dera–Haifa line, and only good luck and a gap in the cordon enabled Lawrence and his party to get away. Then, on 20 November, Lawrence went intelligence-gathering in Dera.

> I went into Dera in disguise to spy out the defences, was caught, and identified by Hajim Bey, the governor, by virtue of Abdul al Qadir's description of me. (I learned all about his treachery from Hajim's

conversation, and from my guards.) Hajim was an ardent paederast and took a fancy to me. So he kept me under guard till night, and then tried to have me. I was unwilling, and prevailed with some difficulty. Hajim sent me to hospital, and I escaped before dawn, being not hurt as he thought. He was so ashamed of the muddle he had made that he hushed the whole thing up, and never reported my capture and escape.

Three significant points emerge from this narrative: Hajim knew that his captive was Major Lawrence (he had been promoted after Aqaba), a British intelligence officer, interrogated him about his mission and, after his escape, successfully hid his blunder from his Turkish and German colleagues. Lawrence too covered up the business, which was less understandable since, however frightful his treatment, he had discovered evidence of al Qadir's treachery at a time when his superior, Clayton, was anxious about a spy among Faisal's advisers. It was also odd that Lawrence, an officer with a high sense of professionalism, chose to say nothing about what other details he may have discovered during his interrogation.

Lawrence wrote two further, more elaborate accounts of his misadventures in the 1922 and 1926 versions of the *Seven Pillars* and referred to them in conversations with Robert Graves and Meinertzhagen and in letters to Mrs Bernard Shaw and E.M.Forster.[4] Each account contained important variations of detail. These, and the sheer implausibility of his narrative, have led three biographers to conclude that the entire affair was a creation of his imagination. Others have accepted unquestioningly what passed and interpreted it as a trauma which radically altered Lawrence's personality and view of the world.

There is no direct corroborative evidence to support Lawrence. The Turks certainly tortured British agents; the brave Sarah Aaronsohn managed to shoot herself rather than endure further torment and sexual abuse after her capture in October 1917. British officers, like Woolley and Newcombe, who were taken prisoner during undercover operations, fared much better. Newcombe was transferred to the excellent Pera Palace Hotel in Constantinople, where Townshend of Kut was being kept. By contrast many of the British and Indian other-ranks taken at Kut suffered wanton neglect and ill-usage. At Afium Qarahisar POW camp prisoners were bastinadoed (beaten on the soles of the feet) if they protested about the outrages of the Commandant, a naval officer and a homosexual sadist, who was removed early in 1917 and hanged as a war criminal by the Allies after the war.[5] Whatever Lawrence may have said to the contrary, the Ottoman government was not utterly insensitive to the brutality of its underlings, although remedial action tended to follow protests from German officers and diplomats, who also vainly tried to stop the Armenian massacres.

Turkish conscripts were commonly disciplined by the bastinado, the customary torture which Lawrence was spared.[6] If, as he claimed, he had been recognised as a British officer, his treatment was exceptional.

There is some oblique and inconclusive evidence about Lawrence's movements after his hurried withdrawal from the Yarmuk Valley. Occasional messages were carried by Beduin riders from el Azraq to Aqaba, from where they were relayed by wireless to the Arab Bureau and GHQ intelligence in Cairo. On 11 November, French intelligence heard that Lawrence was at el Azraq with Sharif Nasir, who had left Aqaba five days earlier. They were believed to be preparing for an excursion northwards, possibly towards the outskirts of Damascus. Four days later, GHQ intelligence heard that Lawrence and Nasir were on their way towards Aleppo and had planned an attack on the line between it and Damascus.[7] Nowhere in his narratives did Lawrence mention Nasir.

At the Arab Bureau, Hogarth received a letter from Lawrence on 26 November which had been written twelve days before and in which he said he was 'very well and cheerful'. That same day Lawrence had written to his mother, so both letters must have been relayed by the same carrier. On 29 November, Hogarth said he had had news of Lawrence up to the 20th and knew his whereabouts and purpose.[8] 'So far as I can judge he will be safe,' he told his wife, and added that Lawrence had asked for and been sent supplies of potted meat and milk chocolate.[9] So, by 20 November, Lawrence was no longer facing the immediate risks of capture or death and could well have been on his way back to Aqaba, where no doubt his victuals would be waiting. Fragmentary details of behind-the-lines activities were filtering back from eastern and central Syria; none indicated that Lawrence had been briefly taken or had suffered harm.

Meinertzhagen heard from Lawrence that he had been taken, stripped, bound and 'then sodomized by the Governor of Dera, followed by similar treatment by the Governor's servants'. Afterwards he was flogged. This tale concluded with a general confession of Lawrence's misfortunes and was delivered on 20 July 1919 when the two men were staying at the same Paris hotel. While Lawrence was bathing, Meinertzhagen noted red weals across his ribs that were explained as the result of an accident at el Azraq in which he had been dragged over barbed wire. According to *The Mint*, these weals were commented on by RAF doctors when Lawrence underwent his medical in August 1922; whether they had been suffered in 1917 or September 1918 when he revisited el Azraq, Lawrence did not say. All this is very strange since 'weal' is used rather than 'scar' or 'cicatrix' and therefore suggests a recent origin. Furthermore, Meinertzhagen later confessed to Malcolm Muggeridge that Lawrence was unscarred.[10] Even odder was Lawrence's admission that he dreaded knowledge of his experience at Dera ever becoming public and that he would never publish a true account of what had happened. And yet he had confessed something of what passed to Stirling in June 1919, and a fuller version would be circulated among his friends during 1922 and 1923 when he was seeking critical advice on the *Seven Pillars*. Once subscription copies of the book were available, and copies deposited in the British Museum and Bodleian libraries, anyone could discover the truth. They did and rumours of his capture and imprisonment appeared in the press.[11]

There was much embellishment in the 1922 version of Lawrence's Dera misadventure and much that was inexplicable.[12] Suffering from a broken toe, he had hobbled into the town, a journey which was 'exquisitely painful'. He was seeking low-grade intelligence about the town's layout and the possible existence of a secret means of access which could be used later by Arab raiders. This was an extraordinarily pointless mission since a good topographical description of the town existed in the 1911 Army Handbook for Syria and additional data could have been gathered from native spies or aerial photographs. Lawrence did stumble on the hidden way as he fled the town, but forgot about it since it played no part in his plans to blockade and take Dera in September 1918.

According to the version printed in the *Seven Pillars* of 1922, disguised in ragged clothes, Lawrence and his Arab companion were stopped by a Turkish sergeant, who hauled Lawrence off, saying that the Bey wished to see him. Taken to a barrack hut, Lawrence presented himself to the 'fleshy' officer as Ahmed ibn Bagr, a Quneitra Circassian, and therefore, as he mistakenly imagined, not liable for conscription. The officer charged Lawrence with being a deserter and had him taken to the guard-room where he heard from the soldiers that he would fulfil 'the Bey's pleasure' that evening.

Lawrence soon discovered what this involved. He was bundled across Dera to the Bey's house and taken to his bedroom. The Bey, a stout figure, whom Lawrence thought a Circassian (actually he was an Anatolian Turk), was waiting in his night shirt. He assaulted, wrestled with, fondled and finally propositioned his captive. Lawrence shied away, a sentry was summoned, and he was stripped. Fondled again, Lawrence kneed the Bey in the groin, 'when he got beastly'. The full guard was called and Lawrence was pinioned: the Bey then hit him, kissed him and scratched his ribs with a bayonet point. 'You must understand that I know all about you, and it will be easier for you if you do as I wish,' the Bey warned. Lawrence was obdurate and the Bey ordered his men to remove him and 'teach me till I prayed to be brought back'.

Outside, Lawrence was flogged for over ten minutes with a riding whip.

Semi-conscious, he was then kicked by a corporal. Worse followed. His legs were prised apart 'while a third astride my back rode me like a horse'. The Bey recalled him, but disdained the bleeding, broken figure whom his guards offered. He was sent away and taken to an Armenian dresser for treatment. His escort tried to comfort him, 'saying that men must suffer their officers' wishes or pay for it'. Before they left him, another told Lawrence 'in a Druze accent' (Druzes were exempt from military service) that the dispensary door was unlocked. At sunrise and through this door, Lawrence escaped dressed in a suit of European clothes he had found in the dispensary. Soon after he found his companion and went on his way back to el Azraq.

This was not the whole truth. In March 1924 while telling Mrs Bernard Shaw his reactions to her husband's new play, *St Joan*, Lawrence admitted that, like the heroine, he had broken under torture. 'I'm always afraid of being hurt: and to me, while I live, the force of that night will lie in the agony which broke me, and made me surrender.' To alleviate his ordeal, he offered up 'the only possession we are born into the world with – our bodily integrity' and rendered himself unfit for the company of decent men. Lawrence had more to reveal, which provoked her to exclaim to her husband, 'He is such an INFERNAL liar!' Shaw disagreed. 'He was an actor. But I must add that neither was he a monster of veracity. One of his chapters (LXXXI) tells of a revolting sequel to his capture by the Turks and his attraction for a Turkish officer. He told me that his account of the affair is not true. I forbore to ask him what actually happened.'[13] Another person in Lawrence's confidence, Meinertzhagen, may have heard more since he wrote soon after his friend's death, 'The Dera incident is false. T.E.L. would have recalled the book if possible; therefore how I loathed the unlimited edition published after his death.'[14]

As he presented them, Lawrence's accounts of what befell him in Dera are open to many challenges. Hajim Muhittin Bey, whose name was inexplicably changed to Nahi in the 1926 version of the *Seven Pillars*, was a real person who died in 1965 at Smyrna (Izmir) unaware of his notoriety. He was a promiscuous womaniser and his family and friends strenuously denied that he had ever been a homosexual.[15] Such protests were understandable, but the experience of such incidents in American prisons suggests that many homosexual rapists are heterosexuals whose behaviour in these circumstances is an expression of an urge to dominate and humiliate their victims.[16] Nor would Hajim Bey's treatment of Lawrence have unduly horrified his brother officers or the NCOs and private soldiers who were his accomplices. Custom, if not the law of the mosque, tolerated the active homosexual and invested his activities with qualities of virility and manliness. Hajim Bey's behaviour was both credible and, within its context, even creditable.

Less believable was its sequel, in which Lawrence escaped and by forced rides covered the distance from el Azraq to Aqaba in half the usual time for, according to the *Seven Pillars*, he was there on 26 November. Nowhere in this narrative does Lawrence refer to medical treatment beyond that applied by the dresser at Dera. And yet, within ten days, he had suffered a broken toe, minor flesh wounds, a stabbing with a bayonet, a flogging, kicking, pummelling and homosexual rape. On top of this was a gruelling, four-day camel-back journey. Lawrence's powers of recuperation bordered on the miraculous since, on 9 December, he was fit enough to travel to Jerusalem, where he met Storrs and joined the ceremonial parade on 9 December which officially marked the city's liberation. Five days later he met Hogarth, who reported that he was 'looking much fitter and better than when I saw him last'.[17]

Lawrence mentioned his encounter with Hogarth in a letter of 14 December. He told his family that he had lingered ten days in el Azraq before taking three to reach Aqaba, which was 'good going' on a camel. In passing, he referred to 'a few days motoring' in Aqaba immediately after his return, which indirectly bears out the reference to his excursion in the artillery war diary. Given the solid tyres of the gunners' cars and trucks, jaunts across a rough landscape are further testimony of Lawrence's swift recovery from his supposed ordeal at Dera.

It seems absolutely certain that Lawrence fabricated the incident at Dera, but why? Two explanations offer themselves. First, the tale was a fabrication created to illustrate a purely literary point; secondly, he was making a coded statement about his own sexuality. Something like this had occurred to him, but at another time and in different circumstances.

In literary terms, the shocking business at Dera vindicated observations made by Lawrence at the beginning of the *Seven Pillars*, where he outlined the rottenness of the Ottoman system manifested by the sodomy endemic among its officer caste. Dera proved the point. 'Incidents like these', Lawrence wrote, 'made the thought of military service in the Turkish army a living death for the wholesome Arab peasants, and the consequences pursued the miserable victims all their after life, in revolting forms of sexual disease.' Yet it was a major epidemic of pellagra rather than venereal diseases which really undermined the Turkish army, as Lawrence and the army's medical services knew well.[18]

The wicked men and their system are finally overthrown. Nemesis comes at the end of Lawrence's tale when, in September 1918, the shattered Turkish army drags itself out of the provinces it has profaned. His account of the rout and massacre cannot arouse pity since the reader knows that the retribution is merited. He need not pause long over the fate of the captured Dera policemen who are turned over to the local Arab population. Lawrence did not seek revenge for his treatment at Dera, but what he had endured there reinforces the feeling that the Turks were getting what they deserved.

Lawrence was also giving the lie to that commonplace of the British army which exalted 'Johnny' Turk as a game and honourable adversary. In doing so, he succumbed to that terrible lie of the twentieth century which insists that crimes can be committed by entire nations rather than individuals.

Lawrence had much to say about homosexuality in the *Seven Pillars*, which contains several homoerotic passages. He analyses and expresses sympathy for Beduin homosexuality, approving the warriors' desire 'to slake one another's needs in their own clean bodies'. 'Friends quivering together in the yielding sand with intimate hot limbs in supreme embrace' struck Lawrence as the 'sensual co-efficient of the mental passion which was wielding our souls in one flaming effort'. Other delights were available, but he avoids explaining what they might involve. 'Several, thirsting to punish appetites they could not wholly prevent, took a savage pride in degrading the body, and offered themselves fiercely to any habit which promised physical pain or filth.'

There were strong echoes of the Uranian muse in Lawrence's descriptions of his two Arab servants, Dawd and Farraj, who shared an 'eastern boy and boy affection'. Lawrence had employed them 'because they looked so young and clean' and tolerated their homosexual liaison, for 'Such friendships often led to manly loves of a depth and force beyond our flesh-steeped conceit.' They could be mischievous and earned several beatings and once, on Lawrence's orders, 'a swinging half-dozen each', a phrase and circumstances which recall his undergraduate reading, Corvo's *Don Tarquino*. This contained several examples of chastisement and humiliation; a page-boy given 'vii criss-cross weals on his plunging hams with a cane', another spat upon by his companions, and a slave given 'commodious action on the flesh of his back bulk'.

Corvo devised erotic fantasies: Lawrence recorded what he and others saw. Their reactions were very different from his. 'The whole community is infected and saturated with vices of which nature abominates the idea,' wrote a disgusted Major Vickery.[19] Another of Lawrence's foes, Sir Arnold Wilson, in his review of *Revolt in the Desert*, contemptuously cited passages which he had clearly read in its source, the *Seven Pillars*.[20]

'The bird of Minerva', wrote Landor, 'flies low and picks up its food under hedges.' Lawrence's hermaphrodite deity flies lower than

Landor's bird, and seems to have a preference for the cesspool, but we must be grateful to be spared, in this edition, more detailed references to a vice to which Semitic races are by no means prone. To most English readers his Epipyschidon on this subject will be incomprehensible, to the remainder, unwelcome.

Wilson, a former army boxing champion, had obviously been enraged by what Lawrence had written on Beduin homosexuality. Lawrence's excursions on this subject worried his friends, who successfully persuaded him to remove one passage from the 1922 version of the *Seven Pillars* in which a young British soldier and an Arab are discovered committing a homosexual act. The Arab was given a hundred lashes in accordance with Quranic law, a sentence which Lawrence had halved, and the British other-ranks gave sixty to their countryman rather than have him face a court martial and imprisonment. Lawrence considered the crime loathsome, but he understood the feelings of the miscreants and had the affair covered up.

This stretches credulity to breaking point, for Lawrence would have had to have secured the collusion of Colonel Joyce and other officers who were unlikely to have shared his tolerance of homosexuality. Moreover, there might have been sturdy objections to compounding one offence with another: flogging had been illegal in the British army for over thirty years. No one else present has ever drawn attention to the incident and, fifty years later, Lawrence's surviving brother, Arnold, was anxious that it remain unknown.[21]

Writing in December 1927 to E.M. Forster, after having read his homosexual short-story 'Dr Woolacott', Lawrence admitted that the subject had been treated in a manner which made him reconsider his feelings:

> The Turks, as you probably know (or have guessed, through the references of the *Seven Pillars*) did it to me, by force: and since then I have gone about whimpering to myself Unclean, unclean. Now I don't know. Perhaps there is another side, to the story. I couldn't ever do it, I believe; the impulse strong enough to make me touch another creature has not yet been born in me....[22]

This must have been very puzzling for Forster, who would also have read in the *Seven Pillars* that Lawrence's treatment at the hands of the Turks had triggered a sexual response. 'A delicious warmth, probably sexual, was swelling through me.' The 1922 version concluded with a faltering admission that he felt strangely impelled to seek a repetition of the experience, much as a moth is drawn towards a flame.

To Robert Graves, Lawrence was more explicit. He confessed an urge to be whipped and, after his return to England in December 1921, admitted that he enjoyed being buggered.[23]*

Not long after, if not before, Lawrence was willingly submitting himself to experiences akin to those he said he had had at Dera. The early stages of his addiction remain obscure; not surprisingly, since such behaviour broke the criminal law. At some time during 1922 he was present at flagellation parties held in Chelsea by a German, Jack Bilbo, who was also known as Bluebeard. This pander had offered his confessions to a German magazine and Lawrence, fearful of public exposure, even possibly prosecution, wrote in the autumn of 1922 to Edward Shortt, the Home Secretary, asking for Bluebeard's deportation and the suppression of the magazine.[24]

Contrary to what Lawrence imagined, the Home Secretary possessed no powers of deportation, which could be invoked only by a court after the deportee had been found guilty of an offence. Bilbo was not prosecuted, nor did he attract police attention, since the Metropolitan Police possess no file on him. He seems to have left the country, for in October 1932 he was in Berlin where he was contemplating publishing his memoirs. Somehow aware of his intentions, Lawrence appealed directly to his distant cousin, Sir Robert Vansittart, at the Foreign Office. Backed by a departmental legal adviser, Vansittart agreed to contact the Berlin Embassy and secure the banning of the proposed book.[25] Again it is unclear whether any action was taken, since no reference to Bilbo or what he had in mind to write appears in those Foreign Office files for the winter of 1932/3 which are publicly available.

If, as seems likely, Lawrence had made a foray into that area of the sexual underworld which catered for his tastes, he had taken an enormous risk. Thereafter, he was more circumspect. From the spring of 1923 he chose to be beaten privately and retained a twenty-year-old Aberdeen youth, John Bruce, for the purpose. How this arrangement came about is the subject of some debate. Bruce, who was paid £2,500 for his story by the *Sunday Times* in 1968, claimed that he had been hired in 1922 after an elaborate procedure involving Lawrence's friend Sir Francis Rennell. Lawrence's biographer, Dr Mack, and Arnold Lawrence, who was less than happy with Bruce's revelations, countered by saying that Bruce had first met Lawrence at Bovington in March shortly after they had enlisted.[26]

This was largely immaterial. From 1923 until 1934 Bruce was persuaded to beat Lawrence regularly although, as he knew, others were similarly employed. The proceedings followed a bizarre pattern devised by Lawrence. He had convinced Bruce that the punitive regime was the concoction of an uncle known as the 'Old Man' or 'R', who wished his nephew to be punished on account of various misdemeanours which had brought shame

---

* See Appendix.

on his family. In the guise of the uncle, Lawrence issued letters to Bruce that listed real and fanciful misdeeds such as insolence to the King and falling into the hands of Jewish moneylenders. After the charge-sheet came instructions about punishment, which consisted either of a beating or, on some occasions, of a mixture of beatings and hard physical exercise including horse-riding and swimming. The whippings were delivered on the bare backside and ended in Lawrence's sexual orgasm.

Afterwards, Lawrence reverted to his role as stern mentor and by letter demanded to know precise details of what had occurred during the session. In these letters there was much lingering over the mechanics of chastisement ('the birch is quite ineffective' or 'I was making up my mind to ask you to use your friend's jute whip') and the victim's response ('Hills [Bruce] reports that after the birching Ted [that is, Lawrence] cried out quite loudly and begged for mercy'). This curiously echoes the description of the whip employed at Dera, which was 'of the Circassian sort, a thong of supple black hide, rounded, and tapering from the thickness of a thumb at the grip (which was wrapped in silver) down to the hard fine point finer than a pencil'.

For the psychologist, these exact rehearsals of the instruments and acts of punishment set down by Lawrence suggest a powerful sexual masochism. Before his addiction to flagellation, he had made much of his earlier escapade in which he said he had been arrested, flogged and imprisoned at Urfa in 1912. He talked about the incident, which had become common knowledge in Cairo by the summer of 1917.[27] He may have spoken of this to his friend, the poet James Elroy Flecker, whom he first met in Beirut at the end of 1911. 'Whipping' was once a topic which they discussed, no doubt with some enthusiasm since Flecker was a masochist.[28]

Masochism can be the result of a yearning for degradation and punishment for hidden sins. It can take many forms although, in the broadest sense, the masochist is bedevilled by guilt for which forgiveness can only be obtained through painful abasement. One source of guilt may be self-contempt; another may be secret fantasies which can never be fulfilled because the practices involved run counter to the subject's inner moral code or would shatter his self-esteem. According to Dr Mack and Arnold Lawrence, his brother's 'affliction' was an effort to suppress rather than stimulate his sexuality. Like the ascetics of the medieval church, Lawrence subdued carnality through bouts of pain.

And yet, to judge by what he wrote on the subject, he was never inclined to explore, let alone discover, the sexual attractions of women. He once told Mrs Bernard Shaw that knowledge of his mother made him sure that he would never marry or father children. Heterosexuality remained a mystery to him and one he was glad not to have unravelled. Lawrence could never have required astringents to deter him from sexual adventures which he would never have contemplated.

There was, however, a sexual element to Lawrence. He confessed that what he endured at Dera had given him an erotic sensation and, latterly, his whippings induced orgasm. During and after his lifetime, there were persistent rumours that he was a homosexual; these were so strong that Lowell Thomas took the unusual step of publicly denying them in his contribution to an encomium to Lawrence published in 1936. The charges, Lowell Thomas suggested, had been spread by 'certain of his enemies' and he refuted them by claiming that Lawrence never revealed any of the affectations of speech or mannerism which were imagined to be the hallmarks of the homosexual.[29]

This is not convincing, but then the allegations were also hard to substantiate. A regular Arab officer, Subhi al-Umari, accused Lawrence of homosexual acts with Dahoum at Karkamis, but this may well have been a repetition of local gossip inspired by their indiscretions. Robin Maugham, stationed at Bovington Camp four years after Lawrence's death, heard an NCO describe how he had whipped Lawrence and then buggered him in what must have been a repeat performance of what had happened at Dera.[30] Whispers of Lawrence's beating sessions seem to have circulated among his close friends; John Buchan was shocked by what he considered extreme and 'unwholesome' forms of self-discipline and, according to Bruce, Churchill may have been in the know since, at Lawrence's funeral, he cautioned him, 'Look to duty now, Jock,' which must have meant 'Keep quiet'.[31] Lawrence's appeals to Edward Shortt in 1922 and Vansittart ten years after may have started some hares.

One of these ran after Lawrence's death in the form of a tale which Richard Aldington heard from Somerset Maugham some time before November 1958.[32] Air-Marshal Sir Hugh Trenchard, as Chief Commissioner for Police, had told Maugham that Lawrence's motorbike accident had been suicide prompted by the knowledge that a warrant had been issued for his arrest to answer charges of indecent behaviour with servicemen at Cloud's Hill. No action had been taken against Lawrence while he was in the RAF and he mistakenly believed that his public celebrity had given him immunity from prosecution. Shortly before his death, he had been visited by a plain-clothes police inspector who warned him what was in store if he did not leave the country immediately. Maugham offered no explanation for the official change of heart towards Lawrence. For his friend Trenchard to have issued such a warrant for execution in Dorset, there would first have had to have been a complaint to the Home Secretary, Sir Herbert Samuel, a former commissioner in Palestine with whom Lawrence had worked during 1922. No documentary evidence has ever surfaced among the Home Office papers or in Dorset to support either a complaint or the official response described by Maugham, although, given the extraordinarily sensitive nature of the charge and the fact that it was never brought to court, it is most improbable that the relevant files would have been preserved.

Speculation about Lawrence's sexuality was inevitable after his confession of what had allegedly passed at Dera. His obsession with the incident, his urge to write and speak about it, his ambivalence about women, contempt for his own body and excessive self-loathing are symptoms shared by many victims of homosexual rape. And yet the evidence shows that Lawrence was never in Dera on 20–21 November 1917 and so could not have been raped there. It is possible that his vivid, minutely observed versions of what occurred were homoerotic fantasy. Certainly all the ingredients are there: the fair-skinned, virginal youth; the burly Turkish soldiers; the masterful Bey; the whippings and the final, not altogether unpleasurable, submission. All this may have been in Graves's mind when he admitted that Lawrence indulged in 'diabolical' fantasies, a judgement upheld for him by a handwriting expert who had examined a sample of Lawrence's script.[33]

Dismissing Dera on purely circumstantial grounds, Desmond Stewart imagined that it represented an actual experience which had occurred when Lawrence had been at el Azraq.[34] Overwhelmed by a sense of failure after the aborted Yarmuk raid, Lawrence seeks punishment like a naughty boy. It is offered by the strong, virile Sharif Ali, who whips him and then, overcoming his resistance, buggers him. Already fascinated, perhaps aroused by masochistic submission, Lawrence may have found the experience pleasurable, which explains the lengths he pursued to have it repeated. Yet, in Arab eyes, Lawrence would have been profoundly humiliated for, by playing the woman's part, he would have made himself contemptible. A dangerous loss of standing may have been averted since, when he left el Azraq, Lawrence took his leave of Ali by a public display of warriorly brotherhood: according to the *Seven Pillars*, they exchanged robes and kissed 'like Jonathan and David'.

So much for Stewart's reconstruction. It is indirectly supported by Meinertzhagen, who recalled some horseplay between himself and Lawrence during their stay at the Majestic Hotel in 1919. The burly, six-foot Meinertzhagen grasped his adversary and walloped his bottom. Lawrence 'made no attempt to resist and told me later that he could easily understand a woman submitting to rape once a strong man hugged her'. Not only did Lawrence seem to understand the possible but by no means universal feelings of the rape victim, he showed many of the clinical symptoms of one who had undergone such a trauma. These included a sense of unworthiness and his irresistible impulse to tell all to anyone who would listen or could read what had happened to him. This he managed to do through the invention of the incident at Dera.

A man's sexuality should remain his own concern, save when he chooses to advertise it, or else when its fulfilment breaks the criminal law or flies in the face of common morality. In relating what happened to him at Dera, Lawrence announced something about his own sexuality. He did so through the fabrication of an event which involved actual people, although he circumspectly altered the name of Hajim Bey in the published edition of the *Seven Pillars*, which suggests an insurance against close investigation. This was unnecessary since all who read his narrative accepted it as a record of his experience. But no such incident could have occurred on 20–21 November 1917, since Lawrence was at Aqaba. He may have suffered a violation like that he so carefully remembered, which must have occurred some time before June 1919, in another place and involving other men. Beyond Stewart's conjecture, there are no clear answers to the questions when, where and by whom. Lawrence's Oxford and Syrian circles included homosexuals such as Leonard Green, Flecker and possibly Vyvyan Richards.

While the mainsprings of Lawrence's peculiar sexuality must remain obscure, its manifestations during the 1920s and 1930s meant that he was living dangerously close to scandal. More was at risk than his private reputation; exposure would have bruised those establishment figures closely associated with him and, given his status as a national hero, would have tarnished British prestige. It is not hard to imagine how the French newspapers would have treated the revelation of his addiction to what was jeeringly called 'le vice anglais'.

IV

BETRAYAL

R EAL traumas awaited Lawrence when he returned to Aqaba at the end of November 1917. During the four weeks when he had been behind enemy lines, the British government had issued the Balfour Declaration, which promised a Jewish national home in post-war Palestine. Soon after, Lenin and Trotsky published full details of secret Allied agreements on the partition of the Ottoman empire from papers found in the Russian Foreign Ministry. Both were bonuses for Turco-German propagandists at a time when the Ottoman government was opening a diplomatic offensive designed to entice the Arabs away from Britain and France. Immediately, the terms of the Sykes–Picot agreement and the Balfour Declaration were publicly announced in Lebanon and Syria, where they confirmed many Arabs' misgivings about the Allies' motives. Faisal too heard the revelations, which so disturbed him that he became susceptible to Turkish blandishments.

Lawrence was also troubled, but for other reasons. Since his first involvement in the Arab movement he had felt uneasy about discrepancies between the terms of the Sykes–Picot agreement and what Hussain believed would be his reward at the end of the war. In a suppressed paragraph in his letter to *The Times* of 8 September 1919, Lawrence admitted that he had encouraged the Arabs because he had believed that the British government would honour its wartime pledges to them. Now that it seemed that the government would break these promises which, he alleged, he been 'authorised' to make in its name, he regretted his part in what had been perjury. He shifted his ground slightly in the *Seven Pillars*, where he claimed that the Arabs considered him 'a free agent of the British government' and naturally asked for and got his endorsement of what they imagined it was offering them. In both instances the form of words is deceptive: promises were never made to all the Arabs, at least not before June 1918; they were made to one Arab, Hussain. This is by the way: more important is the fact that Lawrence never possessed the diplomatic power to enter into any engagements with the Arabs.

This matter of authority was understood by Faisal, if not by Lawrence. Nowhere, throughout his extended negotiations with British, French and American officials in 1919, did he refer to any pledge made by Lawrence. Nevertheless, he did from time to time ask Lawrence for explanations of the intended post-war settlement. For instance, in September 1917, Lawrence complained to Clayton that it was difficult to instruct Faisal 'to leave B area, or a blue area, alone if the Turkish army is using it as a military base against him'.[1] It was impossible, when such matters arose, for Lawrence to feign ignorance and so he lied. In the letter written to *The Times* in September 1919, he presented himself as an innocent forced by the circumstances of war to be the agent of deceitful men. He passed on their lies to the trusting Arabs, whose faith in his integrity was absolute. This private guilt, based upon his secret knowledge that he was betraying the trust of his brothers-in-arms, was a thread which Lawrence later wove into the *Seven Pillars*.

Yet when confronted by Allenby and Faisal in Damascus on 3 October 1918, Lawrence denied any knowledge of the provisions of the Sykes–Picot agreement, which gave France full control over the Lebanon and a protectorate in Syria. Moreover, the bewildered Faisal claimed that until a few moments before the meeting he had been under the impression that both provinces were earmarked for the Arabs. This was a charade. Lawrence knew the terms of Sykes–Picot and had shown them to Faisal, who had probably been given them already by his Turkish contacts early in 1918.

Lawrence and Faisal lied to Allenby and Lawrence has been sparing with the truth in the suppressed section of the letter and in the *Seven Pillars*. One explanation for the scene in Damascus, for Lawrence's elaborations and for his sense of guilt is that he deliberately doctored the information he gave Faisal and other Arabs who quizzed him about the future of the Middle East. He imagined that truthful answers would have disheartened his listeners to the point where their fighting spirit could easily have evaporated. At the same time his exaggeration of Arab post-war rewards raised their expectations to a point where it would be dangerous for Britain and France to disappoint them. France, the proposed inheritor of Syria, would obviously be hurt more than Britain, which would have suited Lawrence. Moreover he was determined, whatever the cost, to get his own way. 'He can be ruthless,' Hogarth wrote in 1920, 'caring little what eggs he breaks to make his omelettes and ignoring responsibility either for the shells or for the digestion of the mess.'

French observers suspected that Lawrence was encouraging Faisal's Syrian ambitions, and the Amir's behaviour during 1918–19 indicates that he believed he was entitled to that province. In moral terms, Lawrence exonerated himself by repeatedly arguing that he was dissembling on behalf of the government. Obviously as Britain's paymaster he had to make bargains with would-be adherents of Faisal who were still Ottoman subjects and anxious to know what would befall them after the war. On one occasion, the Rwallah Amir Nuri Shalaan presented Lawrence with 'a file of documents and asked which British pledge was to be believed'. Flummoxed, Lawrence replied that the latest in date could be trusted. Lawrence did not read them so we do not know what they were, or, if he did, he never mentioned it in the *Seven Pillars*.

What mattered in this context was Lawrence's sense of self-esteem. To his readers he was the servant of a national movement, uniting and guiding the Arabs towards historic fulfilment, not a recruiting officer who struck bargains and doled out cash. Yet at the same time as he tapped the springs of national sentiment, Lawrence had to convince the Arabs that he represented a fair-dealing nation whose rulers kept their word. The fact that they did not caused him deep grief. All this assumes that the Arabs were guileless and incapable of recognising that Lawrence was not a properly accredited representative of Great Britain and that what he had to say carried as much weight as the words of Mcmahon, Sykes or Hogarth. But their letters and pledges, not Lawrence's, were cited time and time again by Arabs after the war. Furthermore only the most artless Arab would have ignored the Quranic injunction:

> And as for the unbelievers,
> Their works are a mirage in the desert.
> The thirsty man thinks it water
> Till, coming to it, he finds nothing.

No one, including Lawrence, was clear as to exactly what the Arabs expected after victory. During interviews with Sykes and Picot in May 1917 and Hogarth in January 1918, Hussain showed an exasperating but effective ability to misunderstand what was told him on the delicate matter of post-war boundaries. His Cairo agent, al Faruqi, added to the confusion, since he was 'apt to put into the mouth of Sir Henry [McMahon] things said to him by more junior people' – perhaps Lawrence?[2] Meeting Hussain at the end of July 1917, Lawrence was told that Picot had assured the King that France would never claim suzerainty over Syria and would quickly evacuate the province, which was not what the Frenchman had intended to say.[3] Yet in June 1918 Sykes assured Wingate that 'The King has frequently been given [the] outline and detail of the agreement ... both by myself, Monsieur Picot, Colonel Brémond, and Commander Hogarth.'[4] None could have had an easy time. 'I have been sent to try and persuade the Old Man of Mecca to do things he does not want to do,' Hogarth wrote to his wife on 10 January 1918. It was 'uphill work for all his benignity and hand patting endearments', since Hussain was the 'most obstinate —— old diplomat on earth'.[5] All his cunning was needed, since from the beginning Hussain had placed an unrealistically high price on his assistance to the Allied cause, which he saw as a vehicle for his inflated dynastic ambitions in Arabia, Palestine and Syria.

Certainly Hussain and his sons had good reason to ignore or pretend to misunderstand Anglo-French arrangements for the future of the Middle East. They appreciated that the final form of the post-war settlement would be dictated by the course of the war. So did Lawrence, which is why he clung to the hope that the Arabs would be allowed to keep what they conquered by their own efforts, a consideration which lay behind his scheme for a spasm of pro-Faisal coups in Syria in November 1917. This was pure ingenuousness since 'their own efforts' was an empty form of words, given the extent of Allied financial and military backing for the Arabs.

One unforeseen event, the United States' entry into the war in April 1917, raised Lawrence's hopes, because he believed that the American government might be more receptive than the British to what he believed was the Arabs' moral right to self-determination on their own terms. In March 1918 he appealed directly to American idealism through William Yale, the US Consul in Cairo.[6] He told him that the Arabs had faith in American political honesty and open-handedness in international affairs. A declaration by the American government in favour of Arab national aspirations would be what Lawrence called the 'trump card' that would finally dispel suspicions about the now not so hidden motives of the imperial powers. History was moving in Lawrence's direction. No longer embarrassed by the attachment of autocratic Russia, the alliance of Britain, France and the United States could honestly face the world as the champion of freedom and the national rights of such subject races as the Arabs to choose their own future. Like Lawrence, Sykes sensed the new mood. He invoked American democratic and libertarian ideals as an argument to try and force the stubborn Picot to forgo his country's post-war colonial claims to Syria.[7]

It seemed to Lawrence that gusts of Yankee plain-dealing and high-mindedness could blow away the fog of distrust between the Arabs and their allies. The Arabs were not only apprehensive about the greed of the imperial powers: they felt that their weakness made them expendable. In the autumn of 1917 Lawrence got wind of the secret approaches being made to the British government by Talaat Bey, the new Turkish Grand Vizier, who was angling for a separate, negotiated peace. This was another episode in a long history of furtive diplomacy which stretched back to the spring of 1915. Then, Jamal Pasha, uncomfortably aware that the Syrians and Lebanese were poised to welcome an Allied invasion, secretly offered to manage a coup, take Syria out of the war and make himself Sultan in return for Allied backing and recognition. The French squashed this scheme, which had been taken seriously by the Foreign Office and the Russians, who had been offered the Straits if Jamal took Constantinople and deposed Mehmed V.[8]

Talaat had more on offer: he proposed a coup against Enver, permission for RN submarines to enter the Straits and sink the *Goeben* and *Breslau*, and an immediate armistice which would pave the way for an Anglo-Ottoman accord in the Middle East. The Foreign Office thought something might come from dealing with Talaat since there was still a residual feeling that long-term imperial interests in the region were safest in the hands of a strong Turkey rather than a cluster of successor states. There was some support for this view in the War Office, but Robertson thought the Germans would step in once details of the plot had emerged. The Arab lobby was horrified. 'We must honourably keep faith with the Arabs,' argued

General Macdonogh, or face a violent Muslim backlash in India.[9] Rumours of these hugger-mugger exchanges with Talaat reached Cairo in October 1917 and may have begun to circulate among the Arabs. A troubled Allenby cabled the Foreign Office for an explanation, arguing that 'The question of continued help from the Arabs depends on their continued belief that we shall keep our promises not to conclude any peace which would leave Arab territories under Turkish domination.'[10]

Lawrence admitted in the *Seven Pillars* that he had been informed of these secret manoeuvres by a friend in Cairo, probably a staff or Arab Bureau colleague, and he was despondent. Since there were those within the British government willing to contemplate seriously a rapprochement with Turkey, it was all the more imperative for the Arabs to press ahead into Syria, if necessary on their own. Lawrence's alarm was understandable but ill-founded. The secret negotiations petered out, but they did give him a pretext to excuse the clandestine exchanges between Faisal and the Turkish government from November 1917 to July 1918.[11]

Having failed to crush the Arab Revolt in Hejaz and faced with its possible spread into Syria, the Ottoman government was forced to find ways by which an accommodation could be reached with the Arab nationalists. Their new policy was revealed to a British secret agent in Berne, who heard in September 1917 that the exiled Khedive Abbas Hilmi and his followers were about to leave Switzerland for Damascus. In return for eventual restoration to the Egyptian throne, the Khedive would act as an intermediary between the Turkish government and Hussain. Appeals were to be made to Hussain's sense of Islamic solidarity and he was to be offered terms for Arab self-government in Syria and Iraq.[12] Overall direction of this programme of Turco-Arab reconciliation was in the hands of Jamal Pasha, who, since his crackdown on the Syrian nationalists, had introduced policies designed to convince local opinion that Turkey and not the Allies was the best patron for Arab nationalism. His appeals were reinforced by frequent references to Anglo-French ambitions for the area.

With the backing of Enver, Jamal wrote to Faisal on 13 November 1917, sending him a horse as a token of friendship. The Prince was invited to a conference at Damascus where he, Jamal and Abbas Hilmi would discuss religious unity and explore the possibilities of an alliance between the Arab movement and the Ottoman government. Such an alignment would be in Faisal's interests since Jamal predicted he would get little from his land-hungry allies. Another letter was sent to Jafar al Askari, who was reminded of his honourable service in the Ottoman army and asked to examine his conscience now 'the Allied governments have openly and officially declared' that, after the war, his homeland, Iraq, was to be made a British protectorate, Syria a French, and Palestine an international zone.[13]

Jamal promised Faisal further letters. His first was revealed to Colonel Joyce on 16 December after Faisal had forwarded a copy to Hussain. Eight days later the Arab Bureau alerted Major Basset at Jiddah: he was told to inform Hussain that the message was a mischievous German device. Moreover, he was commanded to remind Hussain that as an ally he was bound not to make a separate peace. Faisal felt under no such legal obligation and said so to Jamal. Secret exchanges between them continued until July 1918 and, as far as possible, were monitored by British officers, including Lawrence.

The episode was dismissed briefly by Lawrence in Chapter 101 of the *Seven Pillars*, where he suggested that Faisal's replies were the means of driving a wedge between the pro-German faction within the Committee of Union and Progress and the Turanian nationalists led by Mustafa Kemal Pasha (Kemal Atatürk). Lawrence added that he showed Faisal a text of the Sykes–Picot agreement but emphasised that his own 'performance' on the battlefield would wipe out its provisions. In other words, Lawrence stuck to the formula that the Arabs would somehow rule wherever they conquered. In any case, he believed that it was wise for Faisal to keep open links with Constantinople as an insurance policy against an Allied defeat in France. This uncharacteristic piece of *realpolitik* made sense, given the uncertain outcome of the Western Front battles during the spring of 1918.

Lawrence did not add that he played a double game during Faisal's flirtation with the Turks. It was his inescapable duty as a British officer to hamper the exchanges (one messenger was taken by a French patrol) or uncover every detail of what passed between Faisal and his Turkish correspondents by direct questions or subterfuge. At least twice he played the spy. Once, in March, he covertly secured a copy of a letter from Faisal to Muhammad Jamal Pasha, the officer commanding at Maan who acted as a go-between for his namesake after his appointment in December 1917 as Minister of Marine in Constantinople. Early in June Lawrence suborned or bribed one of Faisal's secretaries, by whom he was given a copy of a secret letter which revealed the extent of his master's embroilment with the Turks.[14]

As Faisal's courtier and confidant, Lawrence was in an ambiguous position, since he was not entirely unsympathetic towards the Prince's attempts to secure possession of Syria through a bargain with the Turks. He was also under pressure to make clear just what his government's attitude was towards an Arab Syria. In January 1918 Faisal asked Lawrence to procure an unequivocal, official denial of Jamal's statement about the Sykes–Picot Treaty and a proclamation that the British 'would not annex any Arab country themselves or hand any to any aliens [that is, the French]'.[15] If, as Lawrence later wrote, he showed a text of the Anglo-French accord to Faisal, then this may have been the occasion, although no mention of such a revelation appears in the official report of the incident.

Lawrence, departing from his government's policy, encouraged Faisal to trail his coat for the Turks, even to the point of urging him to look favourably on the idea of joining the Turanian nationalists in an anti-German front. He imagined that such a realignment would not injure Britain, since a weak Arab Syria would have to rely on British support against its stronger, northern neighbour. This was a recipe for chaos and the Foreign Office strongly disapproved. On 24 April Lawrence was ordered by Wingate to stick to official policy and warn Faisal that Jamal would ensnare him in a net of German intrigue. As for the Turanian nationalists, they were the architects of the Armenian massacres and Lawrence was to remind Faisal that their secular creed placed nationality before faith.[16]

Again Lawrence was allowing his passion for an independent Arab Syria to cloud his judgement. Far from creating divisions within the Committee of Union and Progress, Faisal was unwittingly assisting its policies. The armistice with Russia in December 1917 had opened the way for a mass Turkish offensive the following spring, directed at the recovery of territory lost between 1914 and 1916, and an invasion of the Russian Caucasus. By July 1918, the Turkish 'Army of Islam', its sights set on Turkestan, had reached the Caspian Sea and occupied the Baku oilfields. Enver intended to create a new Ottoman empire, united by Turanian national sentiment and Islam, which would extend across former Russian provinces in Central Asia. His dream had made him transfer forces from Syria to the Caucasus during the winter and spring of 1917–18 which, in effect, left the province with a reduced and heavily outnumbered garrison. In strategic terms, Syria took second place to the new Central Asian front and, politically, it was all but abandoned. A deal with Faisal would keep the province within the Ottoman orbit as well as cause much mischief for Britain, who would lose her politically valuable patronage of Arab nationalism. Moreover, a rapprochement with Faisal and the Arabs would add weight to Turkish Pan-Islamic propaganda in Central Asia.

Lawrence's tolerance of Faisal's dalliance with the Turkish government was ill considered and potentially dangerous, at least to British interests. Yet British policy, as revealed through the now well-known Sykes–Picot agreement, made it hard for him to reassure Faisal that a kingdom awaited him in Syria. Faisal was aware of this, and he knew too that his freedom of action was restricted by his dependence on Britain. Negotiation with Turkey offered him a means of escape and even possible strategic advantages, as this conversation of February between Faisal and a Turkish envoy suggests.[17] Asked whether he was willing to mediate between the Ottoman government and his father, Faisal was defiant.

> Envoy: Suppose they [the Turks] would evacuate the country and give it to its owner [Hussain]?
> Faisal: They are liars, they will never evacuate, but we will make them by the sword and if they leave our country they may avert the danger we would inflict on them, and if they say the truth let them show their good faith and evacuate Medina and withdraw from the railway to Amman.
> Envoy: The present military situation of Turkey compels them to make friendship with your father ... had it not been for the advance of British forces with you, you could not clear the Turks from Syria and you know whether the capture of the country by the British will be beneficial or harmful.

Securing Syria or any other military advantage without British help was tempting bait for Faisal. He rose to it. On 10 June, Lawrence got hold of a letter to Muhammad Jamal Pasha in which Faisal sought to discover the terms under which the Ottoman government would accept him as ruler of Syria. He asked for what he called the 'form and type of independence of Syria in conformity with the Prussian–Austrian–Hungary type'. What this meant is far from clear. Either Syria would sever political links with the Ottoman empire in the way that Austria had been removed from the German states in 1867 but keep a military alliance, or else, and this is more likely, Syria would enjoy the same independence within the Ottoman empire as Hungary did within the Austrian.

There was no ambiguity about Faisal's military terms. He demanded the transfer of all Arabs within the Turkish army to his service where they would be under Arab operational command. All Turkish (and presumably German) military supplies in Syria were to be delivered to his forces.[18] Lawrence was convinced that these provisions had been dictated by Faisal's Syrian officers and that he was flying a kite to keep Turkish dissidents hopeful. Others in Cairo and London were less sanguine: on 9 August Hogarth assured the Foreign Office that 'our officers are all ready to assume control' in an emergency. Like its Anglo-Turkish equivalent of a year before, the Turco-Arab rapprochement came to nothing. It was overtaken by the events of August and September 1918, in particular the simultaneous reverses suffered by the German army in France and the Turkish in Syria.

In fact, Faisal was grasping at straws. Anxious about the outcome of the war in Europe, which he was following closely, and disheartened by his own lack of progress in southern Jordan, he found the idea of conquest through negotiation plausible. In spite of Lawrence's assurances, he felt by no means certain that his allies would accept him as ruler of Syria. One further factor impelled him towards a form of compromise with the Turks – the prospect that a British-controlled Palestine would be detached from Syria and be peopled by Jewish immigrants from Europe. On 4 June 1918, six days before he delivered his terms to Muhammad Jamal Pasha, Faisal had had his first discussions with the Zionist leader and visionary Dr Chaim Weizmann.

From the earliest stages of the revolt there had been undercurrents of Arab hostility towards the Zionist movement in Europe and the United States. Since the turn of the century, the Ottoman government had permitted small numbers of Jewish immigrants to acquire land in Palestine and set up their own communities. Lawrence had encountered one in 1909 and described it approvingly, although later he expressed hostility towards German Zionist settlers. His revised opinions were a reflection of a wider Arab fear that more and more colonists would arrive from Europe, buy land and edge out the Palestinian Arabs.

The seeds of future disagreements were apparent in November 1916 when *al Qibla* published an article condemning Zionism. It was brought to the attention of Sykes and Macdonogh in London by agent 'Maurice' who had influence with the Sharif, but not it seems with al Faruqi, who was behind the piece. Macdonogh instructed Wingate to reprove al Faruqi and explain to him the 'extreme danger of such ill-advised attacks on a community of such great influence throughout the world'. According to Sykes it was 'a dangerous topic' which Hussain would be wise to leave alone.[19]

The question of a Zionist involvement in the future of the Middle East could not be shelved. Inside the British government there was an influential group of Zionist converts which included the Foreign Secretary, Balfour, and Sykes, who for complex political reasons wanted an official partnership with Zionism. As far as the Middle East was concerned an Arab–Zionist–Armenian front offered a bulwark against Turco-German efforts to regain political leadership in the region. The price was the separation of Palestine from Syria, with its future administration in British hands and open to Jewish immigration. This emerged after the Balfour Declaration, which was in essence a statement of British friendship towards the world's Jews and an acknowledgement of their aspirations for a homeland in Palestine.

Among Lawrence's colleagues there was widespread sympathy for the Zionists, thanks to the missionary efforts of Aaron Aaronsohn, a former Jewish settler and now an officer with British intelligence. Aaronsohn had won over William Ormsby-Gore of the Arab Bureau, Wyndham Deedes and Meinertzhagen who, having once witnessed an anti-Jewish pogrom in Odessa, knew better than many the brutal malevolence of Eastern European anti-Semitism.

Lawrence, aware of the increase in Zionist pressure on the British government, approached Aaronsohn to discuss the effects which the proposed Jewish homeland might have in Palestine. They met on 12 August 1917 in Cairo, and Aaronsohn, detecting hints of anti-Semitism, found Lawrence hostile and inflexible. 'If the Jews will favour the Arabs they shall be spared, otherwise they will have their throats cut' was his response to the question of how the immigrants would fare in an Arab state.[20] He was speaking with the voice of Faisal, as he revealed in a letter to Clayton of 9 September:

You know of course the differences between the Palestine Jew and the Colonist Jew: to Faisal the important point is that the former speak Arabic, and the latter, German Yiddish. He is in touch with the Arab Jews (their HQ at Safid is in his sphere) and they are ready to help him, on conditions. They show a strong antipathy to the colonist Jews, and have even suggested repressive measures against them. Faisal has ignored this point hitherto and will continue to do so. His attempts to get in touch with the colonist Jews have not been very fortunate. They say they have made their arrangements with the great powers, and wish no contact with the Arab Party. They will not help the Turks or the Arabs.[21]

This final point was unfair since Lawrence knew that many Jews controlled by Aaronsohn were risking their lives gathering intelligence in Turkish-occupied Syria. What Faisal and Lawrence ('I like to make my mind up before he does') wanted to know from Clayton was the nature of the agreements which had been made with the Zionist settlers. Lawrence had been disturbed by Aaronsohn's hopes that, in time, the Jews would secure all land rights from Gaza to Haifa as a preliminary to getting 'practical autonomy' within this coastal area. He predicted future conflict, since the Palestinian tenant farmers, who 'may be ground down but have fixity of tenure', would be evicted by the colonists and end up as landless labourers. Past experience, Lawrence rightly claimed, revealed that the Jewish communities were unwilling to employ Arab labour. Knowing something of the harshness of land wars from what he must have heard of his father's Irish memories, Lawrence foretold that 'the expelled peasantry of Philistria are going to get their own back on the colonists if the Turkish Government breaks down before the British get in.' In conclusion he warned Clayton, 'I see a situation arising in which the Jewish influence in European finance might not be sufficient to deter the Arabs from refusing to quit – or worse!'

In the aftermath of the Balfour Declaration, Arab feeling became more embittered. Lawrence shared their resentment which he explained to William Yale in two interviews in February and March 1918. There was, he had observed, a marked upsurge in anti-Semitism across southern Palestine in both Christian and Muslim communities once the Balfour Declaration had become known. Further concessions to Zionism worsened matters and Lawrence sensed that the waves of ill-feeling would shortly agitate the rest of Syria. At the heart of the problem was the Jewish leadership. 'If, as in the past, the Zionists in Palestine have as leaders that disagreeable arrogant type of their race' as well as 'dishonest and ignorant adventurers' (all presumably Polish, Russian and German Jews), the situation would deteriorate further. The 'broad-minded, liberal type of Jew' with a Western European or American background was needed to win Arab confidence. He foresaw turmoil: it was ironic, he observed, that the prospect of Jewish immigration was now acting as a catalyst for Arab nationalism that was unfriendly to Britain, the author of the Balfour Declaration. This sentiment was being exploited for all it was worth by Turco-German propagandists.

Feelings had reached such a pitch that Lawrence felt certain that 'if it were announced that a Jewish state and Government were to be established in Palestine the Arab movement would come to an end.' Lawrence also warned Yale that the combination of a German victory in France (the expected spring offensive was three weeks off) and continued Allied attachment to the Zionists would dissolve the entire Arab movement. Britain's 'unwise and foolhardy' patronage of Zionism had jeopardised her alliance with the Arabs. His government's motives were beyond Lawrence's understanding, for he could not find any emotional sympathy with the Jewish movement. 'I suppose that we are supporting the Zionists for the help it was thought they could be to us in Russia and because they brought America into the war,' a comment which was not entirely mistaken.[22]

Lawrence's views were expressed in the hope that Yale might persuade his government to temper its enthusiasm for Zionism and offer some comfort to the Arabs. While they contain unmistakable undercurrents of that brand of anti-Semitism which permeated his class at that time, his objections to the Jews were based on his anxieties about the future of the Middle East. What he feared was the incursion of immigrants from the ghettos of Central and Eastern Europe whom he saw as overbearing intruders bent on uprooting the native Palestinian Arabs. Romantically attached to the concept of a Middle East which was hierarchical and rural, Lawrence was instinctively hostile towards a race that represented the cosmopolitan and capitalist and which, if allowed to settle in large numbers, would introduce the sort of modernisation which he detested. The Balfour Declaration was for Lawrence an unwelcome and unsettling factor that threatened to overturn the Anglo-Arab alliance which he had helped to preserve and promote.

The Jewish question was also dividing Lawrence's colleagues. As Meinertzhagen observed, there was a clear-cut preference for the Arabs among British officers then and after the war. Working alongside Hubert Young and Lawrence in the Colonial Office during 1921, he noticed that they 'do their utmost to conceal their dislike and mistrust of the Jews', even though they faithfully worked to implement policies based upon the Balfour Declaration.[23]

Matters arising from the Balfour Declaration were a distraction for Lawrence during 1918: his main concern was the Arab war effort. He and others realised that the British government's new alignment with Zionism could weaken its ties with the Arabs, and diplomatic efforts were made to bring Arabs and Jews together. Speaking at Manchester in December 1917, Sykes felt obliged to 'warn Jews to look through Arab glasses'. United, the two races could exploit the 'man-power, virgin soil, petroleum and brains' which were the untapped assets of the Middle East, a possibility which Lawrence would have abhorred.

As a first stage in this process of conciliation Weizmann, accompanied by Ormsby-Gore and carrying a letter of recommendation from Clayton, visited Aqaba on 6 June 1918 for a meeting with Faisal. Faisal, who could speak English, preferred to conduct the talks through an interpreter, a task which fell to Joyce. Lawrence was present in Aqaba but he did not offer his services, even though he was probably a better Arabist. According to Joyce's recollection of the discussions, Faisal expressed a view that Arab–Jewish co-operation was necessary but refrained from offering any political opinions since he was just an agent of his father. Weizmann explained how the creation of a Jewish Palestine would assist the development of an Arab kingdom which would have Jewish backing. Turning to the knotty problem of Palestine, Weizmann hoped that under British protection it would be colonised by Jews.

Faisal was uneasy about this: as an Arab he could not speak on the future of Palestine, which had already been widely bruited by the Turco-German propaganda machine 'and would undoubtedly be misinterpreted by the uneducated Beduins if openly discussed'. Only when the Arab military and political position had been consolidated could the business be aired. Faisal personally accepted 'a future Jewish claim to Territory in Palestine' and Weizmann promised to get United States Jews to support the Arab movement. Joyce felt that Faisal was sincere in his wish for Arab–Jewish co-operation and he noted that he and Weizmann agreed that 'outside Jews and Arabs no one else had any territorial claim on Syria'.[24] Weizmann met Lawrence and left Aqaba with the impression that he was the mainstay of the military side of the Arab movement. Six months later they met again in London, where Lawrence, convinced that an Arab–Jewish accord was essential for Middle Eastern equilibrium, reintroduced him to Faisal and chaired discussions between them.

Just after he had spoken to Weizmann, Faisal returned to his secret negotiations with the Turks. On this occasion Lawrence intercepted his message and delivered a copy to Cairo, although in principle he approved of Faisal keeping his options open. The underhand exchanges with the Turks, the Arab reaction to the Balfour Declaration, and Britain's earlier moves towards a peace with Turkey were all reminders of the precariousness of the Arabs' position in the world. Lawrence knew this better than most, just as he realised that what he considered their moral rights counted for very little with his government. Their only chance to escape the thicket of diplomacy was to hack themselves out. Victory on the battlefield, Lawrence believed, not only gained land for the conquerors but bestowed on them moral rights which he believed could not be lightly tossed aside by the world.

V

WAR'S MISCHANCES: NOVEMBER 1917–JULY 1918

THE face of the Arab campaign changed rapidly during the winter of 1917/18. What Major Hubert Young called 'the picturesque days of lone-handed enterprise and dashing raids' gave way to a new style of warfare which was more calculated, conventional and tightly controlled from above. Lawrence's influence was still all pervasive, although since July he had followed Allenby's orders and worked in conjunction with a steadily expanding group of staff officers who were being assigned to service with the Arab forces. This body was titled the Hejaz Operations Staff, which was quickly abbreviated to 'Hedgehog'. Hedgehog also embraced the numerous specialists who ran signals, supply and transport and the officers in charge of the ancillary RAF, armoured-car and motorised artillery units concentrated at Aqaba and the forward bases at el Quweira and Bir el Lasan.

These support detachments brought with them British other-ranks: aircraftsmen, mechanics, armourers, drivers, gunners, instructors and wireless operators. There was also Captain Pisani's mountain and machine-gun company of 146 French Algerians which took an important part in nearly every major engagement until the end of the campaign. Aqaba was guarded by an Egyptian infantry battalion and the unloading and movement of supplies was undertaken by the Egyptian Transport Corps. More Egyptian troops appeared in Aqaba at the beginning of April, the 160-strong company of the Egyptian Camel Corps, commanded by Bimbashi [Major] F.G. ('Fred') Peake, which was destined for service as mounted infantry with the railway raiding parties. In total there were over 1,000 Egyptians attached to Faisal's army, many openly pro-Turkish and all contemptuous of the Arabs. Their presence along with the British and French forces was a clear indication that Lawrence's dream of running the campaign with minimal outside help had long evaporated.

A powerful sense of community soon developed among the band of British officers of Hedgehog. It was an exciting, adventurous form of service completely unlike anything they had experienced before. Veterans of Gallipoli and the Western Front found themselves wonderfully free of the regulations and restrictions which governed large-scale operations. They waged war riding across the desert alongside wild tribesmen, grew beards and dressed as they pleased, sometimes like Lawrence in Beduin robes. The subterranean billet was replaced by the camp under the stars. It was all very romantic and intoxicating.

Everyone was mesmerised by Lawrence, whose behaviour and attitudes were a refreshing if sometimes exasperating novelty. Major Stirling, a swashbuckler who turned up at Aqaba in the summer along with a large green Vauxhall car ordered for Faisal, knew what to expect. He had worked with Lawrence and Woolley in Cairo and remembered a couple of 'individualists who laughed at the military machine' and 'said things that we longed to, but on account of upbringing did not say'.[1] Stirling, Joyce, Young, Major Lord 'Eddie' Winterton, Lieutenant-Colonel Alan Dawnay all fell under Lawrence's spell, remained his friends after the war and contributed to the spread of his reputation. Young, an aristocratic and strong-minded professional, found Lawrence a prickly colleague and, although sincere in his admiration, was never blind to his friend's faults. These also surfaced in the memoirs of another colleague, Lieutenant Alec Kirkbride, who first met Lawrence in February 1918. Kirkbride was bowled over by his charm yet sensed its limitations, commenting that 'He was capable of kindness, particularly to those whose youth and inexperience excluded them from the category of possible rivals.'[2]

Kirkbride was not taken in by the glamour which surrounded Lawrence and delighted the Arabs, and he was unconvinced by what he wrote afterwards: 'He made no secret of the fact that he loved fame and it was, no doubt, this longing for notoriety that led him to exaggerate and embroider his versions of the happenings in which he played a part.'[3] There were plenty who took Lawrence and his stories at face value. In his absence, some members of the group entertained the American journalist Lowell Thomas in their mess at el Quweira, and fed him yarns which he believed unreservedly.[4] When Lowell Thomas had worked over this and other material and on the stage and in print had made Lawrence a celebrity, Stirling believed that none who had served with him felt envy or resentment. Young regretted the post-war ballyhoo, but never allowed it to obscure the fact that Lawrence had been indispensable.

The British other-ranks soon learned to respect and admire him. For the first time in his life, Lawrence came into close daily contact with working men. They were initially puzzled by his habits and attitudes, which were very different from what they had come to expect from officers. Air Mechanic Birkinshaw of X Flight heard of Lawrence from his mates after he had been ordered to drive him up country in a Crossley tender. '"Who's Captain Lawrence and how am I going to take him?" And somebody said, "He's the wizard Lawrence, he is. He looks you in the face and you do what he likes."' When their wagon broke down, Lawrence went off to fetch some camels, leaving Birkinshaw with a copy of *Hamlet* to read and some advice. 'Interesting story. Better read it. Hamlet was like me, somehow. Always got himself into trouble without any reason.'[5]

Men like Birkinshaw were unaccustomed to such familiarity from their officers. 'It was already amusing me to think of Lawrence as a severe military colonel,' recalled Driver Rolls. 'In our corps [Armoured Cars], as in others, orders were snapped out like curses, and salutes were exacted in the fullest measure. Lawrence's orders were directions, and he cared nothing about saluting, except he preferred to dispense with it.' Lawrence's manner of command was donnish and reminiscent of the tutorial. 'Instead of an order he usually seemed to raise, first of all, a question for discussion; giving the impression, a true one, that he wanted to have one's opinion of what was best, before he decided on the course to be followed.'[6] It was a style of leadership which fitted the circumstances and was ideally suited to small teams of specialists; and it worked.

Officers and men with the Hejaz force had the opportunity to watch Lawrence as he carried out his principal duty, liaison with the Arabs. His authority with them was now at its height and it was undertaken with consummate skill:

He was beautifully robed in a black aba with a deep gold border, a
kaftan of finest white Damascus silk with wide flowing sleeves bound
at the waist with a belt containing a large curved gold dagger. A qalifah
or head cloth of rich embroidered silk kept in place by an agal of white

and gold. Sandals on his bare feet. In every detail a truly distinguished figure from any nobles of the Royal House of Hussain seated around us. At this, as at dozens of other conferences we attended together, Lawrence rarely spoke. He merely studied the men around him and when the arguments ended as they usually did, in smoke, he then dictated his plan of action which was usually adopted and everyone went away satisfied. It was not as is often supposed by his individual leadership of hordes of Beduin that he achieved success in his daring ventures, but by his wise selection of Tribal leaders and by providing the essential grist to the mill in the shape of golden rewards for work well done.[7]

Joyce's comments were echoed by Stirling, who was aware of Lawrence's 'uncanny ability to sense the feelings of a group of men in whose company he found himself'.[8]

The trappings of rich costume served a practical purpose as well as satisfying Lawrence's vanity. He knew that fine clothes and ostentatious displays of gold were the conventional, outward marks of a man's standing and authority which commanded the immediate respect and obedience of the Beduin tribesman. He usually kept his sharifian robes for such formal occasions as conferences with Faisal, although he could never resist dressing up in them at British HQ, where he attracted much attention. On active service he wore a sombre brown aba, sometimes khaki kit, but once, during the attack on Tal as Shahm station in April 1918, he graced the battlefield in his full white regalia. As he rode across country, his dramatic appearance was heightened by his twenty or so bodyguards. Like Lawrence, who owned a stable of such beasts, they were mounted on richly caparisoned, thoroughbred she-camels prized for their stamina. Each man was chosen by Lawrence, mostly from the Agayl tribe which had a tradition of mercenary service, and was paid six sovereigns a month. As befitted a warrior elite and to sustain the prestige of their master, the bodyguards wore coats of many colours. Seeing them, one British officer was reminded of the multi-coloured costumes of Diaghilev's Russian ballet.

With his escort of camelry, dressed in Arab robes but, on close inspection, clearly an Englishman, Lawrence was a striking figure in camp and on campaign. British officers and other-ranks who encountered him were intrigued. He made his own rules and was always elusive, coming and going without notice either into the hinterland or by boat and aeroplane to Cairo or HQ at Ramleh. He was adored by the Arabs, whose appreciative shouts at his approach were in part a reminder that he paid their generous wages, but he could also bend their will to his. Behind the flamboyant façade was a formidable reputation for courage created by reports of his activities deep inside enemy territory during the past year. Even as the nature of the Arab campaign changed, Lawrence continued to dominate it.

One significant feature of the Arab campaign remained unchanged. Faisal's Arab army was still under the overall direction of Allenby and was expected to assist his operations in southern Palestine. Their central objective was also the same, the elimination of Turkish communications between Syria and Medina. After the fall of Jerusalem in December and with the onset of the wet season, Allenby's aims had been confined to consolidation of his front in preparation for the next stage of his Palestinian offensive. For this to be successful it was of paramount importance that the Hejaz railway was permanently ruptured, leaving the Medina garrison isolated and incapable of intervention in the fighting to the north. Plans devised in November for raids as far north as Damascus and Aleppo were put aside.[9] The high hopes which Lawrence had entertained of large-scale, mobile raids with Druze and Rwallah support faded. During February and March disquieting intelligence reached Cairo which suggested that Druze enthusiasm for Faisal was waning and that they were veering towards the Turks after the disclosure of the Sykes–Picot agreement and reports of the Balfour Declaration.[10]

Realising that long-range sorties in the Damascus region were risky and impractical, Allenby demanded that Faisal's forces confine their efforts to a general advance into southern Jordan and attacks on the railway north and south of Maan. The occupation of a string of weakly held Turkish outposts in southern Jordan had a double purpose. If the Arabs could take them, they would be able to link up with Allenby's forces in the Jordan valley and deny to the Turks a valuable corn-growing region.

The campaign in southern Jordan opened on a successful note. On 3 January 1918, Nasir attacked Jurf ed Darawish station, occupied it for three days, destroyed two trains and fell back towards Aqaba. On the way back his Bani Sakhr tribesmen surprised and captured Tafila on 15 January, taking prisoner its eighty-man garrison.[11] A few days later the hilltop town was reinforced by a larger force of regulars, irregulars and French Algerian gunners commanded by Faisal's brother Zaid. He was a poor choice for general, lacking both experience and resolve, but his inadequacies were offset by Lawrence and Jafar al Askari, who acted as his advisers. Their clear heads and stout hearts were soon needed. Probably under the illusion that Tafila had been the victim of a tribal raid, the Turks sent a column of 100 cavalry and 600 infantry equipped with two howitzers and twenty machine-guns to recover the town.

Zaid panicked when warned of the column's approach. On the morning of 22 January he withdrew his forces from the town and placed them in a defensive position on high ground to the south. The local villagers showed more spirit and engaged the cavalry pickets, temporarily slowing down the Turkish advance. At this stage Lawrence intervened. In his own words, he had scoured his memory for 'old maxims and rules of the military text books', although his instinct dictated that he could check the Turks 'by manoeuvre'. Instead he used his eye for ground and urged Zaid to take advantage of his opponents' delay and shift his men to new positions on a ridge which overlooked the plateau where the Turks were about to deploy. From their new position, the Arab and Algerian machine-gunners were able to hinder the Turks' deployment. Directed by Lawrence, a small party of Arabs, using ground hidden from enemy view, were able to get round the Turks' southern flank. The Turks then faced an attack on their northern flank where armed villagers were able to surprise their machine-gun positions. Pressed from three sides and under heavy machine-gun fire, the Turks broke and scattered. The bitter cold and snow prevented an Arab pursuit.

It was a heartening victory for the Arabs and earned Lawrence a DSO. Liddell Hart made much of Lawrence's skill as a tactician, so elevating Tafila from a skirmish into a battle. By the standards of the time it was a small affair, involving less than 2,000 men and with few casualties. Nevertheless by his quick-wittedness, judgement and courage Lawrence had averted a disaster. In retrospect he felt that he had betrayed his principles by standing and fighting rather than outmanoeuvring his opponents and he considered the seven Arab dead a high price to pay for success. It is, however, hard to imagine what alternative existed: Zaid had abandoned the town, the Arab forces were far from their bases and the weather was harsh so a siege would have been folly. There was no choice but to offer battle.

Zaid and Tafila soon gave Lawrence further cause for heartache. On the day of the battle, he had written to Clayton for 30,000 gold sovereigns with which to fund further operations in southern Jordan, scheduled to begin when the weather improved. Zaid took this money and disbursed it to various tribal sheiks for past services. His treasury exhausted and full of self-reproach for having trusted Zaid, Lawrence returned to HQ. He blamed himself for what had occurred and protested to Hogarth and Clayton that the free hand which Allenby had given him in dealing with the Arabs was too much for him. What he wanted were strict orders which could be obeyed, rather than continuously having to make his own decisions. The older men pointed out that Lawrence could not sidestep his responsibilities, especially as the entire Middle Eastern campaign was entering a crucial phase. Lawrence alone could procure and deliver the Arab assistance that would be vital for Allenby's next offensive. He accepted his fate and recovered his equanimity. 'He is very well and very much at the top of the pole,' Hogarth reported on 25 February.[12] He was certainly in a jaunty and flippant mood when he met Young in Cairo:

> 'They asked me to suggest someone who could take my place in case anything happened to me,' said Lawrence, with his mischievous smile, 'and I told them I thought no one could. And when they pressed me, I said I could only think of Gertrude Bell and yourself, and they seemed to think you would be better for this particular job than she would. It is quite amusing, and there is plenty of honour and glory to be picked up without any great difficulty.'[13]

Soon after, news arrived which confirmed his commanders' judgements about his irreplaceability. Without him, the Arab command at Tafila had disintegrated and the town was evacuated in a pell-mell retreat. On 3 March while Lawrence was at HQ, three strong Turco-German columns which had detrained at Qatraní, Hasa and Jurf ed Darawish prepared to encircle the town. The timid Zaid, who had had ample warning of their approach, fell back under the threat of howitzer fire. Some regulars retreated 'too fast', which saved them since they escaped the claws of the enemy's pincer movement, although the Algerian machine-gunners held their ground to the last moment. 'The Turks profited from the lack of enterprise shown by the Sharifian command [Zaid] at Tafila' was Hedgehog staff's terse diagnosis of the débâcle. Lawrence may have anticipated something of this kind since, before he left Tafila, he had written a message to be delivered to X Flight asking for bombing sorties against the Turkish camps at Hasa and Jurf ed Darawish. Muddle or slackness delayed its arrival until 5 March, a day after Tafila had fallen.[14]

This setback had unforeseen consequences. After their easy triumph at Tafila, the Turco-German columns, alerted to a British offensive across the Jordan, were able to return to Qatrani to reinforce Amman.[15] Although some German and Turkish troops travelled by motor trucks, trains were readily available for their outward and return journeys. The campaign to disrupt the Hejaz railway was simply not yielding any useful tactical results.

It was the inability of the Arabs to make any headway in the railway war which led Allenby to propose a sequence of Anglo-Arab offensives against Amman and Maan at the end of March and the beginning of April. These operations were a preliminary to the big push northwards into Syria which had been sanctioned by Lloyd George in January. Before he could contend with the main concentrations of Turkish, German and Austrian forces (there were 25,000 Germans serving with the Ottoman army by November 1918), Allenby needed to have a secure eastern flank. The March–April operations were designed to achieve this by a permanent scission of the Hejaz railway at Maan and Amman and the elimination of Turkish strongholds south and east of the Dead Sea. Salt was to be occupied by British forces and would serve as the point of contact between Allenby's army and Faisal's. Since the co-operation of Arab forces was vital in this campaign, Lawrence was closely involved in its planning. Between 21 February and 3 March he was variously at Allenby's HQ at Ramleh, Beersheba and Cairo; on 4 March he briefly returned to Aqaba, where he consulted Faisal; and from 8 to 15 March he was back in Egypt.

This was the first occasion when Arab forces were expected to contribute materially to a major operation. To ensure thorough planning beforehand, Lieutenant-Colonel Alan Dawnay was detached from Allenby's staff and sent to Faisal's HQ at el Quweira to advise and co-ordinate preparations. He had 'wanted a little fun' according to Young, but his real purpose was to ensure rigorous professional standards were adhered to before and during the operation. Lawrence was singularly impressed by this elegant, intelligent and open-minded Etonian who, alone of British senior officers, shared his vision of the Arab Revolt. 'He married war and rebellion in himself; as, of old in Yanbu, it had been my dream every regular officer would.' In the *Seven Pillars* Lawrence described Dawnay as a man who charmed and instructed: 'His perfect manner made him friends with all races and classes. From his teaching we began to learn the technique of fighting in matters we had been content to settle by rude and wasteful rules of thumb.'

Lawrence's part in the operation was to bring irregular forces to a rendez-vous with the British at Salt on 30 March. What followed was a sequence of misfortunes. On 23 March, watched by Queen Victoria's soldier son, the Duke of Connaught, ANZAC units, the 60th Londons and the Imperial Camel Corps crossed the Jordan. A fortnight of heavy rain made the going tough and there was stiff resistance from Turkish and German units in the Moab hills and Amman, including some hurriedly moved from Tafila. Amman was briefly taken during heavy fighting between 27 and 30 March but had to be abandoned. British forces fell back to their original positions, having lost 404 dead and over a thousand wounded. Lawrence was uncharit-able about their efforts in the *Seven Pillars*, where he remarked that it was 'deplorable' that 'we should so fall down before the Arabs'. His own and British prestige had been tarnished. He also censured the inability of British and ANZAC detachments to do what the Arabs had so conspicuously failed to do, make the railway unusable.[16]

The Arab contribution to the campaign was negligible. A week after the withdrawal from Amman, Lawrence got news of the reverse, which had travelled with what Liddell Hart called a 'curious slowness'. The Bani Sakhr were quicker off the mark and used the British attack on Amman as an opportunity to seize and plunder two stations north of the town and then ride off.[17] Once it was clear that the British had fallen back beyond Salt, there was nothing for Lawrence to do but return southwards to where the attack on Maan was beginning. In his account of the campaign, published in 1920, *The Times* correspondent W.T.Massey indicated that there was a general disappointment at the poor performance of the Arabs.

> In this Amman enterprise some assistance was expected from the army of the King of the Hijaz. As a matter of fact there was no sign of the sharifian troops north of Karak. We seemed to have more trouble with various Arab tribes east of the Jordan than in obtaining their promises of support.[18]

There was a minor compensation: once the Turco-German detachments pulled out of Tafila, it was reoccupied bloodlessly by the Arabs.

Two minor incidents, one risible, the other rather harrowing, marked Lawrence's return south. As they were about to head south, a bevy of gypsy pedlar–prostitutes arrived at Lawrence's camp seeking business from his bodyguard. Lawrence and Farraj borrowed some of their clothes and, accompanied by three of the whores, entered Amman to examine the state of the town. Importuned by Turkish soldiers they just managed to escape. Soon after, his servant, Farraj, was mortally wounded after a brush with a Turkish patrol, so Lawrence, rather than leave him to fall into Turkish hands, delivered the *coup de grâce* with his revolver.

When Lawrence reached Maan a battle was in full swing. The final arrangements for the attack had been settled by Faisal, Zaid, Jafar and Nuri es Said 'after long and heated debate' on 6 April.[19] It was agreed that a column of regular and irregular forces would occupy Abu el Jurdhan, straddle the line and entrench while a second column attacked Maan. A third, commanded by Dawnay, would assault various targets along the line to the south of Maan and ensure the town's isolation. Nuri es Said dissented and Dawnay doubted whether the untried Arab regulars would be up to the task of storming Maan, but the other Arab commanders were keen to prove their men's mettle in hard fighting. There was further consultation between the commanders of the Maan and Abu el Jurdhan columns at Wahaida on the 13th just before the fighting began when plans were changed.[20]

Throughout the operation Arab forces were given close support by the RAF: aircraft guarded the flanks of the columns, made reconnaissance flights over the battlefields, flew a leaflet raid over Maan and carried out bombing raids on all targets. There was assistance as well from the French gunners, who were attached to the Maan force, and the British motorised artillery, armoured cars and Egyptian Camel Corps, who were with Dawnay.

Lawrence, who had picked up a Model-T Ford and driver at el Quweira, acted throughout as a liaison officer between columns, carried messages back to X Flight's forward airstrip at Decie, and undertook several reconnaissance sorties with Dawnay's force.

After a two-day pause, the central column left Bir el Lasan on 9 April. Commanded by the veteran Iraqi officer Maulud Pasha, it mustered 600 regular infantry, 50 mule-mounted cavalry with artillery and machine-gun support and 400 Huweitat tribesmen under Awda. After a feint towards Ghadir al Haj station, where 1,200 rails were wrenched up, the column turned northwards. On the morning of the following day, 14 April, Maulud's men occupied the Jebel Samna west of Maan, where the newly arrived Lawrence watched them take their positions. The attack on Maan station began with an artillery bombardment on the morning of the 15th, after which Arab regulars advanced and took a low hill 300 yards south-east of their objective, a vital position which 'they evacuated for no reason during the night'.[21] This ground was retaken during the next day after a seven-and-a-half hour bombardment and an air raid. Turkish resistance was stubborn and the final attack on the station was driven off by heavy machine-gun fire.[22]

Under Nuri's direction (Maulud had been wounded), the Arab forces pulled back to the Jebel Samna, dug in and checked a pursuit by the Turkish garrison, which had been reinforced from the north on the 18th. Further north, Jafar's column of 600 regular infantry had attacked and carried Abu el Jurdhan station on 13 April. The approach of a large force of cavalry from Amman forced their withdrawal and the Turks quickly began to repair the line, which was partially open to traffic by the 21st. Six days later trains were operating between Amman and Maan.[23] The ferocity and determination of the Arab attacks had caused consternation among the Turks. Intercepted and deciphered wireless messages revealed that the officer commanding in Maan, Faik Bey, had appealed for 1,000 reinforcements, but the Fourth Army's commander, Muhammad Jamal Pasha, was unmoved.[24] Among the Arab command, there were recriminations. Nuri was contemptuous of Awda, whose irregulars would risk themselves only when it was clear that resistance was crumbling and loot was in the offing. They were 'quite useless', thought Young.[25]

After the Maan attack had been called off, Lawrence was driven to the airstrip at Decie, where he passed on this information. A five-hour drive then took him to Dawnay's HQ where he arrived at ten in the evening of the 18th, just after Dawnay and Hornby had completed their final reconnaissance of Tal as Shahm station. The attack began the next morning. Dawnay had carefully predetermined his units' dispositions and movements, much to the wry amusement of Lawrence. Breakfast was taken at 3.30 a.m.

and at dawn the three Rolls-Royce armoured cars took up their covering positions 4,000 yards west of the station with Lawrence and Dawnay following in a tender. At 9.00 a.m. the Egyptian camelry and Arab irregulars deployed on high ground above the station. As a precaution against a relief train from the south, Lawrence, Dawnay and Hornby blew up a culvert. After an RAF air raid and shelling by the ten-pounders, the thirty-one-strong station garrison surrendered.[26]

Immediately the Arabs surged into the station and pandemonium followed as, 'screaming like Tigers', they fell upon the stores. The Egyptian camelry joined in and Lawrence had to intervene to prevent a brawl. Well satisfied with their plunder, most of the irregulars departed. The rest disappeared the following day after the force found Ramlah station abandoned. Dawnay's depleted force now faced its toughest task, an attack on the well-garrisoned Qalat al Mudawarrah station. The prospects were not good for, on 20 April, a reconnaissance plane from X Flight had reported a train carrying reinforcements moving from Tabuk. As Lawrence later informed staff at Decie airstrip, the train contained two Austrian howitzers with a range of 8,000 yards, which had the advantage over Dawnay's ten-pounders.[27] Both guns were ready for action on the morning of the 21st when Dawnay's armoured cars and artillery deployed before Qalat al Mudawarrah station. Rather than risk heavy losses, Dawnay called off the attack and withdrew. The station was finally attacked and its garrison overwhelmed by two companies of British Imperial Camel Corps on 8 August. 'A beastly indecent performance' was how Dawnay described the operation to Hogarth, thinking no doubt of the Arab contribution.[28] He, the British and Egyptian detachments had accomplished much in four days.

The war of attrition against Maan and the stations to the north continued with intermittent raids during May, June, July and early August. Regular Arab units were now playing an increasingly active role, with the RAF and British and Egyptian ground units providing the essential muscle. Lawrence was never happy about the growing dominance of Arab and non-Arab regular units, nor did he like having to keep in step with Allenby. 'Our movement, clean cut while alone with a simple enemy,' he wrote in the *Seven Pillars*, 'was now bogged in its partner's contingencies,' which meant, one supposes, that the Arabs were having to share some of the burden of fighting the Turks where they were strong, a task hitherto confined to British and Dominion troops.

While Lawrence doggedly stuck to his principles of guerrilla warfare as waged by the Beduin, his colleagues found the Arabs fickle and feckless. Even with substantial support they were unsteady in a crisis. On 21–22 January a force of 2,500 backed by armoured cars and artillery refused to attack Qalat al Mudawarrah and scattered when they heard that a relief force was coming up from Tabuk.[29] At the end of April, Faisal's agent with the Bani Sakhr pledged tribal support for a British incursion which never materialised, causing the operation to miscarry. Lawrence blamed British staff for trusting 'some airy promise' of a handful of sheiks while Wavell, Allenby's biographer, drily remarked, 'it was difficult for G.H.Q. at the time to realize the complete irresponsibility of Arab warfare.'[30] Others with first-hand experience soon learned the lesson. Young was exasperated by the tribesmen's unreliability and Kirkbride felt that they were incapable 'of doing so much damage that the line would be disrupted'. What he and others endured is conveyed in the comments written by Captain Pascoe in the War Diary of the motorised artillery detachment then serving with the Beduin.

8.6.18. Sharif Muhammad Ali of Bani hasn't arrived.

10.6.18. Conference with Hamdi Effendi, commander sharifian forces – decided to await arrival of Muhammad.

30.6.18. Bedu again changed plans and decided would not attack without money. I said unless attack as agreed, the English force would retire.[31]

Sometimes even Lawrence's patience ran out. After a tussle with Zaid in which he failed to persuade him to exploit the victory at Tafila, he wrote angrily to Clayton, 'These Arabs are the most ghastly material to build into a design.'

The regular Arab army contained better material. On 11–12 May a force supported by RAF bombers captured Abu el Jurdhan station and took 200 prisoners, but was forced to retire because of a shortage of water. A second attack on the station five days later was badly mauled by a garrison which had been increased to 400.[32] Sometimes, however, the regular Arabs' inexperience and hurried training gave their allies some awkward moments. During an attack on a station in July, an armoured car officer noticed that 'The first line of Infantry, numbering as I could judge about 50 men, were not reinforced and remained at 600 yards range,' and then followed what was euphemistically called a 'general retirement', leaving the cars to take the full brunt of Turkish fire.[33] Such behaviour must have been particularly galling, considering what Driver Rolls called the 'increasingly lofty attitude' of the Arabs towards the British.

Lawrence advised Rolls and his fellows to show forbearance. He believed that on balance the Arabs had gained the upper hand during the first six months of 1918, although their gains had been modest and the major success of the campaign, the permanent severance of the line between Maan and Medina, had been accomplished by a British unit. Inept leadership, a lack of reserves and muddle had prevented Arab forces from asserting control over the area south of the Dead Sea. Measured in purely strategic terms the Arabs had gained and kept an advantage on the Maan front. Faisal's 3,500 regulars and the fissiparous tribal forces had managed to contain 4,000 men in Maan and a further 1,000 distributed in penny packets guarding stations northwards towards Amman. A further 6,000 Turkish troops were scattered in outposts in southern Jordan and along the line south from Maan. So long as the railway attacks persisted, these units had periodically to be strengthened. Of course this diversion of Turkish forces owed much to the presence with the Arabs of small but powerful Allied auxiliary units. Local aerial supremacy (in February 1918 there were three Rumpler CIs of the Ottoman Air Force stationed at Maan) was a further, perhaps decisive, factor in the Arabs' favour.

Yet Maan still held out, forcing the Arabs to maintain a blockade. During July intelligence decrypts of wireless messages from the commander at Maan revealed food, fodder, fuel and cash shortages and a spate of desertions as morale drooped.[34] Still, the Turkish soldier was amazingly resilient and the Maan garrison could and did take the offensive against outlying Arab pickets. Any relaxation of the pressure of Maan would have invited a Turkish sally which could have endangered the forward posts at el Quweira and Bir el Lasan and communications with Aqaba. There was still plenty of fight left in the Turks on this front: on 21 July an Arab attack on Abu el Jurdhan, well backed by aircraft, armoured cars and artillery was thrown back with eighty dead by the 400-strong garrison.

Lawrence was not present at this action. More and more of his time was taken up with administration and liaison with British HQ, although he still undertook reconnaissance and sabotage missions. On these he commonly travelled by car or lorry, which gave him greater mobility as well as greater comfort (in spite of solid tyres) and his first taste of the excitement of speed. When time pressed, he flew to and from HQ, and on 28 May he went as an observer on a reconnaissance flight over Qalat el Mudawarrah.[35] As the summer progressed, he had less and less time for such diversions; by July Allenby was well into his preparations for an autumn grand offensive against Syria which required closely co-ordinated Arab support. Damascus and Syria now seemed within Lawrence's and the Arabs' grasp.

VI

DAMASCUS: FLAWED TRIUMPH

A T midnight on 19–20 September, General Allenby's Egyptian
Expeditionary Force launched the brilliantly planned and long-awaited
hammer-blow against the Turco-German army in northern Palestine.
Twenty-four hours later, the Turkish 7th and 8th Army Corps and the
German Asian Corps were falling back north-eastwards in disarray with
the 4th Cavalry and Australian Mounted Divisions close on their heels.
Harried by cavalry and harassed by round-the-clock bombing and strafing,
the fragmented and demoralised units rushed helter-skelter towards Dera.
The rout was shortly joined by the remnants of the 4th Army Corps which
had abandoned Maan on 23 September and Amman the day after.

According to Allenby's strategy, those fugitives who escaped their
pursuers would converge on Dera. Lawrence had been instructed to take
an Arab column northwards from Bir el Lasan and seize the town by the
22nd or 23rd, after first having severed its rail links north, south and east.[1]
With Dera in Arab hands, the retreating armies would be jammed into
a bottleneck, cut off from Damascus and with no choice but surrender.
For the first time in the war, Arab forces were fighting as an integral part
of a larger Allied army and had been assigned tactical objectives whose
achievement was essential for the overall success of a major campaign.

Lawrence's sights were set far beyond Dera. As the Turkish army fell
apart the moment was right for a political masterstroke, the occupation
of Damascus by Faisal and the Arabs. Such a coup was for Lawrence
the only possible consummation of the Arab movement; over the past two
years he had goaded and coaxed the Arabs towards this city and made
it for them what Jerusalem had been for the Crusaders. What he had
intended when he had first met Faisal would be accomplished, and the
Arab renaissance could be proclaimed to the world with a dramatic flourish.
The military climax of the Arab Revolt would determine its political future,
because physical possession of Damascus would give substance to Faisal's
flimsy and unassured Syrian pretensions. For Lawrence there was a further
satisfaction since Faisal's occupation of Damascus might prove an insur-
mountable obstacle to French ambitions in the region.

All these elements merge in his narrative of the campaign. The Arab
advance on and capture of Damascus is covered in the closing chapters

of the *Seven Pillars*, and all that Lawrence wrote on the subject seems to justify the book's sub-title, 'A Triumph'. From the start he had presented Damascus as the only goal worthy of the Arabs, for the liberation of a city which had once been the heart of an ancient Arab empire would symbolise the release of the entire Arab world from Ottoman bondage. In purely literary terms the entry into Damascus represents the end of Lawrence's quest; the vindication of his faith in the Arabs; the reward for sacrifice and incontrovertible evidence of what had been achieved by his and their united willpower. All the major and minor themes introduced during the narrative are drawn together in the Damascus chapters to give the work an artistic if not historical completeness. In striving for this artistic effect, satisfying both to himself and to his readers, Lawrence was forced to jettison historical authenticity.

As a result, his account of much that happened before and after the capture of the city was a fabrication and demonstrably so, as he fully appreciated. 'I was on thin ice when I wrote the Damascus chapter,' he later admitted, 'and anyone who copies me will be through it, if he is not careful. S.P. [*Seven Pillars*] is full of half-truth: here.'[2] There was a second reason why Lawrence deliberately tinkered with historical truth. By concocting a version of the Damascus campaign in which the exertions of British, ANZAC and Indian troops are hardly mentioned, even in passing, and those of the Arabs exaggerated to the point where they are transformed into the first emancipators of Damascus, he manufactured potent propaganda which has seldom been challenged. Indeed the distortion has been perpetuated in Rattigan's *Ross* and Lean's film *Lawrence of Arabia*, both of which convey a clear impression that the Arabs took Damascus unaided.

With the Syrian offensive of September 1918, Lawrence's primary task was to ensure that Arab forces fulfilled Allenby's tactical requirements. He was therefore closely involved in each stage of strategic planning and, as the campaign proceeded, he was responsible for liaison between Arab units and British HQ. When detachments from both armies began to converge on Dera he took charge of all arrangements for co-operation between them. On 26 September, Allenby, unaware of his secret schemes, appointed Lawrence political liaison officer under General Sir Harry Chauvel, the commander of the Australian Mounted Division, which had been ordered to advance on Damascus.[3]

The Arab force assigned to the Dera front was led by two able and experienced commanders, Nuri es Said and Nasir. It was small, mobile and well armed. There were 450 regular camelry equipped with twenty light machine-guns, Pisani's Algerian gunners, two Rolls-Royce armoured cars with their tenders, a Gurkha machine-gun company, and Peake's Egyptian camelry. Air cover was provided by two machines detached from X

Flight; for these an airstrip had been levelled at el Azraq, which Lawrence had chosen as the force's rear base. The first phase of the operation was the march from Bir el Lasan to el Azraq, where the column found fresh supplies and was joined by 4,000 or so Beduin already hired by Lawrence. They comprised Rwallah raised by Nuri Shalaan, who was now ready to show his colours openly, Huweitat under Awda and Arab peasantry from the Hawran. Once mustered, the small army would move north-west to Umtaiye, its forward operational base, from where raids would commence on 16 September. These were intended both to disrupt railway communications around Dera and to trick the Turks into thinking that the main thrust of Allenby's offensive would be directed eastwards. Additional measures were taken to decoy the Turks away from central Palestine, including mock camps along the west bank of the Jordan, complete with tents and wicker-work-and-canvas horses.

Detailed operational planning for the attacks on the railway had been devised by Lawrence, who, impatient with regular methods, left the logistics to Joyce and Young. Lawrence imagined that the regular units, which were the pith and essence of his force, could get by in the desert like the Beduin and he was therefore dismissive of his colleagues' meticulous arrangements for transport lines and supply dumps. These had scarcely been completed before the expedition ran into trouble. At the end of August, Hussain snubbed Jafar al Askari by a public denial of his right to the title 'Commander-in-Chief of the Arab armies', an insult which was compounded by a statement that no Arab officer was entitled to a rank beyond captain. Angered by these characteristically boneheaded remarks, the entire officer corps of the Arab army resigned their devalued commissions. The dispute turned ugly on the night of 1/2 September when the rank and file intervened and threatened to turn field-guns on the officers' lines. Fortunately an officer had taken the precaution of removing their breech-blocks. Lawrence, Joyce and Faisal mediated and soothed the hurt officers, whose commissions were validated.[4] The rumpus was a reminder of the gulf which was widening between Hussain and the professional army, whose loyalty had decisively shifted towards Faisal.

The mutiny at Bir el Lasan and el Quweira delayed the Dera force's departure by two days. On 4 September, the advance guard moved off and six days later arrived at el Azraq. The journey was marred by another row, this time between Major Peake and Awda, and again Lawrence had to act as peace-maker. When Peake's camelry reached el Jafr, they were confronted by a testy Awda, who demanded £10,000 as the price for access to their previously stored rations and his wells. In justification for what was outrageous greed, he claimed he had been insulted by a British officer who had refused him a lift. Lawrence was hurriedly summoned and duly delivered the golden placebo. There was further trouble for Peake soon after, when Beduin attached to his unit mutinied for no apparent reason.[5] Neither hitch is mentioned in the *Seven Pillars*.

On 11 September Lawrence was forced to revise his operational plans. He decided that the forces at his disposal were inadequate for an assault on Dera unless it had been heavily bombed first.[6] His request for RAF help was approved at HQ, but the attacks were postponed for five days since Allenby was anxious not to alert the Turks to his forthcoming offensive. On the 16th and 17th DH9s from 144 Squadron dropped 3,000 lbs of bombs on the town, severely damaging a wireless transmitter, the station and rolling-stock.[7] From the beginning, air-power was the key to Arab success.

While Dera was bombed, raiding parties fanned out from Umtaiye towards their targets. The attacks began on the 16th and continued intermittently for six days. Lawrence was omniscient throughout. Travelling by car, he directed and co-ordinated operations, supervised demolitions and, on several occasions, laid charges himself. He commanded the attack on the line north of Jabir station on the 16th and the following day accompanied the force which swung north of Dera and fell upon the line between it and Samakh. Two stations were destroyed and a section of track was put out of action for six days.[8] A third raid on the 18th ran into difficulties when Peake's camelry and the Gurkhas were misled by their Rwallah guides. Taken to Zerka rather than Mafraq, the raiding party found its way to the track blocked by Bani Sakhr tribesmen still loyal to the Turks.[9]

Resistance was always stiff and the raiders were always grateful for the mobility and firepower of the armoured cars. General von Sandars, the Commander-in-Chief in Syria, had grasped the importance of Dera as the nodal point of his rail communications and had placed its reinforced garrison under the command of an energetic German, Major Willmer.[10] The first wave of attacks on the railway and the RAF raids on the 16th convinced von Sandars that a major offensive against Dera was imminent and he immediately reinforced its defences with eight aircraft which were flown from Jenin on the 17th.

The arrival of the German planes tipped the balance against Lawrence and the Arabs. One of his machines had been forced down on the 16th and the other was lost four days later, leaving the Arabs at the mercy of the Dera flight. By the 20th German mastery of the air had brought operations against the railway to a standstill. Temporarily checkmated, Lawrence acted swiftly and decisively. A wireless message summoned up an aeroplane which flew him to Allenby's HQ, where he begged Air Commodore Geoffrey Salmond for aerial assistance. He was given a DH9 and two Bristol Fighters from No. 1 Squadron Royal Australian Air Force. Early on the morning of the 22nd, he flew back to Umtaiye in a Bristol piloted by Captain Ross Smith. Finding Umtaiye deserted, they flew south to where the Arabs had moved their camp in the hope that it would be beyond the range of the Dera flight.

It was not and, soon after Lawrence had landed, the Germans attacked. Ross Smith took to the air and was able to drive off two Pfalz scouts and force down a pair of DFW two-seaters, one of which was destroyed. A second sortie was repelled half an hour later when three Pfalzs were sent packing and one shot down. The Germans returned in the afternoon and a DWF was shot down: control of the air was now in British hands. Once again British air-power had got the Arabs out of a tight spot.[11]

The dog-fights over the desert restored Arab morale. It soared the next day when, in response to Lawrence's request, a four-engined Handley Page V 1500 bomber landed at their camp. It carried supplies, including petrol for the fighters, and filled Arab onlookers with wonderment. They imagined that this huge machine was the stallion which had sired the smaller aircraft they were familiar with, and fancied that the food taken on board for its crew was fodder to sustain the flying monster. At HQ Lawrence had persuaded Salmond and the bomber's pilot, Major Amyas ('Biffy') Borton, to employ the Handley Page for attacks on Dera and Mafraq. Six tons of bombs fell on Dera on 23 September and three on Mafraq the day after.[12]

The aircraft which flew to the Arabs' assistance not only rescued the Dera campaign, they brought news of Allenby's victories and the collapse of the Turkish front in Palestine. Further details of the disintegration of the Turkish 7th and 8th Army Corps were picked up by Lawrence at HQ and passed on to Faisal, who had joined his forces at the front. There was more encouraging news from the south where the 4th Army Corps based on Amman had been decisively beaten by Dominion forces commanded by General Sir Edward Chaytor.

The elimination of the Arabs' old adversary, the 4th Army Corps, had been carried out in less than a week. Chaytor's offensive overran Turkish posts in the Moab Hills, and on 25 September Amman was taken by New Zealanders and the hitherto underrated 2nd West Indian Battalion. The railway to the north had been broken by a detachment of the Auckland Horse on the night of 23/24 September. Thanks to their efforts and the bombing of Mafraq, the line was closed and with it the Turkish escape route north to Dera. When detachments of the Australian Light Horse reached Mafraq on the 28th, they found the station in ruins and the line blocked by stranded trains. Several wagons marked with the Red Crescent contained the bodies of Turkish wounded who had been robbed and murdered by Beduin.[13]

Broken Turkish units in disorderly retreat and burdened with wounded were opponents the Beduin could cope with. Confident that the hard fighting was over, they swarmed towards the battlefields to pillage and kill the unarmed and wounded. The Bani Sakhr, hearing that Maan had been abandoned on the 23rd after a year's gallant defence, tried to intercept the 4,000-strong garrison as it hobbled north. Discovered by RAF reconnaissance aircraft and threatened with aerial attack, the garrison commander, Ali Bey Wakkabi, offered to surrender his force to the 5th Australian Light Horse. When his offer was accepted, the Australians, on Chaytor's orders, deployed to protect the Turkish column from Arab marauders, who had already murdered some of the wounded. Deterred by occasional bursts of machine-gun fire, the skulking Bani Sakhr withdrew to seek easier pickings. As the Turkish infantry marched off into captivity, some were permitted to keep their rifles as protection against Arab looters.[14]

Everywhere Arabs killed and plundered indiscriminately. British personnel were not immune. Lieutenant Gitsham of 144 Squadron was threatened and robbed by Beduin after his machine crashed. Another officer from this squadron, Lieutenant Thomas, who was held prisoner in Dera, was robbed and stripped of his tunic by Arabs who must have been attached to Faisal's forces.[15] British officers were appalled by the Arabs' brutal treatment of Turkish fugitives, wounded and unwounded. To many, the Arabs were no more than brigands, whereas the Turks were soldiers like themselves.

Such sentiments were wormwood to Lawrence. For him the maltreatment, robbery and killing of exhausted men or prisoners were retribution for past cruelties. In the *Seven Pillars* he recorded an encounter outside Dera where some Arab irregulars were 'herding a drove of stripped prisoners towards Sheik Saad'. 'They were', he observed, 'driving them mercilessly, the bruises of their urging blue across the ivory backs; but I left them to it, for these were Turks of the police battalion of Dera, beneath whose iniquities the peasant-faces of the neighbourhood had run with tears and blood, innumerable times.' Other British officers did not share this tit-for-tat philosophy. When General Sir George Barrow, commanding the 4th Cavalry Division, entered Dera on the morning of 28 September, he was horrified by what he saw. Anazah tribesmen had moved into the town unopposed the previous evening and, according to Barrow's official report, 'murdered in cold blood every Turk they came across' and stripped the wounded.[16]

When I came they were still at their ghoulish work, tearing the clothes off the wounded men in an indescribably brutish manner. I did my business with the sharifian commander [Nuri al Said] and cleared out of the town with all my troops as soon as possible.

He rightly feared that many of the Turkish left behind would be slaughtered and concluded, 'Napoleon has been held up to execration for having shot his prisoners in this country. I wish our laws and customs allowed me to do the same. The misery of these poor Turks left to their fate and to the mercy of these cut-throat Beduins cannot easily be described.'

Barrow refrained from including an account of his brusque exchange with Lawrence, whom he had met earlier in the day and had accompanied to Dera. It was, however, set down in his memoirs along with a graphic description of the sufferings of the Turkish wounded.

I asked Lawrence to remove the Arabs. He said he couldn't 'as it was their idea of war'. I replied, 'It is not our idea of war, and if you can't remove them, I will.' He said, 'If you attempt to do that I shall take no responsibility for what happens.' I answered, 'That's all right; I will take the responsibility,' and at once gave orders for our men to clear that station. This was done and nothing untoward happened. All Arabs were turned off the train and it was piqueted by our sentries.[17]

Lawrence never referred either to the cruelties inflicted on the Turks or to this conversation, but the memory of the encounter rankled and Barrow was roughly treated in the *Seven Pillars*. He was charged with showing disappointment when he heard that Arabs had taken Dera and of imagining that they were 'a conquered people'. Barrow's Indian cavalry were, ironically, accused of looting Dera and were compared unfavourably with the Beduin.

My mind felt in the Indian rank and file something puny and confined; an air of thinking themselves mean; almost a careful, esteemed subservience, unlike the abrupt wholesomeness of the Beduin. The manner of the British officers toward their men struck horror into my bodyguard, who had never seen personal inequality before.

They and Lawrence had clearly forgotten about the slaves far away in Aqaba and Hejaz.

By stubbornly refusing to write anything which showed the Arabs in an unfavourable light, Lawrence was forced to condone or excuse sickening brutality. He did so by adopting an elastic morality which exculpated Arab cruelty towards the Turks on the grounds that it was retributive justice. He employed this blanket dispensation in his official report on the killing of German and Turkish prisoners during an engagement north-west of Dera on 27 September. Forewarned that two Turkish columns, one 6,000 strong from Dera, the other numbering 2,000 from el Muzeirib, were escaping northwards, Arab units chose to intercept the smaller. As they proceeded through Tura and Tafas, Turkish soldiers raped Arab women and, at Tafas, the Lancer rearguard massacred the inhabitants, including women and children. The hideous sight of the bodies unhinged Talal, the Sheik of Tafas, who rode alone against the retreating Turks to be shot down.

The Arabs pressed home their attacks and sliced the column into three sections. The one which included German machine-gunners in cars and Muhammad Jamal Pasha and his staff fought its way out; the others succumbed.[18]

> The second and leading portions after a bitter struggle, we wiped out completely. We ordered 'no prisoners' and the men obeyed, except that the reserve company took a hundred and fifty men (including many German A[rmy] S[ervice] C[orps] alive. Later, however, they found one of our men with a fractured thigh who had been afterwards pinned to the ground by two mortal thrusts with German bayonets. Then we turned our Hotchkiss on the prisoners and made an end of them, they saying nothing. The common delusion that the Turk is a clean and merciful fighter led some of the British troops to criticise Arab methods a little later – but they had not entered Tura or Tafas, or watched the Turks swing their wounded by the hands and feet into a burning railway truck, as had been the lot of the Arab army at Jerdun. As for the villagers, they and their ancestors have been for five hundred years ground down by the tyranny of these Turks.

This official report was written within ten days of the massacre and the final sentence indicates that Lawrence was well aware of his fellow officers' loathing for such barbarism. The episode is described in extended and gruesome detail in the *Seven Pillars*: 'In the madness born of the horror of Tafas we killed and killed, even blowing in the heads of the fallen and of the animals; as though their death and running blood could slake our agony.' These words were taken at face value by David Lean, who in his film *Lawrence of Arabia* portrayed Lawrence as infected with the Arabs' dementia. He runs amok among the fleeing Turks, wildly firing his revolver and slashing with his dagger.

There were certainly massacres of villagers at Tafas and Tura by the retiring Turkish column, although to judge from the war diaries of British units that were following up the Turkish retreat such behaviour was uncharacteristic. Worn out and under constant pressure from their mounted and aerial pursuers, most Turkish soldiers were solely concerned with saving themselves. Prisoners taken during the fighting near Tafas were definitely killed in the way described by Lawrence, but whether he gave the order or was even in a position to influence events is another matter. By this stage, as Kirkbride noticed, 'the Arab side could not be said to be under control'. His observation was confirmed by Peake who, fifty years later, recalled his arrival at Tafas where he found Lawrence vainly trying to restrain the Arabs and stop the massacre of prisoners. Immediately and at Lawrence's request, he sent 100 dismounted camelry into the village with fixed bayonets. This ended the killing, for the Beduin, unwilling to tangle with the Egyptians, rode off to harry fragments of the column which had escaped northwards. Then, on Lawrence's orders, Peake and his troopers rounded up those Turks who had survived and put them under guard.[19]

This version of Lawrence's conduct is upheld by Young who, while not present at Tafas, heard later from an eyewitness how he had attempted to rescue the prisoners. Young also revealed that the slaughter of Turkish prisoners had become indiscriminate. He and Kirkbride pleaded with Nuri es Said to order his regulars to stop murdering men captured before the Tafas incident.[20] Pisani, the only other European present throughout the Tafas engagement, and Captain, the Earl of Winterton, both protested to Nuri about the outrages on behalf of their governments.

It is clear from this evidence and what Barrow saw the next day that regular and irregular Arab forces were murdering their prisoners at random. Many who died were clearly innocent of the war crimes which had been committed at Tafas and Tura. Lawrence's attitude to this spate of killing was ambivalent. What he wrote and said in the *Seven Pillars* indicated that he shared the Arabs' purblind fury against the Turks who had carried out massacres and accepted his responsibility for the order to take no prisoners and the shooting of those who were believed to have bayoneted a wounded Arab. On the other hand, Peake's testimony shows that this vengeful passion, generated by the sight of slaughtered and outraged women and children, was soon spent. Lawrence's compassion was also easily exhausted. A day later in Dera he swept aside Barrow's protest about the Arabs' abuse of their prisoners with the excuse that this was how they made war. This was his attitude on 28 September when Young asked him to intervene and save 200 POWs who were suspected of having massacred villagers at Sheik Saad. Lawrence parried by saying that the Arabs would settle the soldiers' fate by public debate among their leaders.[21] Young spoke eloquently in Arabic, followed by Winterton, whose words were translated by Lawrence. The Earl's statement that he was an MP amused the Arabs, and Lawrence explained that their laughter was the consequence of pre-war visits by British MPs whom they considered comic. Winterton agreed and added that they were also bores, as he knew from having had to listen to many of them, which caused further amusement. Comedy averted tragedy and the Turks were spared.

From 26 September until the fall of Damascus, regular and tribal Arab forces killed and robbed prisoners indiscriminately and against the usages of war. Their behaviour constitutes a war crime equal to any committed by the Turkish army during the war. It was possible for Lawrence to exculpate himself and the Arabs for what had occurred at Tafas on the grounds that it avenged a specific atrocity, but this excuse could never cover the promiscuous brutality displayed elsewhere. The Arabs were out of control and neither Lawrence nor his fellow officers could restrain them. To have publicly admitted this would have injured Lawrence's self-esteem. Afterwards he ignored or glossed over these terrible incidents: they had no place in a narrative of the fortunes of the heroic servants of a lofty and noble cause.

The Arab army, if not the nationalist ideal, was now drawing more and more adherents. The decisive British victories, the dissolution of the Ottoman administration, the opportunities for plunder and the prospect of the fall of Damascus attracted hordes of new recruits. There were some convinced Syrian nationalists, but they were outnumbered by looters, camp followers and fellahin from the Hawran villages. Unlike Lawrence, Massey, the *Times* correspondent, had no illusions about their motives. They were 'like vultures which hover about a dying animal' ready to steal from friend and foe. Their behaviour disturbed divisional commanders, who were forced to detach small units to suppress brigandage behind the lines.[22]

Lawrence's mind was concentrated on the political gains now within Faisal's grasp. He had ridden from Tafas to Dera with a 'fixed look', telling his companion Kirkbride, 'We must get there before the [Anglo-Indian] cavalry.' He felt certain that Dera's occupation by Arabs would automatically give Faisal the right to appoint a governor and assume political authority over the town and its hinterland. Both he and Faisal knew that there had been a significant shift in British policy towards the Middle East which made it easier for Faisal to secure Damascus and possibly a Syrian kingdom. In June, the War Cabinet's Middle Eastern Committee had agreed that the circumstances of the war demanded a revision of the Sykes–Picot agreement. As Lawrence had anticipated, America's entry into the war had dictated a change of Allied war aims, which were now to be injected with fresh idealism. Out went the old-world imperialist principle of carving up the spoils which was embodied in the Sykes–Picot agreement, and in came policies based upon granting measures of self-determination to such peoples as the Arabs. For them the benefits were limited. Modified British policy still insisted that any post-war Arab state would have to accept an as yet undefined measure of European tutelage.

The change in British policy was announced to Syrian exiles in Cairo on 8 June. They heard that henceforward the Arabs were permitted to set up their own governments in any area they liberated, save Palestine. This had not yet been approved by the French and was still being argued over as the British army approached Damascus. Nor was Allenby informed. Still believing that the provisions of the Sykes–Picot agreement would prevail in Syria and unaware of what Lawrence had in mind, Allenby had on 25 September informed Lawrence of his intention to move against Damascus, adding that he had 'no objection' to Arab forces entering the city.[23]

The message was dropped to Lawrence from an aeroplane. Once he received it he pressed Faisal to move as swiftly as possible towards Damascus where forewarned Hashemite partisans would be ready to declare for him. This coup would, according to the new lines of British policy, give Faisal the right to establish his own administration and forestall the French. Lawrence knew that the British, Indian and Australian cavalry earmarked for the capture of Damascus were exhausted and running short of rations and fodder. He may also have known that the two divisional commanders, Generals Chauvel and Barrow, were ignorant of the numbers of Damascus's defenders. They chose therefore to move carefully; first a cordon was to be thrown around the city and then an advance would be made into the suburbs.

Allenby was ignorant of what Lawrence and Faisal had in mind. On 22 September he had decided to take Damascus and three days later outlined his plans to his divisional commanders at Jenin. Overall operational command was handed to Sir Harry Chauvel, who was given the Desert Mounted Corps, which consisted of the 5th Cavalry Division and the Australian Mounted Corps, and Barrow's 4th Cavalry Division, to which Faisal's Arabs were attached. According to Allenby's strategy, Barrow's Anglo-Indian horsemen would move eastwards, take Dera and then turn north along the old pilgrim road to Damascus. Accompanied by Arab units, they were to mop up remnants of the Turkish 4th Army Corps and approach Damascus from the south. Simultaneously Chauvel's two cavalry divisions would ride northwards to Quneitra and then advance on Damascus from the east, sweeping north of the city to cut off any retreat by its Turco-German garrison.

Briefing Chauvel, Allenby indicated the political procedures which would follow the capture of Damascus. In essence they were the same as those taken when Jerusalem fell. 'Send for the Turkish Vali [Governor] and tell him to carry on, giving him what extra police he requires.' 'What about the Arabs?' Chauvel queried; 'There is a rumour that they are to have the administration of Syria.' 'Yes, I believe so,' answered Allenby, 'but you must wait until I come and, if Faisal gives you any trouble, deal with him through Lawrence, who will be your liaison officer.'[24] Neither man had the smallest inkling of Faisal's ambitions or Lawrence's willingness to bring them to fruition.

In fact Allenby did not tell Chauvel everything he knew. Four weeks before, General Wilson, the new Chief of Imperial General Staff, had reminded him that Syria was 'of special interest' to the French, who would be aggrieved if the region passed under British military administration. Allenby was therefore advised to act in accordance with whatever the French suggested when he made his arrangements for the administration of Syria. Further guidelines, cabled from London on 25 September, made it clear that both the War and Foreign Offices understood that, once conquered, Syria would become a French sphere of influence. 'They [the French] think that both in France and elsewhere [that is, Syria] this policy should be made perfectly clear,' General Macdonogh explained, and the Foreign Office insisted that French officials alone were to be appointed advisers to any Arab government which might emerge in that area allocated to France by Sykes–Picot. Once Allenby took Damascus 'it would be desirable in conformity with [the] Anglo-French agreement of 1916 [that] he could if possible work through an Arab administration by means of a French liaison.'[25] An interim arrangement of this kind was possible since Allenby's army included 9,000 French troops, among them the Armenian Légion d'Orient and colourful regiments of spahis and Chasseurs d'Afrique attached to Chauvel's division.

Had he known their details, Lawrence would have found these arrangements anathema. He wanted an Arab government in Damascus, backed by the people's will, directed by Faisal and free from French advisers. To keep the French out, he and Faisal contrived a coup in which, once it was clear that the Turks and Germans would evacuate the city, Damascus's Hashemite supporters would declare themselves the new government. Then, on cue, Faisal's tribal and regular forces would enter the city.

The plan misfired. By the night of 30 September, both Chauvel's Desert Mounted Corps and Barrow's 4th Cavalry Division were on the outskirts of Damascus and ready to encircle the city. Brigadier-General Lachlan Wilson of the Australian 3rd Light Horse, under orders to close the Homs road and unable to find a way around the city's northern boundary, decided to cut across the city just before daybreak on 1 October. So Australian cavalrymen, led by a former Brisbane barrister, were the first Allied troops into Damascus. Unopposed save by a handful of snipers, the horsemen encountered passive Turkish soldiers and thousands of excited and welcoming Damascenes.[26] At the town hall, Major Olden, the commander of the advance guard, found authority in the hands of Lawrence's old adversary, Abdul al Qadir, and his brother Muhammad Said. Al Qadir gave Olden a guide and then the cavalrymen cantered off towards the Homs road amid enthusiastic crowds. 'They clung to the horses' necks, they kissed our men's stirrups; they showered confetti and rosewater over them; they shouted, laughed, cried, sang and clapped hands,' Olden recalled.[27] It was fitting that Allied regular troops liberated Damascus, since it was their hard fighting which had made it possible. There was more ahead and by seven in the morning the Australians were out of the city in pursuit of the fleeing Turks.

Lawrence is mute about this and much else which followed, offering instead fudge and fabrication in his version of the events of 1 October and their aftermath. According to the *Seven Pillars*, 4,000 Beduin from Faisal's army had infiltrated the city during the night of 30 September/ 1 October but, afflicted by an inexplicable shyness, they did not make themselves known to its inhabitants, the Australians or the remnants of the Turkish garrison.

Attached as liaison officer to Barrow's HQ, Lawrence became aware that the city would be undefended on the 29th when the pro-Hashemite General Aziz al Ridha al Rikabi surrendered. This 'cheery old boy' had a good breakfast and told Barrow that the city was undefended.[28] Lawrence, aware that the circumstances and the time were now right, slipped away from Barrow's camp early on 1 October and drove towards Damascus with Young. On the way he was encountered by Major White, of the 16th Cavalry Brigade who gave him an escort of Indian lancers. 'This', White wrote, 'was about the same time as the Australians were entering Damascus from the North West'.[28] Perhaps not wishing to remember that he had driven into Damascus protected by Indian cavalrymen, Lawrence later claimed that he had been arrested by them! Once inside the city he made straight for the town hall.

Inside there was pandemonium. Everywhere Syrians and Arabs were shouting and scuffling; Awda was fighting with al Atrash, the Druze leader whose people until a few hours before had been pocketing German gold in return for not harassing retreating columns.[29] Lawrence's forerunners, Nasir and Nuri Shalaan, like Major Olden had found al Qadir and Muhammad Said in charge. They had swapped sides and joined forces with Shukri al Ayyubi, a local pro-Hashemite nationalist, and had declared themselves the city's rulers in Hussain's name.

Whatever the truth of this description found in the *Seven Pillars*, Lawrence appeared at the town hall in his finest sharifian robes to receive his commanding officer, Chauvel.[30] First, he excused his sudden disappearance from Barrow's HQ on the ground that he had wished to discover exactly what was happening in Damascus so that he could report to Chauvel. As it was, the General had come to him and so he presented him to al Ayyubi, whom he introduced as Damascus's new Governor. Realising that al Ayyubi was an Arab, not a Turk, Chauvel demanded, 'I want to see the Turkish Vali. Will you send for him at once.' This was impossible since he had fled, but Lawrence assured Chauvel that al Ayyubi had been legally elected by a majority of the Damascenes, which was a lie. Chauvel was temporarily taken in, but he turned down Lawrence's suggestion that he set up his HQ in the former British Consulate. Chauvel, disliking what he had seen of the city, preferred 'a clean orchard' for his camp.

Not long after he had established his HQ, Chauvel heard the true story of Lawrence's manoeuvres. This was revealed to him by Hubert Young, who had ostensibly called to discuss commissariat business.

He proceeded to inform me of the mistakes I had made. Shukri Pasha had not been elected by a majority of the residents, but only a small faction, i.e. Hejaz supporters, and that, by putting him in, I had virtually admitted the rule of King Hussain over Syria. He said 'they are out to make as little as possible of the British and make the populace think that it is the Arabs who have driven out the Turk. That is why Lawrence asked you to keep men out of the city (which he had done) and they have no intention of asking you for any police.' He also said, 'They are getting the British Consulate ready for you. If you go there you are not defining yourself as Conqueror of this country, but rather as a contributory ally. You should take possession of Jamal Pasha's house, which is the best one in the place, and which they are reserving for Faisal.' He said there was absolute chaos in the city, the Bazaars were closed and all the better class of people were terrified at the idea of the Hejaz crowd being in charge. Faisal's followers were already looting freely. He advised a show of British force as soon as possible. On that, I decided to have a march through the city on the following day, and I did, practically every unit being represented; guns, armoured cars, everything, and I also took possession of Jamal's house.[31]

In essence, Young was correct. He had been a shocked eyewitness to a charade devised by Lawrence to give the impression that Damascus was now a Hashemite city. He had edged out the untrustworthy trimmers, al Qadir and his brother, and nominated al Ayyubi as governor. Then matters got out of hand, for his new administration found itself unable to govern. Within hours a city of 300,000 slid into anarchy. Lawrence's hopes that the few hundred Arab regulars in Damascus could act as a police force were soon dashed; they were insubordinate and joined in the general looting. Lawrence, who shortly before had pleaded with Chauvel to keep Indian cavalry out of the city, was forced to borrow a scrap of notepaper from Massey and write to the General with a request for troops to restore order.[32] During the afternoon, units of Australian cavalry under Colonel Bourchier moved into

Damascus and were posted as guards on public buildings, consulates and hospitals. Barrow's troops were ordered to stem the flow of Druze and Beduin into the city and shoot any who offered resistance or were caught pillaging.[33]

One of the major problems was the hospitals, where 1,800 wounded Turks were languishing untended. Lawrence was prompted to take action by an Australian medical officer and, accompanied by Kirkbride, he went to see what was required. It was a grim excursion, as Kirkbride recalled: 'When we found anyone butchering Turks he went up and asked them in a gentle voice to stop, while I stood by and brandished my firearm. Occasionally, someone turned nasty and I shot them at once before the trouble could spread. Lawrence got quite cross and said, "For God's sake stop being so bloody-minded." '[34] In his version of what passed, Lawrence described how he discovered a Turkish barracks guarded by Australians posted to keep out Arab marauders who would kill the sick and wounded. Astonishingly, given what had occurred during the past week, Lawrence remarked that this pre-caution had been based upon 'a misapprehension of the Arab fashion of making war'. Inside were 600 Turks, dead and dying in their own dung. All that Lawrence could do for their relief was to prod a handful of Turkish doctors into action and command the walking wounded to bury the dead.

Conditions in the city's hospitals were hellish. When they were inspected by a doctor from the 5th Cavalry on 2 October, he reported an 'indescribable state of filth and neglect' everywhere with patients on bare floors dying from neglect and starvation.[35] He alerted Lawrence to the 'grave dangers' of the situation and demanded help with burying the dead. Lawrence is silent about this exchange, but he did recall an incident on the following day when he toured a hospital. Satisfied that matters were improving, he was suddenly confronted by a 'medical major'.

With a frown of disgust for skirt and sandals he said, 'You're in charge?' Modestly I smirked that in a way I was, and then he burst out, 'Scandalous, disgraceful, outrageous, ought to be shot . . .' At this onslaught I cackled out like a chicken, with the wild laughter of strain; it did feel extraordinarily funny to be cursed just as I was pluming myself on having bettered the apparently hopeless.

The major had not entered the charnel house of yesterday, nor smelt it nor seen us burying bodies of ultimate degradation, whose memory had started me up in bed, sweating and trembling, a few hours since. He glared at me muttering 'Bloody brute.' I hooted out again, and he smacked me over the face and stalked off, leaving me more ashamed than angry, for in my heart I felt he was right, and that anyone who pushed through to success a rebellion of the weak against the strong must come out of it so stained in estimation that afterward nothing in the world would make him feel clean.

While Lawrence indulged in self-pity, Chauvel took the initiative over the hospitals, which were placed in the capable hands of Colonel Rupert Downes, the Deputy Director of Medical Services for the Australian Divisions. With a team of Australian, British and Syrian doctors he soon managed to get proper services running again.

As Lawrence admitted, 'Damascus was normal' by 3 October. Order and tranquillity were restored by Chauvel and his soldiers, not by Faisal's administration, for which the task was too great. The impressive parade of British, French, Australian and Indian troops with their artillery and armoured cars on the 2nd reminded the Damascenes of the true identity of their liberators, although, to satisfy Lawrence's vanity, Chauvel permitted an Arab unit to lead the march. Even so the display showed clearly where real power lay.

For the time being, disposal of that power was in the hands of Allenby, who arrived in Damascus at one o'clock on the afternoon of 3 October, two hours before Faisal was due. Allenby's first job was to clarify the political situation in the city and lay the foundations of a local administration. He would be guided by the provisions of the Sykes–Picot Treaty. 'As regards the "A" area, notably the city of Damascus,' he had cabled the War Office on 30 September, 'I shall recognise the local Arab administration which I may expect to find in existence, and shall appoint [a] French liaison officer as required.'[36] British advisers would direct the Arab administration in 'B' area, which embraced the region east of Jordan. Just before he reached Damascus, Allenby heard from Balfour that Hejaz had been granted full belligerent rights and that regions which had fallen to its armed forces would have 'the status of an independent state'. The Foreign Secretary added that Arab flags could be permitted to fly over Amman and Damascus, even though (and he may have been unaware of this) they had been captured by British and Dominion forces.[37]

There remained the problem of Faisal and Lawrence. By now Allenby knew that Lawrence was Faisal's accomplice and could not be relied upon to act as a disinterested liaison officer. Hitherto Lawrence and Allenby had enjoyed cordial relations. For all his instinctive hostility towards senior professional soldiers, Lawrence was in awe of Allenby's forceful personality and powerful presence—he was over six feet tall with a massive frame and was nicknamed 'the Bull'. In conversation Lawrence had found the General imaginative and flexible and their talks were punctuated by extended digressions about wild birds, roses, French literature and Crusader castles, which both found more agreeable than the strategic matters in hand.[38]

For his part, Allenby tolerated Lawrence's whimsicality and quirkiness, respected his courage and appreciated his value as the only officer on his staff who could procure and organise Arab assistance. Most importantly, in the light of what happened when they met in Damascus, Lawrence obeyed Allenby unquestioningly.

From the moment he arrived in Damascus, Allenby asserted his authority. Told that Faisal had in mind a grand entry into the city, he briskly retorted, 'Triumphal entry be damned, I cannot wait till three as I have to go back to Tiberias tonight. You must send a car for him at once. He can go out again for his triumphal entry.' Faisal did as he was bid and was driven to the Victoria Hotel where Allenby, Chauvel and their chiefs of staff were waiting together with Lawrence, Cornwallis, Young, Stirling, Joyce, Nuri es Said and Nasir. Civilities over, Allenby bluntly explained realities to Faisal. As Hussain's representative he would govern Syria with French guidance and financial backing. His authority was excluded from the Lebanon and Palestine, which would be directly controlled by France and Britain. Day-to-day decisions would be taken by Faisal in co-operation with a French officer who, for the time being, would work in harness with Lawrence.[39]

So Lawrence's dream was shattered. 'Faisal objected very strongly' and said 'he knew nothing of France in the matter.' Furthermore 'he understood from the Adviser that Sir Edmund Allenby had sent him [that is, Lawrence] that the Arabs were to have the whole of Syria including Lebanon but excluding Palestine.' Allenby turned to Lawrence and asked, 'Did you not tell him that the French were to have the Protectorate over Syria?' 'No, Sir, I know nothing about it' was the answer. 'But you knew definitely that he, Faisal, was to have nothing to do with the Lebanon,' Allenby replied. 'No Sir, I did not.'

Lawrence, with Faisal's connivance, was either bluffing or else he had in the past misled the Prince about what had been set down in the Sykes–Picot agreement. Allenby was now forthright. Faisal, as a lieutenant-general under his command, would do as he was told like any other soldier. 'He must accept the situation as it was' an when the war had ended the entire business would be settled. Faisal acquiesced and, followed by his entourage, departed for the triumphal parade. This was a limp affair since the spectators had got tired of waiting and had gone off to their homes.

A slight, haggard figure in Arab robes, Lawrence stayed behind. He told Allenby that he would not co-operate with a French liaison officer and that he was due for some leave, which he wished to take in England. 'Yes! I think you better had' was Allenby's comment, and Lawrence left. The next morning he set off for Cairo on the first stage of his journey. Allenby, whose rages like summer storms passed quickly, smoothed his passage by promoting him to full colonel, which ensured Lawrence greater comfort on his journey. He also wrote two letters for Lawrence. One, for a royal audience, was to Sir Clive Wigram, George V's Assistant Private Secretary, and the other was to the Foreign Office, where Lawrence could present his version of the Arab case.

Lawrence's war had ended on a note of acerbity and disappointment. A new one was beginning. He was poised to enter public affairs as the champion of the Arabs. On 8 October, he paused in Cairo to write a piece for *The Times* which outlined the activities of the Arab army over the past six weeks. Otherwise a straightforward narrative, Lawrence's account included assertions that the Arabs had been first into Damascus and that, once there, they had restored order. Legend was already taking over from history.

Five

THE LEGEND OF
LAWRENCE OF ARABIA

I

ACHIEVEMENT

Lawrence's life after 1918, what he wrote and did, and his special place
in the public consciousness of Britain and America were all the direct
result of his wartime career. He arrived in Britain in October 1918 determined to get justice for Faisal and the Arabs. His publicity campaign stimulated immense public interest which concentrated on him and his deeds
rather than on the rights and wrongs of the Arab cause. Within a year,
he was an international celebrity, which he remained until his death. To
the man in the street he was 'Lawrence of Arabia' (the title used by his
fellow officers in Cairo as early as December 1917), 'the Uncrowned King
of Arabia', or 'the Mystery Man of Europe and Asia'.[1] The world never
wearied of stories about him and newspapermen satisfied its need with
a heady mixture of sensation, half-truth and fantasy.

Truth is, proverbially, the first casualty of war: in Lawrence's case it
was a victim of peace. Before looking at the genesis of the legend, it is
worthwhile to pause and summarise just what Lawrence and the Arabs
had achieved during their two years in the field, not least because the
exact details of their campaigns were soon buried under an avalanche of
hyperbole and invention.

The Arab Revolt had secured its primary objective. A civil war had been
provoked between the Turks and the Arabs that had weakened both the
Ottoman empire and its Pan-Islamic propaganda offensive. This point was
pressed home by Lawrence in a report on current Syrian politics composed
for the Arab Bureau in February 1918, was mentioned in passing in the
Seven Pillars and was taken up by Hogarth when he defended the Bureau's
policies before an audience of the Central Asia Society in 1927.[2] This view
was endorsed by Indian officials, who were grateful for a device which
many believed had reduced tension among Muslims and averted civil disorders. Judged as a purely wartime measure, the Arab movement had been
successful, since it had temporarily neutered jihadic militancy. Still, Turco-
German appeals for Pan-Islamic solidarity did not cease the moment Hussain rebelled. In the spring of 1918 Enver Pasha was beating the jihadic
drum as 'the Army of Asia' began its advance towards the Caspian. He
was sure that its victories would stir up religious passions, which they did,
at the expense of the Armenians of eastern Turkey and the Caucasus,
and that Muslims in Turkestan would join in a projected invasion of India.

His expectations in this region were shared by nervous British and Indian intelligence officers, who feared that a recrudescence of fanaticism would sap the loyalty of Muslim sepoys and create new waves of unrest in India. They were not mistaken; Pan-Islamic uprisings erupted across the North-West Frontier in 1919 and flickered on for three years.

Even after Turkey's surrender at the end of October 1918, there were many in the Middle East who thought that there was plenty of latent jihadic passion waiting for the right catalyst to transform it into action. In September 1918 a spy reported to a British intelligence officer in Adana a conversation he had had with a Turkish official who told him that 'special Indians, who were here before the war, have been sent back to India to encourage the Muslims there to rise against the unbelievers.' He added, 'We have also sent agents to Persia, Arabia and the Caucasus.'[3] Four months before, there had been disturbing rumours that Enver Pasha was promoting a jihad in Afghanistan.[4] The Arab Revolt had already passed into history and Muslims, bewildered by Allied plans for the abolition of the caliphate and the annexation of Turkey, were again striving for strength through religious unity. Lawrence's assertion made in February 1918 that the Arab Revolt had 'drawn the teeth of the Caliphate for a generation and killed the jihad' was premature and optimistic.

So too were his hopes that the Hejaz rebellion would signal a sequence of mutinies and massed desertion by Arabs in the Turkish service. Arabs in Turkish uniforms fought their kinsmen along the Hejaz railway and in Syria. When Medina surrendered in February 1919 many Syrians and Arabs were taken prisoner. Hitherto loyal to their sultan, many of these men accepted the judgement of history and chose to join Hussain's army and were no doubt soon engaged in a war against another Arab, his local rival Ibn Saud. Arab nationalism never evolved in the way which Lawrence had hoped. His and Britain's Arab nationalists were Hashemite partisans whose dynastic loyalties cut them off from those who did not see Arab nationhood being achieved by essentially conservative princes whose power rested on the tribal sheiks of the desert and whose political thought was shaped by antique custom. There were dissenters who were unhappy with the Hashemite connection with Britain. One Syrian sheik, Salah Abdullah, spoke for them when he told a British officer in June 1918 that, since Faisal was hand in glove with Britain, 'he had no wish to be ruled by an independent Sharifian government.'[5] In Syria the Druze, Christians, Jews and Shiite Muslims, who made up a third of the population, were likewise extremely uneasy about the replacement of a Turkish with a Hashemite government and voiced their fears to the Crane–King Commission sent out by the Versailles Conference in the summer of 1919. The commissioners also discovered that the new Arab government relied upon former Turkish officials who kept up their corrupt practices.[6]

By his own admission, Lawrence had strained himself to breaking point to get the Arabs to work with a common resolve. His efforts were widely appreciated. 'We have good reason to be thankful to Colonel Lawrence,' Massey wrote in 1919. 'His is one of the most romantic careers of the whole war, and by his staunch advocacy of British friendship for the Arabs, he kept our allies in Arabia actively championing our cause.'[7] It had been a Herculean, often Sisyphean task: the raw material was poor, Faisal wobbled, tribal sheiks and their followers squabbled, brawled and sometimes ran away. Somehow the Beduin and regular units held together and sustained an intermittent harassment of their adversaries. The Northern Arab Army's will to fight owed much to Lawrence's persistence, persuasiveness and forbearance. By contrast the Southern Army under Abdullah remained inert. It was, Kirkbride considered, 'useless for any military purpose', a judgement amply supported by its lacklustre performance during the siege of Medina.

Tribal harmony had been vital and Lawrence had always found it hard to secure. It did not outlast the war and, within months of the armistice, feuds had been reopened. During the spring and summer of 1919, the military administration in Syria was plagued by a revival of internecine warfare among the Beduin. A raiding party 1,000 strong mustered in the Hawran, tribal warfare broke out in western Jordan and there were fears that non-Muslim minorities in this region would be persecuted.[8] Interestingly, in January 1920 Beduin threatened army engineers, commanded by Newcombe, as they were surveying the Hejaz line which, it was hoped, could be repaired and reopened.[9] In short, there was a return to the endemic disorder of Ottoman days, which may have suited many sheiks who had customarily supplemented their revenues by brigandage.

In terms of winning the world war, Lawrence later admitted that his campaign was a sideshow attached to a sideshow. This was a modification of his wartime opinion that the defeat of Turkey would be a blow from which Germany could not recover. Turkey asked for and was granted an armistice on 30 October at the moment when German armies were retreating across Belgium and their generals had already decided to seek terms from the Allies. At the same time the Allied High Command was making calculations which assumed that Germany might continue to fight on in 1919. These were not seriously affected by the news that Turkish forces in Syria and Iraq had been decisively beaten.

As to the campaign in Palestine and Syria, one fact is central. Final victory was gained by Allenby's Allied army in a series of battles during the second part of September 1918 sometimes called 'Armageddon'. These successes were the culmination of a process of piecemeal conquest which had started in Sinai back in 1916 and included the taking of Jerusalem in November 1917. At each stage the enemy's forces were engaged in pitched battles where Allied forces bore the brunt of the fighting. When Damascus fell, Allenby had at his disposal 458,000 men, of whom 176,000 were British, 93,000 Indian, 23,000 Australian, New Zealanders and South Africans and 152,000 Egyptian labourers. Against them were Turco-German units, depleted by the demands of the Caucasus front, which totalled just over 100,000. Most were underfed, ill-clothed and war-weary. Not only did Allenby's army outnumber von Sandars's by four to one; the Allies enjoyed overwhelming air superiority. Air-power clinched victory; between 21 and 23 September retreating columns endured ferocious harassment from the air which was so terrible in its effect that many pilots were sickened and a few refused to fly further missions. This strafing and bombing, combined with the close cavalry pursuit, made it impossible for the Turco-German forces either to regroup or to resist.

Readers of Lawrence's account of the Syrian campaign and of the biographies of Graves and Liddell Hart could be excused ignorance of these vital details since they are pushed into the background by each writer. Those who take their history from the cinema will be completely taken aback since the film *Lawrence of Arabia* excludes any mention of non-Arab forces from its narrative.

Arab eyewitnesses were in no doubt as to how and by whom the Turks had been overcome. 'They could have done it without us!' was the comment of Nuri es Said as he watched the endless flow of British cavalrymen ride into Damascus. What, if anything, did the Arab armies achieve? First, it was better, as Robertson had wisely remarked in 1916, that they were allies rather than opponents who danced to a German tune. Progress on the Iraq front had been hindered by Arab hostility which forced commanders to divert troops to guard lines of communication or serve in punitive columns. In Palestine and Syria the British suffered no such distractions. As von Sandars enviously noted, they 'were fighting under conditions as though in their own country, while the Turks in defence of their own country had to fight amongst a population directly hostile'.[10]

A second and more important benefit of the Arab alliance was that it forced the Turkish High Command to maintain an over-large garrison along the Hejaz railway once it came under Arab attack. According to the figures in the British *Official History*, the Medina garrison was 12,000 (in fact over 16,000 surrendered) and a further 10,000 were deployed along the track from Tabuk to Maan. Intelligence assessments compiled during the winter of 1917/18 added a further 34,000 stationed between Dera and

Maan. So the Arabs were tying down upwards of 30,000 men, a quarter of local Turkish strength. The War Office, Allenby and Lawrence assumed that, if these men had not been sitting in barracks or blockhouses, they would have been used on the Syrian front where their intervention in the 1917–18 campaigns would have upset Allenby's chances of success. For this reason Allenby gave Lawrence his wholehearted support.

What neither man realised was that, in Constantinople, Enver refused to consider redeploying his railway garrisons on the Syrian front. Political arguments overrode military considerations. Possession of Medina, one of the three holy cities of Islam, gave credibility to Turkey's claim to lead the Muslim world. Furthermore, Enver and the Committee of Union and Progress appreciated that a toehold in Arabia could be used to advantage when a final peace settlement was negotiated. For these reasons, Enver was determined to hang on to Medina and defend the lifeline which linked it to the Ottoman heartlands. Even if he had changed his mind, there is nothing to suggest that those troops released would have been automatically transferred to Syria and Palestine. During 1916 and 1917 surplus Turkish troops were loaned for service in the Balkans and on the Eastern Front and, from the winter of 1917/18, all spare men were being drafted to the Caucasus, much to von Sandars's dismay. There were some strategists for whom Arabia was a burden of which Turkey could be well rid. 'Too much was made of the Hejaz and the Yemen,' Ali Said Pasha, Commander-in-Chief in the Yemen, told his British opposite number in Aden. 'Not a single Turkish soldier should hazard his life in these areas,' he added, for 'they brought no financial return to Turkey and were a continual source of religious unrest.'[11] Paradoxically, Lawrence's Arabs were tying down Turkish troops in a region which some senior Turkish officers considered worthless.

Measured by political and military yardsticks and stripped of subsequent romantic ornament, the Arab Revolt was a propaganda coup for Britain which upset Turco-German plans for Pan-Islamic subversion in India and the Sudan. In the long term the movement fulfilled Lord Hardinge's prophecy that it would become a Frankenstein's monster which would torment its begetters. This certainly happened since there was a fundamental divergence of interests between Britain and France, both acquisitive powers, and a national movement which aimed at the creation of independent Arab states, even universal Arab unity. Until 1918 the supranational Ottoman empire had stood in the way of this goal. Once it fell apart, Britain, France and much later Israel and the United States would successively take its place as the focus for Arab nationalist passions.

As for the Arab armed forces, their contribution to the Allied war effort had been useful but marginal. At moments of crisis they had been rescued by British air- and sea-power and were constantly kept alive by injections of British gold, weaponry, ammunition and the loan of Allied specialist units. With this assistance, regular and irregular Beduin forces accomplished what was asked of them. They pinned down Turkish forces along the Damascus-to-Medina line and disrupted the already ramshackle Turkish railway services. At the closing stages of the campaign, a battalion of Arab regulars and several thousand Beduin created a diversion around Dera and hampered the evacuation of Turco-German forces. Their performance on the battlefield varied enormously, although Allied officers, with the exception of Lawrence, soon learned to place little faith in the Beduin, who were primarily concerned with their wages and what they could steal.

This summary, or something very like it, would have been history's verdict on the Arab campaign had Lawrence died in 1918 or slipped back unobtrusively to his former life as an archaeologist.

II

THE MAKING OF THE LEGEND, 1918–1935

THE legend of Lawrence of Arabia was a confection of historical truth, rumour and invention put together between 1918 and 1935. It did not materialise by chance. At each stage in its evolution it was a deliberate creation in which Lawrence himself was closely involved, although never in control. He was able to feed information to his biographers, Robert Graves and Liddell Hart, and he censored what they wrote, but, much to his irritation, his efforts to bridle the press failed.

At first, Lawrence's motive for telling his story had been selfless. 'He wanted no publicity for himself, all he desired was that the Arab cause should be understood' was the journalist Evelyn Wrench's immediate reaction after his first meeting with Lawrence at the end of 1918. This must have seemed strange, since Wrench had already been told by his friend Lord Winterton that Lawrence would 'in future be regarded as one of the great figures of the war'.[1] Once it was clear that this prophecy would be fulfilled, Lawrence took a keen interest in his own reputation and was anxious that his accomplishments should be properly recorded and under-stood. He read closely all reviews of books by or about himself.

At the same time, he was still a slave of his old urge to dress up or add counterfeit details to any story in which he was the central figure. This wantonness with the truth made life awkward for Robert Graves and Liddell Hart when they plied him for information. 'Tangles seem a charac-teristic and inevitable part of anything connected with our subject,' Graves complained to Liddell Hart and wondered whether Lawrence's Irish genes had given him 'a vein of unseriousness which easily becomes treachery'.[2] Several years before he became Lawrence's biographer, Liddell Hart had heard his false boast that he had been the sole begetter of the 1915 Alexan-dretta invasion project and this, together with the suspicion that Lawrence's reputation was overblown, made him cautious of other claims.[3] Graves had been misled into writing that Lawrence had first gone to Jiddah in 1916 as a free agent whereas he had been sent there under specific orders, and later he heard from Lawrence that he had been less than honest in his account of the fall of Damascus.[4]

In the post-war years Lawrence was still in full possession of that facility of imagination which made him concoct extravagant stories about himself. In 1929 he told Francis Yeats-Brown, the literary editor of the *Spectator*, that before the war he had been a secret agent, had infiltrated the Turkish High Command and during the Balkan Wars had served briefly as Enver Pasha's ADC.[5] A fellow aircraftman heard how, during the war, Lawrence without any instruction had flown and landed an aircraft for a £20 wager.[6] Neither anecdote found its way into any biography, but their circulation as gossip added substance to the public stereotype of Lawrence the enigmatic man of derring-do.

In 1918, when the foundations of the Lawrence legend were laid, he had wanted no more than to awaken the British public and government to the sacrifices made by the Arabs and so secure for them the political rewards which he believed were their rightful due. In short, he was the Arabs' public relations man, and he made good headway. Lawrence was co-opted to the Cabinet's Eastern Committee as an Arab expert and he used the introductions given him by Winterton to canvass politicians, news-paper owners and editors. He soon gained the co-operation of the editor of *The Times*, Geoffrey Dawson. Putting his case to Dawson in November, Lawrence emphasised that throughout the war the Arabs had behaved honourably, they had fought without the assurance of an alliance, had spurned the blandishments of other powers and had fought hard; now they wanted political freedom.

This was a highly partial gloss on the truth, but Lawrence's three articles in *The Times* of 26, 27 and 28 November 1918 were vivid but factual.

Described as reports from 'a Correspondent who was in close touch with the Arabs throughout their campaign', the pieces concentrate on the hardships faced by the Arabs and how they were overcome. They outline Arab guerrilla tactics, the help given by the Royal Navy, the taking of Aqaba and various individual skirmishes. Lawrence remained silent about his own and other British officers' activities with the Arabs.

What Lawrence wrote had the attraction of novelty. Here, for the first time, was the thrilling story of an unknown war on a remote front in which colourfully dressed warriors charged on camels and blew up railway engines. This was indeed news. The Egyptian Expeditionary Force censors had blue-pencilled war correspondents' copy which referred to the work done by Allied officers with the Arabs and overall coverage of their activities had been limited to occasional official bulletins. During September and October 1918 Massey had contributed a few lines about the Arab army in his despatches from Syria. Only on 17 October, when *The Times* printed Lawrence's anonymous summary under the headline 'The Arab March to Damascus', did the British public learn any details about the part played in the war by the forces of this hitherto obscure ally.

Even if such stories had been available earlier, their impact would have been very slight. Throughout the summer and autumn of 1918 every British newspaper was dominated by stories of the great victories on the Western Front. Names such as Le Cateau and Saint Quentin filled the headlines, and reports from Syria took second, often third place in column inches, squeezed out by accounts of Allied successes in Italy and the Balkans. Here and there a scattered handful of short paragraphs and official photographs advertised the existence of an Arab army. On 13 June the *Illustrated London News* printed a stock-in-trade war artist's drawing of Arab soldiers, dressed in shorts and *qalifehs*, storming a Turkish gun battery urged on by a British officer in sun helmet who wields a riding crop. Palms indicate an Oriental landscape and underneath a caption announces, 'The Arab forces have accounted for 40,000 Turkish troops.' Over the next five months this magazine and its rival, *The Sphere*, included the occasional photograph of Arab soldiers.

So as the war came to an end, the British public knew little about the Arabs. They, their war and the part played by Lawrence were an exotic story waiting to be told.

By this time, Lawrence had returned to London, and official circles were ringing with gossip about the intriguing figure who was being called 'the Hejaz General'. He came sharply and suddenly into focus on 30 October when rumours began to spread about his extraordinary behaviour during a private audience with George V. As he was about to be invested with his CB and DSO, Lawrence spurned both honours with the excuse that he could not honourably accept such decorations because of the government's refusal to keep faith with the Arabs. The King was discountenanced by this outburst, although he did accept Lawrence's own .303 rifle as a gift. It had a strange history: an Essex Regiment weapon, it was captured at Gallipoli, was then engraved and gold-mounted by Enver Pasha, who gave it to Faisal, who in turn passed it to Lawrence. (This handsome gun is now displayed in the Imperial War Museum.) There were soon reports that Lawrence had been so graceless as to tell the King that he might even fight alongside the Arabs against British troops if official policy were not changed. Such impertinence shocked, but those who tut-tutted may later have been puzzled to see that this brazen fellow still claimed his French honours in the 1919 edition of *Who's Who*. All in all, Lawrence had made a gesture which did nothing to promote the Arab cause and earned him much censure. Its insensitivity was surpassed when he used the ribbon of his Croix de Guerre as a collar for Hogarth's dog.

Lawrence reappeared at Buckingham Palace on 12 December with Faisal, the man on whose behalf he had made his protest, for a short audience with George V. As was standard procedure with potentates from backward countries, Faisal was given a glimpse of the wealth and power of Britain. With Lawrence in tow as his interpreter, he was welcomed as a guest aboard a battleship in the Forth and then was shown something of British industrial sinew during a four-day tour of Glasgow and Clydeside. Reporting the visit of the party in 'picturesque Arabian costume', the *Glasgow Herald* noted that Lawrence held 'the rank of amir'. At a civic dinner, Glasgow's Lord Provost admitted that like most of his countrymen he had 'had little idea that amongst our Allies there was the brave king of Hejaz and the brave Arabs'. A year later such ignorance would have been rare and by then it would have been Lawrence, not an Arabian prince, whom the Glaswegians would have flocked to see.

Lawrence, the national hero and public celebrity, was the creation of Lowell Thomas, an American who had been successively a newspaperman, Professor of Oratory at a Chicago law school and a lecturer in English at Princeton. He had an eye for a good news story, an instinct for what the public wanted, and he was ambitious. Just after America entered the war in April 1917, he was sent to Europe, on the instructions of the United States government and with cash backing from a group of Chicago businessmen, to bring back news stories which would stimulate enthusiasm for the war. There was nothing heartening to be found on the Western Front, quite the contrary, so John Buchan, Director of the new Department of

Information, guided Lowell Thomas towards the Middle East where Allenby was about to capture Jerusalem.

Here, as Buchan rightly guessed, Lowell Thomas found just what he had been looking for, a story with direct emotional appeal for Americans. There were three potent ingredients: a modern 'crusade' for the liberation of the Holy Land; the emancipation of its Arab, Jewish and Armenian communities; and human interest in the form of Lawrence, whom Lowell Thomas called 'Britain's modern Coeur de Lion'. Religious and political idealism were nicely interwoven. Before the war, there had been extensive American missionary activity in Lebanon, Syria and Palestine and the region attracted a steady flow of American Christian pilgrims. Once the war was under way, Americans (many of them Armenian and Jewish immigrants) were deeply concerned about the plight of the non-Muslim communities in the region and became involved in famine relief work there. A war waged to emancipate Middle Eastern races had wider implications. Its aims accorded with the humane and liberal spirit of President Wilson's Fourteen Points, which emphasised post-war freedom and self-determination for races under the domination of the old multi-national empires.

All these themes merged in Lawrence, the new Richard Lionheart. Lowell Thomas heard all about his deeds in Cairo and Aqaba, and in Jerusalem Storrs introduced him to the 'Uncrowned King of Arabia'. Lawrence's story inspired, reassured, and above all appealed to the romantic imagination. Furthermore, Lowell Thomas had on hand the means to give his story the immediacy and vividness which American and British audiences relished – Harry Chase, a film-cameraman and photographer.

It was appropriate that Lawrence, a twentieth-century hero, first secured fame through a film, although he appeared briefly in the background among various Allied officers in the official propaganda newsreel *Allenby's Entry into Jerusalem*, which was released in March 1918. Chase's footage on the Arab campaign was later shown in cinemas in Britain, the United States, India, Singapore, New Zealand and Australia. In July 1918, Wingate asked the Foreign Office for a print to be sent to Cairo, where, he imagined, its screening would help win over local opinion to the Allies.[7] Chase's newsreel sequences formed part of Lowell Thomas's two-hour presentation on the Palestine and Arabian campaigns which opened at New York's Century Theatre in March 1919. The lecture and film (accompanied by a symphony orchestra) was a great success, and a British impresario, Percy Burton, backed its transfer to London, where it opened on 14 August at the Royal Opera House, Covent Garden under the title 'With Allenby in Palestine'. This was quickly altered to 'With Allenby in Palestine and Lawrence in Arabia', which was a truer reflection of the subject matter. Originally scheduled to run for a fortnight, the programme was a sell-out

Turkey's lifeline: Rolling stock on the Damascus–Medina line guarded by
German troops, 1918.

A lifeline destroyed: Damaged station and wagons, Ghadir al Haj, 1918, a picture
possibly taken by Lawrence after a raid.

Master of Damascus: Lawrence is driven through Damascus in a Rolls Royce; British other ranks and Damascenes, wearing traditional fezes, watch his progress, October 1918.

Sir Ronald Storrs: Proconsul and aesthete who befriended Lawrence in Cairo and became a life-long admirer.

Lord Lloyd of Dolobron: Imperialist and Tory MP, he joined Military Intelligence in Cairo with Lawrence in 1914 where they became close friends.

Medina falls, February 1919: Taken after the final surrender of Fakhri Pasha, this picture shows Major Henry Garland (far left), the Amirs Ali and Abdullah, the future King of Jordan, (fifth and sixth from left) and Arab and Turkish officers.

Warriors turned peacemakers: The Amir Faisal (centre), Nuri al Said (second left), Captain Pisani, the commander of the Algerian artillery battery attached to the Arabs during 1917 and 1918 (behind Faisal) and Lawrence; Paris 1919. Faisal's negro slave stands respectfully back from the rest.

Gentleman ranker: Lawrence poses at the RAF base, Miramshah, North-West Frontier, India, 1928.

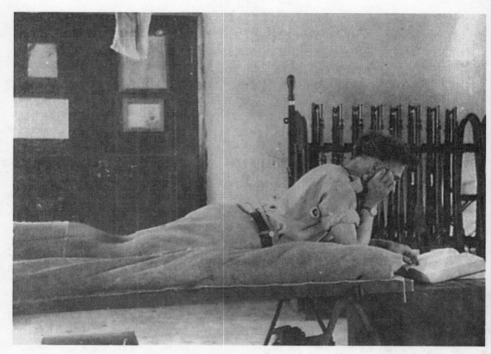

Man of letters: Lawrence reading on his camp bed, Miramshah. The chained rifles behind are a reminder that he was stationed in a region which was a perpetual war-zone.

WHAT 50 YEARS ON STAGE HAS TAUGHT ME—MARIE TEMPEST

WIRELESS: P. 28

DAILY SKETCH

THINGS I HATE
BERNARD SHAW

No. 8,131 [Registered as a newspaper]   MONDAY, MAY 20, 1935   ONE PENNY

TOO BIG FOR WEALTH AND GLORY

Lawrence the Soldier Dies to Live for Ever

Having lingered for six days, Lawrence of Arabia (Mr. T. E. Shaw) died in hospital at Bovington Camp, Dorset, yesterday from injuries received when he crashed with his powerful motor-cycle at Moreton. He was 46. In the year 1914 Lawrence was commissioned fifteen miles near Carchemish on the Euphrates. Two years later he arrived and virtually commanded the Arab Army that in such powerful help to the British campaign in Palestine. In this rôle he became famous the world over as Lawrence of Arabia knight. Spurning opportunity and wealth, he declined an offer of £100,000 to appear in a film.

Death of a hero: Lawrence's death was headline news. Here the familiar icon of him in Arab robes, first used by Lowell Thomas, shares space with that of gentleman ranker astride his Brough 'Superior' motor bike.

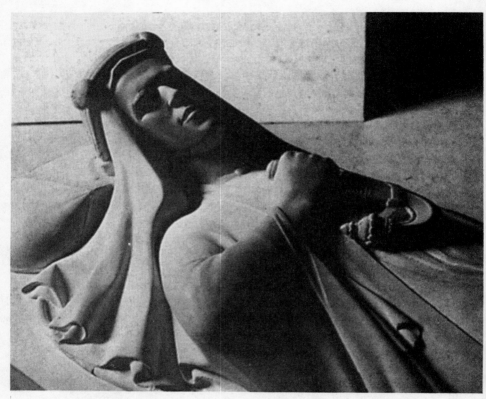

Sleeping Galahad: Lawrence's friend, Eric Kennington, carved this memorial which was originally intended for Salisbury Cathedral. After disagreements between the Bishop, Dean and Lawrence's brother Arnold, the figure was placed in Wareham Church, Dorset, where it remains. Kennington deliberately imitated the style and pose of the carved effigies and brasses of medieval warriors which, as a boy, Lawrence had studied and whose legendary deeds he hoped to emulate.

and was transferred to the Royal Albert Hall, where it ran for six months. Lowell Thomas believed that in London alone at least a million people watched his presentation.

What they saw was a dramatic extravaganza. The Covent Garden production utilised a set left over from the moonlight-on-the-Nile scene from the opera *Joseph and his Brethren* and the show opened with a performance of the Dance of the Seven Veils. Then Mrs Thomas sang her own setting of the muezzin's call to prayer. On this characteristically bogus Oriental note, her husband entered and began his monologue.

At this moment, somewhere in London, hiding from a host of feminine admirers, book publishers, autograph fiends and every species of hero-worshipper, is a young man whose name will go down in history beside those of Sir Francis Drake, Sir Walter Raleigh, Lord Clive, Charles Gordon, and all the other famous heroes of Great Britain's glorious past.

This was Lawrence.

Then followed what Lowell Thomas called 'the most romantic story of the war', illustrated by slides and film and with music provided by the band of the Welsh Guards. The playbills described the production as 'America's Tribute to British Valour'. In fact it was something more. When Burton had brought the production to London he had the encouragement and blessing of the English Speaking Union, of which Lowell Thomas was a member and whose committee included Churchill, Curzon and the newspaper proprietor, Lord Northcliffe. The Union was part of a broader movement which in the early twentieth century aimed to draw Britain and the United States more closely together. The cement with which such organisations hoped to bind the so-called Anglo-Saxon nations was a compound of their shared racial background, language, culture and history. With widespread support in newspaper, business and political circles, bodies such as the English Speaking Union hoped to achieve more than merely reminding Britons and Americans of their inheritance: they also sought to foster a common sense of future destiny.

Lowell Thomas's show was part of this process and was designed to boost Anglo-American understanding. Lawrence was deliberately presented as both an old-style hero and a representative of the new, benevolent imperialism. His life and needs were used to dispel the traditional American misgivings about Britain as a greedy and oppressive imperial power. Lawrence was not a conqueror, but a liberator who led the Arabs towards a better future, Or, in Lowell Thomas's words, 'the wild sons of Ishmael regarded the quiet, fair-haired leader as a sort of supernatural being who had been sent from heaven to deliver them from oppression.' Through Lawrence, American audiences understood enlightened imperialism. In 1919 the United States was being urged by Britain to take up the challenge of this new imperialism as a mandatory power with responsibility for the government of former Ottoman provinces. At the Paris Peace Conference, Lawrence himself pressed the United States to accept the mandates for Constantinople and Armenia.[8]

While Lowell Thomas may have set his listeners thinking about how Lawrence's vision might be fulfilled politically, his underlying purpose was to entertain with an adventure story of guerrilla warfare set against an exotic background. If his subsequent articles in *The Strand Magazine* and his *With Lawrence in Arabia* are anything to go by, his style was vivid and cinematographic. One enthralling incident follows another and everything is larger than life, including of course Lawrence.

London audiences were clearly captivated by the story and its hero. For those who watched and listened, the war was still an overpowering and often nightmarish memory. Peace had been signed at Versailles at the end of June 1919 and, on 11 November 1920, the dead were symbolically laid to rest as the Unknown Warrior was lowered into his grave at Westminster Abbey. There was a duty to remember and, at the same time, to push to the back of the mind recollections of mass suffering and death. There was also a need to get back to what the Americans called 'normalcy'. A contemporary advertisement for Kensitas cigarettes caught the mood nicely. A returned officer and his wife are smoking and relaxing. 'You've seen it through! You don't want to talk about it. You don't want to think about it.'

Yet books about the war were pouring from the presses. Releases for November 1919 included *The Story of our Submarines*, *Green Balls: The Adventures of a Night Bomber* and *How I Filmed the War*. There was a marked public interest in hearing hitherto untold stories, especially when they concerned the more unusual or glamorous aspects of the war. For this reason, men and women flocked to listen to what was advertised as 'the Strange Story of Colonel Lawrence, the leader of the Arab Army' and clearly found it enthralling.

Lowell Thomas's showmanship first produced the Lawrence legend and rendered its hero in the likeness of a superman. What was remarkable was the staying power of the story and the depth and intensity of public interest. This was kept alive by contemporary biographies, by Lawrence's own version of his exploits, *Revolt in the Desert*, which appeared in 1927, and by intermittent newspaper stories. In the widest sense, Lawrence had become a form of public property, a celebrity whose ideas and behaviour were thought to be of concern to newspaper readers. On one level he joined a select band of aviators, explorers, socialites and film stars whose features appeared in the popular press and about whom journalists wrote, usually with a blind disregard for truth. Even Robert Graves felt forced to include a brief section in his biography which included Lawrence's views on children and animals, just the sort of trivia which the popular press relished, as presumably its readers did as well.

The power of the Lawrence legend was more than mere public curiosity about a wartime hero. He was, in simple terms, a hero who fitted perfectly with the temper of his times and possessed qualities which appealed to people of widely different backgrounds and attitudes. But first, he fulfilled a deeply felt national need to have at least one outstanding individual hero from a war which had been fought by the masses. At the same time as he had to represent those masses, this hero had to display the recognisable features which fitted traditional concepts of personal heroism. During and after the conflict there had been a strange ambivalence towards modern war which was most clearly seen in the early 1920s when war memorials were appearing across the country. Many included statues or bronze-cast figures which either showed modern soldiers, clothed and equipped for the trenches with steel helmets, capes and packs like the gunners on the Royal Artillery Memorial at Hyde Park Corner or else armoured knights from the chivalric past, like the figure on the Cavalry Memorial nearby in Hyde Park. An extreme but fascinating example of this genre is at Sledmere, Sir Mark Sykes's Yorkshire estate village, where the memorial includes mock-medieval brasses of Crusaders – perhaps an allusion to Sir Mark's work in the Middle East. The armoured knight, used by propagandists on both sides, embodied the traditional martial virtues of courage, service and personal honour.

In essence, Lawrence belonged to this older strain of heroism. The point was made by Lowell Thomas when he described the lives of Lawrence's brother officers. 'Each man had his own task and went his own way. Each was a free-lance and conducted himself with much the same freedom as did knights of old.' A similar comparison was drawn by Winterton in his articles in *Blackwood's*, when he likened desert campaigning to schoolboy escapades or Elizabethan adventures. The warriors were free agents. This was a world and an age away from the commonplace experience of the First World War battlefield where soldiers fought as part of a vast machine which set their goals, dictated their tactics and minutely regulated every aspect of their lives. Moreover, as Lowell Thomas, Lawrence and others would demonstrate, the desert war was one of continual incident. By contrast, everyday life in the trenches was marked by extended periods of inactivity and boredom.

The desert battleground was, as Lawrence admitted, a clean landscape where fighting men moved freely rather than having to scurry about or hide in holes. This, and the fact that the individual still counted, must have had enormous appeal to those generations which had come to manhood before and during the war. They had been weaned on the adventure stories of G.A.Henty and the *Boy's Own Paper* or the verses of Kipling and Newbolt, in which heroes fought on the open hillsides of India, the wastes of the Sudan or the South African veldt. If there was any ideal of war for the pre-1914 generations, this was it and it closely matched the experience of Lawrence. Furthermore, between 1914 and 1918, nearly every soldier measured his achievement in terms of day-to-day survival or a small share in the defence or capture of some sector of the line often known just by its map reference. Even without Lowell Thomas's hyperbole, Lawrence could have claimed that he had helped liberate a people. Unlike those who stuck it out in the trenches, his cause had been clear and he could look back and see real gains from his exertions.

So, paradoxically, the hero who emerged from the First World War and captured public imagination was a man who was a stranger to the common experience of modern war, although, as he made clear, he knew its horrors. An essentially romantic warrior, his deeds belonged to another age. He wore flowing Arab robes while most men wore khaki, and he rode rather than ran or crawled across the battlefield. He was his own master, not another's pawn. To cross the desert with Lawrence was to take a flight of fancy and forget the reality of modern war. It was an indulgence which, from the 1920s onwards, many were pleased to enjoy. Yet, as C.E.Edmonds (C.E.Carrington), who had seen service on the Western Front, remarked in a short posthumous biography of Lawrence in 1935, he was 'the archetype of the Lost Generation' and like them had passed the post-war years in 'cynical retirement'.

Among the generals of the First World War, no Wellington emerged to command public respect and admiration. The walrus-moustached, rotund, florid generals (Lawrence called them 'red soldiers') like Haig lacked charisma and were collectively unattractive to a post-war generation which distrusted their attitudes and loathed the brutal militarism they appeared to represent. Lionised during the war by government propaganda, such men shrank during the inter-war years when they were mocked as Blimps and the poverty of their strategic thinking was exposed by younger officers like Liddell Hart. Lawrence had little time for them or any professional officer. 'They do their best,' he told Liddell Hart, 'not their fault it's such a rotten best.'

Lawrence was untainted by any connection with the old military caste. Slightly built, short and with almost virginal features, he was the physical antithesis of the old-style bullish general. Unlike them, as Liddell Hart insisted, he was an instinctive soldier who used his brains to save his men's lives rather than unthinkingly squander them as Haig had done. Lawrence belonged to a military tradition, but it was a distant one which embraced men of ideas and letters like Raleigh or Sir Philip Sidney for whom soldiering was a part but not the whole of their existence.

Throughout the war Lawrence, like millions of others, had been a civilian in arms who had tenaciously clung to his independence of habit and thought. Like many young men of his intellectual background, he filled his spare time with re-reading his favourite classics, symbolic links with his pre-war life as well as sheet-anchors of former civilised values. The figure who emerges from Robert Graves's and Liddell Hart's biographies is a rebellious anti-militarist. According to Graves, Lawrence 'is very much hated by government officials, regular soldiers, old-fashioned political experts and such like'. 'To those who were solidly buttressed by dignity and orthodoxy,' Liddell Hart wrote, 'the idea of a temporary second-lieutenant indulging in military criticisms and sitting in judgement was revolting.'

Lawrence, a young man, was on the side of youth and against the oppressive, fuddy-duddy generation of boneheads who had mishandled the war and were, during the 1920s, set upon reimposing pre-war ideas and conventions. His attitudes would have been applauded by many former junior officers and other-ranks who had found themselves and their lives in the hands of the military dullards of the type he had twitted. Moreover a new generation, growing up and coming of age during the 1920s and 1930s, approved Lawrence's individualism and rejection of worn-out men and stale ideas. Graves placed him very firmly on the side of youth and approvingly retold a Lawrentian anecdote in which the young man clashed with that patrician embodiment of the old order, Curzon. Lawrence's use of the expression 'fed up' in an official telegram had irritated the Foreign Secretary, who asked an underling its meaning. 'I believe, my lord, that it is equivalent of disgruntled' was the answer. 'Ah,' said Curzon, 'I suppose it is a term in use among the middle classes.' He then begged an explanation of Lawrence's phrase 'carry on'. (This has all the hallmarks of one of those self-mocking tales which Curzon made up about himself; still, as recounted by Graves, it vindicated Lawrence as 'the common man', a creature which the Marquess would have found incomprehensible.)

Lawrence was not only a figure with which an impatient and rebellious younger generation could identify, he was also used as the example of the Victorian and Edwardian manly virtues which the old wanted the young to emulate. He appears in this role in Lowell Thomas's *The Boy's Life of Colonel Lawrence*, which appeared in Britain and America in 1927, and two ripping yarns for schoolboys by Gurney Slade (Stephen Bartlett), *In Lawrence's Bodyguard* (1930) and *Led by Lawrence* (1934). In the first, Slade imagined that he would be the first of many since 'By his exploits Lawrence has delivered himself into the hands of fiction writers for all time, and by weaving a few of the incidents of his campaign into the plot of a boys' book, I am only one of the forerunners of a mighty horde.' This legion of authors never materialised; boys' tastes changed and, while Biggles held his ground, the comic adventure paper superseded the older Hentyesque genre which Slade practised.

In fact Lawrence has a walk-on part in *In Lawrence's Bodyguard*, which runs true to the usual pattern with the adventures of Irwin Baxter, captain of the first fifteen at Garchester, who, like Lawrence, is an archaeologist working in the Middle East. During the war he uses his skills as an Arabist in various ways and ends up among the tribesmen of Faisal's and then Lawrence's bodyguard. Lawrence himself is an idealised cipher.

> The fame of Lawrence had now flown through all Arabia. From military adviser he had now evolved into the recognised military head of the Revolt. The army had now had time to test his character thoroughly, and it was to their liking. Unselfish, generous to a rare degree, careless of his own life, but extremely careful of his followers', he seemed to them to be possessed of all the virtues of the ideal Arab.

This description probably coincided more or less exactly with the public's knowledge of Lawrence's character and deeds. Robert Graves noticed that in some quarters there was a haziness about his identity. When Lawrence's *Revolt in the Desert* appeared in the bookshops, some customers mistook it for a sequel to *Son of the Sheik*. E.M.Hull's pulp-fiction desert romances enjoyed great popularity, as did their filmed versions starring Valentino, so confusion was inevitable. The popularity of Valentino's desert films may have contributed accidentally to Lawrence's continued fame and vice versa.

The public appetite for Lawrence books stayed strong. Lowell Thomas's *With Lawrence in Arabia* was a British and American bestseller, as was Lawrence's own *Revolt in the Desert*. Within eight years this had been translated into a dozen languages including Russian, Icelandic and Lettish. The *Seven Pillars*, which appeared within two months of Lawrence's death in May 1935, sold well and editions in eight other languages were published within four years.

The simple explanation for these high sales was a universal desire to be entertained by a collection of exciting adventures in a distant land. Their central character also exerted an equally strong fascination, thanks in large part to his post-war behaviour. In 1922, the public was astonished by his enlistment in the RAF, although this could easily be explained in terms with which many war veterans would have sympathised. As Robert Graves had written in his biography, Lawrence had been keen to shed 'the mask of a popular hero' and become one of a crowd, in his case among ordinary servicemen. Such anonymity gave Lawrence the chance for undisturbed self-discovery and the fulfilment of private literary ambitions which had been interrupted by the war. The choice of a barrack hut may have been unusual, but Lawrence's sentiments would have been understood by many who, after the trauma of war, wished to return to a secluded, tranquil and normal life. For them, like Lawrence, the war had been an aberration to be forgotten.

Lawrence's RAF career was carefully charted by the press. It was an essential part of an artificial air of mystery which hung about him. Lowell Thomas had explained his urge for anonymity in terms of modesty, but this did not satisfy either newspapermen or their readers. Robert Graves had aroused their curiosity about the secret Lawrence by intriguing references to his wartime Military Intelligence activities and Lowell Thomas had mentioned his cunning disguises and escapades as a spy. These details added a new dimension to Lawrence and his legend at a time when popular fiction and the cinema were exploiting the public's taste for secret-service adventures. Among the most successful was John Buchan's sequence of Hannay novels, written between 1908 and 1934, in which one of the heroes, Sandy Clanroyden, although based on Aubrey Herbert, shared distinct features with Lawrence.

Like every convincing thriller-writer, Buchan contrived plots that were immediately recognisable to his audience, with incidents and backgrounds adapted from contemporary events. Just after the war, his heroes squared up to the Bolsheviks and in *The House of Four Winds* (1935) the plot revolves around a thinly disguised neo-Fascist youth movement in a central European country, recalling the contemporary Iron Guard in Roumania. Throughout the world of thriller fiction, plucky secret agents, who had learned their trade during the war, played new gambits in a modern version of the 'Great Game' to preserve Britain and her empire. In the public imagination, Lawrence appeared a living example of such a figure and the power of his reputation fuelled speculation that his humble aircraftman's uniform was just another disguise of Britain's masterspy.

Reality appeared to be imitating fiction when, in 1928, Lawrence was posted to Miramshah, an outpost on the North-West Frontier in the heart of the empire's most turbulent province. The coincidence was too much for the popular press, which exploited it to the full with a sheaf of sensational but utterly unfounded reports during the autumn and winter of 1928–9. The *Evening News* opened the sequence with the revelation that Lawrence, masquerading as a messianic holy man, was on the track of Bolshevik conspirators in the volatile city of Amritsar. Next, other papers revealed how, still using the same cover, he had cropped up over the border in Afghanistan where he was organising tribal resistance to the pro-Soviet, reforming Amir, Amanullah. There had been much recent unrest in Afghanistan and this story, which the *Empire News* validated with the eyewitness reports of a bogus missionary, was taken seriously by the world's press. Government denials could not stop the political ruckus. On 6 February 1929, Shapurji Saklatvala, the Communist MP for Battersea North and leading activist in the League Against Imperialism, asked Austen Chamberlain, the Foreign Secretary, whether he would refute the charges against Lawrence which had been made by the Afghan government. By then Lawrence had been ordered back from India at the suggestion of the embarrassed British Minister in Kabul. At his disembarkation at Southampton, he was faced by hordes of pressmen, photographers and newsreel cameramen.

For a few weeks he was the bogeyman of the left. Saklatvala, sure that he had uncovered an agent of imperialist oppression, presided over a meeting at Tower Hill where Lawrence was burned in effigy. Further vexation waited for Lawrence. After he had visited the House of Commons to explain his innocence to the Labour MPs Jimmy Maxton and Ernest Thurtle, some newspapers trumped up the story that he had joined or was about to join the Labour Party, something as far from his mind as spying in the bazaars of Amritsar.

There was a bizarre sequel to the Afghan farrago. The Soviet government, realising its propaganda potential, produced a film, *Visitor from Mecca*, which was shown in Moscow cinemas at the end of 1930. The film's hero, a young Russian engineer, is working on a rail tunnel which will link Russia and Gulistan (presumably Afghanistan) and unite their peoples in friendship. He is hampered by the machinations of the decadent British Resident, who controls the country's ruler and represents imperialism, and an Arab holy man who stands for religious obscurantism and reaction. In the end the forces of progress triumph: the Resident is assassinated and the holy man is revealed to be Lawrence wearing a false beard.[9]

Muscovites would have already been aware of Lawrence's identity. His name was mentioned in 1930 during the trial of a group of British engineers from Vickers and their Russian accomplices on charges of economic sabotage. One of the accused admitted that he had been recruited by Lawrence, who had approached him in London's Savoy Hotel. Lawrence told this man that he was acting for the British General Staff, which wanted to overthrow the Russian government by force. Since Lawrence was in India when this alleged conversation occurred, the Foreign Office was able to deny the tale. What is interesting is that the Russian government clearly believed that the use of Lawrence's name would give credibility to its propaganda. This was a sensible assumption, given his wartime reputation and the groundswell of speculation in the British press which hinted that he was still a key figure in the British secret service.

Rumours of Lawrence the super-spy proliferated. In 1932 he was allegedly back in his old haunts, the borders of Syria and Jordan. At the same time, the Chinese government was alarmed by a German wireless report that the British government had sent Lawrence to Tibet, where he was running arms and ammunition to local resistance groups. Again the Foreign Office had to explain that Lawrence, then based at Plymouth, was an ordinary airman and suggested that the canard was probably Soviet-inspired. Official denials did nothing to stem the flood of such Lawrence stories, as one India Office official ruefully noted.

> During the last few years his wraith has appeared in Kurdistan, Southern Persia, Afghanistan, and, I think, Soviet Turkestan, and in fact almost anywhere where there was trouble which could be attributed to the machiavellian designs of the Imperialistic British government. If the legend has struck deep in proportion to its branches, it seems likely to enjoy quite a respectable spell of immortality.[10]

It did; shortly after Lawrence's funeral in May 1935, *L'Oeuvre* claimed that he was still alive and on a secret mission on the banks of the Nile in southern Sudan. Such speculation was understandable since Mussolini's invasion of Ethiopia was under way and, in the autumn, George Orwell picked up rumours that Lawrence was in that country and organising native forces. Orwell, who had little time for Lawrence, hoped the story might be true. It was another will-o'-the-wisp like the rest of the post-war secret-service tales fabricated about Lawrence.

Alongside make-believe Lawrence mysteries, there was a genuine one which from time to time intrigued the public. It concerned the long personal narrative of the Arab campaign that Lawrence wrote between 1919 and 1925 and which he published privately in 1926. The saga of its composition, including the disappearance of one draft on Reading station, was related by Hogarth in *The Times Literary Supplement* of 13 December 1926. Hogarth had been consulted by Lawrence throughout the book's preparation and he added a few details about the contents of the *Seven Pillars* which contained a 'horrible description' of Lawrence's capture at Dera. What Lawrence called a 'sugar and butter' résumé of the book appeared in *Blackwood's* at the end of 1925 written by Edmund Candler, a former war correspondent with the army in Iraq. Candler had looked through the 1922 draft and was full of praise for 'a war book more exciting than a novel, a code of philosophy, and a manual of irregular desert warfare' together with 'an immense Arabian canvas of peoples and scenes, all individual and unlike one another, and portraits and landscapes by anyone else, yet essentially true.'

This masterpiece was deliberately withheld from the public on Lawrence's instructions. So too was *The Mint*, his later account of his experiences in the RAF, although it circulated in manuscript among his friends. Through copies available in the Bodleian Library, the British Museum and those loaned by subscribers to their friends, many details of the *Seven Pillars* filtered through to the public. The *New Statesman*'s review of its abridgement, *Revolt in the Desert*, referred to this 'mysterious' book which included an account of how Lawrence had been taken prisoner, flogged and left for dead. This was common knowledge by the time of Lawrence's death when an obituary article in the *Daily Sketch* of 20 May 1935 stated that Lawrence had been 'flogged by the Turks till he fainted'. Eight weeks later everyone could read the full details of the hero's ordeal.

The Lawrence legend flourished during a period of passionate political partisanship. In Britain, both the right and the left attempted to kidnap Lawrence and secure his endorsement of their philosophies. It was a futile task, remarked Sir Herbert Read, who thought that Lawrence's deep-rooted masochism disinclined him to total rebellion.[11] The Communist writer Christopher Caudwell detected in Lawrence a fatal weakness which prevented him from assuming a truly heroic role.

> The Great War had no hero. . . . In the twentieth century millions of deaths and mountains of guns, tanks and ships are not enough to make a bourgeois hero. The best thing they achieved was a might-have-been, the pathetic figure of T.E.Lawrence.[12]

Yet Lawrence was not, Caudwell thought, a bourgeois. His RAF life was a rebellion against the bourgeois way of life, but he was not mentally tough enough to rid himself of bourgeois habits of mind. He was 'too intellectual' to become the Communist man of action, the leader of the masses.

Like many other intellectuals and men of letters, Caudwell followed the heroic course of action and died, aged twenty-nine, fighting with the International Brigade in Spain. He, like so many of his generation both of the left and the right, was looking for a leader, a heroic figure who could combine charisma, ideology and action to save his people. Such figures interested Lawrence as well; Lenin won his admiration not for his political theories, but because of his energy and ability to get things done.

Such men were needed, or so it seemed, during the last years of Lawrence's life, which were marked by extended crises in Britain and abroad. Economic disintegration and the failure of conventional politicians and their systems to engage, let alone solve, the problems of industrial recession and mass unemployment drove many into the arms of 'men of destiny' with revolutionary solutions. Lawrence seemed admirably qualified to fulfil this role; he was a man of unconventional but formidable intellect, possessed a strong will, and had proved himself as a man of courage and action. This was Caudwell's view and that of Lawrence's friend, the novelist Henry Williamson, an ardent supporter of Sir Oswald Mosley's British Union of Fascists.

Williamson, who shared Lawrence's passion for speed and the air, imagined he had discovered the ideal Fascist. Lawrence appeared to belong to that new breed of supermen such as D'Annunzio, the Italian poet aviator and Mussolini supporter, who were intoxicated with speed and tested themselves to destruction to prove their superior courage. The similarities between Lawrence and the proto-heroes of Italian Fascism and German Nazism were more apparent than real. Lawrence's self-imposed tests of courage and stamina were a legacy from his youth, which found its final expression in a reckless infatuation with fast motorbikes. On one level this behaviour represented an urge to gain domination over his own body and, remembering his obsession with the codes of medieval chivalry, it was a reminder that blind courage and a debonair disregard for death were marks of knightly prowess.

Nevertheless, Williamson believed that he could induce Lawrence to commit himself to the radical right. There were good reasons for thinking such a conversion possible, even though Lawrence revealed little outward interest in the political issues of the day. Strong men such as Churchill attracted him on a personal level, but he was unmoved by their ideologies. His own seemed a mish-mash of anarchism and nihilism. Yet in conversation with the Labour MP Ernest Thurtle, and in several passages of the *Seven Pillars*, Lawrence indicated his sympathies with the Nietzschean concept of the superman. He told Thurtle, 'I think the planet is in a damnable condition, which no change of party, or social reform, will do more than palliate insignificantly. What is wanted is a new master species – birth control for us, to end the human race in fifty years – and then a clear field for a cleaner mammal. I suppose it must be a mammal.'

Such opinions may have induced Williamson to think that Lawrence might look sympathetically on others who sought a replacement of human beings by a new super-race. He hoped that Lawrence might, on retirement from the RAF, put himself at the head of an anti-war and anti-Jewish league of ex-servicemen. In a wilder flight of fancy, Williamson considered that Lawrence should go to Germany and convince Hitler that Britain did not seek a war. On the day that Lawrence suffered his fatal motorbike accident, he had just wired Williamson with an invitation to Cloud's Hill. Shortly before, a newspaperman had asked him whether he had plans to make himself Britain's dictator, which indicates that the thought, however absurd, had occurred to others. Still, it was highly improbable that, had he lived, Lawrence would have agreed to participate in Williamson's hare-brained schemes or have offered his prestige to the British Fascist movement.

Nevertheless, Lawrence was conscious that his reputation gave him considerable power, even if he was uncertain how he might assert it publicly. Francis Yeats-Brown, who later joined Mosley's British Union of Fascists, wrote in conclusion to a 1929 *Spectator* article on Lawrence, 'He might do greater things in England if the need arose, than he did in Arabia.' Lawrence amended this sentence to, 'Perhaps he might do greater things in England if the need arose, than he did in Arabia.'

These 'greater things' continued to occupy his thoughts. Whatever their nature, they were passing through his mind shortly before his retirement from the RAF. 'Not so long ago,' Liddell Hart wrote to Robert Graves, 'when I was arguing that the publicity he had been getting was his own fault, he retorted that he might need all he had and more, as an aid to his future efforts.' It was all very mysterious, since Lawrence did not elaborate. Still, Liddell Hart noted that 'every now and then' Lawrence suggested 'that he might be coming back to do something bigger than before'. In the same enigmatic vein he would compare himself to the Byzantine General, Belisarius, who had been pushed into obscurity by the jealous Emperor Justinian, but who, when crisis threatened, was recalled and achieved fresh glories. After what he called a 'fascist conversation', Robert Graves was perturbed by Lawrence's views on political freedom, which he thought 'equivocal'. Equally equivocal was Lawrence's resolution for, on the last day of 1934, he confessed that he was looking forward to a future of 'true leisure'. This was hardly the manifesto of a man whose heart was set on 'greater things'.

Yet he was also under pressure from his friends Churchill and Lady Astor to engage himself in 'greater things'. In 1935 both pleaded with Lawrence to turn his talents towards public affairs where his influence and prestige would add weight to Churchill's campaign for speedy rearmament. Lawrence, like many of his countrymen, was disturbed by the growth of the German air force and, as an insider in the RAF, was aware of the need for Britain to keep abreast of Germany in technical research. Moreover, since Churchill was in the political wilderness and commonly branded a war-monger, Lawrence's presence at his side would give him much needed publicity and credibility.

It is clear that several of Lawrence's closest friends and admirers expected him to return to the centre of the public stage and that, during the last year of his life, Lawrence's thoughts were moving fitfully in that direction. What is interesting is that figures of such widely different views as Churchill, Lady Astor, Williamson and Caudwell felt that Lawrence was a force to be reckoned with and that his name and reputation would add lustre to any cause he espoused. 'If he roused himself to action,' Churchill wrote in 1937, 'who should say what crisis he could not surmount or quell? If things were going badly, how glad one would be to see him round the corner.' This was of course the man whom Churchill knew as a friend, not the figure of popular legend.

It was inevitable that Lawrence's exploits should attract the interest of film-makers. Their attentions worried him and he was relieved on hearing, in 1929, that plans for a film of his adventures had been dropped. They were revived in May 1934 when Sir Alexander Korda purchased the film rights of *Revolt in the Desert* from the book's trustees.

Korda wanted to begin filming in 1936 and had in mind a vast desert epic in which Leslie Howard would play Lawrence, an excellent piece of casting. Lawrence was uneasy about the business and in January 1935 explained to Korda 'the inconveniences' which he would suffer when the film appeared. He found the Hungarian 'quite unexpectedly sensitive' and agreeable to proceed only when Lawrence consented. There matters rested until Lawrence's death five months later. Almost immediately Korda began operations. Colonel Stirling, once Lawrence's colleague and lately military adviser to King Zog of Albania, was in charge of preliminary arrangements and on 23 July approached the Foreign Office for help. In essence the film would be action with bombing raids and massed camel charges by Beduin which would be filmed on location on the border between Saudi Arabia and Jordan, with Jerusalem serving for Damascus.

This created problems for, while Stirling assured the Foreign Office that the demolitions would be undertaken in the studio, there were fears that the 'suspicious and savage Saudis' might mistake mock battles for real ones and join in seriously. Nevertheless the Foreign Office saw the film as a chance for some good Hashemite propaganda, although sections of the script which dealt with the government's promises to Hussain would have to be vetted.[13] The outbreak of the Arab Revolt in Palestine during the spring of 1936 ruled out any filming in Jordan which involved gatherings of tribesmen as extras. By now there were strong and insistent objections from the Turkish government about proposed scenes of Turkish atrocities.

Korda was forced to bow to pressure from the censors of the British Board of Film Control and the Foreign Office, which were both anxious not to upset Turkey. In June 1939 after extended negotiations, Korda proposed a new, completely revised script which included Lawrence's Oxford career, the war and, for the final half of the film, an account of his time in the RAF. This, Korda insisted, was to be 'by far the most important part of the picture'. This satisfied the censors and the Foreign Office, but the war and Korda's departure for Hollywood terminated the project.

The new film would have entertained and uplifted audiences. Korda knew that now Britain was facing war, an idealised story of Lawrence would serve to inspire her people. 'My associates and myself', he wrote, 'are fully convinced that the making of a picture about Lawrence's life is today very greatly in the National Interest, as nothing could have such a good propaganda effect as the example of his life.'[14] Had it been made, Korda's film with Leslie Howard in the title role would have been shown in wartime cinemas alongside others which depicted the heroes of Britain's past such as Drake, Pitt the Younger and Nelson. No doubt it would have moved audiences, reminded them of their country's greatness and exemplified the path of duty. It would have been the apotheosis of the Lawrence of legend.

What Korda called the 'unique climax' of the film was to have been Lawrence's service in the RAF. This seemed paradoxical as Lawrence had often represented his enlistment in the ranks as a deliberate effort to discard his former public self and find anonymity. Yet he had chosen obscurity in a service which was at the centre of public attention throughout the 1920s and 1930s and which was widely associated with adventure and glamour. This was the age of the Empire Air Days, Kingsford-Smith, Lindbergh and Amy Johnson and the breaking of aerial records for speed and endurance.

Air was the new frontier, waiting to be overcome, and its conquest stirred the public imagination. Lawrence was swept along by the general enthusiasm. It was, he told Wing-Commander Sydney Smith in 1921, 'the most important development of the future' and he was full of excitement about the new cross-desert air routes which were being planned. Two years later at Farnborough and now a new RAF recruit, Lawrence was overwhelmed by the possibilities ahead. 'I grew suddenly on fire with the glory which the air should be.' Six years later and soon after he had taken part in the management of the Schneider Trophy Race at Plymouth, he still saw himself as involved in 'the greatest adventure that awaits mankind'.

The challenge of the air excited and fascinated contemporaries and Lawrence's association with it, through his RAF service, added a new dimension to his public persona. It aroused the interest of intellectuals who drew comparisons between him and André Malraux and Antoine de Saint Exupéry, both men of letters who risked their lives as fliers. For Auden, Isherwood and their circle, Lawrence's apparent fusion of thought and physical action and daring exerted a peculiar fascination. He was, wrote Auden in 1934, one of those men who 'exemplify most completely what is best and significant in our lives, our nearest approach to a synthesis of feeling and reason, act and thought'. His life had been 'an allegory of the transformation of the Truly Weak Man into the Truly Strong Man, an answer to the question "How shall the self-conscious man be saved?"' Small, neurotic and riddled with self-doubt, Lawrence had still made himself the man of action. It might be possible, Auden imagined, for men like himself to follow the same course. Certainly the external circumstances of their age demanded that weak men made themselves strong.

After Lawrence's death, Auden and Isherwood revised their judgements and concluded that Lawrence had always been a 'Truly Weak Man'. There was something lacking in the hero, not least a sense of purpose and high seriousness:

> A Bristol Fighter which flew overhead
> Swooped down as the pilot leaned out of his seat
> 'It's Lawrence of Arabia', somebody said
> And a typist tittered, 'Isn't he sweet!'

She would no doubt have enjoyed the Lowell Thomas show and, if it had been screened, the Korda film.

Robert Graves suspected that Lawrence had an ability to be all things to all men. This was certainly true of the legend which grew up around him during the last sixteen years of his life. To the man in the street he was a war hero who hated war, despised militarism, scoffed at old-guard generals and politicians and sought only to live quietly on his own terms. He was presented to the country's youth as an example of steadfastness in duty and courage. For the film industry his life and exploits were the basis for an epic which would inspire and thrill audiences. Outspoken and unconventional, he was on the side of the coming generation in its struggle against its elders. As an intellectual he was a model for contemporary writers hesitant about how they should behave in a world which demanded deeds from them as well as ideas. He was in the forefront of efforts to conquer the air, and he might even have been a secret agent as cunning and resourceful as any fictional hero. Churchill could write to him in 1927 and ask him not to wait till the 'Bolshevik Revolution entitles me to summon you to the centre of strife by an order from the Imperial Stirrup!' At the same time a Communist could speculate whether this instinctive enemy of the bourgeois might be the revolutionary leader who would overthrow capitalism. For Williamson and a few Fascists, Lawrence was the lost leader who had to be persuaded to mount his white horse and bring salvation to his people. Anything seemed possible with a man whose legend, Noël Coward recalled, 'was too strong to be gainsaid'.

For Lawrence himself it was something which gave him pleasure or torment according to his mood.

III

LIVING WITH A LEGEND

TOWARDS the end of D.H.Lawrence's *Lady Chatterley's Lover*, Connie Chatterley tries to get her artist father's approval for her marriage to the gamekeeper Mellors. He had been, she reminded him, an officer and was 'like Colonel C.E.Florence, who preferred to become a private soldier again'. Her father was unmoved. 'Sir Malcolm, however, had no sympathy with the unsatisfactory mysticism of the famous C.E.Florence. He saw too much advertisement behind all the humility. It looked just like the sort of conceit the knight most loathed, the conceit of self-abasement.' This fictional reaction to a lightly disguised Lawrence reflected the actual feelings of many of his friends and all his critics.

The charitable view, taken by Sir Lewis Namier, the historian, who knew Lawrence intermittently between 1914 and 1930, was that he was the victim of an inner struggle which he never satisfactorily resolved. 'He was retiring', Namier recalled, 'and yet craved to be seen, he was sincerely shy and naively exhibitionist. He had to rise above others and then humble himself and in self-inflicted humiliation demonstrate his superiority.' Lawrence revealed something of his dualism to Meinertzhagen during the 1919 Paris Peace Conference. 'He told me that ever since childhood he had wanted to be a hero, that he was always fighting between rushing into the limelight and hiding in utter darkness but the limelight had always won.'[1]

Lowell Thomas was yet to appear and in the spring of 1919 Lawrence was enjoying striking poses in his Arab costume. It seemed very bad form, coming so soon after his contretemps with the King, about which he boasted, saying that he had torn off his decorations. His flourishes upset professional diplomats; they made Harold Nicolson uneasy and angered Henry Channon, who thought Lawrence displayed all the hallmarks of a 'bounder'. Cleverness, eccentricity and flamboyance were naturally distasteful to those with much to be modest about. Sir Robert Vansittart, Lawrence's cousin on his father's side and a man of some literary pretensions, took it more calmly with the remark that he was 'A show-off with something to show.'[2]

The devoted Storrs accepted Lawrence's mannerisms, although noting that 'No one could have been more remote from the standard of the public school', which at that time fiercely deprecated displays of individuality, considered harmful to the ideal of team spirit. Storrs also suspected that in Lawrence there was an internal conflict between the hermit and the exhibitionist, in which the latter invariably came out on top. 'He himself never despised, sometimes even encouraged, his legendary saga, particularly for eccentric inconsistency; reserving, however, the right (which the great and particularly the creative artist can rarely afford) of occasional self-belittlement.'[3]

At the heart of these contradictions lay Lawrence's reaction to what he had become in the eyes of the world. Towards Lowell Thomas, his attitude was ambivalent: the American was a 'born vulgarian', 'a mountebank' and an 'intensely crude and pushful fellow'. 'I could kick his card-house down if I got annoyed,' he assured General Murray, who was probably annoyed that all credit for the Middle Eastern war was being shared between Allenby and Lawrence. Still, Lawrence reminded him, Lowell Thomas was 'a very decent fellow – but an American journalist scooping'. Lawrence had been a discreet onlooker at Lowell Thomas's show on several occasions and had seen Chase's film accompanied by Young. Young took exception to one sequence in which footage of British officers was preceded by a caption which stated that only Lawrence was allowed beyond Aqaba for service at the front. This was a lie, and Lawrence assured Young that he would see if it could be changed. Later, when Young again saw the film nothing had been altered, although in fairness it may well have been beyond Lawrence's powers to have the print adjusted.[4]

During the winter of 1919/20, Lawrence needed publicity. France had secured the Syrian mandate and in June 1920 her army drove Faisal and his adherents out of Damascus into exile. Lawrence, while continuing to produce newspaper and magazine articles which highlighted the part played by the Arabs during the war, was now whipping up support for Faisal's adoption as King of Iraq. In broadcasting his views, Lawrence did not disdain such popular newspapers as the *Daily Express*. Without the Lowell Thomas ballyhoo, it is hard to be sure whether what Lawrence had to say would have carried the same weight or been so readily acceptable to editors.

Yet, as he discovered to his irritation, the attention of the press was not like water from a tap, it could not just be turned off. Nor could figures who had aroused public interest be quietly forgotten and allowed to disappear. It was in the nature of human affairs that, when a man known as the 'Uncrowned King of Arabia' chose to become an aircraftman, there would be much public curiosity. The legend dogged Lawrence and brought frequent inconvenience. 'My past has intervened and spoilt my present,' Lawrence complained to Lloyd in January 1929 after his precipitate removal from Miramshah.[5] It continued to do so, provoking in him different reactions. 'I am a local curio,' he told Namier not long after he had settled in Plymouth, where fellow airmen pointed out 'Colonel Lawrence's hut' to visiting friends.[6] This was bearable, but he found snooping newspapermen around Cloud's Hill intolerable and he landed one a haymaker which knocked him over. These intrusions become particularly irksome in 1935 and forced Lawrence to beg Churchill to intervene with his friends among the press barons.

Lawrence was plagued by journalists, who gave him public exposure when he no longer wanted it. It could be equally troublesome when he moved in unfamiliar circles and what he called his 'false reputation' made him feel like an uncaged zoo animal. Meeting George Lloyd's son on his way back from India, Lawrence found the boy embarrassed and asked whether his father had 'been stuffing the poor child with Lowell Thomas stories'. Everything had changed, for now, Lawrence insisted, 'The contrast between my person and my reputation is grotesque.'[7] There was an irony in all this since it was his reputation, with or without ornamentation, which provided him with his entrée into the society of accomplished men and women. It was just because he was Lawrence of Arabia that Lady Astor singled him out from other airmen, hailed him in Plymouth and later added his name to her Cliveden guest list.

Lawrence could not escape what the war had made him, even when he wanted to. Nevertheless, his renunciations of his past were frequent and clamorous. On the publication of Lowell Thomas's book in 1924, Lawrence told Mrs Bernard Shaw, 'It rankles in my mind to be called proud names for qualities which I'd hate to possess ... or for acts of which I'm heartily ashamed.' 'The Arab thing is finished,' he remarked after publication of Robert Graves's biography, which he considered over-dramatic and 'not to be taken seriously', even though he had collaborated in its production. 'Reading it', he told Mrs Bernard Shaw, 'is like the memory of last night's sardine which sometimes comes to a man, unasked, just before breakfast when the day is clean.'

Changing his name by deed poll to Shaw in 1927 was for Lawrence an outward symbol of his wish for a new identity, although no one was fooled by it. The entry in *Who's Who* for T.E.Lawrence reappeared under T.E.Shaw, with a recital of his military and diplomatic services and publications, but without details of his career after 1922. A different surname and allusions to the fact that 'Lawrence' was dead but 'Shaw' lived and was happy could not sever Lawrence from his past nor erase the memory of his deeds from the public mind. The obscure Blair could become the famous Orwell, but the famous Lawrence could not become the obscure Shaw. Once the Afghan imbroglio was over and Lawrence found work to his liking at Plymouth, he came to terms with the inevitable. He learned to coexist with his legend, even to the point of authorising Liddell Hart to start work on a fresh biography in 1934. Its publication would revive public interest, but at least Lawrence felt assured that his life and exploits were in the hands of a man he liked and respected, who enjoyed a high reputation as a serious and disinterested military historian.

There were reasons, apart from convenience, which drove the legendary Lawrence to conceal himself. During his several admissions of personal guilt and self-loathing made to Meinertzhagen in Paris during July 1919, he had confessed that his fame was falsely based and that he was scared of being exposed as a fraud. 'He hates himself and is having a great struggle with his conscience,' Meinertzhagen wrote in his diary. 'His self-deception filled him with bitterness. Shall he run away and hide, confess his sins and become completely discredited – or carry the myth into the limelight in the hopes of not being exposed?'[8]

This outburst seems strange since, at the time, the 'myth' (was this Lawrence's word?) was as yet unformed. The public was still largely unaware of what Lawrence had done during the war, and there is nothing to suggest that he knew that, within a few weeks, Lowell Thomas would parade him and his deeds before the theatre-goers of London. He was, however, engaged in the preparation of the first draft of the *Seven Pillars*, which he discussed with Meinertzhagen on several occasions. It was taking shape as a work of propaganda and polemic and, as such, reflected Lawrence's rage at the way in which the Arabs were being treated at the Peace Conference. What he may have realised was that some of the claims he was making for himself and the Arabs would invite challenge and, with it, his exposure as a charlatan.

Hubert Young found Lawrence's attitude to historical truth capricious. At some date in the early 1920s he and Lawrence looked over a passage in the draft *Seven Pillars* in which Young, under a pseudonym, was unfairly treated. Young demanded either an alteration in line with the truth or else his appearance under his own name. Lawrence refused. Young riposted, 'But the correct account may appear some day.' 'Oh no, it won't,' answered Lawrence. 'But it will,' insisted Young, 'because I'm writing it, and it may perhaps be said that you put me in under a false name in these pages because you knew you were telling lies about me.' Lawrence shifted his ground, explaining that that was why Young appeared under an invented name.[9]

In spite of such juggling with truth Lawrence found himself more or less immune from criticism as a chronicler of historical events. Shortly after Liddell Hart's biography appeared, he remarked, 'He makes it all fit in: afterwards; it didn't happen like that: but who will believe it now?' He did not consider it worthwhile to refute the more outrageous tales about himself. 'Where it was merely one of those idle stories which every man collects about him as a ship collects barnacles – well, then I haven't often bothered,' he told Robert Graves. The analogy was ill-chosen; an encrustation of barnacles makes a ship less seaworthy, whereas the fables which attached to Lawrence increased his public stature, if not his self-esteem.

There was of course no reason why Lawrence should have blamed himself for stories invented by others, but where did the moral responsibility rest for the fictions of his own making? In the *Seven Pillars* he described in some detail the destruction of a bridge north of Nasib station on the night of 17/18 September, adding that it was 'my seventy-ninth'. It was also described as 'my seventy-ninth bridge' in his official report, prepared for and published in the Arab Bureau's bulletin. It was not. An analysis from all available sources gives Lawrence's total of bridge demolitions as twenty-three, an honourable score. Battle fatigue may excuse the original slip, but not its translation from an official file to Lawrence's narrative. Quite simply, he lied twice, and he allowed Graves and Liddell Hart to repeat the falsehood.[10]

This small, but significant, detail is doubly revealing. It shows that Lawrence could fake Arab Bureau records and explains why those biographers who consulted them came away thinking that the *Seven Pillars* was an accurate military history of the Arab campaign. On a larger scale, Lawrence misrepresented what occurred when Damascus fell, but here he was constructing propaganda devised to substantiate Arab political pretensions. Tripling the number of bridges he blew up is altogether a different matter. Here he was indulging in self-glorification and myth-making.

The swollen figure of seventy-nine serves only to exaggerate Lawrence's prowess to a point of distortion. It was a pointless exercise in fraud, since his courage and energy in the field were beyond doubt and required no gloss. This mendacity can partly be explained in literary terms: throughout the *Seven Pillars* there are passages which reflect Lawrence's earlier addiction to chivalric romance, in particular the medieval author's love of overstatement as a device to secure dramatic effect. Figures were particularly vulnerable to this treatment, with digits added or subtracted from the tallies of casualties or prisoners to emphasise either the ferocity of a battle or the totality of a victory. This was also Lawrence's way. Writing about Allenby's final victory in 1918, he assures his readers that, because of Arab assistance, it was won 'with less than four hundred killed'. Yet the sum of deaths among Allied forces during September and October was over 1,400 and for the entire Palestine and Syrian campaigns, 16,000.

For Lawrence, the *Seven Pillars* was a work of high art and not a historical record. Yet, together with *Revolt in the Desert* and the biographies of Robert Graves and Liddell Hart, it was accepted by the public as an accurate account of recent historical events. Lawrence knew this and, while he dismissed Lowell Thomas's flights of fancy, he was acutely aware that he himself had embroidered and twisted the truth. He had done so because he was vain: as he admitted towards the end of the *Seven Pillars*, he had a 'craving for good repute among men'. This was at times so powerful that it drove him to add artificial lustre to his reputation, as Vansittart suspected. 'Lawrence', he remembered, 'was always having his biography written, and filled it with flourishes better forgotten for sake of the rest.'[11]

Lawrence was too intelligent not to appreciate that limelight not only illuminated, it probed. Fear of what it might expose made him wary about remaining too long in its glare. Furthermore, the knowledge of his own complicity in adding false touches to his legend may have contributed to his spasms of grotesque self-abasement which occurred during the 1920s. In September 1925, when the Lowell Thomas biography was on sale, he wrote to Mrs Bernard Shaw:

> I've changed, and the Lawrence who used to go about, and be friendly and familiar with that sort of person, is dead. He's worse than dead. He is a stranger I once knew. From henceforward my way will be with these fellows here, degrading myself (for in their eyes, and your eyes, and Winterton's eyes I see that it is degradation) in the hope that some day I will really feel degraded, be degraded, to their level. I long for people to look down upon me and despise me, and I'm too shy to take the filthy steps which would publicly shame me, and put me into their contempt. I want to dirty myself outwardly, so that my person may properly reflect the dirtiness which it conceals.

Another extraordinary outburst in this vein coincided with the appearance of Graves's biography and his own *Revolt in the Desert*. Again Mrs Bernard Shaw was the recipient: 'I am now an airman, a common airman, dirty in person, living in a barrack, eating badly, off dirty tables, the roughest of mishandled food.... everything about me is cheap, and most things are nasty.'

A deep guilt lurks behind these outpourings. They are not simply a reaction against that vanity which made Lawrence seek and luxuriate in the limelight or enjoy public esteem. He could, as he made clear in his first letter, take 'steps' which would reverse the public's feelings towards him, changing admiration to 'contempt'. What he must have had in mind was that, if he revealed that he had tampered with the truth, even in comparatively trivial matters, to enhance his reputation, he would be transformed from a hero to a charlatan. Yet he could never bring himself to undermine his own reputation, for to have denied one part of the legend would surely have shaken the whole. Worse, he would have betrayed his own friends who had believed implicitly all he had said and written.

No one ever questioned Lawrence's basic integrity and those who knew him interpreted his equivocation towards public notoriety in terms of an inner struggle between polarities in his nature. Shyness, occasional social awkwardness, a dread of failure and, perhaps strongest of all, a residual Puritan conscience were thought to be the reasons why Lawrence shrank from public acclaim. His self-effacement appeared neither natural nor sincere. This had been the judgement both of D.H.Lawrence, who observed his namesake from a distance, and of Young, who knew him well. 'His attitude to publicity', Young remarked, 'was that of Brer Rabbit to the briar-patch. "Don't throw me in that briar-patch, Brer Fox," he would protest, and all the time the briar-patch was where he longed to be.' Young added that when public attention 'became embarrassing and even shameful to him' he genuinely wished to shun it.[12]

Lawrence could never escape what he had become through his own and other people's efforts. The best he could manage was publicly to admit he had cut himself off from his past and sought only obscurity and tranquillity. This plea did not convince many, who sensed that he still adored being the centre of attraction, and it was ignored by journalists for whom any story, real or imaginary, about the 'Uncrowned King of Arabia' was good copy. His eremetical existence added to the curiosity, as it did with Greta Garbo, the film star recluse, with whom Lawrence sympathised – 'The poor soul. I feel for her.'

There were compensations which Lawrence was less than willing to acknowledge. It was because he was Lawrence of Arabia, war-hero, that All Souls College, Oxford granted him a fellowship. In the same guise he first penetrated the society of men of letters like Bernard Shaw and Thomas Hardy. The label was also a passport for social and political circles into which he might otherwise not have been invited. People he mixed with there soon discovered a remarkably intelligent, complex, charming but sometimes insufferable fellow determined to live life on his own terms.

Six

MAKING THE BEST OF IT

November 1918–May 1935

I

DIPLOMAT, 1918–1919

FOR many of his contemporaries, the last part of Lawrence's life seemed an untidy anticlimax to the glorious two years of adventure in the desert. Robert Graves, who knew him intimately from 1919, considered that his friend was 'an intuitive, affectionate Galahad-like man of action who came a frightful crash before his war was over, and is to be judged hereafter a broken hero who tried to appear whole and make the best of it'. Vansittart, who observed Lawrence closely but from a distance, detected in him an ageless schoolboy who 'did not grow up but grew older', having lost his 'vital spark'.[1] Something more might have been expected after the promise of the early years, but it never materialised. Lawrence may have felt this and blamed it on the fact that he was part-Irish. 'Irishmen are disappointing men,' he told his friend, the writer Edward Garnett. 'They go so far, magnificent, and cease to grow. They bring forth promise and less fruition than the rest of the English world massed against them.'

Yet Lawrence had retained his physical strength. Although he had 'over-exerted himself' during the war, he proudly informed John Buchan that the 'wreckage of his body' had been judged fit for the rigours of service life by three doctors. Furthermore, his fragmented career as an author, translator, civil servant and aircraft mechanic confirmed that he possessed his former powers of concentration and quickness of mind.

Lawrence's post-war collection of occupations was unplanned. Until at least October 1917 he had seen his future in terms of picking up old threads, such as his much postponed scheme to found a printing press. Looking beyond the war, he revealed to George Lloyd that 'there was so much for him to do in the world, places to dig, peoples to help', and discussed the possibility of a joint camel trek across Arabia. By now Lawrence's foremost ambition was to write a book about his experiences. Lloyd heard something of this and thought his friend perfectly fitted to the task. 'Generally,' he wrote to Storrs, 'the kind of man capable of these adventures lacks the pen and wit to record them adequately. Luckily Lawrence is gifted with both.'[2] Lawrence started work on the *Seven Pillars* in Paris during the spring of 1919.

Unfinished business made it impossible for Lawrence to give all his attention to writing. His war had ended unsatisfactorily. Faisal's position in Damascus was precarious, he depended upon British money and the kingdom Lawrence had promised him was occupied by an Allied army including a growing French contingent which, by the end of 1918, controlled the Lebanon. Worst of all, events had shown Lawrence that the British government was still inclined to implement the Sykes–Picot agreement and install the French in Syria, establish direct rule over Palestine and annex Iraq, leaving the Arabs with Hejaz.

All this was wormwood to Lawrence and, for the next four years, he hurled himself into the world of international diplomacy solely to help the Arabs achieve what he passionately believed was their rightful reward. It was more than a matter of natural justice: he felt personally affronted by the government's apparent abandonment of the Arabs, whom he had led to expect more for their efforts. The promises which he had made to Faisal and others, perhaps rashly and certainly illicitly, were now exposed as worthless. They never had any substance, as the Arabs probably realised, for no mention of them was ever made to members of the Crane–King Commission in Syria during the summer of 1919, nor by Faisal when he confronted Lloyd George soon after in London. What mattered for Lawrence in what he called his 'dog-fight' in the corridors of power was that he vindicate his own integrity as well as secure Arab political rights.

The intensity and one-sidedness of Lawrence's feelings made it impossible for him to think or act dispassionately. Vansittart, with whom he crossed swords several times during the Paris Peace Conference, recalled him as 'too big for a cherub, too small for an angel, too angry for either'. Lawrence was never a natural civil servant, as Storrs recognised. 'He was an individual force of driving intelligence, yet nothing of an administrator; having as much of the team spirit as Alexander the Great or Lloyd George'. As ever, routine bored him and throughout the Paris conference he did as he pleased, much to the irritation of more punctilious officials. 'Lawrence', Lord Hardinge complained, 'used to come and go irrespective of any authority.'[3]

Curzon (who acted as Foreign Secretary while Arthur Balfour was in Paris) was exasperated by Lawrence's uncritical, pro-Arab partisanship and at least once he was reduced to tears by his abrasiveness. Although Lawrence later thought this was something to crow about, it had been a petty triumph, since the Marquess often wept publicly. In this case he had good reason, because Lawrence's intemperate language constantly threatened to drive a wedge between Britain and France at a time when co-operation between the two powers was vital for a European peace settlement. Lawrence never understood this. 'He has no belief in an Anglo-French understanding in the East,' wrote the diplomat George Kidston after hearing Lawrence's views on the subject. 'He regards France as our natural enemy in those parts and acts accordingly.' Lawrence had not shed the francophobia he had first picked up in Cairo in 1914 and, characteristically, he never missed a chance to vent his prejudice. His exchanges with the French and those Foreign Office officials whose job it was to reach an accord with France were stormy, as Vansittart remembered. 'Lawrence regarded perfidy to our Allies [the French] due to his protégés [the Arabs] and looked askance at those concerned in the dirty work of keeping our word.'[4]

Curzon feared that Lawrence encouraged Faisal's stubbornness and made him unreceptive to French offers over Syria. In July 1919, when Faisal was expected to return to Paris, Curzon insisted that he be kept apart from Lawrence since 'further co-operation between these two will cause serious embarrassment with the French.' Officials who had watched Lawrence at work were more forthright. Archibald Kerr of the Foreign Office's Eastern Department had 'grave misgivings' about his participation in future negotiations with Faisal. 'We and the War Office feel strongly that he is to a large extent responsible for our troubles with the French over Syria,' he told Vansittart. He concluded that if Lawrence again 'bear lead him [Faisal] there is sure to be a recrudescence of our troubles with the French over Syria'. Sir Arthur Hirtzel of the India Office agreed and hoped that Lawrence would never be re-employed by any department. Vansittart was willing to concede that Lawrence could be useful. 'If there is a settlement,' he told Curzon, 'the only way of reaching it – without bloodshed – is through Faisal and Lawrence alone could bring him to his senses.' This was also Kidston's view. If Lawrence was 'properly handled' he could make Faisal tractable.[5]

The root of the trouble was Lawrence's divided loyalty. From Faisal's arrival in London at the end of November 1918 until his departure from Paris the following April, Lawrence was his confidential counsellor, bursar (managing his cash grant from the Foreign Office) and translator. Lawrence was also a servant of the British government from January 1919, holding the position of a technical adviser to the British delegation in Paris. As in the desert, he faced a clash of loyalties, although now his position was more exposed since, as the conference progressed, it was clear to everyone that he was out of step with his government's Middle Eastern policies.

There was another parallel between Lawrence's military and diplomatic careers. In both he took part in a sideshow, since Arab affairs were peripheral to the Paris negotiations. The conference sessions, which ended with the signing of the Versailles Treaty on 28 June 1919, were primarily concerned with European matters. The admission of the small Hejaz delegation to the conference was no more than a formal acknowledgement that it was a belligerent power. Like Portugal and Brazil, its status was marginal. The power to make decisions rested with the 'Big Four': Presidents Clemenceau of France and Wilson of the United States and Prime Ministers Lloyd George of Britain and Orlando of Italy.

The Arab case for self-determination was laid before the full conference on 6 February by Lawrence, acting as Faisal's interpreter and commanding attention in his Arab headdress. He spoke first in English and then, at the unexpected request of the French and Italians, delivered an impromptu version in French. According to the correspondent of *Petit Parisien*, he spoke 'with much patriotism', presumably Arab.

The arguments advanced by Lawrence then and later during the intensive lobbying of influential delegates were as much his own as Faisal's. Their outline had been contained in a memorandum written by Lawrence and presented to the Cabinet's Eastern Committee on 4 November 1918. After a preamble in which he lauded the wartime steadfastness of the Hashemite princes (conveniently forgetting how close Faisal had come to an accord with Turkey a few months earlier), Lawrence proposed him as King of Syria with total freedom in his choice of foreign advisers. On the thorny subject of Palestine, Lawrence indicated that the Arabs would allow Jewish immigration, but correctly prophesied that they would resist attempts to create a Zionist state. Two weeks later he devised a new and radical scheme for the partition of the Arab world into three Hashemite kingdoms under British guidance: Faisal would rule Syria, Abdullah Lower Iraq and Zaid Upper Iraq.

Lawrence had every reason to feel confident that these plans would be treated seriously by the government. When he had visited the Foreign Office on 28 October and discussed Arab matters with Lord Robert Cecil, Assistant Secretary for Foreign Affairs, he had been shown the draft of an Anglo-French proclamation which embodied a completely new approach to the Arabs. The key statement was the admission that Britain and France sought 'the complete and definitive liberation of the peoples so long oppressed by the Turks and the establishment of national Governments and Administrations drawing their authority from the initiative and free choice of indigenous populations'. Britain and France would stand godparent to these new governments and lend them every practical assistance they needed to follow humane and modernising policies. It seemed to Lawrence that at last the Allies had abandoned the Sykes–Picot agreement.[6]

What Lawrence failed to understand was that a formidable body of French public and official opinion wanted the Lebanese and Syrian provisions of the Sykes–Picot agreement to be honoured. It was an emotional issue: the deaths and mutilation of over 2 million Frenchmen demanded compensation in excess of Alsace and Lorraine. Catholics sought to extend their already extensive missionary and teaching activities in Syria and the Lebanon and right-wing nationalists and the colonial lobby trumpeted France's historic rights in the region. When General Henri Gouraud,

France's Commander-in-Chief and Civil Commissioner in Syria, took up his duties in January 1920 he spoke proudly of 'the memories and interests which unite France and Syria' and recalled the 'knightly prowess' of the French crusaders who had once conquered in the region. The allusion was popular among right-wing Catholics, although Faisal often asked who had won the Crusades.

Faisal may have scored a debating point, but both he and Lawrence had no strong cards to play against the French. Throughout the conference, Clemenceau and his Foreign Minister, Aristide Briand, were willing to have private discussions with Faisal in the hope that an accommodation could be reached. Their aim was to persuade him to concede French paramountcy in a zone which encompassed Damascus according to the terms set down in the Sykes–Picot agreement. The scope for manoeuvre was severely limited, since the French government wanted to control Syria as tightly as it did Morocco and Tunisia. Furthermore, there was a fear that any bargain struck with Faisal, however advantageous to France, would stir up restlessness in these protectorates.

Discussions about Syria's future were further complicated by French fears that Britain was giving covert encouragement to Faisal. His choice as the head of the Hejazi delegation had been influenced by the Foreign Office, with Lawrence's support. The French immediately and rightly concluded that Faisal would use the conference to publicise his claims to Syria. Unable to keep him away, French officials made a fuss about the validity of Hejaz's claim to seats at the conference. Lawrence, after badgering Balfour, was able to arrange seats for the Arabs. The French press concluded that Faisal was Britain's stooge: on 7 February *Gaulois* described him as a 'zealous adherent of the British empire' and, shortly after, *Petit Parisien* suggested that he was a party to a British conspiracy by which France would be swindled out of Syria as she had been out of India in the eighteenth century. As Lawrence had predicted four years before in Cairo, old imperial jealousies were breaking surface and throughout the conference he did what he could to exacerbate them, believing such behaviour would assist Faisal.

Faisal had already sensed undercurrents of French hostility during his journey from Marseilles to Boulogne in November. Once installed in the Hejazi delegation's lodgings at 72 Avenue du Bois de Boulogne, Faisal faced more officially instigated slights and unpleasantness. On 20 January he complained to Lawrence that the French had deciphered, censored and delayed his telegrams to Mecca. Lawrence sympathised and asked whether in future they could be transmitted by the Foreign Office, but was told that such an arrangement would deepen French suspicions about Anglo-Arab collusion. Incidentally, as Lawrence knew well, British intelligence had regularly intercepted and deciphered all secret Arab telegrams for the past twelve months.[7] The French were also spreading disinformation about affairs in Hejaz, issuing a communiqué on 28 January with details of a signal defeat of Hussain's army by Ibn Saud's Wahabbis at Taif. This news alarmed Faisal, who immediately considered returning to Hejaz to assist his father, which was just what the French wanted.[8]

These and other affronts were reminders that France would not willingly relinquish overlordship of Syria nor accept Faisal as the independent sovereign. Lawrence believed that this intransigence might collapse under Anglo-American pressure and so he encouraged Faisal to cultivate the goodwill of both powers. This would be more easily forthcoming if Faisal first came to a cordial accommodation with the Zionists, whom Lawrence knew were a powerful lobby in America. Lawrence was too conscious of the possibility of future clashes of Arab and Jewish political and economic interests in Palestine to be a wholehearted Zionist. (When they worked together in the Colonial Office in 1921, Meinertzhagen detected Lawrence's hostility towards Jewish immigration in Palestine.) Nevertheless, in 1919, he was enough of a realist to appreciate that the Balfour Declaration was irrevocable and that continued Arab–Jewish bickering would damage Faisal's cause.

So, with strong Foreign Office backing, Lawrence arranged a series of London meetings between Faisal and Weizmann which concluded with a joint declaration on 3 January. Faisal accepted Palestine's permanent separation from Syria and the principle of Jewish immigration, and both parties pledged themselves to future co-operation. The signed statement was in Lawrence's handwriting.[9] This accord opened the way for approaches to American Zionists, one of whom, Stephen Wise, arranged through Lawrence a meeting between Faisal and President Wilson on 21 January. No notes survive of their conversation.

American sympathy for the Arabs was useful, but what really counted were the views of the British and French governments, which were preoccupied with European affairs. In spite of the Anglo-French declaration of 8 November, which seemingly guaranteed popular self-determination in the Middle East, Lloyd George was primarily concerned with keeping on good terms with France and achieving traditional imperial goals in the Middle East. When he and Clemenceau met in London at the beginning of December 1918, the French President had conceded British control over the oil-rich Mosul district of northern Iraq and offered no objections to continued British rule over Palestine. In making this private agreement both statesmen behaved as if the Sykes–Picot agreement still held, since Mosul had previously been allocated to France.

Once in Paris, Lawrence quickly discovered that the French government believed that the Sykes–Picot agreement was the only basis for a Middle

Eastern settlement. France was strong, one official warned Faisal soon after his arrival and advised him to ignore the clamour of Arab nationalists in Damascus. Briand took a more compromising line when he, Faisal and Lawrence discussed Syria's future on 25 February.[10] Briand opened with an apology for the antipathy shown towards Faisal by sections of the French press and proceeded to prepare the way for a Franco-Arab understanding. 'Our Foreign Office has made a hopeless muddle of its eastern policy,' he candidly admitted, but past errors would be corrected. Faisal, probably at Lawrence's bidding, probed for the means to set the French against the British. 'You are always harping on my anglophile attitude,' he challenged. 'Please understand that there is an Arab–English entente as a result of their help towards us during the war *and peace* [my italics]. This entente is too strong for you to break; but it would be possible to make it triple.' 'That is our dearest wish,' Briand replied. Faisal was not placated and questioned the honesty of French policy. Compromise, Briand insisted, would have to be reached eventually to save France's face.

Lawrence translated during this exchange and passed on his notes to the Foreign Office. Quite clearly Faisal imagined himself the ally of Britain who might expect special consideration from the British government. Lawrence had gone further in his memorandum of 4 November and emphasised a moral obligation owed by Britain to the Arabs. 'I hope', he argued, 'that in dividing the common spoils we will not descend to commercial arguments of the exact participating contingents of British, French, Indian, Arab or Armenian troops.' In other words, Faisal's claim to Syria might seem an excessive return on his wartime investment of men and effort. If Faisal, encouraged by Lawrence, had any illusions on this score they were swept away by the magisterial remarks of Curzon in a letter of 9 October 1919. The Foreign Secretary reminded Faisal that 'His Majesty's Government cannot forget that infinitely the larger share of the burden of the defeat of Turkey was carried by the British Empire.' Furthermore, he added, France had lost heavily in the struggle to defeat Germany, 'which was the power behind Turkey'.[11] Faisal had clearly learned nothing from what had been told him during his brief tour of the Western Front battlefields. Neither, it seemed, had Lawrence.

The British government was not prepared to ditch France in order to show favour to Faisal, even though he and Lawrence believed otherwise. Nevertheless, the Syrian question was a distraction which could easily create a rift between Britain and France and so undermine their efforts to solve Europe's problems. Yet Britain could not afford to wash its hands of Faisal and so provoke widespread unrest in Syria, which was still under British military administration. The answer was a form of compromise, devised on one level to satisfy Faisal and on another to postpone the resolution of Syria's difficulties. On 25 March, Britain, France and the United States agreed to send a commission to Syria which would investigate local opinion, especially on the crucial question of which power would be most welcome as the region's protector.

Faisal regarded this decision as a triumph and he celebrated it by breaking a lifetime of orthodox Muslim abstinence and drinking champagne. Confident that he would be wholeheartedly supported by local opinion, he felt certain that the commission would recommend that either Britain or the United States should be awarded the mandate (the current word used instead of the colonialist-sounding 'protectorate') and that he would be installed as Syria's ruler. A few days later he told Colonel House, President Wilson's adviser, that his recent experiences had taught him that the only powers trustworthy enough to be given the mandate were Britain and the United States.

Aware that the Crane–King commission might return with unfavourable findings, the French increased their efforts to reach a private agreement with Faisal. He, sure that all the Syrians would spurn France as a mandatory power, was uncompromising. On 13 April, two days before Faisal returned to Damascus, he had talks with Clemenceau in which the French President offered Syria independence 'in a form of a federation of local communities corresponding to the traditions and wishes of their populations', which would satisfy the Christian, Jewish and Druze minorities who feared Arab domination. Clemenceau also promised 'material and moral assistance in the emancipation of Syria'.

Lawrence was party to these negotiations and he urged Faisal to accept the French conditions. Lawrence instinctively disliked compromise, but he was by now aware that his government would never jeopardise its good relations with France in order to satisfy Faisal. This had been made plain by Lloyd George, who urged Faisal to accept Clemenceau's terms, which were the best he could ever hope for. Lawrence also pleaded moderation, persuading Faisal to surrender control of his foreign policy to France. 'On the advice of Lawrence', Faisal orally promised Clemenceau that once in Syria he would do his utmost to persuade her people to accept a French mandate ruler in return for recognition as king. This was what Faisal told Clayton six weeks later in Damascus, adding that he never intended to keep his word. Someone's memory was flawed since Lawrence told the Foreign Office that, despite what was being claimed by Clemenceau and the French press, Faisal had refused everything offered him including the Syrian throne.[12]

From this tangle of misunderstanding and contradiction everyone concerned went away believing whatever suited them. At the centre of the confusion was Lawrence. He mischievously encouraged Faisal to reject whatever the French suggested; he also filled Faisal's head with rash ideas of armed resistance. In a conversation with Allenby, Faisal recalled that Lawrence had passed on to him the advice of General Sir Henry Wilson, the Chief of the Imperial General Staff, which had been: 'if you want independence recruit soldiers and be strong.' Allenby was appalled and commented that no British general would have made such a foolish remark. In private Wilson hoped that the French would forgo their claims to Syria and so avert a Franco-Arab war, which would destabilise the whole Middle East.[13] Yet, if Faisal is to be believed, Lawrence also urged him to make a bargain with the French.

All of the muddle and most of the recrimination generated by the Syrian question during the Peace Conference were the direct result of misunderstandings about what exactly had been said during negotiations. Everything hung on the translation and here Lawrence's role was crucial. There were misgivings among Foreign Office officials about the tone and precision of his renderings from and into Arabic after Faisal had claimed that Allied recognition of Arab belligerent rights in October 1918 had distinguished between his own 'Syrian' army and his father's, based in Hejaz. Young was asked to recollect what exactly had been said in Damascus and he replied that he was 'under the impression that Lawrence's translation (*on that occasion*) [my italics] could not have been interpreted to imply separate recognition'.[14] The French too had doubts about the accuracy of Lawrence's translations and during the session on 6 February had their own Arabist listening and ready to pick up any chicanery. None was found and later another Arabist told Meinertzhagen that Lawrence had given a faithful version of Faisal's words.

Harry St John Philby considered Lawrence's Arabic 'rather poor stuff' because of his accent, but otherwise he was fluent enough. Storrs's servant-cum-spy, Ruhi, who coached Lawrence in 1917, was struck by his mispronunciation of many words. Lawrence claimed that by the end of the war his vocabulary stood at 12,000 words but admitted that his grammar and syntax were shaky. Listening to Lawrence's Arabic was 'a perpetual adventure' for Faisal: whether it was adequate for the sophistries and nuances of diplomatic exchanges is another matter. The confused outcome of the vital talks between Faisal and Clemenceau in April indicate that all involved, including Lawrence, departed with widely differing impressions of what had passed.

Faisal remained convinced that France was his enemy; he confided to Lawrence that he drew up his will just before embarking on a French cruiser at Marseilles on 14 April. It had been intended that Lawrence accompany him back to Beirut, but the Foreign Office decided that it would be wiser and probably safer for him to remain in Paris. However, Lawrence may have briefed Faisal on how to handle Crane and King, the two Americans in charge of the Syrian commission. This alone explains why Faisal told them of his enlightened intention to establish an American college for women in Mecca. This and much more left the Americans with the wholesome impression that the Arab Prince was 'a confirmed believer in the Anglo-Saxon race'.

Not only did Faisal reveal himself to be a modern and liberal thinker, he orchestrated popular demonstrations and petitions and stage-managed the Syrian National Assembly (elected on the 1908 Turkish franchise) to give the impression that all Syrians wanted him as their king and either Britain or the United States as the mandatory power. This was in fact the conclusion reached by the commissioners at the end of August, although their findings no longer had any relevance. External events had overtaken Faisal and Syria, and the United States was on the verge of withdrawing from international affairs into isolation.

January to April 1919 had been months of intense activity and strain for Lawrence in an unfamiliar world. They were marked by a personal tragedy when his father died suddenly on 7 April. Thomas Lawrence had suffered from bronchial disorders for several years and finally fell victim to the Spanish 'flu epidemic which was sweeping Western Europe. Since the death of his cousin in 1914 he had been, in secret, Sir Thomas Chapman Bt, the last of his line. His son had been alerted to his illness by a telegram from Robert Lawrence and had flown to England, but he arrived too late.

Lawrence stoically withheld the news of his father's death from Meinertzhagen, with whom he was sharing lodgings at the Continental Hotel. The robust warrior–ornithologist had become Lawrence's companion and father confessor during the conference and in his diary kept a record of their intimate conversations. During April, Lawrence confided that he was tormented by fears that what he was writing would be exposed as mendacious and he admitted to feeling shame about his illegitimacy. These extemporaneous confessions have been challenged by several biographers who suspected that Meinertzhagen may have later adjusted entries in his diaries to highlight either his importance or his percipience. Nevertheless the weight of evidence indicates that, while he could be careless with dates, the substance of his anecdotes is beyond question.

Why Lawrence chose this time to make these revelations and to this man, with whom previously he had only a passing acquaintance, is hard to explain. It is also difficult to understand why he chose to lay bare his sense of guilt about his birth and the supposed falsehoods he had written in a book which was not destined for general circulation. He had other, more immediate worries: his father's death; his ambiguous and far from honourable role as the servant both of his country and of a foreign prince; the knowledge that Faisal's cause was making little headway and the likelihood that his Arab brothers-in-arms were about to be denied their rewards. Lawrence was facing possible failure and this may have triggered penitential confessions about his wider unworthiness. Yet his disclosure of his shortcomings fell short of an admission that he had failed the Arabs; instead, he transferred his sense of guilt to other areas.

He also found time for schoolboy pranks. Looking down the stairwell of the Astoria Hotel, he and Meinertzhagen noticed Lloyd George, Balfour and Hardinge huddled in conversation. Lawrence fetched two packets of Bronco lavatory paper and showered the sheets on to the great men. Then he and Meinertzhagen scurried back to their offices. Later Meinertzhagen overheard Hardinge comment, with a pomposity which must have delighted Lawrence, 'There is nothing funny about toilet paper.' Maybe this jape was another of Lawrence's ways of reminding the world that he was still his own man who, while he moved familiarly among the great and powerful, did not belong to them. On other occasions he disregarded patrician forms of conduct. Vansittart considered him a banner-bearer for a novel and regrettable trend in manners after overhearing a dinner-party exchange. 'I'm afraid my conversation doesn't interest you much,' a lady remarked to Lawrence. 'It doesn't interest at all' was his answer. In spite of such tartness (a feature of his conversation noticed by Isherwood), Lawrence was greatly in demand for social occasions during the conference. There was a strong hint of the exotic about him and the Arab delegation, and rumours of his desert adventures ensured him considerable social attention.

Quite suddenly and inexplicably, on 3 May, he left Paris and hitched a lift to Cairo in a Handley Page o/400 bomber. (This departure may have provoked Hardinge's later remarks about his perverse habit of coming and going as he wished.) The bomber was one of fifty-one which were flown to Egypt between March and October 1919, first to assist in the suppression of an anti-British insurrection and later to overawe the disaffected Egyptians. During the journey, Lawrence told one pilot that he was making the trip to collect his gear from Cairo, but the officer was unconvinced. 'Everything was supposed to be very hush-hush,' he remembered, but 'Knowing Lawrence and talking to him, it was fairly obvious this was not the real reason.'

The real reason was connected with recent events in Hejaz which had concerned Lawrence and the British government since the end of December. The kingdom was coming under increasing pressure from Ibn Saud and his Wahabbi zealots. Members of a Muslim fundamentalist brotherhood whom Lawrence had once likened to Cromwell's Roundheads (the Knights Templar might have been a more apposite comparison), the

Wahabbis were fanatic warriors dedicated to Islamic regeneration. Armed with rifles supplied to Ibn Saud by his patrons in the India Office, the Wahabbis were more than a match for Hejazi troops, a fact they proved at the battle near the Khurma oasis in August 1918.

In the final week of December 1918, Lawrence informed the Foreign Office that he could eliminate the Wahabbis with tanks. The idea was probably Faisal's since he had already asked Lawrence to procure tanks and armoured cars for his father's army. Lawrence obliged and on 3 February had persuaded the War Office to allow forty Hejazi infantrymen to undertake a tank-training course in Egypt.[15] The tanks themselves were withheld on the grounds that they might easily be passed from Hussain to Faisal for use in Syria. Convinced that Hussain's kingdom was imperilled, Lawrence assumed that the British government would intervene if the danger to its client state became too great. In March he casually invited William Yale, then a delegate with the American mission in Paris, to join him in May as an observer with British forces in the Nejd desert, where presumably they would be fighting Ibn Saud. A month later Lawrence suggested to the Foreign Office that Indian Muslim troops could be employed to eject the Wahabbis from Mecca if they managed to take the city.[16]

Together these exchanges indicated that Lawrence believed that a British-backed campaign would be needed to prop up Hussain and remove the threat of the Wahabbis. Still a serving officer, he left for Egypt under the impression that his services would be required at least as an adviser to Hussain. They were: early in May news was received that Abdullah and the Hejazi army had been trounced by the Wahabbis at Tubarah, 100 miles from Mecca. This forced the War Office to capitulate and, on 22 May, GHQ Cairo was instructed to allocate six Mark VI tanks, their spares and a team of instructors for immediate service in Hejaz. A specific order, addressed to Lawrence, warned him to be careful how he deployed the tanks and not to use them too far from their operational base or a railway line.[17] At the same time six aircraft were crated and despatched to Jiddah.

Lawrence briefly touched on the incident in an article in the *Daily Express* of 28 May 1920 in which he censured the War Office for its slowness in making the tanks available to Hussain. Admitting that his advice had been sought over how best to secure peace between Hussain and Ibn Saud, Lawrence was silent about his own participation in the expected war, although it was clear at the time that the War Office intended him to supervise the hurriedly formed Hejazi tank corps. There was, much to Lawrence's pleasure, a droll element in this affair. Ibn Saud was the India Office's man while Hussain danced to a Foreign Office tune and so, for a few weeks, there was the bizarre possibility of a war between two foreign princes sponsored by two British departments of state and entirely paid for by British taxpayers.

Unforeseen circumstances prevented Lawrence from joining in another desert war. After leaving Pisa, his aircraft struck a tree when its pilot, Lieutenant Prince, unwisely attempted to land on Centocelle airfield near Rome as night was falling. He was killed in the crash and his co-pilot was fatally injured. Lawrence, with a broken collar-bone and fractured ribs, gamely helped other wounded crewmen from the wreckage. He was taken to hospital where he was visited by King Victor Emmanuel and the British Ambassador, Sir James Rennell. Rennell's son Francis, a friend and fellow intelligence officer in Egypt, invited Lawrence to convalesce in the Embassy.

After a few days and not yet recovered, Lawrence continued his journey which was dogged by further mischances. Uncertain weather forecasts and a sequence of mechanical hitches forced the bomber flight to follow a serpentine route with stopovers at Taranto, Valona, Albania, Athens and Sollum on the Libyan coast. The delays gave Lawrence the unexpected chance to look over antiquities in Athens and explore the Aegean islands. On Crete he encountered Harry St John Philby, who since 1916 had been the Indian government's representative to Ibn Saud. For three years he had kept Ibn Saud a benevolent neutral and procured him a trickle of modern firearms with which to wage war against the pro-Turkish Ibn Rashid. Philby was as fiercely partisan for Ibn Saud as Lawrence was for the Hashemites. When they met, Philby was on his way by plane to Cairo, the first stage of his mission to Riyadh where he was under orders to dissuade Ibn Saud from further forays into Hejaz. Philby and Lawrence got on well, although each was pugnacious, dogmatic and, for different reasons, at odds with their government's Middle Eastern policies. They travelled together for the final leg of their journey to Heliopolis aerodrome.

When they arrived in Cairo in the middle of June, they found they were no longer needed. Ibn Saud had pulled his forces out of Hejaz as he feared the loss of his £60,000 annuity from Delhi, and had turned his attention towards the conquest of Nejd and, with it, the final overthrow of Ibn Rashid. The crisis over, Lawrence stayed with the Allenbys, where he and Philby enlivened dinner with furious exchanges over the merits of their rival Arab protégés, much to the discomfort of Lady Allenby, who sat between them.

Lawrence lingered in Cairo for several days and sifted through his old reports in Arab Bureau files in search of material for his book. He paused on 28 June to write Stirling, now Deputy Chief Political Officer in Damascus, a report which exposed the treachery of Abdul al Qadir and of his Pan-Islamist brother, Muhammad Said. Intended as evidence for Said's arrest, which would have suited Faisal, the letter included Lawrence's first revelation of the Dera incident. On 17 July, when he was back in Paris, he said more about this to Meinertzhagen.

In Paris, Lawrence continued his routine work on Arab business. On 15 June he advised Faisal to postpone his return for six weeks, since there would be no discussion of Arab affairs until the beginning of September. With the future of Syria in limbo, Lawrence decided to take unofficial leave and return to Oxford, where he could give his full attention to his book. He was also keen to reactivate plans for his printing press and, as an aspirant author, seek out the society and guidance of distinguished men of letters. His way had already been smoothed by Geoffrey Dawson, whose influence had secured him a six-year fellowship of All Souls College.

With typical casualness in such matters, Lawrence announced that he had demobilised himself from the army, somewhat to the astonishment of War Office staff who discovered that he had ignored all the relevant formalities. Meanwhile, the equally exasperated Foreign Office still believed he was a member of the Paris delegation and due to return to assist Balfour when the Syrian question came up for review.[18] It was a prospect which dismayed nearly all his colleagues, who hoped that this reckless amateur would never return to Paris as a member of their profession.

II

KINGMAKER, 1919–1922

THROUGHOUT the Paris conference, Lawrence miscalculated his own powers of persuasion and the British government's willingness to jeopardise its friendship with France on behalf of Faisal. His prickly manner, francophobia and unpredictability irritated colleagues, leaving him without influential allies. His only asset was an ability to sway Faisal, but fears that he would use this talent to hinder rather than advance British interests led to his exclusion from policy-making and negotiations after September 1919. From then until December 1920, when Churchill invited him to join the Colonial Office's new Middle Eastern Department, Lawrence held no official post.

During this period he was a spectator who stood on the touchline, alternately shouting encouragement and abuse to those playing the diplomatic game. As their efforts faltered, his clamour and his audience grew. Lowell Thomas had made his name a household word so that what he had to say about the Middle East commanded the attention of the public, newspaper editors and politicians. His finger remained on the pulse of Middle Eastern affairs: former colleagues made information available to him and, by May 1920, when the government's policies in the region were clearly foundering, he was able to entice old friends such as Aubrey Herbert and Philby into an influential lobby.

New factors were shaping events during this period. Lloyd George, in order to fulfil pledges made in 1917, actively encouraged a Greek invasion of the Turkish mainland which began with landings in Smyrna (Izmir) in May 1919. Soon after, Italian forces landed near Adana and the French pressed into Cilicia, where they hoped to sponsor an Armenian state. These threefold incursions drove the Turks into the arms of Kemal Atatürk, who, backed by the former Turkish army of the Caucasus, was rallying the nationalists. By July 1920 his forces menaced Aleppo and in October 1921 they finally forced the French to withdraw from Cilicia. On the Greek front, Atatürk, with Soviet assistance, began to make headway during the summer and autumn of 1920. As Lawrence had predicted, Ottoman defeat had released the forces of Turkish nationalism, which were given dynamism by Atatürk's leadership and ill-judged Anglo-French efforts to partition Turkey by force.

British policies of meddle and muddle were running into trouble elsewhere in the Middle East. In May 1920 Anglo-Indian troops were rushed to the shores of the Caspian after the Russians had seized Enzeli in support of Persian nationalists who were resisting Britain's efforts to impose a new treaty on their country. Turkey and Persia were peripheral to Lawrence's interests, which centred on Syria, Iraq and Palestine, but events there supported his thesis that it was foolhardy for Britain to rush into headlong collision with popular national movements. 'You cannot make war on a rebellion,' he remarked, with reference to Ireland, where the British government was trying to do just that in its efforts to keep the lid on popular nationalism.[1]

The Cabinet was also coming to the same conclusion but for different reasons. From the summer of 1919 onwards, ministers were increasingly alarmed by the spiralling costs of foreign and imperial commitments. British forces underpinned anti-Bolshevik regimes in northern and southern Russia and provided garrisons for the Rhineland, Constantinople, Syria, Iraq and Persia. They were also waging a war on India's North-West Frontier and suppressing insurgency in the Punjab, Egypt and Ireland. Manpower was stretched to breaking point and matters were made worse by the unwillingness of many conscripts and volunteers, men who had joined up to fight Germany, to stay in the forces and defend the empire. A few weeks before Lawrence's visit to Egypt in June 1919 there had been a number of serious mutinies by British troops in support of swift demobilisation.

Entrenchment was the Cabinet's first response to these problems. Expenses had to be pruned and inessential commitments terminated. At the beginning of September, Lloyd George took the first step with the announcement that the Anglo-Indian army of occupation in Syria would commence evacuation on 1 November. It was costing £9 million annually and served no useful purpose, since Britain would never accept the Syrian mandate, earmarked for France. Faisal would be left the isolated ruler of the inland districts of Damascus, Homs, Hama and Aleppo. Faisal, already on his way to London, was stunned by the news, although he hoped he might still wriggle out of accepting French supervision by an appeal to British and American sympathy.

Lawrence, fearing that Faisal was about to be left in the lurch, attempted to remind the British public that they were under a moral obligation to him. He did this through a contrived leak in a letter to *The Times* of 11 September in which he outlined the details of the hitherto obscure wartime negotiations between Britain and the Arabs. He summarised four vital documents which he claimed to have read while serving on Faisal's staff. One was the Sykes-Picot agreement (of which he had claimed ignorance a year before in Damascus); the other three were Mcmahon's letter to Hussain of 24 October 1915 with its offer of Arab independence south of latitude 37°, saving Basra, Baghdad and regions where French interests predominated, and the declarations of 11 June and 8 November 1918. The last two were interpreted by Lawrence as charters for Arab self-determination in Iraq and Syria with loose British and French surveillance. As for Sykes–Picot, it was no longer workable and Arab representatives should be allowed to share in its revision. Whatever the result of this, Faisal had full rights to rule Damascus, Homs, Hama and Aleppo, where he now governed in co-operation with political officers of Allenby's army of occupation, as well as Mosul, which unknown to Lawrence was now attached to Iraq.

The rest of Lawrence's letter was censored by Wickham Steed, the editor of *The Times*. He cut out Lawrence's repudiation of his own role in the Arab campaign in which he claimed to have been the innocent agent of a deceitful government whose untruths he had passed on to the Arabs. This bitter statement, which would be expanded in the *Seven Pillars*, was soon known in official circles where it caused consternation and confirmed opinions about the author's utter unreliability. On 1 October, William Yale heard from Colonel Walter Gribbon of the General Staff that 'all unofficial statements made to the Arabs by British officers would be disregarded or denied'. Such disavowals were unnecessary since no Arab spokesman then or later ever mentioned pledges specifically made by Lawrence or any other officer during the war. Nevertheless, Lawrence had started a hare which has run ever since. It was chased first by Aubrey Herbert, who on 20 October 1920 asked for a Commons statement about promises made by the government to Faisal. Andrew Bonar Law replied in the Prime Minister's absence to say that none existed. Lawrence had successfully sown suspicions about gross British duplicity towards the Arabs.

But his letter proved a damp squib. The government never wavered in its policy towards Faisal. His protests about past promises were brushed aside and instead he was given a lesson in the stark realities of international power broking. When he met Lloyd George and members of his Cabinet on 19 and 23 September he was firmly told that Britain had no further interest in Syrian affairs and he was advised to go to Paris and get the best terms he could from Clemenceau.

Lawrence did what he could in an attempt to salvage something for his friend. In a memo to the Foreign Office of 15 September he warned that Faisal's abandonment to the French would generate waves of nationalist agitation which would rebound on Britain. In a letter written twelve days later to Curzon, he pleaded with him to keep Faisal in Britain's orbit by procuring concessions from the French, including a free port on the Mediterranean coast, vital for his landlocked principality. He even offered to return to Syria and arrange the transfer of Faisal's government from Damascus to Dera, which lay within Britain's sphere. Curzon was unmoved and refused to consider any course which might imperil Anglo-French cooperation.

In putting his case for Faisal, Lawrence showed a commanding grasp of current developments in the Middle East and some of his evidence, including references to possible Russian involvement, suggests that he was in unofficial contact with former military and diplomatic colleagues who shared his anxieties about government policy. Chief of these was the fear that Faisal, who was now regarded as a champion of Arab nationalism throughout the Middle East, might turn his back on Britain and seek allies elsewhere. During the Paris Peace Conference, his Druze adherent Shakib Arslan had secretly extended feelers to the former Turkish Vizier, Talaat Bey, to explore the possibilities of Russian backing for a Turco-Arab alliance.[2] This must have been in Lawrence's mind when he warned the Foreign Office of the mischief which might follow a pact between Faisal and Atatürk or Russian penetration of the region. In both instances he was correct. Cast adrift by Britain and forced to bargain with France, Faisal fruitlessly sought a common front with Turkish, Kurdish and Egyptian nationalists.[3]

Unable to alter the course of the government's Middle Eastern policy, Lawrence turned his attention away from public affairs. During the winter of 1919–20 he concentrated on his own writing and plans for the republication of Charles Doughty's lengthy and previously obscure *Arabia Deserta*, which he profoundly admired. Meanwhile events in the Middle East followed a course which he had predicted and by the spring of 1920 circumstances favoured a fresh assault on government policy there.

Faisal had been forced to bow to French pressure and acknowledge France as the mandatory power for the whole of Syria. French plans for Syria's future rested upon the creation of a network of small administrative units which followed the racial and religious divisions of the region and entailed close co-operation with local notables. Ultimate authority would rest with French officials, as Faisal quickly learned when he returned to Beirut in January 1920. General Gouraud reminded him that he would have to give formal justification of his claims as ruler of Damascus, Homs, Hama and Aleppo and ordered him to suppress the brigandage endemic in these districts and punish the corruption of his officials.

In Damascus, Faisal found that extreme nationalists had taken control of the Syrian National Assembly, which had rejected the French mandate and branded him a turncoat for accepting it. To reassert his authority, he threw in his lot with the nationalists. On 9 March he redeemed himself and his nationalist credentials by a public repudiation of the French mandate and was duly elected king. This gave the French the excuse they had been looking for. On the pretext of imposing stability, which was ardently sought by the Syrian upper classes and non-Muslim minorities (there had been an Armenian massacre in Aleppo in March 1919), Gouraud marched on Damascus. Arab forces were beaten at Maysalun and after a four-day war Damascus was occupied on 26 July. Faisal fled from his crumbling kingdom and sought sanctuary in British Palestine.

The Franco-Syrian war of July 1920 was one of a series of violent upheavals in the Middle East. In April there had been a murderous riot in Jerusalem in protest against Jewish immigration. Rioters, who included veterans of Faisal's army, held his picture aloft and shouted, 'Long live our King – King Faisal! In the name of our King we urge you to fight the Jews!' There were also calls for the immediate amalgamation of Palestine and Syria. Further south, the news of Faisal's expulsion from Damascus provoked his brother Abdullah to collect an army of Hejazi Beduin and move northwards. By January 1921 he had occupied Maan in the British zone and declared that he would soon reconquer Syria.

The most serious trouble was in Iraq, where the announcement that the country was to receive a British mandate sparked off a general Arab revolt in May. Shortly before, Iraqi nationalist exiles in Damascus had elected Abdullah as their king. This new Arab revolt was the result of uncertainty and disappointment throughout the Middle East: the collapse of the Turkish empire in October 1918 and the public statements of the Allies had raised the hopes of local nationalists to a peak. But the eagerly anticipated new era was stillborn thanks to Anglo-French plans to partition the region. As Lawrence wrote in a letter to *The Times* of 22 July:

> The Arabs rebelled against the Turks during the war not because the Turk government was notably bad, but because they wanted independence. They did not risk their lives in battle to change masters, to become British subjects or French citizens, but to win a show of their own.

This had been denied them and now former allies were enemies and liberators had become oppressors.

This letter marked Lawrence's return to the political arena. He entered it as the champion of both Arab nationalism and liberal imperialism. The two were compatible. 'My own ambition', he told Curzon in September 1919, 'is that the Arabs should be our first brown dominion, and not our last brown colony'. The idea was radical for its time, but not novel since the government had just announced plans for the gradual introduction of self-government in India. Taking this as his cue, Lawrence concluded his *Times* letter, 'I shall be told that the idea of brown Dominions in the British Empire is grotesque,' but India was already on such a course. Furthermore, Lawrence was sure that 'Arabs in these conditions would be as loyal as anyone in the Empire.' Sympathetically handled, Arab national sentiment could be harnessed by Britain to produce a stable and tractable Middle East.

At this moment the Middle East was volatile and the Arabs considered Britain to be their foe thanks to the ineptitude of Lloyd George's coalition. Through a series of newspaper articles and letters published between May and August 1920, Lawrence excoriated the government's policies, suggested cheap and effective alternatives and publicised the good sense and moderation of Faisal.

In two pieces for the Conservative *Daily Express* on 22 and 23 May, he showed how muddled policies were the consequence of having given responsibility for Middle Eastern affairs to three, often conflicting departments of state, the Foreign, India and War Offices. Armed repression was a brittle basis for imperial government in Asia since 'Asiatics have fought in the war, not for us, but for their own interests.' Again, in a *Sunday Times* article on 30 May, he contended 'that brown peoples who had chosen to fight beside the Allies would receive their meed of friendship in the work of peace, that new age of freedom of which victory was the dawn'. What followed was bitter alienation created by the fumbling, out-of-date imperial policies of annexation and coercion.

As baleful news of the Iraqi uprising and its suppression appeared in the press, Lawrence concentrated his attack on official policy there. In the *Observer* of 8 August and the *Sunday Times* of a fortnight later, he rebuked the Indian administration in Iraq for its misjudgements, arrogance and short-sightedness, all of which had been exposed by the Arab revolt. Since 1914, the soldiers and civil servants imported from India to govern the province had been guided by the principle that the Arabs were unfitted for responsibility and needed generations of firm but enlightened rule. The administration was provided by a cadre of ex-officers who acted as district commissioners under the direction of Colonel Arnold Wilson, who hoped to encourage the eventual colonisation of Iraq by what he called 'stalwart Muhammadan cultivators'. To Lawrence this had seemed a recipe for calamity and the events of 1920 had proved him right. There was an irony, he noted, in British officials hanging Arabs 'for political offences, which they call rebellion' even though those executed were still nominally Turkish subjects. This point was taken up on 15 December by the ex-Prime Minister, Asquith, when he asked in the Commons, 'Why are Arabs rebels? To whom traitors?'

Such cruel ambiguities might easily have been avoided, if, as Lawrence argued, the government had sought a partnership with the Arabs rather than insisting that they submitted to the India Office's satraps. At the very end of the war he had proposed the partition of Iraq into two kingdoms under Abdullah and Zaid. This appealed to Hussain, who in January 1919 suggested Abdullah as king of all Iraq, and to Faisal who tolerated the use of Damascus as a base for pro-Hashemite subversion in Iraq. In March 1919 Faisal had asked the British government to permit the repatriation of those Iraqi officers attached to his army. Lawrence supported the request, admitting that, while these men were Abdullah's partisans, they were 'mostly very pro-British'.[4] Wilson was convinced that once in Iraq these men would throw themselves into pro-Hashemite agitation.

He was correct. General Mawlud Mukhlis, Faisal's ex-Chief of Staff and pre-war al Ahd activist, advocated a Hashemite kingdom in Iraq and favoured a nationalist alliance with Atatürk, and Nuri es Said hoped for a Syrian-Iraqi federation under Hashemite rule. Both were involved in anti-government, Hashemite scheming in Iraq and ultimately would be rewarded by high office when Faisal was made king. (Nuri was murdered in 1958 during the coup which overthrew Faisal's grandson, Faisal II.) During the war, as Lawrence knew, these men had been anglophiles and afterwards, like the other Iraqis who had fought alongside Faisal, they were anxious to find outlets for their talents in the new Iraqi government. These were denied them under the Indian policy which severely restricted official posts opened to Arabs. As Lawrence recognised, this stubborn refusal to rule in harness with local men turned old friends into enemies and contributed to the present mess in Iraq. Repeating Sir Mark Sykes's wartime gibe, Lawrence stigmatised the Indian administration as worse than the Turkish. It was loathed, it wasted soldiers' lives and squandered money.

Lawrence not only castigated the government's policy in print; behind the scenes he was gathering support from former friends in the army, civil service and House of Commons. From his All Souls base, he approached eminent and experienced men whom he thought would be sympathetic to his ideas. On 21 May, he invited Philby to join a knot of Middle East experts which included Hogarth and Arnold Toynbee, a historian who had been attached to the Middle East section at the Peace Conference. Their purpose was to persuade Lloyd George to create a new Middle East Department with sole responsibility for the area which, with a complement of 'new men', could devise and implement fresh policies. The India Office would be the loser since, as Lawrence warned Philby, 'Curzon is of course the enemy; but he's not a very bold enemy.'

Pressure on the government was maintained by an all-party group of MPs including the Conservatives Lord Robert Cecil and Aubrey Herbert, and the left-wing Labour MP Colonel Wedgwood, who had served as a RNAS seaplane pilot during operations in support of the Arabs in the Red Sea during 1916. They kept up a steady pressure on the government and the thrust of their attacks followed closely the lines laid down by Lawrence. On 15 July, Herbert enquired whether Iraq could be returned to the pre-war system which had relied on Arab officials and cost £3 million. A week later, George Lambert, a senior Liberal MP, asked about the establishment of the Arab state in Iraq which General Maude had promised when he had taken Baghdad in 1917. Lord Robert Cecil also pressed this matter when he asked for an explanation of the delays in setting up the promised Arab state. Lambert returned to the offensive on 9 August and demanded an Arab government in line with the November 1918 Declaration. Colonel Wedgwood interrupted, 'Why not send Colonel Lawrence to Baghdad?' – which prompted a Tory backbencher to respond, 'Why not send Colonel Wedgwood?'

Lawrence and his allies encountered some opposition. On 3 August *The Times* published a letter from Captain Tytler, who had served in Iraq during the previous three years. Lawrence, he argued, knew little about the region, and his proposal to place it in charge of a Sunni Muslim prince would offend the large Shiite Muslim community which had been protected from Sunnite exactions by the Turkish government. Another Iraq veteran and a Conservative MP, Colonel Freemantle, queried what local support there was in favour of a Sunni chief from Hejaz as King of Iraq.

Such objections did little harm to Lawrence and the pro-Hashemite lobby. The political tide was now flowing fast in their direction. On 22 July Lloyd George told the House that the government accepted the creation of an Arab state in Iraq and four days later he announced that the local Chief Commissioner, Sir Percy Cox, had been ordered to prepare for a transfer of power.

This was a reverse for Curzon, the India Office and the Iraqi administration. The ill-will generated during and after Lawrence's 1916 visit to Iraq intensified. Colonel Arnold Wilson, Cox's deputy, had been singled out by Lawrence as chiefly responsible for much that had gone wrong in the country and he never forgave Lawrence. Afterwards he never missed a chance to denigrate his adversary and his achievements. In a sour but not entirely unjustified review of *Revolt in the Desert*, Wilson belittled the Arabs as soldiers and administrators. Their wartime sponsor, the Arab Bureau, 'died unregretted' in 1920; its members, 'amply mirrored in these pages, appear to constitute a mutual admiration society – almost a cult of which Lawrence is the chief priest and Lowell Thomas the press agent'.[5]

Wilson interpreted the government's change of policy towards Iraq as the result of pressure exerted by Lawrence and his allies. In fact their success owed much to good timing. During the summer of 1920 the government's foreign and imperial policy was looking threadbare. It had been discredited by the futile intervention in Russia, which had finally been abandoned a few months before; the situation in Ireland was worsening; the scandal of General Dyer and the Amritsar shootings spluttered on, and there was growing chaos in the Middle East. Wrong-headed policies meant extra bills which a burdened Treasury duly passed on to the taxpayer at a time of economic slump. Lawrence, catching the current political mood, pressed the point that the public purse could no longer meet the expenses of unending repressive wars which also affronted the national conscience. Rethinking was urgently needed. 'We are big enough to admit a fault, and turn a new page,' he wrote in the *Observer*, 'and we ought to do it with a hoot of joy, because it will save us a million pounds a week.'

New thinking required new men. The central figure in the recasting of Britain's policy in the Middle East was Winston Churchill, who moved from the War Office to become Secretary of State for the Colonies in January 1921. He was assisted in his task by a newly created Middle East Department of experts with local experience and knowledge. On 4 December, Churchill's secretary, Eddie Marsh, approached Lawrence and asked if he would join the department to advise on Arabian affairs. Lawrence accepted and, on

7 January, Churchill met the new member of his staff. He had had to overcome considerable opposition from officials who argued that Lawrence was temperamentally unsuited to the post. Lawrence agreed, but Churchill prevailed. After the crucial interview, he told his wife that Lawrence 'has at last consented to have a bit put in his mouth and saddle fastened to his back'.

Churchill had high ambitions for Lawrence. It has been suggested that in 1922 and in 1925, when Allenby resigned as High Commissioner in Egypt, Churchill recommended Lawrence as his successor. Lawrence certainly imagined that he was a candidate and was both flattered and amused. In September 1934, he wrote to George Lloyd, 'My statement, when they offered me the succession to Allenby – close the residency and take a room in Shepheard's and ride about on a bike', and so 'run the Government of Egypt from underneath'. These suggestions could hardly have reassured the Foreign Office, which appointed the High Commissioner, although its officials may have taken more seriously Lawrence's recommendation of his old friend George Lloyd. At other times Churchill may have dangled various colonial governorships, including Cyprus, in front of Lawrence.[6]

Before 1921, the two men had been casual acquaintances even though each was aware of the other's reputation. Friendship quickly followed and was sustained by mutual admiration. Churchill and Lawrence were very alike, not least in the violent reactions they provoked among the less talented. Both were physically brave; both believed themselves instruments of historical destiny; both were visionaries; both sought to dominate whatever circle they found themselves in; both possessed demonic energy which alternated with moods of inert despair; both enjoyed reputations for wayward brilliance and both aspired to the mastery of English prose. In 1921 Churchill had yet to enjoy the worldwide adulation which followed his wartime triumphs. Then he aroused widespread and deep suspicion among his countrymen; he had entered politics as a Tory, crossed the Commons to become a Liberal and the agent of radical reforms which enraged his former colleagues. A masterful First Lord of the Admiralty, his career had foundered on the shores of Gallipoli, for which débâcle he took much of the blame. There had been recriminations about his recent crusade against Bolshevism which had drawn British armies into Russia for no purpose and confirmed fears that Churchill was both a warmonger and an implacable enemy of the working classes.

None of this mistrust of Churchill or his ideals rubbed off on Lawrence. In so far as such a creature ever existed for him, Churchill came close to Lawrence's ideal of a public man. On hearing of his electoral defeat at Dundee in March 1922, he sent a note of consolation. 'In guts and power and speech you can roll over anyone bar Lloyd George,' he wrote, and later he told Eddie Marsh, 'What bloody shits the Dundeans must be.' Lawrence defended him vigorously to the socialist Shaws with an explanation of his friend's mental anatomy. Churchill, he observed, has 'a Tory instinct; a Liberal intellect: give him time and atmosphere to think, and he takes as gently broad a view of subjects as ordinary human kind can expect.' He had supported Irish Home Rule, and his colonial reforms 'did more solid good to our native clients than all the good wishes of their loudest adversaries'. 'Winston in office does a great deal,' he concluded, 'and he is as fond of his friends as they are of him.' On another occasion Lawrence recalled his former chief as 'a great man' for whom he felt 'not merely admiration, but a very great liking'. He had been a sensitive and sympathetic colleague who had shown himself 'considerate as a statesman can be: and several times I've seen him chuck the statesman-like course and do the honest thing instead'.[7]

Churchill returned Lawrence's affection and regard. Working alongside them in the Colonial Office, Meinertzhagen noticed Churchill's open and profound admiration for Lawrence, which no doubt made him susceptible to whatever he advised. Churchill clearly believed himself in contact not only with a very remarkable man, but with a tangible link with Britain's heroic past and a living example of the finest qualities latent within his countrymen. In 1937 he wrote:

> The fury of the Great War raised the pitch of life to the Lawrence
> standard. The multitudes were swept forward till their pace was the same
> as his. In this heroic period he found himself in perfect relation both
> to men and events.

Maybe that harmony was never recovered in peacetime, but Churchill sensed that, for all his reservations, 'he was a man who held himself ready for a new call'. In August 1943, his imagination stirred by reports of Brigadier Orde Wingate's exploits behind Japanese lines in Burma, Churchill thought another Lawrence had been found. Closer acquaintance with Wingate did not confirm his hopes and he soon lost interest.[8]

Churchill's hero-worship of Lawrence was coupled with a profound respect for his opinions on all aspects of Middle Eastern policy. Moreover, Lawrence enjoyed the goodwill and trust of the Hashemites, who were now destined to play a central part in British designs for the region. Churchill had taken over the Colonial Office and secured unshackled control over Iraqi, Palestinian and Arabian affairs with a mandate to establish stability and make the area what it had once been under Ottoman government, a safe buffer zone between India and Europe. All this had to be achieved at the smallest possible charge to the British taxpayer. In effect, the solutions which Lawrence had continually demanded for the past two years had become official policy. In Paris he had dissented from the government's policy: now it accorded with his private views.

Lawrence had never been a voice crying in the wilderness. His general principle of indirect rule through pliant, dependable local princes had always enjoyed support among many soldiers, diplomats and politicians who were aware of its success in India and northern Nigeria. The application of this system to Iraq was backed by Gertrude Bell, Sir Percy Cox's Oriental Secretary, Cornwallis (who had been Faisal's adviser in Damascus until November 1919) and Hubert Young, another of Churchill's recruits to the Middle Eastern Department. They recognised that Faisal was pro-British and could rule with the assistance of his former Iraqi staff such as Jafar al Askari and Nuri es Said, who were all proven anglophiles.

One of Lawrence's first tasks in January 1922 had been to sound out Faisal about his views and intentions. He proved willing to co-operate with Britain and, on 17 January, Lawrence reported to Churchill with the encouraging news that Faisal would repudiate his father's claims to Palestine and would ignore 'all question of pledges and promises, fulfilled or broken'. In return he hoped that an Arab state might be established on the Jordan, wanted British help to control Ibn Saud and intended to maintain his 'watching brief' for Iraq.[9]

Discovering Faisal's political attitudes was part of the preparations for a conference scheduled by Churchill to open in Cairo on 12 March. Its agenda embraced all the problems then facing the British government in the Middle East, and everyone involved had been invited. Churchill took with him Lawrence and Young; the RAF was represented by Air Marshal Sir Hugh Trenchard, the Chief of Air Staff, and the army by Lieutenant-General Sir Walter Congreve, the Commander-in-Chief in Egypt and Palestine, and General Sir Edmund Ironside, who commanded in Persia. Spokesmen for the civil administrations included Sir Herbert Samuel, the High Commissioner in Palestine, and Sir Percy Cox, who held that office in Iraq and was accompanied by Gertrude Bell. Among Lawrence's former brothers-in-arms were Deedes, now Civil Secretary to the Palestine government, Cornwallis, Jafar al Askari, who represented Faisal, and Joyce, who had been appointed adviser to the Iraqi Ministry of Defence.

General policy lines had already been laid down in London: what the conference had to work out was how best they could be translated into action. First came Iraq, where Cox had already undertaken the business of setting up the machinery of a new, Arab-dominated administration. The government now wanted Faisal as the country's king, but Cox had discovered that the Iraqis were far from unanimous in his favour. Abdullah. chosen a year before by nationalist exiles, was considered unsuitable. Lawrence urged Faisal as the only man who could 'pull together the scattered elements of a backward and half-civilized country', and, unlike his indolent brother, he was active. Furthermore, Lawrence added, his experiences at the Paris Peace Conference had given him the necessary sophistication to sustain the dignity of his office. Cox agreed, but on the ground that Faisal was the only candidate who might secure the backing of the majority of Iraqis. The next problem was one of window-dressing, since it had to appear that Faisal had been chosen by the Iraqis rather than imposed on them by the British. This was handled by Cox; he would return to Iraq, pardon imprisoned or exiled rebels and then Faisal would cable his supporters from Mecca and announce his candidacy for the throne together with acceptance of the terms of the British mandate. He would then proceed to Iraq where, it was hoped, he would find a groundswell of popular support.

The next matter in hand concerned the troublesome Kurds of northern Iraq, who, since the war, had twice rebelled against British authority and demanded a state of their own. Lawrence, who had known the Kurds intimately when he had lived in Karkamis, had initially dismissed their claims to national identity. In September 1919 he had written that the 'Kurds have no corporate feeling and no capacity for autonomy or nationality,' an opinion he subsequently revised, presumably in the light of the continued resistance in Kurdistan. At Cairo he argued against the Kurds being placed under Arab rule and was supported by Major Edward Noel, a political officer with first-hand knowledge of local conditions.[10] Kurdish feelings towards the Arabs were summed up in two sayings: 'Don't encourage an Arab or he will come and commit a nuisance on the skirt,' and 'The Arab is like a fly; the more you shoo him away the more insistent he becomes.' Cox overrode Lawrence and Churchill, who was also sympathetic to the creation of a Kurdish buffer state between Iraq and Turkey. The pro-consul considered that feud-ridden tribesmen were not the stuff of nations and that British money would be wasted trying to make them one. For the Kurds it was a woefully mistaken decision which led to over seventy years of intermittent war and, in the 1980s, genocide.

Administrative costing dominated the thinking of every delegate. The Cabinet expected Churchill to pare spending to the bone, which meant massive cuts in the military budget. It was a matter which deeply interested Lawrence, who had become an enthusiastic apostle of Trenchard's new creed of air control. In essence this consisted of using RAF bombers, supported by armoured-car units, as an overwhelming force with which to overawe and, when necessary, chastise tribesmen who refused to keep the peace. These methods had already been tried on isolated occasions in Iraq, Egypt, Somaliland and India, and Trenchard had been heartened by the results. The army looked askance at air control which, if officially adopted, would jeopardise its traditional role as the empire's police force. Cox also objected to it, for he wrongly believed it would be unable to handle large-scale insurgency in such inaccessible areas as Kurdistan.

Lawrence stuck up for Trenchard during the debate over air control. His opinions carried weight for he had had first-hand experience of Turkish air raids against the Arabs in Hejaz and had later witnessed the havoc wrought by RAF bombers against Turkish units to fight back. 'Sir Hugh is right, the rest of you wrong,' he told the conference in his customary, quiet, emphatic manner. The RAF presence in the Middle East would be discreet, unlike conventional garrisons of troops, which would arouse nationalist fears of alien domination. Air-power, Lawrence believed, was the natural medium for controlling vast regions of waterless terrain where armies could only move slowly, shackled to vulnerable supply lines. A dozen years later, Lawrence told Liddell Hart that he had converted Churchill, although he had been convinced of the advantages of air control long before the Cairo conference.[11]

But by March 1923 Lawrence had had a change of heart. He told Colonel Wavell that air-power was useless against guerrillas and that 'Bombing tribes was ineffective.' This may have been what Wavell, a soldier, wanted to hear and at the time Lawrence was out of love with the RAF. He returned to his former opinions once he was back in the RAF and stationed at Miramshah on the North-West Frontier, where he saw air control in action. He was full of its praises and informed Bernard and Charlotte Shaw, both pacifists, that the warplanes were 'doves' which kept the peace among fractious tribesmen. He had no moral qualms about the system since 'Destroying those few poor villages hurt no one' (warning leaflets were dropped before a punitive raid) and the raj was spared the cost of a ground war. Others, including some RAF officers, were less sanguine about methods which did in fact kill many tribesmen and their families, but air control continued in the Middle East until the late 1950s. It was one of Lawrence's lasting legacies to the region.

Air control was designed to underpin British paramountcy in the Middle East. Politically, this rested on tractable Hashemite rulers, Faisal in Iraq and Abdullah in Jordan. In March 1921 Abdullah was still a thorn in Britain's flesh. In January he had occupied Maan with 2,000 Hejazi Beduin, advertised himself as a champion of Arab nationalism and promised to throw the French out of Syria. He also clung to his empty pretensions to be king of Iraq, which were taken seriously by his brother Faisal, who, when asked in December whether he would accept the Iraqi crown, refused on the ground of his brother's rights. Lawrence knew Abdullah and after the Cairo conference broke up it was his job to bring him to his senses.

Lawrence had already suggested the creation of a state for Abdullah by the partition of the British zone in Palestine. The region east of a line running northwards from Aqaba along the Jordan would be separated from Palestine and offered to Abdullah, who would rule it as Amir with British guidance and an annual cash subsidy. This suited Churchill. Abdullah's personal ambitions would be satisfied, general peace in the region would be restored, and he would keep the lid on anti-Zionist agitation.

The proposition was delivered to Abdullah by Lawrence, who, finding him amenable, conducted him to Churchill at Jerusalem. On 27 March, Churchill, Samuel and Abdullah discussed the future over tea. Abdullah was warned that he would have to stamp out Beduin brigandage, renounce his claims to Iraq, Syria and Palestine, and discourage anti-Jewish propaganda. In return he would get a Treasury annuity, British officers to train his army (the newly formed Arab Legion) and the use of RAF armoured cars to bring the recalcitrant Beduin to heel and keep out Wahabbi raiders. Abdullah agreed to the bargain.

On the surface Lawrence and Churchill had triumphed; the Cairo conference had brought a semblance of stability and order to the Middle East. Lawrence had played the kingmaker, procuring two thrones for Faisal and Abdullah, and he had redeemed what he considered a debt of honour incurred during the war. There remained one insoluble problem, Palestine. During 1920 and 1921 Arab antipathy to Jewish settlement had increased. When Lawrence and Churchill landed at Haifa, they were confronted by a noisy anti-Zionist demonstration. At Gaza, where Churchill insisted on an impromptu tour of the battlefield, there was a riot. Lawrence, who throughout the conference had worn a clerkly suit and Homburg hat, conducted Churchill through a crowd of gesticulating Arabs. 'I say, Lawrence, are these people dangerous?' asked Churchill. 'They don't seem too pleased to see us. What are they shouting?' Lawrence thought they were not dangerous, but neither were they welcoming, since they were shouting, 'Down with the British and down with Jewish policy!'

Two months later when Lawrence was back at his desk in the Colonial Office, he again faced the problem of bringing together the irreconcilable. Several thousand Arabs had attacked a Jewish settlement at Petach Tikuah and he had been asked for his views on a Jewish defence force. He was pessimistic and predicted further violent incidents which might culminate in all-out racial war. 'The success of Zionism' might eventually bring peace, but this would need at least fifty years. 'Popular' as opposed to mandatory government could reduce tension but, as Lawrence knew, this would mean complete Arab domination since the 150,000 Palestinians outnumbered the Jewish settlers.[12]

Privately, Lawrence's sympathies were with the Arabs. Meinertzhagen recalled a heated row not long after between himself, Lawrence and Churchill on the matter. Lawrence, 'grinning from ear to ear and clearly very pleased with himself', was discussing Faisal's and Abdullah's affairs with Churchill. Meinertzhagen had no time for either man, rating Faisal as no more than 'a stranger, a Hashemite, one of Lawrence's creations' and Abdullah as 'another upstart' to whom Lawrence had delivered a kingdom hacked out of land which should have been given to the Jews. Incensed, Lawrence retorted that 'Transjordan was Arab territory and had nothing to do with Palestine.' Meinertzhagen foresaw the eviction of the Hashemites and the emergence of a Jewish state encircled by hostile Arabs. Abdullah had been given the right to exclude Jews from his kingdom, a fact which angered many Zionists, and Meinertzhagen insisted that more land would be needed for settlers. 'At the expense of the Arabs?' Lawrence queried. 'No,' answered Meinertzhagen, 'there are thousands of acres in Transjordan lying fallow and unoccupied owing to Arab laziness.' It would remain so since, as Churchill commented, nothing could now be done about Transjordan for Abdullah was there to stay. This pleased Lawrence.[13]

Less pleasing to Lawrence were his final two assignments for the Colonial Office. On 30 June he was ordered to Jiddah as a special envoy to Hussain, who, unlike his sons, still refused to accept British control over Palestine. It was Lawrence's job to make him change his mind and behave like an obedient client of the British government. This proved impossible, as Lawrence discovered on his arrival in Hejaz at the end of August.

On 2 August, Lawrence cabled the Foreign Office: 'Old man is conceited to a degree, greedy, and stupid, but very friendly, and protests devotion to our interests.' Two days later, angered by Hussain's swollen-headedness, he delivered a sharp assessment of his character which reduced the King and his Foreign Minister to tears. This gave Lawrence hope and he told the Foreign Office, 'The King is weaker than I thought, and could, I think, be bullied into nearly complete surrender.' He mistook his man and it was soon Lawrence's turn to throw a tantrum. He stormed out of one meeting after Hussain again refused to ratify the Versailles Treaty. This 'fluttered them; the King saying he thought no one could treat royalty so'. The histrionics continued but to no avail. Lawrence briefly left Jiddah and returned on 7 October to find Hussain as adamant as ever, making wild demands for the overlordship of the entire Arabian peninsula, Palestine, Iraq and Syria.[14]

Lawrence gained a respite from this pointless exercise on 16 October when he was ordered to Jordan for discussions with Samuel over difficulties which were cropping up.[15] Abdullah was finding kingship too much for him and indicated that he might quit Jordan. Lawrence was needed to inject some resolution into him, as well as persuade him to hand over Syrian exiles implicated in a recent attempt to assassinate General Gouraud.

Lawrence left Hejaz for the final time, certain that Hussain's days were numbered. Shortly before he departed, he told the Foreign Office that the King's new Italian aircraft were 'rubbish' and that his army could easily be overcome by no more than 1,000 Wahabbis. It was, in 1925, when Hussain fled to exile in Amman and the Ibn Saud made himself King of Hejaz.

Until December 1921 Lawrence stayed in Jordan reassuring and assisting Abdullah. Here the love affair between him and the Arab world finally faded. He abominated routine administration, as Peake, his companion during these days, noticed. 'Lawrence was not an office man and he was no believer in the system of obtaining information from files, returns and reports.' Instead he rode across country on camel back or in an unreliable Model-T Ford and saw for himself what needed to be done. Old acquaintances flocked to see him and he was greeted with frenzied enthusiasm by former Beduin brothers-in-arms. Eric Kennington, then in Jordan preparing illustrations for the *Seven Pillars*, was moved by their devotion, but it was tinged with disappointment, since many who hailed Lawrence hoped that he had come to lead them again to Damascus. This he could not do: rather he had to warn Abdullah that British backing depended on his leaving Syria alone. Such advice must have gone against the grain, since Lawrence privately sympathised with the Syrian nationalists and he believed that the terrorists who had tried to kill Gouraud were merely paying the French back in their own coin.[16]

Peake found Lawrence unsettled. His moods were mercurial, swinging between silent depression and bouts of volubility during which he recalled old adventures. His duties certainly irked him. Once, in a fit of frustration, he damned offices as manifestations of a national vice. 'If you must have an office, put clerks in it only and keep officials outside,' he argued, and put theory into practice by limiting his own staff to an Arab clerk. Paperwork vexed him greatly and he avoided much of it by hurling files into his wastepaper basket. Included in this purge were some passports whose irritated owners later turned up to claim them. Philby, whom he had nominated his successor, discovered him clearing his desk in characteristic manner. 'Every paper in the office was torn up and consigned to an enormous wastepaper basket.' This was the same Lawrence who, in 1916, when asked for certain intelligence reports, had replied that they existed only in his head.

On 6 December, Lawrence left Jordan, determined to resign from the Colonial Office. The past four months had been gruelling and marked by disappointments. Hussain defied the British government and Abdullah's state was still precarious. Administration bored him, he was weary, and the Middle East's attractions had withered. On 1 October he had told Kennington, 'The War was good by drawing over our depths that hot surface wish to do or win something.' Then goals had been obvious and could be achieved. Now they were elusive and obtainable only through the uncongenial and tedious processes of negotiation and administration. Robert Graves found Lawrence, back in England, worn out, unable to sleep and inexplicably, given his £500 All Souls allowance and £1,200 Colonial Office salary, short of money. He had already been granted six months' leave from the Colonial Office and, despite Churchill's pleas, he formally resigned on 4 July 1922. He had always considered his appointment a temporary, emergency measure and promised Churchill that he was 'always at his disposal if ever there is a crisis, or any job, small or big, for which he can convince me that I am necessary'.

Peake wondered whether Lawrence's moods of despair owed something to a sense that he had failed in the Middle East. If this was so, Lawrence soon recovered his conviction that what he had done had been right. In retrospect, he felt great pride in his achievements. 'My policy is succeeding in the Arab world,' he told Mrs Bernard Shaw in 1927, momentarily forgetting the contributions then and later of others. A year later, when he congratulated Sir Gilbert Clayton on his appointment as High Commissioner in Iraq, he was optimistic about the future of the Middle East.

> As I get further and further away from things, the more completely do I feel that our efforts during the war have justified themselves, and are proving happier and better than I'd ever hoped. . . . Give Faisal my regards, when you see him. Tell him I thought a great deal of him during the war: and that I think more of him now. He has lasted splendidly. . . . The only essential thing is that the show should go along its proper road, after all. So long as that happens the personalities it uses or breaks are trifles.[17]

The show did run off the road, as it was bound to. With hindsight, the events in the Middle East between 1914 and 1922, in which Lawrence was so closely involved, were a minor episode in the twilight years of Britain's global supremacy. His prescriptions for a stable Middle East, which emphasised cheapness and dependence on client rulers, can now be seen as signs that Britain was already overladen with international responsibilities.

Lawrence had striven for an impossible objective, the reconciliation of British imperialism and Arab nationalism. As an agent of a British government, he had helped awaken an Arab national spirit and encouraged Arabs to believe that their future would be in their own hands. He had said and promised more than he should. If allowed to run free, such ideas would inevitably collide with British interests, and so Lawrence, while claiming that he was repaying a debt of honour to the Arabs, implemented policies designed to restrain Arab nationalism. It was not surprising that a man riddled with internal contradictions should have urged policies which were contradictory. This was recognised by Faisal, who by the time of his death in 1932 had managed to wriggle free of Britain's grasp and secure for Iraq some measure of political independence.

A further and potentially more dangerous contradiction lay at the heart of British policy. How could Britain balance sponsorship of Jewish immigration into Palestine with the need to keep the goodwill of the Arabs? Immediately after the Balfour Declaration Lawrence had predicted unending conflict and his pessimism was confirmed during 1921 when, briefly, he became entangled in the problems of Palestine. Knowledge of their intractability may well have helped him decide to quit his Colonial Office post. He had attempted to procure an accommodation between Faisal and the Zionists, not out of conviction but because such a course would assist the Arabs. Meinertzhagen sensed Lawrence's anti-Semitism when they worked together and it was evident in a 1927 *Spectator* review of a book by Philip Guedalla.[18] The showiness of Guedalla's style struck Lawrence as a manifestation of a racial vice which embraced 'Disraeli's spangled sense of colour, Zangwill's foppery, Rosenberg's electric storms: and the commoner manifestation of Mrs Goldstone, wife of the celebrated banker, upon whose ample front last night at dinner long ranks of pearl were paraded'.

Unforeseen and, during the 1920s, unforeseeable circumstances dictated the future of Palestine. Hitler's seizure of power in 1933 and the spread of virulent anti-Semitism in Central Europe quickened the pace of Jewish immigration. This, in turn, led to the Arab revolt in April 1936, less than a year after Lawrence's death. This upheaval acted as a new and potent stimulus for Arab nationalism and gave Arabs a sense of burning grievance which still remains strong. Arab feelings were as intense as they had been between 1916 and 1918, but now Britain and not the Ottoman empire was the focus of anger.

The Palestinian imbroglio weakened Britain's influence in the Middle East; the Second World War destroyed it. After the Munich crisis of 1938, a reinforced army in Palestine ruthlessly crushed the Arab revolt. Force was needed again in 1942 when British forces overthrew the pro-German nationalist government of Rashid Ali in Iraq. Another wartime emergency, this time in Syria, threw Britain into alliance with Arab nationalists against the pro-Vichy government in Damascus. In 1941 Britain pledged post-war independence to Syria, which was later endorsed by the United States and Russia. French imperialists suspected a conspiracy devised to secure British control over Syria and so accomplish the 'vast designs of T.E.Lawrence' which had been checked twenty years before. Lawrence's ghost was also raised by nationalists in the Lebanon where, in 1940, popular opinion likened him to Hitler. The German leader was 'on a par with Lawrence of Arabia' since 'the latter brought freedom and independence to the Arabs ... and Hitler was going to drive out the French, wipe out the Zionists and give lots of money and gold to the Arabs'.[19] Memories of Lawrence's sovereigns were clearly evergreen. The next generation of Arab nationalists branded Lawrence as the servant of the Zionists and British imperialism.[20]

By 1945 the British empire was no longer the fearsome and vigorous beast it had been in 1918 and French imperial pretensions were in tatters. After a world war fought for high ideals, it was no longer possible for the old imperial powers to brush aside wartime slogans about political freedom and the independence of small nations. France grudgingly evacuated Syria and the Lebanon in 1946 and in the same year Britain relinquished her mandate over Jordan. Unable to suppress the Jewish revolt, Britain gave up Palestine a year later. The immediate result was the establishment of Israel and the first Arab–Israeli war of 1948–9. Retreat was the order of the day in Egypt and Iraq, which lost their garrisons, and in Jordan, where in 1956 Abdullah's grandson, Hussain, severed links made in Lawrence's time by sacking the British officers who commanded the Arab Legion.

The post-war storms dealt harshly with Lawrence's Hashemite kingdoms. The Arab world was looking to new leaders, forceful army officers like Nasser of Egypt who, in many ways, resembled the Young Turks of Lawrence's generation. They were the ideological descendants of the educated Arabs he had known and despised in Syria. Like them, the new generation of Arab nationalists drew their ideas from Western philosophies, including Marxism, and were driven by an implacable antipathy towards France and Britain, the weakened imperial powers which seemed unable to give up their domineering ways. Furthermore, both nations, in association with the United States, were almost universally thought of as the sponsors of Israel and therefore enemies of Arab nationalism. Many of the new nationalists were apostles of economic and social revolution and so wished to overturn traditional hierarchies. The Hashemites were therefore isolated on two counts: they were conservative monarchs and stooges of the Western powers.

The Hashemite kingdom of Iraq fell in 1958, a belated casualty of the Anglo-French invasion of Egypt two years before, after a coup by Young Turk-style nationalist officers. Faisal's grandson, Faisal II, was murdered with his family, as was Lawrence's old comrade Nuri es Said. As Lawrence had recognised, he was a trusty anglophile; in 1954 Selwyn Lloyd, the Foreign Secretary, had called him a 'wise and true friend of Britain', qualities which were anathema to the new Arab nationalists.

Abdullah's grandson and successor, Hussain, proved more durable thanks to his good sense in courting American as well as British favours. True to Lawrence's assurances, Britain pledged armed help in 1956 if Israel invaded Jordan. Two years later, the United States helped out. The Sixth Fleet, with marine paratroopers, stood by in readiness to save Hussain from a repetition of the coup which had recently ousted his cousin in Iraq. He and his kingdom, now shorn of the west bank of the Jordan, still survives, a lasting legacy of Lawrence.

The Middle East of today seems very distant from that which Lawrence knew and believed he understood. In the early 1980s, recalling his efforts to foster Arab–Jewish reconciliation, the Foreign Secretary Lord Carrington regretted that it was so hard for 'moderate' Arab politicians to flourish in the face of extremists and demagogues. Such creatures had been fewer in Lawrence's time and he could dismiss them and their borrowed philosophies. As Gertrude Bell had warned in 1908, 'the great catchwords of revolution, fraternity and equality' were inflammatory in the Middle East, not least because, taken to their logical conclusions, they challenged a world order in which Europeans were supreme. But nationalism could not be ignored; indeed, properly guided and under safe leadership, it was a useful weapon in the war against Turkey.

The war over, Lawrence was able to build on his friendship with the Hashemites and entice them into Britain's orbit after their alarming flirtation with anti-European nationalism in Syria and Iraq. They were conservatives who owed everything, including their thrones, to Britain and were accustomed to working in concert with British officials such as Lawrence. In time, their sons would be sent to English public schools and universities, where connections with Britain's ruling caste would be strengthened and they would learn how to see things the British way. Such arrangements ignored the gathering forces of social and economic change of which Lawrence had been uneasily aware in pre-war Syria.

Lawrence's public policies were indelibly stamped with his private prejudices. As a romantic Tory, he was entranced by the traditional, natural and seemingly timeless order of Middle Eastern society, which he hoped could be preserved through the institution of monarchy. This view remained constant: in 1934 he wrote to his old friend George Lloyd and speculated on what might have happened if he had joined him in Cairo during his term of office as High Commissioner in Egypt. 'Your dignity, with a merry devil of an assistant on the Staff', could have generated an agrarian movement among the Egyptian fellahin 'which would have sidetracked politics', by which Lawrence meant the clamour of the urban, educated nationalists who demanded Britain's disengagement from their country.[21] As during the Arab Revolt, Lawrence the medievalist dreamed of an alliance between lord and peasant to stem the alien forces of capitalism and democracy.

Lawrence was also an imperialist who, like so many others of his generation, embodied the internal dilemma of this creed. He represented the
British Empire as a benign force which would broadcast enlightenment,
and he prophesied the emergence of self-governing coloured states within
the Commonwealth. Yet this seemingly benevolent institution ultimately
rested on force, and he strongly urged the application of the most modern
technology of war to coerce its less biddable subjects.

Beyond the sphere of politics, Lawrence offered his countrymen an intoxicating but deceptive vision of the Middle East. He wrote about an empty
land peopled by romantic warrior chieftains, about their codes of honour
and their hosts of fighting men. He inspired Sir James Lunt to follow
a career in the Arab Legion. Like others who followed him and served
as professional soldiers or civil servants in the Middle East, Lunt felt drawn
by his hero's ability to establish a peculiar personal rapport with the Beduin.
Lawrence's colleague Kirkbride, recalling how Glubb Pasha, the Arab
Legion's commanding officer, had been able to penetrate the mind of his
soldiers, remarked that, like Lawrence, he was a Celt. This was understood
by the Arabs, who believed that the Celts possessed some mysterious quality
which made for an easy empathy between their two races.[22] Be this as
it may, Lawrence glamorised the nomadic Arabs and left a lasting impression
that they had a distinct affinity with the British. Moreover, he insisted,
Britain had some kind of moral debt to these people, a claim which still
exercises a strong hold over many Foreign Office officials.

To return then to the 1980s and to Lord Carrington, who believes that
Britain has a special part to play in the affairs of the Middle East: this
conviction owes much to Lawrence, who, through his life and writing,
taught his countrymen that they could command the affection and trust
of Arabs. Those who now travel across the Middle East are following in
Lawrence's footsteps and their habits of mind have in some way been shaped
by his. As for Lawrence, he said goodbye to the Middle East when the
going was good. He once described its history as a succession of tidal
waves, one of which he 'raised and rolled' towards Damascus. What he
never understood were the deep and strong eddies which flowed beneath
the wave. In time, these became a flood which has swept away the dykes
and breakwaters he had helped build.

III

MAN OF LETTERS

LAWRENCE wanted to be a respected figure of English letters; E.M.
Forster believed that his literary ambitions surpassed all others. Robert
Graves mockingly warned him against deliberately making himself an 'Eminent Literary Person', one of that breed of master wordsmiths whose style
wins academic approval but little else. Lawrence was unmoved. He saw
himself as an artist: words were his pigments and a masterpiece his goal.
He revealed his priorities to Liddell Hart, to whom he once remarked,
'I think that why you write must be because you really have something
to say.'[1] For Lawrence, content took second place to style.

For this reason, his output was limited. *Seven Pillars of Wisdom* appeared
in a private edition in 1926 and, abridged, as *Revolt in the Desert* the following
year. The initial field work for *The Mint*, his worm's-eye view of the RAF
rankers' world, was undertaken during 1922–3. The project was discarded,
and then taken up again in 1927 when a final draft was produced. In accordance with his wishes, and in deference to Lord Trenchard and the current
laws of obscenity and libel, it was not published until 1955. Between 1928
and 1932, he translated *The Odyssey*, which appeared as a lavishly printed
limited edition in Britain and a public edition in the USA. Apart from
a manual of motorboat engine maintenance, this was Lawrence's last full-
length work.

The gestation of the *Seven Pillars* and *The Mint* was slow and painful.
Lawrence started work on the former early in 1919 while he was attending
the Paris Peace Conference and, by April of that year, he was showing
draft chapters to Meinertzhagen. This version was completed by November,
when the manuscript was stolen while Lawrence was changing trains at
Reading station. Perhaps injudiciously, he carried the draft in a bank messenger's case, which tempted a thief. Some people, Robert Graves among
them, cynically imagined that Lawrence, deeply dissatisfied with what he
had written, had jettisoned the manuscript and concocted the theft story.

Almost immediately, Lawrence launched himself into a second draft,
much of which was composed while he was undertaking his official duties
in the Middle East or in a Barton Street attic room that had been placed
at his disposal by his architect friend Sir Henry Baker. The second *Seven
Pillars* was completed by the spring of 1922. Remembering the misadventure

which had befallen the first, he prudently had six copies of the new draft printed and bound by the *Oxford Times*. These were circulated among his former brothers-in-arms and literary friends for comment, criticism and correction.

Save for Rudyard Kipling, who strongly disapproved of the book, Lawrence's first readers were impressed and urged him to publish. He procrastinated, protesting that the book was wretched and unworthy. Finally, at the end of 1923 and under pressure, he relented and agreed to a small private edition of 400 copies, finely printed, elegantly bound, richly illustrated and very expensive. Artists (non-Academicians at Lawrence's insistence) were commissioned and he proceeded to make cuts and revisions to the text. The costs soon ran out of control and he had to settle a bill that finally totalled £13,000, of which £7,000 was borrowed. Lawrence agreed to undertake an abridgement, and *Revolt in the Desert* was published by Jonathan Cape and serialised in the *Daily Telegraph*.

There was no question of publication for *The Mint*, although Edward Garnett, Lawrence's friend and editorial adviser to Jonathan Cape, wanted to produce a bowdlerised edition. Trenchard, fearful of the harm the book would do to the RAF, successfully persuaded Lawrence to postpone its appearance until 1950. Cape were fended off with an absurd demand for a £1 million advance and Lawrence's anxieties about a pirated American edition were dispelled by a legal stratagem: a run of fifty copies of *The Mint* was printed, of which ten were offered for sale at a wildly prohibitive price. In Britain and in the United States a number of typescript copies circulated among Lawrence's circle.

Underlying these elaborate procedures, which incidentally stimulated much press curiosity, were Lawrence's recurrent misgivings about his talents as a writer. He was also deeply apprehensive at having revealed so much of his inner nature and conflicts in the *Seven Pillars*. 'It is not for present publication,' he told Gilbert Clayton in August 1922, 'partly because it's too human a document for me to disclose, partly because of the personalities, partly because it is not good enough to fit my conceit of myself. The last is a weak point, but the first in my mind: though it's difficult to judge one's own work.'[2] Would Lawrence's ambitions outstrip his talents and the gap be exposed by general publication? The question tormented him throughout the six years he took to complete the *Seven Pillars*. 'Hitherto,' he told Edward Garnett, 'I've always managed, usually without trying my hardest, to do anything I wanted in life: and it has bumped me down, rather, to have gone wrong in this thing, after three or four years of top-effort.'

It seemed worth the effort since Lawrence knew that 'The story I have to tell is one of the most splendid ever given a man for writing,' but he dreaded that it might prove 'too big' for him. He wanted to be more than a narrator of an exciting tale; he wished to stamp the book with his own personality and produce a psychological epic of one man at war, both with himself and with his country's foes. Furthermore, this saga had to demonstrate the author's accomplishments as an artist with language. Somehow he wanted to emulate his beloved Malory, who 'passed all his stuff through the mill of his own personality, and gave us a miracle of goodness'.[3] In the end, the *Seven Pillars* would stand comparison with the author's chosen models, Melville's *Moby Dick*, Rabelais' *Pantagruel* and Nietzsche's *Thus Spake Zarathustra*.

Another guide was Doughty: Lawrence admired him as a stylist, regarding his *Travels in Arabia Deserta* (published in 1888) as an artistic triumph and a literary classic. He had been introduced to the man and his book before his first journey to the Middle East in 1909 and, during the war, *Travels in Arabia Deserta* had been used as a handbook by the Arab Bureau. In 1919 Lawrence persuaded Jonathan Cape to reprint the book, for which he wrote an introduction, and he unsuccessfully asked Arthur Balfour to obtain a government pension for Doughty. Lawrence had much in common with him: both men aspired to be poets, cherished ambitions to write a literary epic and were obsessed with the form and structure of language. Trained as a geologist, Doughty had wanted to penetrate the deepest strata of language laid down by the Anglo-Saxons and Chaucer and adapt their usages to write an epic. Despising the language of his Victorian contemporaries, Doughty followed his quest in the wastes of Arabia and *Travels in Arabia Deserta* was the outcome.

Lawrence shared Doughty's regrets about the direction taken by English prose. Reviewing the works of W.H.Hudson in the *Spectator* for 20 August 1928, he remarked that the Elizabethans had crippled Malory's prose with dependent clauses, but he praised the 'limpidity and simpleness' of Bunyan, Swift and Defoe, all inheritors of the older tradition. Lawrence was fascinated and frightened by the demands of creative writing. He desperately wanted to find a style which was his own and which would convey the reality of his experience; he wished to evolve, like his heroes Malory and Doughty, the words and rhythms which would make his desert saga a masterpiece.

Lawrence craved success. In February 1920 he told General Murray that, while the *Seven Pillars* was 'unfit for publication', it was a long and often exciting story and 'would enjoy success' when offered to the public. Moreover viewed as pure history, he believed his version of what had happened in the Middle East 'will probably last a long time, and influence other accounts in the future'. This was what he had intended in 1919 when he set down his first draft. His mood had been sour after what he considered to be the betrayal of the Arabs by the Allies, so much of what he wrote was polemical propaganda which exposed official chicanery and his unwilling part in it. This element remains in muted form in the 1922 and 1925 versions.

Yet it was as literature, not as history, that Lawrence wanted his work to be assessed. Shortly before his death, he told Robert Graves, 'My aim was to create intangible things' and he felt he had succeeded. 'I know that it's a good book: in the sense that it's better than most which have been written lately,' he added rather lamely. As ever, his confidence in his abilities as an artist was fragile.

Feelings of confidence and inadequacy ebb and flow through his letters from the moment he began writing the *Seven Pillars* until his death. This equivocation made life very hard for those he had chosen as critics, since Lawrence's artistic self was inextricably bound up with Lawrence the human being determined to achieve perfection in everything he set his hand to. After a conversation at All Souls towards the end of 1919, L.P.Hartley felt sure that only a masterpiece could satisfy his pretensions.[4] This was so, but Lawrence had no way of knowing whether what he had written was a masterpiece. Mrs Bernard Shaw, whose husband had been sent a copy of the 1922 edition of the *Seven Pillars* together with a sycophantic request for criticism, was puzzled by Lawrence's diffidence. 'If you don't know it is a "great book", what is the use of anyone telling you so?' she asked. Then and later Lawrence desperately needed the assurance of those he thought fit to judge his work. He told an admiring Siegfried Sassoon that when he had completed the *Seven Pillars* he had been crushed by a sense of failure.

Lawrence's approach to Sassoon was a reminder of the high store he set by poetry and the judgements of poets, whom he considered consummate artists with words. There was, Robert Graves believed, a boundary between poetry and prose which Lawrence, the worshipper of poets, would have liked to cross. Such a trespass would have angered Graves, who once wrote, 'Anything that wanders between in an ambitious way and boasts about artistry and style makes me sick.' It was an area where he and Lawrence could not agree. 'The spavined team of T.E.'s literary friends' and his preference for the 'second rate' which embraced D.H.Lawrence and W.H.Auden nauseated Graves.[5] When Lawrence sought respect, criticism and friendship from other writers he was intruding on a world riven by faction, jealousy and backbiting.

It was natural for a writer, particularly one so ambitious as Lawrence, to seek out the company of men and women of letters. Conversations with poets, novelists and professional critics offered him the means to learn about the techniques of writing and the yardsticks needed to measure his own work. So, from the moment he returned to London in October 1918, he made it his business to chase and exploit contacts in the world of *belles lettres*. Excursions into Bohemia were a novel and not uncongenial task for a man whose previous society had been confined to those by and large his intellectual inferiors. His wartime experiences had taught him that for fighting men 'conduct is a very grave matter', whereas creative artists spurned rules and largely tolerated what he called 'human oddness'.

He soon built up a wide and eclectic circle. His first base was All Souls College, Oxford, where he encountered Ezra Pound and Robert Graves. He had enthused over Pound's verse before the war (he may have encouraged his brother Will to invite Pound to talk at St John's in 1913), and had been reading Graves's poetry since 1917. Graves became Lawrence's intimate friend, poetic mentor (he helped him write the dedicatory verse 'To S.A.' for the *Seven Pillars*) and sexual confidant. Graves also gave him the chance to play the patron since, after Graves's Boar's Hill shop went bankrupt in 1922, Lawrence gave him £50 and two chapters from the *Seven Pillars* which were sold to an American magazine for £800. Lawrence was instrumental in getting Graves a lectureship in English at Cairo University and assisted him in preparing his biography *T.E. Lawrence and the Arabs*.

Through Edward ('Eddie') Marsh, Churchill's Private Secretary and patron of the Georgian poets, Lawrence met Thomas Hardy and Siegfried Sassoon, who on first acquaintance could not believe he really was a colonel. By the end of 1922, he was on close terms with Bernard Shaw, E.M.Forster and John Buchan.

Unlike other prominent literary figures, Lawrence avoided attachment to a specific group. While other writers banded together, frequented various haunts in central London or joined circles such as the Bloomsbury set, Lawrence remained, as ever, a freelance. As Christopher Caudwell observed, although he was part of contemporary 'bourgeois culture', Lawrence was an individual who prized his individuality and shunned labels. So, while he was admired by the younger generation of writers, such as Auden and Isherwood, his political neutrality kept him outside their coterie. The left held no attractions for him, nor did he give any attention to the social and economic problems of his own country, which increasingly occupied the thoughts of other contemporary writers.

In essence, Lawrence was a courtier in the 'Palace of Art' where those around him were a source of purely literary ideas and sometimes an appreciative audience. 'All his life he remained an Oxford don,' remarked Isherwood, who noticed his addiction to talking 'shop' and his severity towards those whose ignorance he uncovered. At gatherings of intellectual equals, his moods were unpredictable; he was by turns humble, arrogant or good-humoured. Noël Coward thought him an 'inverted show-off' who could talk 'the most inconceivable balls', a judgement which is supported by an extract from Lawrence's review of Philip Guedalla's *A Man of Letters*.[6]

> Between page 1 and page 42 I could find no return for my labour; but the third line of page 42 was made up of the single word 'No'. Succinct, as a judgement, everybody will agree: but also it was sufficient and final and witty and yet tender.

Yet, as Coward realised, 'his legend was too strong to be gainsaid and I, being a celebrity snob, crushed down my wicked suspicions. He was charming to me anyhow.'[7]

From August 1922, when he first enlisted in the RAF, Lawrence became an intermittent exile from the society of artists and writers. He was a bird of passage who came and went as he pleased, calling unexpectedly on his friends and then leaving suddenly and without explanation. He was fortunate to have friends who accepted his irregularities without question or complaint.

Late in 1923, he found himself a new base, a dilapidated cottage at Cloud's Hill, Dorset, conveniently close to Bovington, where he was then stationed, and to Thomas Hardy's house at Max Gate, where he was a frequent visitor from April 1924 onwards. At first, he rented the cottage from a neighbouring squire, Henry Frampton, who by chance was a distant kinsman to his father. In 1929 he bought the property for £450 and four years later he undertook major improvements which included the provision of running water, a boiler and an iron bath. At Cloud's Hill there were uncomfortable reminders of the self-inflicted Spartan regime of Lawrence's youth and wartime camp life. Alcohol was banned and the cuisine was minimalist, with guests being offered tins of preserved meat and can openers. But black pottery cups were available for Lawrence's own brand of China tea and there was a gramophone.

Exile, whether at Cloud's Hill or on various provincial and Indian airfields, never left Lawrence in complete isolation from the literary world. He was a prolific letter-writer, although he thought correspondence a poor substitute for conversation. He distrusted accomplished letters which were the products of careful revision, so his were often a flow of uninterrupted consciousness, although he admitted that they aspired to literary merit. They 'try very hard to be good', but he doubted whether they or, for that matter, anyone else's letters could ever be 'an art form'. His own output of correspondence far exceeded his production of what he would have regarded as 'art forms' and, probably more than the *Seven Pillars* or *The Mint*, they later attracted readers keen to discover what sort of man Lawrence really was.

Neither the *Seven Pillars* nor *The Mint* fits comfortably into any literary category, although Lawrence never saw himself as an experimental writer. They cannot be considered fiction, since each is rooted in what the author had seen, heard and done. To this extent, they are autobiographical fragments, which is how Lawrence once described *The Mint*, but in neither does he reveal anything about his origins, upbringing or background. The *Seven Pillars* contains much history, which many readers have understandably accepted as authentic. 'The book leaves from first to last an impression of absolute truth,' concluded Hogarth, and such an endorsement from one who, like Lawrence, was at the heart of events has naturally led to the *Seven Pillars* being considered as an objective and exact historical record.

This it was not. Rather, what Lawrence wrote was closer in spirit to the history he had absorbed as a boy, that found in medieval chivalric chronicles where authors, such as Froissart, adapted and embellished the raw material of men and events.

When Lawrence had first encountered medieval romances, he had dreamed of producing them in beautifully printed editions full of rich illustrations. His ambition was fulfilled by the subscribers' edition of the *Seven Pillars*. Decorative initial letters open paragraphs; woodcuts and pen-and-ink drawings are scattered through the text as chapter tailpieces and, in the manner of a medieval illuminated manuscript, there are full-page coloured pictures. While his overall intent was to create a book which would combine the richness of medieval illumination with the elegance of Renaissance printing, Lawrence deliberately chose modern artists such as Paul Nash, Eric Kennington and William Roberts as illustrators. The result is a book true to traditions of good printing and page design which is ornamented with abstract and cubist images, reminders that the subject and author are contemporary.

The abstract pieces complement metaphysical passages. Reading them, Siegfried Sassoon felt convinced that their author owned 'one of the most intensely real minds of my experience'. Other critics concurred; Lawrence was a man of action and philosopher who seemed able to draw a universal significance from what he had done and discovered about himself. As he admitted, Nietzsche's *Thus Spake Zarathustra* had been his philosophical guide when he had been writing the *Seven Pillars*.

Lawrence had much in common with his mentor. Both men, after a conventionally pious upbringing, had lost faith in God and a moral system based upon Christianity. Lawrence and Nietzsche were therefore forced to justify existence in purely human terms. Each replaced 'I will' for 'Thou shalt' as the mainspring of values and behaviour. In the dedicatory verse, Lawrence affirmed the power of his will, 'I drew these tides of men into my hands and wrote my will across the sky in stars'. Later, in less assured mood, he confessed that this remarkable exercise had been accidental. 'Always I grew to dominate those things into which I had drifted, but in none of them did I voluntary engage.'

Although Sassoon regarded him as an 'infallible superman', Lawrence admitted that the costs of serving his will were unbearably heavy. At times he yearned to escape from a regime of hunger, isolation, extremes of temperature and 'the beastliness of living among the Arabs', but 'there lurked always that Will uneasily waiting to burst out.' It alone was the 'sure guide' along the path which ascended 'from purpose to achievement'.

Such passages of introspection and their outcome, Lawrence's urge for abasement, made H.G.Wells categorise the *Seven Pillars* as a 'human document', a judgement the author endorsed. So too did Laurence Durrell, although he had nothing but contempt for the human being who emerged from the pages of an otherwise 'great book'. As its story unfolded, Lawrence was diminished: 'He seemed nothing but a tedious adolescent applying the thumbscrews of denial to himself. Yes, a sort of nasty child. There's not one healthy straightforward emotion or conviction in the whole thing.'[8]

All too aware of his own suffering, the Lawrence of the *Seven Pillars* seemed unmoved by that which he had helped to create. He appears unconcerned when faced with violent death. He is an accessory to the murder of Turkish POWs; an onlooker during other acts of brutality; he kills his servant Farraj to spare him a lingering death; and he is the executioner of Hamed the Moor, whom he shoots to forestall a blood feud. Conventional law and morality are suspended by war, but Lawrence appears untroubled by their absence. 'Blood was always on our hands: we were licensed to it,' he wrote, and the circumstances of the desert war, together with the purity of his own and his followers' ideals, left no room for moral sensibility.

The humane reader, following Lawrence's stark renderings of these horrific events, may feel that, like so many others who have recollected their feelings in war, he was simply revealing its barbarism. Moral indignation is superfluous since the deeds speak for themselves. There is no need for Lawrence to intrude himself when describing such matters. Even so, one might question the innate compassion of a man who could write:

> Next a group of Austrians, officers and non-commissioned officers, appealed to me quietly in Turkish for quarter. I replied with my halting German; whereupon one, in English, begged for a doctor for his wounds. We had none: not that it mattered, for he was mortally hurt and dying.

There is a callousness here, but was it always present, or was it the product of war? The *Seven Pillars* offers no answer, since it contains no pre- or post-war portrait of Lawrence for guidance. Perhaps neither seemed necessary, for when he wrote Lawrence had in mind a limited audience, many of whom knew him intimately and could make their own judgements about how he had been changed by war. Those unable to make the comparison were disturbed by his lack of moral reaction, and wondered whether he was a spokesman for the new ruthlessness which was edging out whatever had survived of the old gentlemanly codes of war.[9]

Not that this mattered too much for Lawrence: his goal was a work of art, not a textbook of morality, strategy and politics. When he embarked on the *Seven Pillars*, he believed that in himself and his experiences he possessed raw materials equal to any available to Malory. All he needed was the technical skill to produce a masterpiece which would measure up to his own merciless standards. Having imposed his will on history, it was the turn of art. In war everything was secondary to the fulfilment of the imagined ideals of the Arab movement; afterwards he concentrated all his energies and will on the acquisition of literary skills and techniques.

One result of this single-minded pursuit of style is mannerism – self-conscious, exhibitionist prose – and there is plenty of that in the *Seven Pillars*. While writing about himself and the triumph of his own will, Lawrence was also telling the story of real men and events. The consequent blend of high style, imagination and reality creates a work which is aesthetically satisfying, but deceptive. This was understood by Professor Elie Kedourie, who in 1977 chose the *Seven Pillars* as the most overrated book of the century.

> As history it is riddled with falsehoods, while as literature it is spoilt by high-flown conceits and modish preciosities. Lastly, in making popular and attractive the confusion between the public world of politics and the private dramas of the self, I judge it to be profoundly corrupting.[10]

None of this can be denied. And yet when, in July 1935 and less than eight weeks after Lawrence's death, the *Seven Pillars* went on public sale it became a bestseller and has remained in print ever since. Many, perhaps most, readers discovered and enjoyed an adventure story set in an exotic land and crammed with exciting incidents, all vividly recorded. There was also the challenge of a puzzle since the book could be taken as a coded document about an enigmatic man with clues as to the real Lawrence and plenty of false trails.

Lawrence thought *The Mint* was a better book than the *Seven Pillars*, although, characteristically, he had second thoughts. He started it at a time when he was disappointed with the *Seven Pillars* and he hoped that a new and totally different subject, service life, might redeem him as an artist. When he finished writing he thought it the equivalent to a second volume of his life, even though, as he warned E.M.Forster, it was 'A bit of a come down' after the first. Packed with 'crude, unsparing, faithful stuff; very metallic and uncomfortable', *The Mint* was saved by its 'restraint, and dignity, and form and craftsmanship'. In other words, Lawrence felt he had at last achieved a technical masterpiece.

Before enlistment at the end of August 1922, Lawrence knew nothing of how ordinary servicemen lived beyond what he had observed at a distance during the war. Within two months he had begun to compile notes at night in his barrack hut, writing under a blanket and apparently unnoticed by his colleagues. 'Artlessly photographic' was how he described the result, which was a prose equivalent of *cinéma vérité*, an unedited sequence of scenes and voices. Its realism distressed Eddie Marsh, who after reading it complained of having been 'battered and oppressed by the monstrous thudding hailstorm of *gros mots*' (for example 'fuck'). Anyone who has undergone National Service or worked on a factory floor or building site will not be surprised by the relentless flow of harsh sexual language but, for many of Lawrence's circle who read *The Mint*, such places and what passed there were a mystery.

The Mint is the RAF depot at Uxbridge in west London where Lawrence and his brother recruits are the ore, melted down and refined in the furnace of training to emerge die-stamped as RAF personnel. This transformation from civilian to serviceman is minutely detailed in the first two parts of the book. The last takes up the adventures of one newly minted coin, Lawrence, when in 1925 he is posted to the officers' training college at Cranwell.

By the time Lawrence finally completed his story in 1928 he regretted the harshness of his first impressions of the RAF, an institution he had since learned to love and where he now enjoyed contentment. His loyalty to the force and to its visionary father-figure, Trenchard, ruled out immediate publication. A bowdlerised version appeared in 1955 ('shit cart' became 'garbage cart') and an unexpurgated one in 1973, by when the British public was all too familiar with words which twenty years before had been thought to be unprintable.

The Mint is Lawrence's last major essay as a writer. When he had put the final touches to the typescript, he felt he had no more to say. There were no experiences left for him to exploit, although other subjects briefly presented themselves only to be abandoned. One was the possibility of doing something on his career between 1918 and 1922 which he called his 'dog fight in Downing Street'.

Lawrence thought most seriously about writing a biography of Sir Roger Casement, the Irish nationalist who had been tried, found guilty and hanged for treason in 1916 after his failed attempts to muster an Irish Legion from

Irish POWs in Germany and to ship arms to Sinn Fein. 'As I see it,' Lawrence told Mrs Bernard Shaw in December 1934, 'his was a heroic nature I should like to write upon subtly, so that his enemies would think I was with them till they had finished my book and rose from reading it to call him the hero. He had the appeal of a broken archangel.' What stood in Lawrence's way was lack of access to Casement's diary in which he had recorded a string of homosexual encounters. The diary had been circulated by British intelligence to deflect efforts to secure Casement a reprieve, but Lawrence believed only a Labour Prime Minister would release it to the public. He was happy to wait. 'I am only 46, able, probably to wait for years: and very determined to make England ashamed of itself if I can.'

With the *Seven Pillars* and *The Mint* Lawrence achieved his ambition to be recognised as an accomplished stylist. Other men of letters, both apprentices and masters, were sufficiently impressed to seek his opinion on their own work. Evelyn Wrench, on becoming editor of the *Spectator* in 1927, invited Lawrence to review books, which he did for eight months under the initials 'CD', which stood for 'Colin Dale', a name based on the last Underground station he had used before his departure to India. Since Lawrence was utterly preoccupied by style, his pieces were one-dimensional. For his first assignment he covered D.H.Lawrence's novels and concentrated heavily on Lawrence's language. 'He is a poet, and a thinker, a man of plane-modulation of the envelope of flesh,' he concluded, without even a hint of how these qualities were reflected in the treatment of human emotions and behaviour. This was understandable since, in some ways, D.H.Lawrence was writing about worlds and human relationships which were beyond his ken. After reading *Lady Chatterley's Lover,* he commented to Eddie Marsh, 'Surely the sex business isn't worth all this fuss. ... I've only met a handful of people who care a biscuit for it.'

In considering material presented to him for consideration by others, including the playwright Noël Coward and the poet Maurice Baring, Lawrence showed himself a sensitive and constructive critic. By contrast, many of the literary judgements scattered through his correspondence were jejune stuff, no more than clever undergraduate fatuity. Richard Aldington and W.B.Yeats were 'no good', Pepys 'a poor earth-bound lack-lustre worm', and Disraeli's novels 'nearly as sad stuff as Chesterton's'. Belloc was castigated for having written for money ('Caddish I call it') and women authors were summarily dismissed in a letter of 1924 to Sydney Cockerell: 'All the women who ever wrote original stuff could have been strangled at birth, and the history of English literature (and my bookshelves) would be unchanged.'

This may have been pure mischievousness coupled with the petulant partisanship which Lawrence quickly picked up from his new literary companions, but behind it lay his continuing urge to intrude his inner self into areas where dispassion was vital. This had always been his way; his private animosity to women as a species was so overwhelming that it was impossible for him to assess them as creative writers. The compass of his knowledge and his cleverness could not hide what others recognised as a symptom of intellectual immaturity. Bernard Shaw detected this, as did Isherwood, who discerned an 'adolescent mind' behind Lawrence's brilliance.

IV

GENTLEMAN RANKER, 1922–1935

O N 28 August 1922, Lawrence presented himself at the RAF recruiting office in Henrietta Street near Covent Garden. According to *The Mint*, he looked like a man for whom enlistment was a final resort, since his suit was frayed and his shoes worn out. He was nervous to the point where he had to hurry off to a nearby public lavatory where he relieved himself and his fears. Inside the office he was received by Captain W.E.Johns, the future author of the Biggles adventure yarns who, alerted by a vigilant NCO, became suspicious. The odd-looking recruit was sent off to fetch some references while enquiries were made about him at the Registry of Births, Deaths and Marriages in Somerset House. Here it was discovered the Lawrence's *nom de guerre*, John Hume Ross, was bogus.

In the meantime, he had reappeared, accompanied by an Air Ministry messenger carrying an order for his immediate enlistment signed by Air Vice-Marshal Sir Oliver Swann. Johns was still uneasy and asked the advice of his immediate superior, who told him to do as he was ordered. 'For heaven's sake, watch your step. This man is Lawrence of Arabia. Get him into the Force or you'll get your bowler hat.' Johns obeyed, but there was more trouble when two doctors turned down Lawrence as unfit. A third was less scrupulous and Lawrence, certified fit for his new duties, was packed off to the training depot at Uxbridge where Johns had already alerted the officer in charge of recruit reception that Lawrence of Arabia was on his way.

Nothing of this hugger-mugger affair appears in *The Mint*, where

Lawrence's passage from civilian to serviceman passes smoothly. So it would have done had the orders of Air Marshal Sir Hugh Trenchard, the Chief of Air Staff, been properly carried out. Detailed arrangements for Lawrence's induction had been left to his assistant Swann, but his instructions had been mislaid in Henrietta Street. This had caused embarrassment and Lawrence later apologised to Swann for his physical debility. 'If I'd known I was such a wreck,' he wrote, 'I'd have gone off and recovered.'

The reasons for this elaborate charade were complex. Lawrence had first openly admitted an urge to join the RAF in March 1921 when he raised the matter informally with Trenchard during the Cairo conference.[1] The exchange had been brief and inconclusive:

> 'I'd like to join this air force of yours some day.'
> 'And I'd be glad to have you.'
> 'Even as a ranker.'
> 'Certainly not. As an officer or nothing.'

There seemed no obvious explanation for this request, which Trenchard may have seen as a piece of typical Lawrentian whimsy. Certainly at Cairo and after, Lawrence was under Trenchard's spell, sharing his dreams for the future of the RAF. During conference sessions, he argued strongly for Trenchard's scheme of air control in Jordan and Iraq and he was fascinated by plans for trans-desert imperial air routes.

Lawrence's intoxication with the air was part of a wider public excitement about the possibilities of aviation, both as a means of fast, efficient transport and as an instrument of war. During the 1920s and 1930s powered flight occupied a prominent place in the public consciousness in the same way as space travel would a generation later. For Lawrence, the conquest of the air was an exhilarating challenge and one which he wished to respond to, but in an unexpected way. As master and guide of the Arab movement he had, to use his own metaphor, ridden the crest of a wave. Now he wished to be a drop of water within another wave, a vital but submerged element within what seemed to him another great surge of history. Authority over men and affairs no longer attracted him since it brought unbearable burdens of responsibility and disappointment. Better, he thought, to be a cog in a machine.

Joining in the conquest of the air as an ordinary mechanic also satisfied that strong vein of evangelicalism instilled into Lawrence as a child. He would not only tend the machines, but use his influence to animate his fellow rankers with a sense of pride in their duties. While Trenchard led from the top, Lawrence would enthuse from below those who performed what he called their 'inarticulate duty'. 'You can see better at the bottom of the ladder than at the top,' he remarked to one of his commanding officers. Early in 1935, he expanded on his philosophy to Robert Graves: 'It is the airmen, the mechanics, who are overcoming the air.... The genius raids, but the common people occupy and possess.' In the same letter he expressed satisfaction that he had done something to make them aware of the value of their work and future inheritance.

Lawrence never bothered to learn to fly. He had enjoyed being flown during the war and continued to make trips; his flight from Miramshah to Karachi at the end of 1928 had been some compensation for expulsion from India and a year later he flew in a dual-control Moth. His need for risk and speed was satisfied by his succession of high-power Brough motorbikes – 'Boanerges' and 'Georges I to VII' – which he rode throughout the 1920s and 1930s, often at great speed. 'Voluntary danger' as he called it, such as racing a Bentley along the serpentine country roads of south-western England, gave him a 'melancholy joy' compounded of the knowledge that his life was in jeopardy. Friends noticed that he never liked the stability of the motor car.

Gadgetry had always fascinated Lawrence and he rightly thought himself a good mechanic. Service to and mastery of machines was for him part of the essence of maleness. 'No woman, I believe, can understand a mechanic's happiness in serving his bits and pieces,' he told Robert Graves, adding that joining the world of men so employed was a modern form of monastic withdrawal. This admission suggests that Lawrence was yearning for those all-male brotherhoods he had shared during his childhood and youth. Those who devotedly tended machines inhabited a separate world.

Lawrence always recognised that service as a craftsman in the RAF was a form of social degradation: he never forgot that he had chosen to live among those whom he considered his inferiors. Once he wrote, 'I backed out of the race, and sat down among people who were not racing,' and often he elaborated on what, for such correspondents as Mrs Bernard Shaw and Lionel Curtis, were the coarse horrors of day-to-day working-class existence. Yet throughout his years as a ranker, Lawrence alternated the roughness of the barrack hut with the refinement of the college high table or the country-house party. It could be confusing; once at Miramshah in 1928, he was overcome with anxiety about whether he would remember which knife and fork he should use when dining as a guest at the mess of the Guides Cavalry. Such niceties never troubled his fellow aircraftmen.

The chasm which separated All Souls, the Colonial Office and the literary salons of the 1920s from the barrack huts filled with what Lawrence described as 'a cross section of unemployed England' was vast, perhaps as wide as that which divided the Englishman from the Beduin. The war fought in the trenches had whittled away some of the barriers which, before

1914, had cut off the upper and middle from the working classes. Some of Lawrence's friends hoped that they could continue this process: Robert Graves became a Labour councillor and, like Edmund Blunden, joined a village cricket team. Others, whom Lawrence had known during the war, went further: Sir Wyndham Deedes gave up a post-war diplomatic career to settle in Bethnal Green, where he became a Labour councillor working tirelessly for the poor, and Colonels Wedgwood and L'e Malone became radical Labour MPs.

E.M.Forster thought that, like them, Lawrence may have 'wanted to get in touch with people' and share their life and work.[2] There may have been an element too of returning to his roots, for his mother had come from the artisanal class. In making this journey, he took with him the intellectual baggage which he had collected in his early life and a strong urge to share it with those who might be interested. While his mother and elder brother Robert undertook missionary work in China, Lawrence went among the unenlightened in the barracks spreading a cultural gospel. His proselytising was often fruitful. In August 1928 he told Mrs Bernard Shaw how gratifying it was to listen to 'People who belong to the News of the World class discuss Beethoven and Mozart at meals.'

Such exchanges were commoner at Cloud's Hill, where Lawrence had set up a small salon to which converts from the Tank Corps at Bovington and RAF friends came to relax, read literature and listen to classical music on the gramophone. Lawrence had grown to love fine music late in life and he once told Meinertzhagen that listening to it was gradually softening the 'hard' side of his nature. His tastes were romantic and melodic: Holst's suite, 'The Planets', in particular the Saturn movement, was an early favourite and later he developed a profound admiration for the music of Elgar. In December 1933 he wrote to the composer:

> This is from my cottage and we have just been playing your 2nd Symphony. Three of us, a sailor, a Tank Corps soldier, and myself. So there are all the Services present: and we agreed that you must be written to and told (if you are well enough to be bothered) that this Symphony gets further under our skins than anything else in the record library at Clouds Hill. We have the Violin Concerto, too; so that says quite a lot. Generally we play the Symphony last of all, towards the middle of the night, because nothing comes off very well after it.

Lawrence discovered that men whose education had been truncated and who lived by manual labour possessed sensitivity and responded to it in others. There were setbacks. On leaving the Drigh Road depot at Karachi, he bequeathed his collection of classical records to his fellow aircraftmen who, soon after, exchanged them for an officer's Sophie Tucker discs.

This news must have disheartened Lawrence, who detested the alien dishar-monies of jazz.

Mixing two worlds gave Lawrence amusement at the expense of others. His appearance in khaki alongside the Hardys at Glastonbury prompted a Frenchwoman to comment, 'Very democratic aren't we.' Lawrence answered in French, 'Sorry, Mr Hardy doesn't understand French. May I offer myself as an interpreter?' Playing the same game in reverse, Lawrence irritated Robert Graves by saying he had become a 'simple fitter' who read *Tit Bits* and *Happy Magazine* and by shamming ignorance of simple academic matters. These remarks, and what Graves called Lawrence's 'garage English', may have been symptoms of a mutual disenchantment during the early 1930s. It owed much to Lawrence's hostility towards Graves's mistress, the poet Laura Riding, whom he considered an 'intellectual freak' and whose verses displeased him.[3]

Graves, like many of Lawrence's friends, found his enlistment inexplic-able, not least because he seemed to have exchanged a familiar and comfort-able world for one which was hostile and incommodious. The sections of *The Mint* which cover the two months of his induction at Uxbridge are a chronicle of shock and disillusionment. The aspirant pioneers of the air are overwhelmed by a regime of menial chores and drill supervised by hectoring officers and NCOs. None of this seemed necessary or useful for men destined to serve machines.

When, in January 1922, he had renewed his appeal to Trenchard for permission to join as a ranker, Lawrence insisted that the lives of his fellow aircraftmen would provide the raw material for a projected book. He out-lined his literary ambitions and explained that they had not been achieved by the *Seven Pillars*, but might be realised through the RAF. The demands of the Colonial Office were too great to give Lawrence the time he needed to write and routine administration bored him.

Trenchard liked and understood Lawrence. 'He was the sort of man', Trenchard recollected, 'who, on entering a roomful of people, would have contrived to be sick on the spot had everyone stood up to applaud him. Yet if, on entering the same room, nobody stirred or showed the faintest sign of recognition, Lawrence might well have reacted by standing on his head.'[4] After much cajolery and some histrionics on Lawrence's side, Tren-chard relented. (During one meeting at Trenchard's house, when Lawrence threatened suicide, the Air Marshal riposted, 'All right, but please go into the garden. I don't want my carpets ruined.') Churchill agreed, so too did Sir Frederick Guest, the Secretary for Air, although his successor Sir Samuel Hoare was kept in ignorance of the plot.

One further factor may have influenced Lawrence and possibly swayed his fellow conspirators. As mentioned earlier, he was being menaced by an underworld figure, Jack Bilbo, who was considering making public Lawrence's attendance at flagellation parties in Chelsea. In May 1922, Lawrence took steps to hire John Bruce, an eighteen-year-old Scot from Aberdeen, who was retained for £3 a week without any clear indication of what his duties might be. This is what Bruce recalled over forty years later and his memory for dates has been called into question. What is beyond doubt is that on 19 March 1923 Lawrence signed on for seven years in the Royal Tank Corps as a private soldier and Bruce, also lately enlisted, joined him in Hut F12 at Bovington camp. According to Bruce, he had been in contact with Lawrence during January and February and had joined up at his suggestion. Within a month of their arrival at Bovington, Lawrence had asked Bruce to perform the first of many ritual beatings.[5]

If, as seems possible, during 1922 Lawrence could have become connected with a homosexual scandal (in an approach to the Admiralty for a store-keeper's job, he had suggested a foreign posting), this would have had grave repercussions for his high-ranking friends and provoked ridicule abroad. Unlike Oscar Wilde some twenty-five years before, Lawrence was an admired and respected national hero whose fall from grace would discompose the establishment. The beatings delivered by Bruce indicate that he was unable to break completely with this addiction. How much of this was known to those in authority is not clear, but if even a hint of it had come their way, it would have been a good reason not to object too strongly to Lawrence's strange urge for anonymity within the armed services.

Two days after Christmas 1922, Lawrence's cover was blown by the *Daily Express* under the headline '"Uncrowned King" as Private Soldier'. His identity had been known to many of his colleagues since his arrival at Uxbridge, but they had shown discretion and, when Farnborough camp was swamped with pressmen, did what they could to fend them off. Lawrence rightly believed that he had been betrayed by an officer who had been paid for his tip. The publicity and revelation of how he had been admitted to the service embarrassed the Air Ministry and left Hoare with no choice but to insist on his immediate discharge.

Lawrence was distraught. Having survived the unwelcome and, for him, pointless regime of drill and bull at Uxbridge, he was looking forward to his new duties as part of the photography unit at Farnborough. The cocoon of service life suited him and he was furious at being forced to shed it. In desperation he appealed to the War Office, where the Adjutant-General, Sir Philip Chetwode, who had served with him in the Middle East, permitted him to join the Royal Tanks Corps under the name T.E.Shaw.

On acceptance into the army, Lawrence had been promised that, if he conducted himself properly, a transfer to the RAF might be sanctioned later. Determined to accelerate this process and disturbed by the harshness of his new environment, Lawrence was soon writing to his influential friends with accounts of his misfortunes. Between March and June 1923 Lionel Curtis, Fellow of All Souls, received a series of baleful letters in which Lawrence outlined the physical and mental horrors of life in Hut F12.[6]

As he told Robert Graves, he had now struck 'bedrock' among the lumpenproletariat. When he remarked to one of his new companions, tactlessly perhaps, that he was now with men who instinctively hurled stones at cats, he got the reply, 'What do you throw?' For Lawrence the nightly bedtime chatter about sex was excruciating. 'Bollocks' and 'twats' were the staple of conversation before lights out and he was nauseated by its baseness. He may also have felt utterly excluded; five years later, he wrote to Robert Graves, 'about fucking ... I haven't ever and don't much want to.'[7] As described in Hut F12, or for that matter in RAF huts, it can hardly have seemed pleasurable.

In despair, Lawrence was forced to admit that he could never find it in himself to deploy his talents for 'moulding men and things' on such unresponsive clay as he found at Bovington. There was a 'moral difference' between the inhabitants of what he called a 'Rowton House [doss-house] without cubicles' and the men he had briefly encountered in the RAF. Yet for all this, his life at Bovington was not irredeemably bleak.

He still had the means of escape to a more agreeable milieu. He had obtained and renovated the cottage at Cloud's Hill where he spent every weekend and two or three evenings each week. He gathered there a handful of rankers who were susceptible to enlightenment and with whom he could discuss art, literature and music. His motorbike gave him swift access to his new friends, the Hardys, with whom he regularly took tea on Sunday afternoons. One fellow ranker noticed that Lawrence seemed to enjoy a somewhat charmed life in camp. He avoided parades with impunity (excused perhaps on account of his duties as a Quartermaster's clerk in charge of recruits' clothing and equipment), managed to secure an abundance of leave passes, had free access to the civilian canteen and had his hut chores magically undertaken by others, presumably by Bruce.[8]

Lawrence, or 'Broughie Shaw' as he was nicknamed, was well liked. His past came to be known, but it was his Brough Superior bike which drew admiration from men for whom it represented two years' pay. He was, one recalled after his death, 'a real gentleman,' generous with his time and sometimes with his cash. At Bovington, he discovered that a sergeant who had fractured his ankle had received inadequate treatment. 'The MO's do not always do the best for their non-commissioned patients,' he told Mrs Bernard Shaw, and asked her to procure an appointment in Harley Street for the man for which he would discreetly foot the bill. His openhandedness extended to buying extra provisions for his mates; once an extensive larder of jam, tinned milk, fruit salad, and cheeses turned up at Bovington, bought by Lawrence to supplement the hut's diet. Later, when back in the RAF, he shared the contents of Fortnum and Mason's hampers sent him by Mrs Bernard Shaw.

Always Lawrence stood apart. 'He was, possibly unique,' one fellow ranker remembered; 'he neither drank, smoked, gambled, nor took any interest in women; he played no games, backed no horses, and filled in no football coupons'. Yet he commanded affection, even deference; at Bovington it was noticed that some men moderated their sexual language in his presence and did what they could to ward off prying journalists.

One reason for Lawrence's acceptance was the knowledge that he possessed power. For a while after his discovery at Farnborough, it was believed that he was a spy under orders from the Air Ministry to uncover what the other ranks thought. In fact, his behaviour revealed the opposite: Lawrence repeatedly acted as the champion of the underdogs with whom he had chosen to live and he proved a valuable ally. He had direct access to a wide range of powerful men within and outside the services with whom he was on intimate terms, and so he was well placed to vent the grievances of his fellow rankers. He complained about the regulation swagger sticks which were then part of walking-out dress, bayonets on rifles which he thought a needless encumbrance for airmen, and, with less success, for the abolition of compulsory Sunday Church Parades. And he was suspected of having been instrumental in the removal of at least one unpopular NCO.

No doubt his brother airmen were reassured by the sight of him walking with Trenchard across Farnborough golf course or by the knowledge that he could lay their grievances in person before him, Churchill or Lady Astor. He was an asset in other ways. Once when his training squad was under crude verbal assault from an NCO at Uxbridge, a voice from the ranks called to him, 'Give him a gob of your toffology.' None came, but it was heartening that 'toffology', that compound of superior knowledge and command of language which was invariably the coercive weapon of 'them', could be pressed into the service of 'us'. It was a situation which satisfied many who served alongside Lawrence and created some entertaining stories, perhaps fresh Lawrence 'legends', in which he turned the tables on authority.

One airman remembered how Lawrence, then thirty-four, had been asked by an Uxbridge NCO why he wore no war-service medal ribbons. The next day Lawrence appeared on parade with his ribbons stitched to his tunic – including presumably the immediately recognisable DSO – which discountenanced the NCO.[9] Whether or not such an incident occurred cannot be known for certain, although in *The Mint* Lawrence mentioned that he had once been questioned about what he had done in the war and claimed that he had been interned at Smyrna by the Turks for the duration.

There was genuine affection for Lawrence from many who served with him and in some cases lasting friendship. Between 1922 and 1924 he created a new circle from his RAF and RTC hutmates which frequently assembled as a kind of salon at Cloud's Hill. At Farnborough he had discovered A.E.('Jock')Chambers and the strikingly handsome R.A.M.Guy, whom he addressed as 'my rabbit' and 'Poppet' and to whom he was a benevolent patron. At the end of March 1923, he paid a Savile Row tailor £16 1s for a fine Cheviot overcoat for Guy and £33 8s for two blue cashmere suits, one for Guy, the other for himself.[10] Leaving the RAF severed Lawrence from Guy just as their friendship was deepening. In December 1923, he wrote to him, 'People aren't friends till they have said all they can say, and are able to sit together, at work or rest, hour-long without speaking. We never got quite to that, but were near it daily ... since S.A.[Salim Ahmed, that is Dahoum, died in September 1918 at Karkamis, probably from typhus] I haven't any risk of that happening.'

After Guy's transfer to the aircraft-carrier HMS *Hermes*, which was based at Plymouth, he occasionally visited Cloud's Hill, joining Lawrence's new friends from Bovington, Arthur ('Posh') Palmer and Arthur Russell. During 1924 this circle widened to include from time to time E.M.Forster, David Garnett, Robert Graves, Siegfried Sassoon and Augustus John. In spite of the consolation of this company, Lawrence continued to hanker after the RAF and early in 1925 stepped up his efforts to win over Trenchard.

These pleas to rejoin the RAF, increasingly morose and self-pitying in tone, began to trouble his friends. Bernard Shaw, who thought that 'the private soldier business is a shocking tomfoolery', wrote to the Prime Minister, Stanley Baldwin, in May 1923 and requested a state pension for Lawrence.[11] 'Lawrence is not normal in many ways,' he explained, 'and it is extraordinarily difficult to do anything for him. . . . He will not work in any harness unless this is padlocked on him. He enlisted in order to have the padlocks riveted on him.' A year later, having failed to persuade Lawrence to accept a commission and the post of official historian of the wartime RFC and RAF, Trenchard relented and promised to support his transfer to the RAF.

But he was unable to sway Sir Samuel Hoare, who remained as adamant as ever, and Lawrence's hopes were shattered. He despaired and hinted that he might take his own life. This was more than emotional blackmail since, at this time, Jock Bruce was sufficiently alarmed by his mood to secretly unload Lawrence's revolver and hide the ammunition. Later he found Lawrence with the gun in his hand searching for the cartridges and, after a scuffle, managed to disarm him.[12] Soon after, Lawrence bucked up, certain, as he told Bruce, that 'the big wheels are grinding for me, and I'll be back in the Royal Air Force soon.' This was indeed the case: Shaw and John Buchan took Lawrence's suicide threat seriously and warned Baldwin. With the publication of Lowell Thomas's book due, Lawrence was again the centre of public attention and so Baldwin, rather than risk a scandal, overrode Hoare. On 19 August, Lawrence was taken back into the RAF and posted to its officers' training college at Cranwell in Lincolnshire.

Lawrence remained in the Air Force until February 1935, the official termination of his original enlistment. There were a few storms which threatened his position. During the winter of 1928/9 the fuss about his alleged undercover work in Afghanistan forced his return to Britain. He faced further trouble during the autumn of 1929 when the new Labour Minister for Air, Lord Thomson, made disapproving noises about his behaviour during the Schneider Trophy race. The Minister was irritated by the fact that Lawrence, an ordinary airman, was on familiar terms with famous and influential public figures. He suspected, correctly, that Lawrence had a penchant for intrigue which might lead to future awkwardness. Thomson was dissuaded from sacking Lawrence, but Lawrence was ordered to cease his contacts with the likes of Lady Astor, who like many of his political friends was a Tory. The restriction, which seems never to have been rigorously enforced, lapsed after Thomson's death in 1930 in the R101 airship accident.

There was a minor squall in March 1933 when Lawrence threatened to quit the RAF after he had been shifted from duties that involved the development and testing of high-speed launches. His part in this work had been noticed by the press and, anxious to avoid publicity about secret work, his commanding officer thought it prudent to remove the main source of interest, Lawrence. Two former friends, Sir Philip Sassoon, the Under-Secretary of State for Air, and Air Marshal Sir Geoffrey Salmond, the Chief of Air Staff, intervened and Lawrence persuaded them of his special fitness to continue work on the speedboat prototypes. 'Lawrence of Arabia has decided to stay on in the Air Force' ran the official memo, and in future he would act as its technical representative touring various commercial suppliers of engines and parts.

Fast boats had become Lawrence's new passion. His interest developed quickly after March 1929 when he had been posted to the Flying Boat Squadron at Mount Batten, Plymouth. Soon after, he became a part-owner of a two-seater speedboat, *Biscuit*, which he refurbished and piloted on excursions around Plymouth Sound. What had been a private pastime was transformed into something more significant after Lawrence had been an eyewitness to the crash of an Iris III flying-boat in February 1931. Nothing could be done to prevent nine of the crew from drowning.

Lawrence was affected by what he had seen and at the inquest spitefully and unjustly blamed the plane's pilot for the accident, saying that the men were unwilling to fly with him. After this mishap he threw himself into work on the sea trials of the new fast tender, the RAF 200. He had a natural aptitude for engines, and his experience tinkering with the *Biscuit*, and a revival of his dormant sense of purposefulness made him indispensable. As in previous endeavours, he soon came to dominate those working around him by a combination of energy and single-mindedness. Even officers bowed before his knowledge and competence. One, Flight-Lieutenant Sims, remembered Lawrence at Bridlington expounding the virtues of the new, fast speedboats being tested there for towing targets.

A slight upright blue-clad figure stood high up in the bows of a boat, with one electric light turning his hair into gold. He was giving a masterly lecture on the major features of the boats. The officer was listening in rapt silence, supported by two other Air Ministry officers. Behind them stood the contractor and engineer, one or two workmen with bared heads stood hushed on each side, and a couple of odd airmen formed the rest of the congregation.[13]

The Air Ministry was now keen to exploit Lawrence's blossoming talents. Wearing his standard mufti (slacks, polo-necked sweater and hacking jacket), he was detailed to tour various civilian contractors in the Midlands as the Air Ministry's representative, discussing problems and laying down standards. The final two years of his service career were marked by a revived vitality and satisfaction in his duties; as in Arabia, he showed himself to be the brilliant amateur, able to penetrate and master a new world into which chance had thrown him. He faced the final days of his RAF life with many regrets.

Outwardly there seemed to be tranquillity and order in Lawrence's existence after 1929, although within two years of his return from India he was seeking and receiving beatings from Bruce and others, as well as other forms of 'discipline'. This pattern of behaviour appears to have continued until at least January 1935, if not beyond. And yet, those people unaware of his secret addiction portrayed him during these years as acquiring stability and apparently coming near to an accord with himself. Reading *The Golden Reign* (1940), the affectionate testament of Clare Sydney Smith, the wife of Lawrence's commanding officer at Mount Batten between 1929 and 1931, it is difficult to believe that she is writing about the man who submitted to a whipping so ferocious that it made one onlooker physically sick.

Mrs Smith's memory was of a different, almost avuncular Lawrence. When she, her husband and Lawrence had first met in Cairo in 1921 they had been equals. Eight years later this familiarity was revived, even though Lawrence, the one-time Colonial Office official, was now Wing-Commander Sydney Smith's clerk. Very quickly 'Tes', as they called him, became a frequent and welcome intruder into the Sydney Smiths' family circle of one daughter and two dogs. Lawrence joined in family occasions such as picnics, was a favourite with the dogs, and Mrs Smith was a regular passenger and sometimes pilot of *Biscuit*. Still the occupant of a serviceman's hut, where he installed his gramophone and wireless set, Lawrence's intimacy with the Smiths brought him back into more familiar social circles. With them he attended luncheon parties and moved among the local gentry.

Another acquaintance from the past, Lady Astor, was MP for Plymouth and she was anxious to cultivate the hero-turned-airman she had once met at All Souls. Something of a lion-hunter, she considered Lawrence 'a beau' and was able to draw him into her circle of the great and famous based at Cliveden. Their reintroduction had been accomplished through their mutual friends, the Shaws. While other distinguished acquaintances, such as Churchill and John Buchan, moved in and out of Lawrence's life, his link with the Shaws had remained unbroken since their first meeting in 1922.

Lawrence was always flattered by Bernard Shaw's attention, but Mrs Shaw came to mean much more to him. As their regular exchange of letters developed, she became a kind of mother-confessor, the willing and understanding recipient of a series of candid revelations about Lawrence's inner self. It was a two-way process, although Lawrence destroyed most of her letters. A few survive, such as that of May 1927, which was a response to Lawrence's earlier exposure of his feelings about his own mother. Mrs Shaw, too, admitted to a 'managing and domineering' mother and a feeling that she had inherited these unattractive qualities. She also echoed Lawrence's admission that knowledge of his own parents' union had made him certain he would never have children – 'My own home life made me firmly resolve never to be the mother of a child who might suffer as I had suffered.'

The intimacy and empathy which grew up between Mrs Shaw and Lawrence suggest that he may have seen her as a surrogate mother. After 1922 he was determined to place a distance between himself and his mother and to resist her emotional demands, a task made easier after 1925 by her prolonged absences in China as the helpmate of her missionary son Robert. Mrs Shaw's care and concern in sending Lawrence food hampers, looking after his affairs in Dorset while he was in India and, on his return, joining with her husband to give him a new Brough motorbike suggest a maternal concern for his well-being. On the other hand, the content and tone of their correspondence clearly indicate that both parties were driven by an urge to find a sympathetic listener. Neither seeks guidance, but rather each delivers autobiographical fragments which, by their nature, could not pass between kinsfolk. 'Homes are ties,' Lawrence once wrote, 'and with you I am quite free, somehow.' At other times, he had felt similarly free to unburden himself to Meinertzhagen and Robert Graves.

Clare Sydney Smith, Lady Astor and Mrs Shaw all represented 'safe' women from whom Lawrence need never have feared any demands for the sexual intimacy which so repelled him. Once, when busy on the *Biscuit*'s engines, he remarked to Clare Sydney Smith that machines needed 'constant attention like an exacting female'. Later at the very end of his mechanical career he assured Robert Graves, 'There are no women in the machines, in any machine,' which was very much in their favour. What lay behind these seemingly incompatible claims was Lawrence's knowledge that the machine possessed reassuring predictability and that he, its master, was always in control.

In the same letter to Graves, Lawrence endorsed his view that RAF life was essentially monastic. He had, by enlisting in 1922, followed a course of action which would have been more understandable and understood in the Middle Ages than in the twentieth century. Yet while an aspirant monk completely abandoned his former life and its trappings, Lawrence clung to much of what he had left behind. He never totally submitted himself to all the discipline that his new life demanded of him; rather, he lived it, according to his own terms, both as ranker and as gentleman.

V

DEATH OF A HERO

IN February 1935 Lawrence was cast adrift from the RAF. He was forty-six years old and uneasily aware that he was ageing. Past exertions, recurrent malaria and injuries from minor bike accidents had taken their toll. Harold Nicolson, who had known him during the Paris Peace Conference, met him again in August 1933 and was struck by how he had changed. 'He has become stockier and squarer. The sliding lurcher effect is gone. A bull terrier in place of a saluki.'[1]

Yet Lawrence's charisma was undiminished. On the eve of his retirement, Montagu Norman, the Governor of the Bank of England, asked Sir Francis Rennell to discover whether he might consider an appointment as the Bank's secretary. No knowledge of routine banking would be needed since the post was an administrative one, requiring what Norman believed were the 'Elizabethan' qualities of 'leadership and inspiration', qualities which Lawrence possessed in plenty. Lawrence was flattered but refused.[2]

He was in no clear mind about what he might do next. He considered several projects: the composition of an apologia to be called 'Confession of Faith'; the revival of a thirty-year-old dream to run his own press on which he could print *The Mint*; or a leisurely rediscovery of the English countryside on his bicycle. There were outside pressures as well. He was concerned about the adequacy of the country's defences against aerial attack, and Churchill and Lady Astor wanted him to join them and alert Britain to the need for rearmament. Henry Williamson wanted him as a recruit for Fascism.

On the morning of 13 May Lawrence wired Williamson to suggest a meeting. Returning on his Brough to Cloud's Hill from the post office at Bovington camp, he was thrown over the handlebars, struck the road and fractured his skull. He was taken, in a coma, to the hospital at Bovington camp, where he died without regaining consciousness six days later. The cause of death was congestion of the lungs and an autopsy revealed that, had he survived, he would have been paralysed and without the powers of reason or speech.

There were no eyewitnesses to the crash and this, coupled with the ham-fisted reaction of the authorities, created the conditions for rumour to flourish. First, all troops in Bovington camp were cautioned about the Official

Secrets Act, and the fathers of Frank Fletcher and Albert Hargreaves, two boy cyclists whom Lawrence seems to have swerved to avoid, were told to see that they did not talk to newspapermen. A pair of detectives maintained a vigil by Lawrence's bedside and other policemen were placed as a guard over Cloud's Hill, as a deterrent against headstrong journalists who might have tried to get in. All communiqués concerning Lawrence were issued by the War Office.

The inquest was held inside the camp in the normal way, with a civilian coroner and jury. Evidence was heard from Frank Fletcher, who, with his companion, had been cycling in the same direction as Lawrence. He heard a crash, was struck by his friend's bike, and then saw the motorbike lying on its side. Too scared to approach Lawrence, who was lying with blood over his face, Fletcher was joined within minutes by another cyclist and some soldiers. Corporal Catchpole of the RAOC, who had been walking his dog nearby, believed he had seen a black car or van travelling towards Lawrence. A dip in the ground prevented him from seeing what followed, but he saw the motorbike swerving, having passed the car. He was officially told not to refer to this car in his evidence and neither boy remembered seeing any motor vehicle. A subsequent examination of Lawrence's Brough revealed that it had jammed in second gear, which indicated that he could not have been doing more than 38 m.p.h.

Neither then nor later was anything more established about the black vehicle: if it existed (and Corporal Catchpole stuck resolutely to his story) its driver never came forward, not surprisingly perhaps. Its disputed existence troubled the coroner and at least one juryman, but their uncertainties did not prevent a verdict of 'accidental death'. This fudge and the furtiveness of the camp authorities led to wild speculation about a cover-up, although of just what no one seemed willing to say.[3]

At the core of the business were rumours that Lawrence had been involved with preparations for Britain's aerial defence, a matter very much in the public mind at the time, and that secret documents had been taken from his cottage. If, as Desmond Stewart suggests, police or military officials did go through Cloud's Hill, they would have found a day book and letters with details of Lawrence's ritual floggings. What they would have made of such material can only be guessed.

Following his wishes, Lawrence was buried in the graveyard of Moreton church, not far from Cloud's Hill. Arnold Lawrence led the mourners, who included Churchill, Lady Astor, Lord Lloyd, Lionel Curtis and Augustus John. Lawrence's coffin was carried by Eric Kennington, Aircraftman Bradbury, Private Russell of the Tank Corps, Pat Knowles (Lawrence's neighbour) and, from another world, Sir Ronald Storrs and Colonel Newcombe. A message came from George V (who had celebrated his Silver

Jubilee a fortnight before) to Arnold Lawrence: 'Your brother's name will live in history and the King gratefully recognizes his distinguished services to his country and feels that it is tragic that the end should have come in this manner to a life still so full of promise.'

There were many other tributes. 'A fine comrade, courteous, though reserved, and he had a rare sense of humour' was the judgement of one who had served alongside him at Uxbridge. Old adversaries were forgiving. *Le Temps* wrote:

> Lawrence had in him the cold violence of the Conquistador, the fierceness of the Irishman, the honest Puritanism of the Scot, the sangfroid of the Anglo-Saxon and the keen intelligence and contemplative spirit of the *savant*.

The official Nazi news agency was more fulsome with praise for 'a man of exemplary devotion to duty, disinterestedness, and self-sacrifice, and an almost mythical figure among British heroes'. Within four years, Dr Goebbels's filmmakers had produced *Uprising in Damascus*, in which Lawrence is portrayed as the devious agent of British imperialism and Zionism. He was universally lamented in the United States, where the *New York Herald Tribune* linked his name with Gordon's. 'Millions of Americans have delighted in Lawrence,' claimed its obituarist, 'and will sincerely mourn his untimely end which robs the whole world of the most romantic figure that the world has brought forth in modern times.' The only sour note came, predictably, from Turkey, where one newspaper remarked on the death of 'a notorious spy' who in his time had been 'King of the Desert'.

Seven

THE BUBBLE
REPUTATION

Chaos of thought and passion, all confused;
Still by himself abused, or disabused;
Created half to rise, and half to fall;
Great lord of all things, yet prey to all;
Sole judge of truth, in endless error hurled:
The glory, jest, and riddle of the world!
                    Alexander Pope 'Essay On Man'

'RIDDLE' and 'enigma' were words which came easily to hand when newspapermen wrote their obituaries of Lawrence. His life was a sequence of contrasting incidents and his behaviour defied easy explanation. He was simply 'Lawrence of Arabia', a unique creature who had held a generation spellbound and whose deeds had already become part of national mythology.

And yet, as an anonymous reviewer of the *Seven Pillars* remarked, 'without the War and without the Arabs it is unlikely he would have known great fame'.[1] This 'artist man-of-action' was 'a story writer who had found the divinely right subject-matter'. The description 'artist' would have pleased Lawrence, for it represented his greatest ambition. With 'story writer' he would have been less happy. He had been driven to do more than narrate a sequence of exciting events: he had wanted to tell the world about himself. The same revelatory urge ran through his vast correspondence and *The Mint*. In offering posterity this mass of autobiographical material, he seemed consciously preparing the way for those who, after his death, would 'rattle my bones'.

This was not a service to history, rather the contrary. 'He loved fantasy', wrote E.M.Forster, 'and leg-pulling and covering up his tracks, and threw a great deal of verbal dust, which bewilders the earnest researcher.'[2] This dust had blinded both Robert Graves and Liddell Hart, as they freely admitted. Much later, the Middle East scholar Elizabeth Monroe commented on Lawrence's 'evil delight in baffling the world'.[3] The red herrings, contradictions and falsehoods which litter Lawrence's letters and published work ensured that he would remain an enigma and that future historians and belletrists would be kept busy seeking keys to the riddle

365

he had created. After death, as in life, Lawrence would command attention.

On one level, this desire to fox posterity was an extension of Lawrence's pleasure in perplexing his friends and contemporaries. On another, it was a form of revenge on academic history undertaken by someone who, as an undergraduate, had cocked a snook at his stuffy, fact-bound tutors. In the same vein, Lawrence had enthralled fellow Jesus men with stories of how he had been bushwhacked by bandits in Syria and escaped by the skin of his teeth. The habit grew and in time became uncontrollable. But, did Yeats-Brown really believe that Lawrence had once penetrated Turkish army HQ during the Balkan Wars? Or did James Hanley, the novelist, accept Lawrence's equally far-fetched claim that he had spent a month in Q-boats during the war?[4] Most probably not but, like Robert Graves and Liddell Hart, they were willing to forgive the tale-teller his flights of fancy. More important is whether Lawrence forgave himself such indulgences.

The extended periods of melancholic brooding which marked Lawrence's later life owed much to his frequently admitted sense of guilt and self-loathing. His Evangelical upbringing would have taught him to set the highest value on truthfulness. By his mother's canon, lying was quite simply a sin. But Lawrence had released himself from such orthodoxy and was free to legislate his own moral code.

Deception could be excused on the ground that it was committed in the cause of art. Art lay at the centre of Lawrence's life and supplanted conventional Christianity as his religion. As a young historian he was captivated by the literature and visual arts of the Middle Ages. As boy and man he dreamed of being a printer of fine books; and in his final years he transformed his experiences in war and peace into two books which he hoped would be admired as creations of a genius.

There was always something distinctly Evangelical about Lawrence's approach to art and his own creative life. The achievement of perfection, like the search for spiritual grace, was a struggle which could consume the soul. Here too was an element of the quest, so familiar from his reading of medieval romance. Both the seeker after oneness with God and the knight errant knew that the pursuit of their goals entailed suffering. This was accepted by Lawrence. Although he looked back on his pre-war existence as an archaeologist as the happiest time of his life, it had not satisfied his deep urge to create. This re-emerged with even stronger force when the war ended and, to a greater or lesser degree, dominated the last years of his life, bringing with it much inner pain.

From childhood, Lawrence had seen himself as different, perhaps even a creature of destiny, although then and later he was tormented by doubt about whether he really possessed the inner power and fixity of purpose of one who could make history on a grand scale. To compensate, he manu-factured embellishments which made himself and his life even more remark-able, exciting and different. This process of constant adornment continued until he died and, by it, he consciously made his life into a work of art and himself into a superman.

Doing so may have triggered those bouts of self-reproach which so dis-tressed his friends. But were Lawrence's sense of unworthiness and self-hatred the products of guilt and shame? Nietzsche, one of his favourite authors, suggested another source for such emotions. 'Solitary man,' Zara-thustra prophesied, 'you are going the way of the lover: *you love yourself and for that reason you despise yourself as only lovers can* [my italics].' The internal recriminations of the narcissist are as bitter as those between lovers.

Vanity, if not self-love, alone explains why Lawrence, the medievalist, merged in his person the roles of warrior-hero and troubadour, continually adding fresh flourishes to his own legend. Yet what Lawrence did as a young explorer in the Levant or as an officer in the field commands respect and required no ornament. Why Lawrence felt impelled to embellish his achievement and then repudiate the fame they offered him remains inexplic-able. This, as much as his many inner contradictions, remains the most enduring Lawrence enigma.

While they were unable to solve the puzzles Lawrence set, those who knew him closely appreciated other and more attractive sides to his person-ality. He was a man of extraordinary sensitivity who could reveal an uncanny knack of knowing the mood and feelings of those around him. This quality was also present in his understanding of language, music, landscape and the artefacts of the past. He could be compassionate, and he moved with ease in many different societies. As a companion he could be charming and affable; those who met him usually recalled his conversation with delight. Testimony of the loyalty he could inspire came, twenty years after his death, when Storrs, Robert Graves and Philby rushed to defend him from denigration. Humbler men who shared barrack huts with Lawrence remembered, quite simply, a decent comrade.

Such defenders were needed. By contriving to make his life into a work of art, Lawrence had invited the attention of posterity. As a one-time student of medieval art he knew that his own life, like a painting or sculpture, would undergo unending examination and interpretation by future gener-ations. To make certain of this attention, he offered them an abundance of ambiguities. There was, as he once remarked, 'no absolute'.

APPENDIX

Since the publication of this book in Britain, I have received further information about T.E. Lawrence's private life through the kindness of Mrs. Elspeth Huxley.

T.E. Lawrence had made a more revealing confession of his homosexuality in May 1921 during a conversation with Kathleen Scott, the widow of Sir Robert Scott, the Antarctic explorer. Lady Scott was a talented sculptress who produced a full-length statue of Lawrence in Arab costume and imagined that her subject had become infatuated with her. On 25 February she discussed Lawrence with Colonel C.E. Vickery, who had served with him during the winter of 1916–1917. What passed between them she recorded in her diary:

> 25 February [1921] Well, well. Heard the most hair-raising stories from Vickery (Gunner) about L [awrence]. He was in Arabia at the same time. According to him, L [awrence] took credit for a great landing [i.e., at al Wajh on 23 November 1917] that took place when in reality he and [obliterated] arrived the following day saying they'd lost their way, but as they had the sea for a flank it seems that was impossible. Says that it is common knowledge that he is a 'royal mistress', that is the reason you never hear him spoken of in Arabia. When V [ickery] referred Hussein to him once, he replied 'Don't talk about that boy to me'. Once a rather beautiful young Arab came to him for a passport in a hurry for Egypt and said he could pay, and produced a slab of gold as big as two man's hands and said 'That is the price of a night with Faisal' and so on. Countless savoury tales! Well, well.

When Lawrence had returned from the Cairo Conference, she confronted him with Vickery's allegations and received a confession:

> 11 May [1921] Colonel Lawrence. He had a drunken father. Whilst drunken, first, dull, son was born. Reformed and then had another; killed; then one in India very remarkable; and a younger one

369

consumptive. Admitted his proclivities, but didn't affect his life. Said Vickery was a medal hunter and only out for himself.[1]

There had been profound disagreements between Lawrence and Vickery when they served together and to judge from his remarks quoted earlier, Vickery found Arab homosexuality repugnant. He was a forthright man who did not suppress his feelings. Writing to the compilers of the official history of the war, he described his superiors at the battle of Arras (April 1917) as 'the worst type of Horse Artillery commanders and both the laughing stock of the regiment'.[2] His allegations against Lawrence were more serious and, given the context in which they were made were, in pure legal terms, slanderous. Furthermore they were a gross breach of the code of honour to which Vickery, as an officer and gentleman, was bound. A professional soldier with a distinguished record and a Durham squire active in county affairs, Vickery would not have spoken carelessly of such matters.

What is most important about Vickery's remarks is that it suggests that, in the eyes of one who had the opportunity to observe him closely on campaign, Lawrence was openly homosexual in his behaviour with the Arabs, and Faisal in particular. There is, of course, only Vickery's word for this; others present during the Arab campaign remained silent on this subject, perhaps out of a sense of loyalty or decorum. Lawrence's activities, while potentially scandalous, were not unusual; throughout the history of the British Empire there were a number of homosexual proconsuls and commanders who found Eastern tolerance offered them wide opportunities for indulgence.[3]

SELECT BIBLIOGRAPHY

OFFICIAL ARCHIVES

Public Record Office, Kew.

Admiralty: Adm 53; Adm 137 [Telegrams].

Air Ministry: Air 1.

Cabinet: Cab 42, Cab 45.

Home Office: HO 42.

Foreign Office: FO 141; FO 371; FO 686 [Jiddah Consulate Files]; FO 800 [Sir Edward Grey Papers]; FO 861 [Aleppo Consular Files]; FO 882 [Arab Bureau Files].

War Office: WO 33 [Telegrams]; WO 95 [War Diaries]; WO 106 [Intelligence Files]; WO 157 [Intelligence Diaries and Reports]; WO 158.

Kitchener Papers: PRO 30.

Indian Office Library, Blackfriars, London. L. Mil 17 [War Diaries]; L.P. & S. 10 [Various files].

Service Historique pour L'Histoire de l'Armée de la Terre, Château de Vincennes, Paris. 16N 3200; 17N 498–9 [Reports and Telegrams of French Military Mission to Hejaz].

PRIVATE ARCHIVES

Field-Marshal Lord Allenby, various papers [St Antony's College, Oxford].

F.T.Birkinshaw, memorandum on T.E.Lawrence [Imperial War Museum].

General Sir Harry Chauvel, various papers [St Antony's College, Oxford].

General Sir Gilbert Clayton, letters and papers [Sudan Archive, University of Durham].

Sir Gerard Clauson, papers [Imperial War Museum].

Major-General Guy Dawnay, letters, papers and diaries [Imperial War Museum].

Sir Wyndham Deedes, letters and diaries [St Antony's College, Oxford].

Major Henry Garland, letters and memoranda [Imperial War Museum].

Commander David Hogarth, letters [St Antony's College, Oxford].

Colonel Pierce Joyce, memoranda on T.E.Lawrence [St Antony's College, Oxford].

Phillip Knightley and Colin Simpson, research notes for *The Secret Lives of Lawrence of Arabia* [Imperial War Museum].

T.E.Lawrence, various papers and letters [St Antony's College, Oxford].

T.E.Lawrence, letters to Mrs Bernard Shaw [British Museum, Additional Manuscripts 56,495–6].

Lord Lloyd, letters and diaries [Churchill College, Cambridge].

General Sir Archibald Murray and Field-Marshal Sir William Robertson, corre-spondence 1916–17 [British Museum, Additional Manuscripts 52,461–2].

General Sir Francis Wingate, letters and papers [Sudan Archive, University of Durham].

William Yale, Reports to the State Department, 1917–20 [St Antony's College, Oxford].

PUBLISHED WORKS

All books are published in London unless stated otherwise.

A.Aaronson, *With the Turks in Palestine* (1917).

U.P.Abd-Allah, *The Islamic Struggle for Syria* (Berkeley, California, 1983).

C.F.Adam, *The Life of Lord Lloyd* (1948).

R.Adelson, *Mark Sykes: Portrait of an Amateur* (1975).

N.Z.Ajay, 'Political Intrigue and Suppression in the Lebanon during World War I', *International Journal of Middle East Studies*, 5 (1974).

Richard Aldington, *Lawrence of Arabia: A Biographical Enquiry* (1955).

W.E.D.Allen and P.Muratoff, *Caucasian Battlefields: A History of the Wars on the Turco-Russian Border, 1828–1921* (Cambridge, 1953).

R.S.Amery, *My Political Life*, vol. II: *1914–29* (1953).

Anon, review of *Seven Pillars of Wisdom, London Mercury*, 188 (June 1935).

G.Antonius, *The Arab Awakening* (1938).

Sir George Arthur, *General Sir John Maxwell* (1932).

W.H.Auden, *The Orators* (1932).

——, *Look Stranger* (1936).

A.J.Barker, *The Mesopotamian Campaign of 1914–1918* (1967).

G.W.Barrow, *The Fire of Life* (1943).

M.Barrows, 'Mission Civilisatrice: French Colonial Policy in the Middle East', *Historical Journal*, 29 (1986).

Gertrude Bell, *From Amurath to Amurath* (1911).

Lady Bell (ed.), *The Letters of Gertrude Bell* (2 vols, 1927).

N. and H.Bentwich, *Mandate Memories* (1963).

G.Blake and R.King, 'The Hejaz Railway and the Pilgrimage to Mecca', *Asian Affairs*, 59 (1972).

A.Boyle, *Trenchard: Man of Vision* (1962).

N.N.E.Bray, *Shifting Sands* (1934).

——, *A Paladin of Arabia* (1936).

E.Brémond, *Le Hedjaz dans la Guerre Mondiale* (Paris, 1931).

E.A.W.Bridge, *A History of Ethiopia* (2 vols, 1927).

John Buchan, *Memory Hold-The-Door* (1940).

R.Bullard, *The Camels Must Go* (1961).

B.C.Busch, *Britain, India and the Arabs, 1914–1921* (Berkeley, California, 1971).

P.R.Butler, 'T.E.Lawrence', *Quarterly Review*, 266 (April 1938).

C.E.Callwell (ed.), *Field-Marshal Sir Henry Wilson: His Life and Diaries* (2 vols, 1927).

E.Candler, 'Lawrence in the Hejaz', *Blackwood's*, 243 (December 1925).

Christopher Caudwell [C.St John Sprigg], *Studies in a Dying Culture* (1938).

C.W.Ceram, *Narrow Pass, Black Mountain* (1956).

J.Charmley, *Lord Lloyd and the Decline of the British Empire* (1987).

W.J.Childs, *Across Asia Minor on Foot* (1918).

Winston S.Churchill, *Great Contemporaries* (1941 edn).

D.Commins, 'Religious Reformers and Arabists in Damascus, 1885–1914', *International Journal of Middle East Studies*, 18 (1986).

V.Cunningham, *British Writers in the Thirties* (1988).

Daily Review of the Foreign Press (Foreign Office, 1914–20).

J.E.Dayton, 'Tracking the Train Lawrence Wrecked', *The Times*, 4.12.64.

Documents on British Foreign Policy, 4th Series, IV (1952).

Laurence Durrell, *The Spirit of the Place* (1969).

Halidé Edib, *Memoirs of Halidé Edib* (New York, n.d.).

C.E.Edmonds [C.E.Carrington], *Lawrence of Arabia* (1935).

L.Einstein, *Inside Constantinople* (1917).

A.Emin, *Turkey in the World War* (New Haven, 1930).

L.Evans, *United States Policy and the Partition of Turkey, 1914–24* (Baltimore, 1965).

C.Falls, *Armageddon, 1918* (1964).

C.R.L.Fletcher, 'David George Hogarth', *Geographical Journal*, 11 (April 1928).

C.V.Fordley, *Bureaucratic Reform in the Ottoman Empire* (Princeton, 1980).

E.M.Forster, 'Cloud's Hill', *Listener*, 1.9.38.

——, '"The Mint" by T.E.Lawrence', *Listener*, 17.2.55.

——, *Abinger Harvest* (Penguin edn, 1967).

I.Friedman, *The Question of Palestine* (1973).

B.Gardner, *Allenby* (1965).

David Garnett (ed.), *The White–Garnett Letters* (1968).

Martin Gilbert, *Winston S.Churchill*, vol. IV: *1916–22*, and companion volumes (1975).

L.Gillet, 'Comment Fut Inventé L'Emir Fayçal', *Révue des Deux Mondes*, 15.7.27.

J.Goldberg, 'Philby as a Source of Early-Twentieth-Century Saudi History: A Critical Examination', *Middle East Studies*, 21 (1985).

——, 'Captain Shakespeare and Ibn Saud: A Balanced Reappraisal', *Middle East Studies*, 22 (1986).

Philip Graves, *Briton and Turk* (1941).

——, *The Life of Sir Percy Cox* (1941).

Robert Graves, *Lawrence and the Arabs* (1927).

Lord Hankey, *The Supreme Command* (2 vols, 1961).

J.Hart, *A Levantine Log-Book* (1905).

Rupert Hart-Davies (ed.), *Sassoon Diaries, 1915–18* (1983), *Sassoon Diaries, 1920–22* (1981), *Sassoon Diaries, 1923–25* (1985).

L.P.Hartley, '"The Mint": A Failed Masterpiece', *Listener*, 14.4.55.

Christopher Hassall, *Edward Marsh* (1959).

A.Herbert, *Mons, Anzac and Kut* (1919).

A.J.Hill, *Chauvel of the Light Horse* (Melbourne, 1978).

D.G.Hogarth, *Accidents of an Antiquary's Life* (1911).

——, *The Ancient East* (1914).

——, 'Lawrence of Arabia: The Story of His Book', *The Times*, 13.12.26.

——, 'Lawrence and the Arabs', *The Times Literary Supplement*, 10.3.27.

—— (ed.), [L.Woolley and T.E.Lawrence], *The Wilderness of Zin* (Palestine Exploration Fund, 1915).

H.M.Hyde, *Solitary in the Ranks* (1977).

D.Ingrams (ed.), *Palestine Papers* (1972).

Christopher Isherwood, *Exhumations* (1966).

R.R.James, *Gallipoli* (1965 edn).

—— (ed.), *Chips: The Diaries of Sir Henry Channon* (1967).

C.T.Jarvis, *Arab Command: The Biography of Lieutenant-Colonel Peake Pasha* (1946 edn).

W.E.Jennings Bramley, 'The Bedouin of the Sinai Peninsula', *Palestine Exploration Fund Proceedings* (1914).

H.A.Jones, *The War in the Air*, vol. V (Oxford, 1935).

T.Jones, *A Diary with Letters, 1931–50* (Oxford, 1954).

E.Kedourie, *England and the Middle East* (Cambridge, 1956).

——, *The Chatham House Version* (1970).

——, *In the Anglo-Arab Labyrinth: The Mcmahon Correspondence and its Interpretation, 1914–39* (Cambridge, 1976).

M.Kent (ed.), *The Great Powers and the Ottoman Empire* (1984).

P.S.Khoury, 'Factionalism among Syrian Nationalists during the French Mandate', *International Journal of Middle East Studies*, 13 (1981).

——, 'The Tribal Shaykh, French Policy and the Nationalist Movement in Syria between two World Wars', *Middle East Studies*, 18 (1982).

A.Kirkbride, *A Crackle of Thorns* (1958).

——, *An Awakening* (1971).

Phillip Knightley and Colin Simpson, *The Secret Lives of Lawrence of Arabia* (1969).

D.H.Lawrence (ed.), *Bernard Shaw: Collected Letters, 1911–1925* (1984).

A.W.Lawrence (ed.), *T.E.Lawrence by His Friends* (1957).

——, (ed.), *Secret Dispatches from Arabia* (1939).

——, *Letters to T.E.Lawrence* (1956).

M.R.Lawrence (ed.), *The Home Letters of T.E.Lawrence and His Brothers* (1954).

T.E.Lawrence, *The Seven Pillars of Wisdom: A Triumph* (1926).

——, *Revolt in the Desert* (1927).

——, *Oriental Assembly* (1939).

——, *The Mint* (1973).

——, *The Letters of T.E.Lawrence*, ed. David Garnett (1938).

——, *The Letters of T.E.Lawrence*, ed. M.Brown (1988).

——, *Letters to His Biographers, Robert Graves and Basil Liddell Hart* (1938).

S.Leslie, *Mark Sykes: His Life and Letters* (1923).

N.N.Lewis, *Nomads and Settlers in Syria and Jordan, 1800–1980* (1987).

B.Liddell Hart, *T.E.Lawrence: In Arabia and After* (1934).

A.L.Macfie, 'The Straits Question in the First World War', *Middle East Studies*, 19 (1983).

J.Mack, *A Prince of Our Disorder: The Life of T.E.Lawrence* (1976).

Compton Mackenzie, *Extremes Meet* (1928).

——, *Gallipoli Memories* (1929).

——, *Athenian Memories* (1931).

——, *My Life and Times: Octave 5 (1915–23)* (1966).

Sir George MacMunn, 'Lawrence in Full', *Saturday Review*, 19.3.27.

—— and C.Falls, *Military Operations: Egypt and Palestine* (4 vols, 1928–30).

A.MacPhail, *Three Persons* (1929).

W.G.Macpherson, *History of the Great War Based on Official Documents: Medical Services General History*, vols III and IV (1924).

—— (ed.), *History of the Great War Based on Official Documents: Diseases of the Great War*, vol. I (1924).

A.Mandelstam, *Le Sort de L'Empire Ottoman* (Paris, 1917).

W.T.Massey, *Allenby's Final Triumph* (1920).

J.C.Masterman, *On The Chariot Wheel* (1975).

Robin Maugham, *Escape from the Shadows* (1972).

R.Meinertzhagen, *Middle East Diary, 1917–56* (1956).

J.L.Miller, 'The Syrian Revolt of 1925', *International Journal of Middle East Studies*, 8 (1977).

F.J.Moberley, *The Campaign in Mesopotamia* (3 vols, 1923).

Lord Moran, *Churchill: The Struggle for Survival* (1968 edn).

H.Morganthau, *Secrets of the Bosphorus* (1918).

S.Moussa, *T.E.Lawrence: An Arab View*, trans. A.Butros (Oxford, 1967).

——, 'A Matter of Principle: King Hussain of the Hijaz and the Arabs of Palestine', *Middle East Studies*, 19 (1983).

L.Namier, *In the Margin of History* (1939).

S.E.Newcombe, 'Report on the Survey of Sinai and Southern Palestine', *Palestine Exploration Fund Proceedings* (1914).

Harold Nicolson, *Diaries and Letters, 1930–39* (1966).

P.M.O'Brien, *T.E.Lawrence: A Bibliography* (Winchester, 1988).

P.O'Prey (ed.), *In Broken Images: Selected Letters of Robert Graves, 1914–46* (1982).

——, *Between Moon and Moon: Letters of Robert Graves, 1946–72* (1984).

Papers Relating to the Foreign Relations of the United States: 1919, The Paris Peace Conference, vols XI, XII (New York, 1969).

G.Payn and S.Morley, *The Noël Coward Diaries* (1982).

Earl Percy, *Highlands of Asiatic Turkey* (1901).

H.StJ.Philby, *Arabian Days* (1948).

——, *Forty Years in the Wilderness* (1956).

B.de Pocock, *Dead Men Tell No Tales* (1943).

Y.Porath, 'Abdullah's Greater Syria Programme', *Middle East Studies*, 20 (1984).

J.Presland, *Deedes Bey* (1942).

A.G.Prÿs-Jones, 'Recollections of T.E.Lawrence', *Jesus College Record* (1986).

Sir Herbert Read, 'Self Portrait of a Misfit', *Listener*, 8.12.38.

J.Rennell Rodd, *Social and Diplomatic Memories, 1902–1919* (1925).

J.Richards and J. Hulbert, 'Censorship in Action: The Case of *Lawrence of Arabia*', *Journal of Contemporary History*, 19 (1983–4).

Vyvyan Richards, *Portrait of T.E.Lawrence of the Seven Pillars of Wisdom* (1936).

W.Robertson, *From Private to Field-Marshal* (1921).

S.C.Rolls, *Steel Chariots in the Desert* (1937).

S.Roskill, *Hankey: Man of Secrets*, vol. II: *1919–31* (1972).

H.W.Sachar, *The Emergence of the Middle East, 1914–24* (1969).

——, *Europe Leaves the Middle East, 1936–54* (1974).

E.W.Said, *Orientalism* (1987 edn).

L.von Sandars, *Five Years in Turkey* (United States Navy Institute, Annapolis, 1927).

Martin Seymour-Smith, *Robert Graves* (1982).

G.B.Shaw, 'The Latest From Colonel Lawrence', *Spectator*, 13.2.27.

J.Sherwood, *No Golden Journey* (1973).

C.K.Shorter, 'The Unknown King of Arabia', *Sphere*, 8.8.28.

G.Slade [Stephen Bartlett], *In Lawrence's Bodyguard* (1930).

——, *Led by Lawrence* (1934).

J.Springhall, B.Fraser and M.Hoare, *Sure and Steadfast: A History of the Boys' Brigade, 1883–1983* (1984).

Statistics of the Military Effort of the British Empire during the Great War (1922).

D.Stewart, *T.E.Lawrence* (1979 edn).

W.F.Stirling, 'Tales of Lawrence of Arabia', *Cornhill Magazine*, 74 (1933).

R.Storrs, *Orientations* (1944 edn).

——, 'Lawrence of Arabia', *Listener*, 3.2.55.

C.Sydney Smith, *The Golden Reign* (1940).

A.J.A.Symons, *The Quest for Corvo* (1935).

L.J.Tarver, 'In Wisdom's House: T.E.Lawrence and the Near East', *Journal of Contemporary History*, 13 (1978).

L.Thomas, *With Lawrence in Arabia* (1962 edn).

A.L.Tibawi, 'T.E.Lawrence, Faisal and Weizmann: The 1919 Attempt to Secure an Arab Balfour Declaration', *Journal of the Royal Central Asian Society*, 56 (1969).

A.P.Townshend, *My Campaign in Mesopotamia* (1920).

U.Trumpener, *Germany and the Ottoman Empire* (Princeton, 1968).

Lord Vansittart, *The Mist Procession* (1958).

C.Vickery, 'Arabia and the Hejaz', *Journal of the Central Asian Society*, 10 (1923).

B.Wasserstein, *The British in Palestine: The Mandatory Government and the Arab–Jewish Conflict, 1917–29* (1978).

T.Waugh, 'The German Counter to Revolt in the Desert', *Journal of the Royal Central Asian Society*, 24 (1937).

Lord Wavell, *The Palestine Campaigns* (1928).

F.J.Weber, *Eagles on the Crescent* (Ithaca, 1970).

S. and R.Weintraub (eds), *Evolution of a Revolt* (Pittsburgh, 1968).

Chaim Weizmann, 'Arabs and Zionists: The Pact of 1919', *The Times*, 10.6.36.

L.B.Weldon, *'Hard Lying': The Eastern Mediterranean, 1914–19* (1925).

Lady Wester-Wemyss, *The Life and Letters of Lord Wester-Wemyss* (1935).

M.O.Williams, 'Syria: The Landlink of History's Chain', *National Geographic Magazine*, 36 (November 1919).

Sir Arnold Wilson, 'Revolt in the Desert', *Journal of the Central Asian Society*, 14 (1927).

——, *Loyalties: Mesopotamia 1914–1917* (2 vols, Oxford, 1930–1).

J.Wilson, *T.E.Lawrence* (National Portrait Gallery T.E.Lawrence Exhibition Catalogue, 1988).

T.Wilson (ed.), *The Political Diaries of C.P.Scott, 1911–1928* (1970).

R.Wingate, *Wingate of the Sudan* (1955).

H.V.F.Winstone, *Leachman: 'OC Desert'* (1982).

W [Earl Winterton], 'Arabian Nights and Days', *Blackwood's*, 207 (May 1920).

——, *Orders of the Day* (1953).

——, *Fifty Tumultuous Years* (1955).

Sir Leonard Woolley, *Dead Towns and Living Men* (1920).

Evelyn Wrench, *Struggle, 1914–20* (1935).

F.Yeats-Brown, 'Lawrence As I Knew Him', *Spectator*, 24.5.35.
H.Young, *The Independent Arab* (1933).
Z.N.Zeine, *Turkish–Arab Relations and the Emergence of Arab Nationalism* (Beirut, 1958).

NOTES

All notes refer to manuscripts and books cited in the bibliography.

ABBREVIATIONS

H.L.: *The Home Letters of T.E.Lawrence and His Brothers.*
K.S.: Knightley and Simpson Files.
L.T.B.: *Letters to His Biographers Robert Graves and B.Liddell Hart.*
S.P.: *Seven Pillars of Wisdom.*

PART 1: FROM BIRTH TO MANHOOD: 1888–1914

I *Ancestry and Inheritance*

1. A.W.Lawrence (ed.)., *T.E.Lawrence by His Friends*, 81; R.R.James (ed.), 34.
2. K.S., Box 2: Celandine Kennington to Lady Hardinge, 30.7.54.
3. *H.L.*, 630; 718.
4. Meinertzhagen, 32: O'Prey, *Between Moon and Moon*, 133.

II *Boyhood and Schooling, 1888–1907*

1. Mack, 33–4.
2. T.Jones, 174.
3. V.Richards, 25.
4. Hogarth, 14.10.17.

III *Oxford and the Orient, 1907–1910*

1. Hogarth, *Accidents*, 1; Fletcher, 343.
2. Prŷs-Jones, 8.
3. K.S., Box 1, Letter from V.Richards, 4.3.65.
4. *Ibid.*, Interview of 12.12.64; Lawrence to Mrs Bernard Shaw, 29.3.27.

5. O'Prey, *In Broken Images*, 202.
6. V.Richards, 30.
7. FO 861/59, 1.6.10.
8. Trumpener, 44 ff.
9. Knightley and Simpson, chs 2 and 3; Stewart, 39–42.
10. R.Graves, 36–7.
11. *Briton and Turks*, 83–93; WO 106/1570, I, 4–5.
12. Mackenzie, *Athenian Memories*, 255; Hogarth, 24.7.15, 9.8.15.
13. Stewart, 54–6.
14. Prŷs-Jones, 10; R.Graves, 19–20.

IV Wandering Scholar: The Middle East, 1910–1913

1. *Letters*, ed. Garnett, 97.
2. Clauson, Clauson to Crocker, 9.10.17.
3. FO 861/61, 10 and 29.3.12.; *H.L.*, 194–5.
4. *H.L.*, 211.
5. Stewart, 95–6.
6. FO 861/60, 19.6.11, 30.10.11.
7. Childs, vii: Young, 14–16; *H.L.*, 170, 190, 447.
8. FO 861/62, 24.2.13; *Letters*, ed. Garnett, 151.
9. FO 861/62, 18.3.13.
10. *Letters*, ed. Garnett, 322.
11. Fletcher, 322.
12. *Ibid.*, pp. 250–1.
13. *Hansard*, 5th Series, 59, 18.4.14.
14. Barrows, 110, 129–30.
15. Ajay, 151; *Hansard*, 5th Series, 59, 18.4.14.
16. Percy, 8; *H.L.*, 146–7, 169–70, 265.
17. Stewart, 108–12.
18. Williams, 457; Rolls, 249–50; *L.T.B.*, 154.
19. Knightley and Simpson, 155–7.
20. Goldberg, 'Captain Shakespeare', 74; Storrs, 122–3.
21. FO 882/10, 30.
22. Zeine, 79, 85; Khoury, 'Divided Loyalties', 325.
23. Commins, 411–12.
24. Macpherson, III, 465, 477, 482–3; IV, 254, 301–3, 393; Macpherson (ed.), 120, 244–5; WO 95/4391 [Inspector of POW camps, Egypt]; Emin, 243–5.

V For King and Country, 1914

1. Hogarth, *Palestine Exploration* (1915), 61, 63.
2. *Ibid.*, 121 [Annual General Meeting Report].
3. Brémond, 60–1; Wingate, 140/3, 37–8.
4. Hogarth (ed.), 75.
5. *Ibid.*, 57, 69–70; *Palestine Exploration Fund Proceedings* (1916), 97–100.

6. Adm 137/97/13, 31.
7. Williams, 457.
8. Young, 22; *H.L.*, 638.
9. *Ibid.*, 303–4.
10. Hogarth, 3.2.17, 4.10.17.
11. *H.L.*, 638.

PART 2: INTELLIGENCE OFFICER: DECEMBER 1914–JUNE 1916

I War and Duty

1. Information from Mrs Marshall, General Clayton's daughter.
2. WO 157/658, 8.11.14.
3. Wingate 137/2; Clayton to Colonel Symes, 10.6.16; Murray to Robertson, 26.5.16.
4. WO 157/702, Director of Military Intelligence to GHQ Cairo, 25.3.16; Clauson, Clauson to Crocker, 9.10.17; Wingate 144/2, 17. The Clauson and Wingate papers contain many deciphered Turkish wireless messages.
5. Weldon, 110, 185 [Erskine Childers, the novelist and Irish nationalist, served on the *Ann Rickmers* with Weldon]; Ajay, *passim*.
6. Statement by Colonel Watson at the annual general meeting of the Palestine Exploration Fund, 22.6.15 (*Proceedings* [1915] 121). See also Jones, V, 161–2.
7. MacMunn and Falls, I, 155; Murray to Robertson, 14.7.16; Jones, V, 178; Adm 137/97, 728.
8. WO 157/689.
9. *Ibid.*
10. L.P. & S. 10/586/548, 51.
11. WO 157/694.
12. WO 157/688, 8.11.14.
13. WO 157/690, 3.4.15; 691, 1.5.15, 4.5.15.
14. WO 157/711, 20.12.16; Wingate 144/1, 1–2.
15. Adm 137/156, 1126; Adm 137/183, 31; MacMunn and Falls, I, 71.
16. Rolls, 109–10.
17. Knightley and Simpson, 42–4.
18. Lloyd 9/4, 11.3.15.
19. *H.L.*, 305.
20. WO 157/711, 'Notes on the Interrogation of Ottoman Prisoners of War, 1.12.16'.
21. Mackenzie, *Extremes Meet*, 50.
22. Mackenzie, *My Life and Times*, V, 29–30; WO 157/793 4 and 9.8.15; WO 158/922, 'R' [Major Sampson] to Newcombe, 3.8.15.
23. FO 371/2489/90222.
24. WO 95/4437 App. H [Intelligence Reports]. Native agents on the Western Desert Front were controlled by Bimbashie A.J. Tweedie of the Egyptian Customs Service.
25. Adm 137/334, 142; Adm 137/335, 20; see also Arthur, 234–6; MacMunn and Falls, I, 133; WO 33/747/2009.
26. Adm 137/97, 122A; Weber, 87. Turkish plans for a campaign of subversion in Egypt had been first laid in July 1914.

II Men and Ideas

1. *L. T.B.*, i, 37.
2. *H.L.*, 301.
3. Murray to Robertson, 26.1.16.
4. WO 95/4360 [G.S. Ops. Cairo] 8.1.16; Deedes, 8.1.16; Hogarth, 12.5.17; Bray, *Paladin*, 296–7; Presland, 235.
5. Robertson to Murray, 5.4.16.
6. Hogarth, 23.12.17.
7. Murray to Robertson, 5.4.16.
8. Mackenzie, *Gallipoli Memories*, 62, 321–2.
9. *Letters*, ed. Brown, 74.
10. Deedes, letter to his mother, 31.12.15; Mackenzie, *Life and Times*, V, 17–18.
11. Hogarth, 7.11.7.
12. Wemyss, 268.
13. Mackenzie, *Athenian Memories*, 139–40; Dawnay, letter to his wife, 11.4.15.
14. Mackenzie, *Gallipoli Memories*, 50–1; Dawnay, letter to his wife, 14.4.15.
15. Adam, 64.
16. Lloyd, 4/1A.
17. Dawnay, letter to his wife, 17.12.15; Wemyss, 265.
18. Busch, 22.
19. *Ibid.*, 40–1.
20. Adm 137/97, 1096.
21. 'Fragmentary Notes of 1915' in Yale, 25.2.18. On 15 February 1915, Storrs sent a report on the 'Syrian Problem' to Kitchener for editing or suppression along with the Field-Marshal's Freemasonic regalia [PRO 30/57/47].
22. *L. T.B.*, ii, 17.
23. Arthur, 153–4; MacMunn and Falls, I, 20–1.
24. Adm 137/97, 1075; 'Notes on Alexandretta and Syria by Catoni and Kennedy' [WO 157/689].
25. WO 106/1570, I, 9, 18; Clayton 694/3, 9.
26. WO 157/698, Intelligence Report 5.1.15, 4.
27. Clayton, 694/3, 10; WO 157/689, 'Notes on Alexandretta', 4.
28. WO 157/698, 'Notes on Alexandretta', 3; Lloyd favoured British annexation of the entire province [Lloyd 9/4, 15.3.15].
29. Clayton 694/3, memo 3.1.15.
30. *Ibid.*, 56–7.
31. Dawnay [Box 3], Dawnay to Aspinall, 5.2.32; James, 330.
32. MacMunn and Falls, I, 79–81; Arthur, 196, 199–200; WO 33/747/2774A, 2790A, 2792B, 2800B, 2798A.

III A Secret War

1. The Sultan's proclamation is printed in full in Mandelstam, 371–4.
2. Einstein, 2.
3. L. Mil 17/5/203; L. Mil 17/5/3250 App 397; see also von Sandars, 45.
4. Einstein, 2.
5. Waugh, 314; Weber, 182.

6. WO 33/748, 3590, 3594.
7. WO 175/701, 24.2.16: *Daily Review of Foreign Press*, 18.5.16, p. 4.
8. Von Sandars, 46, 134–5; Weber, 169; L. Mil 17/5/2403, 13.
9. PRO 30/75/69, 5.3.15: Cab 42/11, 7.4.16, pp. 3–4.
10. WO 157/701, 12.2.16.
11. MacMunn and Falls, I, 67; Wingate 141/1, 19.
12. WO 157/701, 12.6.16; WO 157/702, 14.3.16. Just how the U-boat had managed to get into the Red Sea did not cross the minds of Cairo's intelligence staff!
13. De Pocock, 42.
14. Wingate to Murray, 17.10.16.
15. Waugh, 314; WO 157/698, 7.12.15.
16. Adm 137/333, 621, 705, 765, 868; Adm 137/510, 223, 517; Wingate 140/3, 72–4; WO 95/4361, App 1, 25. WO 33/780, 4145.
17. Robertson, 176–7.
18. Adm 137/334, 1087.
19. Presland, 176–7.
20. Busch, 80.
21. FO 141/461/391; FO 371/2771, fos 150 ff.
22. Kedourie, *Chatham House Version*, 14.
23. WO 33/760, 4425.
24. Adm 137/97/1096.
25. WO 157/700, 27.1.16.
26. Weber, 183.
27. Mackenzie, *My Life and Times*, 5, 17; *Gallipoli Memories*, 243; FO 371/2271, 379.
28. Leslie, 243.
29. L.P. & S., 10/586, 323.

IV Adventures in Blunderland: Iraq, April 1916

1. Lloyd 9/8, 24.5.16.
2. L.P. & S., 10/576, 100.
3. Lloyd 9/8, 29.5.16.
4. WO 33/747, 2021, 2407; WO 158/668, 75; WO 95/5094, App 28.
5. Busch, 74; FO 882/15, 18 ff.
6. Clauson, Box 2.
7. Busch, 58–9.
8. PRO 30/57/48.
9. Cab 42/11, 28.4.16.
10. L. Mil 17/5, 3249.
11. *Ibid.*, 744.
12. *Ibid.*, 3250, App 37; L. Mil 17/5, 3249.
13. James, 46; Weber, 153–4.
14. Knightley and Simpson, 48.
15. P. Graves, *Percy Cox*, 200–1.
16. *Ibid.*, 201; FO 882/15, 72–7; FO 371/2771, 372.
17. *S.P.*, 35.
18. Herbert, 225.

19. L. Mil 17/5, 3250, App 39; *ibid.*, 3251, App 397; WO 33/768/3832, 3989.
20. Robertson to Murray, 15.3.16.
21. WO 33/768, 3749.
22. Wemyss, 298.
23. Herbert, 235; WO 158/668, 75; Wingate 137/1, 19.
24. L. Mil 17/5, 3251, App 475.
25. Wingate 137/1, 12.
26. L. Mil 17/5, App 458; WO 33/768, 4016; Townsend, 295, 335.
27. L. Mil 17/5, 3251, Apps 475, 480.
28. *Ibid.*, 475; WO 33/768, 4279.
29. L. Mil 17/5, 3249; WO 33/768, 4016, 4019, 4072.
30. WO 33/768, 4287.
31. L. Mil 17/5, App 460; WO 33/768/4288.
32. Cab 42/11, 28.4.16.
33. L. Mil 17/5, 8251, Apps 558, 575, 592; WO 33/768, 4350.
34. WO 33/768, 4351; L. Mil 17/5, Apps 519, 556–7.
35. WO 33/768, 4375. The Kaiser ordered a school holiday on the announcement of the surrender of Kut; German propaganda gave it second place to the Easter Rising in Dublin.
36. Herbert, 255.
37. *L.T.B.*, i, 83: Lawrence's report of the exchange is in FO 371/2771, 496–7, and *Letters*, ed. Garnett, 208–10.
38. FO 882/15, 72.
39. *Ibid.*, 369–70; Wingate 137/7 [Lawrence's Report on Iraq] 9, 13.
40. FO 882/15, 70–3; Wingate 137/7, 9; P. Graves, *Percy Cox*, 202–3.
41. Lloyd 9/8, Lloyd to Deedes, 26.5.16.
42. FO 371/2771, 392.
43. Wingate 137/1, 1, 18–19.
44. Wingate 136/6, 153. The Sirdar found Lawrence's report 'very good and interesting' [*ibid.*, 3].
45. Murray to Robertson, 9.3.16; Wingate 137/2, 38–9.
46. FO 882/15, 73.
47. Moberley, II, 296–7; III, 25, 50, 367–8; L. Mil 17/5, 3381, 14.4.16.
48. Goldberg, 'Philby', *passim*; 'Captain Shakespeare', 81.
49. WO 95/4361, App 1, 19; *ibid.*, 4365, App A; *ibid.*, 4380, 8 and 20.11.14; Adm 137/183, 73.
50. WO 33/760, 459.
51. WO 157/690, 23.4.15.
52. MacMunn and Falls, I, 277 n.1.
53. Von Sandars, 191.
54. Moberley, II, 83.

PART 3: WITH THE ARABS AT AQABA: JUNE 1916–JULY 1917

I A Man of Destiny

1. *S.P.*, 43–4.
2. WO 157/702, 21.3.16; *ibid.*, 705, 21.6.16.

3. FO 882/2, 332: WO 33/820, 5746, 5762; Wingate 140/6, Clayton to Wingate, 14.9.16.
4. Weldon, 134–5; WO 33/820, 5758.
5. Wingate 141/4, 24–6.
6. Murray to Robertson, 17.10.16.
7. Lloyd 8/9, Clayton to Lloyd, 28.12.16.
8. Adm 137/548, 39; Lloyd 8/9, Clayton to Lloyd, 28.12.16.
9. *Ibid.*
10. Wingate 141/3, 35; 143/2, 190–2.
11. 17N 499, 14.10.16.
12. Adm 137/334, 597, 615; Jones, V, 219–20; FO 371/2773, 116639.
13. *S.P.*, 88.
14. Von Sandars, 144–5.
15. WO 33/905, 5815, 5821, 6454, 6175.
16. Clayton 693/11 [Lawrence's Report of 18.10.16].
17. 17N 499, 1.6.17.
18. Clayton 693/11.
19. Clayton 470/5, 7.
20. Joyce, 1.
21. Storrs, 172; Clayton 693/11.
22. 17N 499, 3.11.16.
23. Brémond, 9–10, 42, 45 n.3, 59,61; Wingate 143/3, 70; 17N 498, Carton 2, dossier 2; FO 686/1/1, 127 ff.
24. Wingate 141/4, 93.
25. *Ibid.*, 3, 13.
26. WO 33/905, 6024.
27. Wingate 141/2, 42.
28. Lawrence's views are taken from his reports in: Wingate 143/9, 93; 143/6, 8–10, 48–51; Clayton 693/11; WO 33/905, 6156.
29. 17N 499, 14.10.16.
30. Wingate 143/3, 106.
31. *S.P.*, 68.
32. *Letters*, ed. Garnett, 219–20; FO 686/1/1, 123–4; Waugh, 314.
33. Wingate 143/2, 28–31.
34. WO 33/905, 6089; Clayton 694/4, 28.
35. Adm 137/397, 581, 588, 617; Adm 137/548, 40.
36. Wingate 143/6, 53–4.
37. WO 33/905, 6179; Wingate 143/6, 53.
38. Hogarth, 21.1.17. According to Captain Doynal St Quentin, Lawrence converted Hogarth and the Arab Bureau to his views. The Frenchman also believed that it had been Wemyss's assessment of the Hejaz situation which had carried the greatest weight in London [17N, 499, 18.11.16].
39. WO 33/905, 6047; Wingate 143/6, 53.
40. WO 33/905, 6047, 6060, 6065, 6118; Jones, V, 220–1.
41. Wingate 143/2, 190–2, 193.

II Lawrence and the Arabs

1. Clayton 693/11, Lawrence to Clayton, 9.9.17.

2. K.S., Box 6, interview with Gunner Beaumont.
3. Mack, 271.
4. Lloyd 9/13, Lloyd to Clayton, 20.10.17.
5. Wingate 143/7, 40–2.
6. Young, 150.
7. Meinertzhagen, 28–9.
8. Young, 156.
9. *Letters*, ed. Garnett, 490–1.
10. Wingate 141/4, 56.
11. FO 882/2, 50–1.
12. *Ibid.*, 4.
13. Vickery, 59.
14. Rolls, 192, 221, 235–6, 238.
15. WO 95/4415 [A.C. Section], 10.5.18; *ibid.* [O.C. Northern Hejaz], 11.5.18.
16. *Ibid.*, 12.6.18.
17. FO 882/2, 5.
18. Yale, 5.11.17.
19. Clayton 693/11, Lawrence to Clayton, 18.10.16.
20. WO 95/4415 [A.C. Section], 14.9.18.
21. Lewis, 233–4.
22. Khoury, 'Tribal Shaykh', 183–4; Mandelstam, 338–40, 340 n.2.
23. Wingate 149/8, 46.
24. WO 95/4415 [O.C. Northern Hejaz], 10–11.5.18. There was a further mutiny – see 16N 3200, 4.10.18.
25. WO 158/630, 22A, 32A.
26. *Ibid.*, 64A.
27. 17N 498, 'Situation au Hedjaz: Exposé Sommaire des Principaux Evénements Militaires et Politiques, 7.1.18'.
28. *Ibid.*, Cornwallis to Brémond, 26.10.17.
29. WO 158/629, 31A.
30. WO 158/630, 6A.
31. *Ibid.*, 16A.
32. Jarvis, 29–30.
33. Young, 156–7.
34. Khoury, 'Tribal Shaykh', 183–4. After the war Lawrence's Beduin 'patriots' continued to sell their allegiance to the highest bidder. In 1925 the French mandatory authorities paid 800,000 francs to the Syrian nomads in return for their neutrality during a rebellion by the Druze and Damascenes [Miller, 558 n.].
35. FO 686/1, I, 65.
36. Yale, 11.3.18.
37. Wingate 145/1, 18; FO 686/1, I, 1 ff.
38. 17N 498, 9.3.17, 24.8.17; WO 33/946, 9084, 9265; Brémond, 231.
39. Brémond, 106–7; 17N 498, 6.4.17; 17N 499, Carton 2, dossier 2 [9.6.17]. In January 1917 Captain Raho, sabre in hand, led a charge of Abdullah's camelry.
40. WO 106/1417, 19.
41. Presland, 271; Brémond, 185 ff.; Kirkbride, 41–6; 17N 499, Carton 13, dossier 4 (for Aden mutiny).

42. Clayton 693/11, 4.
43. A.W.Lawrence (ed.), *Secret Dispatches*, 155.

III Triumph at Aqaba

1. Mack, 151.
2. Joyce, 2.
3. 16N 3200 ['Le Raid du Major Lawrence et L'Action Anglaise à Akaba'], p. 3.
4. Lloyd 9/13, 20.10.17.
5. *Letters*, ed. Garnett, 238.
6. *Ibid.*
7. MacMunn and Falls, II, ii, 233 n.1.
8. Wingate 144/1, 42; 144/2, 32; Adm 137/548, 83.
9. Adm 137/548, 78.
10. I.e., Arab Bureau decrypts of 12–13.12.16 [Wingate 143/3, 99] which detail Fakhri's forces, their dispositions and the lack of aeroplane spare parts and an epidemic of dysentery at Medina [*ibid.*, 17, 15]. Lawrence knew of this and advised Faisal accordingly. He also summoned up RNAS seaplanes to harass the Turkish forward positions [*ibid.*, 14, 40, 51]. The intelligence information was later passed to Brémond's mission [17N 498, 30.12.16 and 17N 499, 13.12.16]. The Turks suspected that their wireless messages were being intercepted by warships in the Red Sea [WO 157/711, 19.12.16].
11. 17N 498, 12.2.17; the evacuation of women and supernumeraries was also reported [FO 686/1, I, 9].
12. Von Sandars, 207–8; 17N 498, 14.2.17.
13. Garland.
14. Adm 137/150, 207.
15. Bray, *Shifting Sands*, 101. For other views in favour of guerrilla warfare see: WO 33/905/5989A; Wingate 137/5, 1; 140/3, Wingate to Murray 9.6.16; 141/2, 78, and Lloyd 9/8, 22.4.16.
16. Lloyd 9/8, Clayton to Lloyd, 28.12.16.
17. Wingate 143/2, 103, 190–3, 248; 143/3, 106; 16N 3200 ['Le Raid'], p. 2.
18. WO 33/905, 5989A; 17N 499, 18.11.16.
19. For what happened at el Wajh: Garland; Vickery, 51–2; Weldon, 157–8; Adm 137/150, 251; Adm 137/548, 114. All disagree with Lawrence's account.
20. FO 686/1, I, 57.
21. For Lawrence on Vickery and Garland: *L.T.B.* ii, 36, 63, 94, 96 [Lawrence objected to Garland on account of his being a former NCO]; Vickery, 54–6.
22. Clayton 470/6, 22. Wilson thought Bray had a 'kink' about the Arab business; Lawrence cared little for Bray or his critical book – see *Letters*, ed. Garnett, 828 and *Letters*, ed. Brown, 508.
23. WO 157/711, 8.12.16; 17N 499, 15.11.16.
24. *Letters*, ed. Brown, 77; Wingate 143/2, 28–31; Lloyd 9/9, Lloyd to Clayton, 1.1.17; WO 33/905, 7116, 6826; 17N 498, 3.4.17. The Rwallah were desperate for gold with which to buy corn and were willing to hawk their loyalty about – see a report by 'Maurice' (WO 33/935, 7477) of May 1917. Rwallah duplicity

must have been known to Hussain since 'Maurice' enjoyed his confidence [Wingate 144/1, 2]. Lawrence and Faisal must presumably have known something of their potential ally's flexible loyalty.

25. 17N 498, 7.5.17; 17N 499, 25.5.17.
26. 17N 499, 25.5.17; Brémond was deeply disturbed by Lawrence's Syrian machinations, although he had told him that his aim was solely to divide the Islamic world [Brémond, 161 n.].
27. Wingate 145/1, 19.
28. 17N 499, Carton 12, dossier 1.
29. WO 95/4367 [GHQ Ops], 6.2.17 [Notes on the meeting with Brémond]; Clayton 694/4, 8 [Memo on French Mission]; 17N 499 21, 25.1.17; Brémond, 132.
30. Brémond, 133; 17N 498, 22.2.17.
31. Murray to Robertson, 14.7.16; Robertson to Murray, 29.8.16; FO 800/48, 496; 17N 499, 5.11.16.
32. Air 1/2284/209/75, 8 [Report of aerial survey undertaken on 7.8.16].
33. Wingate 145/1, 55, 60.
34. Adm 137/510, 223; Adm 137/548, 167, 182.
35. Lloyd 9/9, Newcombe to Clayton, 20.5.17; Brémond, 132 [Brémond heard that Newcombe and Faisal were discussing plans to take Aqaba at the end of January soon after the occupation of el Wajh]; 17N 498, 26.6.17.
36. WO 33/905, 7116.
37. *Ibid.*, 6826.
38. 17N 499, 19.5.17; WO 158/634, 65A, p. 2.
39. Clayton 694/4, 28.
40. Copies are in: Lloyd 9/9; WO 158/634, 3A, 4A; Wingate 146/5, 71 [with map]; *Letters*, ed. Garnett, 225–36.
41. *Letters*, ed. Brown, 111.
42. Wingate 141/3, Wilson to Wingate, 5.10.16; 17N 498, 30.10.16.
43. Wingate 146/1, 17; WO 158/634, 9A.
44. Stewart, 166–7.
45. 16 N 3200 'Le Raid', p. 1.
46. WO 33/935/7753.
47. 17N 498, 8.6.17, 4.7.17, 18.7.17.
48. Falls, 8.
49. 16N 3200, 'Le Raid', p. 3.

PART 4: THE ROAD TO DAMASCUS: JULY 1917–OCTOBER 1918

I *The Railway War*

1. 16N 3200, 'Le Raid', p. 1.
2. Young, 140.
3. Wingate 146/1, 17.
4. *Ibid.*, 146/5, 54.
5. Barrow, 215.
6. WO 33/935, 7767; WO 158/634, 4A.

7. *Ibid.*, 10A.
8. *Ibid.*; WO 33/935, 7767, 7782.
9. WO 158/629, 2A, 31A.
10. WO 106/1515, 29; *ibid.*, 1516, 15.
11. WO 33/956, 8547.
12. Intelligence estimates on 28.11.17 [WO 33/946, 8622].
13. WO 158/629, 2A, 26A.
14. *Letters*, ed. Brown, 112.
15. Garland; 17N 499, 1.1.17, 13.3.17, 9.8.17; FO 686/1, II, 13, 63, 80.
16. Garland; FO 882/2, 46 ff., 70.
17. WO 33/960, 1005.
18. Von Sandars, 176, 183, 195, 206–7.
19. FO 686/1, II, 80.
20. FO 882/2, 70.
21. Kirkbride, 17–18, 43.
22. 17N 499, 14.10.17 [Lawrence gave Pisani £70 for his expenses]; Brémond, 215–17; WO 158/634, 43B; for Lawrence's objections, *ibid.*, 38A.
23. WO 158/634, 113A.
24. 17N 498, 10.9.17. The would-be assassin was flogged.
25. WO 158/634, 91A; see also *ibid.*, 65A.
26. WO 158/635, 1A, 2A.
27. Wingate 146/6, 68–9.

II A Covert Operation

1. Clayton 692/12, Clayton to Joyce, 24.10.17.
2. Lloyd 9/13, 25.10.17.
3. Lloyd 9/10; another copy is in Clayton 694/4, 30–4.
4. FO 371/3384, 181025.
5. Yale, 12.11.17.
6. Clayton 693/12, 44; 693/11, 9. Wingate agreed [Wingate 146/6, 82].
7. WO 33/935, 8366, 8371.
8. Wingate 146/8, 81.
9. Clayton, 693/11, Lawrence to Clayton, 17.9.17.
10. 17N 498, 6.19.17.
11. Lloyd 9/10.
12. Von Sandars, 208.
13. 17N 498, 23.12.17.
14. WO 33/748, 3570, 3590.

III Dera: Degradation or Deception?

1. WO 95/4415 [RFA Motor Section]. The entry reads, '21.11.17 Carried out recon-naissance with Col. P. Joyce and Col. Lawrence up Wadi Yetm'; for Dzarka, see Adm 53/44609, 20.11.17. Unloading the cars began at 12.50 p.m.
2. A.W.Lawrence (ed.), *T.E. Lawrence by His Friends*, 163–4. Brodie described how he had first met Lawrence at Colonel Joyce's tent the morning after his unit had

disembarked i.e. 21 November. The unit War Diary was written up in April 1918 so the early entries are fragmentary and the date of disembarkation is given as 21 rather than 20 November, although the former may indicate when all equipment and supplies were ashore.

3. Knightley and Simpson, 90–2; the letter remained in Colonel Stirling's possession and was later sold to the University of Texas.

4. Meinertzhagen, 32; Seymour-Smith, 108–9; O'Prey, *Between Moon and Moon*, 140; *Letters*, ed. Brown, 131, 201–2, 260, 261–2, 360–1. Jock Chambers, one of Lawrence's RAF colleagues, heard that he had escaped from Dera by killing a sentry with a stone [Knightley and Simpson, 215].

5. Barker, 295–6.

6. Aaronson, 52–3.

7. WO 33/946/8547. On 25 November GHQ intelligence received written reports from Aqaba of bridge destruction west of Dera and low-grade topographical information from the Dera–Afule region [WO 157/721].

8. Hogarth, 26.11.17.

9. Hogarth, 29.11.17.

10. Malcolm Muggeridge heard this from Meinertzhagen [*Observer*, 29.8.68].

11. E.g. MacMunn in *Saturday Review*, 19.3.27.

12. Knightley and Simpson, 207–13.

13. *Ibid.*, 214–15. The remarks are on a note attached to Shaw s copy of the *Seven Pillars* now in New York Public Library.

14. Meinertzhagen, 38–9.

15. Knightley and Simpson, 215–17.

16. I am indebted to Dr Schild for this point.

17. Hogarth, 16.12.17.

18. See p. 63.

19. Vickery, 53.

20. Wilson, 'Revolt', 282.

21. K.S., Box 4.

22. *Letters*, ed. Brown, 260, 360–1.

23. Seymour-Smith, 108–9.

24. Stewart, 275 332. This letter was seen by Colin Simpson among the Lawrence papers held in the Bodleian Library, Oxford. In a letter to the *Sunday Times* [26.6.77] he claimed that it was removed shortly after and that he had been persuaded to exclude its contents from his biography, having heard from Arnold Lawrence and the Lawrence Trustees that Lawrence had been hounded unjustly by the German magazine. Publication by Stewart dismayed the Trustees. No copy of Lawrence's letter was kept in the Home Office files concerning deportations during 1922–3. No mention of this strange tale was made in Wilson's *Lawrence of Arabia.*

25. K.S., Box 6, Colin Simpson's transcript.

26. Knightley and Simpson, 169–71, 199–201; Mack, 415–41, which includes Bruce's testimony together with copies of the letters concerning Lawrence's beating sessions. Others were involved, apart from Bruce, and the sessions occurred at Cloud's Hill, Edinburgh, Aberdeen and Perth and once included sea-bathing at Collieston during the late autumn. In his conversations with Knightley and Simpson, Bruce revealed he was unaware of the sexual connotations of

the exercises he performed. It need hardly be added that at the time Lawrence's behaviour would have rendered him liable to criminal prosecution.

27. 16N 3200, 'Le Raid', p. 1.
28. Sherwood, 146. Flecker was bisexual and interested in masochism; unlike Lawrence he had attended a public school (Uppingham) where homosexual behaviour had been commonplace.
29. A.W.Lawrence (ed.), *T.E.Lawrence by His Friends*, 214.
30. Maugham, 116.
31. K.S., Box 3: Maugham seems to have told Philip Kerr, one of Lawrence's acquaintances, and Aldington.
32. I am indebted to Dr Schild for these observations.
33. O'Prey, *Between Moon and Moon*, 132–3.
34. Stewart, 188–9, 253; Dr Schild agrees that in clinical terms, Lawrence had endured homosexual rape and believes that the scenario suggested by Stewart may be correct [Letter to author, 21.9.89].

IV Betrayal

1. Clayton, 693/11, 7.
2. Kedourie, *Chatham House version*, 23.
3. Friedman, 298; *Letters*, ed. Brown, 112.
4. FO 371/3381, 123686.
5. Hogarth, 10.1.18.
6. Yale, 25.2.18, 11.3.18.
7. FO 371/3381, 115783.
8. FO 371/2492, 201112, 201528; Weber, 136, 153–4.
9. WO 106/1514; *ibid.*, 1516, 5; Friedman, 218–20.
10. WO 33/935, 8350.
11. *S.P.*, 543.
12. FO 141/430/5411; Yale Report, 21.1.18, 3, 5–6.
13. Yale Report, 21.1.18, 3, 5–6; FO 141/430/5411.
14. FO 141/430/5411, Wingate to Foreign Office, 23.3.18; FO 371/3381, 146256.
15. FO 141/430/5411, Joyce to Arab Bureau, 9.1.18.
16. *Ibid.*, Foreign Office to Wingate, 24.4.18.
17. *Ibid.*, Wingate to Foreign Office, 8.4.18.
18. FO 371/3381, 143456.
19. Wingate 144/1, 2, 3; FO 882/14, 72.
20. Friedman, 219.
21. Clayton 693/11, 4–5.
22. Yale, 25.2.18, 11.3.18.
23. Meinertzhagen, 99.
24. Tabawi, 158–9; FO 882/14, 364–5. For Lawrence's movements; WO 95/4415 [O.C. Northern Hejaz] 4.6.18, 12.6.18.

V War's Mischances, November 1917–July 1918

1. Stirling, 494.
2. Kirkbride, *Awakening*, 19.

3. *Ibid.*, 118–19.
4. Young, 163.
5. Birkinshaw.
6. Rolls, 155.
7. Joyce, 2.
8. Stirling, 497.
9. WO 33/946, 8547; Dawnay, Arab Bureau to DMI, 15.11.17.
10. Yale, 4.3.18, 6; 11.3.18, 4–5.
11. WO 33/946, 8899.
12. Hogarth, 25.2.18.
13. Young, 142.
14. WO 95/4415 [O.C. Northern Hejaz]; Ops summary, March 1918; WO 33/946, 9209; 17N 498 Sommaires &c., 7.3–7.4.18; Brémond, 237; WO 158/635, 21A.
15. WO 33/946, 9308.
16. Liddell Hart, 289–90.
17. WO 33/946, 9413.
18. Massey, 58.
19. WO 95/4415 [O.C. Northern Hejaz], 6.4.18.
20. *Ibid.*, 13.4.18; Young, 164–5; Brémond, 236.
21. WO 95/4415 [O.C. Northern Hejaz], 15.4.18.
22. *Ibid.*, 13.4.18; MacMunn and Falls, II, ii, 406–7.
23. Air 1/2360/226/6/3, 27.4.18.
24. WO 33/946, 9485.
25. Young, 173, 175.
26. WO 95/4415 [A.C. Section], 18–22.4.18; MacMunn and Falls, II, ii, 408.
27. Air 1/2360/6/3, 21.4.18.
28. Hogarth, 4.5.18.
29. WO 33/946, 8935A; WO 95/4415 [RFA], 21–22.1.18; Kirkbride, *Awakening*, 51.
30. Wavell, 253.
31. WO 95/4415 [RFA].
32. FO 882/2, 70.
33. WO 95/4415 [A.C. Section], 26.7.18.
34. WO 33/960, 9977, 9886.
35. Air 1/2360/226/6/4, 25.5.18.

V Damascus: Flawed Triumph

1. Falls, 103; Kirkbride, *Awakening*, 57.
2. Kedourie, *Chatham House version*, 34–5.
3. Hill, 174–5.
4. WO 33/960, 10099; WO 95/4371 [GS Ops], App B, 2.9.18.
5. Jarvis, 41–2, 44.
6. Jones, V, 212–13.
7. *Ibid.*; WO 95/4371 [GS Ops], App B, 16.9.18.
8. Jarvis, 49; Kirkbride, *Awakening*, 66.
9. *Ibid.*, 45–6.
10. MacMunn and Falls, II, ii, 565; von Sandars, 288–9.

11. Air 1/2329/226/1/16.
12. Jones, V, 230, 232; Air 1/2329/226/1/16; Massey, 323–4.
13. MacMunn and Falls, II, ii, 555.
14. Massey, 217; MacMunn and Falls, II, ii, 555–9; WO 95/4371 [GS Ops], 29.9.18.
15. Air 1/2329/226/1/16.
16. WO 95/4510 [4th Cavalry GS], Narrative, pp. 9–10; WO 95/4511 [20th RHA Battery], 28.9.18. For other instances: Massey, 193–4, 233–4; von Sandars, 297–8; WO 95/4725 [Lines of Communication] MP Reports March and June 1918; WO 95/4515 [5th Cavalry GS], 22, 22.9.18.
17. Barrow, 210–11.
18. *Letters*, ed. Garnett, 253–4.
19. Mack, 237–8.
20. Kirkbride, *Awakening*, 81–2.
21. Winterton, *Fifty Tumultuous Years*, 71–2.
22. Massey, 234.
23. Hill, 174–5.
24. *Ibid.*, 175.
25. Busch, 198–9; FO 371/3381, 123868; FO 371/3384, 171564; WO 33/960, 10218.
26. Kedourie, *Chatham House version*, 38; see also WO 33/960, 10185; WO 95/4371 [GS Ops] Apps M, O.
27. Hill, 178.
28. WO 95/4510 [4th Cavalry GS], Narrative, p.11; Cab 45/80 [G. White].
29. Von Sandars, 195–6.
30. Hill, 178–9, quoting Chauvel's account written in 1923.
31. *Ibid.*, 179.
32. *Ibid.*, 180–1; Massey, 261–3; Cab 45/80 [G. White: who says that Lawrence denied the indiscipline of Lawrence regulars.]
33. Hill, 182–3.
34. Kirkbride, *Awakening*, 96–7; *Crackle*, 8–9.
35. WO 95/451 [Asst Director of Medical Services], 2.10.18.
36. WO 33/960, 10166.
37. *Ibid.*, 10177, 10166, 10178.
38. Gardner, 200–11.
39. *Ibid.*, 189–91; Hill, 184–5; Allenby, Chauvel to Allenby, 22.10.29, and attached narrative.

PART 5: THE LEGEND OF LAWRENCE OF ARABIA

I *Achievement*

1. Butler, 219.
2. FO 882/14, 205, 4 ff.; Vickery, 62–3.
3. FO 371/4159, 146374; WO 33/981, 11234.
4. *Ibid.*, 11124. See also WO 33/969 *passim*.
5. WO 95/4515 [5th Cavalry GS], Intelligence Report, 7–12.7.18.
6. *Papers Relating to the Foreign Relations of the US*, XII, 778.
7. Massey, 61. This balanced account of the 1918 Palestine and Syrian campaigns also gives credit to Lawrence's brother officers [250–1].

8. *Papers Relating to the Foreign Relations of the US*, XII, 727; WO 95/4373 [GS Ops], July 1919, App A [2.7.19]; *ibid.*, 4374, Apps 20.9.19, 20.12.19.
9. WO 33/981, 11686.
10. Von Sandars, 145, 263.
11. FO 141/430/5411.

II The Making of the Legend, 1918–1935

1. Wrench, 361.
2. O'Prey, *In Broken Images*, 262.
3. *Ibid.*, 248–9, 252, 257.
4. *Ibid.*, 251.
5. *Spectator*, 24.5.35.
6. Sergeant W.C.Noble, quoted in *Edinburgh Evening News*, 22.5.35.
7. Wingate 148/12, 29.
8. Sachar, 294–5.
9. Bullard, 158. A short newsreel with wartime footage was distributed in British cinemas soon after Lawrence's death with a commentary by Storrs.
10. FO 371/16188, 87–8.
11. Read.
12. Caudwell, 101.
13. FO 371/18925, 224, 227, 230–1, 236A.
14. Richards and Hulbert, 166–7.

III Living with a Legend

1. Meinertzhagen, 32.
2. Vansittart, 205.
3. Storrs, 451.
4. A.W.Lawrence (ed.), *T.E.Lawrence by His Friends*, 105.
5. Lloyd 1/22, Lawrence to Lloyd, 22.1.29.
6. Namier, 380.
7. Lloyd 1/22, Lawrence to Lloyd, 22.1.29.
8. Meinertzhagen, 31.
9. A.W.Lawrence (ed.), *T.E.Lawrence by His Friends*, 106–7.
10. Tarver, *passim*, but especially p. 599, which quotes the entry from the Arab Bureau's official bulletin of 22.10.18.
11. Vansittart, 166.
12. A.W.Lawrence (ed.), *T.E.Lawrence by His Friends*, 106.

PART 6: MAKING THE BEST OF IT: 1918–1935

I Diplomat, 1918–1919

1. O'Prey, *Between Moon and Moon*, 137; Vansittart, 60–1.
2. Lloyd 9/13.
3. FO 608/92, 382–3.
4. *Ibid.*, 382; *Documents on British Foreign Policy*, 370–1; Vansittart, 205.
5. Vansittart, 354–5, 370.

6. Busch, 199–200; FO 371/3384, 181025.
7. FO 608/92, 225, 227, 343; WO 95/4374 [GS Ops], 30.11.19; Kirkbride, *Awakening*, 46.
8. FO 608/93, 73, 94.
9. Weizmann; Tibawi, 151 ff.
10. FO 608/93, 192.
11. *Documents on British Foreign Policy*, 447–8.
12. FO 608/93, 195; WO 33/981, 11138; Evans, 148; Sachar, *Emergence*, 261.
13. Callwell, II, 168–9, 193; WO 33/981, 11098.
14. *Documents on British Foreign Policy*, 265 n.1; FO 608/92, 306.
15. FO 608/93, 76.
16. *Papers Relating to the Foreign Relations of the US*, XI, 123.
17. WO 33/981, 11144, 11232.
18. FO 608/92, 383; *Documents on British Foreign Policy*, 315, 370.

II *Kingmaker, 1919–1922*

1. *Letters*, ed. Garnett, 322.
2. WO 33/969.
3. WO 33/981, 11390, 11512, 11671; FO 371/4159, 139090.
4. *Letters*, ed. Brown, 163.
5. Wilson, 'Revolt', 282.
6. Gilbert, 534; Lloyd 1/22, Lawrence to Lloyd, 30.9.34.
7. Gilbert, companion volume 2, 895.
8. Moran, 124–5.
9. Gilbert, 515–16.
10. *Letters*, ed. Garnett, 290: Noel's views of Kurdish national feeling are in FO 608/95; several items have been officially removed from this file.
11. *L.T.B.*, I, 190–1.
12. Ingrams (ed.), 127.
13. Meinertzhagen, 127.
14. Lawrence's despatches are in FO 686/93; some are quoted in *Letters*, ed. Brown, 188–91.
15. FO 686/93, 12–13.
16. *Letters*, ed. Garnett, 336.
17. Clayton 693/11, Lawrence to Clayton, 9.10.28.
18. *Spectator*, 27.8.27.
19. Sachar, *Europe Leaves the Middle East*, 159, 289, 292.
20. Abd-Allah, 38.
21. Lloyd 1/22, Lawrence to LLoyd, 30.9.34.
22. Kirkbride, *Crackle*, 62. The Arabs noticed that Glubb Pasha, commander of the Jordanian Arab Legion, was half Irish, half Scottish; Lawrence of course was half Anglo-Irish as opposed to Gaelic Irish.

III *Man of Letters*

1. O'Prey, *In Broken Images*, 298.
2. Clayton 693/11, Lawrence to Clayton, 22.8.22.

3. Lawrence in review of an edition of Hakluyt's *Voyages, Spectator,* 10.9.27.
4. Hartley.
5. O'Prey, *In Broken Images,* 260, 262.
6. *Spectator,* 27.8.27.
7. Payn and Morley, 261.
8. Durrell, 36.
9. MacPhail, 195–235.
10. *The Times Literary Supplement,* 21.1.77.

IV Gentleman Ranker, 1922–1935

1. Boyle, 384.
2. Forster, "The Mint".
3. Seymour-Smith, 258–9.
4. Boyle, 428.
5. See p. 217–18.
6. *Letters,* ed. Brown, 227–8, 232–4, 236–7, 239–43.
7. *Ibid.,* 389.
8. Stewart, 284.
9. W.C.Noble in *Edinburgh Evening News,* 21.5.35.
10. Stewart, 276.
11. D.H.Lawrence (ed.), 829.
12. Knightley and Simpson, 196–7.
13. A.W.Lawrence (ed.), *T.E.Lawrence by His Friends,* 557–8.

V Death of a Hero

1. Nicolson, 124–5.
2. Lord Rennell to Liddell Hart, 5.4.34 [Lawrence Collection, St Antony's College, Oxford].
3. Stewart gives an examination of the evidence and hints at foul play or at least the suppression of evidence after suggesting that Lawrence was seriously flirting with Fascism. This is highly unlikely and, even if he had been, who would have had him killed and how? No answers are given nor could they be found outside the world of thriller fantasy [pp. 300–5].

PART 7: THE BUBBLE REPUTATION

1. *London Mercury,* 188 (June 1935).
2. Forester, "The Mint".
3. *The Times Literary Supplement,* 2.10.68.
4. *Letters,* ed. Garnett, 728.

APPENDIX

1. These diaries are reproduced by kind permission of Lady Scott's son, Lord Kennet. The originals are in Cambridge University Library.
2. Cab 45/116, C.E.Vickery.
3. See R.Hyam, Empire and Sexual Opportunity, *Journal of Imperial and Commonwealth History,* 14 (1985–6) for examples.

INDEX